CIMA

OPERATIONAL

PAPER F1

FINANCIAL REPORTING AND TAXATION

Our text is designed to help you study **effectively** and **efficiently**.

In this edition we:

- **Highlight** the **most important elements** in the syllabus and the **key skills** you will need

- **Signpost** how each chapter links to the syllabus and the learning outcomes

- Use **overview and summary diagrams** to develop understanding of interrelations between topics

- **Provide** lots of **exam alerts** explaining how what you're learning may be tested

- **Include examples** and **questions** to help you apply what you've learnt

- **Emphasise key points** in **section summaries**

- **Test your knowledge** of what you've studied in **quick quizzes**

- **Examine your understanding** in our **practice question bank**

SUITABLE FOR EXAMS IN 2015 AND 2016

PUBLISHED MAY 2015

BPP
LEARNING MEDIA

Second edition 2015

ISBN 9781 4727 3412 9

e-ISBN 9781 4727 3646 8

British Library Cataloguing-in-Publication Data
A catalogue record for this book
is available from the British Library

Published by

BPP Learning Media Ltd
BPP House, Aldine Place
142-144 Uxbridge Road
London W12 8AA

www.bpp.com/learningmedia

Printed in the United Kingdom by

Polestar Wheatons
Hennock Road
Marsh Barton
Exeter
EX2 8RP

Your learning materials, published by BPP Learning Media Ltd, are printed on paper sourced from sustainable, managed forests.

We are grateful to the Chartered Institute of Management Accountants for permission to reproduce past examination questions. The suggested solutions in the exam answer bank have been prepared by BPP Learning Media Ltd.

Contents

How our Study Text can help you pass

Streamlined studying	• We show you the best ways to study efficiently • Our Text has been designed to ensure you can easily and quickly navigate through it • The different features in our Text emphasise important knowledge and techniques
Exam expertise	• **Studying F1** on page xvi introduces the key themes of the syllabus and summarises how to pass • We highlight throughout our Text how topics may be tested and what you'll have to do in the exam • We help you see the complete picture of the syllabus, so that you can answer questions that range across the whole syllabus • Our Text covers the syllabus content – no more, no less
Regular review	• We frequently summarise the key knowledge you need • We test what you've learnt by providing questions and quizzes throughout our Text

Our other products

BPP Learning Media also offers these products for the F1 and Operational integrated case study exams:

i-Pass	Providing computer-based testing in a variety of formats, ideal for self-assessment
Exam practice Kit	Providing helpful guidance on how to pass the objective test and more question practice
Passcards	Summarising what you should know in visual, easy to remember, form
Integrated case study Kit	Providing help with exam skills and question practice for the integrated case study exam

You can purchase these products by visiting www.bpp.com/cimamaterials

CIMA Distance Learning

BPP's distance learning packages provide flexibility and convenience, allowing you to study effectively, at a pace that suits you, where and when you choose.

Online classroom live	Through live interactive online sessions it provides you with the traditional structure and support of classroom learning, but with the convenience of attending classes wherever you are
Online classroom	Through pre-recorded online lectures it provides you with the classroom experience via the web with the tutor guidance & support you'd expect from a face to face classroom

You can find out more about these packages by visiting www.bpp.com/cima

Features in our Study Text

Chapter Overview Diagrams illustrate the connections between the topic areas you are about to cover

 Section Introductions explain how the section fits into the chapter

 Key Terms are the core vocabulary you need to learn

KEY TERM

 Key Points are points that you have to know, ideas or calculations that will be the foundations of your answers

KEY POINT

 Exam Alerts show you how subjects are likely to be tested

 Exam Skills are the key skills you will need to demonstrate in the exam, linked to question requirements

 Exam formulae are formulae you will be given in the exam

EXAM

 Examples show how theory is put into practice

 Questions give you the practice you need to test your understanding of what you've learnt

 Case Studies link what you've learnt with the real-world business environment

CASE STUDY

 Links show how the syllabus overlaps with other parts of the qualification, including Knowledge Brought Forward that you need to remember from previous exams

 Website References link to material that will enhance your understanding of what you're studying

 Further Reading will give you a wider perspective on the subjects you're covering

Chapter Summary Diagrams allow you to review each Chapter

Streamlined studying

What you should do	In order to
Read the Chapter and Section Introductions and look at the Chapter Overview diagram	See why topics need to be studied and map your way through the chapter
Go quickly through the explanations	Gain the depth of knowledge and understanding that you'll need
Highlight the Key Points, Key Terms and Formulae To Learn	Make sure you know the basics that you can't do without in the exam
Focus on the Exam Skills and Exam Alerts	Know how you'll be tested and what you'll have to do
Work through the Examples and Case Studies	See how what you've learnt applies in practice
Prepare Answers to the Questions	See if you can apply what you've learnt in practice
Review the Chapter Summary Diagram	Remind you of, and reinforce, what you've learnt
Answer the Quick Quiz	Find out if there are any gaps in your knowledge
Answer the Questions in the OTQ Question Bank and the Practice Question Bank	Practise what you've learnt in depth

Should I take notes?

Brief notes may help you remember what you're learning. You should use the notes format that's most helpful to you (lists, diagrams, mindmaps).

Further help

BPP Learning Media's *Learning to Learn Accountancy* provides lots more helpful guidance on studying. It is designed to be used both at the outset of your CIMA studies and throughout the process of learning accountancy. It can help you **focus your studies on the subject and exam**, enabling you to **acquire knowledge, practise and revise efficiently and effectively**.

Syllabus and learning outcomes

Paper F1 Financial Reporting and Taxation

The syllabus comprises:

Topic and Study Weighting

		%
A	Regulatory environment for financial reporting and corporate governance	10
B	Financial accounting and reporting	45
C	Management of working capital, cash and sources of short-term finance	20
D	Fundamentals of business taxation	25

Learning outcomes		
Lead	**Component**	**Indicative syllabus content**
A Regulatory Environment for Financial Reporting and Corporate Governance (10%)		
1. Explain the need for and the process of regulating the financial reporting information of incorporated entities.	(a) Explain the need for the regulation of the financial reporting information of incorporated entities and the key elements of an ethical regulatory environment for such information	(i) The need for the regulation of financial reporting information. (ii) Key elements of the regulatory environment for financial reporting including local corporate law, local and international conceptual frameworks, local and international financial reporting standards and other regulatory bodies. (iii) Sources of professional codes of ethics. (iv) Provisions of the CIMA Code of Ethics for Professional Accountants of particular relevance to the preparation of financial reporting information. (v) Rules-based versus principles-based approaches to accounting regulation.
	(b) Explain the roles and structures of the key bodies involved in the regulation of financial reporting information	(i) Role and structure of: • The IFRS Foundation. • The International Accounting Standards Board (IASB). • IFRS Advisory Council. • IFRS Interpretations Committee. • International Organisation of Securities Commissions (IOSCO).

Learning outcomes		
Lead	**Component**	**Indicative syllabus content**
	(c) Explain the scope of International Financial Reporting Standards and how they are developed	(i) Interaction of local GAAP bodies with the IASB.
		(ii) *Scope of specific standards in specialised circumstances – IAS 26 Accounting and Reporting by Retirement Benefit Plans, IAS 41 Agriculture, IFRS4 Insurance Contracts, IFRS6 Exploration for and Evaluation of Mineral Resources and IFRS for SMEs (specific knowledge of these standards will not be tested).*
		(iii) The standard setting process for IFRS.
	(d) Describe the role of the external auditor in the context of the financial reporting information of incorporated entities and the content and significance of the audit report	(i) Powers and duties of external auditors.
		(ii) Content of the audit report.
		(iii) Types of audit report.
		(iv) Significance of the audit report.
2. Discuss the need for and key principles of corporate governance regulation.	(a) Discuss the need for and scope of corporate governance regulation	(i) The need for corporate governance regulation.
		(ii) Scope of corporate governance regulation.
	(b) Compare and contrast the approach to corporate governance in different markets	(i) Approach to corporate governance regulations in primary markets around the world, in particular the US and UK.
		(ii) Key differences in approach across these markets
B Financial Accounting and Reporting (45%)		
1. Explain the main elements of and key principles underpinning financial statements prepared in accordance with international financial reporting standards.	(a) Describe the main elements of financial statements prepared in accordance with IFRS	(i) Content of financial statements as specified in: • *preface to IFRS* • *IAS 1 Presentation of Financial Reporting* • *IAS 8 Accounting Policies, Changes in Accounting Estimates and Errors* • *IAS 34 Interim Financial Reporting* • *IFRS 8 Operating Segments.*
	(b) Explain the key principles contained within the IASB's Conceptual Framework for Financial Reporting	(i) Key principles of the Conceptual Framework for Financial Reporting.
		(ii) Broad principles of accounting for fair values (contained in IFRS13 Fair Value Measurement).

Learning outcomes		
Lead	**Component**	**Indicative syllabus content**
2. Produce the primary financial statements of an individual entity incorporating accounting transactions and adjustments, in accordance with relevant international financial reporting standards, in an ethical manner.	(a) Produce the primary financial statements from trial balance for an individual entity, in accordance with International Financial Reporting Standards	(i) Production of the: • statement of financial position • statement of comprehensive income • statement of changes in equity • statement of cash flows for a single incorporated entity in accordance with *IAS 1 Presentation of Financial Reporting* and *IAS7 Statement of Cash Flows.*
	(b) Apply the rules contained in International Financial Reporting Standards to generate appropriate accounting entries in respect of reporting performance, accounting for taxation, employee benefits, non-current assets, accounting for government grants, impairment, inventories and events after the reporting period	(i) Reporting performance – *IFRS 5 Non-current Assets Held for Sale and Discontinued Operations and IAS21 The Effects of Changes in Foreign Exchange Rates* (individual transactions only). (ii) Accounting for taxation – *IAS 12 Income Taxes (not deferred tax).* (iii) Employee benefits – *IAS 19 Employee Benefits.* (iv) Non-current assets – *IAS 16 Property, Plant and Equipment, IAS 23 Borrowing Costs, IAS 38 Intangible Assets, IAS 40 Investment Property,* and *IFRS 5 Non-current Assets Held for Sales and Discontinued Operations.* (v) Accounting for government grants – *IAS 20 Accounting for Government Grants and Disclosure of Government Assistance.* (vi) Impairment – *IAS 36 Impairment of Assets.* (vii) Inventories – *IAS 2 Inventories.* (viii)Events after the reporting period – *IAS 10 Events after the Reporting Period.*

Learning outcomes		
Lead	**Component**	**Indicative syllabus content**
	(c) Discuss the ethical selection and adoption of relevant accounting policies and accounting estimates	(i) Ethics in financial reporting in respect of selection and adoption of accounting policies and estimates.
3. Produce the consolidated statement of financial position and consolidated statement of comprehensive income in accordance with relevant international financial reporting standards, in an ethical manner.	(a) Explain whether an investment in another entity constitutes a subsidiary or an associate relationship in accordance with relevant International Financial Reporting Standards	(i) Provisions of *IFRS 10 Consolidated Financial Statements* and *IAS 28 Investments in Associates* in respect of power to control and significant influence.
	(b) Explain situations where a parent entity is exempt from preparing consolidated financial statements	(i) Exemptions from preparing consolidated financial statements, in accordance with *IFRS 10 Consolidated Financial Statements* and the requirements of *IAS 27 Separate Financial Statements.*
	(c) Produce the consolidated statement of financial position and statement of comprehensive income in accordance with relevant International Financial Reporting Standards for a group comprising one or more subsidiaries (being either wholly or partially directly owned) or associates, including interests acquired part way through an accounting period	(i) Principles of full consolidation and equity accounting in accordance with *IFRS 3 Business Combinations and IAS 28 Investments in Associates.* (ii) Production of: • consolidated statement of financial position • consolidated statement of comprehensive income. (iii) Including the adoption of both full consolidation and the principles of equity accounting, in accordance with the provisions of *IAS 1 Presentation of Financial Statements, IAS 28 Investments in Associates, IFRS3 Business Combinations and IFRS 10 Consolidated Financial Statements. Note: fair value adjustments in respect of assets and liabilities at acquisition will not be tested, however non-controlling interests at either fair value or share of net assets will be tested.*

Learning Outcomes

Lead	Component	Syllabus content
C Management of Working Capital, Cash and Sources of Short-term Finance (20%)		
1. Describe the sources of short-term finance and cash investment.	(a) Describe the sources of short term finance and methods of short-term cash investment available to an entity	(i) Types of short-term finance including trade payables, overdrafts, short-term loans and debt factoring. (ii) Types of cash investment including interest-bearing deposits, short-term treasury bills and other securities.
2. Evaluate the working capital position of an entity.	(a) Analyse trade receivables, trade payables and inventory ratios	(i) Calculation of trade receivable, trade payable and inventory days. (ii) Interpretation of the ratios either in comparison to prior periods, competitors or to the industry as a whole, taking into account the nature of the industry.
	(b) Discuss policies for the management of the total level of investment in working capital and for the individual elements of working capital	(i) Working capital cycle. (ii) Policies for the management of the total level of investment in working capital – aggressive, moderate and conservative. (iii) Methods of trade receivables management, including credit control procedures. (iv) Methods of trade payables management and significance of trade payables as a source of finance and how this affects the relationship with suppliers. (v) Methods of inventory management, including calculations of the economic order quantity (EOQ).
	(c) Evaluate working capital policies	(i) Financial impact of changing working capital policies. (ii) Impact and risks of overtrading. (iii) Identification of areas for improvement.
	(d) Discuss approaches to the financing of working capital investment levels	(i) Approaches to the financing of the investment in working capital – aggressive, moderate and conservative.
3. Analyse the short-term cash position of an entity.	(a) Discuss measures to manage the short-term cash position of an entity	(i) Preparation of short-term cash flow forecasts. (ii) Identification of surpluses or deficits from cash flow forecasts. (iii) Selection of appropriate short-term solutions. (iv) Principles of investing short term including maturity, return, security and liquidity.

Learning Outcomes		
Lead	Component	Syllabus content
1. Discuss the types of taxation that typically apply to an incorporated entity and the regulatory environment for taxation.	(a) Discuss the features of the types of indirect and direct taxation that typically apply to an incorporated entity	(i) Definitions of direct taxation, indirect taxation, taxable person, incidence and competent jurisdiction.
		(ii) Types of taxation – progressive, proportional and regressive.
		(ii) Features of the following types of indirect taxation: • unit taxes • ad valorem taxes • excise duties • property and wealth taxes • consumption taxes • mechanism of value added tax in the context of an incorporated entity.
		(iv) Features of the following types of direct taxation: • tax on trading income • capital taxes.
		(v) Impact of employee taxation.
	(b) Discuss the regulatory environment for taxation, including the distinction between tax evasion and tax avoidance.	(i) Sources of taxation rules such as domestic legislation, court rulings, domestic interpretations and guidelines, EU guidelines and taxation agreements between different countries.
		(ii) Administration of taxation including the principles of record keeping, deadlines and penalties.
		(iii) Powers of taxation authorities.
		(iv) Distinction between tax evasion and tax avoidance and the ethical considerations faced by an entity in respect of tax avoidance.

Learning Outcomes		
Lead	**Component**	**Syllabus content**
2. Explain the taxation issues that may apply to an incorporated entity that operates internationally.	(a) Explain the taxation issues that may apply to an incorporated entity that operates internationally	(i) International taxation issues: • the concept of corporate residence and the key bases of determining residence • types of overseas operations: subsidiary or branch and the implications of each on taxation • issue of double taxation and the methods of gaining relief • types of foreign taxation and the distinction between withholding tax and underlying tax (calculations will not be tested) • transfer pricing and related, ethical and taxation issues.
3. Produce computations for corporate income tax and capital tax.	(a) Produce corporate income tax computations from a given set of rules	(i) Distinction between accounting profit and taxable profit and the reconciliation between them. This will include (based upon a set of rules given in the examination): • identification and treatment of exempt income or income taxed under different rules • identification and treatment of disallowable expenditure • replacement of accounting depreciation with tax depreciation • calculation of tax depreciation allowances • calculation of corporate income tax liability • relief for trading losses.
	(b) Produce capital gains tax computations from a given set of rules	(i) Principle of a capital tax computation on the sale of an asset. (ii) Allowable costs. (iii) Methods of relieving capital losses. (iv) Concept of rollover relief.

Studying F1

1 What's F1 about

F1 covers the **regulation and preparation of financial statements** and how the information contained in them can be used.

It provides the competencies required to produce financial statements for both individual entities and groups using appropriate international financial reporting standards. It also gives insight into how to effectively **source and manage cash and working capital**, which are essential for both the survival and success of organisations.

The final part focuses on the **basic principles and application of business taxation**.

The competencies gained from F1 form the basis for developing further insights into producing and analysing complex group accounts (covered in F2) and formulating and implementing financial strategy (covered in F3).

Aims

The syllabus aims to test the student's ability to:

- Explain the need for and the process of regulating the financial reporting information of incorporated entities

- Discuss the need for and key principles of corporate governance regulation

- Explain the main elements of and key principles underpinning financial statements prepared in accordance with International Financial Reporting Standards

- Produce the primary financial statements of an individual entity incorporating accounting transactions and adjustments, in accordance with relevant International Financial Reporting Standards, in an ethical manner

- Produce the consolidated statement of financial position and consolidated statement of comprehensive income in accordance with relevant International Financial Reporting Standards, in an ethical manner

- Describe the sources of short-term finance and cash investment

- Evaluate the working capital position of an entity

- Analyse the short-term cash position of an entity

- Discuss the types of taxation that typically apply to an incorporated entity and the regulatory environment for taxation

- Explain the taxation issues that may apply to an incorporated entity that operates internationally

- Produce computations for corporate income tax and capital tax

Links with other papers

F1 – Financial Reporting and Taxation is the first paper in the Financial Pillar. It feeds into F2 – Advanced Financial Reporting, and introduces students to some of the key financial accounting techniques they will return to in their Strategic Level studies.

The paper draws on many of the basic techniques covered in the Certificate Level C2 paper, Financial Accounting Fundamentals, such as double entry, tangible non-current assets, inventory and company transactions such as the issue of shares.

2 What's required

2.1 Explanation

As well as testing your knowledge and understanding in the Integrated Case Study (ICS), you are asked to demonstrate the skill of explaining key ideas, techniques or approaches. Explaining means providing simple definitions and covering the reasons **why** these approaches have been developed. You'll gain higher marks if your explanations are clearly focused on the question and you can supplement your explanations with examples. You could try using the PEA approach. Point, Explain, Apply. Make your point in a sentence. Explain that point in another sentence by answering the reader's 'so what?' or 'why?'. Then apply it to the scenario so that your point relates to the organisation or specific situation in the question.

2.2 Interpretation and recommendation

You will probably have to interpret the results of calculations in the ICS. You must understand that interpretation isn't just saying figures have increased or decreased. It means explaining **why** figures have changed and also the consequences of the changes. You will also have to provide recommendations.

3 How to pass

3.1 Study the whole syllabus

You need to be comfortable with **all areas of the syllabus,** as questions in the objective test exam will cover all syllabus areas. **Wider reading** will help you understand the main risks businesses face, which will be particularly useful in the integrated case study exam.

3.2 Lots of question practice

You can **develop application skills** by attempting questions in the Practise Question Bank. While these might not be in the format that you will experience in your exam, doing the questions will enable you to answer the exam questions.

However, you should practice OT exam standard questions, which you will find in the BPP Exam Practice Kit.

4 Brought forward knowledge

The examiner may test knowledge or techniques you've learnt at lower levels. CIMA C02 *Fundamentals of Financial Accounting* are particularly important for this paper.

5 The Integrated Case Study and Links with E1 and P1

The integrated case study exam is based on the expectation that students are developing a pool of knowledge. When faced with a problem students can appropriately apply their knowledge from any syllabus. Students will avoid a historical problem of partitioning their knowledge and accessing, for example, their knowledge of IFRS only when faced with a set of financial statements.

6 What the examiner means

The table below has been prepared by CIMA to help you interpret the syllabus and learning outcomes and the meaning of questions.

You will see that there are 5 levels of Learning objective, ranging from Knowledge to Evaluation, reflecting the level of skill you will be expected to demonstrate. CIMA Certificate subjects only use levels 1 to 3, but in CIMA's Professional qualification the entire hierarchy will be used.

At the start of each chapter in your study text is a topic list relating the coverage in the chapter to the level of skill you may be called on to demonstrate in the exam.

Learning objectives	Verbs used	Definition
1 Knowledge What are you expected to know	• List • State • Define	• Make a list of • Express, fully or clearly, the details of/facts of • Give the exact meaning of
2 Comprehension What you are expected to understand	• Describe • Distinguish • Explain • Identify • Illustrate	• Communicate the key features of • Highlight the differences between • Make clear or intelligible/state the meaning or purpose of • Recognise, establish or select after consideration • Use an example to describe or explain something
3 Application How you are expected to apply your knowledge	• Apply • Calculate/ compute • Demonstrate • Prepare • Reconcile • Solve • Tabulate	• Put to practical use • Ascertain or reckon mathematically • Prove with certainty or to exhibit by practical means • Make or get ready for use • Make or prove consistent/compatible • Find an answer to • Arrange in a table
4 Analysis How you are expected to analyse the detail of what you have learned	• Analyse • Categorise • Compare and contrast • Construct • Discuss • Interpret • Prioritise • Produce	• Examine in detail the structure of • Place into a defined class or division • Show the similarities and/or differences between • Build up or compile • Examine in detail by argument • Translate into intelligible or familiar terms • Place in order of priority or sequence for action • Create or bring into existence
5 Evaluation How you are expected to use your learning to evaluate, make decisions or recommendations	• Advise • Evaluate • Recommend	• Counsel, inform or notify • Appraise or assess the value of • Propose a course of action

Competency Framework

CIMA has developed a competency framework detailing the skills, abilities and competencies that finance professionals need. The CIMA syllabus has been developed to match the competency mix as it develops over the three levels of the professional qualification. The importance of the various competencies at the operational level is shown below.

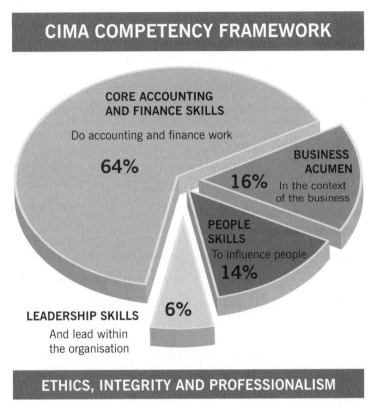

CIMA COMPETENCY FRAMEWORK

CORE ACCOUNTING
AND FINANCE SKILLS

Do accounting and finance work

64%

BUSINESS
ACUMEN
16% In the context
of the business

PEOPLE
SKILLS
To influence people
14%

LEADERSHIP SKILLS **6%**
And lead within
the organisation

ETHICS, INTEGRITY AND PROFESSIONALISM

OPERATIONAL LEVEL

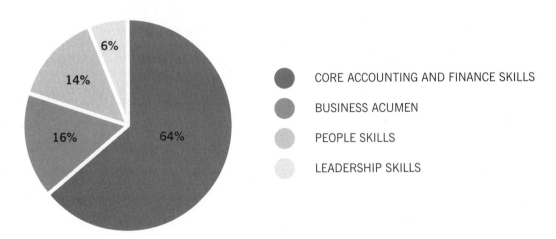

- CORE ACCOUNTING AND FINANCE SKILLS
- BUSINESS ACUMEN
- PEOPLE SKILLS
- LEADERSHIP SKILLS

Assessment

The CIMA assessment is a two-tier structure with objective tests for each subject and an integrated case study at each level.

Objective test

The objective tests are computer based and can be taken on demand. The student exam preparation on the CIMA website has additional information and tools to help you become familiar with the test style. Make sure you check back regularly as more information may be added.

The web link is: http://www.cimaglobal.com/Students/2015-syllabus/Assessment/

The objective tests will test all levels in the CIMA hierarchy of verbs.

Integrated case study

Candidates must pass or receive exemptions from the three objective tests at each level, before attempting the integrated case study exam for that level.

The integrated case studies are available four times a year.

The integrated case study exams combine the knowledge and learning from all the pillars. They will be set in the context of a preseen fictional organisation based on a real business or industry.

REGULATORY ENVIRONMENT FOR FINANCIAL REPORTING AND CORPORATE GOVERNANCE

Part A

REGULATION AND CORPORATE GOVERNANCE

 Accounting is regulated by local statute (such as company law), by Stock Exchange requirements and by accounting standards.

In this chapter we first examine the role of the International Accounting Standards Board (IASB), the development of International Financial Reporting Standards and some criticism of the IASB.

We also look at corporate governance and consider some of the approaches to providing guidance on this issue.

topic list	learning outcomes	syllabus references
1 The need for regulation	A1	A1 (a)
2 The need for a regulatory framework	A1	A1 (a)
3 The International Accounting Standards Board (IASB)	A1	A1 (b)
4 Setting of International Financial Reporting Standards	A1	A1 (c)
5 Progress towards global harmonisation	A1	A1 (c)
6 Conceptual framework and GAAP	A1	A1 (c)
7 Corporate governance	A2	A2 (a) (b)

Chapter Overview

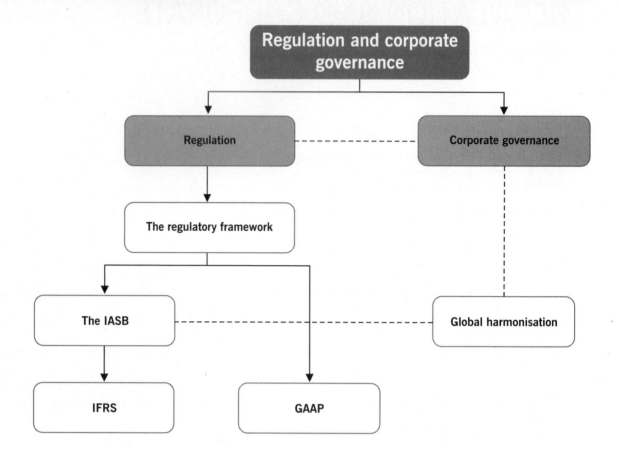

1 The need for regulation

Introduction

In this section we consider the need for regulation of financial reporting.

1.1 The need for regulation

The purpose of financial statements is to provide useful information about the performance and financial position of an entity. Accounting regulations ensure that financial statements actually do provide useful information.

(a) Users of the financial statements need to be able to compare the financial statements of different entities and financial statements of the same entity over time. If preparers of financial statements were able to adopt whatever accounting practices they chose it would be impossible to do this in any meaningful way.

(b) Managers normally wish to show the performance of a company in the best possible light. Without regulation, information might be deliberately presented in such a way as to mislead users.

(c) The owners or providers of finance to a company are often external to the company and separate from its management. They depend on financial statements for information about a company's performance and position. Accounting regulations ensure that the financial statements provide all the information that users need in order to make decisions.

1.1.1 Sources of regulation

In most countries, accounting is regulated by local statute (such as company law), by local stock exchange requirements and by accounting standards. However, different social, political, economic or legal pressures in each country have led to variations in accounting practice.

The main pressures come from:

(a) **National company law** such as the UK Companies Act. Accounting regulations can be codified in law and companies must comply with the legal requirements.

(b) **National accounting standards**. Many countries have their own local standards. In the UK, entities which are not listed can apply UK standards.

(c) **Tax laws**. Some countries accounting requirements are driven by what is required for tax purposes, so accounting profit largely mirrors taxable profit.

(d) **Sources of finance and capital markets**. There is a greater demand for information and disclosure when finance is raised from external sources such as shareholders. Local stock exchange regulations may also specify certain information that has to be disclosed.

(e) **Cultural differences**. The culture of a country and the values that society has can have an influence on accounting regulations and disclosures required by entities.

1.1.2 The need for harmonisation of accounting standards

Businesses increasingly operate across national boundaries and users need to be able to make comparisons between the financial statements of entities located in different countries. It follows that there is a need for a 'common language' of accounting practice, so that all companies throughout the world follow broadly similar accounting regulations. This is known as harmonisation of accounting standards.

Question 1.1   International harmonisation

Learning outcome A1

In accounting terms what do you think are:

(a)   The advantages to international harmonisation?

(b)   The barriers to international harmonisation?

There is a difference between **harmonisation** of accounting standards, which tends to mean increasing the compatibility of accounting practices eg by basing accounting standards on a common underlying set of principles, and **standardisation** of accounting standards, which tends to mean imposing a rigid and narrow set of rules. Given the differences that exist in accounting standards across the world, harmonisation is more likely to happen than standardisation on an international level.

1.2 International accounting standards

The CIMA F1 syllabus focuses on International Financial Reporting Standards (IFRSs), which are produced by the International Accounting Standards Board (IASB). IFRSs have gone a long way in helping to harmonise accounting standards across the globe as we will see later in this chapter.

2   The need for a regulatory framework

Introduction

The regulatory framework is the most important element in ensuring relevant and faithfully presented financial information and thus meeting the needs of shareholders and other users.

Without a single body overall responsible for producing financial reporting standards (the IASB) and a framework of general principles within which they can be produced (the *Conceptual Framework*), there would be no means of enforcing compliance with Generally Accepted Accounting Practice (GAAP). Also, GAAP would be unable to evolve in any structured way in response to changes in economic conditions

2.1 Principles-based versus rules-based systems

KEY POINT

A principles-based system works within a set of laid down principles. A rules-based system regulates for issues as they arise. Both of these have advantages and disadvantages.

The *Conceptual Framework* provides the background of principles within which standards can be developed. This system is intended to ensure that standards are not produced which are in conflict with each other and also that any departure from a standard can be judged on the basis of whether or not it is in keeping with the principles set out in the *Conceptual Framework*. This is a **principles-based** system.

In the absence of a reporting framework, a more **rules-based** approach has to be adopted. This leads to a large mass of regulation designed to cover every eventuality, as in the US. As we have seen over the past few years, a large volume of regulatory measures does not always detect or prevent financial irregularity. One presumed advantage of rules-based systems is that the exercise of judgement is minimised. Auditors who fear litigation tend to prefer rules-based systems. It could be that a rules-based approach is appropriate for controversial areas in accounting.

Section summary

In order to provide useful information the preparation of financial statements needs to be regulated through the use of accounting standards.

3 The International Accounting Standards Board (IASB)

Introduction

In this section we cover the role and structure of the IASB.

3.1 The IASB

The **International Accounting Standards Board (IASB)** is an independent, privately funded body based in London. From April 2001 the IASB assumed accounting standard setting responsibilities from its predecessor body, the International Accounting Standards Committee (IASC).

KEY POINT

The IASB adopted the 41 International Accounting Standards (IASs) issued by its predecessor body, the IASC. All new standards issued by the IASB are now called International Financial Reporting Standards (IFRSs). The term 'IFRSs' is commonly used to refer to all international standards in issue, which currently comprises 41 IASs and 13 IFRSs.

The IASB has complete responsibility for all technical matters concerning IFRSs, including the development and publication of IFRSs, exposure drafts and discussion papers, withdrawal of IFRSs and final approval of interpretations issued by the IFRS Interpretations Committee.

The members of the IASB come from nine countries and have a variety of backgrounds with a mix of auditors, preparers of financial statements, users of financial statements and an academic.

The IASB operates under the oversight of the **IFRS Foundation**.

3.2 The IFRS Foundation

The IFRS Foundation was known as the IASC Foundation until its name was changed in 2010. In March 2001 the IASC Foundation was formed as a not-for-profit corporation incorporated in the USA.

The structure of the IFRS Foundation and related bodies is shown below.

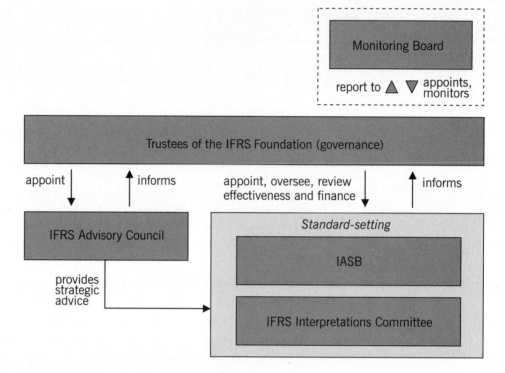

The formal objectives of the IFRS Foundation are to:

(a)   Develop a single set of high quality, understandable, enforceable and globally accepted
       international financial reporting standards (IFRSs) through its standard setting body, the IASB

(b)   Promote the use and rigorous application of those standards

(c)   Take account of the financial reporting needs of emerging economies and small and medium-sized
       entities

(d)   Bring about convergence of national accounting standards and IFRSs to high quality solutions

The IFRS Foundation is currently made up of 21 Trustees, who essentially monitor and fund the IASB, the
IFRS Advisory Council and the IFRS Interpretations Committee. The Trustees are appointed from a variety
of geographic and functional backgrounds.

The IFRS Foundation Trustees have a wide range of responsibilities, including the following.

(a)   Appointing the members of the IASB, the IFRS Advisory Council and the IFRS Interpretations
       Committee.

(b)   Reviewing annually the strategy of the IFRS Foundation and the IASB and its effectiveness.

(c)   Approving annually the budget of the IFRS Foundation and determine the basis for funding.

(d)   Reviewing broad strategic issues affecting financial reporting standards, promoting the IFRS
       Foundation and its work and promoting the objective of rigorous application of IFRSs.

(e)   Establishing and amending operating procedures, consultative arrangements and due process for
       the IASB, the IFRS Interpretations Committee and the IFRS Advisory Council.

3.2.1 The IFRS Advisory Council

The IFRS Advisory Council (formerly called the Standards Advisory Council or SAC) is essentially a forum
used by the IASB to consult with the outside world. Members are appointed by the Trustees and meet
three times a year.

The IFRS Advisory Council consults with national standard setters, academics, user groups and a host of
other interested parties and informs the IASB of their views on a range of issues.

The IASB consults the IFRS Advisory Council on:

- its technical agenda
- project issues related to application and implementation of IFRSs
- its project priorities
- possible benefits and costs of particular proposals

3.2.2 The IFRS Interpretations Committee

The IFRS Interpretations Committee (formerly called the International Financial Reporting Interpretations Committee or IFRIC) was set up in March 2002 and provides guidance on specific practical issues in the interpretation of IFRSs. (Note: despite the name change, interpretations issued by the IFRS Interpretations Committee are still known as *IFRIC Interpretations*.)

The IFRS Interpretations Committee assists the IASB by improving existing IFRSs. It was established in March 2002 to replace the Standards Interpretations Committee (SIC). Where before SIC Interpretations were issued, now **IFRIC Interpretations** are issued.

The IFRS Interpretations Committee has two main responsibilities:

- Review, on a timely basis, newly identified financial reporting issues not specifically addressed in IFRSs.

- Clarify issues where unsatisfactory or conflicting interpretations have developed, or seem likely to develop in the absence of authoritative guidance, with a view to reaching a consensus on the appropriate treatment.

The IFRS Interpretations Committee also helps the IASB move towards international harmonisation by working with its equivalent national-level bodies (such as the Urgent Issues Task Force, or UITF, in the UK).

The IFRS Interpretations Committee develops its interpretations through a due process of consultation and debate which includes making **Draft Interpretations** available for public comment. The IFRIC Interpretations that it makes publicly available are the consensus views that it has reached as a result of this process.

3.3 Benchmark and allowed alternative treatment

Many of the IASs produced by the old IASC allowed entities to make a choice between 'benchmark treatments' and 'allowed alternatives'. By contrast, the IASB has shifted the emphasis away from allowing entities a choice between accounting treatments, and is reconsidering all those IASs where choices are permitted. Its objective is either to reduce the number of options available to choose from, or to eliminate the element of choice altogether. This is in line with the IASB's emphasis on reporting like transactions and events in a like way, and reporting different transactions and events differently.

Section summary

The IASB is responsible for setting International Financial Reporting Standards (IFRSs).

4   Setting of International Financial Reporting Standards

Introduction

This section looks at the process of developing an IFRS and the impact this has on different countries.

4.1 IFRS due process

IFRSs are developed through an international due process that involves accountants, financial analysts and other users of financial statements, the business community, stock exchanges, regulatory and legal authorities, academics and other interested individuals and organisations from around the world. The IASB consults the IFRS Advisory Council in public meetings on major projects, agenda decisions and work priorities, and discusses technical matters in meetings that are open to public observation.

The overall agenda of the IASB will initially be set by discussion with the IFRS Advisory Council. The process for developing an individual standard generally involves the following steps.

 During the early stages of a project, the IASB may establish an **Advisory Committee** to give advice on issues arising in the project. Consultation with the Advisory Committee and the IFRS Advisory Council occurs throughout the project.

 The IASB may develop and publish **Discussion Papers** for public comment. These give an overview of the issues involved and possible ways to address the issues. The public are invited to comment on the views put forward.

 Following the receipt and review of comments, the IASB develops and publishes an **Exposure Draft** for public comment.

 Following the receipt and review of comments, the IASB issues a final International Financial Reporting Standard.

When the IASB issues a standard, it also issues a 'Basis for Conclusions' setting out how it reached the conclusions it did.

4.1.1 Comment periods

The IASB issues each Exposure Draft and Discussion Paper for public comment, with a normal comment period of 120 days. In certain circumstances, the IASB may expose proposals for a much shorter period. However, such limited periods would be used only in extreme circumstances. Draft IFRIC Interpretations are exposed for a 60-day comment period.

4.2 Co-ordination with national standard setters

Close co-ordination between the IASB due process and due process of national standard setters is important to the success of the IASB's mandate.

The IASB is exploring ways in which to integrate its due process more closely with national due process. Such integration may grow as the relationship between IASB and national standard setters evolves.

4.2.1 IASB liaison members

Seven of the full-time members of the IASB have formal liaison responsibilities with national standard setters in order to promote the convergence of national accounting standards and IFRSs. The IASB envisages a partnership between the IASB and these national standard setters as they work together to achieve convergence of accounting standards world-wide.

In addition all IASB members have contact responsibility with national standard setters not having liaison members and many countries are also represented on the IFRS Advisory Council.

4.3 Other international influences

4.3.1 European Commission (EC)

The EC regulations form one part of a broader programme for the harmonisation of company law in member states. The commission is uniquely the only organisation to produce international standards of accounting practice which are legally enforceable, in the form of directives which must be included in the national legislation of member states.

However, the EC has also acknowledged the role of the IASB in harmonising world-wide accounting rules.

Prior to the EC adoption of IFRSs in 2005 the IASB undertook an improvements project, dealing with revisions to IFRSs, for example in the area of materiality, presentation, leases, related parties and earnings per share. This has been matched in, for example, the UK, by a convergence project, bringing UK accounting standards into line with IFRSs where these are better.

4.3.2 International Organisation of Securities Commissions (IOSCO)

IOSCO is the representative of the world's securities markets regulators. IOSCO has been active in encouraging and promoting the improvement and quality of IFRSs over the last ten years. This commitment was evidenced by the agreement between IASC and IOSCO to work on a programme of 'core standards' which could be used by publicly listed entities when offering securities in foreign jurisdictions.

The 'core standards' project resulted in fifteen new or revised standards and was completed in 1999 with the issue of IAS 39 *Financial instruments: recognition and measurement.* IOSCO spent a year reviewing the results of the project and released a report in May 2000 which recommended to all its members that they allow multinational issuers to use IFRSs, as supplemented by reconciliation, disclosure and interpretation where necessary, to address outstanding substantive issues at a national or regional level.

IASB staff and IOSCO continue to work together to resolve outstanding issues and to identify areas where new IASB standards are needed.

4.3.3 Financial Accounting Standards Board (FASB)

The US standard setter, the FASB and the IASB have been undertaking a project of harmonisation between US accounting standards and IFRSs.

In September 2002, both parties acknowledged their commitment to the process of developing accounting standards that can be used for domestic and international purposes. Both the FASB and the IASB have worked together to make amendments to current accounting standards in the short term, and to work together on a long term basis to ensure new standards issued are compatible.

The IASB is currently involved in a joint project with the FASB to develop a common conceptual framework. This would provide a sound foundation for developing future accounting standards. The aim is that future standards should be principles based and internationally converged. This represents a movement away from the rules based approach which has characterised US accounting standards. The new framework will build upon the existing IASB and FASB frameworks and take into account subsequent developments.

The FASB is an important influence on the current and future work of the IASB.

4.4 Specialised industries

Accounting standards issued by the IASB are designed so that they can be applied in most circumstances. Some types of entity, however, are quite specialised in their activities and so the IASB has developed certain accounting standards which relate to these specialised sectors or industries.

These include:

(a)   IAS 26: *Accounting and Reporting by Retirement Benefit Plans*
(b)   IAS 41: *Agriculture*
(c)   IFRS 4: *Insurance Contracts*
(d)   IFRS 6: *Exploration for and Evaluation of Mineral Resources* and
(e)   *IFRS for SMEs* (small and medium entities).

Please note that the syllabus for CIMA F1 states that specific knowledge of these standards will not be tested.

Section summary

IFRSs are set in a similar manner to the previous setting of IASs in accordance with the IASB's due process.

5 Progress towards global harmonisation

Introduction

This section first looks at the arguments for and against having accounting standards, then moves on to consider the global effect of IFRSs and the progress towards global harmonisation of accounting standards.

5.1 Accounting standards and choice

It is sometimes argued that companies should be given a choice in matters of financial reporting on the grounds that accounting standards are detrimental to the quality of such reporting. There are arguments on both sides.

In favour of accounting standards (both national and international), the following points can be made.

*   They **reduce or eliminate confusing variations** in the methods used to prepare accounts.

*   They provide a **focal point for debate** and discussions about accounting practice.

*   They oblige companies to **disclose the accounting policies** used in the preparation of accounts.

*   They are a less rigid alternative to enforcing conformity by means of **legislation**.

*   They have obliged companies to **disclose more accounting information** than they would otherwise have done if accounting standards did not exist.

Many companies are reluctant to disclose information which is not required by national legislation. However, the following arguments may be put forward **against standardisation** and **in favour of choice**.

*   A set of rules which give backing to one method of preparing accounts might be **inappropriate in some circumstances**. For example, IAS 16 on depreciation is inappropriate for investment properties (properties not occupied by the entity but held solely for investment), which are covered by IAS 40 on investment property.

*   Standards may be subject to **lobbying or government pressure** (in the case of national standards). For example, in the USA, the accounting standard Financial Accounting Standard (FAS) 19 on the accounts of oil and gas companies led to a powerful lobby of oil companies, which persuaded the SEC (Securities and Exchange Commission) to step in. FAS 19 was then suspended.

*   Unlike IFRSs, many national standards are not based on a **conceptual framework of accounting**.

*   There may be a **trend towards rigidity**, and away from flexibility in applying the rules.

5.2 Criticisms of the IASB

Any international body, whatever its purpose or activity, faces enormous political difficulties in attempting to gain **international consensus** and the IASB is no exception to this. How can the IASB reconcile the financial reporting situation between economies as diverse as third-world developing countries and sophisticated first-world industrial powers?

Developing countries are suspicious of the IASB, believing it to be dominated by the **USA.** This arises because acceptance by the USA listing authority, the Securities and Exchange Commission (SEC), of IFRS is seen as the priority. For all practical purposes it is the American market which must be persuaded to accept IFRSs, and a lot of progress has now been made in this direction.

Developing countries have been catered for to some extent by the development of IAS 41 on **agriculture**, which is generally of much more relevance to such countries.

There are also tensions between the **UK/US model** of financial reporting and the **European model**. The UK/US model is based around investor reporting, whereas the European model is mainly concerned with tax rules, so shareholder reporting has a much lower priority.

The break-up of the former USSR and the move in many **Eastern European countries** to free-market economies has also created difficulties. It is likely that these countries will have to 'catch up' to international standards as their economies stabilise.

5.3 Global effect of IFRSs and the IASB

As far as Europe is concerned, the consolidated financial statements of many of Europe's top multinationals are already prepared in conformity with national requirements, European Commission (EC) directives and IFRSs. These developments have been given added impetus by the internationalisation of capital markets. IFRSs have been implemented in the European Union since 2005 for the consolidated financial statements of public listed companies.

In Japan, the influence of the IASB had, until recently, been negligible. This was mainly because of links in Japan between tax rules and financial reporting. The Japanese Ministry of Finance set up a working committee to consider whether to bring national requirements into line with IFRSs. The Tokyo Stock Exchange has announced that it will accept financial statements from foreign issuers that conform to home country standards, which would include IFRS.

The Japanese standpoint was widely seen as an attempt to attract foreign issuers, in particular companies from Hong Kong and Singapore. As these countries base their accounting on international standards, this action is therefore implicit acknowledgement by the Japanese Ministry of Finance of IFRS requirements. In December 2009 the Japanese FSA announced that Japanese listed companies would be allowed to use IFRS from 31 March 2010.

In the USA, the Securities and Exchange Commission (SEC) agreed in 1993 to allow foreign issuers (of shares, etc) to follow IFRS treatments on certain issues, including statements of cash flows under IAS 7. The overall effect is that, where an IFRS treatment differs from US GAAP, these treatments will now be acceptable.

In certain countries, the application of IFRSs is mandatory for all domestic listed companies. The following provides an example of some of the countries, but the schedule is not exhaustive: Barbados, Cyprus, Georgia, Jamaica, Jordan, Kenya, Kuwait, Malawi, Mauritius, Nepal, Peru, Serbia and Trinidad and Tobago.

Countries that implemented IFRSs for the 2005 European ruling in respect of the consolidated financial statements of public listed companies include Austria, Belgium, Czech Republic, Denmark, Estonia, Finland, France, Germany, Greece, Hungary, Iceland, Ireland, Italy, Liechtenstein, Lithuania, Luxembourg, Netherlands, Norway, Poland, Portugal, Slovenia, Slovak Republic, Spain, Sweden and the United Kingdom.

Many non-European counties also require their listed companies to adopt IFRSs. These include Australia, Bahamas, Bahrain, Chile, Costa Rica, Egypt, Hong Kong, Kenya, Kuwait, Mauritius, New Zealand, and South Africa.

There are some countries where the implementation of IFRSs is not mandatory but discretionary. These include Aruba, Bermuda, Bolivia, Cayman Islands, Dominica, El Salvador, Gibraltar, Laos, Lesotho, Swaziland, Switzerland, Turkey, Uganda and Zimbabwe.

However, there are several countries where the use of IFRSs is not currently permitted. The following are some of the countries, but the list is not exhaustive: Bangladesh, Cuba, Indonesia, Iran, Senegal, Taiwan, Thailand, Tunisia and Vietnam.

5.4 Approaches to implementation of IFRSs

There are generally three ways a country choosing to adopt international standards can go about it.

(a) **Adoption as local accounting standards**. Some countries choose to adopt IFRSs with little or no amendments for their particular countries.

(b) **Model for local accounting standards**. Other countries adopt IFRSs, but adapt them to suit local needs. This is the case in Australia.

(c) **Persuasive influence in formulating local accounting standards**. Some countries already had accounting standards which pre-dated IFRSs. Many of these countries have been working for may years to narrow the gap between their local standards and IFRSs. This is the case in the UK.

Section summary

In its attempt to formulate standards which are accepted internationally, the IASB has met opposition over various issues from companies, interest groups and countries.

Some progress has been made towards global harmonisation of accounting standards, with many countries, including EU member states, requiring mandatory use of IFRSs for listed entities.

6 Conceptual framework and GAAP

Introduction

In this section we introduce the idea of a conceptual framework.

6.1 The search for a conceptual framework

KEY TERM

A CONCEPTUAL FRAMEWORK in the field we are concerned with, is a statement of generally accepted theoretical principles which form the frame of reference for financial reporting.

These theoretical principles provide the basis for the development of new accounting standards and the evaluation of those already in existence. The financial reporting process is concerned with providing information that is useful in the business and economic decision-making process. Therefore a conceptual framework will form the **theoretical basis** for determining which events should be accounted for, how they should be measured and how they should be communicated to the user. Although it is theoretical in nature, a conceptual framework for financial reporting has highly practical final aims.

The **danger of not having a conceptual framework** is demonstrated in the way some countries' standards have developed over recent years; standards tend to be produced in a haphazard and fire-fighting

approach. Where an agreed framework exists, the standard-setting body act as an architect or designer, rather than a fire-fighter, building accounting rules on the foundation of sound, agreed basic principles.

The lack of a conceptual framework also means that fundamental principles are tackled **more than once** in different standards, thereby producing **contradictions and inconsistencies** in basic concepts, such as those of prudence and matching. This leads to ambiguity and it affects the true and fair concept of financial reporting.

Another problem with the lack of a conceptual framework has become apparent in the USA. The large number of **highly detailed standards** produced by the Financial Accounting Standards Board (FASB) has created a financial reporting environment governed by specific rules rather than general principles. This would be avoided if a cohesive set of principles were in place.

A conceptual framework can also bolster standard setters **against political pressure** from various 'lobby groups' and interested parties. Such pressure would only prevail if it was acceptable under the conceptual framework.

6.2 Advantages and disadvantages of a conceptual framework

6.2.1 Advantages

(a)   The situation is avoided whereby standards are developed on a patchwork basis, where a particular accounting problem is recognised as having emerged, and resources are then channelled into **standardising accounting practice** in that area, without regard to whether that particular issue was necessarily the most important issue remaining at that time without standardisation.

(b)   As stated above, the development of certain standards (particularly national standards) have been subject to considerable **political interference** from interested parties. Where there is a conflict of interest between user groups on which policies to choose, policies deriving from a conceptual framework will be **less open to criticism** that the standard-setter buckled to external pressure.

(c)   Some standards may concentrate on the **statement of profit or loss and other comprehensive income** whereas some may concentrate on the **valuation of net assets** (statement of financial position).

6.2.2 Disadvantages

(a)   Financial statements are intended for a **variety of users**, and it is not certain that a single conceptual framework can be devised which will suit all users.

(b)   Given the diversity of user requirements, there may be a need for a variety of accounting standards, each produced for a **different purpose** (and with different concepts as a basis).

(c)   It is not clear that a conceptual framework makes the task of **preparing and then implementing** standards any easier than without a framework.

Before we look at the IASB's attempt to produce a conceptual framework, we need to consider another term of importance to this debate: generally accepted accounting practice; or GAAP.

6.3 Generally Accepted Accounting Practice (GAAP)

KEY TERM

GAAP signifies all the rules, from whatever source, which govern accounting.

In individual countries this is seen primarily as a **combination** of:

- National company law
- National accounting standards
- Local stock exchange requirements

Although those sources are the basis for the GAAP of individual countries, the concept also includes the effects of **non-mandatory sources** such as IFRS or statutory requirements in other countries.

In many countries, like the UK, GAAP does not have any statutory or regulatory authority or definition, unlike other countries, such as the USA. The term is mentioned rarely in legislation, and only then in fairly limited terms.

There are different views of GAAP in different countries. The IASB convergence programme seeks to reduce these differences.

6.3.1 Rules based versus principles based GAAP

GAAP can be based on legislation and accounting standards that are either:

(a) Rules based, or
(b) Principles based

The USA operates a **rules based** system, where standards are very detailed, attempting to cover all eventualities. Accounts which do not comply in all details are presumed to be misleading. This has the advantage of clear requirements which can be generally understood and it removes any element of judgement. Other advantages of a prescriptive system are that it can be taught and learnt more easily, therefore it should ensure that similar items are treated in a similar way and it should be more obvious if a entity does not follow GAAP.

The IASB's *Conceptual Framework* is a **principles based** system which does not specify all the details but seeks to obtain adherence to the 'spirit' of the regulations. This does leave room for some element of professional judgement, but it also makes it harder for entities to avoid applying a standard as the terms of reference are broader. The *Conceptual Framework* is covered in Chapter 4.

Other advantages of having a principles based system include the following.

(a) Standards based on principles **don't go out of date** in the same way as those based on rules. For example if a prescriptive standard includes a list of common items that would qualify for specific treatment, the list may go out of date as economies progress and develop.

(b) It is more difficult for a company to **manipulate information** to avoid applying a standard based on principles than it is for a prescriptive standard.

(c) Standards based on principles are **less likely to contradict each other** than those based on rules as they are all based on the same basic principles.

(d) Standards based on rules require that many detailed standards covering all possible situations have to be produced. This can result in **complexity in financial reporting** as there are a considerable number of standards to be followed. Having standards based on principles avoids this.

6.3.2 GAAP and a conceptual framework

A conceptual framework for financial reporting can be defined as an attempt to codify existing GAAP in order to reappraise current accounting standards and to produce new standards.

 Section summary

A conceptual framework provides the basis for the formulation of accounting standards.

7 Corporate governance

7.1 Definitions of corporate governance

 Corporate governance, the system by which organisations are directed and controlled, is based on a number of concepts including transparency, independence, accountability and integrity.

KEY POINT

7.1.1 What is corporate governance?

KEY TERM

CORPORATE GOVERNANCE is the **system** by which organisations are directed and controlled. (Cadbury report)

CORPORATE GOVERNANCE is a **set of relationships** between a company's directors, its shareholders and other stakeholders. It also provides the structure through which the objectives of the company are set, and the means of achieving those objectives and monitoring performance, are determined. (OECD)

A number of comments can made about these definitions of corporate governance.

(a)   The **management, awareness, evaluation and mitigation of risk** are fundamental in all definitions of good governance. This includes the operation of an **adequate and appropriate system of control**.

(b)   The notion that **overall performance is enhanced** by **good supervision** and **management** within **set best practice guidelines** underpins most definitions.

(c)   Good governance provides a **framework** for an organisation to pursue its strategy in an **ethical and effective** way and **offers safeguards against misuse of resources**, human, financial, physical or intellectual.

(d)   Good governance is not just about externally established codes, it also requires a willingness to **apply the spirit** as well as the letter of the law.

(e)   Good corporate governance can **attract new investment** into companies, particularly in developing nations. It should mean that shareholders can **trust** those responsible for running and monitoring the company.

(f)   **Accountability** is generally a major theme in all governance frameworks, including accountability not just to shareholders but also other **stakeholders,** and accountability not just by directors but by auditors as well.

(g)   Corporate governance **underpins capital market confidence in companies** and in the government/regulators/tax authorities that administer them. It helps **protect the value of shareholders' investment.**

7.2 Corporate governance concepts

One view of governance is that it is based on a series of underlying concepts.

7.2.1 Fairness

The directors' deliberations and also the systems and values that underlie the company must be **balanced** by taking into account everyone who has a legitimate interest in the company, and respecting their rights and views. In many jurisdictions, corporate governance guidelines reinforce legal protection for certain groups, for example minority shareholders. It should mean the company deals **even-handedly** with others.

7.2.2 Transparency/openness

Transparency means **open and clear disclosure** of relevant information to shareholders and other stakeholders, also not concealing information when it may affect decisions. It means open discussions and a default position of information provision rather than concealment.

7.2.3 Independence

Independence is the avoidance of being unduly influenced by vested interests and being free from any constraints that would prevent a correct course of action being taken. It is an ability to stand apart from

inappropriate influences and be free of managerial capture, to be able to make the correct and uncontaminated decision on a given issue.

Independence is a quality that can be possessed by individuals and is an essential component of professionalism and professional behaviour.

An important distinction generally with independence is **independence of mind and independence of appearance**.

- **Independence of mind** means providing an opinion without being affected by influences compromising judgement

- **Independence of appearance** means avoiding situations where an informed third party could reasonably conclude that an individual's judgement would have been compromised

7.2.4 Probity/honesty

Hopefully this should be the most self-evident of the principles. It relates not only to telling the truth, but also not misleading shareholders and other stakeholders. Lack of probity includes not only obvious examples of dishonesty such as taking bribes, but also reporting information in a slanted way that is designed to give an unfair impression.

7.2.5 Responsibility

Responsibility means management accepting the credit or blame for governance decisions. It implies clear definition of the roles and responsibilities of the roles of senior management.

7.2.6 Accountability

Corporate **accountability** refers to whether an organisation (and its directors) is **answerable** in some way for the consequences of their actions.

Directors being answerable to shareholders have always been an important part of company law, well before the development of the corporate governance codes. For example companies in many regimes have been required to provide **financial information** to shareholders on an **annual basis** and hold **annual general meetings**. However, particularly because of the corporate governance scandals of the last 30 years, investors have demanded greater assurance that directors are acting in their interests. This has led to the development of corporate governance codes.

7.2.7 Reputation

Reputation is determined by how others view a person, organisation or profession. Reputation includes a reputation for **competence,** supplying good quality goods and services in a timely fashion, and also being managed in an orderly way. However a **poor ethical reputation** can be as serious for an organisation as a poor reputation for competence.

7.2.8 Judgement

Judgement means that the board **making decisions that enhance the prosperity** of the organisation. This means that board members must acquire a broad enough knowledge of the business and its environment to be able to provide meaningful direction to it. This has implications not only for the attention directors have to give to the organisation's affairs, but also the way the directors are recruited and trained.

7.2.9 Integrity

'**Integrity** means straightforward dealing and completeness. What is required of financial reporting is that it should be honest and that it should present a balanced picture of the state of the company's affairs. The integrity of reports depends on the integrity of those who prepare and present them.'   *(Cadbury report)*

'**Integrity** [means that] holders of public office should not place themselves under any financial or other obligation to outside individuals or organisations that might influence them in the performance of their official duties.'   *(UK Nolan Committee Standards on Public Life)*

Integrity can be taken as meaning someone of **high moral character**, who sticks to strict moral or ethical principles no matter the pressure to do otherwise. In working life this means adhering to the highest standards of professionalism and probity. **Straightforwardness, fair dealing and honesty in relationships** with the different people and constituencies whom you meet are particularly important. Trust is vital in relationships and belief in the integrity of those with whom you are dealing underpins this.

7.3 Basis of corporate governance guidance

KEY POINT

Globalisation, the **treatment of investors** and **major corporate scandals** have been major driving forces behind corporate governance developments.

Many governance codes have adopted a **principles-based approach** allowing companies flexibility in interpreting the codes' requirements and to explain if they have departed from the provisions of the code.

Insider systems are where listed companies are owned by a small number of major shareholders.

Outsider systems are where shareholdings are more widely dispersed, and the management-ownership split is more of an issue.

7.3.1 Principles or rules?

A continuing debate on corporate governance is whether the guidance should predominantly be in the form of principles, or whether there is a need for detailed laws or regulations.

UK guidance has generally suggested that a voluntary code coupled with disclosure would prove more effective than a statutory code in promoting the key principles of **openness, integrity and accountability**.

Nevertheless the UK guidance has also gone beyond broad principles and provided some specific guidelines. These have aimed to promote an **understanding of directors' responsibilities** and **openness about the ways they have been discharged**. Specific guidelines also help in **raising standards of financial reporting** and **business conduct,** aiming to remove the need for statutory regulation.

7.3.2 Characteristics of a principles-based approach

(a)   **Focus on aims**

The approach focuses on **objectives** (for example the objective that shareholders holding a minority of shares in a company should be treated fairly) rather than the **mechanisms** by which these objectives will be achieved. Possibly therefore principles are easier to integrate into strategic planning.

(b)   **Flexibility**

A principles-based approach can lay stress on those elements of corporate governance to which rules **cannot easily be applied**. These include overall areas such as the requirement to maintain sound systems of internal control, and 'softer' areas such as organisational culture and maintaining good relationships with shareholders and other stakeholders.

(c)   **Breadth of application**

Principles-based approaches can applied across **different legal jurisdictions** rather being founded in the legal regulations of one country. The OECD guidelines are a good example of guidance that is applied internationally.

(d)   **Comply or explain**

Where principles-based approaches have been established in the form of corporate governance codes, the specific recommendations that the codes make have been enforced on a **comply or explain basis**.

(e)   **Role of capital markets**

Principles-based approaches have often been adopted in jurisdictions where the governing bodies of **stock markets** have had the prime role in setting standards for companies to follow.

Listing rules include a requirement to comply with codes, but because the guidance is in a form of a code, companies have more flexibility than they would if the code was underpinned by legal requirements.

7.3.3 Characteristics of a rules-based approach

(a)   **Emphasis on achievements**

Rules-based systems place **more emphasis** on definite **achievements** rather than underlying factors and control systems. The European Union's Eco-Management and Audit Scheme (EMAS) is a good example of a system based on rules, with requirements for **targets to be set** and disclosure requirements of whether or not targets have been achieved. However there may be little incentive to **achieve more** than is required by the rules.

(b)   **Compulsory compliance**

Rules-based approaches allow no leeway. The key issue is whether or not you have **complied with the rules.** There is no flexibility for different circumstances, for organisations of varying size or in different stages of development.

(c)   **Visibility of compliance**

It should in theory be **easy to see** whether there has been compliance with the rules. Comparison between companies should be straightforward. However that depends on whether the rules are **unambiguous**, and the **clarity of evidence** of compliance or non-compliance.

(d)   **Limitations of rules**

Enforcers of a rules-based approach (regulators, auditors) may find it difficult to deal with **questionable situations** that are not covered sufficiently in the rulebook. This was a problem with Enron. The company kept a number of its financial arrangements off its balance sheet. Although this approach can be seen as not true and fair, Enron could use it because it did not breach the accounting rules then in existence in America. Keeping legislation up-to-date to keep loopholes closed is a reactive and probably costly process.

(e)   **Criminal sanctions**

Rules-based approaches to corporate governance tend to be found in legal jurisdictions and culture that lay great emphasis on **obeying the letter of the law** rather than the spirit. Serious breaches will be penalised by criminal sanctions. They often take the form of legislation themselves, notably the Sarbanes-Oxley Act. The amount of legislation for businesses in these jurisdictions may give rise to **significant compliance costs**.

7.4 Corporate governance codes

7.4.1 The Cadbury report

The Cadbury committee in the UK was set up because of the perceived lack of confidence in financial reporting and in the ability of auditors to provide the independent assurances required by the users of financial statements. The main difficulties were considered to be in the relationship between **auditors and boards of directors**. In particular, the commercial burdens on both directors and auditors caused pressure to be brought to bear on auditors by the board, and the auditors often capitulated. Problems were also perceived in the ability of the board of directors to control their organisations.

(a) **Corporate governance responsibilities**

The roles of those concerned with the financial statements are described in the Cadbury report, published in 1992.

(i) The **directors** are responsible for the corporate governance of the company and for producing the financial statements.

(ii) The **shareholders** are linked to the directors via the financial reporting system. The financial statements are addressed directly to the shareholders.

(iii) The **auditors** provide the shareholders with an external objective check on the directors' financial statements.

(iv) Other concerned **users**, particularly employees (to whom the directors owe some responsibility) are indirectly addressed by the financial statements.

(b) **Code of Best Practice**

The **Code of Best Practice** included in the Cadbury report and subsequently amended by later reports was aimed at the directors of all UK public companies, but the directors of all companies were encouraged to use the Code.

7.4.2 The Greenbury code

In 1995, the **Greenbury committee** published a code which established principles for the determination of **directors' pay** and detailing disclosures to be made in the annual reports and accounts.

7.4.3 The Hampel report

The **Hampel committee** followed up in 1998 matters raised in the Cadbury and Greenbury reports, aiming to restrict the regulatory burden on companies and substituting principles for detail whenever possible. Under Hampel:

(a) The accounts should contain a **statement** of how the company applies the corporate governance principles.

(b) The accounts should **explain their policies**, including any circumstances justifying departure from best practice.

7.4.4 Combined Code and UK Corporate Governance Code

The London Stock Exchange subsequently issued a combined corporate governance code in 1998, which was derived from the recommendations of the Cadbury, Greenbury and Hampel reports.

Since the publication of the Combined Code a number of reports in the UK have been published about specific aspects of corporate governance.

- The **Turnbull report** (1999, revised 2005) focused on risk management and internal control.
- The **Smith report** (2003) discussed the role of audit committees.
- The **Higgs report** (2003) focused on the role of the non-executive director.

The Combined Code was revised a number of times after its original publication in 1998. The May 2010 revision changed the name of the code to the **UK Corporate Governance Code**.

The main provisions as of 2012 can be summarised as follows:

UK Corporate Governance Code 2012

A Leadership

A1 Role of the board

All listed companies should be led by an **effective board**, responsible for providing **entrepreneurial leadership**, within a **framework of prudent** and **effective controls**, enabling **risk to be assessed** and **managed**. The board is responsible for setting strategic aims, ensuring sufficient resources are available, setting values and standards and ensuring obligations to shareholders. The board should **meet regularly**, with a **formal schedule of matters** reserved for it. The annual report should explain how the board operates, and give details of members and attendance.

A2 Division of responsibilities

A **clear division of responsibilities** should exist so that there is a balance of power, and no one person has unfettered powers of decision. The roles of **chairman** and **chief executive** should not be exercised by one person.

A3 The chairman

The chairman is responsible for leading the board and ensuring its effectiveness. The chairman should establish the board's agenda, and ensure there is **adequate time for discussion**, particularly of strategic matters. The chairman should promote **openness and debate**, help non-executive directors contribute effectively and promote constructive relations between executives and non-executives. The chairman should ensure that the board receives **accurate, timely and clear information** and should ensure communication with shareholders is effective. The chairman should meet the independence criteria for non-executive directors. A chief executive should not go on to become chairman.

A4 Non-executive directors

Non-executive directors should scrutinise management's performance and constructively challenge strategy. They should obtain assurance about the integrity of financial information and that financial controls and risk management systems are **robust** and **defensible**. Other important tasks include **determining executive remuneration** and playing a significant role in decisions about **board changes**. One of the independent non-executives should be appointed as senior independent director, to act as an intermediary with other directors and shareholders. The chairman should hold meetings with the non-executives without the executives being there, and the non-executives should meet without the chairman to appraise the chairman's performance. Directors should ensure that concerns they have that cannot be resolved are formally recorded.

B Effectiveness

B1 Composition of the board

The board and its committees should have a balance of **skills, experience, independence and knowledge** of the company. The board should be of sufficient size to **operate effectively**, but not so large as to be **unwieldy.** The board should have a **balance** of **executive and non-executive directors** so that no individual or small group is dominant. Decisions on committee membership should take into account the need to avoid undue reliance on particular individuals. At least half the board of FTSE 350 companies should be **independent non-executive directors**. Smaller listed companies should have at least **two independent non-executive directors**.

B2 Appointments to the board

There should be a **clear, formal procedure** for appointing new directors. A nomination committee should make recommendations about all new board appointments. The majority of members of this committee should be independent non-executives. Directors should be appointed **on merit**, against objective criteria, and considering the value of diversity, including gender diversity. The annual report should include a section on the board's policy on diversity and its success in achieving those policy objectives. There should be an **orderly succession process** in place.

B3 Commitment

Directors should allocate sufficient time to the company to **discharge their duties effectively**. In particular the nomination committee should assess the **time commitment expected** of the chairman, and the chairman's other commitments should be disclosed to the board and shareholders. Non-executives' letters of appointment should set out the expected time commitment and non-executives should undertake to have sufficient time to fulfil their responsibilities. Their other significant commitments should be disclosed to the board. A full time executive director should not take on more than one non-executive directorship of a FTSE 100 company, nor the chairmanship of a FTSE 100 company.

B4 Development

All directors should be properly inducted when they join the board and regularly update their skills and knowledge. The chairman should **agree training and development needs** with each director.

B5 Information and support

The board should be **promptly supplied** with **enough information** to enable it to carry out its duties. Information volunteered by management will sometimes need to be supplemented by information from other sources. The chairman and secretary should ensure good information flows. Directors should be able to obtain independent professional advice and have access to the services of the company secretary. The company secretary is responsible for **advising the chairman** on **all governance matters**. The whole board should be responsible for appointing and removing the company secretary.

B6 Evaluation

There should be a **vigorous annual performance evaluation** of the board as a whole, individual directors (effective contribution and commitment) and board committees. Evaluation of the board of FTSE 350 companies should be externally facilitated at **least once every three years**. The chairman should take action as a result of the review, if necessary proposing new board members or seeking the **resignation of directors**.

B7 Re-election

All directors should submit themselves for **re-election regularly**, and at least once every three years. Directors of FTSE 350 companies should be subject to **annual election by shareholders**.

C Accountability

C1 Financial and business reporting

The board should present a **fair, balanced and understandable assessment** of the **company's position and prospects** in the annual accounts and other reports such as interim reports and reports to regulators. The board should ensure that narrative sections of the annual report are consistent with the financial statements and the assessment of the company's performance. The directors should explain their responsibility for the accounts, and the auditors should state their reporting responsibilities. The directors should explain the basis on which the company **generates or preserves value** and the **strategy for delivering the company's longer-term objectives**. The directors should also report on the going concern status of the business.

C2 Risk management and internal control

The board is responsible for determining the **nature and extent of the significant risks** it is willing to take to achieve objectives. Good systems of **risk management and control** should be maintained. The directors should **review effectiveness** annually and report to shareholders that they have done so. The review should cover all controls including financial, operational and compliance controls and risk management.

C3 Audit committee and auditors

There should be **formal and clear arrangements** with the **company's auditors**, and for applying the financial reporting and internal control principles. Companies should have an **audit committee** consisting of independent non-executive directors. One member should have **recent and relevant financial experience**. The committee should **monitor the accounts**, review **internal financial controls** and also other **internal controls and risk management systems** if there is no risk committee. The audit committee should make recommendations for the **appointment and remuneration of the external auditor**, and consider the auditor's **independence and objectivity,** the **effectiveness of the audit process** and whether the external auditor should **provide non-audit services**. FTSE 350 companies should put the external audit contract out to tender at least every ten years. The audit committee should also **review internal audit's work**. If there is no internal audit function, the audit committee should consider annually whether it is needed. The audit committee should also review 'whistleblowing' arrangements for staff who have **concerns about improprieties**. Audit committees should report to shareholders on how they have carried out their responsibilities, including how they have assessed the effectiveness of the external audit process.

D Directors' remuneration

D1 Level and components of remuneration

Remuneration levels should be sufficient to attract directors of **sufficient calibre** to run the company effectively, but companies should not pay more than is necessary. A proportion of remuneration should be based on **corporate and individual performance**. Comparisons with other companies should be used with caution. When designing performance-related elements of remuneration, the remuneration committee should consider annual bonuses and different kinds of long-term incentive schemes. Targets should be stretching. Levels of remuneration for non-executive directors should reflect **time commitment and responsibilities**, and should not include share options or performance-related options.

Boards' ultimate objectives should be to set **notice periods at one year or less**. The remuneration committee should consider the appropriateness of compensation commitments included in the contracts of service.

D2 Procedure

Companies should establish a formal and clear procedure for **developing policy** on **executive remuneration** and for fixing the remuneration package of individual directors. **Directors should not be involved** in **setting their own remuneration**. A **remuneration committee**, staffed by independent non-executive directors, should make **recommendations** about the framework of executive remuneration, and should determine remuneration packages of executive directors and the chairman. The board or shareholders should determine the remuneration of non-executive directors.

E Relations with shareholders

E1 Dialogue with shareholders

The board should keep up a dialogue with shareholders, particularly **major (institutional) shareholders**. The board should try to understand issues and concerns, and discuss governance and strategy with major shareholders.

E2 Constructive use of the AGM

The AGM should be a **means of communication** with **investors**. Companies should count all proxies and announce proxy votes for and against on all votes on a show of hands, except when a poll is taken. Companies should propose a **separate resolution** on each substantially separate issue, and there should

be a resolution covering the **report and accounts**. The chairmen of the audit, nomination and remuneration committees should be available to answer questions at the AGM. Papers should be sent to members at least 20 working days before the AGM.

Compliance with the Code

The UK Corporate Governance Code requires listed companies to include in their accounts:

(a) A narrative statement of how they **applied** the **principles** set out in the UK Corporate Governance Code. This should provide explanations which enable their shareholders to assess how the principles have been applied.

(b) A statement as to whether or not they **complied throughout** the **accounting period** with the provisions set out in the UK Corporate Governance Code. Listed companies that did not comply throughout the accounting period with all the provisions must specify the provisions with which they did not comply, and give **reasons** for **non-compliance**.

7.5 OECD Guidance

The Organisation for Economic Co-operation and Development (OECD) has carried out an extensive consultation with member countries, and developed a **set of principles of corporate governance** that countries and companies should work towards achieving. The OECD has stated that its interest in corporate governance arises from its concern for **global investment**. Corporate governance arrangements should be credible and should be understood across national borders. Having a common set of accepted principles is a step towards achieving this aim.

The OECD developed its Principles of Corporate Governance in 1998 and issued a revised version in April 2004. They are non-binding principles, intended to assist governments in their efforts to evaluate and improve the legal, institutional and regulatory framework for corporate governance in their countries.

They are also intended to provide guidance to stock exchanges, investors and companies. The focus is on stock exchange listed companies, but many of the principles can also apply to private companies and state-owned organisations.

The OECD principles deal mainly with governance problems that result from the **separation of ownership and management** of a company. Issues of ethical concern and environmental issues are also relevant, although not central to the problems of governance.

7.5.1 The OECD principles

The OECD principles are grouped into five broad areas:

(a) **The rights of shareholders**

Shareholders should have the right to **participate and vote in general meetings** of the company, **elect** and **remove members of the board** and **obtain relevant and material information** on a timely basis. Capital markets for corporate control should function in an **efficient and timely manner**.

(b) **The equitable treatment of shareholders**

All shareholders of the same class of shares should be treated equally, including **minority shareholders** and **overseas shareholders**. **Impediments** to **cross-border shareholdings** should be **eliminated**.

(c) **The role of stakeholders**

Rights of stakeholders should be **protected**. All stakeholders should have **access to relevant information** on a regular and timely basis. **Performance-enhancing mechanisms** for employee participation should be **permitted to develop**. Stakeholders, including employees, should be able to **freely communicate their concerns** about illegal or unethical relationships to the board.

(d)   **Disclosure and transparency**

Timely and accurate disclosure must be made of all material matters regarding the company, including the financial situation, foreseeable risk factors, issues regarding employees and other stakeholders and governance structures and policies. The company's approach to disclosure should promote the provision of analysis or advice that is relevant to decisions by investors.

(e)   **The responsibilities of the board**

The board is responsible for the **strategic guidance** of the company and for the **effective monitoring** of management. Board members should act on a fully informed basis, in good faith, with due diligence and care and in the **best interests of the company and its shareholders**. They should treat **all shareholders fairly**. The board should be able to exercise **independent judgement**. This includes assigning independent non-executive directors to appropriate tasks.

7.6 Enron

The most significant scandal in the USA in recent years has been the Enron scandal, when one of the country's biggest companies filed for bankruptcy. The scandal also resulted in the disappearance of Arthur Andersen, one of the Big Five accountancy firms who had audited Enron's accounts. The main reasons why Enron collapsed were over-expansion in energy markets, too much reliance on derivatives trading which eventually went wrong, breaches of federal law, and misleading and dishonest behaviour. However enquiries into the scandal exposed a number of weaknesses in the company's governance.

7.6.1 Lack of transparency in the accounts

This particularly related to certain investment vehicles that were kept off balance sheet. Various other methods of inflating revenues, offloading debt, massaging quarterly figures and avoiding taxes were employed.

7.6.2 Ineffective corporate governance arrangements

The company's management team was criticised for being arrogant and over ambitious. The Economist suggested that Enron's Chief Executive Officer, Kenneth Lay, was like a cult leader, with his staff and employees fawning over his every word and following him slavishly. The non-executive directors were weak, and there were conflicts of interest. The chair of the audit committee was Wendy Gramm. Her husband, Senator Phil Gramm, received substantial political donations from Enron.

7.6.3 Inadequate scrutiny by the external auditors

Arthur Andersen failed to spot or failed to question dubious accounting treatments. Since Andersen's consultancy arm did a lot of work for Enron, there were allegations of conflicts of interest.

7.6.4 Information asymmetry

This is the agency problem of the directors/managers knowing more than the investors. The investors included Enron's employees. Many had their personal wealth tied up in Enron shares, which ended up being worthless. They were actively discouraged from selling them. Many of Enron's directors, however, sold the shares when they began to fall, potentially profiting from them. It is alleged that the Chief Financial Officer, Andrew Fastow, concealed the gains he made from his involvement with affiliated companies.

7.6.5 Executive compensation methods

These were meant to align the interests of shareholders and directors, but seemed to encourage the overstatement of short-term profits. Particularly in the USA, where the tenure of Chief Executive Officers is fairly short, the temptation is to inflate profits in the hope that share options will have been cashed in by the time the problems are discovered.

7.7 The Sarbanes-Oxley Act 2002

In the US the response to the breakdown of stock market trust caused by perceived inadequacies in corporate government arrangements and the Enron scandal was the **Sarbanes-Oxley Act 2002.** The Act applies to all companies that are required to file periodic reports with the Securities and Exchange Commission (SEC). The Act was the most far-reaching US legislation dealing with securities in many years and has major implications for public companies. Rule-making authority was delegated to the SEC on many provisions.

Sarbanes-Oxley shifts responsibility for financial probity and accuracy to the board's **audit committee**, which typically comprises three independent directors, one of whom has to meet certain financial literacy requirements (equivalent to non-executive directors in other jurisdictions).

Along with rules from the Securities and Exchange Commission, Sarbanes-Oxley (Sarbox) requires companies to increase their financial statement **disclosures**, to have an internal **code of ethics** and to impose **restrictions on share trading** by, and **loans to**, corporate officers.

7.8 Detailed provisions of the Sarbanes-Oxley Act

7.8.1 Oversight Board

The Act set up a new regulator, **The Public Company Accounting Oversight Board (PCAOB),** to oversee the audit of public companies that are subject to the securities laws.

The Board has powers to set **auditing, quality control, independence and ethical standards** for registered public accounting firms to use in the preparation and issue of audit reports on the financial statements of listed companies. In particular the board is required to set standards for registered public accounting firms' reports on listed company statements and on their internal control over financial reporting. The board also has **inspection and disciplinary powers** over audit firms.

7.8.2 Separation of Chairman and CEO roles

Separation of the roles of Chairman and Chief Executive is important for a number of reasons. The board of directors votes on executive pay. A chairman who was also chief executive could therefore be voting to increase his own pay, giving rise to a conflict of interest. Good corporate governance requires the board to monitor the operations of the company and ensure that it is being properly run. This is more likely to happen if the board is led by an independent chair, rather than by the officer responsible for running the company. Also the audit committee, which can consist only of external board members, reports to the board. Having the CEO in the chair limits the effectiveness of the audit committee.

Separation of these two roles is therefore important to strengthen the overall integrity of the company.

7.8.3 Auditing standards

Audit firms should **retain working papers** for at least seven years and have **quality control standards** in place, such as second partner review. As part of the audit they should review internal control systems to ensure that they **reflect the transactions** of the client and provide **reasonable assurance** that the transactions are recorded in a manner that will **permit preparation** of the **financial statements** in accordance with **generally accepted accounting principles**. They should also review records to check whether **receipts** and **payments** are being made **only in accordance with management's authorisation**.

7.8.4 Non-audit services

Auditors are expressly prohibited from carrying out a number of services including internal audit, bookkeeping, systems design and implementation, appraisal or valuation services, actuarial services, management functions and human resources, investment management, legal and expert services. **Provision of other non-audit services** is only allowed with the **prior approval** of the **audit committee**.

7.8.5 Quality control procedures

There should be **rotation** of lead or reviewing audit partners every five years, and other procedures such as independence requirements, consultation, supervision, professional development, internal quality review and engagement acceptance and continuation should be in place.

7.8.6 Auditors and audit committee

Auditors should discuss **critical accounting policies**, **possible alternative treatments**, the management letter and unadjusted differences with the audit committee.

7.8.7 Audit committees

Audit committees should be established by all listed companies.

All members of audit committees should be **independent** and should therefore not accept any **consulting** or **advisory fee** from the company or be affiliated to it. At least one member should be a financial expert. Audit committees should be responsible for the **appointment, compensation** and **oversight** of auditors. Audit committees should establish mechanisms for dealing with complaints about accounting, internal controls and audit.

7.8.8 Corporate responsibility

The **chief executive officer** and **chief finance officer** should **certify the appropriateness of the financial statements** and that those **financial statements fairly present the operations and financial condition** of the issuer. If the company has to prepare a restatement of accounts due to material non-compliance with standards, the **chief finance officer and chief executive officer** should **forfeit their bonuses**.

7.8.9 Off balance sheet transactions

There should be **appropriate disclosure of material off-balance sheet transactions** and other relationships (transactions that are not included in the accounts but that impact upon financial conditions, results, liquidity or capital resources).

7.8.10 Internal control reporting (the section 404 requirement)

S404 of the Act states that annual reports should contain **internal control reports** that state the responsibility of management for establishing and maintaining **adequate internal control over financial reporting.** Annual reports should contain an **assessment** of the **effectiveness** of the **internal control over financial reporting**, and a statement identifying the framework used by management to evaluate the effectiveness of the company's internal control over financial reporting.

External auditors should report on this assessment, having carried out independent testing of the control system.

To carry out their review effectively, management is likely to have to rely on internal audit work on the control systems. Internal auditors' work would include:

- Identifying controls at an entity and operational level

- Reviewing the completeness of documentation

- Testing controls

- Advising on the contents of the statement of effectiveness of the internal control system and the disclosure of material weaknesses

Companies should also report whether they have adopted a **code of conduct** for senior financial officers and the content of that code.

7.8.11 Whistleblowing provisions

Employees of **listed companies** and **auditors** will be granted whistleblower protection against their employers if they **disclose private employer information** to parties involved in a fraud claim.

7.9 Impact of Sarbanes-Oxley in the USA

The biggest expense involving compliance that companies are incurring is fulfilling the requirement to ensure their **internal controls** are properly documented and tested, and there is better communication about controls to shareholders. US companies had to have efficient controls in the past, but they now have to document them more comprehensively than before, and then have the external auditors report on what they have done. This has arguably resulted in greater market confidence in American companies.

The Act also formally stripped accountancy firms of almost all non-audit revenue streams that they used to derive from their audit clients, for fear of conflicts of interest. The Act makes clear that there needs to be distance between companies and external auditors. External auditors' position has also been strengthened by the requirement for listed companies to operate effective audit committees.

For auditors the Act strengthens requirements on them to whistleblow internally on any wrongdoing they uncover at client companies, right up to board level.

7.10 International impact of Sarbanes-Oxley

The Act also has a significant **international dimension**. About 1,500 non-US companies, including many of the world's largest, list their shares in the US and are covered by Sarbanes-Oxley. There were complaints that the new legislation conflicted with local corporate governance customs, and following an intense round of lobbying from outside the US, changes to the rules were secured. For example, German employee representatives, who are non-management, can sit on audit committees, and audit committees do not have to have board directors if the local law says otherwise, as it does in Japan and Italy.

As also the US is such a significant influence worldwide, arguably Sarbanes-Oxley may influence certain jurisdictions to adopt a more rules-based approach.

Section summary

Guidance on governance is provided by the UK Corporate Governance Code and the OECD principles. Many UK companies will also have to comply with Sarbox.

Chapter Summary

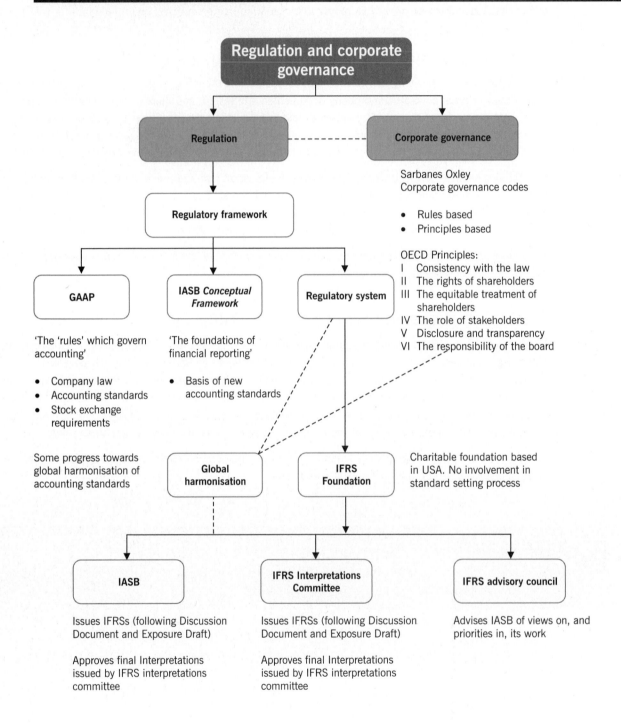

Regulation and corporate governance

Regulation — — — — — — **Corporate governance**

Regulatory framework

GAAP

'The 'rules' which govern accounting'

- Company law
- Accounting standards
- Stock exchange requirements

Some progress towards global harmonisation of accounting standards

IASB *Conceptual Framework*

'The foundations of financial reporting'

- Basis of new accounting standards

Regulatory system

Global harmonisation

IFRS Foundation

Charitable foundation based in USA. No involvement in standard setting process

Sarbanes Oxley
Corporate governance codes

- Rules based
- Principles based

OECD Principles:
I   Consistency with the law
II   The rights of shareholders
III The equitable treatment of shareholders
IV The role of stakeholders
V   Disclosure and transparency
VI The responsibility of the board

IASB

Issues IFRSs (following Discussion Document and Exposure Draft)

Approves final Interpretations issued by IFRS interpretations committee

IFRS Interpretations Committee

Issues IFRSs (following Discussion Document and Exposure Draft)

Approves final Interpretations issued by IFRS interpretations committee

IFRS advisory council

Advises IASB of views on, and priorities in, its work

Quick Quiz

1   Which of the following arguments is not in favour of entities being required to comply with accounting standards?

    A   They reduce variations in methods used to produce accounts
    B   They oblige companies to disclose their accounting policies
    C   They are a less rigid alternative to legislation
    D   They may tend towards rigidity in applying the rules

2   A conceptual framework is:

    A   A theoretical expression of accounting standards
    B   A set of concepts used by the IASB
    C   A theoretical basis for the development of accounting standards
    D   The pro-forma financial statements

3   Corporate governance can be defined as:

    A   The system by which organisations are directed and controlled
    B   The behaviour required of company directors
    C   Statutory requirements imposed on all listed companies
    D   A means of safeguarding against fraud

Answers to Quick Quiz

1   D   The other arguments are all in favour of entities being required to comply with accounting standards.

2   C   A conceptual framework provides the basis within which standards can be updated and new standards formulated.

3   A   This is the definition from the Cadbury report.

Answers to Questions

1.1 International harmonisation

(a)   Advantages of global harmonisation

The advantages of harmonisation will be based on the benefits to users and preparers of accounts, as follows.

(i)   Investors, both individual and corporate, would like to be able to compare the financial results of different companies internationally as well as nationally in making investment decisions.

(ii)   Multinational companies would benefit from harmonisation for many reasons including the following.

(1)   Better access would be gained to foreign investor funds.

(2)   Management control would be improved, because harmonisation would aid internal communication of financial information.

(3)   Appraisal of foreign entities for take-overs and mergers would be more straightforward.

(4)   It would be easier to comply with the reporting requirements of overseas stock exchanges.

(5)   Preparation of group accounts would be easier.

(6)   A reduction in audit costs might be achieved.

(7)   Transfer of accounting staff across national borders would be easier.

(iii)   Governments of developing countries would save time and money if they could adopt international standards and, if these were used internally, governments of developing countries could attempt to control the activities of foreign multinational companies in their own country. These companies could not 'hide' behind foreign accounting practices which are difficult to understand.

(iv)   Tax authorities. It will be easier to calculate the tax liability of investors, including multinationals who receive income from overseas sources.

(v)   Regional economic groups usually promote trade within a specific geographical region. This would be aided by common accounting practices within the region.

(vi)   Large international accounting firms would benefit as accounting and auditing would be much easier if similar accounting practices existed throughout the world.

(b)   Barriers to harmonisation

(i)   Different purposes of financial reporting. In some countries the purpose is solely for tax assessment, while in others it is for investor decision-making.

(ii)   Different legal systems. These prevent the development of certain accounting practices and restrict the options available.

(iii)   Different user groups. Countries have different ideas about who the relevant user groups are and their respective importance. In the USA investor and creditor groups are given prominence, while in Europe employees enjoy a higher profile.

(iv)   Needs of developing countries. Developing countries are obviously behind in the standard setting process and they need to develop the basic standards and principles already in place in most developed countries.

(v)   Nationalism is demonstrated in an unwillingness to accept another country's standard.

(vi)   Cultural differences result in objectives for accounting systems differing from country to country.

(vii)   Unique circumstances. Some countries may be experiencing unusual circumstances which affect all aspects of everyday life and impinge on the ability of companies to produce proper reports, for example hyperinflation, civil war, currency restriction and so on.

(viii) The lack of strong accountancy bodies. Many countries do not have strong independent accountancy or business bodies which would press for better standards and greater harmonisation.

Now try this question from the OTQ Question Bank	Number
	Q8

EXTERNAL AUDIT

Here we look at the role of the external auditor. If you work for an organisation which is audited (internally or externally), try to talk to the auditors about the audit. Because it is the audit of an organisation you know well, you should gain some insight into the role of the auditor.

The external auditors are employed to check the good **stewardship** of the directors of the company and the truth and fairness of the financial statements. To enable them to do this they have certain **rights and duties**.

When the audit is completed and the auditors are satisfied with the information and explanations provided, an **audit report** is issued. The audit report is the instrument by which the auditors express an **opinion** on the truth and fairness of the financial statements. In Sections 3 and 4 we look at the standard audit report and its **modification** when the auditors are not completely satisfied with the results of the audit.

topic list	learning outcomes	syllabus references
1 External audit	A1	A1 (d)
2 Duties and rights of auditors	A1	A1 (d)
3 The audit report	A1	A1 (d)
4 Types of audit opinion	A1	A1 (d)

Chapter Overview

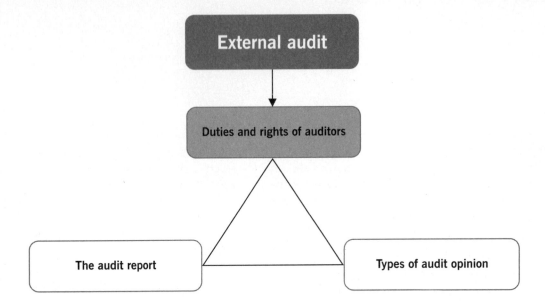

1   External audit

Introduction

If you work in an organisation you may have come across the auditors and even been asked questions by them. In this section we look at what an audit is and why it is necessary.

1.1 Why is an audit needed?

In the modern commercial environment, businesses which are operated as companies with limited liability need to produce accounts to indicate how successfully they are performing. However the owners of a business require something more than accounts because the managers responsible for preparing them may, either unintentionally or by deliberate manipulation, produce accounts which are misleading. An independent examination of the accounts, an **audit**, is needed so that the owners of the business can assess how well management have discharged their **stewardship**.

1.2 Objective of an audit

The objectives of an audit are given in **International Standard on Auditing**, ISA 200 *Overall objectives of the independent auditor and the conduct of an audit in accordance with international standards on auditing* and can be summarised as follows.

KEY TERM

The objective of an AUDIT of financial statements is to enable the auditor to express an opinion on whether the financial statements are prepared, in all material respects, in accordance with an identified financial reporting framework.

The phrases used to express the auditor's opinion are **'give a true and fair view'** or **'present fairly, in all material respects'**, which are equivalent terms.

The phrase 'presented fairly' is interpreted as meaning:

*   Factual
*   Free from bias
*   Reflecting the commercial substance of the business's transactions.

The auditor's opinion enhances the credibility of the financial statements by providing **reasonable assurance** from an independent source that the financial statements taken as a whole are free from **material misstatement**.

KEY TERM

A matter is MATERIAL 'if its omission or misstatement could influence the economic decisions of users taken on the basis of the financial statements'.   (*Conceptual Framework*)

The concept of materiality is very important to auditors as they do not report on anything which is not material. However, they do have to decide whether something is material or not. They may use guidelines such as treating anything which exceeds 5% of profit or 1% of revenue as material.

Reasonable assurance is a high level of assurance, however, it is not absolute assurance because there are inherent limitations of an audit which result in the auditor forming an opinion on evidence that is **persuasive** rather than **conclusive**.

1.3 Responsibilities of management

Responsibility for the preparation and presentation of the financial statements rests firmly with the **management of the entity**. An audit of the financial statements does not relieve management of this responsibility. Many members of the public fail to realise this.

Other responsibilities of management include ensuring that proper accounting records are maintained, and preventing and detecting fraud and errors. Management are also responsible for establishing a system of internal controls within the company.

1.4 The expectations gap

There are some common misconceptions in relation to the role of the auditors, even among 'financially aware' people, including the following examples.

(a)   Many people think that the **auditor's report** is to the **directors** of a company, rather than the shareholders

(b)   Some think that a **qualified audit report** is **more favourable** than an unmodified audit report, whereas the opposite is true

(c)   There is a perception that it is the auditor's duty to detect fraud, when in fact the detection of fraud is the **responsibility** of the **directors**

These findings highlight the 'expectations gap' between what auditors do and what people in general think that they do. Add the fact that many 'financially aware' people do not look at the report and accounts of a company they are considering investing in, and you have some sobering facts for the auditors to contemplate!

Public concern at large company failures has highlighted problems with the expectations gap. This has formed part of a general debate on corporate governance (ie how companies are governed) in many countries. Corporate governance developments have aimed to make the role of the auditor clearer and to regulate the relationship between the auditors and the management of the entity being audited.

1.5 Advantages and disadvantages of having an audit

There are several **advantages** to a company of having an audit, including the following:

(a)   An audit may act as a fraud deterrent as employees know their work will be audited by someone else

(b)   An audit adds credibility to the accounts so may assist the entity in obtaining external finance or with mergers and acquisitions

(c)   The auditor may be able to give advice to management on improvements to internal systems or controls

However, there are **disadvantages**, including:

(a)   The cost of an audit. Countries often legally require companies of a certain size to be audited, so the cost is unavoidable.

(b)   Disruption caused to employees' normal work as they have to provide information to the auditor.

1.6 An overview of the audit process

Very briefly, the key stages of an audit are as follows.

(1)   The auditor is usually appointed by the shareholders at an annual general meeting of the entity.

(2)   The auditor issues to the entity an 'engagement letter' which is a **contract** that sets out the terms of the audit.

(3)   The auditor **plans the audit**, which includes obtaining a detailed understanding of the entity and its accounting systems, assessing the risk of material misstatement and selecting audit procedures to respond to the risk and gather evidence. The planning will also identify which individuals from the audit team will carry out the audit procedures.

(4)   The audit team will then carry out the planned audit procedures and **gather evidence** about whether the accounts are true and fair.

(5)   Once all the evidence has been collected, it will be reviewed by the auditor (usually the audit partner) who will then form **an opinion** on whether the accounts are true and fair.

(6)   Once the opinion has been formed, an **audit report** can be issued. The audit report is addressed to the shareholders of the entity.

Section summary

- An audit is essentially an independent review of the financial statements.

- Audits at best give **reasonable assurance** that the accounts are free from **material misstatement**.

- The **expectations gap** is the difference between the work auditors actually carry out and the work non-auditors think they carry out.

2   Duties and rights of auditors

Introduction

In this section we look at the duties and rights of the auditor. The duties and rights vary according to national law; we focus here on the UK.

2.1 Duties

The auditors should be required to report on every statement of financial position and statement of profit or loss and other comprehensive income laid before the company in general meeting.

The auditors are required to consider the following.

Compliance with legislation	Whether the accounts have been prepared in accordance with the relevant legislation.
Truth and fairness of accounts	Whether the statement of financial position shows a true and fair view of the company's affairs at the end of the period and the statement of profit or loss and other comprehensive income (and a statement of cash flows) show a true and fair view of the results for the period.
Adequate records and returns	Whether adequate accounting records have been kept and proper returns adequate for the audit received from branches not visited by the auditor.
Agreement of accounts to records	Whether the accounts are in agreement with the accounting records.
Consistency of other information	Whether the other information presented with the accounts is consistent with the accounts.

2.2 Rights

The auditors must have certain rights to enable them to carry out their duties effectively.

The principal rights auditors should have, excepting those dealing with resignation or removal, are set out in the table below.

Access to records	A right of access at all times to the books, accounts and vouchers of the company.
Information and explanations	A right to require from the company's officers such information and explanations as the auditors think necessary for the performance of their duties as auditors.
Attendance at/notices of general meetings	A right to attend any general meetings of the company and to receive all notices of, and communications relating to such meetings which any member of the company is entitled to receive.
Right to speak at general meetings	A right to be heard at general meetings which they attend on any part of the business that concerns them as auditors.
Rights in relation to written resolutions	A right to receive a copy of any written resolution proposed.
Right to require laying of accounts	A right to give notice in writing requiring that a general meeting be held for the purpose of laying the accounts and reports before the company.

Rights to information

It is an offence for a company's officer knowingly or recklessly to make a statement in any form to an auditor which:

(a)   Purports to convey any information or explanation required by the auditor

(b)   Is materially misleading, false or deceptive

If auditors have not received all the information and explanations they deem necessary, they should state this fact in their report.

Section summary

Auditor's duties generally include the duties to report explicitly on the **reasonableness** of the accounts audited and their **compliance** with legislation. They should also report on whether adequate accounting records have been kept.

Auditor's rights should include the rights of **access to records** and to receive **information** and **explanations**, also rights relating to **attendance** and **speaking** at **general meetings**.

---

3   The audit report

Introduction

This section looks at the audit report. This is the way that the auditors will report to the shareholders of a company with their opinion on the findings from the audit. In this section we will focus on the structure of the report.

3.1 Preparing the report

International Standard on Auditing, ISA 700 *Forming an opinion and reporting on financial statements*, deals with the auditor's responsibility to form an opinion on the financial statements and provides **guidance on the form and content of the auditor's report**. The auditor's report is the report issued as a result of an audit performed by an independent auditor of the financial statements of an entity.

3.2 Basic elements of the auditor's report

The auditor's report includes the following basic elements, usually in the following layout.

(a)   **Title**

(b)   **Addressee**

(c)   **Introductory paragraph** identifying the financial statements audited

(d)   A **statement** of the **responsibility** of the entity's **management** and the **responsibility** of the **auditor**

(e)   **Scope paragraph** (basis of opinion) including a description of the work performed by the auditor

(f)   **Opinion paragraph** containing an expression of opinion on the financial statements

(g)   **Date** of the report

(h)   **Auditor's address**

(i)   **Auditor's signature**

3.2.1 Unmodified audit opinion

An **unmodified audit opinion** should be expressed when the auditor concludes that the financial statements give a true and fair view (or are presented fairly, in all material respects) in accordance with the applicable reporting framework. An unmodified opinion also indicates implicitly that any changes in accounting principles or in the method of their application, and the effects, therefore, have been properly determined and disclosed in the financial statements.

An illustration of an audit report with an unmodified audit opinion is shown below.

Example: Typical audit report with an unmodified audit opinion

INDEPENDENT AUDITOR'S REPORT

(APPROPRIATE ADDRESSEE)

Report on the Financial Statements

We have audited the accompanying financial statements of ABC Company, which comprise the statement of financial position as at 31 December 20X1, and the statement of profit or loss and other comprehensive income, statement of changes in equity and statement of cash flows for the year then ended, and a summary of significant accounting policies and other explanatory information.

Management's Responsibility for the Financial Statements

Management is responsible for the preparation and fair presentation of these financial statements in accordance with International Financial Reporting Standards, and for such internal control as management determines is necessary to enable the preparation and fair presentation of financial statements that are free from material misstatement, whether due to fraud or error.

Auditor's Responsibility

Our responsibility is to express an opinion on these financial statements based on our audit. We conducted our audit in accordance with International Standards on Auditing. Those standards require that we comply with ethical requirements and plan and perform the audit to obtain reasonable assurance about whether the financial statements are free from material misstatement.

Scope of the audit of the financial statements

An audit involves performing procedures to obtain audit evidence about the amounts and disclosures in the financial statements. The procedures selected depend on the auditor's judgement, including the assessment of the risks of material misstatement of the financial statements, whether due to fraud or error. In making those risk assessments, the auditor considers internal control relevant to the entity's preparation and fair presentation of the financial statements in order to design audit procedures that are appropriate in the circumstances, but not for the purpose of expressing an opinion on the effectiveness of the entity's internal control. An audit also includes evaluating the appropriateness of accounting policies

used and the reasonableness of accounting estimates made by management, as well as evaluating the overall presentation of the financial statements.

We believe that the audit evidence we have obtained is sufficient and appropriate to provide a basis for our audit opinion.

Opinion

In our opinion, the financial statements present fairly, in all material respects, (or *give a true and fair view of*) the financial position of ABC Company as at 31 December 20X1, and (*of*) its financial performance and its cash flows for the year then ended in accordance with International Financial Reporting Standards.

[Auditor's signature]

[Date of the auditor's report]

[Auditor's address]

We will now look in more detail, at the different components of the report.

3.2.2 Title

The auditor's report shall have an appropriate title. The term 'independent auditor' in the title distinguishes the auditor's report from reports that might be issued by others, such as officers of the entity being audited.

3.2.3 Addressee

The auditor's report should be appropriately addressed as required by the circumstances of the engagement. The report is ordinarily addressed to the shareholders of the entity whose financial statements are being audited, but it could also be addressed to those charged with governance of that entity.

3.2.4 Introductory paragraph

The auditor's report should identify the financial statements of the entity that have been audited, including the date of, and period covered by, the financial statements.

3.2.5 Management's responsibility for the financial statements

This section of the auditor's report covers the responsibilities of those in charge of preparing the financial statements. This is often the management of an organisation.

The auditor's report must explain that management are responsible for preparing the financial statements in accordance with an applicable financial reporting framework. It must also describe how management are responsible for internal controls which enable the preparation of financial statements which are free from fraud or error.

3.2.6 Auditor's responsibility

The auditor's report should include a statement that the responsibility of the auditor is to audit and express an opinion on the financial statements in accordance with applicable legal requirements and International Standards on Auditing.

3.2.7 Scope of the audit of financial statements

The auditor's report shall include the description of an audit as in the example at the beginning of this section

3.2.8 Opinion on the financial statements

The opinion paragraph of the auditor's report should clearly state the auditor's opinion as required by the applicable financial reporting framework used to prepare the financial statements, including applicable law.

The terms used to express the auditor's opinion are 'give a true and fair view' or 'present fairly, in all material respects', and are **equivalent**. Both terms indicate, amongst other things, that the auditor considers only those matters that are **material** to the financial statements.

To advise the reader of the context in which 'fairness' is expressed, the auditor's opinion indicates the framework upon which the financial statements are based. The **applicable financial reporting framework** is determined by IFRSs, rules issued by professional bodies, and the development of general practice within a country, with an appropriate consideration of fairness and with due regard to local legislation.

In addition to an opinion of the true and fair view (or fair presentation, in all material respects), the auditor's report may need to include an opinion as to whether the financial statements comply with other requirements specified by **relevant statutes or law**. These other reporting responsibilities must be addressed in a separate section of the auditor's report.

3.2.9 Signature of the auditor

The firm as a whole usually assumes responsibility for the audit, but in some countries an individual partner may be required to take responsibility and sign in his or her own name.

3.2.10 Date of report

The date of an auditor's report on a reporting entity's financial statements should be the date on which the auditor signed the report expressing an opinion on those financial statements.

3.2.11 Location of auditor's office

The report should name the **location** where the auditor is based.

Question 2.1	Unmodified audit opinion

Learning outcome A1

The following is an unmodified audit report, which has been signed by the auditors of Kiln, a limited liability company.

INDEPENDENT AUDITOR'S REPORT

TO THE SHAREHOLDERS OF KILN COMPANY

Report on the Financial Statements

We have audited the accompanying financial statements of Kiln Company, which comprise the statement of financial position as at 31 December 20X3, and the statement of profit or loss and other comprehensive income, statement of changes in equity and statement of cash flows for the year then ended, and a summary of significant accounting policies and other explanatory information.

Management's Responsibility for the Financial Statements

Management is responsible for the preparation and fair presentation of these financial statements in accordance with International Financial Reporting Standards, and for such internal control as management determines is necessary to enable the preparation and fair presentation of financial statements that are free from material misstatement, whether due to fraud or error.

Auditor's Responsibility

Our responsibility is to express an opinion on these financial statements based on our audit. We conducted our audit in accordance with International Standards on Auditing. Those standards require that we comply with ethical requirements and plan and perform the audit to obtain reasonable assurance about whether the financial statements are free from material misstatement.

An audit involves performing procedures to obtain audit evidence about the amounts and disclosures in the financial statements. The procedures selected depend on the auditor's judgment, including the assessment of the risks of material misstatement of the financial statements, whether due to fraud or error. In making those risk assessments, the auditor considers internal control relevant to the entity's preparation and fair presentation of the financial statements in order to design audit procedures that are appropriate in the circumstances, but not for the purpose of expressing an opinion on the effectiveness of the entity's internal control. An audit also includes evaluating the appropriateness of accounting policies used and the reasonableness of accounting estimates made by management, as well as evaluating the overall presentation of the financial statements.

We believe that the audit evidence we have obtained is sufficient and appropriate to provide a basis for our audit opinion.

Opinion

In our opinion, the financial statements present fairly, in all material respects, (or *give a true and fair view of*) the financial position of Kiln Company as at 31 December 20X3, and (*of*) its financial performance and its cash flows for the year then ended in accordance with International Financial Reporting Standards.

[Auditor's signature]

[Date of the auditor's report]

[Auditor's address]

Required

Explain the purpose and meaning of the following phrases taken from the above extracts of an audit report with an unmodified audit opinion.

(a)   '... which comprise the statement of financial position ..., and the statement of profit or loss and other comprehensive income, ... and statement of cash flows ... .'

(b)   '... in accordance with International Standards on Auditing.'

(c)   'In our opinion ...'

Section summary

The audit report is the report used to communicate the auditors' opinion to the shareholders. It has a prescribed layout and must include certain things.

4 Types of audit opinion

Introduction

In the last section we looked at the structure of an audit report which included an unmodified opinion, however, sometimes it will be necessary to issue a modified opinion. In this section, we will look at the different types of audit opinion that can be issued.

4.1 Types of audit opinion

An audit opinion will either be **unmodified** or **modified**.

4.1.1 Unmodified audit opinion

An **unmodified audit opinion** should be expressed when the auditor concludes that the financial statements give a true and fair view (or are presented fairly, in all material respects) in accordance with the applicable reporting framework. The example audit report above contained an unmodified opinion.

4.2 Modified opinions

A modified opinion is required when:

*   The auditor concludes that the financial statements as a whole are not free from material misstatements or

*   The auditor cannot obtain sufficient appropriate audit evidence to conclude that the financial statements as a whole are free from material misstatement

There are three possible types of modifications:

*   A **qualified** opinion
*   An **adverse** opinion
*   A **disclaimer** of opinion

Terminology surrounding audit reports has recently been amended. In real-life examples you might see the following terminology used.

New terminology	Equivalent terminology you may see
Unmodified opinion	Unqualified opinion
Modified opinion	Qualified opinion
Qualified opinion	'Except for' qualified opinion

4.2.1 Types of modifications

The type of modification issued depends on the following:

*   The **nature of the matter** giving rise to the modifications (ie whether the financial statements **are materially misstated** or whether they **may be misstated** when the auditor cannot obtain sufficient appropriate audit evidence)

*   The auditor's judgement about the **pervasiveness** of the effects/possible effects of the matter on the financial statements

At this point we should look again at the concept of **materiality** which is covered in the IASB's *Conceptual Framework*.

A matter is MATERIAL 'if its omission or misstatement could influence the economic decisions of users taken on the basis of the financial statements'.

(Conceptual Framework)

KEY TERM

The concept of materiality is very important to auditors as they do not report on anything which is not material. However, they do have to decide whether something is material or not. They may use guidelines such as treating anything which exceeds 5% of profit before tax or 1% of revenue as material.

Exam skills

Exam questions will make it clear whether or not an item is material. If this is based on amounts, then immaterial amounts will be far less than 5% of profit before tax and material amounts will be far in excess of 10% of profit before tax.

KEY TERM

PERVASIVENESS is a term used to describe the effects or possible effects on the financial statements of misstatements or undetected misstatements (due to an inability to obtain sufficient appropriate audit evidence). There are three types of pervasive effect:

- Those that are not confined to specific elements, accounts or items in the financial statements

- Those that are confined to specific elements, accounts or items in the financial statements and represent or could represent a substantial proportion of the financial statements

- Those that relate to disclosures which are fundamental to users' understanding of the financial statements

4.2.2 Qualified opinions

A qualified opinion must be expressed in the auditor's report in the following two situations:

(1) **The auditor concludes that misstatements are material, but not pervasive, to the financial statements.**

Material misstatements could arise in respect of:

- The appropriateness of selected accounting policies
- The application of selected accounting policies
- The appropriateness or adequacy of disclosures in the financial statements

Example: Qualified opinion due to material misstatement of inventories

The following is an extract from an audit report with a qualified opinion. The qualified opinion has been issued because inventories are materially misstated. Notice the use of the words 'except for' in the Qualified Opinion paragraph.

Basis for Qualified Opinion

The company's inventories are carried in the statement of financial position at xxx. Management has not stated inventories at the lower of cost and net realisable value but has stated them solely at cost, which constitutes a departure from International Financial Reporting Standards. The company's records indicate that had management stated the inventories at the lower of cost and net realisable value, an amount of xxx would have been required to write the inventories down to their net realisable value. Accordingly, cost of sales would have been increased by xxx, and income tax, net income and shareholders' equity would have been reduced by xxx, xxx and xxx, respectively.

> **Qualified Opinion**
>
> In our opinion, **except for** the effects of the matter described in the Basis for Qualified Opinion paragraph, the financial statements present fairly, in all material respects, (or *give a true and fair view of*) the financial position of ABC Company as at 31 December 20X1, and (*of*) its financial performance and its cash flows for the year then ended in accordance with International Financial Reporting Standards.

(2)   **The auditor cannot obtain sufficient appropriate audit evidence on which to base the opinion but concludes that the possible effects of undetected misstatements, if any, could be material but not pervasive.**

The auditor's inability to obtain sufficient appropriate audit evidence is also referred to as a limitation on the scope of the audit and could arise from:

- Circumstances beyond the entity's control (eg accounting records destroyed)

- Circumstances relating to the nature or timing of the auditor's work (eg the timing of the auditor's appointment prevents the observation of the physical inventory count)

- Limitations imposed by management (eg management prevents the auditor from requesting external confirmation of specific account balances)

4.2.3 Adverse opinions

An adverse opinion is expressed when the auditor, having obtained sufficient appropriate audit evidence, concludes that misstatements are both **material and pervasive** to the financial statements.

Example: Adverse opinion due to material misstatement because of non-consolidation of a subsidiary

The following is an extract from an audit report with an adverse opinion. The adverse opinion has been issued because the company has not consolidated a subsidiary and the effect of this on the financial statements is both material and pervasive. Notice the use of the words 'do no present fairly' in the Adverse Opinion paragraph.

Basis for Adverse Opinion

As explained in Note X, the company has not consolidated the financial statements of subsidiary XYZ Company it acquired during 20X1 because it has not yet been able to ascertain the fair values of certain of the subsidiary's material assets and liabilities at the acquisition date. This investment is therefore accounted for on a cost basis. Under International Financial Reporting Standards, the subsidiary should have been consolidated because it is controlled by the company. Had XYZ been consolidated, many elements in the accompanying financial statements would have been materially affected. The effects on the consolidated financial statements of the failure to consolidate have not been determined.

Adverse Opinion

In our opinion, because of the significance of the matter discussed in the Basis for Adverse Opinion paragraph, the consolidated financial statements **do not present fairly** (or *do not give a true and fair view of*) the financial position of ABC Company and its subsidiaries as at 31 December 20X1, and (*of*) their financial performance and their cash flows for the year then ended in accordance with International Financial Reporting Standards.

4.2.4 Disclaimers of opinion

An opinion must be disclaimed when the auditor **cannot obtain sufficient appropriate audit evidence** on which to base the opinion and concludes that the **possible effects** on the financial statements of undetected misstatements, if any, **could be both material and pervasive**.

The opinion must also be disclaimed in situations involving **multiple uncertainties** when the auditor concludes that, despite having obtained sufficient appropriate audit evidence for the individual uncertainties, it is not possible to form an opinion on the financial statements due to the **potential interaction of the uncertainties and their possible cumulative effect** on the financial statements.

If a disclaimer of opinion is issued, the audit opinion paragraph will be replaced with a Disclaimer of Opinion paragraph which will contain the phrase 'we do not express an opinion...'.

4.2.5 Communication with those charged with governance

When the auditor expects to express a modified opinion, the auditor must **communicate with those charged with governance** of the entity (usually the directors) the circumstances leading to the expected modification, and the proposed wording of the modification in the auditor's report.

This allows the auditor to give **notice** to those charged with governance of the intended modification and the reasons for it, to **seek agreement or confirm disagreement** with those charged with governance with respect to the modification, and to give those charged with governance an **opportunity to provide further information and explanations** in respect of the matter giving rise to the expected modification.

At this point, those charged with governance may provide additional information and explanations or may decide to change the accounting for an issue raised by the auditors. The auditors may then conclude that a modified opinion is no longer needed.

Question 2.2	Audit problems

Learning outcome A1

During the course of your audit of the non-current assets of Eastern Engineering, a listed company, at 31 March 20X4 the following problem has arisen.

The company incurred development expenditure of $25,000 spent on a viable new product which will go into production next year and which is expected to last for ten years. The expenditure has been debited in full to the statement of profit or loss and other comprehensive income. The profit before tax is $100,000.

Required

(a) List the general forms of modified opinion available to auditors in drafting their report and state the circumstances in which each is appropriate.

(b) State whether you feel that a modified audit opinion would be necessary for the circumstances outlined above, giving reasons.

(c) On the assumption that you decide that a modified audit opinion is necessary with respect to the treatment of the development expenditure, draft the section of the report describing the matter (the whole report is not required).

(d) Outline the auditor's general responsibility with regard to a statement in the directors' or management report concerning the valuation of land and buildings.

4.3 Emphasis of matter paragraphs in the auditor's report

Emphasis of matter paragraphs are used to draw readers' attention to a matter **already presented or disclosed** in the financial statements that the auditor feels is **fundamental** to their understanding of the financial statements. It is a way for the auditor to emphasise something in the financial statements which they believe to be highly significant. An emphasis of matter paragraph is **not** a modified opinion.

KEY TERM

An EMPHASIS OF MATTER is a paragraph included in the auditor's report that refers to a matter appropriately presented or disclosed in the financial statements, that in the auditor's judgment, is of such importance that it is fundamental to users' understanding of the financial statements.

When an emphasis of matter paragraph is included in the auditor's report, it comes **immediately after the opinion paragraph** and is entitled 'Emphasis of matter' (or appropriate). The paragraph must contain a **clear reference** to the matter being emphasised and to where relevant disclosures that fully describe it can be found in the financial statements. The paragraph must state that **the auditor's opinion is not modified** in respect of the matter emphasised.

The following are examples of situations in which the auditor might include an emphasis of matter paragraph in the auditor's report:

(a) An uncertainty relating to the future outcome of **exceptional litigation or regulatory action**

(b) **Early application of a new accounting standard** that has a **pervasive effect** on the financial statements

(c) A **major catastrophe** that has had, or continues to have, **a significant effect** on the entity's financial position

An example emphasis of matter paragraph is shown below.

Example: Emphasis of matter

Emphasis of matter

We draw attention to Note X to the financial statements which describes the uncertainty related to the outcome of the lawsuit filed against the company by XYZ Company. Our opinion is not qualified in respect of this matter.

Section summary

- A **modified opinion** is required when:
    - The auditor concludes that the financial statements as a whole are not free from material misstatements or
    - The auditor cannot obtain sufficient appropriate audit evidence to conclude that the financial statements as a whole are free from material misstatement

- There are three types of **modified opinion**: a **qualified opinion**, an **adverse opinion** and a **disclaimer of opinion**.

- A **qualified opinion** or a **disclaimer of opinion** may arise if the auditor cannot obtain sufficient appropriate audit evidence.

- A **qualified opinion** or an **adverse opinion** may arise if the auditor concludes that the financial statements are not free from material misstatement.

- **Emphasis of matter paragraphs** can be included in the auditor's report under certain circumstances. Their use does not modify the auditor's opinion on the financial statements.

Chapter Summary

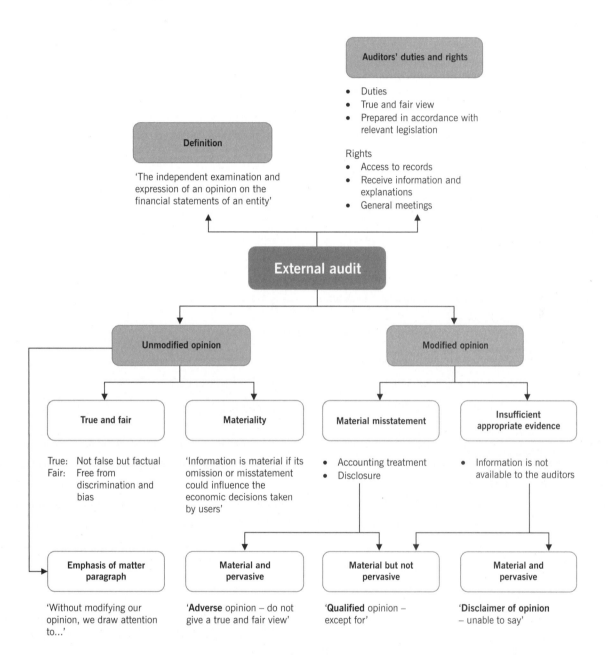

Auditors' duties and rights

- Duties
- True and fair view
- Prepared in accordance with relevant legislation

Rights
- Access to records
- Receive information and explanations
- General meetings

Definition

'The independent examination and expression of an opinion on the financial statements of an entity'

External audit

Unmodified opinion

Modified opinion

True and fair

True: Not false but factual
Fair: Free from discrimination and bias

Materiality

'Information is material if its omission or misstatement could influence the economic decisions taken by users'

Material misstatement

- Accounting treatment
- Disclosure

Insufficient appropriate evidence

- Information is not available to the auditors

Emphasis of matter paragraph

'Without modifying our opinion, we draw attention to...'

Material and pervasive

'**Adverse** opinion – do not give a true and fair view'

Material but not pervasive

'**Qualified** opinion – except for'

Material and pervasive

'**Disclaimer of opinion** – unable to say'

Quick Quiz

1   An audit is the work required to enable the .... to express an .... as to whether the ....
    .... are prepared, in all material respects, in accordance with an identified ....
    ....

2   In no more than **25** words, **explain** the term 'expectations gap'.

3   An audit of PZ's financial statements has shown that inventory is overstated by a material amount due to
    obsolete items being included in the inventory count. Management has refused to change the valuation.
    The auditor does not consider the misstatement to be pervasive. What type of audit opinion should be
    issued in this situation?

    A   Unmodified opinion
    B   Unmodified opinion with an emphasis of matter paragraph
    C   Adverse opinion
    D   Qualified opinion

4   Which of the following is not a statutory right of the auditor?

    A   Access to records
    B   Right to speak at general meetings
    C   Right to amend records
    D   Right to receive a copy of any written resolution proposed

5   **List** the basic elements of the auditors' report.

6   In which of the following situations will a qualified opinion be issued?

    (1)   The auditor concludes that misstatements are material, but not pervasive, to the financial
          statements.

    (2)   The auditor cannot obtain sufficient appropriate audit evidence on which to base the opinion but
          concludes that the possible effects of undetected misstatements, if any, could be material but not
          pervasive.

    (3)   The auditor, having obtained sufficient appropriate audit evidence, concludes that misstatements
          are both material and pervasive to the financial statements.

    A   1 only
    B   1 and 3 only
    C   1 and 2 only
    D   1, 2 and 3

7   ZF is a property rental company and has five properties with similar rental values from which it generates
    all its income. Just after the year end, one of ZF's properties was destroyed in a fire. The effects of the fire
    have been fully disclosed in the financial statements. What type of audit opinion should be issued by the
    auditor in this situation?

    A   Unmodified opinion
    B   Unmodified opinion with an emphasis of matter paragraph
    C   Adverse opinion
    D   Qualified opinion

Answers to Quick Quiz

1　Auditor, opinion, financial statements, financial reporting framework

2　The **expectations gap** is the difference between the work auditors actually carry out and the work non-auditors think they carry out.

3　D　A qualified opinion should be issued as the misstatement is material, but not pervasive.

4　C

5　•　The report should be addressed to its recipients and have a title indicating it is the report of an independent auditor

　　•　Introductory paragraph including identification of the financial statements audited

　　•　Separate sections should deal with the responsibilities of management and the responsibility of the auditors

　　•　Opinion paragraph

　　•　Signature of the auditors

　　•　Date of the auditor's report

　　•　Auditor's address

6　C　(3) would require an adverse opinion to be issued.

7　B　'The financial statements at the year end are not affected by the fire and adequate disclosure has been made, therefore the opinion will be unmodified. However, due to the significant impact on the company's financial performance and position going forward, the burning down of the property is likely to be of such importance that it is fundamental to users' understanding of the financial statements. Therefore the auditors are likely to draw attention to the matter and related disclosure in their audit report by including an emphasis of matter paragraph.'

Answers to Questions

2.1 Unmodified audit opinion

(a)　'... which comprise the statement of financial position ..., and the statement of profit or loss and other comprehensive income, ... and statement of cash flows ... .'

Purpose

The purpose of this phrase is to make it clear to the reader of an audit report the part of a company's annual report upon which the auditors are reporting their opinion.

Meaning

An annual report may include documents such as a five year summary and other voluntary information. However, only the statement of profit or loss and other comprehensive income, statement of financial position and associated notes are required to be audited in true and fair terms. IAS 7 also requires a statement of cash flows for the financial statements to show a true and fair view. Page references (for instance, 8 to 20) may be used instead to cover the statement of profit or loss and other comprehensive income, statement of financial position, notes to the accounts and statement of cash flows. The directors' report, or any equivalent, although examined and reported on by exception if it contains inconsistencies, is not included in these references.

(b)   '...in accordance with International Standards on Auditing ....'

Purpose

This phrase is included in order to confirm to the reader that best practice, as laid down in ISAs, has been adopted by the auditors in both carrying out their audit and in drafting their audit opinion. This means that the reader can be assured that the audit has been properly conducted, and that should he or she wish to discover what such standards are, or what certain key phrases mean, he or she can have recourse to ISAs to explain such matters.

Meaning

ISAs are those standards prepared by the International Auditing and Assurance Standards Board (although local/national standards may be mentioned instead).

These prescribe the principles and practices to be followed by auditors in planning, designing and carrying out various aspects of their audit work, the content of audit reports, both modified and unmodified and so on. Members of professional accountancy bodies are expected to follow all of these standards.

(c)   'In our opinion ...'

Purpose

Auditors are required to report on every statement of financial position, statement of profit or loss and other comprehensive income and statement of cash flows laid before shareholders. In reporting, they are required to state their *opinion* on those accounts. Thus, the purpose of this phrase is to comply with the requirement to report an opinion.

Meaning

An audit report is an expression of opinion by suitably qualified auditors as to whether the financial statements give a true and fair view, and have been properly prepared in accordance with any relevant local legislation. *It is not a certificate*; rather it is a statement of whether or not, in the professional judgement of the auditors, the financial statements give a true and fair view.

2.2 Audit problems

(a)   Auditors may need to modify their audit opinion where they believe the financial statements to be materially misstated.

There are three types of modified opinion:

- Qualified opinion
- Adverse opinion
- Disclaimer of opinion

The following table summarises the different types of modified opinion that can arise.

Nature of circumstances	Material but not pervasive	Material and pervasive
Financial statements are materially misstated	QUALIFIED OPINION	ADVERSE OPINION
Auditor unable to obtain sufficient appropriate audit evidence	QUALIFIED OPINION	DISCLAIMER OF OPINION

(b)   Whether a modification of the audit opinion would be required in relation to the circumstances described in the question would depend on whether or not the auditors considered them to be material. An item is likely to be considered as material in the context of a company's financial statements if its omission, misstatement or non-disclosure would prevent a proper understanding of those statements on the part of a potential user. Whilst for some audit purposes materiality will be considered in absolute terms, more often than not it will be considered as a relative term.

Development costs debited to the statement of profit or loss and other comprehensive income

The situation here is one of misstatement, since best accounting practice, as laid down by IAS 38, requires that development costs should be taken to the statement of profit or loss and other comprehensive income over the useful life of the product to which they relate.

This departure from IAS 38 does not seem to be justifiable and would be material to the reported pre-tax profits for the year, representing as it does 22.5% of that figure.

Whilst this understatement of profit would be material to the financial statements, it is not likely to be seen as pervasive and therefore a **qualified** opinion would be appropriate.

(c)   *Basis for Qualified Opinion*

As explained in note ... development costs in respect of a potential new product have been deducted in full against profit instead of being spread over the life of the relevant product as required by IAS 38; the effect of so doing has been to decrease profits before tax for the year by $22,500.

Qualified Opinion

In our opinion, except for the effects of the matter described in the Basis for Qualified Opinion paragraph, the financial statements present fairly, in all material respects, (or "give a true and fair view of") the financial position of Eastern Engineering as at 31 March 20X4, and of its financial performance and its cash flows for the year then ended in accordance with International Financial Reporting Standards.

(d)   The auditor's general responsibility with regard to the statement in the directors' report concerning the valuation of land and buildings is to satisfy themselves that this is consistent with the treatment and disclosure of this item in the audited financial statements. If the auditors are not satisfied on the question of consistency then they may have to consider qualifying the opinion in their audit report.

Now try these questions from the OTQ Question Bank	Number
	Q4
	Q15
	Q17

ETHICS

This chapter covers ethical codes, in particular the CIMA *Code of Ethics for Professional Accountants*. It begins by discussing the development of ethical codes in general, before spending time on the CIMA Code.

The ethical matters covered in this chapter are very important. As a CIMA student, you are expected to know and apply the Code in your everyday work.

topic list	learning outcomes	syllabus references
1 The need for an ethical code	A1	A1 (a)
2 Sources of ethical codes	A1	A1 (a)
3 Rules or principles based guidance?	A1	A1 (a)
4 Fundamental principles	A1	A1 (a)
5 Threats and safeguards	A1	A1 (a)

Chapter Overview

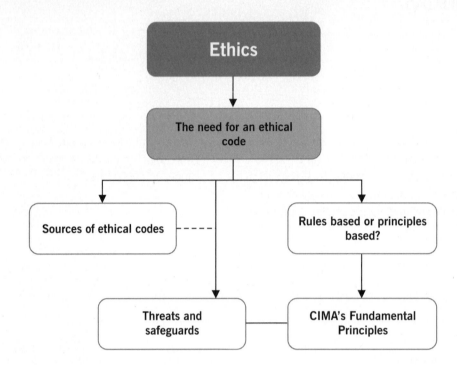

1 The need for an ethical code

Introduction

In this section we discuss the reasons why ethical codes are considered necessary.

KEY TERM

ETHICS is a set of moral principles to guide behaviour.

A professional accountant has a responsibility to act in the public interest, not just to satisfy the needs of a particular client or employer. Different **stakeholders**, for example investors, governments and employees, **rely on accountants** and their expertise. If the information produced by professional accountants cannot be relied upon, financial markets will not operate effectively.

Professional accountants must be qualified but also have an additional obligation to act ethically by following an ethical code. This ethical requirement may be above that required by laws or regulations in some jurisdictions. An ethical code helps **maintain the reputation** of the accounting profession.

Ethics and ethical codes are **constantly evolving** to adapt with changes in business and society. Cases such as Enron and WorldCom in the USA resulted in the perceived integrity of accountants becoming increasingly important. The CIMA Code was most recently revised in October 2010.

Question 3.1	Ethical issues

Learning outcome B2

Briefly explain the main ethical issues that arise in the following situations.

(a)   Dealing with a repressive authoritarian government abroad

(b)   An aggressive advertising campaign

(c)   Employee redundancies

(d)   Payments or gifts to officials who have the power to help or hinder the payees' operations

Section summary

A need for an **ethical code** has developed due to various stakeholders relying on accountants and their reputation. An ethical code must evolve to adapt with changing circumstances.

2 Sources of ethical codes

Introduction

This section covers the variety of sources behind the development of ethical codes.

2.1 Early sources of rules

In prehistoric tribes, there were no laws, no court and no police. Rules would have developed through need. The tribe would have a collective idea of what was right or wrong for the good of the group and would have punished a group member who stepped out of line, for example by taking food from others.

Further sources of rules developed as **society** grew and eventually the first laws were laid down to control the larger populations. **Religion** played a major role in developing the rules for the individual, and many of these rules are still in place today.

Business law is relatively new, and has only developed over the last couple of hundred years with industrialisation and the needs that grew from it. **Professional and corporate codes of conduct** are an even more recent development.

Social attitudes have helped shape ethical codes differently in different countries. For example in some cultures (such as Japan) gifts are regarded as an essential part of civilised negotiation, even in circumstances where to Western eyes they might appear ethically dubious. Globalisation has resulted in a move towards standardisation of ethical codes for accountants across the world.

2.2 IFAC

IFAC (the International Federation of Accountants, of which CIMA is a member) is an international body representing all the major accountancy bodies across the world. Its mission is to develop high standards in professional accountants and enhance the quality of services they provide. To enable this, the IFAC ethics committee, the International Ethics Standards Board of Accountants (IESBA), published the *Code of Ethics for Professional Accountants*.

The IESBA Code sets out the five fundamental principles of professional ethics and it provides a conceptual framework for applying those principles. Members must apply this conceptual framework to identify threats to compliance with the five fundamental principles, evaluate their significance and apply appropriate safeguards to eliminate or reduce them so that compliance with the fundamental principles is not compromised.

For further information visit www.ifac.org.

2.3 Professional bodies

Professional bodies have their own ethical codes. All CIMA members (and registered students) are required to follow the CIMA *Code of Ethics for Professional Accountants* which is based on the IESBA Code. The CIMA Code has sections which apply to both accountants in business and accountants in public practice.

Although CIMA and IESBA have produced detailed ethical guidance for professional accountants, countries may have their own additional ethical guidance. For example, in the UK, the Financial Reporting Council has issued five ethical standards and an ethical standard specific to small entities, which provide an additional source of guidance for UK auditors.

2.4 Employing organisations

Businesses also have ethical values, based on the **norms** and **standards** of **behaviour** that their leaders believe will best help them express their identity and achieve their objectives. Some of these ethical values may be **explicit**, for example, expressed in a mission statement or in employee training programmes. Others may be **unwritten rules and customs** that form part of the organisations' culture.

Business life is a fruitful source of **ethical dilemmas** because its whole purpose is material gain, the making of profit. Success in business requires a constant search for potential advantage over others and business people are under pressure to do whatever yields such advantage.

CASE STUDY

Organisation systems and targets do have ethical implications. The *Harvard Business Review* reported that the US retailer Sears Roebuck was deluged with complaints that customers of its car service centre were being charged for unnecessary work. Apparently this was because mechanics had been given targets of the number of car spare parts they should sell.

In recent times, trust in business has fallen and increasingly more evidence is required to demonstrate it. In recent years, the UK has seen a procession of corporate disasters including Barings Bank, Northern Rock and HBOS. The US has seen scandals concerning WorldCom, Enron, AIG and Lehman Brothers. Europe did not escape and has seen its share of problems with Parmalat and in India, massive corporate fraud was discovered at Satyam computers. All these scandals have severely knocked public confidence and trust in major corporations.

In an attempt to counter this lack of trust, many corporations have developed **ethical strategies** and **policies** to provide **guidance** and **training** for their employees. Increasing numbers of corporations are developing ethical codes for their employees which must be followed during the course of their employment. The strategy is set by the leadership and this will feed into all areas of the business and become part of the culture of the organisation.

Question 3.2	Employee behaviour

Learning outcome B2

How can an organisation influence employee behaviour towards ethical issues?

An ethical strategy is not always visible to outsiders, and many companies now produce **Corporate Responsibility Policies (CRPs)** and **Corporate Responsibility Reports (CRRs)** for their stakeholders to demonstrate their commitment and to manage their relationships in the wider community.

Section summary

Sources of ethical codes include law, religion, social attitudes, IESBA, professional bodies and employing organisations.

3 Rules or principles based guidance?

Introduction

In this section we look at the advantages and disadvantages of principles based guidance.

The CIMA Code is in the form of a principles-based framework. It contains some rules but in the main it is flexible guidance. It can be seen as being a framework of principles rather than a set of rules. There are a number of advantages of a framework of principles over a system of ethical rules.

3.1 Advantages of principles based guidance

(a) A framework of guidance places the onus on the professional to **consider actively** relevant issues in a given situation, rather than just agreeing action with a checklist of forbidden items. It also requires the professional to **demonstrate** that a responsible conclusion has been reached about ethical issues.

(b) The framework prevents professionals interpreting legalistic requirements narrowly to get around the ethical requirements. There is an extent to which rules engender deception, whereas principles encourage compliance.

(c) A framework allows for variations that are found in every individual situation. Each situation is likely to be different.

(d)   A framework can accommodate a rapidly changing environment, such as the one in which auditors operate.

(e)   A framework can contain prohibitions where these are necessary when principles are not enough.

(f)   A code prescribes minimum standards of behaviour that are expected.

(g)   Codes can include examples to illustrate how the principles are applied.

3.2 Disadvantages of principles based guidance

(a)   As ethical codes cannot include all circumstances and dilemmas, accountants need a very good understanding of the underlying principles.

(b)   International codes such as the IESBA Code cannot fully capture regional variations in beliefs and practice.

(c)   The illustrative examples can be interpreted mistakenly as rules to follow in all similar circumstances.

(d)   Principles based codes can be difficult to enforce legally, unless the breach of the code is blatant. Most are therefore voluntary and perhaps therefore less effective.

Section summary

The CIMA Code is a **principles based framework**. There are advantages and disadvantages of a principles based framework over a system of rules.

4   Fundamental principles

Introduction

This section explains the fundamental principles in the CIMA Code, threats to those principles and the safeguards which can be applied to counteract those threats.

4.1 CIMA fundamental principles of professional ethics

CIMA's ethical guidelines are available at **www.cimaglobal.com**. Ensure you read them.

CIMA's *Code of ethics for professional accountants* was last revised in October 2010 and is based on IESBA's *Code of ethics for professional accountants*. It sets out the five fundamental principles of professional ethics and provides a conceptual framework for applying those principles.

CIMA members must not only **know** the fundamental principles, but also **apply** them in their everyday work. There are **serious consequences for failing to follow them**, quite apart from the unacceptability of failure. Whenever a complaint is made against a member, failure to follow the contents of the fundamental principles will be taken into account when a decision is made as to whether a *prima facie* case exists of professional misconduct. The code reflects the standards CIMA expects from both its **members** and **students**.

The five fundamental principles are summarised in the table below.

Fundamental principles	
Integrity	A professional accountant should be straightforward and honest in all professional and business relationships.
Objectivity	A professional accountant should not allow bias, conflict of interest or undue influence of others to override professional or business judgements.
Professional competence and due care	A professional accountant has a continuing duty to maintain professional knowledge and skill at the level required to ensure that a client or employer receives competent professional service based on current developments in practice, legislation and techniques. A professional accountant should act diligently and in accordance with applicable technical and professional standards when providing professional services.
Confidentiality	A professional accountant should respect the confidentiality of information acquired as a result of professional and business relationships and should not disclose any such information to third parties without proper and specific authority unless there is a legal or professional right or duty to disclose. Confidential information acquired as a result of professional and business relationships should not be used for the personal advantage of the professional accountant or third parties.
Professional behaviour	A professional accountant should comply with relevant laws and regulations and should avoid any action that discredits the profession.

4.1.1 Integrity

Integrity is the important principle of honesty and requires accountants to be straightforward in all professional and business relationships. Particular care must be taken when reporting figures and statements. Omitting key information, obscuring the facts or making calculations and decisions without due care could result in false or misleading information being produced and integrity being breached.

Integrity goes further than the work an accountant produces. It also requires the accountant to act in a professional, consistent manner. The accountant must treat everyone the same rather than being friendly to some colleagues but cold to others. It also means that they should not back down over their personal or professional values just to avoid a difficult situation.

4.1.2 Objectivity

Objectivity is a combination of impartiality, intellectual honesty and a freedom from conflicts of interest. Accountants should act fairly and not allow prejudice or bias or the influence of others to affect their judgements. It contrasts with subjectivity which means an individual takes matters into consideration which are important to them, eg friendship and loyalty.

Objectivity is the core value that an accountant brings to their organisation. It is often difficult to separate one's personal interest from a decision, but as accountants it is expected.

Circumstances which may leave accountants in particular risk of breaching this principle include accepting excessive hospitality or forming illicit relationships which could cause embarrassment and the risk of blackmail. Where a threat to objectivity exists, it can be reduced or eliminated by withdrawal, terminating the relationship, involving others in the process and discussing the problem with seniors.

4.1.3 Professional competence and due care

Professional competence and due care means accountants should refrain from performing any services that they cannot perform with reasonable care, knowledge, competence, diligence and a full awareness of the important issues. There is a duty to remain technically up-to-date and apply appropriate technical and professional standards when providing professional services.

Where others perform work on the accountant's behalf, the accountant must ensure that such staff also have adequate experience, qualification and are supervised. Limitations and problems found should be disclosed to those to whom the accountant is reporting. Fact and opinion should be clearly identified to avoid misunderstandings.

4.1.4 Confidentiality

Accountants have a duty to safeguard the security of information in their possession unless there is a legal or professional right or duty to disclose. Also this means not using information obtained in the course of work for personal advantage or for the benefit of others.

Breaches of confidentiality often occur when information is inadvertently disclosed to friends and family and where the accountant has recently changed employers. Care must be taken to keep confidential all information found in the course of performing a professional duty and where a new job is commenced, prior experience may be used in the new role, but not prior information.

CIMA's Code lists circumstances where confidential information may be disclosed. Examples include:

- Disclosure is permitted by law and is authorised by the client or employer.

- Disclosure is required by law, such as providing evidence in legal proceedings or assisting public authorities when legal infringements have occurred.

- Disclosure is permitted by a professional duty or right, such as complying with technical or ethical requirements, protecting the professional interests of an accountant in a legal action, to respond to a professional body in an investigation or to comply with a quality review.

4.1.5 Professional behaviour

Professional behaviour means, in essence, not doing anything that might bring discredit to the profession and to comply with all relevant laws and regulations. This is defined by the profession as 'actions which a reasonable and informed third party, having knowledge of all relevant information, would conclude negatively affects the good reputation of the profession.'

Section summary

The five fundamental principles are **integrity**, **objectivity**, **professional competence and due care**, **confidentiality** and **professional behaviour**.

5 Threats and safeguards

Introduction

This section covers the type of threat that a professional accountant might face and the action that should be taken if such a threat arises.

5.1 Threats to compliance with the fundamental principles

Compliance with the fundamental principles could be threatened by a wide range of circumstances and relationships. These threats can occur whether a professional accountant works in business or in practice (eg as an external auditor). As a professional accountant, you need to be able to identify threats to your compliance with the fundamental principles. If the threat is anything other than trivial, you will need to take steps to reduce it to an acceptable level. The CIMA code identifies the following common categories of threats.

Threat	Description
Self-interest	The threat that a financial or other interest will inappropriately influence the professional accountant's judgement or behaviour (this often results in a **conflict of interest** situation).
Self-review	The threat that a professional accountant will not appropriately evaluate the results of a previous judgement made by themselves or by another individual within their firm.
Advocacy	The threat that a professional accountant will promote a client's or employer's position to the point that the professional accountant's objectivity is compromised.
Familiarity	The threat that due to a long or close relationship with a client or employer, a professional accountant will be too sympathetic to their interests or too accepting of their work.
Intimidation	The threat that a professional accountant will be deterred from acting objectively because of actual or perceived pressures, including attempts to exercise undue influence over the professional accountant.

Examples of these threats for both the professional accountant in business and the professional accountant in practice are given below.

Threat	Examples: Accountant in business	Examples: Accountant in practice (audit)
Self-interest	Financial interests, loans and guarantees, incentive compensation arrangements, personal use of corporate assets, external commercial pressures, acceptance of a gift	Having a financial interest in a client, the possibility of losing a client
Self-review	Business decisions being subject to review and justification by the same accountant responsible for making those decisions or preparing the data supporting them, reporting on the functionality of a system that you helped to create	Auditing financial statements prepared by the firm
Advocacy	Furthering the employer's cause aggressively without regard to reasonableness of statements made. (Furthering legitimate goals of employer organisation would not generally create an advocacy threat provided that statements made are not misleading)	Acting as an advocate in a client's lawsuit or dispute
Familiarity	Long association with business contacts who can influence decisions, long association with colleagues	Audit team member having family at the client, acceptance of gifts or preferential treatment from a client
Intimidation	Threats of dismissal from employment, influence of a dominant personality	Threats of replacement due to disagreement

5.2 Safeguards against threats

As we have seen, compliance with these principles could be threatened by a wide range of circumstances. The professional accountant should apply safeguards to counteract these threats.

There are two general categories of safeguard identified in the CIMA guidance. These are:

(a) Safeguards created by the profession, legislation or regulation. Legal rules and professional codes are specifically designed to support ethical behaviour: a partial solution is therefore to comply with the rules! Potential safeguards include:

- Education and training, as a requirement for entry into the profession

- Continuing professional development whilst within the profession (both of these are safeguards because they help you make the right decisions)

- Corporate governance regulations (eg on internal company controls and financial reporting)

- Professional standards, related monitoring and disciplinary procedures (including complaints procedures and a duty to report breaches of ethical requirements to deter unethical behaviour)

- Third-party review of financial reports and returns produced by members (eg the auditing of accounts)

(b)   Safeguards in the work environment, which increase the likelihood of identifying or deterring unethical behaviour, include:

- Quality controls, and internal audits of quality controls

- Mechanisms to empower and protect staff who raise ethical concerns ('whistleblowers')

- Involvement of, or consultation with, independent third parties (eg non executive directors or regulatory bodies)

- Rotation of personnel to avoid increasing familiarity and opportunities for collusion in fraud

- Opportunities to discuss ethical dilemmas (eg with an ethics officer, committee or forum)

5.3 Dealing with an ethical dilemma

An ethical dilemma exists when you find yourself in a situation where one or more of the fundamental principles of the CIMA Code are threatened.

The CIMA Code provides advice on what to do if you are facing an ethical dilemma: firstly you should consider the relevant facts and relevant parties involved, the fundamental principles related to the matter in question, established internal procedures at your company and the different courses of action you could take.

Once you have considered the above, you then need to decide what to do next. You should:

(1)   Determine an appropriate course of action that is consistent with the fundamental principles in the CIMA Code, weighing the consequences of each possible course of action. You should always consider the law, financial regulations and your organisation's policies when deciding what to do.

(2)   If the matter remains unresolved after taking that course of action, you should consult with your manager or relevant colleagues in your organisation for help in resolving the situation. It might be that you need to consider escalating your concerns, for example with senior managers or the board of directors. You should follow your organisation's internal grievance or whistle blowing procedure if there is one.

(3)   If after raising the issue internally, the matter still remains unresolved and you consider it to be significant, you should consider obtaining professional advice from the relevant professional body or from legal advisers.

(4)   Finally if the conflict remains unresolved, you consider how to remove yourself from the matter creating the conflict. In extreme cases, you may need to consider resigning. Seek advice before you take this step.

The CIMA Code recommends documenting the substance of the issue, the details of any discussions held, and the decisions made concerning that issue so that you can show how you dealt with the issue if you need to. You can always contact the CIMA ethics helpline to help you consider your course of action and to guide you through the CIMA Code.

See **www.cimaglobal.com/Professional-ethics/Ethics/** for help and advice on ethics.

5.4 Specific threats facing an accountant in business

Section 320 of the 2010 CIMA Code deals with the preparation and reporting of information. It specifies that a professional accountant in business should maintain information for which they are responsible so that it describes the true nature of transactions, assets and liabilities, is timely, accurate and complete.

5.4.1 Conflicts between professional and employment obligations

Ethical guidance stresses that a professional accountant should normally support the legitimate and ethical obligations established by the employer. However the professional accountant may be pressurised to act in ways that threaten compliance with the fundamental principles. These include:

- Acting contrary to law, regulation, technical or professional standards
- Aiding unethical or illegal earnings management strategies
- Misleading auditors or regulators
- Issuing or being associated with a report that misrepresents the facts

If these problems are faced, the accountant should either obtain advice from inside the employer, an independent professional advisor, CIMA, lawyers, or use the formal procedures within the organisation.

5.4.2 Preparation and reporting of information

As well as complying with financial reporting standards, the professional accountant in business should aim to prepare information that describes clearly the nature of the business transactions, classifies and records information in a timely and proper manner, and represents the facts accurately. If the accountant faces pressures to produce misleading information, superiors should be consulted, such as an audit committee. The accountant should not be associated with misleading information, and may need to seek legal advice or report to the appropriate authorities.

5.4.3 Acting with sufficient expertise

Guidance stresses that the professional accountant should only undertake tasks for which he or she has sufficient specific training or experience. Certain pressures may threaten the ability of the professional accountant to perform duties with appropriate competence and due care:

- Lack of information
- Insufficient training, experience or education
- Lack of time
- Inadequate resources

Whether this is a significant threat will depend on the other people the accountant is working with, the seniority of the accountant and the level of supervision and review of work. If the problem is serious, the accountant should take steps to remedy the situation including obtaining training, ensuring time is available and consulting with others where appropriate. Refusal to perform duties is the last resort.

5.4.4 Financial interests

Ethical guidance highlights financial interests as a self-interest threat to objectivity and confidentiality. In particular the temptation to manipulate price-sensitive information in order to gain financially is stressed. Financial interests may include shares, profit-related bonuses or share options.

This threat can be countered by the individual consulting with superiors and disclosing all relevant information. Having a remuneration committee composed of independent non-executive directors determining the remuneration packages of executive directors can help resolve the problems at senior levels.

5.4.5 Inducements

Ethical guidance highlights the possibility that accountants may be offered inducements to influence actions or decisions, encourage illegal behaviour or obtain confidential information.

The guidance points out that threats to compliance may appear to arise not only from the accountant making or accepting the inducement, but from the offer having being made in the first place. The guidance recommends that directors or senior managers be informed, and disclosure may be made to

third parties. The accountant should also disclose to senior management whether any close relatives work for competitors or suppliers.

Section summary

Professional accountants may face threats to the fundamental principles in the form of **self-review, self-interest, advocacy, familiarity and intimidation threats**. Appropriate **safeguards** must be put in place to eliminate or reduce such threats to acceptable levels.

The accountant in business may face a variety of difficulties including conflicts between professional and employment obligations, pressure to prepare misleading information, a lack of sufficient expertise, financial interests or inducements.

Chapter Summary

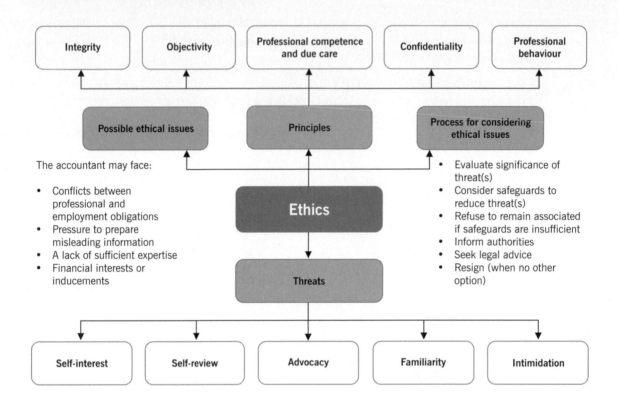

Quick Quiz

1   Which of the following is not an advantage of a principles-based ethical code?

    A   It prevents narrow, legalistic interpretations

    B   It can accommodate a rapidly changing environment

    C   The illustrative examples provided can be followed in all similar situations

    D   It prescribes minimum expected standards of behaviour

2   Fill in the blank.

    .... means that a professional accountant should be straightforward and honest in all business and professional relationships.

3   List **three** examples of a familiarity threat.

4   Which of the following is not a legitimate reason to disclose confidential information?

    A   Disclosure is permitted by law

    B   To protect the professional interests of an accountant in a legal investigation

    C   To assist a family member

    D   To provide information to a bank where disclosure is authorised by your employer

5   Jake has been put under significant pressure by his manager to change the conclusion of a report he has written which reflects badly on the manager's performance.

    Which threat is Jake facing?

    A   Self-interest

    B   Advocacy

    C   Intimidation

    D   Self-review

Answers to Quick Quiz

1   C   Although the examples may be good guides for conduct in many instances, circumstances will vary, so they should not be seen as totally prescriptive.

2   Integrity

3   • Making a business decision that will affect a close family member
    • Long association with a business contact
    • Acceptance of hospitality

4   C   Care should be taken not to disclose confidential information to family members.

5   C   'Significant pressure' indicates an intimidation threat.

Answers to Questions

3.1 Ethical issues

(a)   Dealing with unpleasantly authoritarian governments can be supported on the grounds that it **contributes to economic growth and prosperity** and all the benefits they bring to society in both countries concerned. It can also be opposed as it is **contributing to the continuation of the regime,** and is **fundamentally repugnant**.

(b)   Honesty in advertising is an important problem. Many products are promoted exclusively on image. Deliberately creating the impression that purchasing a particular product will enhance the happiness, success and sex-appeal of the buyer can be attacked as **dishonest.** It can be defended on the grounds that the supplier is actually **selling a fantasy or dream** rather than a physical article.

(c)   Dealings with employees are coloured by the **opposing views of corporate responsibility and individual rights**. The idea of a job as property to be defended has now disappeared from labour relations in many countries, but corporate decisions that lead to redundancies are still deplored. This is because of the obvious **impact of sudden unemployment on aspirations and living standards**, even when the employment market is buoyant. Nevertheless businesses have to consider the cost of employing labour as well as its productive capacity.

(d)   The main problems with payments or gifts to officials are making the distinction between those that should never be made, and those that can be made in certain cultural circumstances.

   (i)   **Extortion**. Foreign officials have been known to threaten companies with the complete closure of their local operations unless suitable payments are made.

   (ii)   **Bribery**. This is payments for services to which a company is not legally entitled. There are some fine distinctions to be drawn; for example, some managers regard political contributions as bribery.

   (iii)   **Grease money**. Multinational companies are sometimes unable to obtain services to which they are legally entitled because of deliberate stalling by local officials. Cash payments to the right people may then be enough to oil the machinery of bureaucracy.

   (iv)   **Gifts**. In some cultures (such as Japan) gifts are regarded as an essential part of civilised negotiation, even in circumstances where to Western eyes they might appear ethically dubious. Managers operating in such a culture may feel at liberty to adopt the local customs.

3.2 Employee behaviour

Here are some suggestions.

- Recruitment and selection policies and procedures
- Induction and training
- Objectives and reward schemes
- Ethical codes
- Threat of ethical audit

Now try these questions from the OTQ Question Bank	**Number**
	Q16
	Q28

THE CONCEPTUAL FRAMEWORK

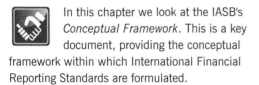

In this chapter we look at the IASB's *Conceptual Framework*. This is a key document, providing the conceptual framework within which International Financial Reporting Standards are formulated.

4

topic list	learning outcomes	syllabus references
1 The IASB *Conceptual Framework*	B1	B1 (b)
2 The objective of general purpose financial reporting	B1	B1 (b)
3 Underlying assumption	B1	B1 (b)
4 Qualitative characteristics of useful financial information	B1	B1 (b)
5 The elements of financial statements	B1	B1 (b)
6 Recognition of the elements of financial statements	B1	B1 (b)
7 Measurement of the elements of financial statements	B1	B1 (b)
8 Fair representation and compliance with IFRS	B1	B1 (b)
9 IFRS 13 *Fair value measurement*	B1	B1 (b)

Chapter Overview

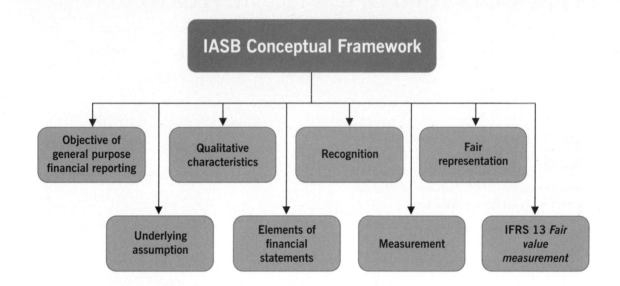

1   The IASB *Conceptual Framework*

Introduction

This section explains the *Conceptual Framework* developed by the IASB.

1.1 A conceptual framework

In July 1989 the old International Accounting Standards Committee (IASC) produced a document called *Framework for the preparation and presentation of financial statements*. In 2010 this was updated to 'The *Conceptual Framework for Financial Reporting*. The *Conceptual Framework* is the basis upon which all IASs and IFRSs are developed and it therefore determines how financial statements are prepared and the information they contain.

The *Conceptual Framework* consists of four chapters, following on after a foreword and introduction. These **chapters** are as follows.

Chapter 1   The objective of general purpose financial reporting

Chapter 2   The reporting entity (to be added at a later date)

Chapter 3   Qualitative characteristics of useful financial information

Chapter 4   The remaining text from the 1989 *Framework*

- Underlying assumption
- The elements of financial statements
- Recognition of the elements of financial statements
- Measurement of the elements of financial statements
- Concepts of capital and capital maintenance

1.2 Preface

The preface to the *Conceptual Framework* points out the fundamental reason why financial statements are produced worldwide, ie to **satisfy the requirements of external users**, but that practice varies due to the individual pressures in each country.

These pressures may be social, political, economic or legal, but they result in variations in practice from country to country, including the form of statements, the definition of their component parts (assets, liabilities etc), the criteria for recognition of items and both the scope and disclosure of financial statements.

1.3 Introduction

The introduction to the *Conceptual Framework* lays out the purpose, status and scope of the document. It then looks at different users of financial statements and their information needs.

1.3.1 Purpose and status

The introduction gives a list of the purposes of the *Conceptual Framework*.

(a)   to assist the Board in the **development of future IFRSs** and in its review of existing IFRSs.

(b)   to assist the Board in **promoting harmonisation** of regulations, accounting standards and procedures relating to the presentation of financial statements by providing a basis for reducing the number of alternative accounting treatments permitted by IFRSs.

(c)   to assist **national standard-setting bodies** in developing national standards.

(d) to assist **preparers of financial statements** in applying IFRSs and in dealing with topics that have yet to form the subject of an IFRS.

(e) to assist **auditors** in forming an opinion as to whether financial statements conform with IFRSs.

(f) to assist **users of financial statements** in interpreting the information contained in financial statements prepared in conformity with IFRSs.

(g) to provide those who are interested in the work of IASB with **information** about its approach to the formulation of IFRSs.

The *Conceptual Framework* is not an IFRS and hence does not define standards for any particular measurement or disclosure issue. Nothing in this *Conceptual Framework* overrides any specific IFRS. In the (rare) cases of conflict between an IFRS and the *Conceptual Framework*, the **IFRS will prevail**. These cases will diminish over time as the *Conceptual Framework* will be used as a guide in the production of future IFRS. The *Conceptual Framework* itself will be revised occasionally depending on the experience of the IASB in using it.

1.3.2 Scope

The *Conceptual Framework* deals with:

(a) The **objective** of financial reporting

(b) The **qualitative characteristics** of useful financial information

(c) The **definition, recognition and measurement** of the elements from which financial statements are constructed

(d) Concepts of **capital and capital maintenance**

The *Conceptual Framework* is concerned with **'general purpose' financial statements** (ie a normal set of annual statements), but it can be applied to other types of accounts. A complete set of financial statements includes:

(a) A statement of financial position

(b) A statement of profit or loss and other comprehensive income

(c) A statement of changes in financial position (eg a statement of cash flow, statement of changes in equity)

(d) Notes, other statements and explanatory material

Supplementary information may be included, but some items are not included, namely commentaries and reports by the directors, the chairman, management etc.

All types of financial reporting entities are included (commercial, industrial, business; public or private sector).

KEY TERM

A REPORTING ENTITY is an entity for which there are users who rely on the financial statements as their major source of financial information about the entity.   *(Conceptual Framework)*

1.3.3 Users and their information needs

Users of accounting information consist of investors, employees, lenders, suppliers and other trade payables, customers, government and their agencies and the public. You should be able to remember enough to do the following exercise.

Question 4.1   Users of financial information

Consider the information needs of the users of financial information listed above.

2 The objective of general purpose financial reporting

Introduction

The *Conceptual Framework* states that:

'The objective of general purpose financial reporting is to provide information about the reporting entity that is useful to existing and potential investors, lenders and other creditors in making decisions about providing resources to the entity.'

These users7 need information about:

- the **economic resources of the entity**;
- the **claims against the entity**; and
- changes in the entity's **economic resources and claims**

Information about the entity's **economic resources and the claims against it** helps users to assess the entity's liquidity and solvency and its likely needs for additional financing.

Information about a reporting entity's financial performance (the **changes in its economic resources and claims**) helps users to understand the return that the entity has produced on its economic resources. This is an indicator of how efficiently and effectively management has used the resources of the entity and is helpful in predicting future returns.

The *Conceptual Framework* makes it clear that this information should be prepared on an **accruals basis**.

KEY TERM

ACCRUALS BASIS The effects of transactions and other events are recognised when they occur (and not as cash or its equivalent is received or paid) and they are recorded in the accounting records and reported in the financial statements of the periods to which they relate.

Financial statements prepared under the accruals basis show users past transactions involving cash and also obligations to pay cash in the future and resources which represent cash to be received in the future.

Information about a reporting entity's cash flows during a period also helps users assess the entity's **ability to generate future net cash inflows** and gives users a better understanding of its operations .

3 Underlying assumption

Introduction

Going concern is the underlying assumption in preparing financial statements.

3.1 Going concern

KEY TERM

GOING CONCERN The entity is normally viewed as a going concern, that is, as continuing in operation for the foreseeable future. It is assumed that the entity has neither the intention nor the necessity of liquidation or of curtailing materially the scale of its operations.   *(Conceptual Framework)*

It is assumed that the entity has no intention to liquidate or curtail major operations. If it did, then the financial statements would be prepared on a **different (disclosed) basis.**

4 Qualitative characteristics of useful financial information

Introduction

The *Conceptual Framework* states that qualitative characteristics are the attributes that make financial information useful to users.

Chapter 3 of the *Conceptual Framework* distinguishes between **fundamental** and **enhancing** qualitative characteristics, for analysis purposes.

Fundamental qualitative characteristics distinguish useful financial reporting information from information that is not useful or misleading.

Enhancing qualitative characteristics distinguish more useful information from less useful information.

The two fundamental qualitative characteristics are **relevance** and **faithful representation**.

4.1 Relevance

KEY TERM

RELEVANCE. Relevant information is capable of making a difference in the decisions made by users. It is capable of making a difference in decisions in decisions if it has **predictive value**, **confirmatory value** or both.   *(Conceptual Framework)*

The relevance of information is affected by its **nature** and its **materiality**.

KEY TERM

MATERIALITY. Information is material if omitting it or misstating it could influence decisions that users make on the basis of financial information about a specific reporting entity.   *(Conceptual Framework)*

4.2 Faithful representation

KEY TERM

FAITHFUL REPRESENTATION. Financial reports represent **economic phenomena** in words and numbers. To be useful, financial information must not only represent relevant phenomena but must **faithfully represent** the phenomena that it purports to represent.   *(Conceptual Framework)*

To be a faithful representation information must be **complete, neutral** and **free from error**.

A **complete** depiction includes all information necessary for a user to understand the phenomenon being depicted, including all necessary descriptions and explanations.

A **neutral** depiction is without bias in the selection or presentation of financial information. This means that information must not be manipulated in any way in order to influence the decisions of users.

Free from error means there are no errors or omissions in the description of the phenomenon and no errors made in the process by which the financial information was produced. It does not mean that no inaccuracies can arise, particularly where estimates have to be made.

4.2.1 Substance over form

This is **not a separate qualitative characteristic** under the *Conceptual Framework*. The IASB says that to do so would be redundant because it is **implied in faithful representation**. Faithful representation of a transaction is only possible if it is accounted for according to its **substance and economic reality**.

4.3 Enhancing qualitative characteristics

4.3.1 Comparability

KEY TERM

COMPARABILITY. Comparability is the qualitative characteristic that enables users to identify and understand similarities in, and differences among, items. Information about a reporting entity is more useful if it can be compared with similar information about other entities and with similar information about the same entity for another period or date. *(Conceptual Framework)*

Consistency, although related to comparability, **is not the same**. It refers to the use of the same methods for the same items (i.e. consistency of treatment) either from period to period within a reporting entity or in a single period across entities.

The **disclosure of accounting policies** is particularly important here. Users must be able to distinguish between different accounting policies in order to be able to make a valid comparison of similar items in the accounts of different entities.

Comparability is **not the same as uniformity**. Entities should change accounting policies if those policies become inappropriate.

Corresponding information for preceding periods should be shown to enable comparison over time.

4.3.2 Verifiability

KEY TERM

VERIFIABILITY. Verifiability helps assure users that information faithfully represents the economic phenomena it purports to represent. It means that different knowledgeable and independent observers could reach consensus that a particular depiction is a faithful representation. *(Conceptual Framework)*

4.3.3 Timeliness

KEY TERM

TIMELINESS. Timeliness means having information available to decision-makers in time to be capable of influencing their decisions. Generally, the older information is the less useful it is. *(Conceptual Framework)*

Information may become less useful if there is a delay in reporting it. There is a **balance between timeliness and the provision of reliable information**.

If information is reported on a timely basis when not all aspects of the transaction are known, it may not be complete or free from error.

Conversely, if every detail of a transaction is known, it may be too late to publish the information because it has become irrelevant. The overriding consideration is how best to satisfy the economic decision-making needs of the users.

4.3.4 Understandability

KEY TERM

UNDERSTANDABILITY. Classifying, characterising and presenting information clearly and concisely makes it understandable. *(Conceptual Framework)*

Financial reports are prepared for users who have a **reasonable knowledge of business and economic activities** and who review and analyse the information diligently. Some phenomena are inherently complex and cannot be made easy to understand. Excluding information on those phenomena might make the information easier to understand, but without it those reports would be incomplete and therefore misleading. Therefore matters should not be left out of financial statements simply due to their difficulty as even well-informed and diligent users may sometimes need the aid of an advisor to understand information about complex economic phenomena.

The cost constraint on useful financial reporting

This is a pervasive constraint, not a qualitative characteristic. When information is provided, its benefits must exceed the costs of obtaining and presenting it. This is a **subjective area** and there are other difficulties: others, not the intended users, may gain a benefit; also the cost may be paid by someone other than the users. It is therefore difficult to apply a cost-benefit analysis, but preparers and users should be aware of the constraint.

5 The elements of financial statements

 Introduction

Transactions and other events are grouped together in broad **classes** and in this way their financial effects are shown in the financial statements. These broad classes are the **elements** of financial statements.

The *Conceptual Framework* lays out these elements as follows.

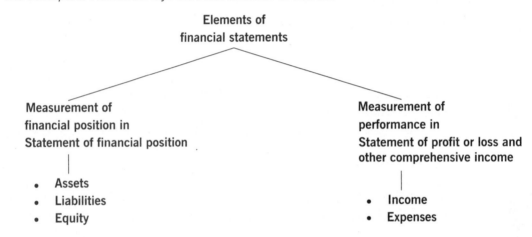

A process of **sub-classification** then takes place for presentation in the financial statements, eg assets are classified by their nature or function in the business to show information in the best way for users to take economic decisions.

5.1 Financial position

We need to define the three terms listed under this heading above.

KEY TERMS

ASSET. A **resource controlled** by an entity **as a result of past events** and from which **future economic benefits** are expected to flow to the entity.

LIABILITY. A **present obligation** of the entity **arising from past events**, the settlement of which is expected to result in an **outflow** from the entity of resources embodying economic benefits.

EQUITY. The **residual interest** in the assets of the entity after deducting all its liabilities.

(Conceptual Framework)

These definitions are important, but they do not cover the **criteria for recognition** of any of these items, which are discussed in the next section of this chapter. This means that the definitions may include items which would not actually be recognised in the statement of financial position because they fail to satisfy recognition criteria particularly the **probable flow of any economic benefit** to or from the business.

Whether an item satisfies any of the definitions above will depend on the **substance and economic reality** of the transaction, not merely its legal form.

5.2 Assets

We can look in more detail at the components of the definitions given above.

KEY TERM

FUTURE ECONOMIC BENEFIT. The potential to contribute, directly or indirectly, to the flow of cash and cash equivalents to the entity. The potential may be a productive one that is part of the operating activities of the entity. It may also take the form of convertibility into cash or cash equivalents or a capability to reduce cash outflows, such as when an alternative manufacturing process lowers the cost of production.

(Conceptual Framework)

Assets are usually employed to produce goods or services for customers; customers will then pay for these. **Cash itself** renders a service to the entity due to its command over other resources.

The existence of an asset, particularly in terms of **control**, is not reliant on:

(a)   **physical form** (hence patents and copyrights); *nor*

(b)   **legal rights** (hence leases).

Transactions or events **in the past** give rise to assets; those expected to occur in the future do not in themselves give rise to assets. For example, an intention to purchase a non-current asset does not, in itself, meet the definition of an asset.

5.3 Liabilities

Again we can look more closely at some aspects of the definition. An essential characteristic of a liability is that the entity has a **present obligation**.

KEY TERM

OBLIGATION. A duty or responsibility to act or perform in a certain way. Obligations may be legally enforceable as a consequence of a binding contract or statutory requirement. Obligations also arise, however, from normal business practice, custom and a desire to maintain good business relations or act in an equitable manner.

(Conceptual Framework)

It is important to distinguish between a present obligation and a **future commitment**. A management decision to purchase assets in the future does not, in itself, give rise to a present obligation.

Settlement of a present obligation will involve the entity giving up resources embodying economic benefits in order to satisfy the claim of the other party. This may be done in various ways, not just by payment of cash.

Liabilities must arise from **past transactions or events**. In the case of, say, recognition of future rebates to customers based on annual purchases, the sale of goods in the past is the transaction that gives rise to the liability.

Question 4.2

Assets and liabilities

Consider the following situations. In each case, do we have an asset or liability within the definitions given by the *Conceptual Framework?* Give reasons for your answer.

(a)   Pat Co has purchased a patent for $20,000. The patent gives the company sole use of a particular manufacturing process which will save $3,000 a year for the next five years.

(b)   Baldwin Co paid Don Brennan $10,000 to set up a car repair shop, on condition that priority treatment is given to cars from the company's fleet.

(c)   Deals on Wheels Co provides a warranty with every car sold

5.4 Equity

Equity is defined above as a **residual**, but it may be sub-classified in the statement of financial position. This will indicate legal or other restrictions on the ability of the entity to distribute or otherwise apply its equity. Some reserves are required by statute or other law, eg for the future protection of creditors. The amount shown for equity depends on the **measurement of assets and liabilities.** It has nothing to do with the market value of the entity's shares.

5.5 Performance

Profit is used as a **measure of performance**, or as a basis for other measures (eg Earnings per share). It depends directly on the measurement of income and expenses, which in turn depend (in part) on the concepts of capital and capital maintenance adopted.

The elements of income and expense are therefore defined.

KEY TERMS

INCOME. **Increases in economic benefits** during the accounting period in the form of inflows or enhancements of assets or decreases of liabilities that **result in increases in equity, other than those relating to contributions from equity participants**.

EXPENSES. **Decreases in economic benefits** during the accounting period in the form of outflows or depletions of assets or incurrences of liabilities that **result in decreases in equity, other than those relating to distributions to equity participants**.   *(Conceptual Framework)*

Income and expenses can be **presented in different ways** in the statement of profit or loss and other comprehensive income, to provide information relevant for economic decision-making. For example, income and expenses which relate to continuing operations are distinguished from the results of discontinued operations.

5.6 Income

Both **revenue** and **gains** are included in the definition of income. **Revenue** arises in the course of ordinary activities of an entity.

KEY TERM

GAINS. Increases in economic benefits. As such they are no different in nature from revenue.
                              (Conceptual Framework)

Gains include those arising on the disposal of non-current assets. The definition of income also includes **unrealised gains**, eg on revaluation of marketable securities.

5.7 Expenses

As with income, the definition of expenses includes losses as well as those expenses that arise in the course of ordinary activities of an entity.

KEY TERM

LOSSES. Decreases in economic benefits. As such they are no different in nature from other expenses.

(Conceptual Framework)

Losses will include those arising on the disposal of non-current assets. The definition of expenses will also include **unrealised losses**, eg the fall in value of an investment.

Section summary

Make sure you learn the important definitions.

- Financial position:

    - Assets
    - Liabilities
    - Equity

- Financial performance:

    - Income
    - Expenses

6 Recognition of the elements of financial statements

Introduction

Items which meet the definition of assets or liabilities may still not be recognised in financial statements because they must also meet certain **recognition criteria**.

KEY TERM

RECOGNITION. The process of incorporating in the statement of financial position or statement of profit or loss and other comprehensive income an item that meets the definition of an element and satisfies the following criteria for recognition:

(a)   it is probable that any future economic benefit associated with the item will flow to or from the entity; and

(b)   the item has a cost or value that can be measured with reliability   *(Conceptual Framework)*

Regard must be given to **materiality** (see above).

6.1 Probability of future economic benefits

Probability here means the **degree of uncertainty** that the future economic benefits associated with an item will flow to or from the entity. This must be judged on the basis of the **characteristics of the entity's environment** and the **evidence available** when the financial statements are prepared.

6.2 Reliability of measurement

The cost or value of an item, in many cases, **must be estimated**. The *Conceptual Framework* states, however, that the use of reasonable estimates is an essential part of the preparation of financial statements and does not undermine their reliability. Where no reasonable estimate can be made, the item should not be recognised, although its existence should be disclosed in the notes, or other explanatory material.

Items may still qualify for recognition **at a later date** due to changes in circumstances or subsequent events.

6.3 Assets which cannot be recognised

The recognition criteria do not cover items which many businesses may regard as assets. A skilled workforce is an undoubted asset but workers can leave at any time so there can be no certainty about the probability of future economic benefits. A company may have come up with a new name for its product which is greatly increasing sales but, as it did not buy the name, the name does not have a cost or value that can be reliably measured, so it is not recognised.

6.4 Recognition of items

We can summarise the recognition criteria for assets, liabilities, income and expenses, based on the definition of recognition given above.

Item	Recognised in	When
Asset	The statement of financial position	It is probable that the future economic benefits will flow to the entity and the asset has a cost or value that can be measured reliably.
Liability	The statement of financial position	It is probable that an outflow of resources embodying economic benefits will result from the settlement of a present obligation and the amount at which the settlement will take place can be measured reliably.
Income	The statement of profit or loss and other comprehensive income	An increase in future economic benefits related to an increase in an asset or a decrease of a liability has arisen that can be measured reliably.
Expenses	The statement of profit or loss and other comprehensive income	A decrease in future economic benefits related to a decrease in an asset or an increase of a liability has arisen that can be measured reliably.

7 Measurement of the elements of financial statements

Introduction

A number of different measurement bases are used in financial statements. They include

- Historical cost
- Current cost
- Realisable (settlement) value
- Present value of future cash flows

Measurement is defined as follows.

KEY TERM

MEASUREMENT. The process of determining the monetary amounts at which the elements of the financial statements are to be recognised and carried in the statement of financial position and statement of profit or loss and other comprehensive income.   *(Conceptual Framework)*

This involves the selection of a particular **basis of measurement**. A number of these are used to different degrees and in varying combinations in financial statements. They include the following.

KEY TERMS

HISTORICAL COST. Assets are recorded at the amount of cash or cash equivalents paid or the fair value of the consideration given to acquire them at the time of their acquisition. Liabilities are recorded at the amount of proceeds received in exchange for the obligation, or in some circumstances (for example, income taxes), at the amounts of cash or cash equivalents expected to be paid to satisfy the liability in the normal course of business.

CURRENT COST. Assets are carried at the amount of cash or cash equivalents that would have to be paid if the same or an equivalent asset was acquired currently.

Liabilities are carried at the undiscounted amount of cash or cash equivalents that would be required to settle the obligation currently.

REALISABLE (SETTLEMENT) VALUE.

REALISABLE VALUE. The amount of cash or cash equivalents that could currently be obtained by selling an asset in an orderly disposal.

SETTLEMENT VALUE. The undiscounted amounts of cash or cash equivalents expected to be paid to satisfy the liabilities in the normal course of business.

PRESENT VALUE. A current estimate of the present discounted value of the future net cash flows in the normal course of business.　　　　　　　　　　　　　　　　　　　　　　　　　*(Conceptual Framework)*

7.1 Measurement bases

Historical cost is the most commonly adopted measurement basis, but this is usually combined with other bases, eg inventory is carried at the lower of cost and net realisable value (NRV).

Recent standards use the concept of **fair value**, which is defined by IFRS 13 as 'the price that would be received to sell an asset or paid to transfer a liability in an orderly transaction between market participants at the measurement date'.

The following examples will demonstrate the different valuation methods:

A machine was purchased on 1 January 20X8 for $3m. That was its original cost. It has a useful life of 10 years and under the **historical cost convention** it will be carried at **original cost less accumulated depreciation**. So in the financial statements at 31 December 20X9 it will be carried at:

$3m – (0.3 x 2) = $2.4m

The current cost of the machine, which will probably also be its fair value, will be fairly easy to ascertain if it is not too specialised. For instance, two year old machines like this one may currently be changing hands for $2.5m, so that will be an appropriate fair value.

The **net realisable value** of the machine will be the amount that could be obtained from selling it, less any costs involved in making the sale. If the machine had to be dismantled and transported to the buyer's premises at a cost of $200,000, the NRV would be $2.3m.

The **replacement cost** of the machine will be the cost of a new model less two year's depreciation. The cost of a new machine may now be $3.5m. Assuming a 10-year life, the replacement cost will therefore be $2.8m.

The **present value** of the machine will be the discounted value of the future cash flows that it is expected to generate. If the machine is expected to generate $500,000 per annum for the remaining 8 years of its life and if the company's cost of capital is 10%, present value will be calculated as:

$500,000 × 5.335* = $2667,500

* Cumulative present of $1 per annum for 8 years discounted at 10%

7.2 Advantages of historical cost accounting

As we are still using historical cost accounting, it may be supposed to have a number of advantages. The most important ones are:

- Amounts used are objective and free from bias.

- Amounts are reliable, they can always be verified, they exist on invoices and documents.

- Amounts in the statement of financial position can be matched with amounts in the statement of cash flows.

- Opportunities for creative accounting are fewer than under systems which allow management to apply their judgement to the valuation of assets.

- It has been used for centuries and is easily understood.

7.3 Disadvantages of historical cost accounting

Historical cost accounting has a number of disadvantages. They arise as particular problems in periods of inflation. The main ones are:

- It can lead to understatement of assets in the statement of financial position. A building purchased 50 years ago will appear at the price that was paid for it 50 years ago.

- Because assets are understated, depreciation will also be understated. While the purpose of depreciation is not to set aside funds for replacement of assets, if an asset has to be replaced at twice the price that was paid for its predecessor, the company may decide that it may have been prudent to make some provision for this in earlier years.

- When inventory prices are rising, and when the company is operating a FIFO system, the cheapest inventories are being charged to cost of sales and the most expensive are being designated as closing inventory in the statement of financial position. This leads to understatement of cost of sales.

- An organisation selling in an inflationary market will see its revenue and profits rise, but this is 'paper profit', distorted by the understated depreciation and cost of sales.

From these disadvantages various issues arise:

- Understatement of assets will depress a company's share price and make it vulnerable to takeover. In practice, listed companies avoid this by revaluing land and buildings in line with market values.

- Understated depreciation and understated cost of sales lead to overstatement of profits, compounded by price inflation.

- Overstated profits can lead to too much being distributed to shareholders, leaving insufficient amounts for investment.

- Overstated profits will lead shareholders to expect higher dividends and employees to demand higher wages.

- Overstated profits lead to overstated tax bills.

During periods where price inflation is low, profit overstatement will be marginal. The disadvantages of historical cost accounting become most apparent in periods of inflation.

7.4 Concepts of capital and capital maintenance

The problem of when profit can be recognised depends on what constitutes an increase in capital. Most entities use a **financial concept of capital** when preparing their financial statements.

First of all, we need to define the different concepts of capital.

> **CAPITAL**. Under a **financial concept of capital**, such as invested money or invested purchasing power, capital is the net assets or equity of the entity. The financial concept of capital is adopted by most entities.
>
> Under a **physical concept of capital**, such as operating capability, capital is the productive capacity of the entity based on, for example, units of output per day.   *(Conceptual Framework)*

The definition of profit is also important.

> **PROFIT** . The residual amount that remains after expenses (including capital maintenance adjustments, where appropriate) have been deducted from income. Any amount over and above that required to maintain the capital at the beginning of the period is profit.   *(Conceptual Framework)*

The main difference between the two concepts of capital maintenance is the treatment of the **effects of changes in the prices of assets and liabilities** of the entity. In general terms, an entity has maintained its capital if it has as much capital at the end of the period as it had at the beginning of the period. Any amount over and above that required to maintain the capital at the beginning of the period is profit.

(a)   **Financial capital maintenance**: profit is the increase in nominal money capital over the period. This is the concept used in Current Purchasing Power, and used under historical cost accounting.

(b)   **Physical capital maintenance**: profit is the increase in the physical productive capacity over the period. This is the concept used in Current Cost Accounting.

7.5 Capital maintenance in times of inflation

Profit can be measured as the **difference between how wealthy a company is at the beginning and at the end of an accounting period.**

(a)   This wealth can be expressed in terms of the capital of a company as shown in its opening and closing statements of financial position.

(b)   A business which maintains its capital unchanged during an accounting period can be said to have broken even.

(c)   Once **capital has been maintained, anything** achieved **in excess represents profit.**

For this analysis to be of any use, we must be able to draw up a company's statement of financial position at the beginning and at the end of a period, so as to place a value on the opening and closing capital. There are particular difficulties in doing this during a **period of rising prices**.

In conventional historical cost accounts, assets are stated in the statement of financial position at the amount it cost to acquire them (less any amounts written off in respect of depreciation or impairment in value). Capital is simply the **difference between assets and liabilities**.

For example, consider the following opening and closing statements of financial position of a company.

	Opening	Closing
	$	$
Inventory (100 items at cost)	500	600
Other net assets	1,000	1,000
Capital	1,500	1,600

Assuming that no new capital has been introduced during the year, and no capital has been distributed as dividends, the profit shown in historical cost accounts would be $100, being the excess of closing capital over opening capital. And yet in physical terms the company is no better off: it still has 100 units of

inventory (which cost $5 each at the beginning of the period, but $6 each at the end) and its other net assets are identical. The 'profit' earned has merely enabled the company to keep pace with inflation.

An alternative to the concept of capital maintenance based on historical costs is to express capital in **physical** terms. On this basis, no profit would be recognised in the example above because the physical substance of the company is unchanged over the accounting period. Capital is maintained if at the end of the period the company is in a position to achieve the same physical output as it was at the beginning of the period. You should bear in mind that financial definitions of capital maintenance are not the only ones possible; in theory at least, there is no reason why profit should not be measured as the increase in a company's **physical** capital over an accounting period.

8 Fair presentation and compliance with IFRS

Financial statements should **present fairly** the financial position, financial performance and cash flows of an entity. **Compliance with IFRS** is presumed to result in financial statements that achieve a fair presentation.

The following points made by IAS 1 expand on this principle.

(a)   **Compliance with IFRS** should be disclosed

(b)   **All relevant IFRS** must be followed if compliance with IFRS is disclosed

(c)   Use of an **inappropriate accounting treatment** cannot be rectified either by disclosure of accounting policies or notes/explanatory material

There may be (very rare) circumstances when management decides that compliance with a requirement of an IFRS would be misleading. **Departure from the IFRS** is therefore required to achieve a fair presentation. The following should be disclosed in such an event.

(a)   Management confirmation that the financial statements fairly present the entity's financial position, performance and cash flows

(b)   Statement that all IFRS have been complied with *except* departure from one IFRS to achieve a fair presentation

(c)   Details of the nature of the departure, why the IFRS treatment would be misleading, and the treatment adopted

(d)   Financial impact of the departure

This is usually referred to as the 'true and fair override'.

8.1 Extreme case disclosures

In very rare circumstances, management may conclude that compliance with a requirement in a Standard or Interpretation may be so **misleading** that it would **conflict with the objective** of financial statements set out in the *Conceptual Framework*, but the relevant regulatory framework prohibits departure from the requirements. In such cases the entity needs to reduce the perceived misleading aspects of compliance by **disclosing**:

(a)   The title of the Standard, the nature of the requirement and the reason why management has reached its conclusion.

(b)   For each period, the adjustment to each item in the financial statements that would be necessary to achieve fair presentation.

IAS 1 states what is required for a fair presentation.

(a)   Selection and application of **accounting policies**

(b)   **Presentation of information** in a manner which provides relevant, reliable, comparable and understandable information

9 IFRS 13: *Fair value measurement*

9.1 Fair value

IFRS 13 *Fair Value Measurement* defines fair value and sets out a framework for measuring the fair value of assets, liabilities and an entity's own equity instruments in a single IFRS.

It **applies to all IFRSs** where a fair value measurement is required except:

- share-based payment transactions (IFRS 2)
- leasing transactions (IAS 17)
- measurements which are similar to, but not the same as, fair value, e.g:
  - net realisable value of inventories (IAS 2)
  - value in use (IAS 36).

KEY TERM

FAIR VALUE. The price that would be received to sell an asset or paid to transfer a liability in an orderly transaction between market participants at the measurement date.

Fair value measurements are based on an asset or a liability's **unit of account**, which is specified by each IFRS where a fair value measurement is required.

For most assets and liabilities, the unit of account is the individual asset or liability, but in some instances may be a group of assets or liabilities.

9.2 Measurement

Fair value is a **market-based measure**, not an entity-specific one. For some assets and liabilities **observable market transactions or observable market information** might be available to provide the fair value. These are known as **observable inputs** and include market share prices for quoted companies, published or quoted interest rates and recent transactions.

Where a price for an identical asset or liability is not observable, an entity should measure fair value using another valuation technique – this may include **unobservable inputs** where the value is not determined by reference to an external/verifiable source.

IFRS 13 states that the valuation techniques used to measure fair value should maximise the use of relevant observable inputs and minimise the use of unobservable inputs ie that it should, as far as possible, be based on quantifiable, external information rather than internal information which can be more subjective.

Chapter Summary

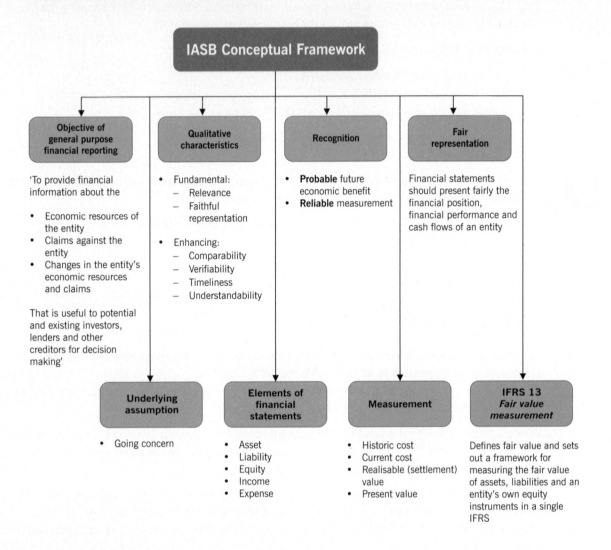

IASB Conceptual Framework

Objective of general purpose financial reporting

'To provide financial information about the

- Economic resources of the entity
- Claims against the entity
- Changes in the entity's economic resources and claims

That is useful to potential and existing investors, lenders and other creditors for decision making'

Qualitative characteristics

- Fundamental:
  - Relevance
  - Faithful representation

- Enhancing:
  - Comparability
  - Verifiability
  - Timeliness
  - Understandability

Recognition

- **Probable** future economic benefit
- **Reliable** measurement

Fair representation

Financial statements should present fairly the financial position, financial performance and cash flows of an entity

Underlying assumption

- Going concern

Elements of financial statements

- Asset
- Liability
- Equity
- Income
- Expense

Measurement

- Historic cost
- Current cost
- Realisable (settlement) value
- Present value

IFRS 13 *Fair value measurement*

Defines fair value and sets out a framework for measuring the fair value of assets, liabilities and an entity's own equity instruments in a single IFRS

Quick Quiz

1   How does the *Conceptual Framework* help promote the harmonisation of accounting standards?

2   **List** the four enhancing qualitative characteristics of financial statements identified in the *Conceptual Framework*.

3   The *Conceptual Framework* recognises that there is a pervasive constraint on the information that can be provided by financial reporting. What is this pervasive constraint?

4   In no more than 35 words, **explain** the objective of general purpose financial reporting according to the *Conceptual Framework*.

Answers to Quick Quiz

1   A conceptual framework provides fundamental principles on which all IFRSs are based and so reduces the number of alternative accounting treatments permitted by IFRSs, thereby helping to promote harmonisation of accounting standards, procedures and regulations.

2   Completeness, verifiability, timeliness and understandability.

3   The pervasive constraint is cost. The providers and users of financial information incur costs either in preparing or analysing financial information. The IASB seeks to ensure that costs are justified by benefits.

4   The objective of general purpose financial reporting is to provide financial information about the reporting entity that is useful to **existing** and **potential investors**, **lenders** and **other creditors** in **making decisions** about providing resources to the entity.

Specifically general purpose financial statements provide information about

- the **economic resources** of an entity

- **claims against the entity** and

- **changes** in the entity's **economic resources** and **claims**.

Answers to Questions

4.1   Users of financial information

(a)   **Investors** are the providers of risk capital

   (i)   Information is required to help make a decision about buying or selling shares, taking up a rights issue and voting.

   (ii)   Investors must have information about the level of dividend, past, present and future and any changes in share price.

   (iii)   Investors will also need to know whether the management has been running the company efficiently.

   (iv)   As well as the position indicated by the statement of profit or loss and other comprehensive income, statement of financial position and earnings per share (EPS), investors will want to know about the liquidity position of the company, the company's future prospects, and how the company's shares compare with those of its competitors.

(b)   **Employees** need information about the security of employment and future prospects for jobs in the company, and to help with collective pay bargaining.

(c)   **Lenders** need information to help them decide whether to lend to a company. They will also need to check that the value of any security remains adequate, that the interest repayments are secure, that the cash is available for redemption at the appropriate time and that any financial restrictions (such as maximum debt/equity ratios) have not been breached.

(d)   **Suppliers** need to know whether the company will be a good customer and pay its debts.

(e)   **Customers** need to know whether the company will be able to continue producing and supplying goods.

(f)   **Government's** interest in a company may be one of creditor or customer, as well as being specifically concerned with compliance with tax and company law, ability to pay tax and the general contribution of the company to the economy.

(g) The **public** at large would wish to have information for all the reasons mentioned above, but it could be suggested that it would be impossible to provide general purpose accounting information which was specifically designed for the needs of the public.

4.2 Assets and liabilities

(a) This is an asset, albeit an intangible one. There is a past event, control and future economic benefit (through cost savings).

(b) This cannot be classified as an asset. Baldwin Co has no control over the car repair shop and it is difficult to argue that there are 'future economic benefits'.

(c) The warranty claims in total constitute a liability; the business has taken on an obligation. It would be recognised when the warranty is issued rather than when a claim is made.

Now try these questions from the OTQ Question Bank	Number
	Q3
	Q5
	Q7
	Q24
	Q32

FINANCIAL ACCOUNTING AND REPORTING

Part B

PRESENTATION OF PUBLISHED FINANCIAL STATEMENTS

This chapter covers preparation of the accounts for limited companies. It lays out the IAS 1 (revised) *Presentation of financial statements* format for the statement of financial position, statement of profit or loss and other comprehensive income, statement of changes in equity and the disclosures required in the notes to the accounts. The best way to gain familiarity with these formats and disclosures is by doing practice questions.

You will cover the financial statements of group companies in later chapters of this Study Text.

topic list	learning outcomes	syllabus references
1 IAS 1 (revised) *Presentation of financial statements*	B1	B1 (a)
2 Statement of financial position	B2	B2 (a)
3 The current/non-current distinction	B1	B1 (a)
4 Statement of profit or loss and other comprehensive income	B2	B2 (a)
5 Statement of changes in equity	B2	B2 (a)
6 Notes to the financial statements	B2	B2 (a)
7 IAS 8 *Accounting policies, changes in accounting estimates and errors*	B1	B1 (a), (c)
8 IFRS 8 *Operating segments*	B1	B1 (a)
9 IAS 34 *Interim financial reporting*	B1	B1 (a)

Chapter Overview

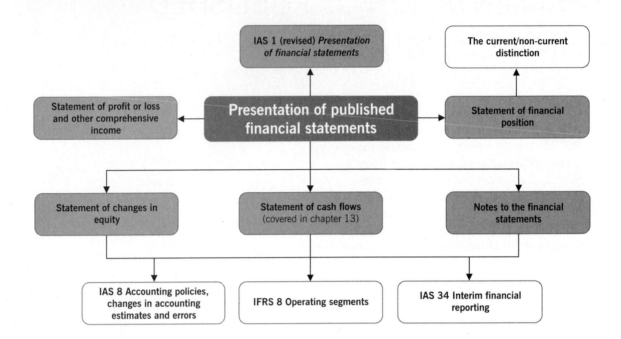

1 IAS 1 (revised) *Presentation of financial statements*

Introduction

In this section we look at the requirements for financial statements given in IAS 1 (revised) *Presentation of financial statements.* This standard gives substantial guidance on the form and content of published financial statements and details the statement of financial position, the statement of profit or loss and other comprehensive income and the statement of changes in equity (the statement of cash flows is covered by IAS 7).

1.1 Purpose of financial statements

The purpose of financial statements is to provide users with information about the financial position, financial performance and cash flows of an entity. They show the results of management's stewardship. Per IAS 1, financial statements provide information about an entity's:

(a)   assets
(b)   liabilities
(c)   equity
(d)   income and expenses, including gains and losses
(e)   other changes in equity
(f)   cash flows

1.2 Responsibility for the financial statements

Responsibility for the preparation and presentation of an entity's financial statements rests with the **board of directors** (or equivalent).

1.3 Components of financial statements

KEY POINT

IMPORTANT NOTE

An amendment to IAS 1 was published in June 2011. This amendment changed the name of the full statement from 'statement of comprehensive income' to 'statement of profit or loss and other comprehensive income'. The statement down to 'Profit (loss) for the year', which had previously been referred to as the 'income statement', then became the 'statement of profit or loss'. We have used the revised terminology in this text, but you will still probably meet 'income statement' and 'statement of comprehensive income' in other publications or articles and possibly in your F1 exam.

You may also see the statement of financial position referred to as the balance sheet and the statement of cash flows referred to as the cash flow statement.

A complete set of financial statements includes the following:

- Statement of financial position

- Statement of profit or loss and other comprehensive income (either as a single statement or as two separate statements: the statement of profit or loss and the statement of other comprehensive income)

- Statement of changes in equity

- Statement of cash flows

- Notes, including a summary of significant accounting policies and other explanatory information

In addition, IAS 1 encourages, but does not require, a **financial review** by management (which is *not* part of the financial statements), explaining the main features of the entity's performance and position. The report may include a review of the following:

(a) **Factors/influences determining performance**: changes in the environment in which the entity operates and the entity's policy for investment, including its dividend policy

(b) The entity's **sources of funding**, the policy on gearing and its risk management policies

(c) **Strengths and resources** of the entity whose value is not reflected in the statement of financial position under IFRSs

1.4 Fair presentation

Financial statements should **present fairly** the financial position, financial performance and cash flows of an entity. This requires:

- Representing transactions in accordance with the recognition criteria for assets, liabilities, income, expenses and equity set out in the *Framework*

- Compliance with applicable IFRSs and a statement of compliance

- Selection, application and disclosure of accounting policies in accordance with IAS 8

- Presentation of information in a way that provides relevant, reliable, comparable and understandable information

- Presentation of additional disclosures when the disclosures required by IFRSs are insufficient to give a full understanding of an event or transaction

In the rare circumstances where management decides that compliance with a standard would not present a true and fair picture, they can **depart** from the requirements of the standard in order to achieve fair presentation. They should disclose:

- That the financial statements are a fair presentation of the entity's position, performance and cash flows

- That the entity has complied with all other relevant IFRSs

- Details of the departure from an IFRS, why it was necessary and the financial impact of the departure

1.5 Going concern

IAS 1 states that an entity should prepare its financial statements on a **going concern basis** unless management either intends to liquidate the entity or to cease trading. The going concern basis assumes that the business will **continue to trade** for the foreseeable future.

1.6 Accruals basis

IAS 1 requires entities to prepare their financial statements, except for the statement of cash flows, on the **accruals basis of accounting**. The accruals basis of accounting recognises income when it is earned and expenses when they are incurred, whether or not any cash has been received or paid.

1.7 Other matters covered by IAS 1

IAS 1 also includes the following requirements for financial statements.

(a) Financial statements should be presented at least **annually** and should be produced **within six months of the end of the reporting period.**

(b)   The presentation and classification of items in the financial statements should be **consistent** from year to year. Changes in presentation and classification are permitted if required by another IFRS or if the change would result in more appropriate presentation or classification.

(c)   **Material** items should be presented separately in the financial statements. Immaterial items can be **aggregated** with similar items.

(d)   Assets and liabilities, and income and expenses should **not be offset** except when it is required or permitted by another IFRS.

(e)   **Comparative information** should be disclosed for the previous period for all numerical information, unless another IFRS permits or requires otherwise. Comparative information should be reclassified when the presentation or classification of items in the financial statements is amended.

Section summary

Financial statements should **present fairly** the financial position, financial performance and cash flows of an entity.

IAS 1 covers the **form and content** of financial statements. The main components are:

*   Statement of financial position
*   Statement of profit or loss and other comprehensive income
*   Statement of changes in equity
*   Statement of cash flows
*   Notes to the financial statements

2 Statement of financial position

Introduction

First of all we will look at the **suggested format** of the statement of financial position (given in an appendix to IAS 1) and then at further disclosures required.

2.1 Statement of financial position example

XYZ CO
STATEMENT OF FINANCIAL POSITION AT 31 DECEMBER 20X9

	$'000	$'000
Assets		
Non-current assets		
Property, plant and equipment	X	
Other intangible assets	X	
Available-for-sale financial assets	X	
		X
Current assets		
Inventories	X	
Trade receivables	X	
Other current assets	X	
Cash and cash equivalents	X	
		X
Total assets		X

Equity and liabilities	$'000	$'000
Share capital	X	
Retained earnings	X	
Other components of equity	X	
Total equity		X
Non-current liabilities		
Long-term borrowings	X	
Deferred tax	X	
Long-term provisions	X	
Total non-current liabilities		X
Current liabilities		
Trade and other payables	X	
Short-term borrowings	X	
Current portion of long-term borrowings	X	
Current tax payable	X	
Short-term provisions	X	
Total current liabilities		X
Total liabilities		X
Total equity and liabilities		X

As a minimum, IAS 1 requires the following items to be shown in the statement of financial position:

(a)   Property, plant and equipment

(b)   Investment property

(c)   Intangible assets

(d)   Financial assets (excluding amounts shown under (e), (h) and (i))

(e)   Investments in associates

(f)   Biological assets

(g)   Inventories

(h)   Trade and other receivables

(i)   Cash and cash equivalents

(j)   Assets classified as held for sale under IFRS 5

(k)   Trade and other payables

(l)   Provisions

(m)   Financial liabilities (other than (j) and (k))

(n)   Current tax liabilities and assets

(o)   Deferred tax liabilities and assets

(p)   Liabilities included in disposal groups under IFRS 5

(q)   Non-controlling interests (group accounts only)

(r)   Issued capital and reserves

The example shown above is shown in full for illustration only; some elements are not examinable in F1. IAS 1 does not prescribe the **order or format** in which the items listed should be presented. It simply states that they **must be presented separately** because they are so different in nature or function from each other.

IAS 1 also requires that any **other line items**, **headings** or **sub-totals** should be shown in the statement of financial position when it is necessary for an understanding of the entity's financial position.

Management must decide whether to present additional items separately. Their decision should consider the following factors:

(a)   **Nature and liquidity of assets and their materiality**. So monetary/non-monetary assets and current/non-current assets will be presented separately.

(b)   **Function within the entity.** Inventories, receivables and cash and cash equivalents are therefore shown separately.

(c)   **Amounts, nature and timing of liabilities**. Interest-bearing and non-interest-bearing liabilities and provisions will be shown separately, classified as current or non-current as appropriate.

IAS 1 also requires separate presentation where **different measurement bases** (eg cost or valuation) are used for assets and liabilities which differ in nature or function.

2.2 Information presented either in the statement of financial position or by note

Further **sub-classification** of the line items listed above should be disclosed either in the statement of financial position or in the notes. The sub-classification details will in part depend on the requirements of IFRSs. The size, nature and function of the amounts involved will also be important.

Disclosures will vary from item to item and IAS 1 gives the following examples.

(a)   **Property, plant and equipment** are classified by class as described in IAS 16, *Property, plant and equipment.*

(b)   **Receivables** are analysed between amounts receivable from trade customers, other members of the group, receivables from related parties, prepayments and other amounts.

(c)   **Inventories** are sub-classified, in accordance with IAS 2 *Inventories,* into classifications such as merchandise, production supplies, materials, work in progress and finished goods.

(d)   **Provisions** are analysed showing separately provisions for employee benefit costs and any other items classified in a manner appropriate to the entity's operations. (NB not examinable in F1)

(e)   **Equity capital and reserves** are analysed showing separately the various classes of paid in capital, share premium and reserves.

IAS 1 lists some **specific disclosures** which must be made, either in the statement of financial position or in the related notes.

(a)   **Share capital disclosures** (for each class of share capital)

    (i)   Number of shares authorised

    (ii)   Number of shares issued and fully paid, and issued but not fully paid

    (iii)   Par value per share, or that the shares have no par value

    (iv)   Reconciliation of the number of shares outstanding at the beginning and at the end of the year

    (v)   Rights, preferences and restrictions attaching to that class including restrictions on the distribution of dividends and the repayment of capital

    (vi)   Shares in the entity held by the entity itself or by related group companies

    (vii)   Shares reserved for issuance under options and sales contracts, including the terms and amounts

(b)   Description of the nature and purpose of **each reserve** within owners' equity

(c)   The amount of any dividends proposed or declared after the reporting date but before the financial statements were authorised for issue

(d)   The amount of any cumulative preference dividends not recognised

Section summary

IAS 1 suggests a format for the statement of financial position and specifies various items which must be shown in the statement.

3   The current/non-current distinction

Introduction

In this section we look at the requirements of IAS 1 to distinguish between current and non-current assets and liabilities in the statement of financial position.

3.1 The current/non-current distinction

An entity should present **current** and **non-current** assets and liabilities as separate classifications in the statement of financial position, except where a presentation based on liquidity provides more relevant and reliable information. If a presentation based on liquidity is used, all assets and liabilities must be presented broadly **in order of liquidity**.

In either case, the entity should disclose any portion of an asset or liability which is expected to be recovered or settled **after more than twelve months**. For example, for an amount receivable which is due in instalments over 18 months, the portion due after more than twelve months must be disclosed.

3.2 Current assets

KEY TERM

An asset should be classified as a CURRENT ASSET when it:

- is expected to be realised in, or is held for sale or consumption in, the normal course of the entity's operating cycle; or
- is held primarily for trading purposes; or
- is expected to be realised within twelve months of the end of the reporting period; or
- is cash or a cash equivalent asset which is not restricted in its use

All other assets should be classified as non-current assets.   *(IAS 1)*

3.3 Current liabilities

KEY TERM

A liability should be classified as a CURRENT LIABILITY when it:

- Is expected to be settled in the normal course of the entity's operating cycle; or
- Is held primarily for the purpose of trading; or
- Is due to be settled within twelve months after the reporting period; or
- The entity does not have an unconditional right to defer settlement of the liability for at least twelve months after the reporting period

All other liabilities should be classified as non-current liabilities.   *(IAS 1)*

Section summary

An entity should present **current** and **non-current** assets and liabilities as separate classifications in the statement of financial position.

4   Statement of profit or loss and other comprehensive income

Introduction

Income and expenses are presented in the statement of profit or loss and other comprehensive income. This section looks at the requirements of IAS 1 for this statement.

4.1 Statement of profit or loss and other comprehensive income – format

IAS 1 allows income and expense items to be presented either:

(a)   in a single **statement of profit or loss and other comprehensive income**; or

(b)   in two statements: a **statement of profit or loss** plus a separate **statement of other comprehensive income**

The suggested format for these statements follows.

XYZ CO
STATEMENT OF PROFIT OR LOSS AND OTHER COMPREHENSIVE INCOME FOR THE YEAR ENDED
31 DECEMBER 20X9

	20X9 *$'000*
Revenue	X
Cost of sales	X
Gross profit	X
Other income	X
Distribution costs	X
Administrative expenses	X
Other expenses	X
Finance costs	X
Profit before tax	X
Income tax expense	X
Profit for the year from continuing operations	X
Loss for the year from discontinued operations	X
Profit for the year	X
Other comprehensive income:	
Gains/(losses) on property revaluation	X
Income tax relating to components of other comprehensive income	X
Other comprehensive income for the year, net of tax	X
Total comprehensive income for the year	X

Companies are given the option of presenting this information in two statements as follows:

XYZ CO
STATEMENT OF PROFIT OR LOSS FOR THE YEAR ENDED 31 DECEMBER 20X9

	20X9
	$'000
Revenue	X
Cost of sales	X
Gross profit	X
Other income	X
Distribution costs	X
Administrative expenses	X
Other expenses	X
Finance costs	X
Profit before tax	X
Income tax expense	X
Profit for the year from continuing operations	X
Loss for the year from discontinued operations	X
Profit for the year	X

XYZ CO
STATEMENT OF OTHER COMPREHENSIVE INCOME FOR THE YEAR ENDED 31 DECEMBER 20X9

	20X9
	$'000
Profit for the year	X
Other comprehensive income:	
Gains on property revaluation	X
Income tax relating to components of other comprehensive income	X
Other comprehensive income for the year, net of tax	X
Total comprehensive income for the year	X

Exam skills

In this Study Text, we have used the term '**statement of profit or loss**' to refer to the section from revenue to profit for the year, whether or not that section is presented as part of a single statement of profit or loss and other comprehensive income or as a separate statement. In exam questions, you should make sure that you always call your statement the same name as the statement the examiner asks for in the question.

As a minimum, IAS 1 requires the following items to be disclosed in the statement of profit or loss and other comprehensive income:

(a)   Revenue
(b)   Finance costs
(c)   Share of profits and losses of associates accounted for using the equity method*
(d)   Pre-tax gain or loss attributable to discontinued operations
(e)   Tax expense
(f)   Profit or loss
(g)   Each component of other comprehensive income classified by nature
(h)   Share of the other comprehensive income of associates
(i)   Total comprehensive income

* These items relate to group accounts.

IAS 1 also requires that any **other line items, headings or sub-totals** should be shown in the statement of profit or loss and other comprehensive income when it is necessary for an understanding of the entity's financial position or if another IFRS requires it.

Management must decide whether to present additional items separately. They should consider factors including materiality and the nature and function of the items of income and expense when making this decision.

4.2 Information presented either in the statement of profit or loss or by note

IAS 1 requires separate disclosure of the nature and amount of items of income and expense if they are material. This disclosure should be in the statement of profit or loss or in the notes. Examples of items which may require separate disclosure are:

- Write downs of inventories or property, plant and equipment
- Disposals of property, plant and equipment
- Disposals of investments
- Discontinued operations
- Litigation settlements

4.3 Analysis of expenses

IAS 1 requires an analysis of expenses to be given either in the statement of profit or loss or by note, using a classification based on *either* the **nature of the expenses** or their **function**.

4.3.1 Nature of expenses method

In this method, expenses are aggregated in the statement of profit or loss **according to their nature** (eg purchase of materials, depreciation, wages and salaries, transport costs). This is by far the easiest method, especially for smaller entities. An example of this classification follows.

	20X9 $'000
Revenue	X
Other operating income	X
Changes in inventories of finished goods and work in progress	(X)
Work performed by the entity and capitalised	X
Raw material and consumables used	(X)
Employee benefits expense	(X)
Depreciation and amortisation expense	(X)
Impairment of property, plant and equipment	(X)
Other expenses	(X)
Finance costs	(X)
Profit before tax	X
Income tax expense	(X)
Profit for the year	X

4.3.2 Function of expenses method

You are likely to be more familiar with this method. Expenses are classified according to their function as part of cost of sales, distribution or administrative activities. This method often gives **more relevant information** for users, but the allocation of expenses by function requires the use of judgement and can be arbitrary. An example of this classification follows.

	20X9 $'000
Revenue	X
Cost of sales	(X)
Gross profit	X
Other income	X
Distribution costs	(X)
Administrative expenses	(X)
Other expenses	(X)
Finance costs	(X)
Profit before tax	X
Income tax expense	(X)
Profit for the year	X

If an entity uses the function of expenses method, additional disclosure should be given on the nature of expenses, including depreciation, amortisation and employee expenses.

Exam alert

The usual method of presentation is expenses by function and this is the format likely to appear in your exam.

Section summary

IAS 1 requires all items of income and expense in a period to be shown in a **statement of profit or loss and other comprehensive income**.

IAS 1 offers **two** possible formats for the statement of profit or loss section or separate statement of profit or loss - by function or by nature. Classification by function is more common.

5 Statement of changes in equity

Introduction

The statement of changes in equity presents the movements in an entity's capital and reserves balances. Changes in an entity's equity over the reporting period reflect the increase or decrease in its net assets, and therefore its wealth, for the period. This section covers the requirements in IAS 1 for this statement.

5.1 Statement of changes in equity example

This is the format of the statement of changes in equity as per IAS 1.

XYZ CO

STATEMENT OF CHANGES IN EQUITY FOR THE YEAR ENDED 31 DECEMBER 20X9

	Share capital $'000	Retained earnings $'000	Share premium $'000	Revaluation surplus $'000	Total equity $'000
Balance at 1 January 20X8	X	X	X	–	X
Changes in accounting policy	–	X	–	–	X
Restated balance	X	X	–	–	X
Changes in equity					
Dividends	–	X	–	–	X
Total comprehensive income for the year	–	X	–	X	X
Balance at 31 December 20X8	X	X	X	X	X
Changes in equity for 20X9					
Issue of share capital	X	–	X	–	X
Dividends	–	X	–	–	X
Total comprehensive income for the year	–	X	–	X	X
Transfer to retained earnings	–	X	–	(X)	–
Balance at 31 December 20X9	X	X	X	X	X

Section summary

IAS 1 requires a statement of changes in equity. This shows the movement in the equity section of the statement of financial position.

6 Notes to the financial statements

Introduction

In this section we will learn about notes to the financial statements, including their function and presentation.

6.1 Structure

Notes to the financial statements provide more detailed analysis and narrative information about items in the financial statements and also give additional information, such as contingent liabilities and commitments.

Per IAS 1, the notes to the financial statements should perform the following functions:

(a)   Provide information about the **basis on which the financial statements were prepared** and which **specific accounting policies** were chosen and applied to significant transactions/events

(b)   Disclose any information, not shown elsewhere in the financial statements, which is **required by IFRSs**

(c)   Show any additional information that is relevant to understanding which is not shown elsewhere in the financial statements

The way the notes are presented is important. They should be given in a **systematic manner** and **cross referenced** to other related information.

IAS 1 suggests a **certain order** for notes to the financial statements, which assists users when comparing the statements of different entities. The suggested order is as follows.

(a)   A statement of **compliance** with IFRSs

(b)   A summary of significant **accounting policies** applied

(c)   **Supporting information** for items in each financial statement in the same order as each financial statement and line item is presented

(d)   Other disclosures, eg:

   (i)   Contingent liabilities, commitments and other financial disclosures
   (ii)   Non-financial disclosures

The order of specific items may have to be varied occasionally, but a systematic structure is still required.

6.2 Presentation of accounting policies

The accounting policies section should describe the following.

(a)   The **measurement basis** (or bases) used in preparing the financial statements

(b)   The **other accounting policies** used, as required for a proper understanding of the financial statements

6.3 Other disclosures

An entity must also disclose in the notes:

(a)   The amount of **dividends proposed or declared** before the financial statements were authorised for issue but not recognised as a distribution to owners during the period, and the amount per share

(b)   The amount of any **cumulative preference dividends** not recognised

Example: Preparing financial statements

USB Co has the following trial balance at 31 December 20X9.

	Debit $'000	Credit $'000
Cash at bank	100	
Inventory at 1 January 20X9	2,200	
Administrative expenses	2,206	
Distribution costs	650	
Non-current assets at cost:		
Land	12,000	
Buildings	10,000	
Plant and equipment	1,400	
Motor vehicles	320	
Accumulated depreciation		
Buildings		4,000
Plant and equipment		480
Motor vehicles		120
Retained earnings		12,360
Trade receivables	876	
Purchases	4,200	
Dividend paid	200	
Sales revenue		11,752
Trade payables		2,440
Share premium		1,000
$1 ordinary shares		2,000
	34,152	34,152

The following additional information is relevant.

(a)   Depreciation is to be provided as follows:

   (i)   Buildings at 5% straight line, charged to administrative expenses
   (ii)   Plant and equipment at 20% on the reducing balance basis, charged to cost of sales
   (iii) Motor vehicles at 25% on the reducing balance basis, charged to distribution costs

(b)   No final dividend is being proposed.

(c)   A customer has gone bankrupt owing $76,000. This debt is not expected to be recovered and an adjustment should be made. An allowance for receivables of 5% is to be set up.

(d)   1 million new ordinary shares were issued at $1.50 on 1 December 20X9. This transaction has been correctly accounted for.

(e)   The land is to be revalued to $18,000,000.

(f)   Closing inventory figure is $1,600,000.

Required

Prepare in a form suitable for publication, the statement of profit or loss and other comprehensive income for the year to 31 December 20X9, a statement of changes in equity and a statement of financial position at that date in accordance with the requirements of International Financial Reporting Standards. Ignore taxation. Notes to the financial statements are not required.

Solution

USB CO
STATEMENT OF PROFIT OR LOSS AND OTHER COMPREHENSIVE INCOME FOR THE YEAR ENDED 31 DECEMBER 20X9

	$'000
Revenue	11,752
Cost of sales (W2)	4,984
Gross profit	6,768
Administrative expenses (W3)	2,822
Distribution costs (650 + 50 (W1))	700
Profit for the year	3,246
Other comprehensive income	
Gain on revaluation of land	6,000
Total comprehensive income	9,246

USB LIMITED
STATEMENT OF CHANGES IN EQUITY FOR THE YEAR ENDED 31 DECEMBER 20X9

	Share capital $'000	Share premium $'000	Retained earnings $'000	Revaluation surplus $'000	Total $'000
Balance at 1 Jan 20X9	1,000	500	12,360	–	13,860
Total comprehensive income	–	–	3,246	6,000	9,246
Dividend paid	–	–	(200)	–	(200)
Share issue	1,000	500	–	–	1,500
Balance at 31 Dec 20X9	2,000	1,000	15,406	6,000	24,406

BPP
LEARNING MEDIA

USB LIMITED
STATEMENT OF FINANCIAL POSITION AS AT 31 DECEMBER 20X9

	$'000	$'000
Non-current assets		
Property, plant and equipment (W1)	6,386	
Land (W1)	18,000	
		24,386
Current assets		
Inventory	1,600	
Trade receivables (876 – 76 – 40)	760	
Cash	100	
		2,460
Total assets		26,846
Equity and liabilities		
Equity		
Share capital		2,000
Retained earnings		15,406
Share premium		1,000
Revaluation surplus		6,000
Current liabilities		
Trade payables		2,440
Total equity and liabilities		26,846

Workings

1   *Depreciation*

	$'000
Buildings (10,000 × 5%)	500
Plant (1,400 – 480) × 20%	184
Motor vehicles (320 – 120) × 25%	50

Property, plant and equipment

	Cost	Acc Dep	Dep chg	Carrying amount
	$'000	$'000	$'000	$'000
Buildings	10,000	4,000	500	5,500
Plant	1,400	480	184	736
Motor vehicles	320	120	50	150
	11,720	4,600	734	6,386

Land is to be revalued to $18m. When the land is revalued, a reserve of $18m – $12m = $6m is created and the increase in value is shown in other comprehensive income.

Tutorial note: revaluations of non-current assets are covered in Chapter 6 of this Study Text.

2   *Cost of sales*

	$'000
Opening inventory	2,200
Purchases	4,200
Depreciation on plant (W1)	184
Closing inventory	(1,600)
	4,984

3   *Administrative expenses*

	$'000
Per trial balance	2,206
Depreciation on buildings (W1)	500
Irrecoverable debt	76
Receivables allowance ((876 – 76) × 5%)	40
	2,822

Question 5.1	Financial statements

Learning outcome B2

Atok Co compiles its financial statements to 30 June annually. At 30 June 20X9, the company's trial balance was as follows:

	$'000	$'000
Sales revenue		14,800
Purchases	8,280	
Inventory at 1 July 20X8	1,390	
Distribution costs	1,080	
Administration expenses	1,460	
Land at valuation	10,500	
Building: cost	8,000	
accumulated depreciation at 1 July 20X8		2,130
Plant and equipment: cost	12,800	
accumulated depreciation at 1 July 20X8		2,480
Trade receivables and payables	4,120	2,240
Cash at bank	160	
Ordinary shares of 50c each: as at 1 July 20X8		10,000
issued during year		4,000
Share premium account: as at 1 July 20X8		2,000
arising on shares issued during year		2,000
Revaluation surplus as at 1 July 20X8		3,000
Retained earnings		3,140
10% loan notes (redeemable 20Y8)		
(issued 1 April 20X9 with interest payable 31 March and 30		2,000
September each year)	47,790	47,790

The following matters remain to be adjusted for in preparing the financial statements for the year ended 30 June 20X9:

(a)   Inventory at 30 June 20X9 amounted to $1,560,000 at cost. A review of inventory items revealed the need for some adjustments for two inventory lines.

(i)   Items which had cost $80,000 and which would normally sell for $120,000 were found to have deteriorated. Remedial work costing $20,000 would be needed to enable the items to be sold for $90,000.

(ii)   Some items sent to customers on sale or return terms had been omitted from inventory and included as sales in June 20X9. The cost of these items was $16,000 and they were included in sales at $24,000. In July 20X9 the items were returned in good condition by the customers.

(b)   Depreciation is to be provided as follows:

Buildings	2% per year on cost
Plant and equipment	20% per year on cost

80% of the depreciation is to be charged in cost of sales, and 10% each in distribution costs and administrative expenses.

(c)   The land is to be revalued to $12,000,000. No change was required to the value of the buildings.

(d)   Accruals and prepayments were:

	Accruals	Prepayments
	$'000	$'000
Distribution costs	190	120
Administrative expenses	70	60

Required

(a)   Prepare the company's statement of profit or loss and other comprehensive income for the year ended 30 June 20X9 and statement of financial position as at that date for publication, complying with the provisions of International Financial Reporting Standards.

(b)   Prepare a statement of changes in equity for the year ending 30 June 20X9, complying with the provisions of International Financial Reporting Standards.

Notes to the financial statements are not required. Ignore taxation.

Section summary

IAS 1 suggests a certain order for notes to the financial statements.

7   IAS 8 *Accounting policies, changes in accounting estimates and errors*

Introduction

IAS 8 deals with accounting policies, the treatment of changes in accounting policies and of changes in accounting estimates, and errors.

7.1 Developing accounting policies

IAS 8 defines accounting policies as follows.

KEY TERM

ACCOUNTING POLICIES are the specific principles, bases, conventions, rules and practices applied by an entity in preparing and presenting financial statements.   (IAS 8)

Accounting policies are determined by **applying the relevant IFRS or IAS**.

Where there is no applicable IFRS or IAS management should use its **judgement** in developing and applying an accounting policy that results in information that is **relevant** and **reliable**. Management should consider IFRSs and IASs that deal with similar and related issues. They should also consider the definitions, recognition criteria and measurement concepts contained in the *Framework*.

An entity must select and apply its accounting policies for a period **consistently** for similar transactions, other events and conditions, unless an IFRS or an IAS specifically requires or permits categorisation of items for which different policies may be appropriate. If an IFRS or an IAS requires or permits categorisation of items, an appropriate accounting policy must be selected and applied consistently to each category.

7.2 Changes in accounting policies

The same accounting policies are usually adopted from period to period, to allow users to analyse trends over time in profit, cash flows and financial position. **Changes in accounting policy will therefore be rare** and should be made only if required by one of three things:

(a)   A new statutory requirement

(b)   A new accounting standard

(c)   If the change will result in a **more appropriate presentation** of events or transactions in the financial statements of the entity

The standard highlights two types of event **which do not constitute changes in accounting policy**.

(a)   Adopting an accounting policy for a **new type of transaction** or event not dealt with previously by the entity

(b)   Adopting a **new accounting policy** for a transaction or event which has not occurred in the past or which was not material

If a policy of revaluation of property, plant and equipment is adopted for the first time then this is treated as a revaluation under IAS 16 *Property, plant and equipment*, not as a change of accounting policy under IAS 8.

Examples of changes in accounting policies include:

(a)   Inventory previously valued on a First In, First Out (FIFO) basis is now to be valued on a weighted average cost basis.

(b)   Depreciation is now classified as administrative expenses rather than cost of sales.

7.2.1 Applying a change in accounting policy

IAS 8 requires **retrospective application** of a change in accounting policy, *unless* it is **impracticable** to determine the cumulative amount of the adjustment.

KEY TERMS

RETROSPECTIVE APPLICATION means to apply a new accounting policy to transactions, other events and conditions as if that policy had always been applied.

Applying a requirement is IMPRACTICABLE when the entity cannot apply it after making every reasonable effort to do so. It is impracticable to apply a change in an accounting policy retrospectively or to make a retrospective restatement to correct an error if one of the following apply.

(a)   The effects of the retrospective application or retrospective restatement are not determinable.

(b)   The retrospective application or retrospective restatement requires assumptions about what management's intent would have been in that period.

(c)   The retrospective application or retrospective restatement requires significant estimates of amounts and it is impossible to distinguish objectively information about those estimates that: provides evidence of circumstances that existed on the date(s) at which those amounts are to be recognised, measured or disclosed; and would have been available when the financial statements for that prior period were authorised for issue, from other information.   *(IAS 8)*

In other words, retrospective application means that all comparative information must be restated **as if the new policy had always been in force**, with amounts relating to earlier periods reflected in an adjustment to opening reserves of the earliest period presented. Comparative information should be restated unless it is impracticable to do so.

Prospective application is allowed only when it is impracticable to determine the cumulative effect of the change.

KEY TERM

PROSPECTIVE APPLICATION of a change in accounting policy means to apply the new accounting policy to transactions, other events and conditions occurring after the date as at which the policy is changed.

In other words, the new accounting policy is applied from the point it is adopted to transactions occurring from that date forwards. No adjustments are made for the treatment of transactions that occurred in the past under the old policy.

7.2.2 Disclosure of a change in accounting policy

Certain **disclosures** are required when a change in accounting policy has a material effect on the current period or any prior period presented, or when it may have a material effect in subsequent periods.

(a)   Reasons for the change

(b)   Nature of the change

(c) Amount of the adjustment for the current period and for each period presented

(d) Amount of the adjustment relating to periods prior to those included in the comparative information

(e) The fact that comparative information has been restated or that it is impracticable to do so

If an entity has chosen to change an accounting policy, rather than this being required by statute or accounting standards, an explanation of why the new policy provides more reliable and relevant information must be given.

An entity should also disclose information relevant to assessing the **impact of new IFRSs** on the financial statements where these have **not yet come into force.**

7.3 Changes in accounting estimates

7.3.1 What are accounting estimates?

Estimates arise in relation to business activities because of the **uncertainties inherent within them**. Judgements are made based on the most up to date information and the use of such estimates is a necessary part of the preparation of financial statements. It does *not* undermine their reliability. Here are some examples of accounting estimates.

- A necessary **doubtful debt provision**
- **Useful lives** of depreciable assets
- Provision for **obsolescence of inventory**

Where circumstances change or more information becomes available, the estimate may need to be revised.

7.3.2 Changes in accounting estimates

When an accounting estimate needs to be changed, the **effect of the change** should be accounted for prospectively, ie, included in the financial statements in the period it arises, and in future periods if the change affects both current and future periods.

An example of a change in accounting estimate which affects only the **current period** is a change in the doubtful debt estimate. However, a revision in the life over which an asset is depreciated would affect both the **current and future periods**, in the amount of the depreciation expense.

Reasonably enough, the effect of a change in an accounting estimate should be included in the **same expense classification** as was used previously for the estimate. This rule helps to ensure **consistency** between the financial statements of different periods.

The **materiality** of the change is also relevant. The nature and amount of a change in an accounting estimate that has a material effect in the current period (or which is expected to have a material effect in subsequent periods) should be disclosed. If it is not possible to quantify the amount, this impracticability should be disclosed.

7.4 Prior period errors

KEY TERM

PRIOR PERIOD ERRORS are omissions from, and misstatements in, the entity's financial statements for one or more prior periods arising from a failure to use, or misuse of, reliable information that:

(a) Was available when financial statements for those periods were authorised for issue, and

(b) Could reasonably be expected to have been obtained and taken into account in the preparation and presentation of those financial statements

Such errors include the effects of mathematical mistakes, mistakes in applying *accounting policies*, oversights or misinterpretations of facts, and fraud. *(IAS 8)*

7.4.1 Accounting treatment for prior period errors

Prior period errors should be corrected retrospectively.

This involves:

(a)   Either restating the comparative amounts for the prior period(s) in which the error occurred, or

(b)   When the error occurred before the earliest prior period presented, restating the opening balances of assets, liabilities and equity for that period

so that the financial statements are presented **as if the error had never occurred**.

Only where it is **impracticable** to determine the cumulative effect of an error on prior periods can an entity correct an error **prospectively**.

Various **disclosures** are required.

(a)   **Nature** of the prior period error

(b)   For each prior period, to the extent practicable, the **amount** of the correction for each financial statement line item affected

(c)   The amount of the correction at the **beginning of the earliest prior** period presented

(d)   If **retrospective restatement is impracticable** for a particular prior period, the **circumstances** that led to the existence of that condition and a description of how and from when the error has been corrected. Subsequent periods need not repeat these disclosures.

Question 5.2	Prior period error

Learning outcome B1

During 20X7 Global discovered that certain items had been included in inventory at 31 December 20X6, valued at $4.2m, which had in fact been sold before the year end. The following figures for 20X6 (as reported) and 20X7 (draft) are available.

	20X6 $'000	20X7 (draft) $'000
Sales	47,400	67,200
Cost of goods sold	(34,570)	(55,800)
Profit before taxation	12,830	11,400
Income taxes	(3,880)	(3,400)
Net profit	8,950	8,000

Reserves at 1 January 20X6 were $13m. The cost of goods sold for 20X7 includes the $4.2m error in opening inventory. The income tax rate was 30% for 20X6 and 20X7.

Required

Prepare the statement of profit or loss for 20X7, with the 20X6 comparative, and a reconciliation of opening and closing retained earnings for 20X6 and 20X7.

Section summary

IAS 8 deals with the treatment of changes in accounting estimates, changes in accounting policies and errors.

Accounting policies must comply with accounting standards and be applied **consistently**

Changes in accounting policy are applied **retrospectively**.

Changes in accounting estimates are **not** applied retrospectively.

Prior period errors will require **retrospective** correction if they are **material**.

8 IFRS 8 *Operating segments*

Introduction

Large entities produce a wide range of products and services, often in several different countries. Further information on how the overall results of entities are made up from each of these product or geographical areas will help the users of the financial statements assess the past performance of the entity, better understand its risks and returns, and make more informed judgments about the entity as a whole. This is the reason for **segment reporting.**

Segment reporting is covered by IFRS 8 *Operating segments*, which replaced IAS 14 *Segment reporting* in November 2006.

8.1 IFRS 8 *Operating segments*

IFRS 8 requires an entity to adopt the 'management approach' to reporting on the financial performance of its operating segments. This 'management approach' has two intended advantages:

(a)   It allows users of the financial statements to view operations through the eyes of management.

(b)   As it is based on information which is being collected anyway, it should not involve too much cost or time to prepare.

In the words of the Standard:

'An entity shall disclose information to enable users of its financial statements to evaluate the nature and financial effects of the business activities in which it engages and the economic environments in which it operates.'

IFRS 8 applies to listed companies only.

8.1.1 Operating segments

An OPERATING SEGMENT is a component of an entity:

(a)   that engages in business activities from which it may earn revenues and incur expenses

(b)   whose operating results are regularly reviewed by the entity's chief operating decision maker to make decisions about resources to be allocated to the segment and assess its performance, and

(c)   for which discrete financial information is available   *(IFRS 8)*

8.1.2 Determining reportable segments

An entity must report separate information about **each operating segment** that:

(a)   Has been identified as meeting the **definition of an operating segment**; and

(b)   Exceeds any of the following thresholds:

(i)   Segment **revenue** (internal and external) is **10% or more** of total revenue, or

(ii)   Segment **profit or loss** is **10% or more** of all segments in profit (or all segments in loss if greater)

(iii)   Segment **assets** are **10% or more** of total assets

At least **75% of total external revenue** must be reported by operating segments. Where this is not the case, additional segments must be identified (even if they do not meet the 10% thresholds).

Two or more operating segments **below** the thresholds may be aggregated to produce a reportable segment if the segments have **similar economic characteristics** and the segments are similar in *each* of the following respects:

- The **nature of the products or services**
- The **nature of the production process**
- The **type or class of customer for their products or services**
- The **methods used to distribute their products or provide their services**, and
- If applicable, the **nature of the regulatory environment**

Operating segments that do not meet **any of the quantitative thresholds** may be reported separately if management believes that information about the segment would be useful to users of the financial statements.

Example: Operating segments

CTU Co has the following operating segments

Segment	Internal revenue $'000	External revenue $'000	Total revenue $'000
Car division	29	61	90
Bike division	–	45	45
Truck division	–	39	39
Tractor division	–	23	23
Van division	–	21	21
Digger division	–	17	15
	29	206	235

The reportable operating segments are the Car, Bike and Truck divisions as each of them has revenue of more than $23,500 (10% of the total revenue of $235,000).

These three divisions between them have external revenue of $145,000. This is less than 75% of the total external revenue (75% × $206,000 = $154,500) so the Tractor division is also a reportable segment. This brings external revenue generated by reportable segments to $168,000, so neither of the two remaining segments need to be reported on.

8.1.3 Decision tree to help identify reportable segments

The following decision tree will assist in identifying reportable segments.

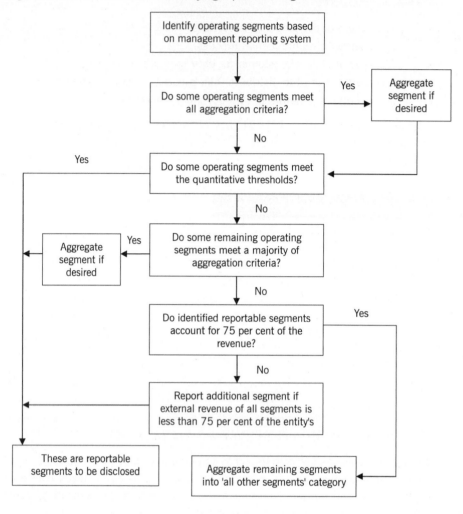

8.1.4 Disclosures

IFRS 8 requires disclosure of:

(a) Factors used to identify the entity's reportable segments
(b) **Types of products and services** from which each reportable segment derives its revenues
(c) Reportable segment **revenues**, **profit** or **loss**, **total assets**, **total liabilities** and other material items

KEY POINT

Reporting of a measure of **profit or loss** by segment is compulsory. Other items are disclosed if included in the figures reviewed by or regularly provided to the chief operating decision maker.

The amount reported for each segment should be the amounts **reported to the chief operating decision maker** for the purpose of allocating resources to the segment and assessing its performance. The entity should explain how segment profit or loss and assets and liabilities are measured. **Geographical disclosures**, including external revenue and non-current assets are required on a **country by country** basis if material.

Section summary

IFRS 8 is a **disclosure standard**, which is applicable to listed companies.

Segment reporting is necessary for a better understanding and assessment of:

- Past performance
- Risks and returns
- Informed judgements

IFRS 8 adopts the **managerial approach** to identifying segments.

IFRS 8 gives guidance on how segments should be **identified** and **what information should be disclosed** for each reportable segment.

9 IAS 34 *Interim financial reporting*

IAS 34 recommends that **entities whose shares are publicly traded should produce interim financial reports**, and for entities that do publish such reports, it lays down principles and guidelines for their production.

The following definitions are used in IAS 34.

KEY TERM

INTERIM PERIOD is a financial reporting period shorter than a full financial year.

INTERIM FINANCIAL REPORT means a financial report containing either a complete set of financial statements (as described in IAS 1) or a set of condensed financial statements (as described in this standard) for an interim period.   *(IAS 34)*

9.1 Scope

The standard does not make the preparation of interim financial reports **mandatory**, taking the view that this is a matter for governments, securities regulators, stock exchanges or professional accountancy bodies to decide within each country. The IASB does, however, strongly recommend to governments, etc, that interim reporting should be a requirement for companies whose equity or debt securities are **publicly traded**.

(a)   An interim financial report should be produced by such companies for **at least the first six months of their financial year** (ie a half year financial report).

(b)   The report should be **available no later than 60 days** after the end of the interim period.

Therefore, a company with a year ending 31 December would be required as a minimum to prepare an interim report for the half year to 30 June and this report should be available before the end of August.

9.2 Minimum components

The proposed standard specifies the **minimum component elements** of an interim financial report.

- Condensed statement of financial position
- Condensed statement of profit or loss and other comprehensive income
- Condensed statement of changes in equity
- Condensed statement of cash flows
- Selected note disclosures

The rationale for requiring only condensed statements and selected note disclosures is that entities need not duplicate information in their interim report that is contained in their report for the previous financial year. Interim statements should **focus more on new events, activities and circumstances**.

9.3 Form and content

Where **full financial statements** are given as interim financial statements, IAS 1 should be used as a guide, otherwise IAS 34 specifies minimum contents.

A entity should use the same **recognition and measurement principles** in its interim financial statements as it does in its year-end financial statements. It is important that figures in interim statements are not 'massaged' to present a favourable picture of the position and performance of the entity.

Note

You will not be required to prepare interim reports in your examination, but should be aware that this standard exists.

Section summary

- IAS 34 in concept makes straightforward proposals for the production of interim financial reports by entities

- It is essential to apply principles of recognition and measurement that will prevent entities from 'massaging' the interim figures

Chapter Summary

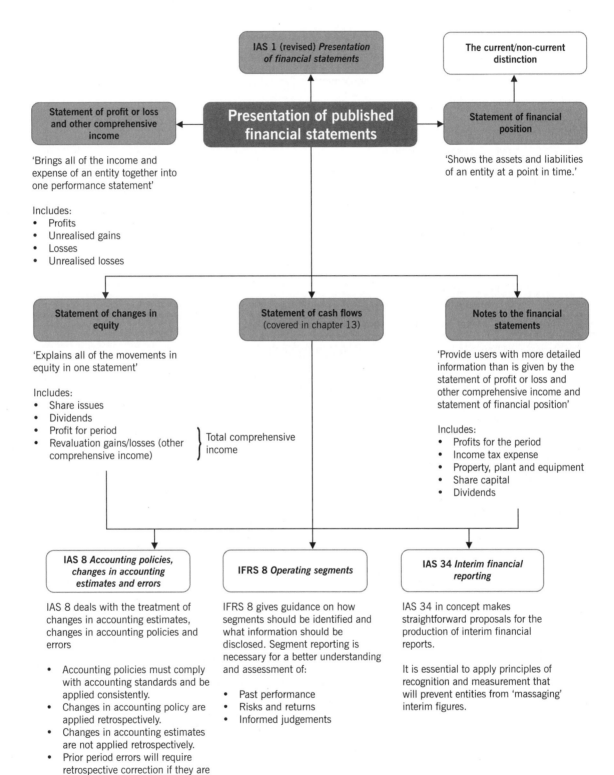

IAS 1 (revised) *Presentation of financial statements*

The current/non-current distinction

Statement of profit or loss and other comprehensive income

Presentation of published financial statements

Statement of financial position

'Brings all of the income and expense of an entity together into one performance statement'

Includes:
- Profits
- Unrealised gains
- Losses
- Unrealised losses

'Shows the assets and liabilities of an entity at a point in time.'

Statement of changes in equity

Statement of cash flows (covered in chapter 13)

Notes to the financial statements

'Explains all of the movements in equity in one statement'

Includes:
- Share issues
- Dividends
- Profit for period
- Revaluation gains/losses (other comprehensive income) } Total comprehensive income

'Provide users with more detailed information than is given by the statement of profit or loss and other comprehensive income and statement of financial position'

Includes:
- Profits for the period
- Income tax expense
- Property, plant and equipment
- Share capital
- Dividends

IAS 8 *Accounting policies, changes in accounting estimates and errors*

IFRS 8 *Operating segments*

IAS 34 *Interim financial reporting*

IAS 8 deals with the treatment of changes in accounting estimates, changes in accounting policies and errors

- Accounting policies must comply with accounting standards and be applied consistently.
- Changes in accounting policy are applied retrospectively.
- Changes in accounting estimates are not applied retrospectively.
- Prior period errors will require retrospective correction if they are material.

IFRS 8 gives guidance on how segments should be identified and what information should be disclosed. Segment reporting is necessary for a better understanding and assessment of:

- Past performance
- Risks and returns
- Informed judgements

IAS 34 in concept makes straightforward proposals for the production of interim financial reports.

It is essential to apply principles of recognition and measurement that will prevent entities from 'massaging' interim figures.

Quick Quiz

1   Financial statements provide users with information about the financial ...., financial
    .... and .... of an entity.

2   Which of the following are examples of current assets?

    (a)   Property, plant and equipment
    (b)   Prepayments
    (c)   Cash equivalents
    (d)   Manufacturing licences
    (e)   Retained earnings

3   Intangible assets must be disclosed as non-current assets in the statement of financial position.

    True   ☐

    False ☐

4   Which of the following must be disclosed on the face of the statement of profit or loss?

    (a)   Tax expense
    (b)   Analysis of expenses
    (c)   Net profit or loss for the period.

5   Where are revaluation gains shown in the financial statements?

Answers to Quick Quiz

1   Position, performance, cashflows

2   (b) and (c) only

3   True

4   (a) and (c) only. (b) may be shown in the notes.

5   In the 'other comprehensive income' section of the statement of profit or loss and other comprehensive income and the statement of changes in equity as a movement between the opening and closing balances.

Answers to Questions

5.1   Financial statements

(a)   ATOK CO
STATEMENT OF PROFIT OR LOSS AND OTHER COMPREHENSIVE INCOME FOR THE YEAR ENDED 30 JUNE 20X9

	$'000
Revenue (14,800 – 24) (W1)	14,776
Cost of sales (W1)	(10,280)
Gross profit	4,496
Distribution costs (1,080 + 272 + 190 – 120)	(1,422)
Administration expenses (1,460 + 272 + 70 – 60)	(1,742)
Finance cost (2,000 × 10% × 3/12)	(50)
Profit for the year	1,282
Other comprehensive income	
Gain on revaluation of land	1,500
Total comprehensive income for the year	2,782

ATOK CO
STATEMENT OF FINANCIAL POSITION AS AT 30 JUNE 20X9

	$'000	$'000
Assets		
Non current assets		
Property, plant and equipment (W3)		25,470
Current assets		
Inventories (W1)	1,566	
Receivables (4,120 + 120 + 60 – 24)	4,276	
Cash and cash equivalents	160	
		6,002
Total assets		31,472
Equity		
Share capital		14,000
Retained earnings		4,422
Share premium account		4,000
Revaluation surplus		4,500
		26,922

	$'000	$'000
Non current liabilities		
10% loan notes 20Y8		2,000
Current liabilities		
Trade payables	2,240	
Accruals (190 + 70 + 50)	310	
Total current liabilities		2,250
Total equity and liabilities		31,472

(b)   ATOK CO
STATEMENT OF CHANGES IN EQUITY FOR THE YEAR ENDED 30 JUNE 20X9

	Share capital $'000	Share premium $'000	Revaluation surplus $'000	Retained earnings $'000	Total $'000
As at 1 July 20X8	10,000	2,000	3,000	3,140	18,140
Issue of shares	4,000	2,000	–	–	6,000
Total comprehensive income for the year	–	–	1,500	1,282	2,782
As at 30 June 20X9	14,000	4,000	4,500	4,422	26,922

Workings

1   *Cost of sales*

	$'000
Opening inventory	1,390
Purchases	8,280
	9,670
Closing inventories ((1,560 + 16 – 10) see below)	(1,566)
	8,104
Depreciation (W2)	2,176
Cost of sales	10,280

Inventory adjustments

(i)   Lower of cost ($80,000) and NRV ($90,000 – $20,000) = $70,000. Therefore $10,000 (80,000 – 70,000) adjustment.

(ii)   Inventory understated by $16,000

Sales overstated by $24,000

Tutorial note: inventories are covered in Chapter 11 of this Study Text.

2   *Depreciation*

	$'000
Buildings (8,000 @ 2%)	160
Plant (12,800 @ 20%)	2,560
	2,720

80% to cost of sales: 2,176. 10% to distribution and 10% to administration: 272

3   *Property, plant and equipment*

	$'000
Land and buildings (12,000 + 8,000 – 2,130 – 160)	17,710
Plant and equipment (12,800 – 2,480 – 2,560)	7,760
	25,470

Tutorial note: remember that land is not depreciated.

5.2 Prior period error

STATEMENT OF PROFIT OR LOSS

	20X6 $'000	20X7 $'000
Sales	47,400	67,200
Cost of goods sold (W1)	(38,770)	(51,600)
Profit before tax	8,630	15,600
Income tax (W2)	(2,620)	(4,660)
Profit for the year	6,010	10,940

RETAINED EARNINGS

	20X6 $'000	20X7 $'000
Opening retained earnings		
As previously reported	13,000	21,950
Correction of prior period error (4,200 – 1,260)	–	(2,940)
As restated	13,000	19,010
Profit for the year	6,010	10,940
Closing retained earnings	19,010	29,950

Workings

1   Cost of goods sold

	20X6 $'000	20X7 $'000
As stated in question	34,570	55,800
Inventory adjustment	4,200	(4,200)
	38,770	51,600

2   Income tax

	20X6 $'000	20X7 $'000
As stated in question	3,880	3,400
Inventory adjustment (4,200 × 30%)	(1,260)	1,260
	2,620	4,660

Now try these questions from the OTQ Question Bank	Number
	Q20
	Q21
	Q23
	Q30

NON-CURRENT ASSETS I

This chapter deals with IAS 16.

IAS 16 should be familiar to you from your earlier studies, as should the mechanics of accounting for depreciation, revaluations of non-current assets and disposals of non-current assets. Some questions are given here for revision purposes.

topic list	learning outcomes	syllabus references	ability required
1 IAS 16 *Property, plant and equipment*	B2	B2 (b)	application

Chapter Overview

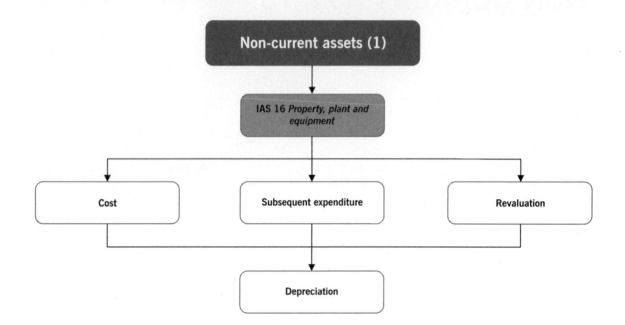

1   IAS 16 *Property, plant and equipment*

Introduction

This chapter looks at IAS 16 *Property, plant and equipment* which covers all aspects of accounting for property, plant and equipment. This represents the bulk of items which are 'tangible' non-current assets. Here we will consider the rules for recognition, derecognition, measurement and depreciation. We will also cover what happens when an asset is revalued.

1.1 Definitions

IAS 16 gives a large number of definitions which you should be familiar with for your exam.

KEY TERMS

PROPERTY, PLANT AND EQUIPMENT are tangible assets that:

- are held for use in the production or supply of goods or services, for rental to others, or for administrative purposes; and

- are expected to be used during more than one period.

CARRYING AMOUNT is the amount at which an asset is recognised in the statement of financial position after deducting any accumulated depreciation and accumulated impairment losses.

COST is the amount of cash or cash equivalents paid or the fair value of the other consideration given to acquire an asset at the time of its acquisition or construction.

DEPRECIATION is the result of systematic allocation of the depreciable amount of an asset over its useful life.

DEPRECIABLE AMOUNT of a depreciable asset is the cost of an asset or other amount substituted for cost, less its residual value.

FAIR VALUE is the price that would be received to sell an asset or paid to transfer a liability in an orderly transaction between market participants at the measurement date.

An IMPAIRMENT LOSS is the amount by which the carrying amount of an asset exceeds its recoverable amount.

RECOVERABLE AMOUNT is the higher of an asset's fair value less costs to sell and its value in use.

The RESIDUAL VALUE is the net amount which the entity expects to obtain for an asset at the end of its useful life after deducting the expected costs of disposal.

USEFUL LIFE is one of two things.

- The period over which an asset is expected to be available for use by an entity
- The number of production or similar units expected to be obtained from the asset by the entity.

(IAS 16)

An 'amount substituted for cost' will normally be a **current market value** after a revaluation has taken place.

1.2 Recognition

In this context, recognition simply means incorporation of the item in the business's accounts, in this case as a non-current asset. The recognition of property, plant and equipment depends on two criteria:

(a)   It is probable that **future economic benefits** associated with the asset will flow to the entity
(b)   The cost of the asset to the entity can be **measured reliably**

These recognition criteria apply to **subsequent expenditure** as well as costs incurred initially.

Property, plant and equipment can amount to **substantial amounts** in financial statements, affecting the presentation of the company's financial position and the profitability of the entity, through depreciation and also if an asset is wrongly classified as an expense and taken to profit or loss.

1.3 Initial measurement

Once an item of property, plant and equipment qualifies for recognition as an asset, it will initially be **measured at cost**.

1.3.1 Components of cost

The standard lists the components of the cost of an item of property, plant and equipment:

- **Purchase price**, less any trade discount or rebate
- **Import duties** and non-refundable purchase taxes
- **Directly attributable costs** of bringing the asset to working condition for its intended use, eg:
    - The cost of site preparation
    - Initial delivery and handling costs
    - Installation costs
    - Testing
    - Professional fees (architects, engineers)
- Initial estimate of the cost of dismantling and removing the asset and restoring the site on which it is located

IAS 16 provides **additional guidance on directly attributable** costs included in the cost of an item of property, plant and equipment.

(a)   These costs bring the asset to the location and working conditions necessary for it to be capable of operating in the manner intended by management, including those costs to test whether the asset is functioning properly.

(b)   These are determined after deducting the net proceeds from selling any items produced when bringing the asset to its location and condition.

The standard also states that income and related expenses of operations that are **incidental** to the construction or development of an item of property, plant and equipment should be **recognised** in profit or loss.

The following costs **will not be part of the cost** of property, plant or equipment unless they can be attributed directly to the asset's acquisition, or bringing it into its working condition.

- Administration and other general overhead costs
- Start-up
- Initial operating losses before the asset reaches planned performance

All of these will be recognised as an **expense** rather than an asset.

In the case of **self-constructed assets**, the same principles are applied as for acquired assets. If the entity makes similar assets during the normal course of business for sale externally, then the cost of the asset will be the cost of its production under IAS 2 *Inventories*. This also means that abnormal costs (wasted material, labour or other resources) are excluded from the cost of the asset. An example of a self-constructed asset is when a building company builds its own head office.

1.3.2 Exchanges of assets

IAS 16 specifies that exchanges of items of property, plant and equipment, regardless of whether the assets are similar, are measured at **fair value**, **unless the exchange transaction lacks commercial substance** or the fair value of neither of the assets exchanged can be **measured reliably**. If the acquired item is not measured at fair value, its cost is measured at the carrying amount of the asset given up.

1.3.3 Subsequent expenditure

Subsequent expenditure can be recognised when

(a)   It is probable that **future economic benefits** associated with the asset will flow to the entity
(b)   The cost of the asset to the entity can be **measured reliably**

Expenditure incurred in replacing or renewing a component of an item of property, plant and equipment must be **recognised in the carrying amount of the item**. The carrying amount of the replaced or renewed component must be derecognised. If part of an item of property, plant and equipment is depreciated separately, when it is replaced, the new part is treated as an acquisition and the replaced part is treated like a disposal.

A similar approach is also applied when an item of property, plant and equipment, such as an aircraft, has to undergo a **major inspection** to enable the continued use of the item, regardless of whether parts of the item are replaced. When each major inspection is performed, its cost is recognised in the carrying amount of the item of property, plant and equipment as a replacement (eg to the previous inspection) if the recognition criteria are met. Any remaining carrying amount of the previous inspection is derecognised. This occurs regardless of whether the cost of the previous inspection was identified in the transaction in which the item was acquired or constructed.

Repairs and maintenance costs should be recognised as an expense when they are incurred.

1.4 Measurement subsequent to initial recognition

IAS 16 allows two possible treatments here, a choice between keeping an asset recorded at **cost** or revaluing it to **fair value**.

(a)   **Cost model.** Carry the asset at its cost less accumulated depreciation and any accumulated impairment losses.

(b)   **Revaluation model.** Carry the asset at a revalued amount, being its fair value at the date of the revaluation less any subsequent accumulated depreciation and subsequent accumulated impairment losses. The revised IAS 16 makes clear that the **revaluation model is available only if the fair value of the item can be measured reliably**. Revaluations are considered below.

1.5 Depreciation

The need to depreciate non-current assets arises from the **accruals assumption**. If money is expended in purchasing an asset then the amount expended must at some time be charged against profits. If the asset is one which contributes to an entity's revenue over a number of accounting periods it would be inappropriate to charge any single period (eg the period in which the asset was acquired) with the whole of the expenditure. Instead, some method must be found of spreading the cost of the asset over its useful economic life.

1.5.1 Requirements of IAS 16 for depreciation

IAS 16 requires the depreciable amount of a depreciable asset to be allocated on a **systematic basis** to each accounting period during the useful life of the asset. Depreciable amount is the cost or valuation of the asset less its residual value. If the residual value is greater than the carrying amount of the asset, then the depreciation charge is zero.

One way of defining depreciation is to describe it as a means of **spreading the cost** of a non-current asset over its useful life, and so matching the cost against the full period during which it earns profits for the business.

There are situations where, over a period, an asset has **increased in value**, ie its current value is greater than the carrying value in the financial statements. You might think that in such situations it would not be necessary to depreciate the asset. The standard states, however, that this is irrelevant, and that depreciation should still be charged to each accounting period, based on the depreciable amount, irrespective of a rise in value.

An entity is required to **begin depreciating** an item of property, plant and equipment when it is **available for use** and to continue depreciating it until it is derecognised even if it is idle during the period.

Some assets require routine repairs and maintenance, however, depreciation should still be charged on these assets.

1.5.2 Depreciation methods

There are various methods of allocating depreciation to accounting periods. An entity should choose the method which best reflects the way the future economic benefits arising from the asset will be consumed by the entity.

You should be familiar with the various **accepted methods of allocating depreciation, which are the straight line, reducing balance and machine hour methods,** and the relevant calculations and accounting treatments. These are revised in the questions below.

Question 6.1	Depreciation I

Learning outcome B2

A lorry bought for a business cost $17,000. It is expected to last for five years and then be sold for scrap for $2,000. Usage over the five years is expected to be:

Year 1	200 days
Year 2	100 days
Year 3	100 days
Year 4	150 days
Year 5	40 days

Required

Work out the depreciation to be charged each year under:

(a) The straight line method
(b) The reducing balance method (using a rate of 35%)
(c) The machine hour method

| **Question 6.2** | Depreciation II |

Learning outcome B2

(a)   What are the purposes of providing for depreciation?

(b)   In what circumstances is the reducing balance method more appropriate than the straight-line method? Give reasons for your answer.

1.5.3 Change in depreciation method

The depreciation method chosen should be reviewed at least every financial year end. If there has been a **significant change** in the way the entity uses the asset, the method of depreciation should be changed to reflect this. A change in the method of depreciation should be accounted for as a **change in accounting estimate under IAS 8** and accounted for **prospectively**, ie the new method should be applied in the current and future accounting periods. No changes to earlier periods are required.

Example: change in depreciation method

Jakob Co purchased an asset for $100,000 on 1.1.X1. It had an estimated useful life of 5 years and it was depreciated using the reducing balance method at a rate of 40%. It had no residual value. On 1.1.X3 the directors decided to change the method to straight line as this would give a fairer presentation.

Show the depreciation charge for each year (to 31 December) of the asset's life.

Solution

Year		Depreciation charge $	Aggregate depreciation $
20X1	$100,000 × 40%	40,000	40,000
20X2	$60,000 × 40%	24,000	64,000
20X3	$\dfrac{\$100,000 - \$64,000}{3}$ *	12,000	76,000
20X4		12,000	88,000
20X5		12,000	100,000

$$* \text{New depreciation charge} = \frac{(\text{Carrying amount} - \text{Re sidual value})}{\text{Re maining useful life}}$$

Note that in this example, there is no residual value.

1.5.4 Change in useful life or residual value of an asset

The depreciation charge on a non-current asset depends not only on the cost (or value) of the asset, but also on its **estimated useful life** and its **residual value**.

Once decided, the useful life should be **reviewed at least every financial year end** and depreciation rates adjusted for the current and future periods, if expectations vary significantly from the original estimates. Residual value should also be reviewed and amended as necessary. Any change to useful life or residual value should be accounted for **prospectively**, ie in the current and future accounting periods. No change should be made to past accounting periods.

Example: change in useful life

A business purchased a non-current asset costing $12,000 with an estimated life of four years and no residual value. If it used the straight line method of depreciation, it would make an annual provision for depreciation of 25% of $12,000 = $3,000.

Now what would happen if the business decided after two years that the useful life of the asset has been underestimated, and it still had five more years in use to come (making its total life seven years)?

Solution

For the first two years, the asset would have been depreciated by $3,000 per annum, so that its carrying amount after two years would be $(12,000 – 6,000) = $6,000. If the remaining life of the asset is now revised to five more years, the remaining amount to be depreciated (here $6,000) should be spread over the remaining life, giving an annual depreciation charge for the final five years of:

$$\frac{\text{Carrying amount at time of life readjustment - residual value}}{\text{New estimate of remaining useful life}} = \frac{\$6,000}{5 \text{ years}} = \$1,200 \text{ per year}$$

Similar adjustments are made when there is a change in the expected residual value of the asset.

1.5.5 Treatment of depreciation in the accounts

Depreciation is usually treated as an **expense**:

DEBIT	Depreciation expense (statement of profit or loss)	X
CREDIT	Accumulated depreciation (statement of financial position)	X

Sometimes depreciation is included in the cost of the new assets produced, for example, depreciation of plant and machinery may be incurred in the production of goods for sale (inventory items).

1.6 Impairment of asset values

An **impairment loss** should be treated in the same way as a **revaluation decrease** (ie the decrease should be **recognised as an expense**). However, a revaluation decrease (or impairment loss) should be charged directly against any related revaluation surplus to the extent that the decrease does not exceed the amount held in the revaluation surplus in respect of that same asset.

A **reversal of an impairment** loss should be treated in the same way as a **revaluation increase**, ie a revaluation increase should be recognised as income to the extent that it reverses a revaluation decrease or an impairment loss of the same asset previously recognised as an expense.

1.7 Retirements and disposals

When an asset is permanently **withdrawn from use, or sold or scrapped**, and no future economic benefits are expected from its disposal, it should be withdrawn from the statement of financial position.

Gains or losses are the difference between the net disposal proceeds and the carrying amount of the asset. They should be recognised as income or expense in profit or loss. This applies also to **revalued assets**.

1.8 Derecognition

An entity is required to **derecognise the carrying amount** of an item of property, plant or equipment that it disposes of on the date the **criteria for the sale of goods** in IAS 18 *Revenue* would be met. This also applies to parts of an asset.

An entity cannot classify as revenue a gain it realises on the disposal of an item of property, plant and equipment.

Question 6.3	Depreciation III

Learning outcome B2

A business purchased two rivet-making machines on 1 January 20X5 at a cost of $15,000 each. Each had an estimated life of five years and a nil residual value. The straight line method of depreciation is used.

Owing to an unforeseen slump in market demand for rivets, the business decided to reduce its output of rivets, and switch to making other products instead. On 31 March 20X7, one rivet-making machine was sold (on credit) to a buyer for $8,000.

Later in the year, however, it was decided to abandon production of rivets altogether, and the second machine was sold on 1 December 20X7 for $2,500 cash.

Required

Prepare the machinery ledger account, provision for depreciation of machinery ledger account and disposal of machinery ledger account for the accounting year to 31 December 20X7.

1.9 Revaluations

The **market value** of land and buildings usually represents fair value, assuming existing use and line of business. Such valuations are usually carried out by professionally qualified valuers.

In the case of **plant and equipment**, fair value can also be taken as **market value**. Where a market value is not available, however, depreciated replacement cost should be used. There may be no market value where types of plant and equipment are sold only rarely or because of their specialised nature (ie they would normally only be sold as part of an ongoing business).

The frequency of valuation depends on the **volatility of the fair values** of individual items of property, plant and equipment. The more volatile the fair value, the more frequently revaluations should be carried out. Where the current fair value is very different from the carrying value then a revaluation should be carried out.

Most importantly, when an item of property, plant and equipment is revalued, **the whole class of assets to which it belongs should be revalued.** A class is a grouping of assets of a similar nature, for example, land, buildings, motor vehicles etc.

All the items within a class should be **revalued at the same time**, to prevent selective revaluation of certain assets and to avoid disclosing a mixture of costs and values from different dates in the financial statements. A rolling basis of revaluation is allowed if the revaluations are kept up to date and the revaluation of the whole class is completed in a short period of time.

1.9.1 Accounting entries for a revaluation

When an asset is revalued, the double entry to account for it is:

DEBIT   Property, plant and equipment (statement of financial position)

CREDIT   Revaluation surplus (statement of financial position)

The revaluation surplus is part of owners' equity and so the credit to the revaluation surplus will be seen as **'other comprehensive income'** in the statement of profit or loss and other comprehensive income. If the revaluation is reversing a previous decrease in value that was recognised as an expense, the increase in value should first be recognised as income up to the value that was previously recognised as an expense, any excess is then taken to the revaluation surplus.

Example: Revaluation surplus

Binkie Co has an item of land carried in its books at $13,000. Two years ago a slump in land values led the company to reduce the carrying value from $15,000. This was taken as an expense in the statement of profit or loss. There has been a surge in land prices in the current year, however, and the land is now worth $20,000.

Required

Account for the revaluation in the current year.

Solution

The double entry is:

DEBIT	Asset value (statement of financial position)	$7,000	
CREDIT	Statement of profit or loss		$2,000
	Revaluation surplus		$5,000

Note: **the credit to the revaluation surplus will be shown under 'other comprehensive income'**.

The case is similar for a **decrease in value** on revaluation. Any decrease should be recognised as an expense, except where it offsets a previous increase taken as a revaluation surplus in owners' equity. Any decrease greater than the previous upwards increase in value must be taken as an expense in the profit or loss.

Example: Revaluation decrease

Let us simply swap round the example given above. The original cost was $15,000, revalued upwards to $20,000 two years ago. The value has now fallen to $13,000.

Required

Account for the decrease in value.

Solution

The double entry is:

DEBIT	Revaluation surplus	$5,000	
DEBIT	Statement of profit or loss	$2,000	
CREDIT	Asset value (statement of financial position)		$7,000

There is a further complication when a **revalued asset is being depreciated**. As we have seen, an upward revaluation means that the depreciation charge will increase. Normally, a revaluation surplus is only realised when the asset is sold, but when it is being depreciated, part of that surplus is being realised as the asset is used. The amount of the surplus realised is the difference between depreciation charged on the revalued amount and the (lower) depreciation which would have been charged on the asset's original cost. **This amount can be transferred to retained (ie realised) earnings** as a direct transfer between reserves. It should **not** be put through the statement of profit or loss.

Example: Revaluation and depreciation

Crinckle Co bought an asset for $10,000 at the beginning of 20X6. It had a useful life of five years. On 1 January 20X8 the asset was revalued to $12,000. The expected useful life has remained unchanged (ie three years remain).

Required

Account for the revaluation and state the treatment for depreciation from 20X8 onwards.

Solution

On 1 January 20X8 the carrying value of the asset is $10,000 – (2 × $10,000 ÷ 5) = $6,000. For the revaluation:

| DEBIT | Asset value | $6,000 | |
| CREDIT | Revaluation surplus | | $6,000 |

The depreciation for the next three years will be $12,000 ÷ 3 = $4,000, compared to depreciation on cost of $10,000 ÷ 5 = $2,000. So each year, the extra $2,000 can be treated as part of the surplus which has become realised:

| DEBIT | Revaluation surplus | $2,000 | |
| CREDIT | Retained earnings | | $2,000 |

This is a movement on owners' equity only, not an item in the statement of profit or loss. It will be disclosed in the statement of changes in equity.

1.9.2 Disposal of revalued items

When a revalued item is disposed of, the gain or loss on disposal is calculated as the sales proceeds less the carrying value of the asset at the date of disposal. This amount is recognised in profit or loss. The revaluation surplus associated with the asset that has been disposed of is transferred directly to retained earnings. This transfer will be seen in the statement of changes in equity.

Example: Revaluation and disposal

Dartford Inc bought an asset for $50,000 at the beginning of 20X3. It had a useful life of five years. On 1 January 20X4 the asset was revalued to $60,000, the useful life remained the same (ie 4 years remaining). On 31 December 20X4, the asset was sold for £63,000. (Note: Dartford does not transfer the excess depreciation to retained earnings.)

Required

Account for the disposal of the asset and show the double entries required.

Solution

On 1 January 20X4 the carrying value of the asset is $50,000 – ($50,000 ÷ 5) = $40,000

For the revaluation:

DEBIT	Asset cost ($60,000 – $50,000)	$10,000	
DEBIT	Accumulated depreciation	$10,000	
CREDIT	Revaluation surplus		$20,000

At 31 December 20X4, the carrying value of the asset is $60,000 – ($60,000 ÷ 4) = £45,000

The gain on disposal is therefore $63,000 - $45,000 = $18,000

To account for the disposal:

DEBIT	Cash	$63,000	
DEBIT	Accumulated depreciation	$15,000	
CREDIT	Asset value		$60,000
CREDIT	Gain on sale (statement of profit or loss)		$18,000

To remove the associated revaluation surplus:

DEBIT	Revaluation surplus	$20,000	
CREDIT	Retained earnings		£20,000

This is a movement on owners' equity only, not an item in the statement of profit or loss. It will be disclosed in the statement of changes in equity.

1.10 Disclosure

The standard has a long list of disclosure requirements, for each class of property, plant and equipment.

(a)   **Measurement bases** for determining the gross carrying amount (if more than one, the gross carrying amount for that basis in each category)

(b)   **Depreciation methods** used

(c)   **Useful lives** or depreciation rates used

(d)   **Gross carrying amount** and accumulated depreciation (aggregated with accumulated impairment losses) at the beginning and end of the period

(e)   **Reconciliation** of the carrying amount at the beginning and end of the period showing:

(i)   Additions

(ii)   Disposals and assets classified as 'held for sale' in accordance with IFRS 5

(iii)   Acquisitions through business combinations

(iv)   Increases/decreases during the period from revaluations and from impairment losses

(v) Impairment losses recognised in profit or loss

(vi) Impairment losses reversed in profit or loss

(vii) Depreciation

The financial statements should also disclose the following.

(a) Existence and amounts of **restrictions on title**, and items pledged as security for liabilities

(b) Amount of commitments to **acquisitions**

Revalued assets require further disclosures.

(a) Basis used to revalue the assets

(b) Effective date of the revaluation

(c) Whether an independent valuer was involved

(d) Carrying amount of each class of property, plant and equipment that would have been included in the financial statements had the assets not been revalued.

(e) Revaluation surplus.

The following format (with notional figures) is commonly used to disclose non-current asset movements.

	Total $	Land and buildings $	Plant and equipment $
Cost or valuation			
At 1 January 20X4	50,000	40,000	10,000
Revaluation surplus	12,000	12,000	–
Additions in year	4,000	–	4,000
Disposals in year	(1,000)	–	(1,000)
At 31 December 20X4	65,000	52,000	13,000
Depreciation			
At 1 January 20X4	16,000	10,000	6,000
Charge for year	4,000	1,000	3,000
Eliminated on disposals	(500)	–	(500)
At 31 December 20X4	19,500	11,000	8,500
Carrying value			
At 31 December 20X4	45,500	41,000	4,500
At 1 January 20X4	34,000	30,000	4,000

 Question 6.4 IAS 16

Learning outcome B2

(a) In a statement of financial position prepared in accordance with IAS 16, what does carrying amount or net book value (NBV), represent?

(b) In a set of financial statements prepared in accordance with IAS 16, is it correct to say that the carrying value figure in a statement of financial position cannot be greater than the market (net realisable) value of the partially used asset as at the end of the reporting period? Explain your reasons for your answer.

Section summary

IAS 16 *Property, plant and equipment* provides the basic rules on **depreciation** including important definitions of depreciation, depreciable assets, useful life and depreciable amount.

When a non-current asset is **revalued**, depreciation is charged on the revalued amount.

When a non-current asset is **sold**, there is likely to be a profit or loss on disposal. This is the difference between the net sale price of the asset and its carrying value at the time of disposal.

Chapter Summary

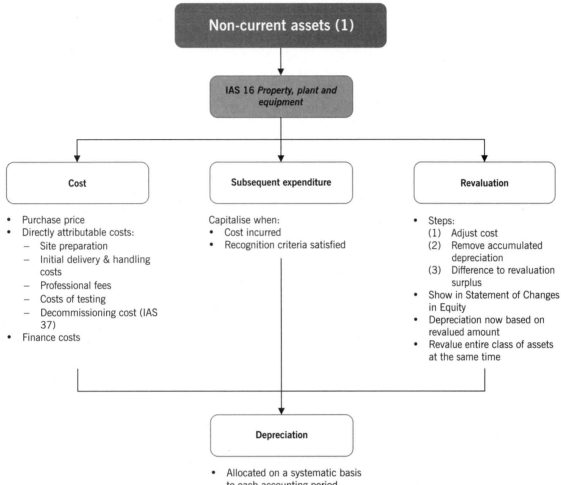

Non-current assets (1)

IAS 16 *Property, plant and equipment*

Cost

- Purchase price
- Directly attributable costs:
  - Site preparation
  - Initial delivery & handling costs
  - Professional fees
  - Costs of testing
  - Decommissioning cost (IAS 37)
- Finance costs

Subsequent expenditure

Capitalise when:
- Cost incurred
- Recognition criteria satisfied

Revaluation

- Steps:
  (1) Adjust cost
  (2) Remove accumulated depreciation
  (3) Difference to revaluation surplus
- Show in Statement of Changes in Equity
- Depreciation now based on revalued amount
- Revalue entire class of assets at the same time

Depreciation

- Allocated on a systematic basis to each accounting period
- Depreciable about is the cost or valuation of the asset less its residual value.

Quick Quiz

1   Define depreciation.

2   Which of the following elements can be included in the production cost of a non-current asset?

    A   Purchase price

    B   Architect's fees

    C   Import duties

    D   Installation costs

3   Market value can usually be taken as fair value.

    True ☐

    False ☐

Answers to Quick Quiz

1   The result of the systematic allocation of the depreciable amount of an asset over its useful life.
2   All of them.
3   True

Answers to Questions

6.1 Depreciation I

(a)   Under the straight line method, depreciation for each of the five years is:

$$\text{Annual depreciation} = \frac{\$(17,000 - 2,000)}{5} = \$3,000$$

(b)   Under the reducing balance method, depreciation for each of the five years is:

Year	Depreciation	
1	35% × $17,000	= $5,950
2	35% × ($17,000 – $5,950) = 35% × $11,050	= $3,868
3	35% × ($11,050 – $3,868) = 35% × $7,182	= $2,514
4	35% × ($7,182 – $2,514) = 35% × $4,668	= $1,634
5	Balance to bring book value down to $2,000 = $4,668 – $1,634 – $2,000	= $1,034

(c)   Under the machine hour method, depreciation for each of the five years is calculated as follows.

Total usage (days) = 200 + 100 + 100 + 150 + 40 = 590 days

$$\text{Depreciation per day} = \frac{\$(17,000 - 2,000)}{590} = \$25.42$$

Year	Usage (days)	Depreciation ($) (days × $25.42)
1	200	5,084.00
2	100	2,542.00
3	100	2,542.00
4	150	3,813.00
5	40	1,016.80
		14,997.80

Note. The answer does not come to exactly $15,000 because of the rounding carried out at the 'depreciation per day' stage of the calculation.

6.2 Depreciation II

(a)   The accounts of a business try to recognise that the cost of a non-current asset is gradually consumed as the asset wears out. This is done by gradually writing off the asset's cost to profit or loss over several accounting periods. This process is known as depreciation, and is an example of the accruals assumption. IAS 16 *Property, plant and equipment* requires that depreciation should be allocated on a systematic basis to each accounting period during the useful life of the asset.

With regard to the accrual principle, it is fair that the profits should be reduced by the depreciation charge; this is not an arbitrary exercise. Depreciation is not, as is sometimes supposed, an attempt to set aside funds to purchase new non-current assets when required. Depreciation is not generally provided on freehold land because it does not 'wear out' (unless it is held for mining etc).

(b) The reducing balance method of depreciation is used instead of the straight line method when it is considered fair to allocate a greater proportion of the total depreciable amount to the earlier years and a lower proportion to the later years on the assumption that the benefits obtained by the business from using the asset decline over time.

In favour of this method it may be argued that it links the depreciation charge to the costs of maintaining and running the asset. In the early years these costs are low and the depreciation charge is high, while in later years this is reversed.

6.3 Depreciation III

MACHINERY ACCOUNT

20X7		$	20X7		$
1 Jan	Balance b/f	30,000	31 Mar	Disposal of machinery account	15,000
			1 Dec	Disposal of machinery account	15,000
		30,000			30,000

ACCUMULATED DEPRECIATION OF MACHINERY

20X7		$	20X7		$
31 Mar	Disposal of machinery account*	6,750	1 Jan	Balance b/f	12,000
			31 Dec	Statement of profit or loss ***	3,500
1 Dec	Disposal of machinery account**	8,750			
		15,500			15,500

* Depreciation at date of disposal = $6,000 + $750

** Depreciation at date of disposal = $6,000 + $2,750

*** Depreciation charge for the year = $750 + $2,750

DISPOSAL OF MACHINERY

20X7		$	20X7		$
31 Mar	Machinery account	15,000	31 Mar	Account receivable (sale price)	8,000
1 Dec	Machinery account	15,000	31 Mar	Provision for depreciation	6,750
			1 Dec	Cash (sale price)	2,500
			1 Dec	Provision for depreciation	8,750
			31 Dec	Statement of profit or loss (loss on disposal)	4,000
		30,000			30,000

You should be able to calculate that there was a loss on the first disposal of $250, and on the second disposal of $3,750, giving a total loss of $4,000.

Workings

1 At 1 January 20X7, accumulated depreciation on the machines will be:

2 machines × 2 years × $\dfrac{\$15,000}{5}$ per machine pa = $12,000, or $6,000 per machine

2 Monthly depreciation is $\dfrac{\$3,000}{12}$ = $250 per machine per month

3   The machines are disposed of in 20X7.

   (a)   On 31 March – after 3 months of the year. Depreciation for the year on the machine = 3 months × $250 = $750.

   (b)   On 1 December – after 11 months of the year. Depreciation for the year on the machine = 11 months × $250 = $2,750

6.4 IAS 16

(a)   In simple terms the carrying value of an asset is the cost of an asset less the 'accumulated depreciation', that is all depreciation charged so far. It should be emphasised that the main purpose of charging depreciation is to ensure that profits are fairly reported. Thus depreciation is concerned with the statement of profit or loss and other comprehensive income rather than the statement of financial position. In consequence the carrying value in the statement of financial position can be quite arbitrary. In particular, it does not necessarily bear any relation to the market value of an asset and is of little use for planning and decision making.

An obvious example of the disparity between carrying value and market value is found in the case of buildings, which may be worth considerably more than their carrying value.

(b)   Carrying value can in some circumstances be higher than market value (net realisable value). IAS 16 *Property, plant and equipment* states that the carrying value of an asset cannot be greater than its 'recoverable amount'. However 'recoverable amount' as defined in IAS 16 is the amount recoverable from further use. This may be higher than the market value.

This makes sense if you think of a specialised machine which could not be sold for much money on the secondhand market but which will produce goods which can be sold at a profit for many years.

Now try these questions from the OTQ Question Bank	Number
	Q6
	Q9
	Q19
	Q34
	Q44
	Q47

NON-CURRENT ASSETS II

This chapter covers some further accounting standards which relate to one of the important items on the statement of financial position, non-current assets.

IAS 20 deals with the government grants, **IAS 40** addresses the accounting for investment properties, and

IAS 23 deals with the treatment of funds used in self-constructed assets.

topic list	learning outcomes	syllabus references
1 IAS 20 *Government grants*	B2	B2 (b)
2 IAS 40 *Investment property*	B2	B2 (b)
3 IAS 23 *Borrowing costs*	B2	B2 (b)

Chapter Overview

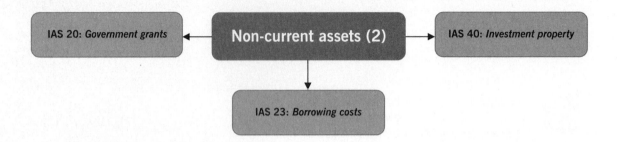

1 IAS 20 *Government grants*

KEY POINT

It is common for entities to receive government grants for various purposes (grants may be called subsidies, premiums, etc). They may also receive other types of assistance which may be in many forms. The treatment of government grants is covered by IAS 20 *Accounting for government grants and disclosure of government assistance.*

1.1 Scope

IAS 20 does **not** cover the following situations.

- Accounting for government grants in financial statements reflecting the effects of **changing prices**
- Government assistance given in the form of **'tax breaks'**
- Government acting as **part-owner** of the entity

1.2 Definitions

These definitions are given by the standard.

KEY TERMS

GOVERNMENT Government, government agencies and similar bodies whether local, national or international.

GOVERNMENT ASSISTANCE Action by government designed to provide an economic benefit specific to an entity or range of entities qualifying under certain criteria.

GOVERNMENT GRANTS Assistance by government in the form of transfers of resources to an entity in return for past or future compliance with certain conditions relating to the operating activities of the entity. They exclude those forms of government assistance which cannot reasonably have a value placed upon them and transactions with government which cannot be distinguished from the normal trading transactions of the entity.

GRANTS RELATED TO ASSETS. Government grants whose primary condition is that an entity qualifying for them should purchase, construct or otherwise acquire non-current assets. Subsidiary conditions may also be attached restricting the type or location of the assets or the periods during which they are to be acquired or held.

GRANTS RELATED TO INCOME. Government grants other than those related to assets.

FORGIVABLE LOANS Loans which the lender undertakes to waive repayment of under certain prescribed conditions.   IAS 20

FAIR VALUE The price that would be received to sell an asset or paid to transfer a liability in an orderly transaction between market participants at the measurement date.   IFRS 13

You can see that there are many **different forms** of government assistance: both the type of assistance and the conditions attached to it will vary. Government assistance may have encouraged an entity to undertake something it otherwise would not have done.

How will the receipt of government assistance affect the financial statements?

(a)   An appropriate method must be found to account for any **resources transferred**.

(b)   The extent to which an entity has **benefited** from such assistance during the reporting period should be shown.

1.3 Government grants

An entity should not recognise government grants (including non-monetary grants at fair value) until it has **reasonable assurance** that:

- The entity will comply with any **conditions** attached to the grant

- The entity will **actually receive** the grant

Even if the grant has been received, this does not prove that the conditions attached to it have been or will be fulfilled.

It makes no difference in the treatment of the grant whether it is received in cash or given as a reduction in a liability to government, ie the **manner of receipt is irrelevant**.

Any related **contingency** should be recognised under IAS 37 Provisions, contingent liabilities and contingent assets, once the grant has been recognised. (IAS 37 is outside the scope of the CIMA F1 syllabus).

In the case of a **forgivable loan** (as defined in key terms above) from government, it should be treated in the same way as a government grant when it is reasonably assured that the entity will meet the relevant terms for forgiveness.

1.3.1 Accounting treatment of government grants

IAS 20 requires grants to be recognised as income over the relevant periods to match them with related costs which they have been received to compensate. This should be done on a systematic basis. **Grants should not, therefore, be credited directly to equity.**

It would be against the accruals assumption to credit grants to income on a receipts basis, so a **systematic basis of matching** must be used. A receipts basis would only be acceptable if no other basis was available.

It will usually be easy to identify the **costs related to a government grant**, and thereby the period(s) in which the grant should be recognised as income, ie when the costs are incurred. Where grants are received in relation to a depreciating asset, the grant will be recognised over the periods in which the asset is depreciated *and* in the same proportions.

| Question 7.1 | Recognition |

Learning outcome B2

Arturo Co receives a government grant representing 50% of the cost of a depreciating asset which costs $40,000. How will the grant be recognised if Arturo Co depreciates the asset:

(a)   over four years straight line; or

(b)   at 40% reducing balance?

The residual value is nil. The useful life is four years.

In the case of **grants for non-depreciable assets**, certain obligations may need to be fulfilled, in which case the grant should be recognised as income over the periods in which the cost of meeting the obligation is incurred. For example, if a piece of land is granted on condition that a building is erected on it, then the grant should be recognised as income over the building's life.

There may be a **series of conditions** attached to a grant, in the nature of a package of financial aid. An entity must take care to identify precisely those conditions which give rise to costs which in turn determine the periods over which the grant will be earned. When appropriate, the grant may be split and the parts allocated on different bases.

An entity may receive a grant as compensation for expenses or losses which it has **already incurred**. Alternatively, a grant may be given to an entity simply to provide immediate financial support where no future related costs are expected. In cases such as these, the grant received should be recognised as income of the period in which it becomes receivable.

1.3.2 Non-monetary government grants

A non-monetary asset may be transferred by government to an entity as a grant, for example a piece of land, or other resources. The **fair value** of such an asset is usually assessed and this is used to account for both the asset and the grant. Alternatively, both may be valued at a nominal amount.

1.3.3 Presentation of grants related to assets

There are two choices here for how government grants related to assets (including non-monetary grants at fair value) should be shown in the statement of financial position.

(a)   Set up the grant as **deferred income.**

(b)   **Deduct the grant** in arriving at the **carrying amount** of the asset.

These are considered to be acceptable alternatives and we can look at an example showing both.

Example: Accounting for grants related to assets

A company receives a 20% grant towards the cost of a new item of machinery, which cost $100,000. The machinery has an expected life of four years and a nil residual value. The expected profits of the company, before accounting for depreciation on the new machine or the grant, amount to $50,000 per annum in each year of the machinery's life.

Solution

The results of the company for the four years of the machine's life would be as follows.

(a)   *Reducing the cost of the asset*

	Year 1 $	Year 2 $	Year 3 $	Year 4 $	Total $
Profit before depreciation	50,000	50,000	50,000	50,000	200,000
Depreciation*	20,000	20,000	20,000	20,000	80,000
Profit	30,000	30,000	30,000	30,000	120,000

*The depreciation charge on a straight line basis, for each year, is ¼ of $(100,000 – 20,000) = $20,000.

Statement of financial position at year end (extract)

	$	$	$	$
Non-current asset	80,000	80,000	80,000	80,000
Depreciation 25%	20,000	40,000	60,000	80,000
Carrying amount	60,000	40,000	20,000	–

(b)   *Treating the grant as deferred income*

	Year 1 $	Year 2 $	Year 3 $	Year 4 $	Total $
Profit as above	50,000	50,000	50,000	50,000	200,000
Depreciation	(25,000)	(25,000)	(25,000)	(25,000)	(100,000)
Grant	5,000	5,000	5,000	5,000	20,000
Profit	30,000	30,000	30,000	30,000	120,000

Statement of financial position at year end (extract)

Non-current asset at cost	100,000	100,000	100,000	100,000
Depreciation 25%	(25,000)	(50,000)	(75,000)	(100,000)
Carrying amount	75,000	50,000	25,000	–
Government grant				
deferred income	15,000	10,000	5,000	–

Whichever of these methods is used, the **cash flows** in relation to the purchase of the asset and the receipt of the grant are often disclosed separately because of the significance of the movements in cash flow.

Deducting the grant from the cost of the asset is simpler, but the deferred income method has the advantage that the non-current asset continues to be carried at cost in the financial statements.

1.3.4 Presentation of grants related to income

These grants are a credit in profit or loss, but there is a choice in the method of disclosure.

(a)   Present as a **separate credit** or under a general heading, eg 'other income'

(b)   **Deduct from the related expense**

Some would argue that offsetting income and expenses in the statement of profit or loss is not good practice. Others would say that the expenses would not have been incurred had the grant not been available, so offsetting the two is acceptable. Although both methods are acceptable, disclosure of the grant may be necessary for a **proper understanding** of the financial statements, particularly the effect on any item of income or expense which is required to be separately disclosed.

1.3.5 Repayment of government grants

If a grant must be repaid it should be accounted for as a **revision of an accounting estimate** (see IAS 8).

(a)   **Repayment of a grant related to income:** apply first against any unamortised deferred income set up in respect of the grant; any excess should be recognised immediately as an expense.

(b)   **Repayment of a grant related to an asset**: increase the carrying amount of the asset or reduce the deferred income balance by the amount repayable. The cumulative additional depreciation that would have been recognised to date in the absence of the grant should be immediately recognised as an expense.

It is possible that the circumstances surrounding repayment may require a review of the **asset value** and an impairment of the new carrying amount of the asset.

1.4 Government assistance

Some forms of government assistance are excluded from the definition of government grants.

(a)   Some forms of government assistance **cannot reasonably have a value placed on them**, eg free technical or marketing advice, provision of guarantees.

(b)   There are transactions with government which **cannot be distinguished from the entity's normal trading transactions**, eg government procurement policy resulting in a portion of the entity's sales. Any segregation would be arbitrary.

Disclosure of such assistance may be necessary because of its significance; its nature, extent and duration should be disclosed. Loans at low or zero interest rates are a form of government assistance, but the imputation of interest does not fully quantify the benefit received.

1.5 Disclosure

Disclosure is required of the following.

- **Accounting policy** adopted, including method of presentation
- **Nature and extent** of government grants recognised and other forms of assistance received
- **Unfulfilled conditions and other contingencies** attached to recognised government assistance

2 IAS 40 *Investment property*

KEY POINT

An entity may own land or a building **as an investment** rather than for use in the business. It may therefore generate cash flows largely independently of other assets which the entity holds. The treatment of investment property is covered by IAS 40.

2.1 Definitions

Consider the following definitions.

KEY TERMS

INVESTMENT PROPERTY is property (land or a building – or part of a building – or both) held (by the owner or by the lessee under a finance lease) to earn rentals or for capital appreciation or both, rather than for:

(a)   Use in the production or supply of goods or services or for administrative purposes, or

(b)   Sale in the ordinary course of business

OWNER-OCCUPIED PROPERTY is property held by the owner (or by the lessee under a finance lease) for use in the production or supply of goods or services or for administrative purposes.

FAIR VALUE is the price that would be received to sell an asset or paid to transfer a liability in an orderly transaction between market participants at the measurement date.

COST is the amount of cash or cash equivalents paid or the fair value of other consideration given to acquire an asset at the time of its acquisition or construction.

CARRYING AMOUNT is the amount at which an asset is recognised in the statement of financial position.

A property interest that is held by a lessee under an OPERATING LEASE may be classified and accounted for as an INVESTMENT PROPERTY, if and only if the property would otherwise meet the definition of an investment property and the lessee uses the IAS 40 FAIR VALUE MODEL. This classification is available on a property-by-property basis.

Examples of investment property include:

(a)   **Land held for long-term capital appreciation** rather than for short-term sale in the ordinary course of business

(b)   A **building** owned by the reporting entity (or held by the entity under a finance lease) and **leased out under an operating lease**

(c)   A building held by a **parent** and leased to a **subsidiary**. Note, however, that while this is regarded as an investment property in the individual parent company financial statements, in the **consolidated** financial statements this property will be regarded as owner-occupied (because it is occupied by the group) and will therefore be treated in accordance with IAS 16.

(d)   Property that is being constructed or developed for future use as an investment property

Question 7.2	Investment property

Learning outcome B2

Rich Co owns a piece of land. The directors have not yet decided whether to build a factory on it for use in its business or to keep it and sell it when its value has risen.

Would this be classified as an investment property under IAS 40?

2.2 IAS 40

IAS 40 *Investment property* was published in March 2000 and has recently been revised. Its objective is to prescribe the accounting treatment for investment property and related disclosure requirements.

The standard includes investment property held under a finance lease or leased out under an operating lease. However, the current IAS 40 does not deal with matters covered in IAS 17 *Leases*. (IAS 17 is outside the scope of the CIMA F1 syllabus).

You now know what **is** an investment property under IAS 40. Below are examples of items that are **not investment property.**

Type of non-investment property	Applicable IAS
Property intended for sale in the ordinary course of business	IAS 2 *Inventories*
Property being constructed or developed on behalf of third parties	IAS 11 *Construction contracts* (outside the scope of the CIMA F1 syllabus)
Owner-occupied property	IAS 16 *Property, plant and equipment*

2.3 Recognition

Investment property should be recognised as an asset when **two conditions** are met.

(a)   It is **probable** that the **future economic benefits** that are associated with the investment property will **flow to the entity**.

(b)   The **cost** of the investment property can be **measured reliably**.

2.4 Initial measurement

An investment property should be measured initially at its **cost,** including transaction costs.

A property interest held under a lease and classified as an investment property shall be accounted for **as if it were a finance lease**. The asset is recognised at the lower of the fair value of the property and the present value of the minimum lease payments. An equivalent amount is recognised as a liability.

2.5 Measurement subsequent to initial recognition

IAS 40 requires an entity to **choose between two models.**

- The fair value model
- The cost model

Whatever policy it chooses should be applied to **all of its investment property**.

Where an entity chooses to classify a property held under an **operating lease** as an investment property, there is **no choice**. The **fair value model must be used** for **all the entity's investment property**, regardless of whether it is owned or leased.

2.5.1 Fair value model

KEY TERM

(a) After initial recognition, an entity that chooses the FAIR VALUE MODEL should measure all of its investment property at fair value, except in the extremely rare cases where this cannot be measured reliably. In such cases it should apply the IAS 16 cost model.

(b) A gain or loss arising from a change in the fair value of an investment property should be recognised in net profit or loss for the period in which it arises.

(c) The fair value of investment property should reflect market conditions at the end of the reporting period.

This was the first time that the IASB has allowed a fair value model for non-financial assets. This is not the same as a revaluation, where increases in carrying amount above a cost-based measure are recognised as revaluation surplus. Under the fair-value model all changes in fair value are recognised in profit or loss.

The standard elaborates on **issues relating to fair value**.

(a) Fair value assumes that an orderly transaction has taken place between market participants, ie both buyer and seller are reasonably informed about the nature and characteristics of the investment property.

(b) A buyer participating in an orderly transaction is **motivated but not compelled** to buy. A seller participating in an orderly transaction is neither an over-eager nor a forced seller, nor one prepared to sell at any price or to hold out for a price not considered reasonable in the current market.

(c) **Fair value is not the same as 'value in use'** as defined in IAS 36 *Impairment of assets*. Value in use reflects factors and knowledge specific to the entity, while fair value reflects factors and knowledge relevant to the market.

(d) In determining fair value an entity **should not double count assets**. For example, elevators or air conditioning are often an integral part of a building and should be included in the investment property, rather than recognised separately.

(e) In those rare cases where the **entity cannot determine the fair value of an investment property reliably**, the cost model in **IAS 16** must be applied until the investment property is disposed of. The **residual value must be assumed to be zero**.

2.5.2 Cost model

The cost model is the **cost model in IAS 16**. Investment property should be measured at **depreciated cost, less any accumulated impairment losses**. An entity that chooses the cost model should **disclose the fair value of its investment property**.

2.5.3 Changing models

Once the entity has chosen the fair value or cost model, it should apply it to all its investment property. It **should not change from one model to the other unless the change will result in a more appropriate presentation**. IAS 40 states that it is highly unlikely that a change from the fair value model to the cost model will result in a more appropriate presentation.

2.6 Transfers

Transfers to or from investment property should **only** be made **when there is a change in use**. For example, owner occupation commences so the investment property will be treated under IAS 16 as an owner-occupied property.

When there is a transfer from investment property carried at fair value to owner-occupied property or inventories, the property's cost for subsequent accounting under IAS 16 or IAS 2 should be its fair value at the date of change of use.

Conversely, an owner-occupied property may become an investment property and need to be carried at fair value. An entity should apply IAS 16 up to the date of change of use. It should treat any difference at that date between the carrying amount of the property under IAS 16 and its fair value as a revaluation under IAS 16.

Example: Transfer to investment property

A business owns a building which it has been using as a head office. In order to reduce costs, on 30 June 20X9 it moved its head office functions to one of its production centres and is now letting out its head office. Company policy is to use the fair value model for investment property.

The building had an original cost on 1 January 20X0 of $250,000 and was being depreciated over 50 years. At 31 December 20X9 its fair value was judged to be $350,000.

How will this appear in the financial statements at 31 December 20X9?

Solution

The building will be depreciated up to 30 June 20X9.

	$
Original cost	250,000
Depreciation 1.1.X0 – 1.1.X9 (250/50 × 9)	(45,000)
Depreciation to 30.6.X9 (250/50 × 6/12)	(2,500)
Carrying amount at 30.6.X9	202,500
Revaluation surplus	147,500
Fair value at 30.6.X9	350,000

The difference between the carrying amount and fair value is taken to a **revaluation surplus** in accordance with IAS 16.

However the building will be subjected to a fair value exercise at each year end and these gains or losses will go to **profit or loss**. If at the end of the following year the fair value of the building is found to be $380,000, $30,000 will be credited to profit or loss.

2.7 Disposals

Derecognise (eliminate from the statement of financial position) an investment property on disposal or when it is permanently withdrawn from use and no future economic benefits are expected from its disposal.

Any **gain or loss** on disposal is the difference between the net disposal proceeds and the carrying amount of the asset. It should generally be **recognised as income or expense in profit or loss.**

Compensation from third parties for investment property that was impaired, lost or given up shall be recognised in profit or loss when the compensation becomes receivable.

2.8 Disclosure requirements

These relate to:

- Choice of fair value model or cost model
- Whether property interests held as operating leases are included in investment property
- Criteria for classification as investment property

- Assumptions in determining fair value
- Use of independent professional valuer (encouraged but not required)
- Rental income and expenses
- Any restrictions or obligations

2.8.1 Fair value model – additional disclosures

An entity that adopts this must also disclose a **reconciliation** of the carrying amount of the investment property at the beginning and end of the period.

2.8.2 Cost model – additional disclosures

These relate mainly to the depreciation method. In addition, an entity which adopts the cost model **must disclose the fair value** of the investment property.

3 IAS 23 *Borrowing costs*

Introduction

IAS 23 looks at the treatment of borrowing costs, particularly where the related borrowings are applied to the construction of certain assets. These are what are usually called 'self-constructed assets', where an entity builds its own inventory or non-current assets over a substantial period of time.

3.1 Definitions

Only two definitions are given by the standard:

KEY TERMS

BORROWING COSTS. Interest and other costs incurred by an entity in connection with the borrowing of funds.

QUALIFYING ASSET. An asset that necessarily takes a substantial period of time to get ready for its intended use or sale.   *(IAS 23)*

3.2 Capitalisation

IAS 23 requires that all eligible borrowing costs must be **capitalised**. Eligible borrowing costs are those borrowing costs which are directly attributable to the acquisition, construction or production of a qualifying asset. These are the borrowing costs that **would have been avoided** had the expenditure on the qualifying asset not been made.

3.2.1 Interest rate

Where specific borrowings have been used to finance the acquisition, construction or production of an asset, it is straightforward to work out the borrowing costs eligible for capitalisation. The interest rate applicable will be that associated with the specific borrowings.

Once the relevant borrowings which relate to a specific asset are identified, then the **amount of borrowing costs available for capitalisation** will be the actual borrowing costs incurred on those borrowings during the period, *less* any investment income on the temporary investment of those borrowings. It would not be unusual for some or all of the funds to be invested before they are actually used on the qualifying asset.

Example: Borrowing costs

On 1 January 20X6 Stremans Co borrowed $1.5m to finance the production of two assets, both of which were expected to take a year to build. Work started during 20X6. The loan facility was drawn down and incurred on 1 January 20X6, and was utilised as follows, with the remaining funds invested temporarily.

	Asset A $'000	Asset B $'000
1 January 20X6	250	500
1 July 20X6	250	500

The loan rate was 9% and Stremans Co can invest surplus funds at 7%.

Required

Calculate the borrowing costs which may be capitalised for each of the assets and consequently the cost of each asset as at 31 December 20X6.

Solution

	Asset A $	Asset B $
Borrowing costs		
To 31 December 20X6 ($500,000/$1,000,000 × 9%)	45,000	90,000
Less investment income		
To 30 June 20X6 ($250,000/$500,000 × 7% × 6/12)	(8,750)	(17,500)
	36,250	72,500
Cost of assets		
Expenditure incurred	500,000	1,000,000
Borrowing costs	36,250	72,500
	536,250	1,072,500

Where no specific borrowings have been used, but the entity has used its general borrowings to finance an asset, the entity must work out an interest rate at which borrowing costs can be capitalised. This is known as the **capitalisation rate** and is calculated as the weighted average of the entity's borrowing costs in the period. This capitalisation rate is applied to the expenditure on the asset to calculate the borrowings costs that can be capitalised.

3.2.2 Period of capitalisation

Three events or transactions must be taking place for capitalisation of borrowing costs to be started.

(a)   Expenditure on the asset is being incurred
(b)   Borrowing costs are being incurred
(c)   Activities are in progress that are necessary to prepare the asset for its intended use or sale

If active development is **interrupted for any extended periods**, capitalisation of borrowing costs should be suspended for those periods. Once substantially all the activities necessary to prepare the qualifying asset for its intended use or sale are complete, then capitalisation of borrowing costs should cease.

Question 7.3		Borrowing costs

Learning outcomes B2

Acruni Co had the following loans in place at the beginning and end of 20X6.

	1 January 20X6	*31 December 20X6*
	$m	*$m*
10% Bank loan repayable 20X8	120	120
9.5% Bank loan repayable 20X9	80	80
8.9% debenture repayable 20X7	–	150

The 8.9% debenture was issued to fund the construction of a qualifying asset (a piece of mining equipment), construction of which began on 1 July 20X6.

On 1 January 20X6, Acruni Co began construction of a qualifying asset, a piece of machinery for a hydro-electric plant, using existing borrowings. Expenditure drawn down for the construction was: $30m on 1 January 20X6, $20m on 1 October 20X6.

Required

Calculate the borrowing costs that can be capitalised for the hydro-electric plant machine.

3.2.3 Disclosure

The following should be disclosed in the financial statements in relation to borrowing costs.

(a)   Amount of borrowing costs capitalised during the period
(b)   Capitalisation rate used to determine the amount of borrowing costs eligible for capitalisation

Section summary

IAS 23 looks at the treatment of borrowing costs, particularly where the related borrowings are applied to the **construction of certain assets.**

Chapter Summary

	Non-current assets (2)	

IAS 20: *Government grants*

Recognise as income over the relevant periods to match with related costs

Grants should not, therefore, be credited directly to equity

IAS 23: *Borrowing costs*

All eligible borrowing costs must be capitalised
- Capitalise during active periods (acquisition, construction, production)
- Suspend capitalisation during periods of interruption
- Specific borrowings: cost incurred less investment income
- General borrowings: use weighted average

IAS 40: *Investment property*

Choose between two models:
- The fair value model
- The cost model

The policy chosen should be applied to all investment property

Quick Quiz

1   Any increase in the value of an investment property held at fair value should go to the ....
    surplus.

Answers to Quick Quiz

1 Profit or loss for the period

Answers to Questions

7.1 Recognition

The grant should be recognised in the same proportion as the depreciation.

(a) Straight line

		Depreciation $	Grant income $
Year	1	10,000	5,000
	2	10,000	5,000
	3	10,000	5,000
	4	10,000	5,000

(b) Reducing balance

		Depreciation $	Grant income $
Year	1	16,000	8,000
	2	9,600	4,800
	3	5,760	2,880
	4 (remainder)	8,640	4,320

7.2 Investment property

Yes. If an entity has not determined that it will use the land either as an owner-occupied property or for short-term sale in the ordinary course of business, the land is considered to be held for capital appreciation and would therefore be classified as an investment property.

7.3 Borrowing costs

Capitalisation rate = weighted average rate = $(10\% \times \frac{120}{120+80}) + (9.5\% \times \frac{80}{120+80}) = 9.8\%$

Borrowing costs = ($30m \times 9.8\%) + ($20m \times 9.8\% \times 3/12)

= $3.43m

NON-CURRENT ASSETS III

We begin our examination of intangible non-current assets with a discussion of a revised IAS on the subject **(IAS 38)**.

Goodwill and its treatment is a controversial area, as is the accounting for items similar to goodwill, such as brands. Goodwill is very important in **group accounts** which we will cover later in this text.

In Section 3 we look in more detail at the IAS 38 provisions covering research and development.

topic list	learning outcomes	syllabus references
1 IAS 38 *Intangible assets*	B2	B2 (b)
2 Goodwill	B2	B2 (b)
3 Research and development	B2	B2 (b)

Chapter Overview

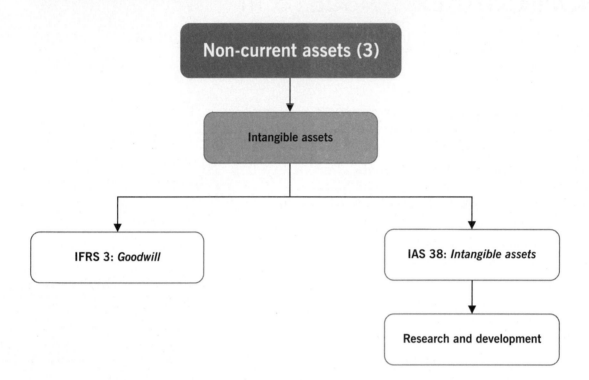

1   IAS 38 *Intangible assets*

Introduction

This section covers IAS 38 *Intangible assets* which was originally published in September 1998. It has been revised to reflect changes introduced by IFRS 3 *Business combinations*.

1.1 The objectives of the standard

(a)   To establish the criteria for when intangible assets may or should be **recognised**

(b)   To specify how intangible assets should be **measured**

(c)   To specify the **disclosure requirements** for intangible assets

It applies to all intangible assets with certain **exceptions**: deferred tax assets (IAS 12), leases that fall within the scope of IAS 17, financial assets, insurance contracts, assets arising from employee benefits (IAS 19), non-current assets held for sale and mineral rights and exploration and extraction costs for minerals etc (although intangible assets used to develop or maintain these rights are covered by the standard). It does *not* apply to goodwill acquired in a business combination, which is dealt with under IFRS 3 *Business combinations*.

1.2 Definition of an intangible asset

The definition of an intangible asset is a key aspect of the standard, because the rules for deciding whether or not an intangible asset may be **recognised** in the accounts of an entity are based on the definition of what an intangible asset is.

KEY TERM

An **INTANGIBLE ASSET** is an **identifiable** non-monetary asset without physical substance. The asset must be:

(a)   **Controlled** by the entity as a result of events in the past, and

(b)   Something from which the entity expects **future economic benefits** to flow

Examples of items that might be considered as intangible assets include computer software, patents, copyrights, motion picture films, customer lists, franchises and fishing rights. IAS 38 gives a significant amount of guidance on the definition of an intangible asset. This is covered in the sections below.

1.2.1 Intangible asset: must be identifiable

An intangible asset must be identifiable in order to distinguish it from goodwill. With non-physical items, there may be a problem with **'identifiability'**.

(a)   If an intangible asset is **acquired separately through purchase**, there may be a transfer of a legal right that would help to make an asset identifiable.

(b)   An intangible asset may be identifiable if it is **separable**, ie if it could be rented or sold separately. However, 'separability' is not an essential feature of an intangible asset.

1.2.2 Intangible asset: must be controlled by the entity

Another element of the definition of an intangible asset is that it must be under the control of the entity as a result of a past event. The entity must therefore be able to enjoy the future economic benefits from the asset, and prevent the access of others to those benefits. A **legally enforceable right** is evidence of such control, but is not always a *necessary* condition.

(a)   Control over **technical knowledge or know-how** only exists if it is protected by a **legal right**.

(b)   The skill of employees, arising out of the benefits of **training costs**, is most unlikely to be recognisable as an intangible asset, because an entity does not control the future actions of its staff.

(c)   Similarly, **market share and customer loyalty** cannot normally be intangible assets, since an entity cannot control the actions of its customers.

1.2.3 Intangible asset: expected future economic benefits

An item can only be recognised as an intangible asset if economic benefits are expected to flow in the future from ownership of the asset. Economic benefits may come from the **sale** of products or services, or from a **reduction in expenditures** (cost savings).

1.3 Recognition of intangible assets

Intangible assets can be **internally generated** or can be **purchased**, either separately or as part of a business combination.

An item should be recognised as an intangible asset if it **fully meets the definition** in IAS 38 and if:

(a)   It is **probable** that the **future economic benefits** that are attributable to the asset will **flow to the entity, and**

(b)   The **cost of the asset can be measured reliably**

Management has to exercise its judgement in assessing the degree of certainty attached to the flow of economic benefits to the entity. External evidence is best.

1.3.1 Purchased intangible assets

How the cost of an intangible asset is measured depends on whether it was purchased or internally generated.

If an intangible asset is **purchased separately**, its cost can usually be measured reliably as its purchase price (including incidental costs of purchase such as legal fees, and any costs incurred in getting the asset ready for use).

When an intangible asset is acquired as **part of a business combination** (ie an acquisition or takeover), the cost of the intangible asset is its **fair value** at the date of the acquisition. **Quoted market prices** in an active market provide the most reliable estimate of the fair value. If no active market exists for an intangible asset, its fair value is the amount that the entity would have paid for the asset, at the acquisition date, in an orderly transaction between market participants, on the basis of the best information available. In determining this amount, an entity should consider the outcome of recent transactions for similar assets. There are techniques for estimating the fair values of unique intangible assets (such as brand names) and these may be used to measure an intangible asset acquired in a business combination.

IFRS 3 *Business combinations* explains that when the fair value of intangible assets acquired in business combinations can be measured reliably, they should be **recognised separately** from goodwill.

In accordance with IAS 20, intangible assets acquired by way of government grant and the grant itself may be recorded initially either at cost (which may be zero) or fair value.

1.3.2 Internally generated intangible assets

It can be difficult to determine whether an internally generated intangible asset meets the IAS 38 recognition criteria. For example, in some cases, the cost of an internally generated intangible asset is difficult to distinguish from the cost of running day-to-day operations.

Therefore IAS 38 provides additional guidance for the recognition of internally generated intangible assets by classifying the generation of the asset into a **research phase** or a **development phase**.

IAS 38 does not allow internally generated goodwill, brands, publishing titles or customer lists to be recognised as intangible assets as their cost cannot be reliably measured.

1.4 Other expenditure

All expenditure related to an intangible asset which does not meet the criteria for recognition either as an identifiable intangible asset or as goodwill arising on an acquisition should be **expensed as incurred**. The IAS gives examples of such expenditure.

- Start up costs
- Advertising costs
- Training costs
- Business relocation costs

Prepaid costs for services, for example advertising or marketing costs for campaigns that have been prepared but not launched, can still be recognised as a **prepayment**.

If tangible asset costs have been expensed in previous financial statements, they may not be recognised as part of the cost of an asset in the future.

1.5 Measurement of intangible assets subsequent to initial recognition

IAS 38 allows two methods of measurement for intangible assets after they have been first recognised.

(a) The **cost model** or **'amortised cost'**: an intangible asset should be **carried at its cost**, less any accumulated depreciation and less any accumulated impairment losses. Expenditure on an intangible asset subsequent to initial recognition rarely meets the definition of an intangible asset in IAS 38 and is usually expensed.

(b) The **revaluation model** allows an intangible asset to be carried at a revalued amount, which is its **fair value** at the date of revaluation, less any subsequent accumulated amortisation and any subsequent accumulated impairment losses. Note that:

(i) The fair value must be able to be measured reliably with reference to an **active market** in that type of asset.

(ii) The **entire class** of intangible assets of that type must be revalued at the same time (to prevent selective revaluations).

(iii) If an intangible asset in a class of revalued intangible assets cannot be revalued because there is **no active market** for this asset, the asset should be carried at its **cost less any accumulated amortisation and impairment losses**.

(iv) Revaluations should be made with such **regularity** that the carrying amount does not differ from that which would be determined using fair value at the end of the reporting period.

KEY POINT

This treatment is **not** available for the **initial recognition** of intangible assets. This is because the cost of the asset must be reliably measured.

The guidelines state that there **will not usually be an active market** in an intangible asset; therefore the revaluation model will usually not be available. For example, although copyrights, publishing rights and film rights can be sold, each has a unique sale value. In such cases, revaluation to fair value would be inappropriate. A fair value might be obtainable however for assets such as fishing rights or quotas or taxi cab licences.

Where an intangible asset is revalued upwards to a fair value, the amount of the revaluation should be credited directly to equity under the heading of a **revaluation surplus**. The increase will be shown as a gain in other comprehensive income.

However, if a revaluation surplus is a **reversal of a revaluation decrease** that was previously charged against income, the increase can be recognised as income in profit or loss for the year.

Where the carrying amount of an intangible asset is revalued downwards, the amount of the **downward revaluation** should be charged as an expense against income, unless the asset has previously been revalued upwards. A revaluation decrease should be first charged against any previous revaluation surplus in respect of that asset.

Question 8.1	Revaluation

Learning outcome B2

An intangible asset is measured by a company at fair value. The asset was revalued by $400 in 20X3, and there is a revaluation surplus of $400 in the statement of financial position. At the end of 20X4, the asset is valued again, and a downward valuation of $500 is required.

Required

State the accounting treatment for the downward revaluation.

When the revaluation model is used, and an intangible asset is revalued upwards, the cumulative revaluation **surplus may be transferred to retained earnings** when the surplus is eventually realised. The surplus would be realised when the asset is disposed of. However, the surplus may also be realised over time as the **asset is used** by the entity. The amount of the surplus realised each year is the difference between the amortisation charge for the asset based on the revalued amount of the asset, and the amortisation that would be charged on the basis of the asset's historical cost. The realised surplus in such cases should be transferred from revaluation surplus directly to retained earnings, and should not be taken through profit or loss. This is the same treatment as is permitted by IAS 16 for property, plant and equipment.

1.6 Useful life

An entity should **assess** the useful life of an intangible asset, which may be **finite or indefinite**. An intangible asset has an indefinite useful life when there is **no foreseeable limit** to the period over which the asset is expected to generate net cash inflows for the entity.

Many factors are considered in determining the useful life of an intangible asset, including: expected usage; typical product life cycles; technical, technological, commercial or other types of obsolescence; the stability of the industry; expected actions by competitors; the level of maintenance expenditure required; and legal or similar limits on the use of the asset, such as the expiry dates of related leases. Computer software and many other intangible assets normally have short lives because they are susceptible to technological obsolescence. However, uncertainty does not justify choosing a life that is unrealistically short.

The useful life of an intangible asset that arises from **contractual or other legal rights** should not exceed the period of the rights, but may be shorter depending on the period over which the entity expects to use the asset.

1.7 Amortisation period and amortisation method

An intangible asset with a finite useful life should be amortised over its **expected useful life**.

(a)   Amortisation should start when the asset is **available for use**.

(b)   Amortisation should cease at the earlier of the date that the asset is classified **as held for sale** in accordance with IFRS 5 *Non-current assets held for sale and discontinued operations* and the date that the asset is **derecognised**.

(c)   The amortisation method used should reflect the **pattern in which the asset's future economic benefits are consumed**. If such a pattern cannot be predicted reliably, the straight line method should be used.

(d)   The amortisation charge for each period should normally be recognised **in profit or loss**.

The **residual value** of an intangible asset with a finite useful life is **assumed to be zero** unless a third party is committed to buying the intangible asset at the end of its useful life or unless there is an active market for that type of asset (so that its expected residual value can be measured) and it is probable that there will be a market for the asset at the end of its useful life.

The useful life and the amortisation method used for an intangible asset with a finite useful life should be **reviewed at each financial year-end**. Any changes to useful life or amortisation method should be accounted for as a **change in accounting estimate** in accordance with IAS 8.

1.8 Intangible assets with indefinite useful lives

An intangible asset with an indefinite useful life **should not be amortised**. IAS 36 *Impairment of assets* requires that such an asset is tested for impairment at least annually.

The useful life of an intangible asset that is not being amortised should be **reviewed each year** to determine whether it is still appropriate to assess its useful life as indefinite. Reassessing the useful life of an intangible asset as finite rather than indefinite is an indicator that the asset may be impaired and therefore it should be tested for impairment.

Question 8.2   Useful life

Learning outcome B2

It may be difficult to establish the useful life of an intangible asset, and judgement will be needed. Consider how to determine the useful life of a *purchased* brand name.

1.9 Disposals/retirements of intangible assets

An intangible asset should be eliminated from the statement of financial position when it is disposed of or when there is no further expected economic benefit from its future use. On disposal the gain or loss arising from the **difference between the net disposal proceeds and the carrying amount** of the asset should be taken to profit or loss as a gain or loss on disposal (ie treated as income or expense).

1.10 Disclosure requirements

The standard has fairly extensive disclosure requirements for intangible assets. The financial statements should disclose the **accounting policies** for intangible assets that have been adopted.

For **each class of intangible assets**, disclosure is required of the following.

- The **method of amortisation** used

- The **useful life** of the assets or the amortisation rate used

- The **gross carrying amount**, the **accumulated amortisation** and the **accumulated impairment losses** as at the beginning and the end of the period

- A **reconciliation of the carrying amount** as at the beginning and at the end of the period (additions, retirements/disposals, revaluations, impairment losses, impairment losses reversed, amortisation charge for the period, net exchange differences, other movements)

- The carrying amount of **internally-generated intangible assets**

The financial statements should also disclose the following.

- In the case of intangible assets that are assessed as having an indefinite useful life, the carrying amounts and the reasons supporting that assessment

- For intangible assets acquired by way of a **government grant** and initially recognised at fair value, the **fair value initially recognised**, the **carrying amount**, and the accounting treatment for subsequent remeasurements

- The carrying amount, nature and remaining amortisation period of any intangible asset that is **material to the financial statements of the entity as a whole**

- The existence (if any) and amounts of intangible assets whose **title is restricted** and of intangible assets that have been **pledged as security** for liabilities

- The amount of any **commitments for the future acquisition of intangible assets**

Where intangible assets are accounted for at revalued amounts, disclosure is required of the following.

- The **effective date of the revaluation** (by class of intangible assets)

- The **carrying amount** of revalued intangible assets

- The carrying amount that would have been shown (by class of assets) **if the cost model had been used**, and the amount of amortisation that would have been charged

- The amount of any **revaluation surplus** on intangible assets, as at the beginning and end of the period, and movements in the surplus during the year (and any restrictions on the distribution of the balance to shareholders)

- The methods and significant assumptions applied in estimating fair values

The financial statements should also disclose the amount of research and development expenditure that has been charged as an expense of the period.

Section summary

- An intangible asset should be recognised if, and only if, it is probable that future economic benefits will flow to the entity and the cost of the asset can be measured reliably.

- An asset is initially recognised at cost and subsequently carried either at cost or revalued amount.

- Costs that do not meet the recognition criteria should be expensed as incurred.

- An intangible asset with a finite useful life should be amortised over its useful life. An intangible asset with an indefinite useful life should not be amortised.

2 Goodwill

Introduction

This section looks at both internally generated and purchased goodwill.

2.1 Internally generated goodwill

Goodwill is **created by good relationships** between a business and its customers

(a)   By building up a **reputation** (by word of mouth perhaps) for high quality products or high standards of service

(b)   By **responding promptly and helpfully** to queries and complaints from customers

(c)   Through the **personality of the staff** and their attitudes to customers

The value of goodwill to a business might be **extremely significant**. However, **internally generated goodwill** is *not* included in the accounts of a business at all, and we should not expect to find an amount for internally generated goodwill in the company's statement of financial position.

KEY POINT

Internally generated goodwill may **not** be recognised as an asset.

IAS 38 deliberately precludes the recognition of internally generated goodwill because it is not an identifiable resource with a cost that is capable of being reliably measured. Therefore any costs associated with generating goodwill in this way are recognised as an expense as they are incurred in the statement of profit or loss and other comprehensive income.

On reflection, we might agree with this omission of internally generated goodwill from the accounts of a business:

(a)   The goodwill is **inherent** in the business but it has not been paid for, and it does not have an 'objective' value. We can guess at what such goodwill is worth, but such guesswork would be a matter of individual opinion, and not based on hard facts.

(b)   Goodwill **changes** from day to day. One act of bad customer relations might damage goodwill and one act of good relations might improve it. Staff with a favourable personality might retire or leave to find another job, to be replaced by staff who need time to find their feet in the job, etc. Since goodwill is continually changing in value, it cannot realistically be recorded in the accounts of the business.

2.2 Purchased goodwill

When an entity purchases another entity, it may generally pay more than the sum total of the assets and liabilities in the entity's financial statements. This is because it expects to generate future economic benefits from the acquisition which are over and above the price paid. The excess amount paid represents the **goodwill** inherent in the business and is known as **purchased goodwill**.

2.2.1 IFRS 3 *Business combinations*

The treatment of purchased goodwill in a business combination is dealt with by IFRS 3 *Business combinations*.

(a)   IFRS 3 defines goodwill as 'an asset representing the future economic benefits arising from other assets acquired in a business combination that are not individually identified and separately recognised'.

(b)   Goodwill is calculated as the difference between the **purchase consideration** and the **fair value** of the identifiable assets and liabilities acquired.

As a result of this calculation, purchased goodwill can therefore be **positive** or **negative**.

Positive goodwill is recognised as an intangible non-current asset in the statement of financial position. After recognition, positive goodwill is measured **at the original amount less any accumulated impairment losses**. It is **not amortised**. Instead it is tested for impairment at least annually, in accordance with IAS 36 *Impairment of assets*.

Negative goodwill acquired in a business combination in effect means that the buyer has got a '**bargain purchase**' as they have paid less for the entity than the fair value of its identifiable assets and liabilities. Negative goodwill could be thought of as a discount on the purchase price. As this is unusual, IFRS 3 requires that the purchaser checks to make sure that the acquired assets and liabilities are correctly identified and valued and that goodwill calculation is correct. Negative goodwill should be **credited to profit or loss** in the year of acquisition.

Goodwill acquired in a business combination is an important part of group accounting which is covered later in this Study Text.

Section summary

If a business has **goodwill**, it means that the value of the business as a going concern is greater than the value of its identifiable net assets. The valuation of goodwill is extremely subjective and fluctuates constantly. For this reason internally generated goodwill is **not** shown as an asset in the statement of financial position.

Purchased positive goodwill arising on a business combination is recognised as an intangible asset under the requirements of **IFRS 3**. It must then be reviewed for impairment annually.

Purchased negative goodwill is credited to profit or loss in the year of acquisition.

3 Research and development

Introduction

As we saw above, it can be difficult to determine whether an internally generated intangible asset meets the IAS 38 recognition criteria. IAS 38 provides additional guidance on when these assets should be recognised by classifying the generation of the asset into a research phase or a development phase. This guidance will be the focus of this section.

3.1 Definitions

The following definitions are given by IAS 38.

KEY TERMS

RESEARCH is original and planned investigation undertaken with the prospect of gaining new scientific or technical knowledge and understanding.

DEVELOPMENT is the application of research findings or other knowledge to a plan or design for the production of new or substantially improved materials, devices, products, processes, systems or services prior to the commencement of commercial production or use.

Although we will concentrate on costs incurred in research and development as defined above, IAS 38 broadens the application to include costs incurred in a **research phase** or **development phase** of an **internal project**.

3.2 Research phase

KEY POINT

Research costs cannot be recognised as an intangible asset and must be **charged to profit or loss** in the year they are incurred.

Research costs by definition do not meet the criteria for recognition under IAS 38. This is because, at the research stage of a project, it cannot be certain that probable future economic benefits will flow to the entity from the project. There is too much uncertainty about the likely success or otherwise of the project. Research costs that have been recognised as an expense cannot be subsequently recognised as an asset in a later period.

Examples of research activities include:

- Activities aimed at obtaining new knowledge
- The search for applications of research findings or other knowledge
- The search for product or process alternatives
- The formulation and design of possible new or improved product or process alternatives

3.3 Development phase

Development activities tend to be much further advanced than the research stage. Where the entity can demonstrate that it is probable that future economic benefits will flow to the entity from the project, the entity may be able to recognise an intangible asset.

Development activities include:

- The design, construction and testing of pre-production prototypes and models
- The design of tools, jigs, moulds and dies involving new technology
- The design, construction and operation of a pilot plant that is not of a scale economically feasible for commercial production
- The design, construction and testing of a chosen alternative for new/improved materials

3.3.1 Recognition of development costs as an intangible asset

Development expenditure must be recognised as an intangible asset (sometimes called 'deferred development expenditure') if, and only if, the business can demonstrate **all** of the criteria in IAS 38 have been met.

The recognition criteria are as follows.

The entity must demonstrate:

- **P** – how the intangible asset will generate **Probable** future economic benefits (this is demonstrated by the existence of an external market or by how the asset will be useful to the business if it is to be used internally)
- **I** – its **Intention** to complete the intangible asset and use or sell it
- **R** – the availability of adequate technical, financial and other **Resources** to complete the development and to use or sell the intangible asset
- **A** – its **Ability** to use or sell the intangible asset
- **T** – the **Technical** feasibility of completing the intangible asset so that it will be available for use or sale
- **E** – its ability to measure reliably the **Expenditure** attributable to the intangible asset during its development

The development costs of a project recognised as an intangible asset should not exceed the amount that it is probable will be **recovered from related future economic benefits**, after deducting further development costs, related production costs, and selling and administrative costs directly incurred in marketing the product.

IAS 38 **prohibits** the recognition of **internally generated brands, mastheads, publishing titles and customer lists** and similar items as intangible assets. These all fail to meet one or more (in some cases all) of the definition and recognition criteria and in some cases are probably indistinguishable from internally generated goodwill.

3.4 Cost of an internally generated intangible asset

The costs allocated to an internally generated intangible asset should be only costs that can be **directly attributed** or allocated on a reasonable and consistent basis to creating, producing or preparing the asset for its intended use. IAS 38 lists the following which may form part of the cost of an intangible asset:

(a) **Salaries, wages** and other employment related costs of personnel arising from the generation of the intangible asset

(b) Costs of **materials and services** consumed in generating the intangible asset

(c) **Overhead costs** that were incurred to generate the intangible asset, such as the depreciation of property, plant and equipment

(d) **Other direct costs**, such as the amortisation of patents and licences that are used to generate the intangible asset or fees to register a legal right

Interest may also be included as an element of cost. IAS 23 *Borrowing costs* specifies criteria for this.

IAS 38 specifically **excludes** the following costs from being recognised as part of the cost:

(a) **Selling** and **administrative** costs
(b) Costs to train staff to operate the asset

The cost of an internally generated intangible asset is the sum of the permitted **expenditure incurred from the date when** the intangible asset **first meets the recognition criteria**. If, as often happens, considerable costs have already been recognised as expenses before management could demonstrate that the criteria have been met, this earlier expenditure should not be retrospectively recognised at a later date as part of the cost of an intangible asset.

Question 8.3	Intangible asset

Learning outcome B2

Doug Co is developing a new production process. During 20X3, expenditure incurred was $100,000, of which $90,000 was incurred before 1 December 20X3 and $10,000 between 1 December 20X3 and 31 December 20X3. Doug Co can demonstrate that, at 1 December 20X3, the production process met the criteria for recognition as an intangible asset. The recoverable amount of the know-how embodied in the process is estimated to be $50,000.

How should the expenditure be treated?

3.5 Amortisation of development costs

Once capitalised as an intangible asset, development costs must be **amortised** and recognised as an expense to match the costs with the related revenue or cost savings. This must be done on a systematic basis, so as to reflect the pattern in which the related economic benefits are recognised.

It is unlikely to be possible to **match exactly** the economic benefits obtained with the costs which are held as an asset simply because of the nature of development activities. The entity should consider either:

(a) the revenue or other benefits from the sale/use of the product/process; *or*

(b) the period of time over which the product/process is expected to be sold/used

KEY POINT

> If the pattern cannot be determined reliably, the straight-line method should be used.

The amortisation will begin when the **asset is available for use**.

3.6 Impairment of development costs

As with all assets, impairment is a possibility, but perhaps even more so in cases such as this. Impairments of intangible assets are covered by IAS 36 *Impairment of assets*. The development costs should be **written down** to the extent that the unamortised balance (taken together with further development costs, related production costs, and selling and administrative costs directly incurred in marketing the product) is no longer probable of being recovered from the expected future economic benefit.

3.7 Disclosure

For **each class of intangible assets** (including development costs), IAS 38 requires the following disclosures.

* The **method of amortisation** used

* The **useful life** of the assets or the amortisation rate used

* The **gross carrying amount**, the **accumulated amortisation** and the **accumulated impairment losses** as at the beginning and the end of the period

* A **reconciliation of the carrying amount** as at the beginning and at the end of the period (additions, retirements/disposals, revaluations, impairment losses, impairment losses reversed, amortisation charge for the period, net exchange differences, other movements)

* The carrying amount of **internally-generated intangible assets**

Question 8.4	Research and development I

Learning outcome B2

Y Co is a research company which specialises in developing new materials and manufacturing processes for the furniture industry. The company receives payments from a variety of manufacturers, which pay for the right to use the company's patented fabrics and processes.

Research and development costs for the year ended 30 September 20X5 can be analysed as follows.

	$
Project A	280,000

New flame-proof padding. Expected to cost a total of $400,000 to complete development. Expected total revenue $2,000,000 once work completed - probably late 20X6. Customers already placed advanced orders for the material after seeing demonstrations of its capabilities earlier in the year.

Project B   150,000

New colour-fast dye. Expected to cost a total of $3,000,000 to complete. The dye is being developed as a cheaper replacement for a dye already used in Y Co's most successful product, cost savings of over $10,000,000 are expected from its use. Although Y has demonstrated that the dye is a viable product, and has the intention to finish developing it, the completion date is currently uncertain because external funding will have to be obtained before the development work can be completed.

Project C   110,000

Investigation of new adhesive recently developed in aerospace industry. If this proves effective then Y Co may well generate significant income because it will be used in place of existing adhesives.

Explain how the three research projects A, B and C will be dealt with in Y Co's statement of profit or loss and other comprehensive income and statement of financial position.

In each case, explain your proposed treatment in terms of IAS 38 *Intangible assets*.

Question 8.5   Research and development II

Learning outcome B2

Y Co had the following balances relating to deferred development expenditure at 30 September 20X4:

	$
Deferred development expenditure (cost)	1,250,000
Amortisation	(125,000)
Carrying value at 30 September 20X4	1,125,000

The existing deferred development expenditure is being amortised over 10 years on a straight line basis.

Show how these balances and the research and development costs in the previous question will be disclosed in the accounts of Y Co at 30 September 20X5.

Show extracts from the:

(a) Statement of profit or loss
(b) Statement of financial position
(c) Notes to the financial statements

Section summary

If the criteria laid down by IAS 38 are satisfied, development costs should be capitalised as an intangible asset. They are then amortised, beginning from the time when the development project is available for use.

Chapter Summary

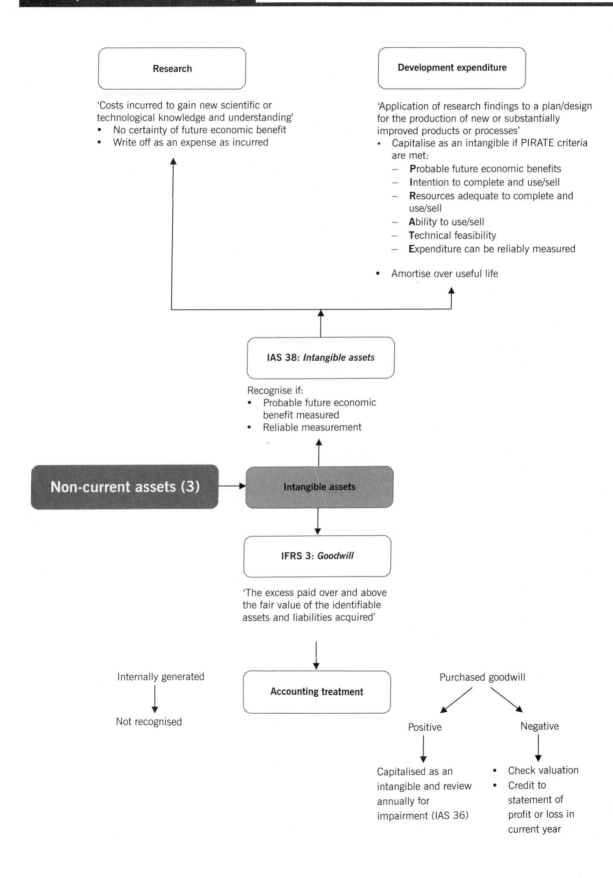

Research

'Costs incurred to gain new scientific or technological knowledge and understanding'
- No certainty of future economic benefit
- Write off as an expense as incurred

Development expenditure

'Application of research findings to a plan/design for the production of new or substantially improved products or processes'
- Capitalise as an intangible if PIRATE criteria are met:
  - **P**robable future economic benefits
  - **I**ntention to complete and use/sell
  - **R**esources adequate to complete and use/sell
  - **A**bility to use/sell
  - **T**echnical feasibility
  - **E**xpenditure can be reliably measured

- Amortise over useful life

IAS 38: *Intangible assets*

Recognise if:
- Probable future economic benefit measured
- Reliable measurement

Non-current assets (3)

Intangible assets

IFRS 3: *Goodwill*

'The excess paid over and above the fair value of the identifiable assets and liabilities acquired'

Internally generated

Not recognised

Accounting treatment

Purchased goodwill

Positive

Capitalised as an intangible and review annually for impairment (IAS 36)

Negative
- Check valuation
- Credit to statement of profit or loss in current year

Quick Quiz

1 Intangible assets can only be recognised in a company's accounts if:

- It is probable that .... will flow to the entity
- The cost can be ....

2 What are the criteria which must be met before development expenditure can be recognised as an intangible asset?

3 Research costs must be expensed.

True ☐

False ☐

4 How is goodwill calculated under IFRS 3?

5 The following statements relate to intangible assets.

1 An intangible asset should be amortised on a systematic basis over the asset's useful life.

2 Internally generated goodwill may be carried in the statement of financial position if the value can be determined with reasonable certainty.

3 Internally generated brands can never be recognised as intangible assets.

Which of the above statements are consistent with IAS 38 *Intangible Assets*?

A 1 and 2 only
B 1 and 3 only
C 2 only
D 3 only

Answers to Quick Quiz

1   Future economic benefits. Measured reliably.

2   **PIRATE** criteria:

    Probable economic benefits will be generated by the intangible asset

    Intention to complete the intangible asset and use or sell it

    Resources (technical, financial) adequate to complete the development and to use or sell

    Ability to use or sell the intangible asset

    Technical feasibility of completing the intangible asset

    Expenditure can be measured reliably.

3   True

4   Goodwill is calculated as the difference between the purchase consideration and the fair value of the identifiable assets and liabilities acquired

5   B   Internally generated goodwill can not be recognised as an intangible asset as its cost cannot be reliably measured.

Answers to Questions

8.1 Revaluation

In this example, the downward valuation of $500 can first be set against the revaluation surplus of $400. The revaluation surplus will be reduced to nil and a charge of $100 made as an expense in 20X4 in the statement of profit or loss.

8.2 Useful life

Factors to consider would include the following.

(a)   Legal protection of the brand name and the control of the entity over the (illegal) use by others of the brand name (ie control over pirating)

(b)   Age of the brand name

(c)   Status or position of the brand in its particular market

(d)   Ability of the management of the entity to manage the brand name and to measure activities that support the brand name (eg advertising and PR activities)

(e)   Stability and geographical spread of the market in which the branded products are sold

(f)   Pattern of benefits that the brand name is expected to generate over time

(g)   Intention of the entity to use and promote the brand name over time (as evidenced perhaps by a business plan in which there will be substantial expenditure to promote the brand name)

8.3 Intangible asset

At the end of 20X3, the production process is recognised as an intangible asset at a cost of $10,000. This is the expenditure incurred since the date when the recognition criteria were met, that is 1 December 20X3. The $90,000 expenditure incurred before 1 December 20X3 is expensed, because the recognition criteria were not met. It will **never** form part of the cost of the production process recognised in the statement of financial position.

8.4 Research and development I

Project A

This project meets the criteria in IAS 38 for development expenditure to be recognised as an asset. These are as follows.

(a) **P** – how the intangible asset will generate **probable** future economic benefits: Customers have already placed advanced orders for the final product after development

(b) **I** – its **intention** to complete the intangible asset and use to sell it: Y Co intends to finish development of the product by late 20X6 and then sell the right to use it to customers

(c) **R** – the availability of adequate technical, financial and other **resources** to complete the development and to use or sell the intangible asset: Adequate resources do exist, the project seems to be in the late stages of development

(d) **A** – its **ability** to use or sell the intangible asset: Customers have already placed advanced orders for the final product, so Y Co's ability to use the asset is clear

(e) **T** – the **technical** feasibility of completing the intangible asset so that it will be available for use or sale: the capabilities of the product were demonstrated to customers, so the technical feasibility is assured

(f) **E** – its ability to measure reliably the **expenditure** attributable to the intangible asset during its development: Y Co has a reliable estimation of costs to date and to complete.

Hence the costs of $280,000 incurred to date should be capitalised as an intangible asset in the statement of financial position. Once the material is ready for use, the intangible asset should be amortised over its useful life.

Project B

This project meets most of the criteria discussed above which would enable the costs to be carried forward, however, it fails on the availability of adequate resources to complete the project. As such, the costs cannot be capitalised and should be recognised as an expense in the statement of profit or loss.

Once funding is obtained the situation can then be reassessed and future costs may be capitalised.

Project C

This is a research project according to IAS 38, ie original and planned investigation undertaken with the prospect of gaining new scientific or technical knowledge or understanding.

There is no certainty as to its ultimate success or commercial viability and therefore it cannot be considered to be a development project. IAS 38 therefore requires that costs be written off as incurred as an expense in the statement of profit or loss.

8.5 Research and development II

(a)   STATEMENT OF PROFIT OR LOSS (EXTRACT)

	$
Research expenditure (Project C)	110,000
Development costs (Project B)	150,000
Amortisation of capitalised development costs	125,000

(b)   STATEMENT OF FINANCIAL POSITION (EXTRACT)

	$
Non-current assets	
Intangible assets – deferred development expenditure (1,125 – 125 + 280)	1,280,000

(c)   NOTE TO THE FINANCIAL STATEMENTS

Note X - *Deferred development costs*

	$
Cost	
Balance b/f	1,250,000
Additions during year (Project A)	280,000
Balance c/f	1,530,000
Amortisation	
Balance b/f	125,000
Charge during year	125,000
Balance c/f	250,000
Carrying value at 30 September 20X5	1,280,000
Carrying value at 30 September 20X4	1,125,000

Now try these questions from the OTQ Question Bank

Number
Q14
Q48

IMPAIRMENT OF ASSETS

 This chapter covers one of the important items on the statement of financial position, non-current assets.

IAS 36 on impairment is an important and very examinable standard.

topic list	learning outcomes	syllabus references
1 IAS 36 *Impairment of assets*	B2	B2 (b)

Chapter Overview

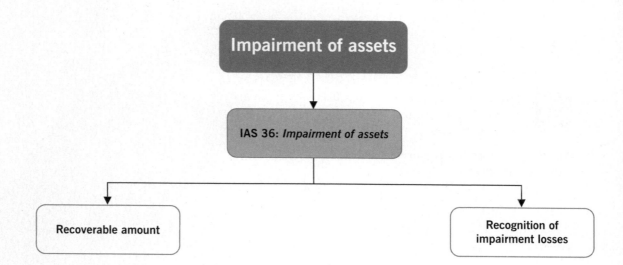

1 IAS 36 *Impairment of assets*

Introduction

There is an established principle that assets should not be carried at above their recoverable amount. An entity should write down the carrying value of an asset to its recoverable amount if the carrying value of an asset is not recoverable in full. IAS 36 was published in June 1998 and was revised in March 2004. It puts in place a detailed methodology for carrying out impairment reviews and related accounting treatments and disclosures. We will look at the standard in this section.

1.1 Scope

IAS 36 applies to all tangible, intangible and financial assets except inventories, assets arising from construction contracts, deferred tax assets, assets arising under IAS 19 *Employee benefits* and financial assets within the scope of IAS 32 *Financial instruments, disclosure and presentation*. This is because those IASs already have rules for recognising and measuring impairment. Note also that IAS 36 does not apply to non-current assets held for sale, which are dealt with under IFRS 5 *Non-current assets held for sale and discontinued operations*.

KEY TERM

IMPAIRMENT: a fall in the value of an asset, so that its 'recoverable amount' is now less than its carrying value in the statement of financial position. *(IAS 36)*

The basic principle underlying IAS 36 is relatively straightforward. If an asset's value in the accounts is higher than its realistic value, measured as its 'recoverable amount', the asset is judged to have suffered an impairment loss. It should therefore be reduced in value, by the amount of the **impairment loss**. The amount of the impairment loss should be **written off against profit** immediately (unless the asset has been revalued in which case the loss is treated as a revaluation decrease).

The main accounting issues to consider are therefore as follows.

(a) How is it possible to **identify when** an impairment loss may have occurred?
(b) How should the **recoverable amount** of the asset be measured?
(c) How should an 'impairment loss' be **reported in the accounts**?

1.2 Identifying a potentially impaired asset

An entity should assess at the end of each reporting period whether there are any indications of impairment to any assets. The concept of **materiality** applies, and only material impairment needs to be identified.

If there are indications of possible impairment, the entity is required to make a formal estimate of the **recoverable amount** of the assets concerned.

IAS 36 suggests how **indications of a possible impairment** of assets might be recognised. The suggestions are based largely on common sense.

(a) **External sources of information**

(i) A fall in the asset's market value that is significantly more than would normally be expected from passage of time or normal use.

(ii) Significant adverse changes in the technological, market, economic or legal environment in which the entity operates.

(iii) An increase in market interest rates or other market rates of return on investments likely to affect the discount rate used in calculating value in use.

(iv) The carrying amount of the entity's net assets being more than its market capitalisation.

(b)   **Internal sources of information**: evidence of obsolescence or physical damage, adverse changes in the use to which the asset is put, or the asset's economic performance

Even if there are no indications of impairment, the following assets must **always** be tested for impairment annually.

(a)   An intangible asset with an **indefinite useful life**
(b)   **Goodwill** acquired in a business combination

1.3 Measuring the recoverable amount of the asset

What is an asset's recoverable amount?

KEY TERM

The RECOVERABLE AMOUNT of an asset should be measured as the *higher value* of:

(a)   the asset's fair value less costs to sell; and
(b)   its value in use.   *(IAS 36)*

An asset's fair value less costs to sell is the amount net of selling costs that could be obtained from the sale of the asset. Selling costs include sales transaction costs, such as legal expenses.

(a)   If there is **an active market** in the asset, the net selling price should be based on the **market value**, or on the price of recent transactions in similar assets.

(b)   If there is **no active market** in the assets it might be possible to estimate a net selling price using best estimates of what market participants might pay in an orderly transaction at the measurement date.

Net selling price **cannot** be reduced, however, by including within selling costs any **restructuring or reorganisation expenses**, or any costs that have already been recognised in the accounts as liabilities.

The concept of '**value in use**' is very important.

KEY TERM

The VALUE IN USE of an asset is measured as the present value of future cash flows expected to be derived from an asset or cash-generating unit.

The cash flows used in the calculation should be **pre-tax cash flows** and a **pre-tax discount rate** should be applied to calculate the present value.

The calculation of **value in use** must reflect the following.

(a)   An estimate of the **future cash flows** the entity expects to derive from the asset
(b)   Expectations about **possible variations** in the amount and timing of future cash flows
(c)   The **time value of money**
(d)   The price for bearing the **uncertainty** inherent in the asset, and
(e)   **Other factors** that would be reflected in pricing future cash flows from the asset

Calculating a value in use therefore calls for estimates of future cash flows, and the possibility exists that an entity might come up with **over-optimistic estimates** of cash flows. The IAS therefore states the following.

(a)   Cash flow projections should be based on '**reasonable and supportable**' assumptions.

(b)   Projections of cash flows, normally up to a maximum period of five years, should be based on the most **recent budgets or financial forecasts**.

(c)   Cash flow projections beyond this period should be obtained by extrapolating short-term projections, using either a **steady or declining growth rate** for each subsequent year (unless a rising growth rate can be justified). The long term growth rate applied should not exceed the average long term growth rate for the product, market, industry or country, unless a higher growth rate can be justified.

1.4 Recognition and measurement of an impairment loss

The rule for **assets at historical cost** is:

KEY POINT

If the **recoverable amount** of an asset is **lower than the carrying amount,** the carrying amount should be **reduced** by the difference (ie the impairment loss) which should be charged as an **expense** in profit or loss.

The rule for **assets held at a revalued amount** (such as property revalued under IAS 16) is:

KEY POINT

The impairment loss is to be treated as a revaluation decrease under the relevant IAS.

In practice this means:

- To the extent that there is a revaluation surplus held in respect of the asset, the impairment loss should be charged to revaluation surplus.

- Any excess should be charged to profit or loss.

The IAS goes into quite a large amount of detail about the important concept of **cash-generating units**. As a basic rule, the recoverable amount of an asset should be calculated for the **asset individually**. However, there will be occasions when it is not possible to estimate such a value for an individual asset, particularly in the calculation of value in use. This is because cash inflows and outflows cannot be attributed to the individual asset.

KEY TERM

A CASH-GENERATING UNIT is the smallest identifiable group of assets for which independent cash flows can be identified and measured.

Question 9.1

Cash-generating unit

Learning outcome B2

Can you think of some examples of how a cash-generating unit would be identified?

Example: Recoverable amount and carrying amount

Fourways Co is made up of four cash-generating units. All four units are being tested for impairment.

(a) Property, plant and equipment and separate intangibles would be allocated to the cash-generating units as far as possible.

(b) Current assets such as inventories, receivables and prepayments would be allocated to the relevant cash-generating units.

(c) Liabilities (eg payables) would be deducted from the net assets of the relevant cash-generating units.

(d) The net figure for each cash-generating unit resulting from this exercise would be compared to the relevant recoverable amount, computed on the same basis.

1.5 Goodwill and the impairment of assets

Goodwill acquired in a business combination does not generate cash flows independently of other assets. It must be **allocated** to each of the acquirer's **cash-generating units** (or groups of cash-generating units) that are expected to benefit from the synergies of the combination.

A cash-generating unit to which goodwill has been allocated is tested for impairment annually. The **carrying amount** of the unit, including goodwill, is **compared with the recoverable amount**. If the carrying amount of the unit exceeds the recoverable amount, the entity must recognise an impairment loss.

The annual impairment test may be performed at any time during an accounting period, but must be performed at the **same time every year**.

1.6 Corporate assets

Corporate assets are group or divisional assets such as a head office building, computer equipment or a research centre. Essentially, corporate assets are assets that do not generate cash inflows independently from other assets, hence their carrying amount cannot be fully attributed to a cash-generating unit under review.

In testing a cash-generating unit for impairment, an entity should identify all the corporate assets that relate to the cash-generating unit. Corporate assets will need to be allocated to cash-generating units on a reasonable and consistent basis.

1.7 Accounting treatment of an impairment loss

An impairment loss has occurred if the recoverable amount of an asset is less than its carrying amount in the statement of financial position. This loss should be **recognised immediately**:

(a)   The asset's **carrying amount** should be reduced to its recoverable amount in the statement of financial position.

(b)   The **impairment loss** should be recognised immediately in profit or loss (unless the asset has been revalued in which case the loss is treated as a revaluation decrease).

After reducing an asset to its recoverable amount, the **depreciation charge** on the asset should then be based on its new carrying amount, its estimated residual value (if any) and its estimated remaining useful life.

An impairment loss should be recognised for a **cash-generating unit** if (and only if) the recoverable amount for the cash-generating unit is less than the carrying amount in the statement of financial position for all the assets in the unit. When an impairment loss is recognised for a cash-generating unit, the loss should be allocated between the assets in the unit in the following order.

(a)   First, to the **goodwill** allocated to the cash-generating unit

(b)   Then to all other assets in the cash-generating unit, on a **pro rata basis**

In allocating an impairment loss, the carrying amount of an asset should not be reduced below the highest of:

(a)   Its fair value less costs to sell

(b)   Its value in use (if determinable)

(c)   Zero

Any remaining amount of an impairment loss should be recognised as a liability if required by other IASs.

Example: Impairment loss I

A company that extracts natural gas and oil has a drilling platform in the Caspian Sea. It is required by legislation of the country concerned to remove and dismantle the platform at the end of its useful life. Accordingly, the company has correctly included an amount in its accounts for removal and dismantling costs, and is depreciating this amount over the platform's expected life.

The company is carrying out an exercise to establish whether there has been an impairment of the platform.

(a) Its carrying amount in the statement of financial position is $3m.

(b) The company has received an offer of $2.8m for the platform from another oil company. The bidder would take over the responsibility (and costs) for dismantling and removing the platform at the end of its life.

(c) The present value of the estimated cash flows from the platform's continued use is $3.3m.

(d) The carrying amount in the statement of financial position for the provision for dismantling and removal is currently $0.6m.

What should be the value of the drilling platform in the statement of financial position, and what, if anything, is the impairment loss?

Solution

Fair value less costs to sell	= $2.8m
Value in use	= PV of cash flows from use less the carrying amount of the provision/liability = $3.3m – $0.6m = $2.7m
Recoverable amount	= Higher of these two amounts, ie $2.8m
Carrying value	= $3m
Impairment loss	= $0.2m

The carrying value should be reduced to $2.8m

Example: Impairment loss II

A company has acquired another business for $4.5m: tangible assets are valued at $4.0m and goodwill at $0.5m.

An asset with a carrying value of $1m is destroyed in a terrorist attack. The asset was not insured. The loss of the asset, without insurance, has prompted the company to estimate whether there has been an impairment of assets in the acquired business and what the amount of any such loss is. The recoverable amount of the business (a single cash-generating unit) without the asset is measured as $3.1m.

Solution

There has been an impairment loss of $1.4m ($4.5m – $3.1m).

The impairment loss will be recognised in profit or loss. The loss will be allocated between the assets in the cash-generating unit as follows.

(a) A loss of $1m can be attributed directly to the uninsured asset that has been destroyed.

(b) The remaining loss of $0.4m should be allocated to goodwill.

The carrying value of the assets will now be $3m for tangible assets and $0.1m for goodwill.

1.8 Disclosure

IAS 36 calls for substantial disclosure about impairment of assets. The information to be disclosed includes the following.

(a) For each class of assets, the amount of **impairment losses recognised** and the amount of any **impairment losses recovered** (ie reversals of impairment losses)

(b)   For each individual asset or cash-generating unit that has suffered a **significant impairment loss**, details of the nature of the asset, the amount of the loss, the events that led to recognition of the loss, whether the recoverable amount is fair value price less costs to sell or value in use, and if the recoverable amount is value in use, the basis on which this value was estimated (eg the discount rate applied)

Section summary

The main aspects of IAS 36 to consider are:

- Indications of impairment of assets
- Measuring recoverable amount, as net selling price or value in use
- Measuring value in use
- Cash-generating units
- Accounting treatment of an impairment loss, for individual assets and cash-generating units

Chapter Summary

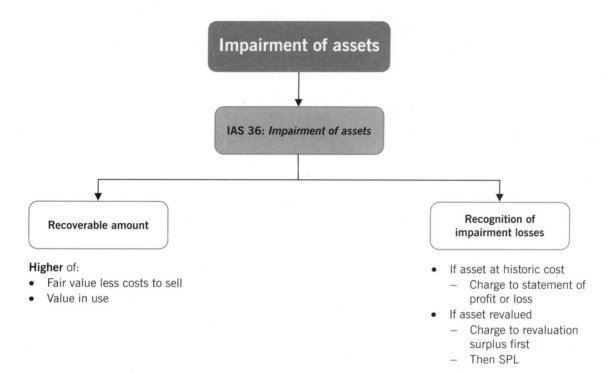

Impairment of assets

IAS 36: *Impairment of assets*

Recoverable amount

Higher of:
- Fair value less costs to sell
- Value in use

Recognition of impairment losses

- If asset at historic cost
  - Charge to statement of profit or loss
- If asset revalued
  - Charge to revaluation surplus first
  - Then SPL

Quick Quiz

1   Define impairment.

Answers to Quick Quiz

1   A fall in value of an asset, so that its 'recoverable amount' is less than its carrying value. Where the 'recoverable amount' of an asset is the higher of its fair value less costs to sell and its fair value in use.

Answers to Questions

9.1 Cash-generating unit

Here are two possibilities.

(a)   A mining company owns a private railway that it uses to transport output from one of its mines. The railway now has no market value other than as scrap, and it is impossible to identify any separate cash inflows with the use of the railway itself. Consequently, if the mining company suspects an impairment in the value of the railway, it should treat the mine as a whole as a cash-generating unit, and measure the recoverable amount of the mine as a whole.

(b)   A bus company has an arrangement with a town's authorities to run a bus service on four routes in the town. Separately identifiable assets are allocated to each of the bus routes, and cash inflows and outflows can be attributed to each individual route. Three routes are running at a profit and one is running at a loss. The bus company suspects that there is an impairment of assets on the loss-making route. However, the company will be unable to close the loss-making route, because it is under an obligation to operate all four routes, as part of its contract with the local authority. Consequently, the company should treat all four bus routes together as a cash-generating unit, and calculate the recoverable amount for the unit as a whole.

Now try these questions from the OTQ Question Bank	Number
	Q13
	Q18
	Q46

REPORTING FINANCIAL PERFORMANCE I

 In this chapter we look at **IFRS 5** which deals with discontinued operations and non-current assets held for sale.

topic list	learning outcomes	syllabus references
1 IFRS 5 *Non-current assets held for sale and discontinued operations*	B2	B2 (b)

Chapter Overview

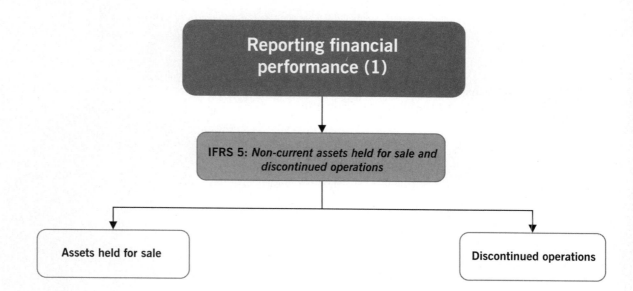

1 IFRS 5 *Non-current assets held for sale and discontinued operations*

Introduction

This section looks at IFRS 5 *Non-current assets held for sale and discontinued operations*. We first look at the objective of IFRS 5 and then move on to examine the necessary presentation and disclosures.

1.1 Objective

IFRS 5 requires assets and groups of assets that are '**held for sale**' to be **presented separately** in the statement of financial position and the results of **discontinued operations** to be presented separately in the statement of profit or loss and other comprehensive income. This is required so that users of financial statements will be better able to make **projections** about the financial position, profits and cash flows of the entity. IFRS 5 also gives guidance on how assets held for sale should be valued.

1.2 Assets held for sale

A non-current asset (or disposal group) should be classified as **held for sale** if an entity plans to **recover the value of the asset by selling it**, rather than **through continuing use**.

IFRS 5 defines a disposal group as follows.

KEY TERM

DISPOSAL GROUP: a group of assets to be disposed of, by sale or otherwise, together as a group in a single transaction, and liabilities directly associated with those assets that will be transferred in the transaction. (In practice a disposal group could be a subsidiary, a cash-generating unit or a single operation within an entity.) *(IFRS 5)*

A non-current asset or disposal group can only be classified as held for sale if it meets **all** of the following criteria:

(a) The asset must be **available for immediate sale** in its present condition.
(b) Its sale must be **highly probable** (ie, significantly more likely than not).

For the sale to be highly probable, the following must apply:

(a) Management must be **committed** to a plan to sell the asset.

(b) There must be an active programme to **locate a buyer.**

(c) The asset must be marketed for sale at a **price that is reasonable** in relation to its current fair value.

(d) The sale should be expected to take place **within one year** from the **date of classification**.

(e) It is unlikely that significant changes to the plan will be made or that the plan will be withdrawn.

An asset (or disposal group) can still be classified as held for sale, even if the sale has not actually taken place within one year. However, the delay must have been **caused by events or circumstances beyond the entity's control** and there must be sufficient evidence that the entity is still committed to sell the asset or disposal group. Otherwise the entity must cease to classify the asset as held for sale.

| **Question 10.1** | Assets held for sale |

Learning outcome B2

On 1 December 20X3, a company became committed to a plan to sell a manufacturing facility and has already found a potential buyer. The company does not intend to discontinue the operations currently carried out in the facility. At 31 December 20X3 there is a backlog of uncompleted customer orders. The company will not be able to transfer the facility to the buyer until after it ceases to operate the facility and has eliminated the backlog of uncompleted customer orders. This is not expected to occur until spring 20X4.

Required

Can the manufacturing facility be classified as 'held for sale' at 31 December 20X3?

1.2.1 Accounting treatment

KEY POINT

A non-current asset (or disposal group) that is held for sale should be measured at the **lower of** its **carrying amount** and **fair value less costs to sell**. Fair value less costs to sell is equivalent to net realisable value.

IFRS 5 gives the following definitions.

KEY TERMS

FAIR VALUE: is the price that would be received to sell an asset or paid to transfer a liability in an orderly transaction between market participants at the measurement date.

COSTS TO SELL: the incremental costs directly attributable to the disposal of an asset (or disposal group), excluding finance costs and income tax expense.

RECOVERABLE AMOUNT: the higher of an asset's fair value less costs to sell and its value in use.

VALUE IN USE: the present value of estimated future cash flows expected to arise from the continuing use of an asset and from its disposal at the end of its useful life.

KEY POINT

If the fair value less costs to sell of the asset is lower than its carrying amount in the financial statements, an **impairment loss** should be recognised.

Note that this is an exception to the normal rule. IAS 36 *Impairment of assets* requires an entity to recognise an impairment loss only where an asset's recoverable amount is lower than its carrying value. Recoverable amount is defined as the higher of net realisable value and value in use. IAS 36 does not apply to assets held for sale.

Non-current assets held for sale **should not be depreciated**, even if they are still being used by the entity. When the asset is disposed of, the profit on disposal is calculated in the normal way, with any profit on disposal being taken to the statement of profit or loss.

If the entity revalues its assets then the asset must be revalued before it is classified as held for sale. The resulting loss on remeasurement to fair value less costs to sell should be shown as an expense in profit or loss.

1.2.2 Presentation in the financial statements

Non-current assets and disposal groups classified as held for sale should be **presented separately** from other assets in the statement of financial position. The liabilities of a disposal group should be presented separately from other liabilities in the statement of financial position. Note that:

(a) Assets and liabilities held for sale **should not be offset**.

(b) The **major classes** of assets and liabilities held for sale should be **separately disclosed** either in the statement of financial position or in the notes.

Example: Measurement of assets held for sale

On 1 July 20X6, RW purchased a building for $250,000. The building had an expected useful life of 10 years and nil residual value. RW uses the straight-line method of depreciation.

On 30 June 20X8, RW decided to sell the building. The market value of the building at that date was $195,000 due to falling property prices. RW had already been approached by two different companies offering to buy the building and was confident that it could be sold quickly. RW estimated that selling costs would be approximately $10,000.

Required

How should the factory be treated in RW's financial statements at 30 June 20X8?

Solution

The building should be classified as 'held for sale' at 30 June 20X8. It should be included in the statement of financial position on its own separate line under non-current assets at the lower of its carrying amount and fair value less costs to sell.

The current carrying value of the building is: $250,000 - (250,000 \times {}^{2}\!/_{10}) = \$200,000$

Fair value less costs to sell: $195,000 - 10,000 = \$185,000$

The building should be valued in the statement of financial position at $185,000. An expense (impairment loss) of $15,000 (= $200,000 - $185,000) should be recognised in the statement of profit or loss.

1.2.3 Additional disclosures

In the period in which a non-current asset (or disposal group) has been either classified as held for sale or sold the following should be disclosed.

(a) A **description** of the non-current asset (or disposal group)

(b) A description of the **facts and circumstances** of the disposal

(c) Any **gain or loss** recognised when the item was classified as held for sale

Where an asset previously classified as held for sale is **no longer held for sale**, the entity should disclose a description of the facts and circumstances leading to the decision and its effect on results.

1.3 Discontinued operations

IFRS 5 defines a **discontinued operation** as follows.

KEY TERMS

DISCONTINUED OPERATION: a component of an entity that has either **been disposed of**, or **is classified as held for sale**, and:

(a) Represents a separate major line of business or geographical area of operations

(b)   Is part of a single co-ordinated plan to dispose of a separate major line of business or geographical area of operations, or

(c)   Is a subsidiary acquired exclusively with a view to resale

COMPONENT OF AN ENTITY: operations and cash flows that can be clearly distinguished, operationally and for financial reporting purposes, from the rest of the entity.

An entity should **present and disclose information** that enables users of the financial statements to evaluate the financial effects of **discontinued operations** and disposals of non-current assets or disposal groups. This allows users to distinguish between operations which will continue in the future and those which will not, and makes it more possible to predict future results.

1.3.1 Presentation and disclosure

An entity should disclose a **single amount** in the statement of profit or loss comprising the total of:

(a)   The **post-tax profit or loss** of discontinued operations and

(b)   The post-tax gain or loss recognised on the **measurement to fair value less costs to sell** or on the disposal of the assets or disposal group(s) constituting the discontinued operation

An entity should also disclose an **analysis** of this single amount into:

(a)   The revenue, expenses and pre-tax profit or loss of discontinued operations

(b)   The related income tax expense

(c)   The gain or loss recognised on the measurement to fair value less costs to sell or on the disposal of the assets or disposal group(s) constituting the discontinued operation

(d)   The related income tax expense

This information may be presented either in the statement of profit or loss or in the notes. If it is presented in the statement of profit or loss it should be presented in a section identified as relating to discontinued operations, ie **separately** from continuing operations. This analysis is not required where the discontinued operation is a newly acquired subsidiary that has been classified as held for sale.

An entity should disclose the **net cash flows** attributable to the operating, investing and financing activities of discontinued operations. These disclosures may be presented either on the face of the statement of cash flows or in the notes.

Gains and losses on the remeasurement of a disposal group that is not a discontinued operation but is held for sale should be included in profit or loss from continuing operations.

Comparative information for the discontinued operation should also be presented.

The following amended illustration is taken from the implementation guidance to IFRS 5. Here the minimum disclosure is given in the statement of profit or loss – just the profit for the year from discontinued operations. The analysis of this profit should be given in the notes.

XYZ
STATEMENT OF PROFIT OR LOSS
FOR THE YEAR ENDED 31 DECEMBER 20X2

Continuing operations	20X2 $'000	20X1 $'000
Revenue	X	X
Cost of sales	(X)	(X)
Gross profit	X	X
Other income	X	X
Distribution costs	(X)	(X)
Administrative expenses	(X)	(X)
Other expenses	(X)	(X)
Finance costs	(X)	(X)
Profit before tax	X	X
Income tax expense	(X)	(X)
Profit for the year from continuing operations	X	X
Discontinued operations		
Profit for the year from discontinued operations	X	X
Profit for the year	X	X

Note that if there were items of 'other comprehensive income' this would be shown as a full 'statement of profit or loss and other comprehensive income' as per the format in the previous chapter.

Question 10.2	Discontinued operation

Learning outcome B2

On 20 October 20X3 the directors of a parent company made a public announcement of plans to close a steel works. The closure means that the group will no longer carry out this type of operation, which until recently has represented about 10% of its total sales revenue. The works will be gradually shut down over a period of several months, with complete closure expected in July 20X4. At 31 December 20X3 output had been significantly reduced and some redundancies had already taken place. The cash flows, revenues and expenses relating to the steel works can be clearly distinguished from those of the subsidiary's other operations.

Required

How should the closure be treated in the financial statements for the year ended 31 December 20X3?

Section summary

IFRS 5 *Non-current assets held for sale and discontinued operations* requires assets 'held for sale' to be presented separately in the statement of financial position. The results of discontinued operations should be presented separately in the statement of profit or loss and other comprehensive income.

Chapter Summary

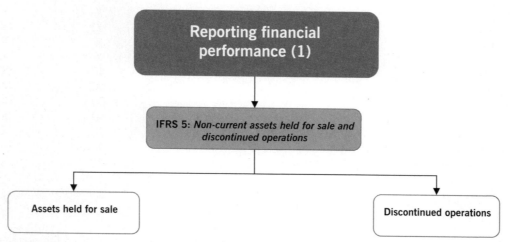

Reporting financial performance (1)

IFRS 5: *Non-current assets held for sale and discontinued operations*

Assets held for sale

- Criteria:
  - Available for immediate sale in its present condition
  - Sale must be highly probable
  - Entity is actively seeking a sale
  - Sale expected within one year of classification as held for sale
- Accounting treatment:
  - Revalue (if asset is revalued)
  - Remeasure to **lower** of:
    - Carrying amount
    - Fair Value less Costs To Sell (impairment loss to SPL)
  - Do not depreciate
  - On disposal treat as a normal disposal (profit/loss on disposal ⟶ SPL)

Discontinued operations

'A component of an entity that either has been disposed of or is classified as held for sale and:
(1) Represents a separate major line of business or geographical area of operations
(2) Is part of a single coordinated plan to dispose of a separate major line of business or geographical area of operations
(3) Is a subsidiary acquired exclusively with a view to resale'

Quick Quiz

1   What aspects of accounting are dealt with by IFRS 5?

2   What are the principal requirements of IFRS 5?

Answers to Quick Quiz

1   IFRS 5 deals with the accounting treatment of non-current assets held for sale and discontinued operations.

2   The principal requirements of IFRS 5 are that assets held for sale are presented separately in the statement of financial position and that discontinued operations are presented separately in the statement of profit or loss and other comprehensive income.

 ## Answers to Questions

10.1 Assets held for sale

The facility will not be transferred until the backlog of orders is completed; this demonstrates that the facility is not available for immediate sale in its present condition. The facility cannot be classified as 'held for sale' at 31 December 20X3. It must be treated in the same way as other items of property, plant and equipment: it should continue to be depreciated and should not be separately disclosed.

10.2 Discontinued operation

Because the steel works is being closed, rather than sold, it cannot be classified as 'held for sale'. In addition, the steel works is not a discontinued operation. Although at 31 December 20X3 the group was firmly committed to the closure, this has not yet taken place and therefore the steel works must be included in continuing operations. Information about the planned closure could be disclosed in the notes to the financial statements.

Now try this question from the OTQ Question Bank	Number
	Q31

REPORTING FINANCIAL PERFORMANCE II

In this, the second chapter on reporting financial performance, we look at three more accounting standards addressing foreign currency, income taxes and how to respond to events that take place after the financial reporting date.

topic list	learning outcomes	syllabus references
1 Foreign currency translation	B2	B2 (b)
2 IAS 21 *The effects of changes in foreign exchange rates*	B2	B2 (b)
3 IAS 12 *Income taxes*	B2	B2 (b)
4 IAS 10 *Events after the reporting period*	B2	B2 (b)

Chapter Overview

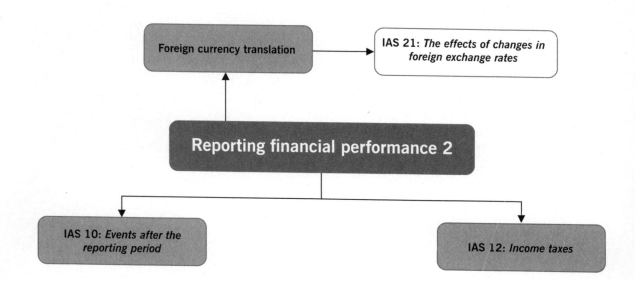

1   Foreign currency translation

Introduction

If a company trades overseas, it will buy or sell assets in foreign currencies. For example, an Indian company might buy materials from Canada, and pay for them in US dollars, and then sell its finished goods in Germany, receiving payment in euros. The purchase and sale must be translated into the company's local currency (here the Indian rupee) to record the double entry in the nominal ledger. If the company owes money in a foreign currency at the end of the accounting year, or holds monetary assets which were bought in a foreign currency, those liabilities or assets must be also translated into the local currency.

A company might have a subsidiary abroad (ie a foreign entity that it owns), and the subsidiary will trade in its own local currency. The subsidiary will keep its nominal ledger and prepare its annual financial statements in its own currency. However, at the year end, the parent company must consolidate the results of the overseas subsidiary into its group financial statements, so that the assets and liabilities and the annual profits of the subsidiary are translated into the parent company's currency.

If foreign currency exchange rates remained constant, there would be no accounting problem. As you will be aware, however, foreign exchange rates are continually changing. It is not inconceivable, for example, that the rate of exchange between the Polish zloty and British sterling might be Z6.2 to £1 at the start of the accounting year, and Z5.6 to £1 at the end of the year (in this example, a 10% increase in the relative strength of the zloty).

There are two distinct types of foreign currency transaction, conversion and translation.

1.1 Conversion gains and losses

Conversion is the process of exchanging amounts of one foreign currency for another.

For example, suppose a US company buys a large consignment of goods from a supplier in Germany. The order is placed on 1 May and the agreed price is €124,250. At the time of delivery the rate of foreign exchange was €2 to $1. The local company would record the amount owed in its books as follows.

DEBIT	Purchases (124,250 ÷ 2)	$62,125	
CREDIT	Payables		$62,125

When the local company comes to pay the supplier, it needs to obtain some foreign currency. By this time, however, if the rate of exchange has altered to €2.05 to $1, the cost of raising €124,250 would be (÷ 2.05) $60,610. The company would need to spend only $60,610 to settle a debt for inventories 'costing' $62,125. As the payable is settled for less than the company originally thought it would have to pay, a profit on conversion or **exchange gain** of $1,515 ($62,125 - $60,610) has arisen.

DEBIT	Payables account	$62,125	
CREDIT	Cash		$60,610
CREDIT	Profit on conversion (exchange gain)		$1,515

Profits (or losses) on conversion would be **included in profit or loss for the year** in which conversion (whether payment or receipt) takes place.

Suppose that another US company sells goods to a Chinese company, and it is agreed that payment should be made in Chinese Yuan at a price of Y116,000. We will further assume that the exchange rate at the time of sale is Y10.75 to $1, but when the debt is eventually paid, the rate has altered to Y10.8 to $1. The company would record the sale as follows.

DEBIT	Receivables (116,000 ÷ 10.75)	$10,791	
CREDIT	Revenue		$10,791

When the Y116,000 are paid, the local company will convert them into $, to obtain (÷ 10.8) $10,741. In this example, there has been a **loss on conversion** of $50 which will be **written off to profit or loss for the year**:

DEBIT	Cash	$10,741	
DEBIT	Loss on conversion (exchange loss)	$50	
CREDIT	Receivables account		$10,791

There are **no accounting difficulties** concerned with foreign currency conversion gains or losses, and the procedures described above are uncontroversial.

1.2 Translation

Foreign currency translation, as distinct from conversion, does not involve the act of exchanging one currency for another. **Translation is required at the end of an accounting period when a company still holds assets or liabilities in its statement of financial position which were obtained or incurred in a foreign currency.**

These assets or liabilities might consist of any of the following.

(a) An individual home company holding individual **assets** or **liabilities** originating in a foreign currency 'deal'.

(b) An individual home company with a separate **branch** of the business operating abroad which keeps its own books of account in the local currency.

(c) A home company which wishes to consolidate the **results of a foreign subsidiary**.

2 IAS 21: *The effect of changes in foreign exchange rates*

Introduction

The questions discussed above are addressed by IAS 21 *The effects of changes in foreign exchange rates*. We will examine those matters which affect single company accounts here.

2.1 Definitions

These are some of the definitions given by IAS 21.

KEY TERMS

FOREIGN CURRENCY. A currency other than the functional currency of the entity.

FUNCTIONAL CURRENCY. The currency of the primary economic environment in which the entity operates.

PRESENTATION CURRENCY. The currency in which the financial statements are presented.

EXCHANGE RATE. The ratio of exchange for two currencies.

EXCHANGE DIFFERENCE. The difference resulting from translating a given number of units of one currency into another currency at different exchange rates.

CLOSING RATE. The spot exchange rate at the year end date.

SPOT EXCHANGE RATE. The exchange rate for immediate delivery.

MONETARY ITEMS. Units of currency held and assets and liabilities to be received or paid in a fixed or determinable number of units of currency. *(IAS 21)*

Each entity – whether an individual company, a parent of a group, or an operation within a group (such as a subsidiary, associate or branch) – should determine its **functional currency** and **measure its results and financial position in that currency**.

For most individual companies the functional currency will be the currency of the country in which they are located and in which they carry out most of their transactions.

An entity can **present** its financial statements in any currency (or currencies) it chooses: in other words, it can have a **presentation currency** that is different from its functional currency. IAS 21 deals with the situation in which financial statements are presented in a currency other than the functional currency.

Most individual companies' presentation currency will normally be the same as their functional currency (the currency of the country in which they operate).

A company's presentation currency may be different from its functional currency if it is listed on a foreign stock exchange or operates within a group.

2.2 Determining functional currency

IAS 21 states that an entity should consider the following factors in determining its functional currency:

(a)   The currency that mainly **influences sales prices** for goods and services (often the currency in which prices are denominated and settled)

(b)   The currency of the **country whose competitive forces and regulations** mainly determine the sales prices of its goods and services

(c)   The currency that mainly **influences labour, material and other costs** of providing goods or services (often the currency in which prices are denominated and settled)

Sometimes the functional currency of an entity is not immediately obvious. Management must then exercise judgement and may also need to consider:

(a)   The currency in which **funds from financing activities** (raising loans and issuing equity) are generated

(b)   The currency in which **receipts from operating activities** are usually retained

2.3 Foreign currency transactions: initial recognition

IAS 21 states that a foreign currency transaction should be recorded, on initial recognition in the functional currency, by applying the exchange rate between the reporting currency and the foreign currency **at the date of the transaction** to the foreign currency amount.

An **average rate** for a period may be used if exchange rates do not fluctuate significantly.

2.4 Reporting at subsequent year ends

The following rules apply at each subsequent year end.

(a)   Report foreign currency **monetary items** (eg receivables, payables, cash, loans) using the **closing rate**

(b)   Report **non-monetary items** (eg non-current assets, inventories) which are carried at **historical cost** in a foreign currency using the **exchange rate at the date of the transaction** (historical rate)

(c)   Report **non-monetary items** which are carried at **fair value** in a foreign currency using the exchange rates that existed **when the values were measured.**

2.5 Recognition of exchange differences

Exchange differences occur when there is a **change in the exchange rate** between the transaction date and the date of settlement of monetary items arising from a foreign currency transaction.

Exchange differences arising on the settlement of monetary items (receivables, payables, loans, cash in a foreign currency) or on translating an entity's monetary items at rates different from those at which they were translated initially, or reported in previous financial statements, should be **recognised in profit or loss** in the period in which they arise.

There are two situations to consider.

(a) The transaction is **settled in the same period** as that in which it occurred: all the exchange difference is recognised in that period.

(b) The transaction is **settled in a subsequent accounting period**: the exchange difference recognised in each intervening period up to the period of settlement is determined by the change in exchange rates during that period.

In other words, where a monetary item has not been settled at the end of a period, it should be **restated using the closing exchange rate** and any gain or loss taken to the statement of profit or loss.

For **non-monetary items carried at fair value** which are retranslated at the date of remeasurement, exchange differences should be **recognised in the same place as the revaluation gain or loss**. If a gain or loss on a non-monetary item is recognised in other comprehensive income (eg revaluation of a property), any exchange component of that gain or loss shall be recognised in other comprehensive income. Where a gain or loss is recognised in profit or loss, any exchange component of that gain or loss shall be recognised in profit or loss.

Question 11.1	Entries

Learning outcome B2

White Cliffs Co, whose year end is 31 December, buys some goods from Rinka SA of France on 30 September. The invoice value is €40,000 and is due for settlement in equal instalments on 30 November and 31 January. The exchange rate moved as follows.

	€= $1
30 September	1.60
30 November	1.80
31 December	1.90
31 January	1.85

Required

State the accounting entries in the books of White Cliffs Co.

2.6 Exchange differences and cash flows

Exchange differences will also affect the working capital adjustments made in preparing a statement of cash flows.

For instance, if a foreign exchange gain has arisen on receivables during the year, the closing balance will include that gain, so the gain must be removed to arrive at the actual movement on receivables.

If the opening balance was $50,000 and the closing balance was $65,000, we would note this as a cash outflow of $15,000. But if the closing balance includes an exchange gain of $5,000, we deduct this from the closing balance to get an actual movement of $10,000.

> ### Section summary
>
> Foreign transactions are initially translated at the **exchange rate at the date of the transaction**. At the year end, **monetary** assets and liabilities are translated at the **closing rate**. **Exchange differences** are recognised in **profit or loss**.
>
> **Non-monetary** assets and liabilities are only **retranslated if they are carried at fair value**. The exchange gain or loss is recognised in the same place as the revaluation gain or loss (either profit or loss or other comprehensive income).

3   IAS 12 *Income taxes*

> ### Introduction
>
> IAS 12 *Income taxes* uses the term *income taxes* to refer to taxes on profits and gains of an entity. IAS 12 considers both current and deferred tax. In this section we will look at current tax. Deferred tax is not examinable in CIMA F1 but is tested in F2.

3.1 Current tax versus deferred tax

Before we go any further, let us be clear about the difference between current and deferred tax.

(a)   **Current tax** is the amount *actually payable* to the tax authorities in relation to the trading activities of the enterprise during the period.

(b)   **Deferred tax** is an *accounting measure*, used to match the tax effects of transactions with their accounting impact and thereby produce less distorted results.

3.2 IAS 12 definitions

These are some of the important definitions given in IAS 12 relevant to current tax.

KEY TERMS

ACCOUNTING PROFIT. Net profit or loss for a period before deducting tax expense.

TAXABLE PROFIT (TAX LOSS). The profit (loss) for a period, determined in accordance with the rules established by the taxation authorities, upon which income taxes are payable (recoverable).

TAX EXPENSE (TAX INCOME). The aggregate amount included in the determination of net profit or loss for the period in respect of current tax and deferred tax.

CURRENT TAX. The amount of income taxes payable (recoverable) in respect of the taxable profit (tax loss) for a period.   *(IAS 12)*

3.3 Accounting entries

You may have assumed until now that accounting for income tax was a very simple matter for companies. You would calculate the amount of tax due to be paid on the company's taxable profits and you would:

DEBIT   Tax charge (statement of profit or loss)
CREDIT   Tax liability (statement of financial position)

with this amount.

However, it may take some time to finalise the company's accounts and therefore its tax liability.

Example: The company's tax charge for 20X5 is estimated at $55,000. The following entry is made in the financial statements:

DEBIT	Statement of profit or loss (tax expense)	$55,000
CREDIT	Statement of financial position (tax payable)	$55,000

When the final tax liability is agreed with the tax authority, the amount payable is $58,000, and this amount is paid and posted as:

DEBIT	Statement of financial position (tax payable)	$58,000
CREDIT	Cash	$58,000

The account on the statement of financial position now has a DR balance of $3,000. This represents an **underprovision** of tax for 20X5. This tax has been paid but not charged to the statement of profit or loss.

In the accounts for 20X6, this underprovision will be accounted for. If the estimated liability for 20X6 is $60,000, the following entries will be made:

DEBIT	Statement of profit or loss	$60,000	*Being current tax*
		$3,000	*Being prior year underprovision*
CREDIT	Statement of financial position	$63,000	

The statement of financial position will now have a balance of $60,000, being the amount payable for the current year.

Complexities also arise when we consider the future tax consequences of what is going on in the accounts now. This is an aspect of tax called **deferred tax**, which is not examinable at F1 level.

Section summary

- Current tax is the amount actually payable to the tax authorities in relation to the trading activities of the entity during the period.

---

4 *IAS 10 Events after the reporting period*

Introduction

In this section we cover the reporting requirements where an event occurs after the end of the reporting period. In some instances, the financial statements will need to be amended for such an event.

4.1 Purpose of IAS 10

The financial statements are significant indicators of a company's success or failure. It is important, therefore, that they include all the information necessary for an understanding of the company's position.

IAS 10 *Events after the reporting period* requires the provision of additional information in order to facilitate such an understanding. IAS 10 deals with events **after** the end of the reporting period which may affect the position at the end of the reporting period.

4.2 Definitions

The standard gives the following definition.

KEY TERM

EVENTS OCCURRING AFTER THE END OF THE REPORTING PERIOD are those events, both favourable and unfavourable, that occur between the end of the reporting period and the date on which the financial statements are authorised for issue. Two types of events can be identified.

- Those that provide evidence of conditions that existed at the end of the reporting period – *adjusting events after the reporting period*
- Those that are indicative of conditions that arose after the end of the reporting period – *non-adjusting events after the reporting period*   *(IAS 10)*

4.3 Adjusting events

KEY POINT

An adjusting event is one which **provides evidence of conditions that existed at the end of the reporting period**. IAS 10 requires the entity to adjust amounts recognised in its financial statements to reflect these adjusting events.

An **example** of additional evidence which becomes available after the end of the reporting period is where a **customer goes bankrupt, thus confirming that the trade account receivable balance at the year end is uncollectable.**

In relation to **going concern**, the standard states that, where operating results and the financial position have deteriorated after the end of the reporting period, it may be necessary to reconsider whether the going concern assumption is appropriate in the preparation of the financial statements.

Other examples of **adjusting events** are:

- Evidence of a permanent diminution in property value prior to the year end
- Sale of inventory after the end of the reporting period for less than its carrying value at the year end
- Insolvency of a customer with a balance owing at the year end
- Amounts received or paid in respect of legal or insurance claims which were in negotiation at the year end
- Determination after the year end of the sale or purchase price of assets sold or purchased before the year end
- Evidence of a permanent diminution in the value of a long-term investment prior to the year end
- Discovery of error or fraud which shows that the financial statements were incorrect

4.4 Non-adjusting events

KEY POINT

A non-adjusting event is one which is **indicative of conditions that arose after the end of the reporting period**. Non-adjusting events do not require adjustment of items in the financial statements, but should be **disclosed** if they are material as they may affect the user's understanding of the financial statements.

The standard gives the following examples of events which are non-adjusting:

- Acquisition of, or disposal of, a subsidiary after the year end
- Announcement of a plan to discontinue an operation
- Major purchases and disposals of assets
- Destruction of a production plant by fire after the end of the reporting period
- Announcement or commencing implementation of a major restructuring
- Share transactions after the end of the reporting period
- Litigation commenced after the end of the reporting period

But note that, while they may be non-adjusting, events that are **material** should be disclosed in the notes to the financial statements.

4.5 Dividends

Dividends on equity shares should only be included as a liability in the financial statements if they have **been declared before the end of the reporting period**. Those dividends declared by the entity **after** the end of the reporting period should not be recognised as a liability at the end of the reporting period, but should be disclosed in the notes to the financial statements.

4.6 Disclosures

The following **disclosure requirements** are given for **material non-adjusting events** which occur after the end of the reporting period.

(a)   The nature of the event
(b)   An estimate of the financial effect, or a statement that such an estimate cannot be made

The financial statements should also state **the date on which they were authorised for issue**.

Question 11.2	Adjusting or not?

Learning outcome B2

State whether the following events occurring after the end of the reporting period require an adjustment to the assets and liabilities of the financial statements.

(a)   Purchase of an investment
(b)   A change in the rate of corporate tax, applicable to the previous year
(c)   An increase in pension benefits
(d)   Losses due to a fire which occurred after the reporting period
(e)   An irrecoverable debt suddenly being paid
(f)   The receipt of proceeds of sales or other evidence concerning the net realisable value of inventory
(g)   A sudden decline in the value of property held as a long-term asset

Section summary

IAS 10 deals with **events occurring after the reporting period**. It distinguishes between **adjusting** and **non-adjusting** events and gives examples.

Chapter Summary

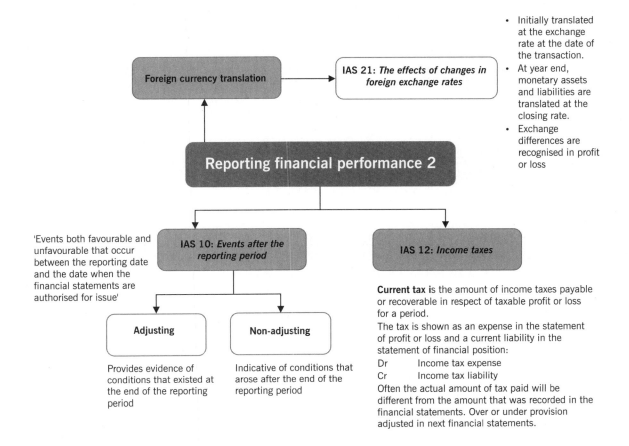

Foreign currency translation → **IAS 21: *The effects of changes in foreign exchange rates***

- Initially translated at the exchange rate at the date of the transaction.
- At year end, monetary assets and liabilities are translated at the closing rate.
- Exchange differences are recognised in profit or loss

Reporting financial performance 2

'Events both favourable and unfavourable that occur between the reporting date and the date when the financial statements are authorised for issue'

IAS 10: *Events after the reporting period*

Adjusting

Provides evidence of conditions that existed at the end of the reporting period

Non-adjusting

Indicative of conditions that arose after the end of the reporting period

IAS 12: *Income taxes*

Current tax is the amount of income taxes payable or recoverable in respect of taxable profit or loss for a period.

The tax is shown as an expense in the statement of profit or loss and a current liability in the statement of financial position:

Dr   Income tax expense
Cr   Income tax liability

Often the actual amount of tax paid will be different from the amount that was recorded in the financial statements. Over or under provision adjusted in next financial statements.

Quick Quiz

1   A customer goes bankrupt after the end of the reporting period and his debt must be written off. Is this an adjusting or non-adjusting event according to IAS 10?

Adjusting event   ☐

Non-adjusting event   ☐

2   Inventory is lost in a fire after the end of the reporting period. Is this an adjusting or non-adjusting event according to IAS 10?

Adjusting event   ☐

Non-adjusting event   ☐

Answers to Quick Quiz

1   Adjusting
2   Non-adjusting

Answers to Questions

11.1   Entries

The purchase will be recorded in the books of White Cliffs Co using the rate of exchange ruling on 30 September.

DEBIT	Purchases	$25,000
CREDIT	Trade payables	$25,000

Being the $ cost of goods purchased for €40,000 (€40,000 ÷ €1.60)

On 30 November, White Cliffs must pay €20,000. This will cost €20,000 ÷ €1.80= $11,111 and the company has therefore made an exchange gain of $12,500 – $11,111 = $1,389.

DEBIT	Trade payables	$12,500
CREDIT	Exchange gains: Profit or loss	$1,389
CREDIT	Cash	$11,111

On 31 December, the year end, the outstanding liability will be recalculated using the rate applicable to that date: €20,000 ÷ €1.90= $10,526. A further exchange gain of $1,974 has been made and will be recorded as follows.

DEBIT	Trade payables	$1,974
CREDIT	Exchange gains: Profit or loss	$1,974

The total exchange gain of $3,363 will be included in the operating profit for the year ending 31 December.

On 31 January, White Cliffs must pay the second instalment of €20,000. This will cost them $10,811 (€20,000 ÷ €1.85).

DEBIT	Trade payables	$10,526
DEBIT	Exchange losses: Profit or loss	$285
CREDIT	Cash	$10,811

11.2 Adjusting or not?

(b), (e) and (f) require adjustment.

Now try these questions from the OTQ Question Bank	**Number**
	Q11
	Q22
	Q50

EMPLOYEE BENEFITS

An increasing number of companies and other entities now provide a **pension and other benefits** in addition to salaries and wages as part of their employees' remuneration package. In view of this trend, it is important that there is standard best practice for the way in which employee benefit costs are **recognised, measured, and presented** in the sponsoring entities' accounts.

Note that IAS 19 was revised in June 2011.

topic list	learning outcomes	syllabus references
1 IAS 19 *Employee benefits*	B2	B2 (b)
2 Short-term employee benefits	B2	B2 (b)
3 Post-employment benefits	B2	B2 (b)
4 Defined contribution plans	B2	B2 (b)
5 Defined benefit plans: recognition and measurement	B2	B2 (b)
6 Defined benefit plans: other matters	B2	B2 (b)

Chapter Overview

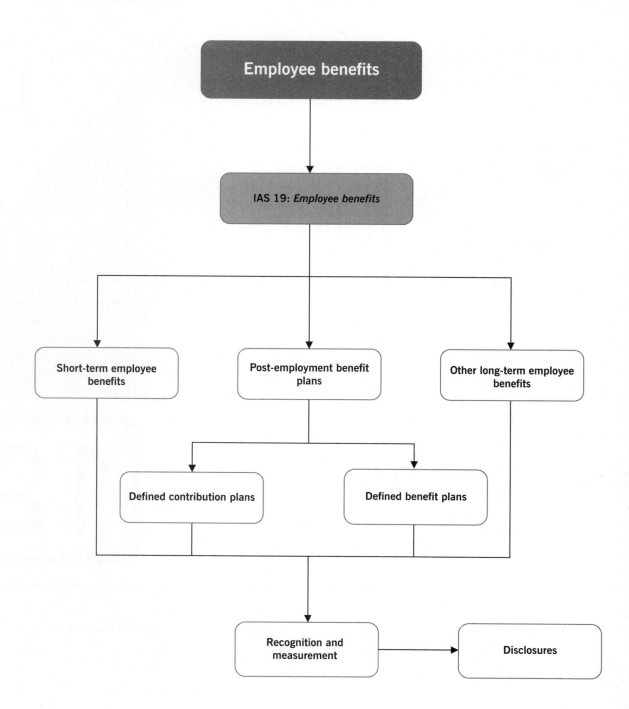

1   IAS 19 *Employee benefits*

Introduction

When a company or other entity employs a new worker, that worker will be offered a **package of pay and benefits**. Some of these will be short-term and the employee will receive the benefit at about the same time as he or she earns it, for example basic pay, overtime etc. Other employee benefits are **deferred**, however, the main example being retirement benefits (ie a pension).

1.1 The conceptual nature of employee benefit costs

The cost of these deferred employee benefits to the employer can be viewed in various ways. They could be described as **deferred salary** to the employee. Alternatively, they are a **deduction** from the employee's true gross salary, used as a tax-efficient means of saving. In some countries, tax efficiency arises on retirement benefit contributions because they are not taxed on the employee, but they are allowed as a deduction from taxable profits of the employer.

1.2 Accounting for employee benefit costs

Accounting for **short-term employee benefit costs** tends to be quite straightforward, because they are simply recognised as an expense in the employer's financial statements of the current period.

Accounting for the cost of **deferred employee benefits** is much more difficult. This is because of the large amounts involved, as well as the long time scale, complicated estimates and uncertainties. In the past, entities accounted for these benefits simply by charging the statements of profit or loss and other comprehensive income of the employing entity on the basis of actual payments made. This led to substantial variations in reported profits of these entities and disclosure of information on these costs was usually sparse.

1.3 IAS 19 *Employee benefits*

IAS 19 is intended to prescribe the following.

(a)   When the cost of employee benefits should be **recognised as a liability or an expense**

(b)   The **amount** of the liability or expense that should be recognised

As a basic rule, the standard states the following.

(a)   A **liability** should be recognised when an employee has provided a service in exchange for benefits to be received by the employee at some time in the future.

(b)   An **expense** should be recognised when the entity enjoys the economic benefits from a service provided by an employee regardless of when the employee received or will receive the benefits from providing the service.

The basic problem is therefore fairly straightforward. An entity will often enjoy the **economic benefits** from the services provided by its employees in advance of the employees receiving all the employment benefits from the work they have done, for example they will not receive pension benefits until after they retire.

1.4 Categories of employee benefits

The standard recognises four categories of employee benefits, and proposes a different accounting treatment for each. These four categories are as follows.

1 **Short-term** benefits including:

- Wages and salaries
- Social security contributions
- Paid annual leave
- Paid sick leave
- Paid maternity/paternity leave
- Profit shares and bonuses
- Paid jury service
- Paid military service
- Non-monetary benefits, eg medical care, cars, free or subsidised goods

2 **Post-employment benefits**, eg pensions and post-employment medical care and post-employment insurance

3 **Other long-term benefits**, eg profit shares, bonuses or deferred compensation payable later than 12 months after the year end, sabbatical leave, long-service benefits and long-term disability benefits

4 **Termination benefits**, eg early retirement payments and redundancy payments

Benefits may be paid to the employees themselves, to their dependants (spouses, children, etc) or to third parties.

1.5 Definitions

IAS 19 uses a great many important definitions. This section lists those that relate to the different categories of employee benefits.

KEY TERMS

EMPLOYEE BENEFITS are all forms of consideration given by an entity in exchange for service rendered by employees or for the termination of employment.

SHORT-TERM EMPLOYEE BENEFITS are employee benefits (other than termination benefits) that are expected to be settled wholly before twelve months after the end of the annual reporting period in which the employees render the related service.

POST-EMPLOYMENT BENEFITS are employee benefits (other than termination benefits and short-term employee benefits) that are payable after the completion of employment.

OTHER LONG-TERM EMPLOYEE BENEFITS are all employee benefits other than short-term employee benefits, post-employment benefits and termination benefits.

TERMINATION BENEFITS are employee benefits provided in exchange for the termination of an employee's employment as a result of either:

(a) an entity's decision to terminate an employee's employment before the normal retirement date, or

(b) an employee's decision to accept an offer of benefits in exchange for

---

Section summary

IAS 19 *Employee benefits* is a long and complex standard covering both short-term and long-term (post-employment) benefits. The complications arise when dealing with **post-employment benefits**.

2   Short-term employee benefits

Introduction

Accounting for short-term employee benefits is fairly straightforward, because there are **no actuarial assumptions** to be made, and there is **no requirement to discount** future benefits (because they are all, by definition, payable no later than 12 months after the end of the accounting period).

2.1 Recognition and measurement

The rules for short-term benefits are essentially an application of **basic accounting principles and practice**.

(a)   **Unpaid short-term employee benefits** as at the end of an accounting period should be recognised as an accrued expense. Any short-term benefits **paid in advance** should be recognised as a prepayment (to the extent that it will lead to, eg a reduction in future payments or a cash refund).

(b)   The **cost of short-term employee benefits** should be recognised as an **expense** in the period when the economic benefit is given, as employment costs (except insofar as employment costs may be included within the cost of an asset, eg property, plant and equipment).

3   Post-employment benefits

Introduction

Many employers provide post-employment benefits for their employees after they have stopped working. **Pension schemes** are the most obvious example, but an employer might provide post-employment death benefits to the dependants of former employees, or post-employment medical care.

3.1 General

Post-employment benefit schemes are often referred to as '**plans**'. The 'plan' receives regular contributions from the employer (and sometimes from current employees as well) and the money is invested in assets, such as stocks and shares and other investments. The post-employment benefits are paid out of the income from the plan assets (dividends, interest) or from money from the sale of some plan assets.

3.2 Definitions

IAS 19 sets out the following definitions relating to classification of plans.

KEY TERMS

DEFINED CONTRIBUTION PLANS are post-employment benefit plans under which an entity pays fixed contributions into a separate entity (a fund) and will have no legal or constructive obligation to pay further contributions if the fund does not hold sufficient assets to pay all employee benefits relating to employee service in the current and prior periods.

DEFINED BENEFIT PLANS are post-employment benefit plans other than defined contribution plans.

There are two types or categories of post-employment benefit plan, as given in the definitions above.

(a)   **Defined contribution plans**. With such plans, the employer (and possibly current employees too) pay regular contributions into the plan of a given or 'defined' amount each year. The contributions are invested, and the size of the post-employment benefits paid to former employees depends on how well or how badly the plan's investments perform. If the investments perform well, the plan will be able to afford higher benefits than if the investments performed less well.

(b) **Defined benefit plans**. With these plans, the size of the post-employment benefits is determined in advance, ie the benefits are 'defined'. The employer (and possibly current employees too) pay contributions into the plan, and the contributions are invested. The size of the contributions is set at an amount that is expected to earn enough investment returns to meet the obligation to pay the post-employment benefits. If, however, it becomes apparent that the assets in the fund are insufficient, the employer will be required to make additional contributions into the plan to make up the expected shortfall. On the other hand, if the fund's assets appear to be larger than they need to be, and in excess of what is required to pay the post-employment benefits, the employer may be allowed to take a 'contribution holiday' (ie stop paying in contributions for a while).

It is important to make a clear distinction between the following.

- **Funding** a defined benefit plan, ie paying contributions into the plan
- **Accounting for** the cost of funding a defined benefit plan

The key difference between the two types of plan is the nature of the 'promise' made by the entity to the employees in the scheme:

(a) Under a **defined contribution** plan, the 'promise' is to pay the agreed amount of contributions, Once this is done, the entity has no further liability and no exposure to risks related to the performance of the assets held in the plan.

(b) Under a **defined benefit** plan, the 'promise' is to pay the amount of benefits agreed under the plan. The entity is taking on a far more uncertain liability that may change in future as a result of many variables and has continuing exposure to risks related to the performance of assets held in the plan. In simple terms, of the plan assets are insufficient to meet the plan liabilities to pay pensions in future, the entity will have to make up any deficit.

3.3 Recap

- There are two categories of **post-retirement benefit plans**:
  - Defined contribution plans
  - Defined benefit plans

- **Defined contribution plans** provide benefits commensurate with the fund available to produce them.

- **Defined benefit plans** provide promised benefits and so contributions are based on estimates of how the fund will perform.

- **Defined contribution plans costs** are easy to account for and this is covered in the next section.

Section summary

There are two types of post-employment benefit plan:

- Defined contribution plans

- Defined benefit plans

4 Defined contribution plans

Introduction

Defined contribution plans produce benefits based on contributions made.

4.1 Accounting

A typical defined contribution plan would be where the employing company agreed to contribute an amount of, say, 5% of employees' salaries into a post-employment plan.

Accounting for payments into defined contribution plans is straightforward.

(a) The **obligation** is determined by the amounts to be contributed for that period.

(b) There are no actuarial assumptions to make.

(c) If the obligation is settled in the current period (or at least no later than 12 months after the end of the current period) there is **no requirement for discounting**.

IAS 19 requires the following.

(a) **Contributions** to a defined contribution plan should be recognised as an **expense** in the period they are payable (except to the extent that labour costs may be included within the cost of assets).

(b) Any liability for **unpaid contributions** that are due as at the end of the period should be recognised as a **liability** (accrued expense).

(c) Any **excess contributions** paid should be recognised as an asset (prepaid expense), but only to the extent that the prepayment will lead to, eg a reduction in future payments or a cash refund.

In the (unusual) situation where contributions to a defined contribution plan do not fall due entirely within 12 months after the end of the period in which the employees performed the related service, then these should be **discounted**. The discount rate to be used is discussed below in paragraph 5.10.1.

4.2 Disclosure requirements

The financial statements must disclose the amount recognised as an **expense** in the period. The entity should disclose information about contributions to defined contribution plans for key management personnel.

Section summary

Defined contribution plans are simple to account for as the benefits are defined by the contributions made.

5 Defined benefit plans: recognition and measurement

Introduction

Defined benefit plans produce benefits set out at the start of the plan. The annual pension will be calculated with a formula. For example:

(Final salary/60) x number of years worked

5.1 Introduction

Accounting for defined benefit plans is much more complex. The complexity of accounting for defined benefit plans stems largely from the following factors.

(a) The future benefits (arising from employee service in the current or prior years) **cannot be estimated exactly**, but whatever they are, the employer will have to pay them, and the liability should therefore be recognised now. To estimate these future obligations, it is necessary to use **actuarial assumptions**.

(b) The obligations payable in future years should be valued, by discounting, on a **present value** basis. This is because the obligations may be settled in many years' time.

(c) If actuarial assumptions change, the amount of required contributions to the fund will change, and there may be **re-measurement gains or losses**. A contribution into a fund in any period is not necessarily the total for that period, due to actuarial gains or losses.

IAS 19 defines the following key terms to do with defined benefit plans.

KEY TERMS

The NET DEFINED BENEFIT LIABILITY (ASSET) is the deficit or surplus, adjusted for any effect of limiting a net defined benefit asset to the asset ceiling.

The DEFICIT OR SURPLUS is:

(a) the present value of the defined benefit obligation less
(b) the fair value of plan assets (if any).

The ASSET CEILING is the present value of any economic benefits available in the form of refunds from the plan or reductions in future contributions to the plan.

The PRESENT VALUE OF A DEFINED BENEFIT OBLIGATION is the present value, without deducting any plan assets, of expected future payments required to settle the obligation resulting from employee service in the current and prior periods.

PLAN ASSETS comprise:

(a) Assets held by a long-term employee benefit fund; and

(b) Qualifying insurance policies

5.2 Outline of the method

An outline of the method used for an employer to account for the expenses and obligation of a defined benefit plan is given below. The stages will be explained in more detail later.

 Determine the deficit or surplus:

(a) An **actuarial technique** should be used to make a reliable estimate of the amount of future benefits employees have earned from service in relation to the current and prior years. The entity must determine how much benefit should be attributed to service performed by employees in the current period, and in prior periods. Assumptions include, for example, assumptions about employee turnover, mortality rates, future increases in salaries (if these will affect the eventual size of future benefits such as pension payments).

(b) The benefit should be **discounted** to arrive at the present value of the defined benefit obligation and the current service cost.

(c) The **fair value** of any **plan assets** should be deducted from the present value of the defined benefit obligation.

The surplus or deficit determined in Step 1 may have to be adjusted if a net benefit asset has to be restricted by the **asset ceiling**.

 Determine the amounts to be recognised in **profit or loss**:

(a) **Current service cost**
(b) Any **past service cost** and **gain or loss on settlement**
(c) **Net interest** on the **net defined benefit liability (asset)**

 Determine the **remeasurements** of the **net defined benefit liability (asset)**, to be recognised in other **comprehensive income** (items that will not be **reclassified to profit or loss):**

(a) **Actuarial gains and losses**

(b) **Return on plan assets** (excluding amounts included in net interest on the net defined benefit liability (asset))

(c) Any change in the effect of the **asset ceiling** (excluding amounts included in net interest on the net defined benefit liability (asset))

5.3 Constructive obligation

IAS 19 makes it very clear that it is not only its legal obligation under the formal terms of a defined benefit plan that an entity must account for, but also any **constructive obligation** that it may have. A constructive obligation, which will arise from the entity's informal practices, exists when the entity has no realistic alternative but to pay employee benefits, for example if any change in the informal practices would cause unacceptable damage to employee relationships.

5.4 The statement of financial position

In the statement of financial position, the amount recognised as a **net defined benefit liability** (which may be a negative amount, ie an asset) should be the following.

(a) The **present value of the defined obligation** at the year end, **minus**

(b) The **fair value of the assets of the plan** as at the year end (if there are any) out of which the future obligations to current and past employees will be directly settled.

5.5 The statement of profit or loss and other comprehensive income

All of the gains and losses that affect the plan obligation and plan asset must be recognised. The **components of defined benefit cost must be recognised as follows** in the statement of profit or loss and other comprehensive income:

Component	Recognised in
(a) **Service cost**	Profit or loss
(b) **Net interest on the net defined benefit liability**	Profit or loss
(c) **Remeasurements of the net defined benefit liability**	Other comprehensive income (not reclassified to profit or loss)

5.6 Service costs

These comprise:

(a) **Current service cost**, this is the increase in the present value of the defined benefit obligation resulting from employee services during the period. The measurement and recognition of this cost was introduced in Section 5.1.

(b)   **Past service cost**, which is the change in the obligation relating to service in **prior periods**. This results from amendments or curtailments to the pension plan, and

(c)   Any **gain or loss on settlement.**

5.7 Net interest on the defined benefit liability (asset)

In Section 5.1 we looked at the recognition and measurement of the defined benefit obligation. This figure is the discounted **present value** of the future benefits payable. Every year the discount must be 'unwound', increasing the present value of the obligation as time passes through an interest charge.

5.7.1 Interest calculation

IAS 19 requires that the interest should be calculated on the **net defined benefit liability (asset)**. This means that the amount recognised in profit or loss is the net of the interest charge on the obligation and the interest income recognised on the assets.

The calculation is as follows:

The **net defined benefit liability/(asset)** should be determined as at the **start** of the accounting period, taking account of changes during the period as a result of contributions paid into the plan and benefits paid out.

Many exam questions include the assumption that all payments into and out of the plan take place at the end of the year, so that the interest calculations can be based on the opening balances.

In the exam, **interest** will need to be **calculated separately** on the opening defined benefit obligation and the opening **plan assets** to be able to find the remeasurement gains/losses as a balancing figure (see paragraph 5.11 below) as follows:

Then the **net interest cost** (or income) is posted to **profit or loss** and represents the **financing effect** of paying for benefits in advance (if there is a net pension asset and surplus ie net interest *income*) or in arrears (if there is a net pension liability and deficit ie net interest *cost*).

5.8 Remeasurements of the net defined benefit liability

Remeasurements of the net defined benefit liability/(asset) comprise:

(a)   Actuarial gains and losses;

(b)   The return on plan assets, (excluding amounts included in net interest on the net defined benefit liability/(asset)); and

(c)   Any change in the effect of the asset ceiling, (excluding amounts included in net interest on the net defined benefit liability/(asset)).

The gains and losses relating to points (a) and (b) above will arise in every defined benefit scheme so we will look at these in this section. The asset ceiling is a complication that is not relevant in every case, so it is dealt with separately, later in the chapter.

5.8.1 Remeasurement gains or losses on defined benefit obligation

At the end of each accounting period, a new valuation, using updated assumptions, should be carried out on the obligation. Remeasurement ('actuarial') gains or losses arise because of the following.

- **Actual events** (eg employee turnover, salary increases) differ from the actuarial assumptions that were made to estimate the defined benefit obligations

- The effect of **changes to assumptions** concerning benefit payment options

- **Estimates are revised** (eg different assumptions are made about future employee turnover, salary rises, mortality rates, and so on)

- The effect of changes to the **discount rate**

Remeasurement gains and losses are recognised in **other comprehensive income (IAS 1)**.

5.8.2 Remeasurement gains or losses on plan assets

A new valuation of the plan assets is carried out at each period end, using current fair values. Any **difference between the new value, and what has been recognised up to that date** (normally the opening balance, interest, and any cash payments into or out of the plan) is treated as a '**remeasurement**' and recognised in other comprehensive income.

This remeasurement gain or loss represents the **difference between the return on the plan assets and the interest income** included in the net defined pension liability (or asset). The **return** on the plan assets is the increase in the value of the investments over time and is defined as **interest, dividends and other income** derived from the plan assets together with **realised and unrealised gains or losses** on the plan assets, less any costs of managing plan assets and tax payable by the plan itself.

Example

At 1 January 20X2 the fair value of the assets of a defined benefit plan were valued at $1,100,000 and the present value of the defined benefit obligation was $1,250,000. On 31 December 20X2, the plan received contributions from the employer of $490,000 and paid out benefits of $190,000.

The current service cost for the year was $360,000 and a discount rate of 6% is to be applied to the net liability/(asset).

After these transactions, the fair value of the plan's assets at 31 December 20X2 was $1,500,000. The present value of the defined benefit obligation was $1,553,600.

Required

Calculate the remeasurement gains or losses on the defined benefit obligation and plan assets and illustrate how this pension plan will be treated in the statement of profit or loss and other comprehensive income and statement of financial position for the year ended 31 December 20X2.

Solution

It is always useful to set up a working reconciling the assets and obligation:

	Assets $	Obligation $
Fair value/present value at 1/1/X2	1,100,000	1,250,000
Interest (1,100,000 × 6%)/(1,250,000 × 6%)	66,000	75,000
Current service cost		360,000
Contributions received	490,000	
Benefits paid	(190,000)	(190,000)
	1,466,000	1,495,000
Remeasurement gain on plan assets through OCI (balancing figure)	34,000	–
Remeasurement loss on defined benefit obligation through OCI (balancing figure)	–	58,600
Closing fair value/present value at 31/1/X2	1,500,000	1,553,600

The following accounting treatment is required.

(a) In the **statement of profit or loss and other comprehensive income**, the following amounts will be recognised:

In **profit or loss**:

	$
Current service cost	360,000
Net interest on net defined benefit liability (75,000 – 66,000)	9,000
	369,000

In **other comprehensive income**:

	$
Remeasurement gain on plan assets	34,000
Remeasurement loss on defined benefit obligation	(58,600)
	24,600

(b) In the **statement of financial position**, the net defined benefit liability of $53,600 (1,553,600 – 1,500,000) will be recognised.

5.9 Recap

The recognition and measurement of defined benefit plan costs are complex issues.

- Learn and understand the definitions of the various elements of a defined benefit pension plan

- Learn the **outline of the method of accounting** (see paragraph 5.2)

- Learn the recognition method for the:

  - Statement of financial position
  - Statement of profit or loss and other comprehensive income

Section summary

Defined benefit plans are much more difficult to deal with as the benefits are promised so they define the contributions to be made.

Discount rates used should be determined by reference to market yields on high-quality fixed-rate corporate bonds.

Actuarial assumptions made should be unbiased and based on market expectations.

Remeasurement gains or losses, which form part of the return on plan assets, arise due to differences between **the year end valuation of the defined benefit obligation and plan assets** and their **accounting value**. They are required to be recognised in **other comprehensive income**.

6 Defined benefit plans: other matters

Introduction

This section looks at the special circumstances of curtailments and settlements. These complications are less likely to appear in exam questions than the matters covered in the earlier sections of this chapter.

We have now covered the basics of accounting for defined benefit plans. This section looks at the special circumstances of past service costs, curtailments and settlements.

6.1 Past service cost and gains and losses on settlement

In paragraph 5.9 we identified that the total service cost may comprise not only the current service costs but other items, past service cost and gains and losses on settlement. This section explains these issues and their accounting treatment.

6.1.1 Past service cost

Past service cost is the change in the present value of the defined benefit obligation resulting from a plan **amendment** or **curtailment**.

A plan **amendment** arises when an entity either introduces or withdraws a defined benefit plan or **changes the benefits payable** under an existing plan. As a result, the entity has taken on additional obligations that it has not hitherto provided for (or reduced its obligation to its employees). For example, an employer might decide to introduce a medical benefits scheme for former employees. This will create a new defined benefit obligation that has not yet been provided for.

A **curtailment occurs when an entity significantly reduces the number of employees covered by a plan**. This could result from an isolated event, such as closing a plant, discontinuing an operation or the termination or suspension of a plan.

Past service costs can be either **positive** (if the changes increase the obligation) or **negative** (if the change reduces the obligation).

6.1.2 Accounting for past service cost

An entity should **remeasure the obligation** (and the related plan assets, if any) using current actuarial assumptions, before determining past service cost or a gain or loss on settlement.

Past service costs are recognised at the earlier of the following dates:

(a)   When the plan amendment or curtailment occurs, and

(b)   When the entity recognises related restructuring costs (in accordance with IAS 37) or termination benefits.

6.1.3 Gains and losses on settlement

A **settlement** occurs either when an employer enters into a transaction to eliminate part or all of its post-employment benefit obligations (other than a payment of benefits to or on behalf of employees under the terms of the plan and included in the actuarial assumptions).

A curtailment and settlement might **happen together**, for example when an employer brings a defined benefit plan to an end by settling the obligation with a one-off lump sum payment and then scrapping the plan.

The gain or losses on a settlement is the difference between:

(a)   The **present value of the defined benefit obligation** being settled, as valued on the date of the settlement; and

(b)   The **settlement price**, including any plan assts transferred and any payments made by the entity directly in connection with the settlement.

6.1.4 Accounting for past service cost and gains and losses on settlement

An entity should **remeasure the obligation** (and the related plan assets, if any) using current actuarial assumptions, before determining past service cost or a gain or loss on settlement.

The rules for recognition for these items are as follows.

Past service costs are recognised at the earlier of the following dates:

(a)   When the plan amendment or curtailment occurs, and

(b)   When the entity recognises related restructuring costs (in accordance with IAS 37) or termination benefits.

6.1.5 Accounting for gains and losses on settlement

An entity should recognise a **gain or loss** on settlement in **profit or loss** when the **settlement occurs**.

6.2 Asset ceiling test

When we looked at the recognition of the net defined benefit liability/(asset) in the statement of financial position at the beginning of Section 5 the term 'asset ceiling' was mentioned. This term relates to a threshold established by IAS 19 to ensure that any defined benefit asset (ie a pension surplus) is carried at **no more than its recoverable amount**. In simple terms, this means that any net asset is restricted to the amount of cash savings that will be available to the entity in future.

6.3 Net defined benefit assets

A net defined benefit asset may arise if the plan has been overfunded or if actuarial gains have arisen. This meets the definition of an asset (as stated in the *Conceptual Framework*) because **all** of the following apply.

(a)   The entity **controls a resource** (the ability to use the surplus to generate future benefits).

(b)   That control is the **result of past events** (contributions paid by the entity and service rendered by the employee).

(c)   **Future benefits** are available to the entity in the form of a reduction in future contributions or a cash refund, either directly or indirectly to another plan in deficit.

The **asset ceiling** is the **present value** of those future benefits. The **discount rate used is the same** as that used to calculate the net interest on the net defined benefit liability/(asset). The net defined benefit asset would be reduced to the asset ceiling threshold. Any related write down would be treated as a **remeasurement** and recognised in **other comprehensive income**.

6.4 Suggested approach and question

The suggested approach to defined benefit schemes is to deal with the change in the obligation and asset in the following order.

Step	Item	Recognition	
1	**Record opening figures:** • Asset • Obligation		
2	**Interest cost on plan liabilities** • Based on discount rate and PV obligation at start of period. • Should also reflect any changes in obligation during period.	DEBIT CREDIT	*Net interest cost (P/L)* *(x% × b/d liabilities)* *Plan liabilities (SOFP)*
3	**Interest on plan assets** • Based on discount rate and asset value at start of period. • Technically, this interest is also time apportioned on contributions less benefits paid in the period.	DEBIT CREDIT	*Plan assets (SOFP)* *Net interest cost (P/L)* *(x% × b/d assets)*
4	**Current service cost** • Increase in the present value of the obligation resulting from employee service in the current period.	DEBIT CREDIT	*Current service cost (P/L)* *Plan liabilities (SOFP)*
5	**Contributions** • As advised by actuary.	DEBIT CREDIT	*Plan assets (SOFP)* *Company cash*
6	**Benefits** • Actual pension payments made.	DEBIT CREDIT	*Plan liabilities (SOFP)* *Plan assets (SOFP)*
7	**Past service cost** • Change in pension liabilities for employee service in prior periods, resulting from a plan amendment or curtailment.	**Positive (increase in obligation):** DEBIT CREDIT **Negative (decrease in obligation):** DEBIT CREDIT	 *Past service cost (P/L)* *Plan liabilities (SOFP)* *Plan liabilities (SOFP)* *Past service cost (P/L)*

Step	Item	Recognition	
8	**Gains and losses on settlement** • Difference between the value of the obligation being settled and the settlement price.	**Gain**	
		DEBIT	*Plan liabilities (SOFP)*
		CREDIT	*Plan assets*
		CREDIT	*Cash*
		Loss	
		DEBIT	*Service cost (P/L)*
		DEBIT	*Plan liabilities (SOFP)*
		CREDIT	*Plan assets*
		CREDIT	*Cash*
9	**Remeasurements: actuarial gains and losses** • Arising from annual valuations of liabilities. • On plan liabilities, differences between actuarial assumptions and actual experience during the period, or changes in actuarial assumptions.	**Gain**	
		DEBIT	*Plan liabilities (SOFP)*
		CREDIT	*Other comprehensive income*
		Loss	
		DEBIT	*Other comprehensive income*
		CREDIT	*Plan liabilities(SOFP)*
10	**Remeasurements: return on assets less interest income** • Arising from annual valuations of plan assets	**Gain**	
		DEBIT	*Plan assets (SOFP)*
		CREDIT	*Other comprehensive income*
		Loss	
		DEBIT	*Other comprehensive income*
		CREDIT	*Plan assets (SOFP)*
11	**Disclose in accordance with the standard**	See comprehensive question.	

Exam skills

It would be useful for you to do a question on accounting for post-employment defined benefit schemes.

Question 12.1

Comprehensive

Learning outcomes B2

For the sake of simplicity and clarity, all transactions are assumed to occur at the year end.

The following data applies to the post employment defined benefit compensation scheme of BCD Co.

Discount rate: 10% (each year)

Present value of plan liabilities at start of 20X2: $1,600,000

Market value of plan assets at start of 20X2: $1,402,000

The following figures are relevant.

	20X2 $'000
Current service cost	150
Benefits paid out	130
Contributions paid by entity	120
Present value of plan liabilities at year end	1,710
Fair value of plan assets at year end	1,610

At the end of 20X2, a decision was taken to make a one-off additional payment to former employees currently receiving pensions from the plan. This was announced to the former employees before the year end. This payment was not allowed for in the original terms of the scheme. The actuarial valuation of the obligation in the table above **includes** the additional liability of $40,000 relating to this additional payment.

Required

Show how the reporting entity should account for this defined benefit plan in 20X2.

Section summary

You should know how to deal with curtailments and settlements.

Chapter Summary

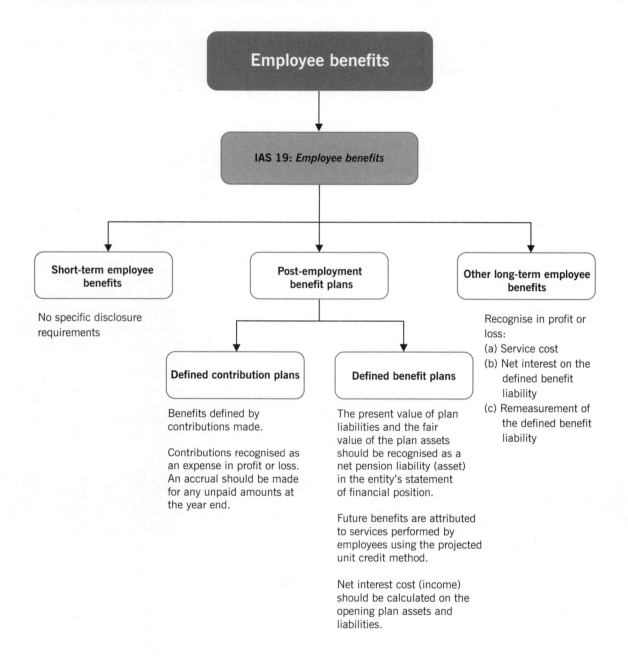

Employee benefits

IAS 19: *Employee benefits*

Short-term employee benefits

No specific disclosure requirements

Post-employment benefit plans

Other long-term employee benefits

Recognise in profit or loss:
(a) Service cost
(b) Net interest on the defined benefit liability
(c) Remeasurement of the defined benefit liability

Defined contribution plans

Benefits defined by contributions made.

Contributions recognised as an expense in profit or loss. An accrual should be made for any unpaid amounts at the year end.

Defined benefit plans

The present value of plan liabilities and the fair value of the plan assets should be recognised as a net pension liability (asset) in the entity's statement of financial position.

Future benefits are attributed to services performed by employees using the projected unit credit method.

Net interest cost (income) should be calculated on the opening plan assets and liabilities.

Quick Quiz

1   What are the four categories of employee benefits covered by IAS 19?

2   What is the difference between defined contribution and defined benefit plans?

3   What is a 'constructive obligation' compared to a legal obligation?

4   How should a defined benefit expense be recognised in the statement of profit or loss and other comprehensive income?

5   What causes remeasurement gains or losses?

Answers to Quick Quiz

1
- Short-term
- Post-employment
- Other long-term
- Termination

2 Under a defined contribution plan, the employer engages to pay an agreed amount of contributions and undertakes no further liability. Under a defined benefit plan, the employer engages to pay an agreed level of benefits – if the plan assets are insufficient to meet the plan liabilities, the employer will have to make up the deficit.

3 A constructive obligation exists when the entity has no realistic alternative than to pay employee benefits.

4 P/L: Current service cost + net interest on net defined asset/liability + past service cost + cost of curtailments or settlements.

OCI: Gains and losses on remeasurement of plan assets or obligation.

5 Remeasurement gains/losses arise as the result of actuarial assumptions about benefit payment options, salary and employee turnover estimates, and discount rates.

Answer to Question

12.1 Comprehensive

The gain or loss on remeasurement is established as a balancing figure in the calculations, as follows.

It is always useful to set up a working reconciling the assets and obligation:

	Assets 20X2 $'000	Liabilities 20X2 $'000
Opening fair value/present value at 1/1/X2	1,402	1,600
Interest (10%)	140	160
Current service cost		150
Contributions received	120	
Benefits paid	(130)	(130)
Past service cost	–	40
	1,532	1,820
Remeasurement gain on plan assets through OCI (balancing figure)	78	–
Remeasurement gain on defined benefit obligation through OCI (balancing figure)	–	(110)
Closing fair value/present value at 31/1/X2	1,610	1,710

In the statement of financial position, the liability that is recognised is calculated as follows.

	20X2 *$'000*
Present value of plan liabilities	1,710
Market value of plan assets	(1,610)
Net pension liability/(asset) in statement of financial position	100

The following will be recognised in profit or loss for the year:

	20X2 *$'000*
Current service cost	150
Past service cost	40
Net interest on defined benefit liability (asset) (160 – 140)	20
Expense recognised in profit or loss	210

The following remeasurements will be recognised in other comprehensive income for the year:

	20X2 *$'000*
Remeasurement gain on plan liabilities	110
Remeasurement gain on plan assets	78
	188

STATEMENTS OF CASH FLOWS

 The importance of the distinction between cash and profit and the scant attention paid to this by the statement of profit or loss has resulted in the development of statements of cash flows.

This chapter adopts a systematic approach to the preparation of statements of cash flows; you should learn this method and you will then be equipped for any problems in the exam itself.

The third section of the chapter looks at the information which is provided by statements of cash flows and how it should be analysed.

topic list	learning outcomes	syllabus references
1 IAS 7 *Statement of cash flows*	B2	B2 (a)
2 Preparing a statement of cash flows	B2	B2 (a)

Chapter Overview

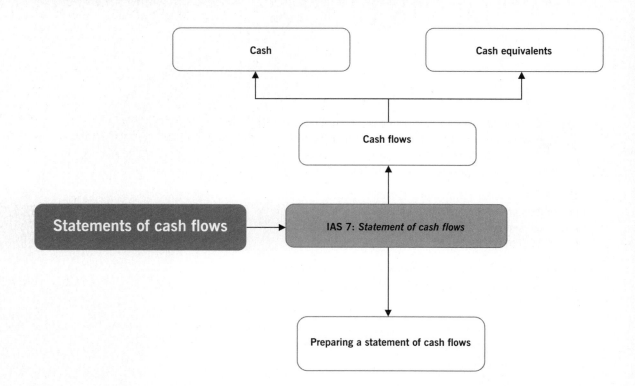

1 IAS 7 *Statement of cash flows*

Introduction

In this section we look at why statements of cash flows are useful. We also cover the required presentation of a statement of cash flows as per IAS 7.

1.1 Cash flow and profit

It has been argued that 'profit' does not always give a useful or meaningful picture of a company's operations. Readers of a company's financial statements might even be **misled by a reported profit figure**.

(a) Shareholders might believe that if a company makes a profit after tax, of say, $100,000 then this is the amount which it could afford to **pay as a dividend**. Unless the company has **sufficient cash** available to stay in business and also to pay a dividend, the shareholders' expectations would be wrong.

(b) Employees might believe that if a company makes profits, it can afford to **pay higher wages** next year. This opinion may not be correct: the ability to pay wages depends on the **availability of cash**.

(c) Survival of a business entity depends not so much on profits as on its **ability to pay its debts when they fall due**. Such payments might include 'revenue' items such as material purchases, wages, interest and taxation etc, but also capital payments for new non-current assets and the repayment of loan capital when this falls due (for example on the redemption of debentures).

From these examples, it may be apparent that a company's performance and prospects depend not so much on the 'profits' earned in a period, but more realistically on liquidity or **cash flows**.

1.2 Funds flow and cash flow

Some countries, either currently or in the past, have required the disclosure of additional statements based on **funds flow** rather than cash flow. However, the definition of 'funds' can be very vague and such statements often simply require a rearrangement of figures already provided in the statement of financial position and statement of profit or loss. By contrast, a statement of cash flows is unambiguous and provides information which is additional to that provided in the rest of the accounts. It also lends itself to organisation by activity and not by classification in the statement of financial position.

Statements of cash flows are frequently given as an **additional statement**, supplementing the statement of financial position, statement of profit or loss and other comprehensive income and related notes. The group aspects of statements of cash flows (and certain complex matters) have been excluded as they are beyond the scope of your syllabus.

1.3 Objective of IAS 7

The aim of IAS 7 is to provide information to users of financial statements about an entity's **ability to generate cash and cash equivalents**, as well as indicating the cash needs of the entity. The statement of cash flows provides *historical* information about cash and cash equivalents, classifying cash flows between operating, investing and financing activities.

1.4 Scope

A statement of cash flows should be presented as an **integral part** of an entity's financial statements. All types of entity can provide useful information about cash flows as the need for cash is universal, whatever the nature of their revenue-producing activities. Therefore **all entities are required by the standard to produce a statement of cash flows.**

1.5 Benefits of cash flow information

The use of statements of cash flows is very much **in conjunction** with the rest of the financial statements. Users can gain further appreciation of the change in net assets, of the entity's financial position (liquidity and solvency) and the entity's ability to adapt to changing circumstances by affecting the amount and timing of cash flows. Statements of cash flows **enhance comparability** as they are not affected by differing accounting policies used for the same type of transactions or events.

Cash flow information of a historical nature can be used as an indicator of the amount, timing and certainty of future cash flows. Past forecast cash flow information can be **checked for accuracy** as actual figures emerge. The relationship between profit and cash flows can be analysed as can changes in prices over time.

1.6 Definitions

The standard gives the following definitions, the most important of which are **cash** and **cash equivalents**.

KEY TERMS

CASH comprises cash on hand and demand deposits.

CASH EQUIVALENTS are short-term, highly liquid investments that are readily convertible to known amounts of cash and which are subject to an insignificant risk of changes in value.

CASH FLOWS are inflows and outflows of cash and cash equivalents.

OPERATING ACTIVITIES are the principal revenue-producing activities of the entity and other activities that are not investing or financing activities.

INVESTING ACTIVITIES are the acquisition and disposal of non-current assets and other investments not included in cash equivalents.

FINANCING ACTIVITIES are activities that result in changes in the size and composition of the contributed equity capital and borrowings of the entity.
(IAS 7)

1.7 Cash and cash equivalents

The standard expands on the definition of cash equivalents: they are not held for investment or other long-term purposes, but rather to meet short-term cash commitments. To fulfil the above definition, an investment's **maturity date should normally be three months from its acquisition date**. It would usually be the case then that equity investments (ie shares in other companies) are *not* cash equivalents. An exception would be where preferred shares were acquired with a very close maturity date.

Loans and other borrowings from banks are classified as financing activities. In some countries, however, **bank overdrafts** are repayable on demand and are treated as part of an entity's total cash management system. In these circumstances an overdrawn balance will be included in cash and cash equivalents. Such banking arrangements are characterised by a balance which fluctuates between overdrawn and credit.

Movements between different types of cash and cash equivalent are not included in cash flows. The investment of surplus cash in cash equivalents is part of cash management, not part of operating, investing or financing activities.

1.8 Presentation of a statement of cash flows

IAS 7 requires statements of cash flows to report cash flows during the period classified by **operating, investing and financing activities.**

Example: Simple statement of cash flows

Flail Co commenced trading on 1 January 20X1 with a medium-term loan of $21,000 and a share issue which raised $35,000. The company purchased non-current assets for $21,000 cash, and during the year to 31 December 20X1 entered into the following transactions.

(a)   Purchases from suppliers were $19,500, of which $2,550 was unpaid at the year end.

(b)   Wages and salaries amounted to $10,500, of which $750 was unpaid at the year end.

(c)   Interest on the loan of $2,100 was fully paid in the year and a repayment of $5,250 was made.

(d)   Sales revenue was $29,400, including $900 receivables at the year end.

(e)   Interest on cash deposits at the bank amounted to $75.

(f)   A dividend of $4,000 was proposed as at 31 December 20X1.

You are required to prepare a statement of cash flows for the year ended 31 December 20X1.

Solution

FLAIL CO
STATEMENT OF CASH FLOWS
FOR THE YEAR ENDED 31 DECEMBER 20X1

	$	$
Cash flows from operating activities		
Cash received from customers ($29,400 – $900)	28,500	
Cash paid to suppliers ($19,500 – $2,550)	(16,950)	
Cash paid to and on behalf of employees ($10,500 – $750)	(9,750)	
Interest paid	(2,100)	
Interest received	75	
Net cash flow from operating activities		(225)
Investing activities		
Purchase of non-current assets		(21,000)
Financing activities		
Issue of shares	35,000	
Proceeds from medium-term loan	21,000	
Repayment of medium-term loan	(5,250)	
Net cash flow from financing activities		50,750
Net increase in cash and cash equivalents		29,525
Cash and cash equivalents at 1 January 20X1		–
Cash and cash equivalents at 31 December 20X1		29,525

Note that the dividend is only proposed and so there is no related cash flow in 20X1.

1.9 Presentation

The manner of presentation of cash flows from operating, investing and financing activities **depends on the nature of the entity**. By classifying cash flows between different activities in this way users can see the impact on cash and cash equivalents of each one, and their relationships with each other. We can look at each in more detail.

1.9.1 Operating activities

This is perhaps the key part of the statement of cash flows because it shows whether, and to what extent, companies can **generate cash from their operations**. It is these operating cash flows which must, in the end pay for all cash outflows relating to other activities, ie paying loan interest, dividends and so on.

Most of the components of cash flows from operating activities will be those items which **determine the net profit or loss of the entity**, ie they relate to the main revenue-producing activities of the entity. The standard gives the following as examples of cash flows from operating activities.

(a)   Cash receipts from the sale of goods and the rendering of services

(b)   Cash receipts from royalties, fees, commissions and other revenue

(c)   Cash payments to suppliers for goods and services

(d)   Cash payments to and on behalf of employees

Certain items may be included in the net profit or loss for the period which do *not* relate to operational cash flows, for example the profit or loss on the sale of a piece of plant will be included in net profit or loss, but the cash flows will be classed as **investing**.

1.9.2 Investing activities

The cash flows classified under this heading show the extent of new investment in **assets which will generate future profit and cash flows**. The standard gives the following examples of cash flows arising from investing activities.

(a)   Cash payments to acquire property, plant and equipment, intangibles and other non-current assets, including those relating to capitalised development costs and self-constructed property, plant and equipment

(b)   Cash receipts from sales of property, plant and equipment, intangibles and other non-current assets

(c)   Cash payments to acquire shares or debentures of other entities

(d)   Cash receipts from sales of shares or debentures of other entities

(e)   Cash advances and loans made to other parties

(f)   Cash receipts from the repayment of advances and loans made to other parties

1.9.3 Financing activities

This section of the statement of cash flows shows the share of cash which the entity's capital providers have claimed during the period. This is an indicator of **likely future interest and dividend payments**. The standard gives the following examples of cash flows which might arise under these headings.

(a)   Cash proceeds from issuing shares

(b)   Cash payments to owners to acquire or redeem the entity's shares

(c)   Cash proceeds from issuing debentures, loans, notes, bonds, mortgages and other short or long-term borrowings

Example: Bank loans

The notes to the financial statements of Hayley Co show the following in respect of bank loans.

Year ended 30 June	20X5 $'000	20X4 $'000
Amounts payable within one year	12	8
Amounts payable after more than one year	96	58
	108	66

Interest paid on bank loans in the year to 30 June 20X5 amounted to $6,000. Hayley Co took out new loans totalling $56,000 in the period.

Required

Calculate the loan repayment to be shown in the statement of cash flows of Hayley Co for the year to 30 June 20X5.

Solution

Loan liabilities

	$'000
Bal b/f at 1.7.X4	66
New loans	56
	122
Loan repayment (bal fig)	(14)
Bal c/f at 30.6.X5	108

Alternative working using T account:

BANK LOANS

	$'000		$'000
Loan repayment (bal fig)	14	Bal 1.7.X4	66
Bal 30.6.X5	108	New loans	56
	122		122

1.10 Reporting cash flows from operating activities

The standard offers a choice of method for this part of the statement of cash flows.

(a) **Direct method:** disclose major classes of gross cash receipts and gross cash payments

(b) **Indirect method:** net profit or loss is adjusted for the effects of transactions of a non-cash nature, any deferrals or accruals of past or future operating cash receipts or payments, and items of income or expense associated with investing or financing cash flows

1.10.1 Using the direct method

There are different ways in which the **information about gross cash receipts and payments** can be obtained. The most obvious way is simply to extract the information from the accounting records. This may be a laborious task, however, and the indirect method below may be easier. The example and question above used the direct method.

1.10.2 Using the indirect method

This method is undoubtedly **easier** from the point of view of the preparer of the statement of cash flows. The net profit or loss for the period is adjusted for the following.

(a)   Changes during the period in inventories, operating receivables and payables

(b)   Non-cash items, eg depreciation, provisions, profits/losses on the sales of assets

(c)   Other items, the cash flows from which should be classified under investing or financing activities.

A **proforma** of such a calculation, taken from the IAS, is as follows and this method may be more common in the exam. (The proforma has been amended to reflect changes to IFRS.)

	$
Cash flows from operating activities	
Net profit before taxation	X
Adjustments for:	
Depreciation	X
Profit (loss) on disposal of a non-current asset	X
Investment income	(X)
Interest expense	X
Operating profit before working capital changes	X
Increase in trade and other receivables	(X)
Decrease in inventories	X
Decrease in trade payables	(X)
Cash generated from operations	X
Interest paid	(X)
Income taxes paid	(X)
Net cash from operating activities	X

It is important to understand why **certain items are added and others subtracted**. Note the following points.

(a)   Depreciation is not a cash expense, but is deducted in arriving at profit. It makes sense, therefore, to eliminate it by adding it back.

(b)   By the same logic, a loss on a disposal of a non-current asset (arising through underprovision of depreciation) needs to be added back and a profit deducted.

(c)   An increase in inventories means less cash – so cash has been spent on buying inventories.

(d)   An increase in receivables means the company's debtors have not paid as much, and therefore there is less cash.

(e)   If payables are paid, causing the payables figure to decrease, the business has less cash.

1.10.3 Indirect versus direct

The direct method is encouraged where the necessary information is not too costly to obtain, but IAS 7 does not require it. In practice, therefore, the direct method is rarely used. It is not obvious that businesses in practice are right in favouring the indirect method. It could be argued that companies ought to monitor their cash flows carefully enough on an ongoing basis to be able to use the direct method at minimal extra cost.

A proforma for the direct method is given below.

	$'000	$'000
Cash flows from operating activities		
Cash receipts from customers	X	
Cash paid to suppliers and employees	(X)	
Cash generated from operations	X	
Interest paid	(X)	
Income taxes paid	(X)	
Net cash from operating activities		X

1.11 Interest and dividends

Cash flows from interest and dividends received and paid should each be **disclosed separately**. Each should be classified in a consistent manner from period to period as either operating, investing or financing activities.

Dividends paid by the entity can be classified in **one of two ways**.

(a)   As a **financing cash flow**, showing the cost of obtaining financial resources.

(b)   As a component of **cash flows from operating activities** so that users can assess the entity's ability to pay dividends out of operating cash flows.

1.12 Taxes on income

Cash flows arising from taxes on income should be **separately disclosed** and should be classified as cash flows from operating activities *unless* they can be specifically identified with financing and investing activities.

Taxation cash flows are often **difficult to match** to the originating underlying transaction, so most of the time all tax cash flows are classified as arising from operating activities.

Example of a statement of cash flows

In the next section we will look at the procedures for preparing a statement of cash flows. First, look at this **example**, adapted from the example given in the standard (which is based on a group and therefore beyond the scope of your syllabus).

Direct method

STATEMENT OF CASH FLOWS (DIRECT METHOD)
YEAR ENDED 31 DECEMBER 20X7

	$m	$m
Cash flows from operating activities		
Cash receipts from customers	30,330	
Cash paid to suppliers and employees	(27,600)	
Cash generated from operations	2,730	
Interest paid	(270)	
Income taxes paid	(900)	
Net cash from operating activities		1,560
Cash flows from investing activities		
Purchase of property, plant and equipment	(900)	
Proceeds from sale of equipment	20	
Interest received	200	
Dividends received	200	
Net cash used in investing activities		(480)
Cash flows from financing activities		
Proceeds from issuance of share capital	250	
Proceeds from long-term borrowings	250	
Dividends paid*	(1,290)	
Net cash used in financing activities		(790)
Net increase in cash and cash equivalents		290
Cash and cash equivalents at beginning of period		120
Cash and cash equivalents at end of period		410

* This could also be shown as an operating cash flow

Indirect method

STATEMENT OF CASH FLOWS (INDIRECT METHOD)
YEAR ENDED 31 DECEMBER 20X7

	$m	$m
Cash flows from operating activities		
Net profit before taxation	3,570	
Adjustments for:		
Depreciation	450	
Investment income	(500)	
Interest expense	400	
Operating profit before working capital changes	3,920	
Increase in trade and other receivables	(500)	
Decrease in inventories	1,050	
Decrease in trade payables	(1,740)	
Cash generated from operations	2,730	
Interest paid	(270)	
Income taxes paid	(900)	
Net cash from operating activities		1,560
Cash flows from investing activities		
Purchase of property, plant and equipment	(900)	
Proceeds from sale of equipment **	20	
Interest received	200	
Dividends received	200	
Net cash used in investing activities		(480)
Cash flows from financing activities		
Proceeds from issuance of share capital	250	
Proceeds from long-term borrowings	250	
Dividends paid*	(1,290)	
Net cash used in financing activities		(790)
Net increase in cash and cash equivalents		290
Cash and cash equivalents at beginning of period		120
Cash and cash equivalents at end of period		410

*   This could also be shown as an operating cash flow
**   The equipment was disposed of at its carrying amount, so no profit or loss arose.

Section summary

Statements of cash flows are a useful addition to the financial statements of companies because it is recognised that accounting profit is not the only indicator of a company's performance.

IAS 7 requires cash flows during the period to be classified by **operating, investing and financing activities**.

Cash flows from operating activities can be reported using the **direct** or **indirect method**.

2 Preparing a statement of cash flows

Introduction

This section will teach you how to prepare a statement of cash flows. This is an important skill for your exam.

2.1 Working capital adjustments

In essence, preparing a statement of cash flows is very straightforward. You should therefore simply learn the format and apply the steps shown below. Note that the following items are treated in a way that might seem confusing, but the treatment is logical if you **think in terms of cash**.

(a)   **Increase in inventory** is treated as **negative** (in brackets). This is because it represents a cash **outflow**; cash is being spent on inventory.

(b)   An **increase in receivables** would be treated as **negative** for the same reasons; more receivables means less cash.

(c)   By contrast an **increase in payables is positive** because cash is being retained and not used to settle accounts payable. There is therefore more of it.

2.2 Step-by-step method

Read the requirements of the question. Scan through the question detail.

Set out the proforma statement of cash flows with the headings required by IAS 7. You should leave plenty of space. Ideally, use three or more sheets of paper, one for the main statement, one for the notes and one for your workings. It is essential to know the formats well.

Transfer items across from the statement of financial position into the proforma (eg cash balances), workings on the face of the proforma (eg changes in working capital) or set up workings (eg property, plant and equipment working).

Transfer items across from the statement of profit or loss into the proforma (eg loss on sale of assets), workings on the face of the proforma or set up workings (eg tax or interest paid).

Deal with the additional information using your workings page and transfer items to the statement of cash flows as you work them out.

Finish off your workings and transfer any outstanding items to the statement of cash flows.

If the direct method is required, do any additional workings needed.

Finish off the statement of cash flows.

Do any notes to the statement of cash flows required in the question.

Now work through the following example and then attempt the questions, using the approach we recommend above.

> **Example: Preparation of a statement of cash flows**
>
> Kane Co's statement of profit or loss for the year ended 31 December 20X2 and statements of financial position at 31 December 20X1 and 31 December 20X2 were as follows.

KANE CO

STATEMENT OF PROFIT OR LOSS FOR THE YEAR ENDED 31 DECEMBER 20X2

	$'000	$'000
Sales		720
Raw materials consumed	70	
Staff costs	94	
Depreciation	118	
Loss on disposal of property, plant and equipment	18	
		300
Operating profit		420
Interest payable		28
Profit before tax		392
Taxation		124
Profit for the year		268

Note: Total dividends paid during the year were $66,000.

KANE CO

STATEMENTS OF FINANCIAL POSITION AS AT 31 DECEMBER

	20X2		20X1	
	$'000	$'000	$'000	$'000
Assets				
Property, plant and equipment				
Cost	1,596		1,560	
Depreciation	318		224	
		1,278		1,336
Current assets				
Inventory	24		20	
Trade receivables	76		58	
Bank	48		56	
		148		134
Total assets		1,426		1,470
Equity and liabilities				
Share capital	360		340	
Share premium	36		24	
Retained earnings	716		514	
		1,112		878
Non-current liabilities				
Long-term loans		200		500
Current liabilities				
Trade payables	12		6	
Taxation	102		86	
		114		92
		1,426		1,470

During the year, the company paid $90,000 for a new piece of machinery.

Required

Prepare a statement of cash flows for Kane Co for the year ended 31 December 20X2 in accordance with the requirements of IAS 7, using the indirect method.

Solution

KANE CO
STATEMENT OF CASH FLOWS FOR THE YEAR ENDED 31 DECEMBER 20X2

	$'000	$'000
Net cash flow from operating activities		
Profit before tax	392	
Depreciation charges	118	
Interest expense	28	
Loss on sale of property, plant and equipment	18	
Increase in inventories	(4)	
Increase in receivables	(18)	
Increase in payables	6	
Cash generated from operations	540	
Interest paid	(28)	
Dividends paid	(66)	
Tax paid (86 + 124 − 102)	(108)	
Net cash flow from operating activities		338
Cash flows from investing activities		
Payments to acquire property, plant and equipment	(90)	
Receipts from sales of property, plant and equipment (W)	12	
Net cash flows from investing activities		(78)
Cash outflow from financing activities		
Issues of share capital (360 + 36 − 340 − 24)	32	
Long-term loans repaid (500 − 200)	(300)	
Net cash outflow from financing activities		(268)
Decrease in cash and cash equivalents		(8)
Cash and cash equivalents at 1.1.X2		56
Cash and cash equivalents at 31.12.X2		48

Working: property, plant and equipment

Cost

	$'000
At 1.1.X2	1,560
Purchases	90
	1,650
Disposals (bal fig)	(54)
At 31.12.X2	1,596

Alternative working using T account

COST

	$'000		$'000
At 1.1.X2	1,560	At 31.12.X2	1,596
Purchases	90	Disposals (balance)	54
	1,650		1,650

Accumulated depreciation

	$'000
At 1.1.X2	224
Charge for the year	118
	342
Depreciation on disposals (bal fig)	(24)
At 31.12.X2	318

Alternative working using T account

ACCUMULATED DEPRECIATION

	$'000		$'000
At 31.1.X2	318	At 1.1.X2	224
Depreciation on disposals (balance)	24	Charge for year	118
	342		342

	$'000
Carrying value of disposals	30
Net loss reported	(18)
Proceeds of disposals	12

Question 13.1	Statement of cash flows

Learning outcome B2

Set out below are the financial statements of Emma Co. You are the financial controller, faced with the task of implementing IAS 7 *Statement of cash flows*.

EMMA CO
STATEMENT OF PROFIT OR LOSS FOR THE YEAR ENDED 31 DECEMBER 20X2

	$'000
Sales revenue	2,553
Cost of sales	1,814
Gross profit	739
Distribution costs	125
Administrative expenses	264
Operating profit	350
Interest received	25
Interest paid	75
Profit before taxation	300
Taxation	140
Profit for the year	160

EMMA CO
STATEMENTS OF FINANCIAL POSITION AS AT 31 DECEMBER

	20X2 $'000	20X1 $'000
Assets		
Non-current assets		
Property, plant and equipment	380	305
Intangible assets	250	200
Investments	–	25
Current assets		
Inventories	150	102
Receivables	390	315
Short-term investments (highly liquid)	50	–
Cash in hand	2	1
Total assets	1,222	948

	20X2	20X1
Equity and liabilities		
Equity		
Share capital ($1 ordinary shares)	200	150
Share premium account	160	150
Revaluation surplus	100	91
Retained earnings	260	180
Non-current liabilities		
Long-term loan	170	50
Current liabilities		
Trade payables	127	119
Bank overdraft	85	98
Taxation	120	110
Total equity and liabilities	1,222	948

The following information is available.

(a)   The proceeds of the sale of non-current asset investments amounted to $30,000.

(b)   Fixtures and fittings, with an original cost of $85,000 and a carrying amount of $45,000, were sold for $32,000 during the year.

(c)   The following information relates to property, plant and equipment.

	31 December	
	20X2	20X1
	$'000	$'000
Cost	720	595
Accumulated depreciation	340	290
Carrying value	380	305

(d)   50,000 $1 ordinary shares were issued during the year at a premium of 20c per share.

(e)   Dividends totalling $80,000 were paid in 20X2.

Required

Prepare a statement of cash flows for the year to 31 December 20X2 using the indirect method in accordance with IAS 7.

Exam skills

Remember that every item in the statement of financial position will have some impact on the statement of cash flows. It will either appear in the statement or be part of an adjustment. When you are doing a question, you should check back through the statement of financial position and make sure everything is accounted for.

Section summary

You need to be aware of the **format** of the statement of cash flows as laid out in **IAS 7**. Setting out the format is an essential first stage in preparing the statement, so this format must be learnt.

Chapter Summary

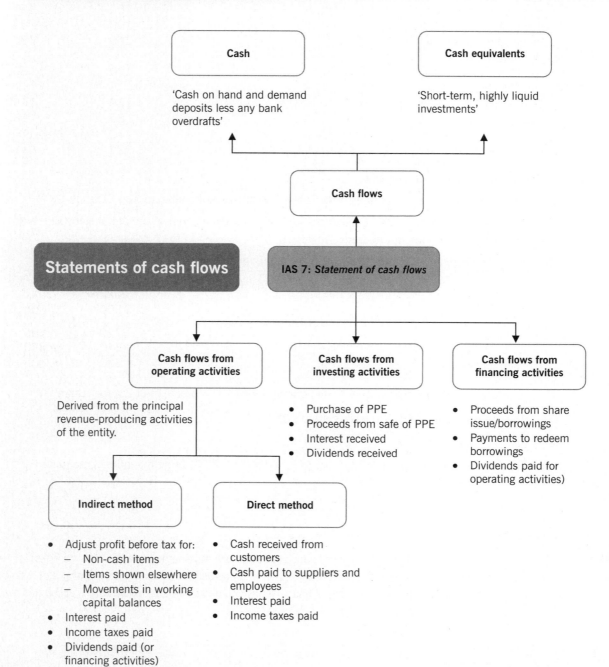

Cash

'Cash on hand and demand deposits less any bank overdrafts'

Cash equivalents

'Short-term, highly liquid investments'

Cash flows

Statements of cash flows

IAS 7: *Statement of cash flows*

Cash flows from operating activities

Derived from the principal revenue-producing activities of the entity.

Cash flows from investing activities

- Purchase of PPE
- Proceeds from safe of PPE
- Interest received
- Dividends received

Cash flows from financing activities

- Proceeds from share issue/borrowings
- Payments to redeem borrowings
- Dividends paid for operating activities)

Indirect method

- Adjust profit before tax for:
  - Non-cash items
  - Items shown elsewhere
  - Movements in working capital balances
- Interest paid
- Income taxes paid
- Dividends paid (or financing activities)

Direct method

- Cash received from customers
- Cash paid to suppliers and employees
- Interest paid
- Income taxes paid

Quick Quiz

1   What is the aim of a statement of cash flows?

2   The standard headings in IAS 7 *Statement of cash flows* are:

- O.................... a.....................
- I.................... a.....................
- F.................... a.....................
- Net.................... in C........................ and ....

3   Cash equivalents are current asset investments which will mature or can be redeemed within three months of the year end. True or false?

4   Why are you more likely to encounter the indirect method as opposed to the direct method?

5   List the steps that should be followed to prepare a statement of cash flows.

Answers to Quick Quiz

1 To indicate an entity's ability to generate cash and cash equivalents.

2 • Operating activities
   • Investing activities
   • Financing activities
   • Net increase (decrease) in cash and cash equivalents

3 False. See the definition in paragraph 1.6 if you are not sure about this.

4 The indirect method utilises figures which appear in the financial statements. The figures required for the direct method may not be readily available.

5

 Read the requirements of the question. Scan through the question detail.

 Set out the proforma statement of cash flows with the headings required by IAS 7. You should leave plenty of space. Ideally, use three or more sheets of paper, one for the main statement, one for the notes and one for your workings. It is essential to know the formats well.

 Transfer items across from the statement of financial position into the proforma (eg cash balances), workings on the face of the proforma (eg changes in working capital) or set up workings (eg property, plant and equipment working)

 Transfer items across from the statement of profit or loss into the proforma (eg loss on sale of assets), workings on the face of the proforma or set up workings (eg tax or interest paid)

 Deal with the additional information using your workings page and transfer items to the statement of cash flows as you work them out.

 Finish off your workings and transfer any outstanding items to the statement of cash flows

 If the direct method is required, do any additional workings needed

 Finish off the statement of cash flows

 Do any notes to the statement of cash flows required in the question

Answers to Questions

13.1 Statement of cash flows

EMMA CO
STATEMENT OF CASH FLOWS FOR THE YEAR ENDED 31 DECEMBER 20X2

	$'000	$'000
Net cash flows from operating activities		
Profit before tax	300	
Depreciation charge (W1)	90	
Net interest charge	50	
Loss on sale of property, plant and equipment (45 – 32)	13	
Profit on sale of non-current asset investments (30 – 25)	(5)	
Increase in inventories	(48)	
Increase in receivables	(75)	
Increase in payables	8	
Cash generated from operating activities	333	
Interest received	25	
Interest paid	(75)	
Dividends paid	(80)	
Tax paid (110 + 140 – 120)	(130)	
Net cash flows from operating activities		73
Cash flows from investing activities		
Payments to acquire property, plant and equipment (W2)	(201)	
Payments to acquire intangible non-current assets	(50)	
Receipts from sales of property, plant and equipment	32	
Receipts from sale of non-current asset investments	30	
Net cash outflow from investing activities		(189)
Cash flows from financing activities		
Issue of share capital	60	
Long-term loan	120	
Net cash flows from financing		180
Increase in cash and cash equivalents		64
Net cash and cash equivalents at 1.1 X2		(97)
Cash and cash equivalents at 31.12.X2		(33)

Workings

1　　Depreciation charge

	$'000	$'000
Depreciation at 31 December 20X2		340
Depreciation 31 December 20X1	290	
Depreciation on assets sold (85 – 45)	40	
		250
Charge for the year		90

2   Purchase of property, plant and equipment

	$'000
Balance b/d 1.1.X2	595
Revaluation (100 – 91)	9
Disposals	(85)
	519
Purchases (bal fig)	201
Balance c/d 31.12.X2	720

Alternative working using T account

PROPERTY, PLANT AND EQUIPMENT

	$'000		$'000
1.1.X2 Balance b/d	595	Disposals	85
Revaluation (100 – 91)	9		
Purchases (bal fig)	201	31.12.X2 Balance c/d	720
	805		805

Now try these questions from the OTQ Question Bank

Number
Q33
Q45

THE CONSOLIDATED STATEMENT OF FINANCIAL POSITION I

Preparing consolidated financial statements is an important area of your syllabus.

In this chapter we will look at the basic principles of consolidation and the definitions given in the relevant IFRSs. These matters are fundamental to your comprehension of consolidation, so make sure you go through them carefully.

We will then look at the basic procedures required to produce a consolidated statement of financial position.

There are plenty of questions and examples in this chapter - work through *all* of them carefully.

Topic list	learning outcomes	syllabus references
1 Groups and consolidation: an overview	B3	B3 (a) (b)
2 The consolidated statement of financial position	B3	B3 (c)
3 Goodwill arising on consolidation	B3	B3 (c)
4 Non-controlling interests	B3	B3 (c)
5 Impairment of goodwill	B3	B3 (c)

Chapter Overview

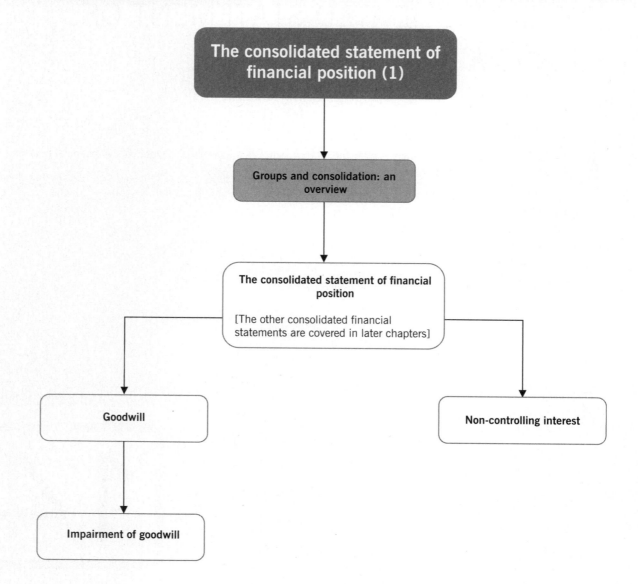

1 Groups and consolidation: an overview

Introduction

Many large businesses consist of several companies controlled by one central or administrative company. Together these companies are called a group. The controlling company, called the parent or holding company, will own some or all of the shares in the other companies, called subsidiaries. There are many reasons for businesses to operate as groups including for the goodwill associated with the names of the subsidiaries and for tax or legal purposes.

IFRS requires that the results of a group should be presented as a whole, in a set of group or 'consolidated' financial statements. This chapter and those following will teach you the principles and mechanics of preparing a set of consolidated financial statements. In this first section, we look at the accounting standards which govern group accounting as well as some important definitions.

1.1 Accounting standards

We will be looking at four accounting standards in this and the next three chapters.

- IAS 27 (revised) *Separate financial statements*
- IFRS 3 *Business combinations*
- IFRS 10 *Consolidated financial statements*
- IAS 28 (revised) *Investments in associates and joint ventures*

These standards are all concerned with different aspects of group accounts, but there is some overlap between them.

IAS 27 (revised) deals with the accounting treatment of subsidiaries and associates in the separate financial statements of an individual parent entity that is not required to produce consolidated financial statements. In this and the next chapter we will concentrate on IFRS 10, which covers the basic group definitions and consolidation procedures of a parent-subsidiary relationship. First of all, however, we will look at all the important definitions involved in group accounts, which **determine how to treat each particular type of investment** in group accounts.

1.2 Definitions

We will look at some of these definitions in more detail later, but they are useful here in that they give you an overview of all aspects of group accounts.

KEY TERMS

CONTROL. An investor controls an investee when the investor is exposed, or has rights, to variable returns from its involvement with the investee and has the ability to affect those returns through power over the investee.   *(IFRS 10)*

POWER. Existing rights that give the current ability to direct the relevant activities of the investee.
(IFRS 10)

SUBSIDIARY. An entity that is controlled by another entity (known as the parent).   *(IFRS 10)*

PARENT. An entity that has one or more subsidiaries.   *(IFRS 10)*

GROUP. A parent and all its subsidiaries.   *(IFRS 10)*

ASSOCIATE. An entity over which an investor has significant influence and which is neither a subsidiary nor a joint venture of the investor.   *(IFRS 10)*

SIGNIFICANT INFLUENCE is the power to participate in the financial and operating policy decisions of an investee or an economic activity but is not control or joint control over those policies.
(IFRS 10)

CONSOLIDATED FINANCIAL STATEMENTS. The financial statements of a group in which the assets, liabilities, equity, income, expenses and cash flows of the parent and its subsidiaries are presented as those of a single economic entity.

(IFRS 10)

SEPARATE FINANCIAL STATEMENTS. Financial statements presented by a parent in which the investments are accounted for at cost or in accordance with IFRS 9 *Financial instruments*.

(IAS 27 (revised))

Exam alert

All the definitions relating to group accounts are extremely important. You must **learn them** and **understand** their meaning and application. You need to be able to identify the nature of an investment, using the definitions of control and significant influence.

We can summarise the different types of investment and the required accounting for them as follows.

Investment	Criteria	Required treatment in group accounts
Subsidiary	Control	Full consolidation
Associate	Significant influence	Equity accounting (see Chapter 16)
Investment which is neither of the above	Asset held for accretion of wealth	As for single company accounts per IAS 39 (not examinable)

As the level of investment increases, the amount of financial information given about the investment in the group accounts also increases. This makes sense as a larger investment will have a bigger effect on the financial results and financial position of the investing entity.

1.3 Investments in subsidiaries

The important point in determining whether an investment is a subsidiary is **control**. In most cases, control will involve the holding company or parent owning a majority of the ordinary shares in the subsidiary (to which normal voting rights are attached). There are circumstances, however, when the parent may own only a minority of the voting power in the subsidiary, *but* the parent still has control.

IFRS 10 provides a definition of control and identifies three separate elements of control:

An investor controls an investee if and only if it has all of the following:

(1)   Power over the investee
(2)   Exposure to, or rights to, variable returns from its involvement with the investee; and
(3)   The ability to use its power over the investee to affect the amount of the investor's returns

If there are changes to one or more of these three elements of control, then an investor should reassess whether it controls an investee.

1.3.1 Power

Power is defined as **existing rights that give the current ability to direct the relevant activities of the investee.** There is no requirement for that power to have been exercised.

Relevant activities may include:

(a)   Selling and purchasing goods or services
(b)   Managing financial assets
(c)   Selecting, acquiring and disposing of assets

(d)   Researching and developing new products and processes

(e)   Determining a funding structure or obtaining funding.

In some cases assessing power is straightforward, for example, where power is obtained directly and solely from having the majority of voting rights or potential voting rights, and as a result the ability to direct relevant activities.

In other cases, assessment is more complex and more than one factor must be considered. IFRS 10 gives the following examples of **rights**, other than voting or potential voting rights, which individually, or alone, can give an investor power.

(a)   Rights to appoint, reassign or remove key management personnel who can direct the relevant activities

(b)   Rights to appoint or remove another entity that directs the relevant activities

(c)   Rights to direct the investee to enter into, or veto changes to transactions for the benefit of the investor

(d)   Other rights, such as those specified in a management contract.

IFRS 10 suggests that the **ability** rather than contractual right to achieve the above may also indicate that an investor has power over an investee.

An investor can have power over an investee even where other entities have significant influence or other ability to participate in the direction of relevant activities.

1.3.2 Returns

An investor must have exposure, or rights, to **variable returns** from its involvement with the investee in order to establish control.

This is the case where the investor's returns from its involvement have the potential to vary as a result of the investee's performance.

Returns may include:

(a)   Dividends

(b)   Remuneration for servicing an investee's assets or liabilities

(c)   Fees and exposure to loss from providing credit support

(d)   Returns as a result of achieving synergies or economies of scale through an investor combining use of their assets with use of the investee's assets

1.3.3 Link between power and returns

In order to establish control, an investor must be able to use its power to affect its returns from its involvement with the investee. This is the case even where the investor delegates its decision making powers to an agent.

1.3.4 Accounting treatment of subsidiaries in group accounts

Where a parent has one or more subsidiaries, IFRS 10 requires the parent to present **consolidated financial statements** (also referred to as **group accounts**), in which the accounts of the parent and subsidiaries are combined and presented **as a single entity**. This presentation means that the substance, rather than the legal form, of the relationship between parent and subsidiaries will be presented.

1.4 Investments in associates

An investment in an associate is something less than a subsidiary, but more than a simple investment. The key criterion here is **significant influence**. This is defined as the 'power to participate', but *not* to 'control' (which would make the investment a subsidiary).

Significant influence can be determined by the holding of voting rights (usually attached to shares) in the entity. IAS 28 states that if an investor holds **20% or more** of the voting power of the investee, it can be presumed that the investor has significant influence over the investee, *unless* it can be clearly shown that this is not the case. Any **potential voting rights** should be taken into account in assessing whether the investor has significant influence over the investee.

Significant influence can be presumed *not* to exist if the investor holds **less than 20%** of the voting power of the investee, unless it can be demonstrated otherwise.

The **existence of significant influence** is evidenced in one or more of the following ways.

(a)   Representation on the **board of directors** (or equivalent) of the investee
(b)   Participation in the **policy making process**
(c)   **Material transactions** between investor and investee
(d)   Interchange of management personnel
(e)   Provision of essential technical information

1.4.1 Accounting treatment of associates in group accounts

IAS 28 requires the use of the **equity method** of accounting for investments in associates. This method will be explained in detail in Chapter 17.

1.5 Trade investments

A trade investment is a simple investment in the shares of another entity, that is held for the accretion of wealth, and is not an associate or a subsidiary.

Trade investments are simply shown as **investments** under non-current assets in the consolidated statement of financial position of the group. Dividends received from trade investments are recorded as investment income in the statement of profit or loss and other comprehensive income.

Question 14.1

Learning outcomes B3

Which TWO of the following investments would be treated as an associate in the consolidated financial statements of Smith Co?

A   Smith Co owns 15% of the ordinary shares of Red Co and has significant influence over Red Co

B   Smith Co owns 45% of the ordinary shares of Pink Co and can appoint 4 out of 5 directors to the Board of Directors of Pink Co

C   Smith co owns 40% of the preference shares (non-voting) and 15% of the ordinary shares of Yellow Co

D   Smith Co owns 60% of the preference shares (non-voting) and 40% of the ordinary shares of Aquamarine Co

1.6 Content of group accounts

It is important to note at this point that consolidated financial statements are an *additional* set of financial statements that are produced. They do not replace the individual financial statements of the parent or its subsidiaries. The group itself has no legal form, the group accounts are produced to satisfy accounting standards and, in some countries, legal requirements.

Consolidated financial statements are issued to the shareholders of the parent and provide information to those shareholders on all the companies controlled by the parent.

Most parent companies present their own individual accounts and their group accounts in a single **package**. The package typically comprises the following.

- **Parent company financial statements**, which will include 'investments in subsidiary undertakings' as an asset in the statement of financial position, and income from subsidiaries (dividends) in the statement of profit or loss and other comprehensive income

- **Consolidated statement of financial position**

- **Consolidated statement of profit or loss and other comprehensive income** (or separate statement of profit or loss)

- **Consolidated statement of cash flows**

1.7 Accounting for subsidiaries and associates in the parent's separate financial statements

A parent company will produce its own single company financial statements. In these statements, investments in subsidiaries and associates are shown as **investments** under non-current assets in the statement of financial position. The investments should be either accounted for at cost or in accordance with IAS 39.

1.8 Exemption from preparing group accounts

IFRS 10 specifies that a parent **need not present** consolidated financial statements if and only if all of the following hold:

(a)   The parent is itself a **wholly-owned subsidiary** or it is a **partially owned subsidiary** of another entity and all its other owners, including those not otherwise entitled to vote, have been informed about, and do not object to, the parent not presenting consolidated financial statements

(b)   Its debt or equity instruments are **not publicly traded**

(c)   It did not file, nor is it in the process of filing, its financial statements with a securities commission or other regulatory organisation for the purpose of issuing any class of instruments in a public market; and

(d)   Its **ultimate or any intermediate parent** publishes consolidated financial statements that are available for public use and comply with International Financial Reporting Standards

A parent that does not present consolidated financial statements must comply with IAS 27 (revised) rules on separate financial statements.

Section summary

IFRS requires that the results of a group should be presented as a whole, in a set of group or 'consolidated' financial statements.

The definition of a subsidiary is based on a 'control' relationship.   The definition of an associate is based on the ability of the investing entity to exercise significant influence.

The different types of investment and the required accounting for them is summarised as follows.

Investment	Criteria	Required treatment in group accounts
Subsidiary	Control	Full consolidation (IFRS 10)
Associate	Significant influence (20%+ rule)	Equity accounting (IAS 28)
Investment which is neither of the above	Asset held for accretion of wealth	As for single company accounts (IAS 39)

IFRS 10 includes some specific exemptions from the preparation of consolidated financial statements.

2 The consolidated statement of financial position

Introduction

How are consolidated financial statements prepared? IFRS 10 lays out the basic procedures and we will consider these in the rest of this chapter.

2.1 Basic consolidation procedure

The preparation of a consolidated statement of financial position, in a very simple form, consists of two procedures.

(a)   Take the individual accounts of the parent company and each subsidiary and **cancel out items** which appear as an asset in one company and a liability in another.

(b)   Add together all the uncancelled assets and liabilities throughout the group on a line by line basis.

Items requiring cancellation may include the following.

(a)   The asset **'shares in subsidiary companies'** (also called 'investment in subsidiary companies') which appears in the parent company's accounts will be matched with the liability 'share capital' in the subsidiaries' accounts.

(b)   There may be **intra-group trading** within the group. For example, Subsidiary Co may sell goods on credit to Parent Co. Parent Co would then be a receivable in the accounts of Subsidiary Co, while Subsidiary Co would be a payable in the accounts of Parent Co.

Example: basic consolidation procedure

Parent Co has just bought 100% of the shares of Subsidiary Co. Below are the statements of financial position of both companies just before consolidation.

PARENT CO STATEMENT OF FINANCIAL POSITION	$'000	SUBSIDIARY CO STATEMENT OF FINANCIAL POSITION	$'000
Assets			
Investment in subsidiary*	50	Receivables	20
Receivables	30	Cash	30
	80		50
Equity and liabilities			
Share capital	80	Share capital*	50
	80		50

* Cancelling items

The consolidated statement of financial position will appear as follows.

PARENT AND SUBSIDIARY

CONSOLIDATED STATEMENT OF FINANCIAL POSITION

	$'000
Receivables (30 + 20)	50
Cash	30
	80
Share capital**	80
	80

**Note. This is the parent company's share capital only. The subsidiary's has been cancelled.

Example: basic consolidation procedure with intra-group trading

P Co regularly sells goods to its one subsidiary company, S Co, which it has owned since S Co's incorporation. The statement of financial position of the two companies on 31 December 20X6 are given below.

STATEMENTS OF FINANCIAL POSITION AS AT 31 DECEMBER 20X6

	P Co $	S Co $
Assets		
Non-current assets		
Property, plant and equipment	35,000	45,000
Investment in 40,000 $1 shares in S Co at cost	40,000	
	75,000	
Current assets		
Inventories	16,000	12,000
Receivables: S Co	2,000	
Other	6,000	9,000
Cash at bank	1,000	
Total assets	100,000	66,000
Equity and liabilities		
Equity		
40,000 $1 ordinary shares		40,000
70,000 $1 ordinary shares	70,000	
Retained earnings	16,000	19,000
	86,000	59,000
Current liabilities		
Bank overdraft		3,000
Payables: P Co		2,000
Payables: Other	14,000	2,000
Total equity and liabilities	100,000	66,000

Required

Prepare the consolidated statement of financial position of the P group at 31 December 20X6.

Solution

The cancelling items are:

(a)   P Co's asset 'investment in shares of S Co' ($40,000) cancels with S Co's liability 'share capital' ($40,000)

(b)   P Co's asset 'receivables: S Co' ($2,000) cancels with S Co's liability 'payables: P Co' ($2,000).

The remaining assets and liabilities are added together to produce the following consolidated statement of financial position.

P GROUP CONSOLIDATED STATEMENT OF FINANCIAL POSITION AS AT 31 DECEMBER 20X6

	$	$
Assets		
Non-current assets		
Property, plant and equipment (35 + 45)		80,000
Current assets		
Inventories (16 + 12)	28,000	
Receivables (6 + 9)	15,000	
Cash at bank	1,000	
		44,000
Total assets		124,000
Equity and liabilities		
Equity		
70,000 $1 ordinary shares (P Co only)	70,000	
Retained earnings (16 + 19)	35,000	
		105,000
Current liabilities		
Bank overdraft	3,000	
Payables (14 + 2)	16,000	
		19,000
Total equity and liabilities		124,000

Note the following.

(a) P Co's bank balance is **not netted off** with S Co's bank overdraft. To offset one against the other would be less informative and would conflict with the principle that assets and liabilities should not be netted off.

(b) The share capital in the consolidated statement of financial position is the **share capital of the parent company alone**. This must *always* be the case, no matter how complex the consolidation, because the share capital of subsidiary companies must *always* be a wholly cancelling item.

2.2 Part cancellation

An item may appear in the statements of financial position of a parent company and its subsidiary, but not at the same amounts.

(a) The parent company may have acquired **shares in the subsidiary** at a price **greater or less than their par value**. The asset will appear in the parent company's accounts at cost, while the liability will appear in the subsidiary's accounts at par value. This raises the issue of **goodwill**, which is dealt with later in this chapter.

(b) The intra-group trading balances may not be equal to each other because of **goods or cash in transit**.

(c) One company may have **issued loan stock** of which a **proportion only** is taken up by the other company.

The following question illustrates the techniques needed to deal with items (b) and (c) above. The procedure is to **cancel as far as possible**. The remaining uncancelled amounts will appear in the consolidated statement of financial position.

(a) **Uncancelled loan stock** will appear as a **liability of the group**.

(b) **Uncancelled balances on intra-group accounts** represent **goods or cash in transit**, which will appear in the consolidated statement of financial position.

Question 14.2

Basic consolidation

Learning outcomes B3

The statements of financial position of P Co and of its subsidiary S Co have been made up to 30 June. P Co has owned all the ordinary shares and 40% of the loan stock of S Co since its incorporation.

P CO STATEMENT OF FINANCIAL POSITION AS AT 30 JUNE

	$	$
Assets		
Non-current assets		
Property, plant and equipment	120,000	
Investment in S Co, at cost		
80,000 ordinary shares of $1 each	80,000	
$20,000 of 12% loan stock in S Co	20,000	
		220,000
Current assets		
Inventories	50,000	
Receivables	40,000	
Current account with S Co	18,000	
Cash	4,000	
		112,000
Total assets		332,000
Equity and liabilities		
Equity		
Ordinary shares of $1 each, fully paid	100,000	
Retained earnings	95,000	
		195,000
Non-current liabilities		
10% loan stock		75,000
Current liabilities		
Payables	47,000	
Taxation	15,000	
		62,000
Total equity and liabilities		332,000

S CO STATEMENT OF FINANCIAL POSITION AS AT 30 JUNE

	$	$
Assets		
Property, plant and equipment		100,000
Current assets		
Inventories	60,000	
Receivables	30,000	
Cash	6,000	
		96,000
Total assets		196,000
Equity and liabilities		
Equity		
80,000 ordinary shares of $1 each, fully paid	80,000	
Retained earnings	28,000	
		108,000
Non-current liabilities		
12% loan stock		50,000
Current liabilities		
Payables	16,000	
Taxation	10,000	
Current account with P Co	12,000	
		38,000
Total equity and liabilities		196,000

The difference on current accounts arises because of goods in transit.

Required

Prepare the consolidated statement of financial position of the P group.

Section summary

- The basic procedure of consolidation combines the financial statements of a parent and its subsidiaries on a **line by line** basis by adding together like items.

- Items which appear as an asset in one company and a liability in another are **cancelled out**.

- The asset '**shares in subsidiary companies**' (also called 'investment in subsidiary companies') which appears in the parent company's accounts will be cancelled with the liability '**share capital**' in the subsidiaries' accounts.

- If an item appears in the statements of financial position of a parent company and its subsidiary at different amounts, the procedure is to **cancel as far as possible**. The remaining uncancelled amounts will appear in the consolidated statement of financial position.

3 Goodwill arising on consolidation

Introduction

In the examples we have looked at so far the cost of shares acquired by the parent company has always been equal to the par value of those shares. This is seldom the case in practice and we must now consider some more complicated examples.

3.1 Goodwill arising on consolidation

Example: Goodwill arising on consolidation

P Co purchased all of the share capital (40,000 $1 shares) of S Co for $60,000. The statements of financial position of P Co and S Co prior to the acquisition are as follows.

STATEMENTS OF FINANCIAL POSITION AS AT 31.12.X1

	P Co $'000	S Co $'000
Non-current assets		
Property, plant and equipment	100	40
Cash at bank	60	
Total assets	160	40
Equity and liabilities		
Share capital	160	40
Total equity and liabilities	160	40

First we will examine the entries made by the parent company in its own statement of financial position when it acquires the shares.

The entries in P Co's books would be:

DEBIT	Investment in S Co	$60,000	
CREDIT	Bank		$60,000

So P Co's statement of financial position will look as follows:

	P Co $'000
Non-current assets	
Property, plant and equipment	100
Investment in S Co	60
Total assets	160
Equity and liabilities	
Share capital	160
Total equity and liabilities	160

Next we will look at the group accounts.

Now when the directors of P Co agree to pay $60,000 for a 100% investment in S Co they must believe that, in addition to its non-current assets of $40,000, S Co must also have **intangible assets** worth $20,000. This amount of $20,000 paid over and above the value of the tangible assets acquired is called the **goodwill arising on consolidation** (sometimes **premium on acquisition**).

Following the normal cancellation procedure the $40,000 share capital in S Co's statement of financial position should be cancelled against $40,000 of the 'investment in S Co' in the statement of financial position of P Co. This would leave a $20,000 debit uncancelled in the parent company's accounts and this $20,000 would appear in the consolidated statement of financial position under the caption 'Intangible non-current assets: goodwill arising on consolidation', as follows.

P GROUP CONSOLIDATED STATEMENT OF FINANCIAL POSITION AS AT 31.12.X1

	$'000
Non-current assets	
Property, plant and equipment (100 + 40)	140
Intangible non-current assets: goodwill arising on consolidation	20
Total assets	160

	$'000
Equity and liabilities	
Share capital (P Co only)	160
Total equity and liabilities	160

3.2 What is goodwill?

Goodwill is created by good relationships between a business and its customers. The goodwill inherent in a business will include intangibles such as a good reputation, a well known brand or a valuable customer list. IAS 38 *Intangible assets* prohibits the recognition of internally generated goodwill.

However, when goodwill arises on consolidation, as we have seen in the example above, IFRS 3 requires the goodwill to be recognised as an intangible asset in the consolidated financial statements.

IFRS 3 defines goodwill as 'an asset representing the future economic benefits arising from other assets acquired in a business combination that are not individually identified and separately recognised'.

3.3 Measurement and treatment of goodwill

Goodwill arising on consolidation is calculated in accordance with IFRS 3 as the difference between the **purchase consideration** and the **value** of the identifiable assets acquired and liabilities assumed.

As a result of this calculation, the goodwill can therefore be **positive** or **negative**.

Positive goodwill is recognised as an intangible non-current asset in the statement of financial position. After recognition, positive goodwill is measured **at the original amount less any accumulated impairment losses**. It is **not amortised**. Instead it is tested for impairment at least annually, in accordance with IAS 36 *Impairment of assets* (impairment of goodwill is discussed later in this chapter).

Negative goodwill acquired in a business combination in effect means that the buyer has got a '**bargain purchase**' as they have paid less for the entity that the fair value of its identifiable assets and liabilities. Negative goodwill could be thought of as a discount on the purchase price. As this is unusual, IFRS 3 requires that the purchaser checks to make sure that the acquired assets and liabilities are correctly identified and valued and that the goodwill calculation is correct. Negative goodwill should be **credited to profit or loss** in the year of acquisition.

3.4 Goodwill and pre-acquisition profits

Up to now we have assumed that S Co had no retained earnings when it was acquired and therefore we have not had to deal with any profits made by S Co before P Co took ownership of it. Assuming instead that S Co was purchased sometime after incorporation and had earned profits of $8,000 in the period before acquisition, its statement of financial position just before the purchase would look as follows.

S CO STATEMENT OF FINANCIAL POSITION	$
Total assets	48,000
Share capital	40,000
Retained earnings	8,000
	48,000

If P Co now purchases all the shares in S Co it will acquire total assets worth $48,000 at a cost of $60,000. Clearly in this case S Co's intangible assets (goodwill) are being valued at $12,000. Any earnings retained by the subsidiary **prior to its acquisition** by the parent company must be **incorporated**

in the cancellation process so as to arrive at a figure for goodwill arising on consolidation. In other words, not only S Co's share capital, but also its **pre-acquisition** retained earnings, must be cancelled against the asset 'investment in S Co' in the accounts of the parent company. The uncancelled balance of $12,000 appears in the consolidated statement of financial position as goodwill.

The consequence of this is that **any pre-acquisition retained earnings of a subsidiary company are not aggregated with the parent company's retained earnings** in the consolidated statement of financial position. The figure of consolidated retained earnings comprises the retained earnings of the parent company plus the **post-acquisition retained earnings only of subsidiary companies**. The post-acquisition retained earnings are simply retained earnings now *less* retained earnings at acquisition.

Other reserves, such as the **revaluation surplus**, are treated in the same way as retained earnings.

Exam alert

If you're confused by this, think of it another way, from the point of view of group reserves. Only the profits earned **by the group** should be consolidated. Profits earned by the subsidiary before it became part of the group are not group profits. They reflect what the parent company is getting for its money on acquisition.

Example: goodwill and pre-acquisition profits

Sing Co acquired the ordinary shares of Wing Co on 31 March 20X1 when the statements of financial position of each company were as follows.

STATEMENTS OF FINANCIAL POSITION AS AT 31 MARCH 20X1

	SING CO $	WING CO $
Assets		
Non-current assets		
Investment in 50,000 shares of Wing Co at cost	80,000	-
Current assets	40,000	60,000
Total assets	120,000	60,000
Equity and liabilities		
Equity		
Ordinary shares of $1 each	75,000	50,000
Retained earnings	45,000	10,000
Total equity and liabilities	120,000	60,000

Required

Prepare the consolidated statement of financial position as at 31 March 20X1.

Solution

The technique to adopt here is to produce a new working: 'Goodwill'. A proforma working is set out below.

Goodwill

	$	$
Consideration transferred		X
Less net assets acquired and liabilities assumed:		
Ordinary share capital	X	
Share premium	X	
Retained earnings at acquisition	X	
		(X)
Goodwill		X

Applying this to our example the working will look like this.

	$	$
Consideration transferred*		80,000
Less net value of identifiable assets acquired and liabilities assumed:		
Ordinary share capital	50,000	
Retained earnings at acquisition	10,000	
		(60,000)
Goodwill		20,000

*This is the cost of the investment in Sing Co's statement of financial position.

SING GROUP
CONSOLIDATED STATEMENT OF FINANCIAL POSITION AS AT 31 MARCH 20X1

	$
Assets	
Non-current assets	
Goodwill arising on consolidation (W)	20,000
Current assets (40,000 + 60,000)	100,000
	120,000
Equity	
Ordinary shares (Sing Co only)	75,000
Retained earnings*	45,000
	120,000

* Retained earnings of Sing Co plus *post-acquisition* retained earnings of Wing Co. At this point, ie the date of acquisition, all Wing Co's retained earnings are *pre-acquisition*.

Example: goodwill and pre-acquisition profits continued

Suppose that a year has passed and you now wish to prepare the consolidated statement of financial position for the Sing group as at 31 March 20X2. The individual statements of financial position are as follows.

STATEMENTS OF FINANCIAL POSITION AS AT 31 MARCH 20X2

	SING CO $	WING CO $
Assets		
Non-current assets		
Investment in 50,000 shares of Wing Co at cost	80,000	-
Current assets	50,000	80,000
Total assets	130,000	80,000
Equity and liabilities		
Equity		
Ordinary shares of $1 each	75,000	50,000
Retained earnings	55,000	30,000
Total equity and liabilities	130,000	80,000

Required

Prepare the consolidated statement of financial position as at 31 March 20X2.

Solution

We can see from the individual statements of financial position that Wing Co has generated profits of $20,000 since being controlled by Sing Co as the retained earnings balance has increased from $10,000 on acquisition to $30,000 at 31 March 20X2. These profits belong to the group and should be consolidated. The technique to adopt here is to produce a new working: *Retained earnings.* A proforma working is set out below.

Retained earnings

	P Co $	S Co $
Per question	X	X
Pre-acquisition retained earnings		(X)
		X
Post-acquisition retained earnings of S Co	X	
Group retained earnings	X	

Applying this to our example the working will look like this.

Retained earnings

	SING CO $	WING CO $
Per question	55,000	30,000
Pre-acquisition retained earnings		(10,000)
		20,000
Post-acq'n ret'd earnings of Wing Co	20,000	
Group retained earnings	75,000	

The goodwill calculation will be the same as before as it is based on the net assets of Wing Co at the **acquisition date**.

SING GROUP
CONSOLIDATED STATEMENT OF FINANCIAL POSITION AS AT 31 MARCH 20X2

	$
Assets	
Non-current assets	
Goodwill arising on consolidation	20,000
Current assets (50,000 + 80,000)	130,000
	150,000
Equity and liabilities	
Ordinary shares (Sing Co only)	75,000
Retained earnings (see working above)	75,000
	150,000

4 Non-controlling interest

In the scenarios we have looked at so far, the parent has owned 100% of the share capital of the subsidiary (ie the subsidiary is **wholly owned** by the parent). However, a parent may own **less than 100%** of the share capital of the subsidiary (ie the subsidiary is **partly-owned**) but still have **control** of it. A proportion of the net assets of such subsidiaries in fact belongs to investors from outside the group which we call the **non-controlling interest (NCI)**.

The consolidated financial statements show the extent to which assets and liabilities are **controlled** by the parent company. So where a subsidiary is partly-owned, the **total** assets and liabilities of the subsidiary are still consolidated, however, the part which is **not owned** by the group, ie the non-controlling interest, is then shown separately in the **equity section** of the consolidated statement of financial position.

IFRS 10 defines NON-CONTROLLING INTEREST as the equity in a subsidiary not attributable, directly or indirectly, to a parent.

KEY TERM

4.1 Measuring non-controlling interest

IFRS 3 allows two alternative ways of calculating non-controlling interest in the group statement of financial position. Non-controlling interest **at the acquisition date** can be valued at:

(a)   Its **proportionate share** of the subsidiary's net assets; or

(b)   **Fair value** (or **'full value'**) (usually based on the market value of the shares held by the non-controlling interest).

IFRS 3 (revised) suggests that the closest approximation to fair value will be the **market price of the shares** held by **non-controlling shareholders** at the **date of acquisition** by the parent.

It is entirely possible that the prices paid for the shares by the parent and NCI will be different, due to the parent paying a premium (**'control premium'**) to obtain control of the company.

IFRS 3 allows a parent to **choose** which method to use on a transaction by transaction basis.

NCI is shown in the equity section of the consolidated statement of financial position and is included in the consolidated financial statements at its **value at the acquisition date** (either at fair value *or* NCI's share of net assets) **plus the NCI's share of post-acquisition retained earnings and other reserves**:

Non-controlling interest at reporting date

	$
NCI at acquisition	X
Plus NCI's share of post-acquisition retained earnings (and other reserves)	X
NCI at reporting date	X

The existence of a non-controlling interest also has an impact on the calculation of group retained earnings as some of the retained earnings are owned by the NCI. Group retained earnings should only reflect the **group's share** of the post-acquisition retained earnings of the subsidiary. The working for group retained earnings working is amended as follows.

Retained earnings

	P Co $	S Co $
Per question	X	X
Pre-acquisition retained earnings		(X)
		Y
Group share of post-acquisition retained earnings:		
S Co (Y × %)	X	
Group retained earnings	X	

4.2 Goodwill and non-controlling interest

In the calculations of goodwill we have looked at so far, the parent company has acquired 100% of the shares in the subsidiary.

Where the parent acquires less than 100%, there is a non-controlling interest, but the **consolidated accounts show 100% of goodwill** even though the group does not 'own' all of it. This is consistent with the treatment of other assets and the concept of **control**. Because this is the case, we need to include NCI in our goodwill calculation.

The proforma calculation for goodwill will now look as follows.

	$	$
Goodwill		
Consideration transferred		X
Plus non-controlling interest at acquisition (either fair value or proportionate share of net assets)		X
Less net assets acquired and liabilities assumed:		
Ordinary share capital	X	
Share premium	X	
Retained earnings at acquisition	X	
		(X)
Goodwill		X

Example: effect of measurement of NCI on goodwill calculation

The example below shows the effect of the different methods of measuring NCI on the goodwill calculation.

P Co acquired 90% of S Co for $10,000,000 on 1 January 20X1. At the acquisition date the value of S Co's net assets was $8,000,000.

Calculate goodwill on the assumption that:

(a)   NCI is valued at the fair value at the date of acquisition which was $1,000,000.
(b)   NCI is valued at the proportionate share of net assets.

Solution

Exam skills

From now on the answers to questions will include a sketch of the group structure as shown below. It is recommended that you do this as a rough working when answering assessment questions as it helps to clarify the question – showing the percentage ownership and the date of acquisition. Although the date of acquisition seems an unnecessary addition at this point, it will become clear in the next chapter when we look at acquisitions part-way through the year.

$$P\ Co$$

$$1.1.X1 \qquad \downarrow \qquad 90\%$$

$$S\ Co$$

(a)   *Goodwill*

	$'000
Consideration transferred	10,000
Fair value of NCI at acquisition	1,000
	11,000
Less net assets acquired and liabilities assumed	(8,000)
Total goodwill	3,000

(b)   *Goodwill*

	$'000
Consideration transferred	10,000
NCI at acquisition (10% × $8,000,000)	800
	10,800
Less net assets acquired and liabilities assumed	(8,000)
Total goodwill	2,800

The difference between goodwill calculated using the fair value method and goodwill calculated using the proportionate share of net assets, ($3,000,000 – $2,800,000 = $200,000), is the goodwill attributable **to the NCI**. **Total goodwill** is recognised in the statement of financial position as the group controls 100% of it. We can also calculate goodwill attributable to the NCI as follows:

	$
Fair value of NCI	1,000
NCI in net assets at acquisition (10% × 8,000)	(800)
Goodwill	200

4.3 Effect of non-controlling interest at fair value

The example below shows the effect of measuring NCI at fair value.

Example: NCI at fair value

P Co purchased 75% of the share capital of S Co on 1 January 20X1 for $60,000 when the retained earnings of S Co were $5,000. P Co values non-controlling interest at fair value. The fair value of the non-controlling interest in S Co at that date was $15,000. The statements of financial position of P Co and S Co as at 31 December 20X1 are given below.

P CO
STATEMENT OF FINANCIAL POSITION

	P Co $	S Co $
Assets		
Non-current assets		
Property, plant and equipment	50,000	35,000
30,000 $1 ordinary shares in S Co at cost	60,000	-
	110,000	35,000
Current assets	45,000	40,000
Total assets	155,000	75,000
Equity and liabilities		
Equity		
$1 ordinary shares	80,000	40,000
Retained earnings	55,000	15,000
	135,000	55,000
Current liabilities	20,000	20,000
Total equity and liabilities	155,000	75,000

Required

Prepare the consolidated statement of financial position at 31 December 20X1.

Solution

All of S Co's net assets are consolidated despite the fact that the company is only 75% owned. NCI is included in the statement of financial position at its fair value plus its share of post-acquisition retained earnings.

P GROUP
CONSOLIDATED STATEMENT OF FINANCIAL POSITION

	$	$
Assets		
Non-current assets		
Property, plant and equipment (50,000 + 35,000)	85,000	
Goodwill (W2)	30,000	
		115,000
Current assets (45,000 + 40,000)		85,000
Total assets		200,000

	$	$
Equity and liabilities		
Equity attributable to owners of the parent		
Share capital (P Co only)	80,000	
Retained earnings (W3)	62,500	
		142,500
Non-controlling interest (W4)		**17,500**
Total equity		160,000
Current liabilities (20,000 + 20,000)		40,000
Total equity and liabilities		200,000

Workings

1 *Group structure*

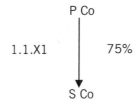

P Co

1.1.X1   75%

S Co

2 *Goodwill*

	$	$
Consideration transferred		60,000
Plus fair value of non-controlling interest at acquisition		15,000
Less net assets acquired and liabilities assumed:		
Ordinary share capital	40,000	
Retained earnings at acquisition	5,000	
		(45,000)
Goodwill		30,000

3 *Retained earnings*

	P Co $	S Co $
Per question	55,000	15,000
Pre-acquisition retained earnings		(5,000)
		10,000
Group share of post-acq ret'd earnings:		
S Co (75% × 10,000)	7,500	
Group retained earnings	62,500	

4 *Non-controlling interest at reporting date*

	$
Fair value of NCI at acquisition	15,000
Plus NCI's share of post-acquisition retained earnings (25% × 10,000)	2,500
NCI at reporting date	17,500

If non-controlling interest was valued instead at proportionate share of net assets, goodwill and non-controlling interest in the example above would be as follows:

5 *Goodwill*

	$
Considered transferred	60,000
Non-controlling interest at acquisition ((40,000 + 5,000) × 25%)	11,250
Net assets of S Co at acquisition (40,000 + 5,000)	(45,000)
	26,250

6   *Non-controlling interest at reporting date*

	$
NCI at acquisition	11,250
Share of post-acquisition retained earnings	2,500
	13,750

Compare these with goodwill and non-controlling interest in the solution above and you will see that both have been reduced by $3,750 – this is the goodwill attributable to the non-controlling interest. So whether non-controlling interest is valued at share of net assets or at fair value, the statement of financial position will still balance.

Question 14.3   Goodwill

Learning outcomes B3

On 31 December 20X8 Pandora Co acquired 4 million of the 5 million $1 ordinary shares of Sylvester Co, paying $10m cash. On that date the carrying value of Sylvester's net assets was $7.5m.

The market price of the shares held by the non-controlling shareholders just before the acquisition was $2.00. What is goodwill in the consolidated statement of financial position?

Section summary

The non-controlling interest (NCI) shows the extent to which net assets controlled by the group are owned by other parties.

5   Impairment of goodwill

Introduction

Goodwill must be tested for impairment annually in accordance with IAS 36 *Impairment of assets*.

Goodwill arising on consolidation is subjected to an annual **impairment review** and impairment may be expressed as an amount or as a percentage. When non-controlling interest is measured using the **proportionate method**, the double entry to write off the impairment is:

DEBIT	Group retained earnings	CREDIT	Goodwill

However, when non-controlling interest is valued **at fair value**, the goodwill in the statement of financial position includes goodwill attributable to the non-controlling interest. In this case the double entry will reflect the non-controlling interest proportion based on their shareholding as follows:

DEBIT	Group retained earnings	CREDIT	Goodwill
DEBIT	Non-controlling interest	CREDIT	Goodwill

Example

In our example above in section 4.3, the non-controlling interest holds 25%. If the total goodwill of $30,000 was impaired by 20% (so impairment is 20% × $30,000 = $6,000) the double entry for this would be:

		$			$
DEBIT	Retained earnings	4,500	CREDIT	Goodwill	6,000
DEBIT	Non-controlling interest	1,500			

The effect on the workings for goodwill, retained earnings and NCI would be as follows.

1   *Group structure*

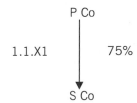

P Co

1.1.X1   75%

S Co

2   *Goodwill*

	$	$
Consideration transferred		60,000
Plus fair value of non-controlling interest at acquisition		15,000
Less net assets acquired and liabilities assumed:		
Ordinary share capital	40,000	
Retained earnings at acquisition	5,000	
		(45,000)
Goodwill at acquisition		30,000
Less impairment		(6,000)
Goodwill at reporting date		24,000

3   *Retained earnings*

	P Co	S Co
	$	$
Per question	55,000	15,000
Pre-acquisition retained earnings		(5,000)
		10,000
Group share of post-acq ret'd earnings:		
S Co (75% × 10,000)	7,500	
	62,500	
Less impairment of goodwill	(4,500)	
Group retained earnings	58,000	

4   *Non-controlling interest at reporting date*

	$
Fair value of NCI at acquisition	15,000
Plus NCI's share of post-acquisition retained earnings (25% x 10,000)	2,500
Less impairment of goodwill	(1,500)
NCI at reporting date	15,000

Section summary

When NCI is measured at the share of net assets, impairment of goodwill must be written off against retained earnings. When NCI is measured at fair value, the NCI's proportion of the impairment must be written off against the NCI balance in the SOFP to reflect the fact that goodwill includes goodwill attributable to the NCI.

Chapter Summary

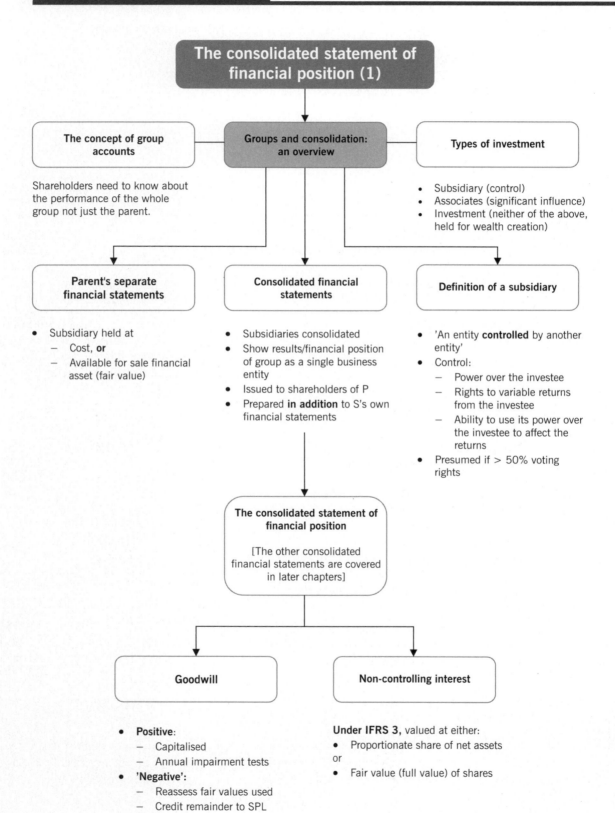

The consolidated statement of financial position (1)

The concept of group accounts

Shareholders need to know about the performance of the whole group not just the parent.

Groups and consolidation: an overview

Types of investment

- Subsidiary (control)
- Associates (significant influence)
- Investment (neither of the above, held for wealth creation)

Parent's separate financial statements

- Subsidiary held at
  - Cost, **or**
  - Available for sale financial asset (fair value)

Consolidated financial statements

- Subsidiaries consolidated
- Show results/financial position of group as a single business entity
- Issued to shareholders of P
- Prepared **in addition** to S's own financial statements

Definition of a subsidiary

- 'An entity **controlled** by another entity'
- Control:
  - Power over the investee
  - Rights to variable returns from the investee
  - Ability to use its power over the investee to affect the returns
- Presumed if > 50% voting rights

The consolidated statement of financial position

[The other consolidated financial statements are covered in later chapters]

Goodwill

- **Positive:**
  - Capitalised
  - Annual impairment tests
- **'Negative':**
  - Reassess fair values used
  - Credit remainder to SPL

Non-controlling interest

Under IFRS 3, valued at either:
- Proportionate share of net assets

or

- Fair value (full value) of shares

Quick Quiz

1   North acquired 100% of the ordinary shares in South on 1 July 20X3 at a cost of $300,000. South's retained earnings at 1 July 20X3 were $36,000, and its issued share capital was $200,000.

At the reporting date of 30 June 20X6, the retained earnings of South were $16,000.

What figure for goodwill should be included in the consolidated statement of financial position of the North Group at 30 June 20X6?

A $64,000
B $84,000
C $123,000
D $138,000

2   The summarised statements of financial position of Falcon and Kestrel at 31 December 20X8 were as follows:

	Falcon	Kestrel
	$m	$m
Net assets	68	25
Share capital	10	10
Reserves	58	20
	68	30

On 1 January 20X8 Falcon purchased 80% of the equity share capital of Kestrel for $28 million when the reserves of Kestrel were $20 million. The goodwill arising on consolidation was $3million.

What was the fair value of the non-controlling interest at the acquisition date?

3   How should trade investments be accounted for in the consolidated financial statements of the investor?

A   They should be consolidated on a line-by-line basis

B   They should be equity accounted for

C   A percentage of the investment's profits and assets and liabilities should be consolidated on a line-by-line basis

D   The amount paid for the investment at cost should be shown in the statement of financial position.

4   Select the correct options to complete the sentence

An investment is classified as a subsidiary if the **investor has [power/control/significant influence]** over an investee. A subsidiary must be included in the consolidated financial statements **[on a line-by-line basis showing 100% of assets and liabilities/on a line-by-line basis showing the investor's share of assets and liabilities/ as a single line item showing the investment and share of profits]**. The excess of consideration over the value of the net assets paid by the investor for the subsidiary is known as **[non-controlling interests/control premium/goodwill]**.

5   According to IFRS 10, which of the following **must** be true for a parent to be exempt from preparing consolidated accounts?

(a)   The ultimate or intermediate parent publishes consolidated financial statements that comply with local GAAP

(b)   The parent's equity shares are not publicly traded

(c)   The parent does not have more than one subsidiary

(d)   The parent only has subsidiaries in foreign countries and those subsidiaries do not report under IFRS

(e)   The parent's debt instruments are not publicly traded

(f)   The parent is a wholly-owned subsidiary or it is a partially owned subsidiary of another entity and its other owners do not object to the parent not presenting consolidated financial statements

(g)   The non-controlling interest arising on consolidation is immaterial

Answers to Quick Quiz

1   A   Goodwill is calculated at the date of acquisition and is only changed if there is an impairment of goodwill

Group structure

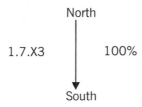

North

1.7.X3   100%

South

	$'000	$'000
Consideration transferred		300
Less net assets acquired:		
Ordinary share capital	200	
Retained earnings at acquisition	36	
		(236)
Goodwill		64

2   Group structure

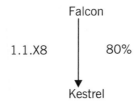

Falcon

1.1.X8   80%

Kestrel

	$	$
Goodwill		
Consideration transferred		28
Fair value of non-controlling interest at acquisition		X
Less net assets acquired and liabilities assumed:		
Ordinary share capital	10	
Retained earnings at acquisition	20	
		(30)
Goodwill		3

Therefore NCI = 3 + 30 − 28 = $5m

3   D   A trade investment is simply shown as an investment in the statement of financial position. The investor will only produce consolidated accounts if they also have subsidiaries.

4   An investment is classified as a subsidiary if the investor has **control** over an investee. A subsidiary must be included in the consolidated financial statements **on a line-by-line basis showing 100% of assets and liabilities**. The excess of consideration over the value of the net assets paid by the investor for the subsidiary is known as **goodwill**.

5   The correct answers are:

(b)   The parent's equity shares are not publicly traded

(e)   The parent's debt instruments are not publicly traded

(f)   The parent is a wholly-owned subsidiary or it is a partially owned subsidiary of another entity and its other owners do not object to the parent not presenting consolidated financial statements

See section 1. 8 for the full list of requirements for exemption from preparing group accounts.

BPP
LEARNING MEDIA

Answers to Questions

14.1

The correct answers are A and D.

Red Co is an **associate** of Smith Co as Smith Co has significant influence over Red Co.

Pink Co is a **subsidiary** of Smith Co as Smith Co's ability to appoint 4 out of 5 directors gives it **control** over Pink Co.

Yellow Co is a trade investment of Smith Co as Smith Co holds less than 20% of the voting rights of Yellow Co, so is assumed not to have significant influence. Note that the preference shares do not have voting rights so do not have any influence over the running of the company. Remember that shareholdings are not the only way of demonstrating control or significant influence. If it could be shown in another way that Smith Co does have significant influence over Yellow Co, Yellow Co would be classified as an associate.

Aquamarine Co is an **associate** of Smith co as Smith Co holds more than 20% of the voting rights of Aquamarine Co and is therefore presumed to have significant influence over Aquamarine Co.

14.2 Basic consolidation

P GROUP CONSOLIDATED STATEMENT OF FINANCIAL POSITION AS AT 30 JUNE

	$	$
Assets		
Non-current assets		
Property, plant and equipment (120,000 + 100,000)		220,000
Current assets		
Inventories (50,000 + 60,000)	110,000	
Goods in transit (18,000 – 12,000)	6,000	
Receivables (40,000 + 30,000)	70,000	
Cash (4,000 + 6,000)	10,000	
		196,000
Total assets		416,000
Equity and liabilities		
Equity		
Ordinary shares of $1 each, fully paid (parent)	100,000	
Retained earnings (95,000 + 28,000)	123,000	
		223,000
Non-current liabilities		
10% loan stock	75,000	
12% loan stock (50,000 × 60%)	30,000	
		105,000
Current liabilities		
Payables (47,000 + 16,000)	63,000	
Taxation (15,000 + 10,000)	25,000	
		88,000
Total equity and liabilities		416,000

Note especially how:

(a)   The uncancelled loan stock in S Co becomes a liability of the group
(b)   The goods in transit is the difference between the current accounts ($18,000 – $12,000)
(c)   The investment in S Co's shares is cancelled against S Co's share capital

---

14.3 Goodwill

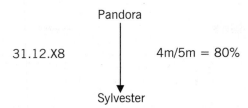

Pandora

31.12.X8   4m/5m = 80%

Sylvester

	$'000
Fair value of consideration transferred	10,000
Fair value of NCI ($2 × 1m)	2,000
	12,000
Less net assets acquired and liabilities assumed	(7,500)
Goodwill	4,500

Now try these questions from the OTQ Question Bank	Number
	Q35
	Q36

THE CONSOLIDATED STATEMENT OF FINANCIAL POSITION II

This chapter continues to look at the consolidated statement of financial position, adding some further complications such as when the acquisition takes place part-way through the year and intra-group trading.

Topic list	learning outcomes	syllabus references
1 Acquisition of a subsidiary part way through the year	B3	B3 (c)
2 Intra-group trading	B3	B3 (c)
3 Intra-group sales of non-current assets	B3	B3 (c)

Chapter Overview

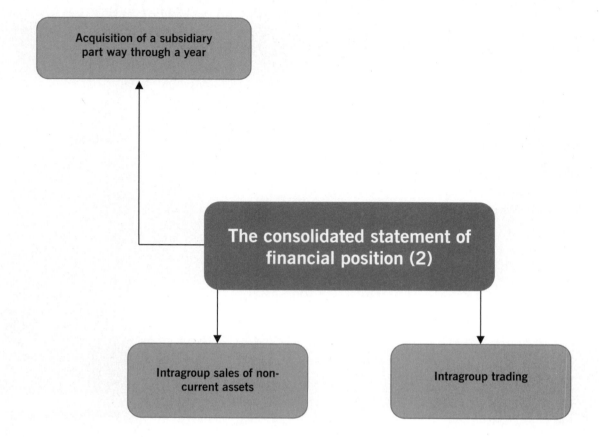

1   Acquisition of a subsidiary part way through the year

Introduction

In the examples we have looked at in the previous chapter, the subsidiary was conveniently purchased on the first or last day of the accounting period. However, in practice this will probably not be the case.

This section considers the effect on consolidation when a subsidiary is purchased part way through the year.

If a parent purchases a subsidiary company during the year, as we have already seen, at the end of the accounting year it will be necessary to prepare consolidated accounts.

The subsidiary's accounts to be consolidated will show the subsidiary's profit or loss for the whole year. For consolidation purposes, however, it will be necessary to distinguish between:

(a)   Profits earned before acquisition – so that we can calculate goodwill

(b)   Profits earned after acquisition – so that we can calculate group retained earnings

To do this, we usually assume that the subsidiary's **profits accrue evenly** over the year. Then we can take the profit for the year and calculate the pre-and post-acquisition profits based on the number of months the parent has owned the subsidiary.

Question 15.1	Acquisition during the year

Learning outcome B3

Hinge Co acquired 80% of the ordinary shares of Singe Co on 1 April 20X5. On 31 December 20X4 Singe Co's accounts showed a revaluation surplus of $4,000 and retained earnings of $15,000. The fair value of the non-controlling interest at acquisition was $7,000. The statements of financial position of the two companies at 31 December 20X5 are set out below.

HINGE CO
STATEMENT OF FINANCIAL POSITION AS AT 31 DECEMBER 20X5

	$	$
Assets		
Non-current assets		
Property, plant and equipment	32,000	
16,000 ordinary shares of 50c each in Singe Co	50,000	
		82,000
Current assets		85,000
Total assets		167,000
Equity and liabilities		
Equity		
Ordinary shares of $1 each	100,000	
Revaluation surplus	7,000	
Retained earnings	40,000	
		147,000
Current liabilities		20,000
Total equity and liabilities		167,000

SINGE CO
STATEMENT OF FINANCIAL POSITION AS AT 31 DECEMBER 20X5

	$	$
Assets		
Property, plant and equipment		30,000
Current assets		43,000
Total assets		73,000
Equity and liabilities		
Equity		
20,000 ordinary shares of 50c each	10,000	
Revaluation surplus	4,000	
Retained earnings	39,000	
		53,000
Current liabilities		20,000
Total equity and liabilities		73,000

Required

Prepare the consolidated statement of financial position of Hinge Co at 31 December 20X5. You should assume that profits have accrued evenly over the year to 31 December 20X5.

Section summary

When a parent acquires a subsidiary part way through the year, the profits for the period need to be apportioned between pre- and post-acquisition. Only post-acquisition profits are included in the group's consolidated statement of financial position.

2 Intra-group trading

Introduction

The consolidated financial statements present the accounts of the parent and subsidiary as a single entity. Therefore the effects of any trading that has happened between the two entities must be eliminated. This section covers how to deal with this situation in a consolidation question.

2.1 Unrealised profit

Any receivable/payable balances outstanding between the companies are cancelled on consolidation. No further problem arises if all such intra-group transactions are **undertaken at cost**, without any mark-up for profit.

However, each company in a group is a separate trading entity and may wish to treat other group companies in the same way as any other customer. In this case, a company (say A Co) may buy goods at one price and sell them at a higher price to another group company (B Co). The accounts of A Co will quite properly include the profit earned on sales to B Co; and similarly B Co's statement of financial position will include inventories at their cost to B Co, ie at the amount at which they were purchased from A Co.

This gives rise to two problems.

(a)   Although A Co makes a profit as soon as it sells goods to B Co, the group does not make a sale or achieve a profit until an outside customer buys the goods from B Co.

(b)   Any purchases from A Co which remain unsold by B Co at the year end will be included in B Co's inventory. Their value in the statement of financial position will be their cost to B Co, which is not the same as their cost to the group.

The objective of consolidated accounts is to present the financial position of several connected companies as that of a single entity, the group. This means that **in a consolidated statement of financial position the only profits recognised should be those earned by the group in providing goods or services to outsiders**. Similarly, inventory in the consolidated statement of financial position should be valued at cost to the group.

Suppose that a holding company P Co buys goods for $1,600 and sells them to its subsidiary S Co for $2,000. The goods are in S Co's inventory at the year end and appear in S Co's statement of financial position at $2,000. In this case, P Co will record a profit of $400 in its individual accounts, but from the group's point of view the figures are:

Cost	$1,600
External sales	NIL
Closing inventory at cost	$1,600
Profit/loss	NIL

If we add together the figures for retained earnings and inventory in the individual statements of financial position of P Co and S Co the resulting figures for consolidated retained earnings and consolidated inventory will each be overstated by $400. A **consolidation adjustment** is therefore necessary as follows.

DEBIT   Group retained earnings
CREDIT   Group inventory (statement of financial position)

with the amount of **profit unrealised** by the group. We call this the '**provision for unrealised profit**' or PUP, as it is a provision against inventory for the unrealised profit generated by the intra-group sale.

Exam skills

You might have to calculate the unrealised profit given either a gross profit margin or a mark-up on cost. Remember that:

- **Mark-up** is the profit as a percentage of **cost**
- **Gross profit margin** is the profit as a percentage of **sales**

2.2 Non-controlling interests in unrealised intra-group profits

A further problem occurs where a subsidiary company which is **not wholly owned is involved in intra-group trading** within the group. If a subsidiary S Co is 75% owned and sells goods to the parent company for $16,000 cost plus $4,000 profit, ie for $20,000 and if these items are unsold by P Co at the end of the reporting period, the 'unrealised' profit of $4,000 earned by S Co and charged to P Co will be partly owned by the non-controlling interest of S Co.

The correct treatment of these intragroup profits is to remove the whole profit, charging the non-controlling interest with their proportion.

DEBIT   Group retained earnings
DEBIT   Non-controlling interest
CREDIT   Group inventory (statement of financial position)

The credit is made on the face of the group statement of financial position and the debit to the **appropriate column** of the retained earnings working. This will then split the unrealised profit between the group and the NCI if the subsidiary made the sale.

If the sale was made by the parent, there is no effect on the NCI.

The retained earnings working will look as follows.

If S Co makes the sale:

	P Co $	S Co $
Per question	X	X
Less unrealised profit		(X)
Pre-acquisition retained earnings		(X)
		Y
Group share of post-acquisition retained earnings:		
S Co (Y × %)	X	
Group retained earnings	X	

If P Co makes the sale:

	P Co $	S Co $
Per question	X	X
Less unrealised profit	(X)	
Pre-acquisition retained earnings		(X)
	—	Y
Group share of post-acquisition retained earnings:		
S Co (Y × %)	X	
Group retained earnings	X	

Example: non-controlling interests and intra-group profits (1)

P Co has owned 75% of the shares of S Co since the incorporation of that company. During the year to 31 December 20X2, S Co sold goods costing $16,000 to P Co at a price of $20,000 and these goods were still unsold by P Co at the end of the year. Draft statements of financial position of each company at 31 December 20X2 were as follows.

	P Co $	P Co $	S Co $	S Co $
Assets				
Non-current assets				
Property, plant and equipment	125,000		120,000	
Investment: 75,000 shares in S Co at cost	75,000		–	
		200,000		120,000
Current assets				
Inventories	50,000		48,000	
Trade receivables	20,000		16,000	
		70,000		64,000
Total assets		270,000		184,000
Equity and liabilities				
Equity				
Ordinary shares of $1 each fully paid	80,000		100,000	
Retained earnings	150,000		60,000	
		230,000		160,000
Current liabilities		40,000		24,000
Total equity and liabilities		270,000		184,000

Required

Prepare the consolidated statement of financial position of P Co at 31 December 20X2. It is the group policy to value the non-controlling interest at acquisition at its proportionate share of the subsidiary's net assets.

Solution

P CO

CONSOLIDATED STATEMENT OF FINANCIAL POSITION AS AT 31 DECEMBER 20X2

	$	$
Assets		
Property, plant and equipment (125,000 + 120,000)		245,000
Current assets		
Inventories (50,000 + 48,000 – 4,000 unrealised profit)	94,000	
Trade receivables (20,000 + 16,000)	36,000	
		130,000
Total assets		375,000
Equity and liabilities		
Equity		
Ordinary shares of $1 each	80,000	
Retained earnings (W2)	192,000	
		272,000
Non-controlling interest (W3)		39,000
		311,000
Current liabilities		64,000
Total equity and liabilities		375,000

Workings

1   *Group structure*

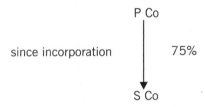

P Co

since incorporation   75%

S Co

2   *Retained earnings*

	P Co	S Co
	$	$
Per question	150,000	60,000
Less unrealised profit (20,000 – 16,000)		(4,000)
Pre-acquisition		–
		56,000
Share of S Co: $56,000 × 75%	42,000	
	192,000	

3   *Non-controlling interest*

	$
NCI at acquisition (25% × 100,000)	25,000
NCI share of post acquisition retained earnings (25% × 56,000)	14,000
	39,000

Note: No goodwill working is necessary as the acquisition was at the date of incorporation. The profit earned by S Co but unrealised by the group is $4,000 of which $3,000 (75%) is attributable to the group and $1,000 (25%) to the non-controlling interest. Remove the whole of the profit charging the non-controlling interest with their proportion. This is done by making the adjustment to profit in S's column in the retained earnings working.

Example: non-controlling interests and intra-group profits (2)

Explain how the answer to the above example would change if the facts remained the same except that the goods were sold by P Co to S Co.

Solution

Note: As above, no goodwill working is necessary as the acquisition was at the date of incorporation. The full unrealised profit is always deducted from group inventories but this time, as P made the sale, the debit is made against P Co's retained earnings $4,000. The full amount is charged to consolidated retained earnings and none to the non-controlling interest.

	P Co $	S Co $
Retained earnings		
Per question	150,000	60,000
Less unrealised profit	(4,000)	
Pre-acquisition		-
		60,000
Share of S Co: $60,000 × 75%	45,000	
	191,000	
Non-controlling interest		
NCI at acquisition (25% × 100,000)		25,000
NCI share of post acquisition retained earnings (25% × 60,000)		15,000
		40,000

Question 15.2   Unrealised profit

Learning outcomes B3

P Co acquired 75% of the shares in S Co on 1 January 20X2 when the retained earnings of S Co stood at $10,000. The fair value of the non-controlling interest at the date of acquisition was $15,000. During the year to 31 December 20X2, S Co sold goods to P Co for $20,000 at a mark-up of 25%. 50% of these goods were still unsold by P Co at the end of the year. At the same date, P Co owed S Co $12,000 for goods bought and this debt is included in the trade payables of P Co and the trade receivables of S Co.

Draft statements of financial position of each company at 31 December 20X2 were as follows.

	P Co $	$	S Co $	$
Assets				
Non-current assets				
Tangible assets	80,000			40,000
Investment in S Co at cost	46,000			
		126,000		
Current assets				
Trade receivables	30,000		25,000	
Inventories	10,000		5,000	
		40,000		30,000
Total assets		166,000		70,000

	P Co		S Co	
	$	$	$	$
Equity and liabilities				
Equity				
Ordinary shares of $1 each	100,000		30,000	
Retained earnings	45,000		22,000	
		145,000		52,000
Current liabilities				
Trade payables		21,000		18,000
Total equity and liabilities		166,000		70,000

Required

Prepare a draft consolidated statement of financial position for P Co.

Section summary

- In a consolidated statement of financial position, the only profits recognised should be those **earned by the group** in providing goods or services to outsiders.

- Inventory in the consolidated statement of financial position should be valued at **cost to the group**.

Unrealised profit must be removed from the consolidated financial statement of financial position and charged against the retained earnings of the company that **made the sale**.

3   Intra-group sales of non-current assets

Introduction

As well as engaging in trading activities with each other, group companies may on occasion wish to **transfer non-current assets**. In this section we will look at how this affects the consolidation process.

3.1 Accounting treatment

In their individual accounts the companies concerned will treat the transfer just like a sale between unconnected parties: the selling company will record a profit or loss on sale, while the purchasing company will record the asset at the amount paid to acquire it, and will use that amount as the basis for calculating depreciation.

On consolidation, the usual **'group entity' principle applies**. The consolidated statement of financial position must show assets at their cost to the group, and any depreciation charged must be based on that cost. Two consolidation adjustments will usually be needed to achieve this.

(a)   An adjustment to alter retained earnings and non-current assets cost so as to remove any element of unrealised profit or loss. This is similar to the adjustment required in respect of unrealised profit in inventory.

(b)   An adjustment to alter retained earnings and accumulated depreciation is made so that consolidated depreciation is based on the asset's cost to the group.

In practice, these steps are combined so that the retained earnings of the entity making the unrealised profit are debited with the unrealised profit less the additional depreciation.

The double entry is as follows.

(a)   Sale by parent

DEBIT	Group retained earnings
CREDIT	Non-current assets

with the profit on disposal, less the additional depreciation.

(b)   Sale by subsidiary

DEBIT	Group retained earnings (P's share of S)
DEBIT	Non-controlling interest (NCI's share of S)
CREDIT	Non-current assets

with the profit on disposal, less additional depreciation

Example: intra-group sales of non-current assets

P Co acquired 60% of S Co on incorporation. On 1 January 20X1 S Co sells plant with a carrying value of $10,000 to P Co for $12,500. The companies make up accounts to 31 December 20X1 and the balances on their retained earnings at that date are:

P Co	after charging depreciation of 10% on plant	$27,000
S Co	including profit on sale of plant	$18,000

Required

Show the working for consolidated retained earnings.

Solution

Retained earnings

	P Co $	S Co $
Per question	27,000	18,000
Unrealised profit on sale of plant (W2)		(2,250)
Pre-acquisition		-
		15,750
Share of S Co: $15,750 × 60%	9,450	
	36,450	

Workings

1   *Group structure*

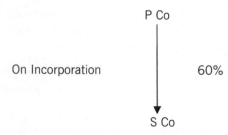

2   *Unrealised profit*

	$
Unrealised profit on transfer ($12,500 – $10,000)	2,500
Less: proportion depreciated by year end ($250/10 years)	(250)
	2,250

Notes

1   The non-controlling interest in the retained earnings of S Co is 40% × $15,750 = $6,300.

2   The asset is written down to cost and depreciation on the 'profit' element is removed. The group profit for the year is thus reduced by a net (($2,250) × 60%) = $1,350.

3   As shown above, the adjustment to retained earnings is made in the company that made the sale.

Section summary

The consolidated statement of financial position must show **non-current assets** at their **cost to the group** and any depreciation charged must be based on that cost.

Chapter Summary

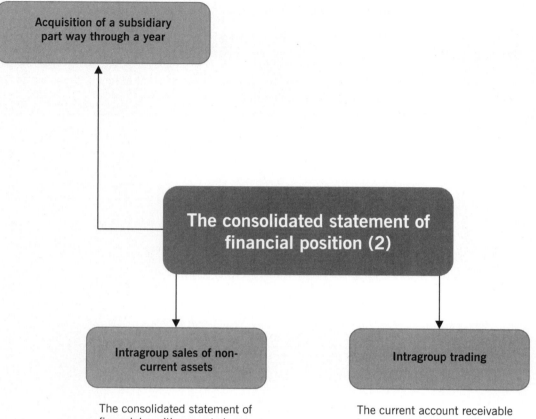

Acquisition of a subsidiary part way through a year

The consolidated statement of financial position (2)

Intragroup sales of non-current assets

The consolidated statement of financial position must show non-current assets at their **cost to the group** and depreciation charged must be based on that cost.

Any profit on sale within the group is unrealised and must be eliminated.

Intragroup trading

The current account receivable in one company's books should equal the current account payable in the other.

These two balances should be cancelled on consolidation as intragroup receivables and payables should not be shown.

Inventories sold within the group at a profit

In substance, the seller as made profit from selling goods to itself (as the goods are still in inventory at the year-end). This unrealised profit must be eliminated

Inventories should be **valued at the lower of cost and NRV to the group**.

Quick Quiz

1   Pretty Co owns 80% of Ugly Co. Ugly Co sells goods to Pretty Co at cost plus 50%. The total invoiced sales to Pretty Co by Ugly Co in the year ended 31 December 20X9 were $120,000 and, of these sales, 50% were held in inventory by Pretty Co at 31 December 20X9.

    What is the provision for unrealised profit?

2   Chicken Co owns 90% of Egg Co. Egg Co sells goods to Chicken Co at cost plus 50%. The total invoiced sales to Chicken Co by Egg Co in the year ended 31 December 20X9 were $900,000 and, of these sales, goods which had been invoiced at $60,000 were held in inventory by Chicken Co at 31 December 20X9.

    What is the provision for unrealised profit? How much of this would be borne by Chicken Co and how much by the NCI?

3   Major Co, which makes up its accounts to 31 December, has an 80% owned subsidiary Minor Co. Major Co sells goods to Minor Co at a margin of 30%. On consolidation at 31 December 20X8, the reduction in group retained earnings related to these goods is $3,600.

    What is the value of the goods purchased from Major Co included in the individual financial statements of Minor Co at 31 December 20X8?

4   Challis Co owns 60% of Glass Co. In the year ended 31 March 20X3, Glass Co sold goods with a cost price of $600,000 to Challis Co at a margin of 40%. Of these goods, 30% were held in inventory by Challis Co at 31 March 20X3. At the same date, the inventory balances in the individual accounts of Challis Co and Glass Co were $1,200,000 and $756,000 respectively.

    What amount for inventory should be included in the consolidated statement of financial position of Challis Co at 31 March 20X3?

    A $1,836,000
    B $120,000
    C $1,956,000
    D $2,076,000

5   Complete the paragraph below by selecting the correct option in each case.

    When part of the consideration paid for a subsidiary is contingent on future events, the **[fair value /the discounted present value]** of that consideration at the acquisition date should be **[excluded from/added to/subtracted from]** the total consideration paid in the calculation of **[non-controlling interests/retained earnings/goodwill]**.

Answers to Quick Quiz

1

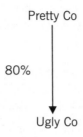

Pretty Co

80%

Ugly Co

Provision for unrealised profit

		$
Sale price	150%	120,000
Cost price	100%	(80,000)
Gross profit	50%	40,000
Unrealised profit (40,000 × 50%)		20,000

2

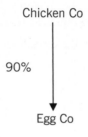

Chicken Co

90%

Egg Co

Unrealised profit: $60,000 × $\dfrac{50}{150}$ = $20,000

The unrealised profit of $ 20,000 would be deducted from the retained earnings of Egg Co at the year end (in the retained earnings working).

This means the amount borne by Chicken Co is 90% × $20,000 = $18,000

3   As the sale is from the parent to the subsidiary, the whole provision for unrealised profit is attributable to the group. Therefore the reduction in group retained earnings is equal to the provision for unrealised profit which is $3,600.

Major Co

80%

Minor Co

Provision for unrealised profit

		$
Sale price	100%	12,000
Cost price	70%	(8,400)
Gross profit	30%	3,600

Sale price = inventory in Minor Co at year end = $12,000

4   A

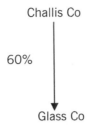

Challis Co

60%

Glass Co

Provision for unrealised profit

		$
Sale price	100%	1,000,000
Cost price	60%	(600,000)
Gross profit	40%	400,000
Unrealised profit (400,000 × 30%)		120,000
Group inventory (1,200,000 + 756,000 − 120,000)		1,836,000

5   When part of the consideration paid for a subsidiary is contingent on future events, the **fair value** of that consideration at the acquisition date should be **added to** the total consideration paid in the calculation of **goodwill**.

 Answers to Questions

15.1   Singe Co has made a profit of $24,000 ($39,000 − $15,000) for the year. This is assumed to have arisen evenly over the year; $6,000 in the three months to 31 March and $18,000 in the nine months after acquisition. The company's pre-acquisition retained earnings are therefore as follows.

	$
Balance at 31 December 20X4	15,000
Profit for three months to 31 March 20X5 ($^3/_{12} \times 24,000$)	6,000
Pre-acquisition retained earnings	21,000

The balance of $4,000 on the **revaluation surplus** is all pre-acquisition.

HINGE CO
CONSOLIDATED STATEMENT OF FINANCIAL POSITION AS AT 31 DECEMBER 20X5

	$	$
Assets		
Non–current assets		
Property, plant and equipment (32,000 + 30,000)	62,000	
Goodwill (W2)	22,000	
		84,000
Current assets (85,000 + 43,000)		128,000
Total assets		212,000

	$	$
Equity and liabilities		
Equity attributable to owners of the parent		
Ordinary shares of $1 each	100,000	
Revaluation surplus (W4)	7,000	
Retained earnings (W3)	54,400	
		161,400
Non-controlling interest (W5)		10,600
Total equity		172,000
Current liabilities (20,000 + 20,000)		40,000
Total equity and liabilities		212,000

Workings

1   *Group structure*

```
                        Hinge
                          |
        1.4.X5            |       80%
                          |
                          v
                        Singe
```

2   *Goodwill*

	$	$
Consideration transferred		50,000
Fair value of non-controlling interest		7,000
Less net assets acquired and liabilities assumed:		
Ordinary share capital	10,000	
Retained earnings at acquisition (as above)	21,000	
Revaluation surplus	4,000	
		(35,000)
Goodwill		22,000

3   *Retained earnings*

	Hinge Co $	Singe Co $
Per question	40,000	39,000
Pre-acquisition retained earnings (W2)		(21,000)
		18,000
Group share of post-acq'n ret'd earnings		
Singe Co: $18,000 × 80%	14,400	
	54,400	

4   *Revaluation surplus*

	$
Hinge Co	7,000
Group share of post-acq'n revaluation surplus: Singe Co	–
	7,000

5   *Non-controlling interest at reporting date*

	$
Fair value of NCI at acquisition date	7,000
NCI share of post-acquisition retained earnings (20% x 18,000)	3,600
NCI	10,600

15.2 Unrealised profit

P CO
CONSOLIDATED STATEMENT OF FINANCIAL POSITION AS AT 31 DECEMBER 20X2

	$	$
Assets		
Non-current assets		
Tangible assets (80,000 + 40,000)		120,000
Goodwill (W2)		21,000
Current assets		
Trade receivables (30,000 + 25,000 – 12,000)	43,000	
Inventories (10,000 + 5,000 – 2,000(W5))	13,000	
		56,000
Total assets		197,000
Equity and liabilities		
Equity attributable to owners of the parent		
Ordinary shares of $1 each	100,000	
Retained earnings (W3)	52,500	
		152,500
Non-controlling interest (W4)		17,500
		170,000
Current liabilities (21,000 + 18,000 – 12,000)		27,000
Total equity and liabilities		197,000

Workings

1   *Group structure*

P Co

1.1.X2   75%

S Co

2   *Goodwill*

	$	$
Consideration transferred		46,000
Plus fair value of NCI at acquisition		15,000
Less net assets acquired and liabilities assumed:		
Share capital	30,000	
Retained earnings	10,000	
		40,000
Goodwill		21,000

3   *Retained earnings*

	P Co $	S Co $
Per question	45,000	22,000
Adjustments (unrealised profit attributable to P (W5))		(2,000)
Pre-acquisition retained earnings		(10,000)
		10,000
Group share of post-acq'n ret'd earnings:		
S Co (75% × 12,000)	7,500	
Group retained earnings	52,500	

4   *Non-controlling interest at reporting date*

	$
Fair value of NCI at acquisition	15,000
Plus NCI's share of post-acquisition retained earnings (25% × 10,000)	2,500
Less unrealised profit attributable to NCI (W5)	(500)
NCI at reporting date	17,500

5   *Provision for unrealised profit*

		$
Sale price	125%	20,000
Cost price	100%	(16,000)
Gross profit	25%	4,000
Unrealised profit (4,000 × 50%)		2,000

Now try these questions from the OTQ Question Bank

Number
Q37
Q38
Q51
Q58

THE CONSOLIDATED STATEMENT OF PROFIT OR LOSS AND OTHER COMPREHENSIVE INCOME

This chapter introduces the basic procedures required to produce a consolidated statement comprehensive income.

We begin by looking at a basic consolidated statement of profit or loss, including the impact of a non-controlling interest. We then move on to look at the effects of intra-group trading and acquisitions of subsidiaries part way through the year.

Finally, we look at the consolidated statement of profit or loss and other comprehensive income, which includes revaluations of property, plant and equipment within the group.

There are plenty of questions and examples in this chapter - work through *all* of them carefully.

Topic list	learning outcomes	syllabus references
1 The consolidated statement of profit or loss	B3	B3 (c)
2 Acquisitions part way through the year	B3	B3 (c)
3 The consolidated statement of profit or loss and other comprehensive income	B3	B3 (c)

Chapter Overview

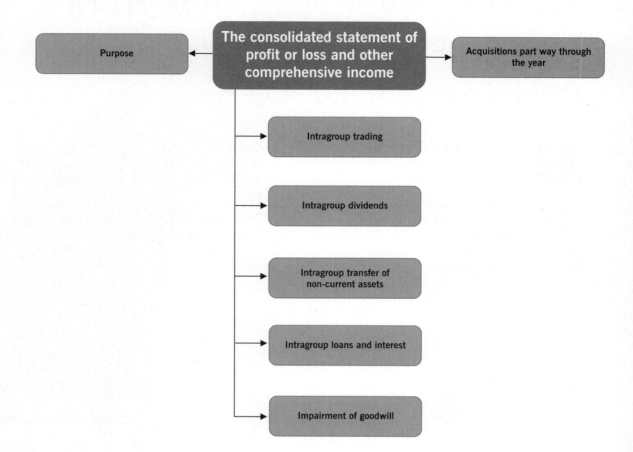

1 The consolidated statement of profit or loss

Introduction

In the previous chapters you studied how to prepare the consolidated statement of financial position. Now you will learn how to apply those techniques to prepare a consolidated statement of profit or loss. The aim of the consolidated statement of profit or loss is to show the results of the group for an accounting period as if it were a **single entity**. Exactly the same philosophy is adopted as for the statement of financial position, ie that of **control**. Accordingly, the consolidated statement of profit or loss shows the profits resulting from the control exercised by the parent entity.

1.1 Consolidation procedure

The consolidated statement of profit or loss must show the profit or loss **controlled** by the group. It must also identify the **ownership** of the profit, splitting it into the portions owned by the parent and the non-controlling interest.

As with the consolidated statement of financial position, the source of the consolidated statement of profit or loss is the individual accounts of the separate companies in the group.

Consider the following example.

Example

P Co acquired 75% of the ordinary shares of S Co on that company's incorporation in 1 January 20X3. The summarised statements of profit or loss of the two companies for the year ending 31 December 20X6 are set out below.

	P Co $	S Co $
Revenue	75,000	38,000
Cost of sales	(30,000)	(20,000)
Gross profit	45,000	18,000
Distribution and administrative expenses	(14,000)	(8,000)
Profit before tax	31,000	10,000
Income tax expense	(10,000)	(2,000)
Profit for the year	21,000	8,000

Required

Prepare the consolidated statement of profit or loss for the year ending 31 December 20X6.

Solution

P CO
CONSOLIDATED STATEMENT OF PROFIT OR LOSS FOR THE YEAR ENDED 31 DECEMBER 20X6

	$
Sales revenue ($75,000 + $38,000)	113,000
Cost of sales ($30,000 + $20,000)	(50,000)
Gross profit	63,000
Administrative expenses ($14,000 + $8,000)	(22,000)
Profit before tax	41,000
Income tax expense ($10,000 + $2,000)	(12,000)
Profit for the year	29,000
Profit attributable to:	
Owners of the parent (balancing figure)	27,000
Non-controlling interest (W2)	2,000
	29,000

Workings

1   *Group structure*

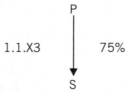

2   *Non-controlling interests*

	$
Profit for the year - per question	8,000
NCI share	× 25%
	= 2,000

Notice how the non-controlling interest is dealt with.

(a)   Down to the line **'Profit for the year,'** the **whole** of S Co's results is included without reference to group share or non-controlling share. A **reconciliation** is then inserted to show the ownership of the profits.

(b)   Complete the reconciliation in this order:

(i)   Fill in the total profit for the year
(ii)   Calculate the NCI share of profit (NCI % × Subsidiary's profit for the year)
(iii) Deduce the amount attributable to the members of the parent as a balancing figure

---

Question 16.1	Consolidated statement of profit or loss

Learning outcome B3

The following information relates to the Wheeler group for the year to 30 April 20X7.

	Wheeler Co $'000	Brookes Co $'000
Revenue	1,100	500
Cost of sales	630	300
Gross profit	470	200
Administrative expenses	105	150
Profit before tax	365	50
Income taxes	65	10
Profit for the year	300	40

Additional information

(a)   Wheeler Co purchased 80% of the issued share capital of Brookes Co in 20X0. At that time, the retained earnings of Brookes amounted to $56,000.

Required

Prepare the consolidated statement of profit or loss and the movement on retained earnings for the Wheeler group for the year to 30 April 20X7.

1.2 Intra-group trading

Like the consolidated statement of financial position, the consolidated statement of profit or loss should deal with the results of the group as those of a single entity. When one company in a group sells goods to another an identical amount is added to the sales revenue of the first company and to the cost of sales of

the second. Yet as far as the group's dealings with outsiders are concerned no sale has taken place. Therefore intra-group sales and purchases are eliminated from the consolidated statement of profit or loss.

The consolidated figures for sales revenue and cost of sales should represent **sales to**, and **purchases from, outsiders**. An adjustment is therefore necessary to **reduce the sales revenue and cost of sales figures by the value of intra-group sales during the year**.

We have also seen in an earlier chapter that any unrealised profits on intra-group trading should be excluded from the figure for group retained earnings. This will occur whenever goods sold at a profit within the group remain in the inventory of the purchasing company at the year end. The best way to deal with this is to **calculate the unrealised profit on unsold inventories at the year end and reduce consolidated gross profit by this amount**. Cost of sales will be the balancing figure.

Example: intra-group trading

Suppose in our earlier example that S Co had recorded sales of $5,000 to P Co during 20X6. S Co had purchased these goods from outside suppliers at a cost of $3,000. One half of the goods remained in P Co's inventory at 31 December 20X6. Prepare the revised consolidated statement of profit or loss.

Solution

The consolidated statement of profit or loss for the year ended 31 December 20X6 would now be as follows.

	$
Sales revenue ($75,000 + $38,000 − $5,000 (W3))	108,000
Cost of sales ($30,000 + $20,000 − $5,000 + $1,000(W3))	(46,000)
Gross profit	62,000
Administrative expenses	(22,000)
Profit before taxation	40,000
Income tax expense	(12,000)
Profit for the year	28,000
Profit attributable to:	
Owners of the parent	26,250
Non-controlling interest (W2)	1,750
	28,000

Workings

1   *Group structure*

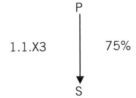

P

1.1.X3   75%

S

2   *Non-controlling interests*

	$
Profit for the year - per question	8,000
Provision for unrealised profit (PUP)	(1,000)
	7,000
NCI share	× 25%
	= 1,750

3   *Intra-group trading*

S → P

- Intra –group revenue and cost of sales:
  Cancel $5,000 out of revenue and cost of sales

- PUP = ½ in inventories × ($5,000 − $3,000) mark up = $1,000
  Increase cost of sales by $1,000 and reduce profit for the year in non-controlling interest working (as subsidiary is the seller)

Note. In this example, the unrealised profit arose on sales made by the subsidiary. This means that it has to be eliminated from the subsidiary's profit before the non-controlling interest is calculated.

Question 16.2 Intra-group trading I

Learning outcome B3

Pumpkin has held 90% of the equity share capital of Squash for many years. Cost of sales for each entity for the year ended 31 December 20X3 was as follows:

	$
Pumpkin	100,000
Squash	80,000

During the year, Squash sold goods costing $5,000 to Pumpkin for $8,000. At the year end, all these goods remained in inventory.

(a) What figure should be shown as cost of sales in the consolidated statement of profit or loss of the Pumpkin group for the year ended 31 December 20X3?

> $

A   172,000

B   175,000

C   180,000

D   183,000

(b) If Squash's profit for the year was $16,000, what is the profit attributable to the NCI?

Question 16.3 Intra-group trading II

Learning outcomes B3

Percy has held 75% of the equity share capital of Mercy for many years.

Draft summarised statements of profit or loss for Percy and Mercy for the year ended 31 December 20X3 are below.

STATEMENTS OF PROFIT OR LOSS AT 31 DECEMBER 20X3

	PERCY	MERCY
	$	$
Revenue	500,000	300,000
Cost of sales	300,000	200,000
Gross profit	200,000	100,000
Administrative expenses	90,000	45,000
Profit before taxation	110,000	55,000
Income taxes	10,000	5,000
Profit for the year	100,000	50,000

During the year, Percy sold goods which cost $20,000 to Mercy at a margin of 20%. At the year end, all of these goods remained in inventory.

Required

Prepare the consolidated statement of profit or loss for the Percy group as at 31 December 20X3.

1.3 Intra-group dividends

In our example so far we have assumed that S Co retains all of its after-tax profit. It may be, however, that S Co distributes some of its profits as dividends. Group retained earnings are only adjusted for dividends paid to the parent company shareholders. Dividends paid by the subsidiary to the parent are cancelled on consolidation.

1.4 Intra-group transfers of non-current assets

As we have seen in the previous chapter, as well as engaging in trading activities with each other, group companies may on occasion wish to transfer non-current assets. If non-current assets are transferred between group companies at a profit, on consolidation the profit on transfer must be eliminated and expenses must be reduced by any additional depreciation arising from the increased carrying value of the asset. The non-controlling interest is adjusted if the asset was sold by the subsidiary.

Example

At the beginning of the year a 75% subsidiary transfers a non-current asset to the parent for $500,000. Its carrying value was $400,000 and it has 4 years of useful life left. How is this accounted for at the end of the year in the consolidated statement of profit or loss?

Solution

	$
Unrealised profit	100,000
Additional depreciation (100 ÷ 4)	(25,000)
Net charge to statement of profit or loss	75,000

	DR $	CR $
Non-current asset		100,000
Additional depreciation	25,000	
Group profit (75%)	56,250	
Non-controlling interest (25%)	18,750	
	100,000	100,000

1.5 Intra-group loans and interest

Loans between a parent and a subsidiary should be eliminated on consolidation as they do not represent finance from the group point of view.

The adjustments required are:

To cancel the loans in the consolidated statement of financial position:

DEBIT	Loan payable
CREDIT	Loan receivable

To cancel the interest payable/interest receivable in the consolidated statement of profit or loss:

DEBIT	Group finance income
CREDIT	Group finance costs

1.6 Impairment of goodwill

Impairment losses on goodwill during the year should be added to expenses in the consolidated statement of profit or loss. Note that **all** of the impairment loss on goodwill recognised for the year to expenses regardless of whether the full or partial goodwill method is used.

Section summary

The consolidated statement of profit or loss is prepared by combining the statements of profit or loss of each group company on a line-by-line basis.

Intra-group sales and purchases are eliminated from the consolidated statement of profit or loss.

2 Acquisitions part way through the year

Introduction

We have seen in the last chapter that retained earnings in the consolidated statement of financial position comprise:

- the whole of the parent company's retained earnings
- the **group's share of post-acquisition retained earnings** in the subsidiary.

From the total retained earnings of the subsidiary we must therefore **exclude** both the **non-controlling interest's share** of total retained earnings and the **group's share of pre-acquisition** retained earnings.

A **similar procedure is necessary in the consolidated statement of profit or loss** if it is to link up with the consolidated statement of financial position.

As we have seen in the last chapter, if the subsidiary is **acquired part way through the accounting year**, it is necessary to split the profits earned between those earned pre-acquisition and those earned post-acquisition.

So we must first split the entire statement of profit or loss of the subsidiary between pre-acquisition and post-acquisition proportions. Only the post-acquisition figures are included in the consolidated statement of profit or loss. Consider the following example.

Example

P Co acquired 60% of the equity of S Co on 1 April 20X5. The statements of profit or loss of the two companies for the year ended 31 December 20X5 are set out below.

	P Co $	S Co $	S Co ($^9/_{12}$) $
Revenue	170,000	80,000	60,000
Cost of sales	65,000	36,000	27,000
Gross profit	105,000	44,000	33,000
Administrative expenses	43,000	12,000	9,000
Profit before tax	62,000	32,000	24,000
Income taxes	23,000	8,000	6,000
Profit for the year	39,000	24,000	18,000
Note			
Retained earnings brought forward	81,000	40,000	
Retained earnings carried forward	108,000	58,000	

Required

Prepare the consolidated statement of profit or loss and movements on retained earnings.

Solution

The shares in S Co were acquired three months into the year. Only the post-acquisition proportion (9 months' worth) of S Co's statement of profit or loss is included in the consolidated statement of profit or loss. This is shown above for convenience, in your assessment, you will have to calculate the proportion to include.

P CO
CONSOLIDATED STATEMENT OF PROFIT OR LOSS FOR THE YEAR ENDED 31 DECEMBER 20X5

	$
Revenue (170 + 60)	230,000
Cost of sales (65 + 27)	92,000
Gross profit	138,000
Administrative expenses (43 + 9)	52,000
Profit before tax	86,000
Income taxes (23 + 6)	29,000
Profit for the year	57,000
Profit attributable to:	
Owners of the parent (bal fig)	49,800
Non-controlling interest (W2)	7,200
	57,000
Movement on retained earnings	
Group profit for year	49,800
Retained earnings brought forward*	81,000
Retained earnings carried forward	130,800

* All of S Co's retained earnings brought forward are pre-acquisition.

Workings

1   *Group structure*

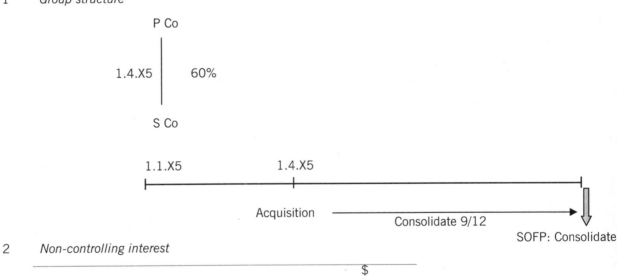

2   *Non-controlling interest*

	$
Profit for the year - per question	18,000
NCI share	× 40%
	= 7,200

Exam skills

When a subsidiary is purchased part-way through a year, you may find it helpful to add to your group structure diagram by drawing a timeline showing when the acquisition happened and how much of the subsidiary's results should be consolidated, as shown above.

Section summary

If a subsidiary is acquired during the year, only the post-acquisition element of the statement of profit or loss balances are included on consolidation.

3 The consolidated statement of profit or loss and other comprehensive income

Introduction

A consolidated statement of profit or loss and other comprehensive income will be easy to produce once you have done the statement of profit or loss. In this section, we take the example from the last section and add an item of comprehensive income to illustrate this.

Example: consolidated statement of profit or loss and other comprehensive income

P Co acquired 60% of the equity of S Co on 1 April 20X5. The consolidated statement of profit or loss for the year ended 31 December 20X5 is shown below.

P CO
CONSOLIDATED STATEMENT OF PROFIT OR LOSS FOR THE YEAR ENDED 31 DECEMBER 20X5

	$
Revenue (170 + 60)	230,000
Cost of sales (65 + 27)	92,000
Gross profit	138,000
Administrative expenses (43 + 9)	52,000
Profit before tax	86,000
Income taxes (23 + 6)	29,000
Profit for the year	57,000
Profit attributable to:	
Owners of the parent (bal fig)	49,800
Non-controlling interest (W)	7,200
	57,000

Working

Non-controlling interests

	$
Profit for the year - per question	18,000
NCI share	× 40%
	= 7,200

Show the consolidated statement of profit or loss and other comprehensive income if S Co made a $20,000 revaluation gain on one of its properties during the year, *after* it had been acquired by P Co.

Solution

P CO

CONSOLIDATED STATEMENT OF PROFIT OR LOSS AND OTHER COMPREHENSIVE INCOME FOR THE
YEAR ENDED 31 DECEMBER 20X5

	$
Revenue (170 + 60)	230,000
Cost of sales (65 + 27)	92,000
Gross profit	138,000
Administrative expenses (43 + 9)	52,000
Profit before tax	86,000
Income taxes (23 + 6)	29,000
Profit for the year	57,000
Other comprehensive income:	
Gain on property revaluation	20,000
Total comprehensive income for the year	77,000
Profit attributable to:	
Owners of the parent (bal fig)	49,800
Non-controlling interest (40% × 18,000)	7,200
	57,000
Total comprehensive income attributable to:	
Owners of the parent (bal fig) (49,800 + 60% × 20,000)	61,800
Non-controlling interest (7,200 + 40% × 20,000)	15,200
	77,000

Notice how the non-controlling interest is dealt with.

Down to the line **'total comprehensive income for the year'** the **whole** of S Co's post-acquisition results
are included without reference to group share or non-controlling interest share. Profit for the year and total
comprehensive income are then split between the group and the non-controlling interest.

Question 16.4	Other comprehensive income

Learning outcome B3

The consolidated statement of profit or loss of Wheeler Co and its 80% owned subsidiary, Brookes Co,
has been prepared for the year ended 30 April 20X7 and is shown below. During the year, Wheeler Co
made a $30,000 revaluation gain on one of its properties and Brookes Co made a revaluation gain of
$10,000 on a piece of land. The accountant at Wheeler Co has yet to prepare the consolidated statement
of profit or loss and other comprehensive income.

WHEELER GROUP

CONSOLIDATED STATEMENT OF PROFIT OR LOSS FOR THE YEAR ENDED 30 APRIL 20X7

	$'000
Revenue (1,100 + 500)	1,600
Cost of sales (630 + 300)	930
Gross profit	670
Administrative expenses (105 + 150)	255
Profit before taxation	415
Income taxes (65 + 10)	75
Profit for the year	340
Profit attributable to:	
Owners of the parent (bal fig)	332
Non-controlling interest (20% × 40)	8
	340

Required

Prepare the consolidated statement of profit or loss and other comprehensive income for the Wheeler Group as at 30 April 20X7.

Question 16.5	Comprehensive example I

Learning outcome B3

The statements of profit or loss and other comprehensive income for two entities for the year ended 30 September 20X5 are presented below:

STATEMENTS OF PROFIT OR LOSS AND OTHER COMPREHENSIVE INCOME
FOR THE YEAR ENDED 30 SEPTEMBER 20X5

	CV $'000	SG $'000
Revenue	5,000	4,200
Cost of sales	(4,100)	(3,500)
Gross profit	900	700
Distribution and administrative expenses	(320)	(180)
Investment income	50	-
Profit before tax	630	520
Income tax expense	(240)	(170)
PROFIT FOR THE YEAR	390	350
Other comprehensive income:		
Gain on revaluation of property (net of deferred tax)	60	20
TOTAL COMPREHENSIVE INCOME FOR THE YEAR	450	370

Additional information

(1) CV acquired a 75% investment in SG on 1 October 20X2. It is group policy to measure non-controlling interests at fair value at acquisition. Goodwill of $250,000 arose on acquisition.

(2) No impairment of goodwill had been necessary up to 1 October 20X4. However, the directors conducted an impairment review at 30 September 20X5 and decided that goodwill on acquisition was impaired by 20%.

(3) During the year ended 30 September 20X5, SG sold goods to CV for $300,000. Two thirds of these goods remain in CV's inventories at the year end. SG charges a mark-up of 25% on cost.

(4) SG paid a dividend of $60,000 to its equity shareholders on 30 September 20X5. CV includes its share of the dividend in investment income.

Requirement

(a) Prepare the consolidated statement of profit or loss and other comprehensive income for the CV group for the year ended 30 September 20X5.

(b) How would non-controlling interests differ if non-controlling interests at acquisition had been measured at the proportionate share of the net assets and if CV had sold the goods to SG in note (3)?

Chapter Summary

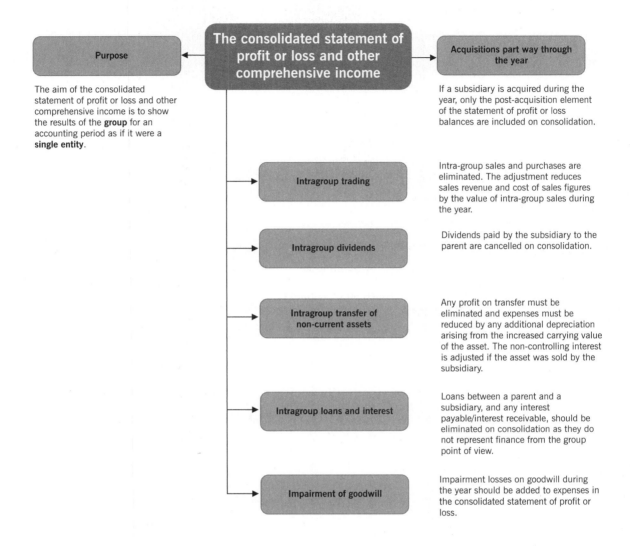

The consolidated statement of profit or loss and other comprehensive income

Purpose

The aim of the consolidated statement of profit or loss and other comprehensive income is to show the results of the **group** for an accounting period as if it were a **single entity**.

Acquisitions part way through the year

If a subsidiary is acquired during the year, only the post-acquisition element of the statement of profit or loss balances are included on consolidation.

Intragroup trading

Intra-group sales and purchases are eliminated. The adjustment reduces sales revenue and cost of sales figures by the value of intra-group sales during the year.

Intragroup dividends

Dividends paid by the subsidiary to the parent are cancelled on consolidation.

Intragroup transfer of non-current assets

Any profit on transfer must be eliminated and expenses must be reduced by any additional depreciation arising from the increased carrying value of the asset. The non-controlling interest is adjusted if the asset was sold by the subsidiary.

Intragroup loans and interest

Loans between a parent and a subsidiary, and any interest payable/interest receivable, should be eliminated on consolidation as they do not represent finance from the group point of view.

Impairment of goodwill

Impairment losses on goodwill during the year should be added to expenses in the consolidated statement of profit or loss.

Quick Quiz

The following information is relevant for questions 1 and 2.

Whales owns 90% of Porpoise. The gross profit for each company for the year ended 31 March 20X7 is calculated as follows:

	Whales	Porpoise
	$	$
Revenue	120,000	70,000
Cost of sales	(80,000)	(50,000)
Gross profit	40,000	20,000

During the year Porpoise made sales to Whales amounting to $30,000. $15,000 of these sales were in inventories at the year end. Profit made on the year end inventories items amounted to $2,000. Porpoise's profit for the year is $17,000.

1   What is group revenue and gross profit?

2   What is the profit attributable to the non-controlling interest?

The following information is relevant for questions 3 and 4.

Barley has owned 60% of the issued share capital of Oats for many years. Barley sells goods to Oats at cost plus 20%. The following information is available for the year.

	Revenue
	$
Barley	460,000
Oats	120,000

During the year Barley sold goods to Oats for $60,000, of which $18,000 were still held in inventory by Oats at the year end. Oats' profit for the year is $53,000.

3   At what amount should total revenue appear in the consolidated statement of profit or loss?

    A $520,000
    B $530,000
    C $538,000
    D $562,000

4   What is the profit attributable to the non-controlling interest?

5   Walcot purchased 90% of Ufton on 1 June 20X3. Extracts from the individual statements of profit or loss and other comprehensive income for the year ended 31 December 20X3 are as follows.

STATEMENTS OF PROFIT OR LOSS AT 31 DECEMBER 20X3

	WALCOT	UFTON
	$'000	$'000
Revenue	70,000	30,000
Gross profit	25,000	10,000
Profit for the year	5,000	3,000
Other comprehensive income:		
Revaluation of property	2,000	500
Total comprehensive income	7,000	3,500

The revaluation of Ufton's property occurred on 31 December 20X3.

What is the total comprehensive income attributable to the NCI?

Answers to Quick Quiz

1   *Group structure*

Whales

90%

Porpoise

	$
Revenue (120 + 70 − 30*)	160,000
Cost of sales (80 + 50 − 30* + 2**)	(102,000)
Gross Profit	58,000

* To remove the intra-group sale

** To remove the unrealised profit

2   *Non-controlling interest*

	$
Profit for the year - per question	17,000
PUP	(2,000)
	15,000
NCI share	× 10%
Profit attributable to NCI	= 1,500

3   A
     Group structure

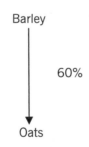

Barley

60%

Oats

Revenue   = 460,000 + 120,000 − 60,000

          = $520,000

4   *Non-controlling interest*

	$
Profit for the year - per question	53,000
PUP (18,000 × 20/120)	(3,000)
	50,000
NCI share	× 40%
Profit attributable to NCI	= 20,000

5 CONSOLIDATED STATEMENT OF PROFIT OR LOSS AND OTHER COMPREHENSIVE INCOME

	$'000
Profit for the year (5,000 + 3,000 × 7/12)	6,750
Other comprehensive income:	
Gain on property revaluation (2,000 + 500)	2,500
Total comprehensive income for the year	9,250
Profit attributable to:	
Owners of the parent (bal fig)	6,575
Non-controlling interest (10% × (3,000 × 7/12))	175
	6,750
Total comprehensive income attributable to:	
Owners of the parent (bal fig)	9,025
Non-controlling interest (175 + [10% × 500])	**225**
	9,250

 ## Answers to Questions

16.1 Consolidated statement of profit or loss

WHEELER GROUP
CONSOLIDATED STATEMENT OF PROFIT OR LOSS FOR THE YEAR TO 30 APRIL 20X7

	$'000
Revenue (1,100 + 500)	1,600
Cost of sales (630 + 300)	930
Gross profit	670
Administrative expenses (105 + 150)	255
Profit before taxation	415
Income taxes (65 + 10)	75
Profit for the year	340
Profit attributable to:	
Owners of the parent (bal fig)	332
Non-controlling interest (W2)	8
	340
Movement on retained earnings	
Group profit for year	332
Retained earnings brought forward (460 + 80% × (106 − 56*))	500
Retained earnings carried forward	832

* Retained earnings at acquisition

Workings

1 *Group structure*

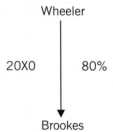

Wheeler

20X0   80%

Brookes

2   *Non-controlling interest*

	$
Profit for the year - per question	40,000
NCI share	× 20%
	= 8,000

16.2 Intra-group trading I

(a)   B

Group structure

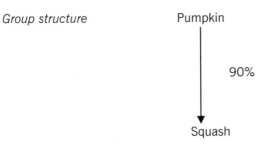

Pumpkin

90%

Squash

	$
Cost of sales	
Pumpkin	100,000
Squash	80,000
	180,000
Less: intra-group sales	(8,000)
Add: provision for unrealised profit (5,000 – 2000)	3,000
Cost of sales	175,000

(b)   *Non-controlling interest*

	$
Profit for the year - per question	16,000
PUP	(3,000)
	13,000
NCI share	× 10%
Profit attributable to NCI	= 1,300

16.3 Intra-group trading II

PERCY GROUP
CONSOLIDATED STATEMENT OF PROFIT OR LOSS AT 31 DECEMBER 20X3

	$
Revenue (500 + 300 – 25(W3))	775,000
Cost of sales (300 + 200 – 25(W3) + 5(W3))	480,000
Gross profit	295,000
Administrative expenses (90 + 45)	135,000
Profit before taxation	160,000
Income taxes (10 + 5)	15,000
Profit for the year	145,000
Profit attributable to:	
Owners of the parent (bal fig)	132,500
Non-controlling interest (W2)	12,500
	145,000

Workings

1   *Group structure*

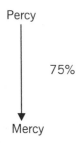

Percy

75%

Mercy

2   *Non-controlling interest*

	$
Profit for the year - per question	50,000
NCI share	× 25%
	= 12,500

3   *Intra-group trading*

P → S

- Intra –group revenue and cost of sales:
  Cancel $25,000 ($20,000 × 100/80 margin) out of revenue and cost of sales

- PUP = all in inventories × ($20,000 × 20/80 margin) = $5,000
  Increase cost of sales by $5,000

Because the sale was made from the parent, Percy, to the subsidiary, Mercy, there is no unrealised profit attributable to the non-controlling interest.

16.4 Other comprehensive income

WHEELER GROUP
CONSOLIDATED STATEMENT OF PROFIT OR LOSS AND OTHER COMPREHENSIVE INCOME
FOR THE YEAR ENDED 30 APRIL 20X7

	$'000
Revenue (1,100 + 500)	1,600
Cost of sales (630 + 300)	930
Gross profit	670
Administrative expenses (105 + 150)	255
Profit before taxation	415
Income taxes (65 + 10)	75
Profit for the year	340
Other comprehensive income:	
Gain on non-current asset revaluation (30 + 10)	40
Total comprehensive income for the year	380
Profit attributable to:	
Owners of the parent (bal fig)	332
Non-controlling interest (20% × 40)	8
	340
Total comprehensive income attributable to:	
Owners of the parent (bal fig) (332 + 30* + (80% × 10))	370
Non-controlling interest (8 + 20% × 10)	10
	380

*Note that the non-controlling interest only has a share in the profits and revaluation gains of Brookes, and not of Wheeler Co, so none of the $30,000 revaluation gain of Wheeler Co is allocated to the NCI.

Working

Group structure

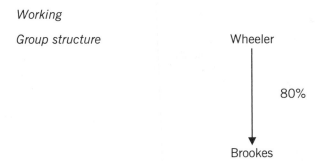

Wheeler

80%

Brookes

16.5 Comprehensive income I

(a)   CV GROUP
CONSOLIDATED STATEMENT OF PROFIT OR LOSS AND OTHER COMPREHENSIVE INCOME
FOR THE YEAR ENDED 30 SEPTEMBER 20X5

	$'000
Revenue (5,000 + 4,200 − 300 (W4))	8,900
Cost of sales (4,100 + 3,500 − 300 (W4) + 40 (W4))	(7,340)
Gross profit	1,560
Distribution and administration expenses (320 + 180 + 50 (W3))	(550)
Investment income (50 − 45 (W5))	5
Profit before tax	1,015
Income tax expense (240 + 170)	(410)
Profit for the year	605
Other comprehensive income:	
Gains on property revaluation (net of tax) (60 + 20)	80
Total comprehensive income for the year	685
Profit attributable to:	
Owners of the parent (615 − 65)	540
Non-controlling interest (W2)	65
	605
Total comprehensive income attributable to:	
Owners of the parent (695 − 70)	615
Non-controlling interest (W2)	70
	685

Workings

1   *Group structure*

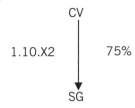

CV

1.10.X2   75%

SG

2   *Non-controlling interest*

	Profit for the year	Total comprehensive income
	$'000	$'000
Per question	350	370
Impairment loss for year (W3)	(50)	(50)
Provision for unrealised profit (W4)	(40)	(40)
	260	280
NCI share	× 25%	× 25%
	= 65	= 70

3   *Impairment of goodwill*

Impairment of goodwill for the year = $250,000 goodwill × 20% impairment = $50,000

Tutorial note: Add $50,000 to 'administration expenses' and deduct from profit for the year/total comprehensive income in NCI working (as full goodwill method adopted here)

4   *Intra-group trading*

SG → CV

- Intra –group revenue and cost of sales:
  Tutorial note: cancel $300,000 out of revenue and cost of sales

- Provision for unrealised profit = $300,000 × 2/3 in inventories × 25/125 mark up = $40,000
  Tutorial note: increase cost of sales by $40,000 and reduce profit for the year/total comprehensive income in NCI working (as subsidiary is the seller)

5   *Intra-group dividend*

CV's share of SG's dividend = $60,000 x 75% = $45,000

Tutorial note: cancel $45,000 out of 'Investment income'

(b)   *Non-controlling interest (under partial goodwill method and if parent sells to subsidiary for intra-group trading)*

Non-controlling interest

	Profit for the year $'000	Total comprehensive income $'000
Per question	350	370
NCI share	× 25% = 87.5	× 25% = 92.5

Tutorial note: the provision for unrealised profit is only deducted when the subsidiary is the seller and the parent is the seller here. Impairment loss for the year is only deducted under the full goodwill method and the partial goodwill method is used in part (b).

16.6 Comprehensive income II

CL GROUP

CONSOLIDATED STATEMENT OF PROFIT OR LOSS AND OTHER COMPREHENSIVE INCOME FOR THE YEAR ENDED 31 DECEMBER 20X8

	$'000
Revenue (43,000 + (26,000 × 6/12) – 6,000 (W4))	50,000
Cost of sales (28,000 + (18,000 × 6/12) – 6,000 (W4) + 1,000 (W4))	(32,000)
Gross profit	18,000
Distribution costs (2,000 + (800 × 6/12))	(2,400)
Administrative expenses (4,000 + (2,200 × 6/12) + 500 (W3))	(5,600)
Finance costs (500 + (300 × 6/12))	(650)
Profit before tax	9,350
Income tax expense (1,400 + (900 × 6/12))	(1,850)
Profit for the year	7,500
Other comprehensive income:	
Gain on property revaluation (200 + 1,000)	1,200
Total comprehensive income for the year	8,700
Profit attributable to:	
Owners of the parent	6,940
Non-controlling interest (W3)	560
	7,500
Total comprehensive income attributable to:	
Owners of the parent	7,740
Non-controlling interest (W3)	960
	8,700

Workings

1   *Group structure*

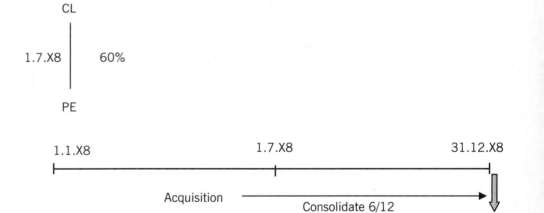

2   *Non-controlling interest*

	Profit for the year $'000	Total comprehensive Income $'000
Per question (3,800 × 6/12 = 1,900)/(1,900 + 1,000)	1,900	2,900
Impairment loss for year (W3)	(500)	(500)
	1,400	2,400
NCI share	× 40%	× 40%
	= 560	= 960

3   *Impairment of goodwill*

Impairment of goodwill for the year = $500,000

Add $500,000 to 'administration expenses' and deduct from profit for year/total comprehensive income in NCI working (as full goodwill method adopted here)

4   *Intra-group trading*

CL → PE

- Intra –group revenue and cost of sales:
  Cancel $6m out of revenue and cost of sales

- PUP = $6m × 20/120 mark up = $1m
  Increase cost of sales by $1m. No impact on NCI as sale from parent to subsidiary

Now try these questions from the OTQ Question Bank	**Number**
	Q39
	Q40
	Q41
	Q59

ASSOCIATES

In this chapter we deal with the treatment of associates in the consolidated financial statements.

Associates have to be included in consolidated financial statements, according to the revised IAS 28, under the **equity method.**

Topic list	learning outcomes	syllabus references
1 Accounting for associates	B3	B3 (a)
2 The equity method	B3	B3 (a)
3 More complex situations	B3	B3 (a) (c)

Chapter Overview

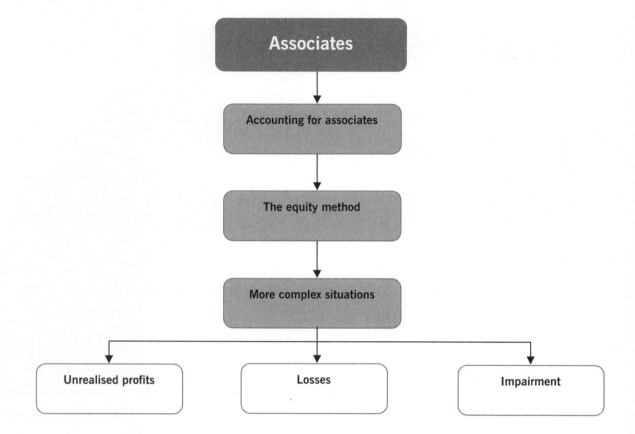

1 Accounting for associates

Introduction

Accounting for associates is covered by IAS 28 (revised) *Investments in associates and joint ventures*. The investing company does not have control, as it does with a subsidiary, but it does have **significant influence**.

1.1 Definitions

These are the important definitions you need to know.

KEY TERMS

- ASSOCIATE. An entity, including an unincorporated entity such as a partnership, over which an investor has significant influence and which is neither a subsidiary nor an interest in a joint venture.

- SIGNIFICANT INFLUENCE is the power to participate in the financial and operating policy decisions of the investee but is not control or joint control over those policies.

- EQUITY METHOD. A method of accounting whereby the investment is initially recorded at cost and adjusted thereafter for the post-acquisition change in the investor's share of net assets of the investee. The profit or loss of the investor includes the investor's share of the profit or loss of the investee.

We have already looked at how the **status** of an investment in an associate should be determined. Go back to Chapter 14 to revise it.

IAS 28 requires all investments in associates to be accounted for in the consolidated accounts using the **equity method**, *unless* the investment is classified as 'held for sale' in accordance with IFRS 5 in which case it should be accounted for under IFRS 5, or the exemption in the paragraph below applies.

An investor is exempt from applying the equity method if:

(a)   It is a parent exempt from preparing consolidated financial statements under IFRS 10, or

(b)   All of the following apply:

    (i)   The investor is a **wholly-owned subsidiary** or it is a **partially owned subsidiary** of another entity and its other owners, including those not otherwise entitled to vote, have been informed about, and do not object to, the investor not applying the equity method;

    (ii)   The investor's debt or equity instruments are **not publicly traded**

    (iii)   It is **not in the process of issuing securities** in public securities markets; and

    (iv)   The **ultimate or intermediate parent** publishes consolidated financial statements that comply with International Financial Reporting Standards

The use of the equity method should be **discontinued** from the date that the investor **ceases to have significant influence.** From that date, the investor shall account for the investment in accordance with IAS 39 *Financial instruments: recognition and measurement*.

The following points are also relevant and are similar to a parent-subsidiary consolidation situation.

(a)   Use financial statements drawn up to the **same reporting date.**

(b)   If this is impracticable, adjust the financial statements for **significant transactions/events** in the intervening period. The difference between the reporting date of the associate and that of the investor must be no more than three months.

(c)   Use **uniform accounting policies** for like transactions and events in similar circumstances, adjusting the associate's statements to reflect group policies if necessary.

1.2 Separate financial statements of the investor

If an investor **issues consolidated financial statements** (because it has subsidiaries), an investment in an associate should be *either*:

(a)   Accounted for at **cost**, or

(b)   In accordance with **IAS 39** (at fair value)

in its separate financial statements.

If an investor that does *not* **issue consolidated financial statements** (ie it has no subsidiaries) but has an investment in an associate this should similarly be included in the financial statements of the investor either at cost, or in accordance with IAS 39.

Section summary

IAS 28 requires that, in consolidated accounts, **associates** should be accounted for using **equity accounting principles**.

2 The equity method

Introduction

In this section we look at how to apply the equity method using a simple example. The equity method reflects the parent's significant influence over the associate. If the consolidated statement of financial position contained only an investment at its cost (or fair value) and the statement of profit or loss and other comprehensive income included only dividend income, this would not be very informative. The parent has an interest in, and shares responsibility for, the associate's performance.

2.1 Consolidated statement of profit or loss and other comprehensive income

The basic principle behind the equity accounting method is that the investing company (X Co) should take account of its **share of the earnings** of the associate, Y Co, whether or not Y Co distributes the earnings as dividends. X Co achieves this by adding to consolidated profit the **group's share of Y Co's profit after tax**.

Under equity accounting, the associated company's sales revenue, cost of sales and so on are **not amalgamated** with those of the group. Any dividend income received from the associate is removed from consolidated income and instead the group share only of the associate's profit after tax is recognised in profit or loss and the **group** share of any other comprehensive income in the associate is recognised as a separate line within other comprehensive income.

Notice the difference between this treatment and the **consolidation** of a subsidiary company's results. If Y Co were a subsidiary X Co would consolidate the whole of its sales revenue, cost of sales etc line by line.

Example: Consolidated statement of profit or loss and other comprehensive income

The following statements of profit or loss and other comprehensive income relate to the P Co group, consisting of the parent company, an 100% owned subsidiary (S Co) and an associated company (A Co) in which the group has a 30% interest. P Co has owned both of these investments for several years.

STATEMENTS OF PROFIT OR LOSS AND OTHER COMPREHENSIVE INCOME

	P Co $'000	S Co $'000	A Co $'000
Sales revenue	600	800	300
Cost of sales	(370)	(400)	(120)
Gross profit	230	400	180
Other expenses	(110)	(180)	(80)
	120	220	100
Finance income	30	-	-
	150	220	100
Finance costs	-	(20)	-
Profit before tax	150	200	100
Income tax expense	(55)	(90)	(40)
Profit for the year	95	110	60
Other comprehensive income:			
Gains on property revaluation, net of tax	30	20	10
Total comprehensive income for the year	125	130	70

Required

Prepare the consolidated statement of profit or loss and other comprehensive income for the P Group.

Solution

P GROUP CONSOLIDATED STATEMENT OF PROFIT OR LOSS AND OTHER COMPREHENSIVE INCOME

	$'000
Sales revenue (600 + 800)	1,400
Cost of sales (370 + 400)	(770)
Gross profit	630
Other expenses (110 + 180)	(290)
	340
Finance income	30
	370
Finance costs	(20)
Group profit	350
Group share of associate's profit (30% × 60)	18
	368
Income tax expense (55 + 90)	(145)
Profit for the year	223
Other comprehensive income:	
Gains on property revaluation, net of tax (30 + 20)	50
Share of other comprehensive income of associate (30% × 10)	3
Total comprehensive income for the year	276

Note the following

(a)   Consolidated sales revenue, group gross profit and expenses **exclude** the sales revenue, gross profit and costs etc of **associates**.

(b)   The group share of the associate's **profit after tax** is credited to the group statement of profit or loss (here, 30% of $60,000 = $18,000). If the associate had been acquired during the year, it would be time apportioned so that only **post-acquisition profits** are included.

(c)   **Taxation** includes only the income tax expense of the **parent company and subsidiaries** in total. (The share of the associate's tax has been dealt with by measuring the share of the associate's profit **net of tax** earlier in the statement.)

(d)   Within other comprehensive income, the amounts relating to the parent and subsidiary are aggregated as usual and the **group share** of the associate's **other comprehensive income** is shown separately.

2.2 Consolidated statement of financial position

A figure for **investment in associates** is shown which at the time of the acquisition must be stated at cost. At the end of each accounting period the group share of the retained reserves of the associate is added to the original cost to get the total investment to be shown in the consolidated statement of financial position.

The investment in the associate must be assessed for any evidence of impairments, in accordance with IAS 39 *Financial Instruments: Recognition and measurement,* and any impairment loss written off against the carrying value of the associate.

A proforma working for the investment in associate figure is as follows.

	$
Cost of associate	X
Share of post-acquisition retained reserves	X/(X)
Less: impairment losses on associate to date	(X)
	X

Example: entries in the consolidated statement of financial position

P Co, a company with subsidiaries, acquires 25,000 of the 100,000 $1 ordinary shares in A Co for $60,000 on 1 January 20X8. In the year to 31 December 20X8, A Co earns profits after tax of $24,000, from which it pays a dividend of $6,000.

How will A Co's results be accounted for in the individual and consolidated accounts of P Co for the year ended 31 December 20X8?

Solution

In the **individual accounts** of P Co, the investment will be recorded on 1 January 20X8 at cost. Unless there is an impairment in the value of the investment, this amount will remain in the individual statement of financial position of P Co permanently. The only entry in P Co's individual statement of profit or loss will be to record dividends received. For the year ended 31 December 20X8, P Co will:

DEBIT	Cash (25% × $6,000)	$1,500	
CREDIT	Income from shares in associates		$1,500

In the **consolidated accounts** of P Co equity accounting principles will be used to account for the investment in A Co. Consolidated profit after tax will include the group's share of A Co's profit after tax (25% × $24,000 = $6,000). To the extent that this has been distributed as dividend, it is already included in P Co's individual accounts and will automatically be brought into the consolidated results. That part of the group's share of profit in the associate which has not been distributed as dividend (25% × (24,000 – 6,000) = $4,500) will be brought into consolidation by the following adjustment.

DEBIT	Investment in associates	$4,500	
CREDIT	Income from shares in associates		$4,500

The asset 'Investment in associates' is then stated at $64,500, being cost of $60,000 plus the group share of post-acquisition retained earnings ($4,500).

Example: consolidated statement of financial position

On 1 January 20X6 the net assets of A Co amount to $220,000, financed by 100,000 $1 ordinary shares and revenue reserves of $120,000. P Co, a company with subsidiaries, acquired 30,000 of the shares in A Co for $75,000. During the year ended 31 December 20X6 A Co's profit after tax is $30,000, from which dividends of $12,000 are paid.

Required

Show how P Co's investment in A Co would appear in the consolidated statement of financial position at 31 December 20X6.

Solution

CONSOLIDATED STATEMENT OF FINANCIAL POSITION AS
AT 31 DECEMBER 20X6 (EXTRACT)

	$
Non-current assets	
Investment in associate	
Cost	75,000
Group share of post-acquisition retained earnings (30% × [$30,000 – $12,000])	5,400
	80,400

Question 17.1   Associates I

Learning outcome B3

Set out below are the draft accounts of Parent Co and its subsidiaries and of Associate Co. Parent Co acquired 40% of the equity capital of Associate Co three years ago when the latter's reserves stood at $40,000.

SUMMARISED STATEMENTS OF FINANCIAL POSITION

	Parent Co & Subsidiaries $'000	Associate Co $'000
Property, plant and equipment	220	170
Investment in associate at cost	60	–
Loan to Associate Co	20	–
Current assets	100	50
Loan from Parent Co	–	(20)
	400	200
Share capital ($1 shares)	250	100
Retained earnings	150	100
	400	200

SUMMARISED STATEMENTS OF PROFIT OR LOSS

	Parent Co & Subsidiaries $'000	Associate Co $'000
Profit before tax	95	80
Taxation expense	(35)	(30)
Profit for the year	60	50

Required

Prepare the summarised consolidated accounts of Parent Co.

Section summary

Under the **equity method**, the investing company should take account of its share of earnings of the associate by adding to consolidated profit the group's share of the associate's profit after tax.

In the consolidated **statement of financial position**, the investment in associates should be shown as:

- Cost of the investment in the associate; plus
- Group share of post-acquisition retained reserves; less
- Any impairment losses on the investment in associate to date

3 More complex situations

Introduction

Here we consider how to deal with unrealised profits, losses made by associates and impairment of the investment in an associate.

3.1 Unrealised profits

A group (made up of a parent and its subsidiaries) may trade with its associates. This introduces the possibility of unrealised profits if goods sold within the group are still in inventories at the year end. This is similar to the examples seen earlier involving unrealised profits arising on trading between a parent and a subsidiary. The important thing to remember is that when an associate is involved, **only the group's share is eliminated**.

The precise accounting entries depend on the direction of the transaction. 'Upstream' transactions are sales from an associate to the investor. 'Downstream' transactions are sales of assets from the investor to an associate.

The entries in the consolidated statement of financial position are as follows, where A% is the parent's holding in the associate, and PUP is the provision for unrealised profit.

For upstream transactions (associate sells to parent/subsidiary) where the parent holds the inventories:

DEBIT	Retained earnings of parent/subsidiary	PUP × A%
CREDIT	Group inventories	PUP × A%

OR

For downstream transactions,(parent/subsidiary sells to associate) where the associate holds the inventories:

DEBIT	Retained earnings of parent/subsidiary	PUP × A%
CREDIT	Investment in associate	PUP × A%

In the statement of profit or loss and other comprehensive income, the precise treatment of the reduction in profit (a debit entry) also depends on the direction of the transaction:

DEBIT	Cost of sales (increases cost of sales)	PUP × A%	if **parent** made the sales
DEBIT	Share of associate's profit (decreases the profit)	PUP × A%	if **associate** made the sales

Example: downstream transaction

A Co, a parent with subsidiaries, holds 25% of the equity shares in B Co. During the year, A Co makes sales of $1,000,000 to B Co at cost plus a 25% mark-up. At the year end, B Co has all these goods still in inventories. What effect does this transaction have on the consolidated statement of financial position?

Solution

A Co has made an unrealised profit of $200,000 ($1,000,000 × 25/125) on its sales to the associate. The group's share (25%) of this must be eliminated:

DEBIT	Group retained earnings	$50,000	
CREDIT	Investment in associate		$50,000

Because the sale was made to the associate, the group's share of the unsold inventory forms part of the investment in the associate at the year-end. If the associate had made the sale to the parent, the adjustment would have been:

DEBIT	Group retained earnings	$50,000	
CREDIT	Inventories (consolidated statement of financial position)		$50,000

3.2 Associate's losses

When the equity method is being used and the investor's share of losses of the associate equals or exceeds its interest in the associate, the investor should **discontinue** including its share of further losses. The investment is reported at nil value. The interest in the associate is normally the carrying amount of the investment in the associate, but it also includes any other long-term interests, for example, long-term receivables or loans.

After the investor's interest is reduced to nil, **additional losses** should only be recognised where the investor has incurred obligations or made payments on behalf of the associate (for example, if it has guaranteed amounts owed to third parties by the associate).

3.3 Impairment losses

IAS 39 sets out a list of indications that a financial asset (including an associate) may have become impaired. Any impairment loss is recognised in accordance with IAS 36 *Impairment of assets* for each associate individually.

Learning outcome B3

The statements of financial position of J Co and its investee companies, P Co and S Co, at 31 December 20X5 are shown below.

STATEMENTS OF FINANCIAL POSITION AS AT 31 DECEMBER 20X5

	J Co $'000	P Co $'000	S Co $'000
Non-current assets			
Property, plant and equipment	2,745	1,625	785
Investments	1,500	–	–
	4,245	1,625	785
Current assets			
Inventory	575	300	265
Trade receivables	330	290	370
Cash	50	120	20
	955	710	655
Total assets	5,200	2,335	1,440
Equity and liabilities			
Equity			
Share capital – $1 shares	2,000	1,000	750
Retained earnings	1,460	885	390
	3,460	1,885	1,140
Non-current liabilities			
12% loan stock	500	100	
Current liabilities			
Trade payables	680	350	300
Bank overdraft	560	–	–
	1,240	350	300
Total equity and liabilities	5,200	2,335	1,440

Additional information

(a) J Co acquired 600,000 ordinary shares in P Co on 1 January 20X0 for $1,000,000 when the retained earnings of P Co were $200,000.

(b) J Co acquired 225,000 ordinary shares in S Co on 1 January 20X4 for $500,000 when the retained earnings of S Co were $150,000.

(c) P Co manufactures a component used by both J Co and S Co. Transfers are made by P Co at cost plus 25%. J Co held $100,000 inventory of these components at 31 December 20X5. In the same period J Co sold goods to S Co of which S Co had $80,000 in inventory at 31 December 20X5. J Co had marked these goods up by 25%.

(d) The goodwill in P Co is impaired and should be fully written off. An impairment loss of $92,000 is to be recognised on the investment in S Co in the individual financial statements of J Co (this has yet to be recorded).

(e) Non-controlling interest is valued at full fair value. P Co shares were trading at $1.60 just prior to the acquisition by J Co.

Required

Prepare, in a format suitable for inclusion in the annual report of the J Group, the consolidated statement of financial position at 31 December 20X5.

Section summary

The **group's share** of **unrealised profit** on intra-group transactions with the associate must be **removed** from the consolidated financial statements. The adjustments required depend on which company made the sale.

When the equity method is being used and the investor's share of losses of the associate equals or exceeds its interest in the associate, the investor should **discontinue including its share of further losses**.

Chapter Summary

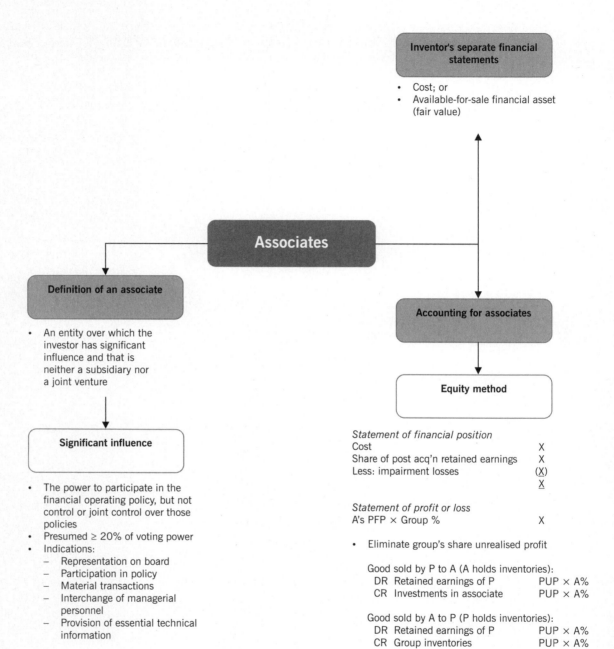

Inventor's separate financial statements

- Cost; or
- Available-for-sale financial asset (fair value)

Associates

Definition of an associate

- An entity over which the investor has significant influence and that is neither a subsidiary nor a joint venture

Significant influence

- The power to participate in the financial operating policy, but not control or joint control over those policies
- Presumed ≥ 20% of voting power
- Indications:
  - Representation on board
  - Participation in policy
  - Material transactions
  - Interchange of managerial personnel
  - Provision of essential technical information

Accounting for associates

Equity method

Statement of financial position

Cost	X
Share of post acq'n retained earnings	X
Less: impairment losses	(X)
	X

Statement of profit or loss

A's PFP × Group %	X

- Eliminate group's share unrealised profit

  Good sold by P to A (A holds inventories):
  DR Retained earnings of P   PUP × A%
  CR Investments in associate   PUP × A%

  Good sold by A to P (P holds inventories):
  DR Retained earnings of P   PUP × A%
  CR Group inventories   PUP × A%

Quick Quiz

1   *Complete the paragraph by selecting the correct options.*

An associate is an entity over which the investor has **[control/power/significant influence]** which can be assumed when the investor holds more than **[20%/50%/10%]** of the equity shares of the investee. An associate should be accounted for in the consolidated accounts **[on a line by line basis/using the equity method]**. Any impairment losses on the associate are deducted from **[the investment in associate balance/non-controlling interest]** in the consolidated statement of financial position.

2   How should associates be accounted for in the separate financial statements of the investor?

A   Full consolidation

B   Equity method

C   A proportion of the associate's assets and liabilities should be consolidated

D   Either at cost or in accordance with IAS 39.

The following information is relevant for questions 3 and 4.

Alfred Co bought a 25% shareholding on 31 December 20X8 in Grimbald Co at a cost of $38,000.

During the year to 31 December 20X9 Grimbald Co made a profit before tax of $82,000 and the taxation charge on the year's profits was $32,000. A dividend of $20,000 was paid on 31 December out of these profits.

3   What amounts for Grimbald should be included in the consolidated statement of profit or loss of the Alfred Group at 31 December 20X9?

4   What amounts for Grimbald should be included in the consolidated statement of financial position of the Alfred Group at 31 December 20X9?

5   Clementine has owned 21% of the ordinary shares of Tangerine for several years. Clementine does not have any investments in any other companies. How should the investment in Tangerine be reflected in the financial statements of Clementine?

A   The revenues and costs and assets and liabilities of Tangerine are added to the revenues and costs and assets and liabilities of Clementine on a line by line basis.

B   An amount is shown in the statement of financial position for 'investment in associate' being the original cost paid for the investment plus Clementine's share of the profit after tax of Tangerine. 21% of the profit after tax of Tangerine should be added to Clementine's profit after tax in the statement of profit or loss each year.

C   An amount is shown in the statement of financial position under 'investments' being the original cost paid for the investment, this amount does not change. Dividends received from Tangerine are recognised in the statement of profit or loss of Clementine.

D   An amount is shown in the statement of financial position under 'investments' being the original cost paid for the investment, this amount does not change. 21% of the profit after tax of Tangerine should be added to Clementine's profit after tax in the statement of profit or loss each year.

Answers to Quick Quiz

1   An associate is an entity over which the investor has **significant influence** which can be assumed when the investor holds more than **20%** of the equity shares of the investee. An associate should be accounted for in the consolidated accounts **using the equity method**. Any impairment losses on the associate are deducted from **the investment in associate balance** in the consolidated statement of financial position

2   D   Either at cost or in accordance with IAS 39.

3

CONSOLIDATED STATEMENT OF PROFIT OR LOSS AT 31 DECEMBER 20X8 (EXTRACT)

	$
Income from shares in associate ($82,000 – $32,000 × 25%)	12,500

4

CONSOLIDATED STATEMENT OF FINANCIAL POSITION AT 31 DECEMBER 20X8 (EXTRACT)

	$
Investment in associate	45,500

Working

	$
Cost of investment	38,000
Share of post-acquisition retained earnings ((82,000 – 32,000 – 20,000) × 25%)	7,500
	45,500

5   C   Tangerine is an associate of Clementine, however because Clementine has no other investments in other companies, it will not produce consolidated accounts. Therefore the investment will appear in the single company accounts of Clementine as a simple investment. The statement of financial position will show an investment at cost and the statement of profit or loss will show dividends received from Tangerine. If Clementine instead did produce consolidated accounts, Tangerine would be accounted for using the equity method and B would instead be correct.

Answers to Questions

17.1 Associates I

PARENT CO
CONSOLIDATED STATEMENT OF PROFIT OR LOSS

	$'000
Net profit	95
Income from shares in associates (50 × 40%)	20
Profit before tax	115
Taxation	(35)
Profit attributable to the members of Parent Co	80

PARENT CO
CONSOLIDATED STATEMENT OF FINANCIAL POSITION

	$'000
Assets	
Property, plant and equipment	220
Investment in associate (see note)	84
Loan to Associate Co	20
Current assets	100
Total assets	424
Equity and liabilities	
Share capital (Parent only)	250
Retained earnings (W)	174
Total equity and liabilities	424

Note

	$'000
Investment in associate	
Cost of investment	60
Share of post-acquisition retained earnings (W)	24
	84

Working – retained earnings

Retained earnings	Parent & Subsidiaries $'000	Associate $'000
Per question	150	100
Pre-acquisition		(40)
Post-acquisition		60
Group share in associate ($60 × 40%)	24	
Group retained earnings	174	

Note the following points about the treatment of the associate in the consolidated statement of financial position:

(a) An extra column is set out in the retained earnings working to calculate the group share of the associate's post acquisition retained earnings (ie exactly the same calculation as for a subsidiary).

(b) The loan balance asset due from Associate in the books of Parent is **not cancelled out**. There is no cancellation of any balances, whether loans or trading balances, due between the group and the associate. This is because the associate is not fully consolidated so there is no corresponding balance to cancel.

17.2 Associates II

J GROUP CONSOLIDATED STATEMENT OF FINANCIAL POSITION AS AT 31 DECEMBER 20X5

	$'000
Non-current assets	
Property, plant and equipment (2,745 + 1,625)	4,370.00
Investment in associate (W3)	475.20
	4,845.20
Current assets	
Inventory (575 + 300 – 20 (W6))	855.00
Receivables (330 + 290)	620.00
Cash (50 + 120)	170.00
	1,645.00
Total assets	6,490.20

	$'000
Equity and liabilities	
Equity	
Share capital	2,000.00
Retained earnings (W4)	1,570.20
	3,570.20
Non-controlling interest (W5)	730.00
	4,300.20
Non-current liabilities	
12% loan stock (500 + 100)	600.00
Current liabilities (680 + 560 + 350)	1,590.00
Total equity and liabilities	6,490.20

Workings

1   Group structure

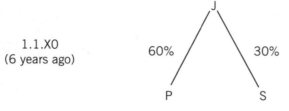

	1.1.X0		60%		30%		1.1.X4	
	(6 years ago)						(2 years ago)	

P   S

2   *Goodwill*

	$'000	$'000
P Co		
Consideration transferred		1,000
Non-controlling interest (400 × $1.60)		640
Net assets acquired		
Share capital	1,000	
Retained earnings	200	
		(1,200)
Goodwill at acquisition		440
Impairment loss		(440)
		0

3   *Investment in associate*

	$'000
Cost of investment	500.0
Share of post-acquisition retained earnings (390 − 150) × 30%	72.0
Less PUP	(4.8)
Less impairment loss	(92.0)
	475.2

4   *Retained earnings*

	J	P	S
	$'000	$'000	$'000
Retained earnings per question	1,460.0	885.0	390.0
Adjustments			
Unrealised profit (W6)	(4.8)	(20.0)	
Impairment loss (P)		(440.0)	
		425.0	390.0
Less pre-acquisition reserves		(200.0)	(150.0)
	1,455.2	225.0	240.0
P: 60% × 225	135.0		
S: 30% × 240	72.0		
Impairment loss (S)	(92.0)		
	1,570.2		

5   *Non-controlling interest at reporting date*

	$'000
Fair value of NCI at acquisition (W2)	640.0
Group share of post-acquisition retained earnings (225 x 40%)	90.0
	730.0

6   *Unrealised profit (PUP)*

	$'000
On sales by P to J (parent co) $100 \times 25/125$	20.0
On sales by J to S (associate) $80 \times 25/125 \times 30\%$	4.8

<table>
<tr><td>Now try these questions from the OTQ Question Bank</td><td>Number</td></tr>
<tr><td></td><td>Q42</td></tr>
<tr><td></td><td>Q43</td></tr>
<tr><td></td><td>Q60</td></tr>
</table>

FUNDAMENTALS OF BUSINESS TAXATION

Part C

GENERAL PRINCIPLES OF TAXATION

 This chapter forms an introduction to taxation and the general principles you need to know for the exam.

In Section 1, we look at the general principles of taxation, such as the sources of rules and the terminology you need to know.

Section 2 covers how tax is administered and in section 3 we look at the collection of tax and the powers of enforcement of the tax authorities.

topic list	learning outcomes	syllabus references
1 General principles of taxation	D1	D1 (a) (b)
2 Administration of tax	D1	D1 (b)
3 Tax enforcement	D1	D1 (b)

Chapter Overview

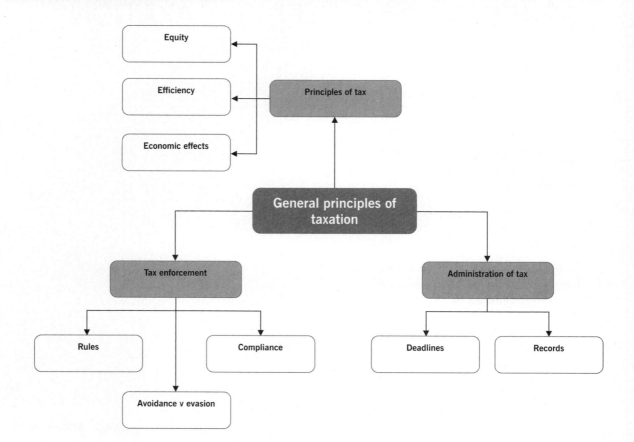

1   General principles of taxation

Introduction

In this section we look at the underlying principles of tax and introduce some general tax concepts and terminology. The general principles of tax are not specific to any one country, but should apply to most countries. We have used the UK tax system to illustrate concepts in this chapter.

1.1 Characteristics of taxation

The economist, Adam Smith, in his book 'Wealth of Nations', proposed that a 'good tax' should have the following characteristics:

(a)   **Equity**: the tax burden should be fairly distributed, eg a higher rate tax for wealthier individuals.
(b)   **Certainty**: an individual should be able to determine the tax implication of their actions.
(c)   **Convenience**: tax should be easy to pay.
(d)   **Efficiency**: tax should be easy and cheap to collect.

In the US, these characteristics are included among the 10 principles that form the American Institute of Certified Public Accountants' 'Guiding Principles of Good Tax Policy':

- Equity and fairness
- Certainty
- Convenience of payment
- Economy of collection
- Simplicity

- Neutrality
- Economic growth and efficiency
- Transparency and visibility
- Minimum tax gap
- Appropriate government revenues

The three **major** principles recognised today are:

(a)   **Equity**: the tax burden should be fairly distributed, eg a higher rate tax for wealthier individuals.
(b)   **Efficiency**: tax should be easy and cheap to collect. This is best achieved by the use of 'unpaid tax collectors', such as employers who have to collect and account for payroll taxes, eg PAYE (pay-as-you-earn) in the UK.
(c)   **Economic effects**: the government must consider the effect of taxation policy on various sectors of the economy. For example, tax allowances on capital expenditure may stimulate growth in the manufacturing sector.

1.1.1 Sources of tax rules

Sources of tax rules include the following:

(a)   Domestic legislation and court rulings, eg in the UK the annual Finance Act. Although the legislators try to think of all possible situations, business is always changing and so the law may have to be interpreted by the courts. This gives rise to court rulings that have the force of law.

(b)   Domestic tax authority practice and guidance statements. Every tax authority develops its own practice on how the law is applied. For example, UK tax law states that employees should be taxed on all 'benefits' supplied by the employer. However, in practice, certain benefits are exempted from the rules because it would be too time consuming to account for them and they yield little in the way of tax.

(c)   Supranational bodies, such as the European Union (EU). The EU has a number of rules on value added tax (sales tax), which have to be applied by all members of the EU.

(d)   International tax treaties. When a company operates in more than one country it may be taxed twice on its profits. In order to avoid this 'double tax', countries enter into tax treaties which set out which country gets to tax the profits and to allow relief for local taxes paid.

Exam alert

In the exam you will be told which tax rules apply. The tax rules are also released on the CIMA website prior to the exam. Make sure you check the website to see what they are in advance.

www.cimaglobal.com/students

The tax rules will be given in the following format.

COUNTRY X - TAX REGIME FOR USE THROUGHOUT THE EXAMINATION PAPER

Relevant Tax Rules for Years Ended 31 March 2007 to 2014

Corporate Profits

Unless otherwise specified, only the following rules for taxation of corporate profits will be relevant, other taxes can be ignored:

- Accounting rules on recognition and measurement are followed for tax purposes.

- All expenses other than depreciation, amortisation, entertaining, taxes paid to other public bodies and donations to political parties are tax deductible.

- Tax depreciation is deductible as follows:

  - 50% of additions to property, plant and equipment in the accounting period in which they are recorded

  - 25% per year of the written-down value (ie cost minus previous allowances) in subsequent accounting periods except that in which the asset is disposed of

  - No tax depreciation is allowed on land

- The corporate tax on profits is at a rate of 25%.

- No indexation is allowed on the sale of land.

- Tax losses can be carried forward to offset against future taxable profits from the same business.

Value Added Tax

Country X has a VAT system which allows entities to reclaim input tax paid.

In country X the VAT rates are:

Zero rated   0%
Standard rated   15%
Exempt goods   0%

1.2 The tax base

Taxes can be classified according to their **tax base** (what is being taxed). They can be based on any or all of the following items.

- **Income or profits** (personal income tax and company income tax)
- **Assets** (tax on capital gains, wealth and inheritance taxes)
- **Consumption** (or expenditure, eg taxes on alcohol, cigarettes or fuel and sales taxes)

1.2.1 Schedular systems of tax

Countries often separate different types of income into different categories and then have separate rules to determine how that income is taxed. This is known as a **schedular system**.

For example, in the UK, the tax system includes the following schedules for company income tax:

(a)   Schedule DI – Trading income

(b)   Schedule DIII – Interest income

(c)   Schedule DV – Income (ie dividends) from overseas subsidiaries

The rules under each schedule are different. When a company completes a tax return, income must be correctly allocated to each schedule.

1.3 Tax terminology

When considering the tax framework, there are a number of terms that you need to be familiar with.

1.3.1 Direct versus indirect tax

Direct taxation is charged directly on the person, or enterprise, who is intended to pay the tax, and is a tax on income. The person or enterprise must pay the tax due directly to the tax authorities. Examples include personal income taxes, company income tax, tax on capital gains.

Indirect taxation is charged indirectly on the final consumer of the goods or services and is a tax on consumption or spending. The more a person spends, the more tax is paid. An example is sales tax, for example VAT in the UK and TVA in France.

1.3.2 Taxable person

The person liable to pay tax is called a **taxable person**. The taxable person can be an individual or a company.

1.3.3 Competent jurisdiction

Jurisdiction relates to the power of a tax authority to charge and collect tax. **Competent jurisdiction** is the authority whose tax laws apply to an individual or a company.

1.3.4 Tax rate structure

A government will structure its tax rates according to where it wishes the burden of taxation to fall. There is a general agreement that people on higher incomes should pay more tax, but governments have learned that punitive rates at the top lead to higher levels of tax avoidance and evasion.

There are three possible tax rate structures.

*   A **proportional** tax rate structure taxes all income at the same rate, so the same proportion of all income is taken in tax.

*   A **progressive** tax rate structure takes a higher proportion in tax as income rises.

*   A **regressive** structure would take a decreasing proportion as income rises.

Most Western countries use a progressive tax rate structure.

1.3.5 Tax gap

This is the gap between the tax theoretically collectable and the amount actually collected. The tax authorities work unceasingly to minimise this gap.

1.3.6 Hypothecation

The government can choose to ring-fence (ie restrict the use of) certain types of tax revenue for the purposes of certain types of expenditure. This prevents the money being spent on anything else and is known as **hypothecation**.

An example in the UK is the revenue from the 'congestion charge' levied on London motorists which can only be spent on transport in the capital.

1.3.7 Incidence/effective incidence

The **incidence** of a tax is on the person or organisation that pays it.

It is important to distinguish between **formal** and **effective** incidence.

- The **formal incidence** of a tax is on the person or organisation who has direct contact with the tax authorities.

- The **effective incidence** of a tax is on the person or organisation who actually bears the end cost of the tax.

For example, the formal incidence of a sales tax is on the entity that is responsible for paying the sales tax to the tax authorities. However, the effective incidence of a sales tax is on the customer who bears the tax burden (ie the cost of the tax) when they make a purchase from the entity.

Section summary

- The three major principles of tax recognised today are **equity, efficiency** and **economic effects**.

- Tax rules arise from a number of sources. There are four main ones:

    - Domestic tax legislation and court rulings
    - Domestic tax authority practice
    - Supranational bodies
    - International tax treaties

- Taxes can be classified according to their **tax base: income or profits, assets,** or **consumption**.

- Taxation can be one of two forms: **direct** or **indirect.**

- There are three possible tax structures: **proportional, progressive** and **regressive**.

- The **incidence** of a tax is on the person or organisation that pays it. It is important to distinguish between **formal** and **effective** incidence.

2 Administration of tax

Introduction

In this section on administration of tax we cover record keeping, tax returns and deadlines.

2.1 Record keeping

Tax authorities require businesses to keep records of the tax they pay. It makes no difference if the tax is a cost to the business (eg tax on business profits or gains) or whether the business acts merely as a tax collector (eg employee tax and social security contributions).

Tax records usually need to be kept in more detail than is strictly necessary than for financial reporting purposes. This is so that the business can satisfy the tax authority that is has complied with the law.

For example, businesses will need to keep detailed records of:

- Supporting documents for company income tax and capital gains tax calculations
- Employee pay, income tax and social security contributions for employee tax
- All sales and purchases subject to VAT or other sales tax, or to excise duties
- Transaction prices for intra-group sales with overseas subsidiaries

2.2 Retention of records

Most tax authorities have the power to inspect business records to ensure compliance. If mistakes are made, the tax authority may be able to re-assess earlier years and collect back taxes owed. Therefore there is usually a minimum period for which tax records must be kept. In the UK this is six years for certain types of tax.

2.3 Deadlines

There are deadlines for reporting and paying outstanding tax to the tax authorities. There may be different deadlines for the different types of tax.

For instance, in the UK, company income tax for small and medium entities has to be paid within 9 months of the end of the accounting period. The company tax return has to be submitted within 12 months of the end of the period. At this point, any adjustment will be made to the amount originally paid. In contrast, large entities must pay the tax due in four instalments, two during the financial year and two after. Both methods allow the government to collect tax before the company's tax liability is finalised.

In the UK, a business also has to file a return on employee taxes within 6 weeks of the end of the tax year.

Similarly, there are deadlines for the submission of records of VAT (sales tax) and other excise duties. The business may be fined for submitting returns late.

Tax due to, or collected on behalf of the tax authorities must be paid within a time limit. In the UK, employee taxes must be paid to HM Revenue and Customs on a monthly basis by a specified date. Interest is charged for late payment and there may also be penalties charged for persistent late payment.

Section summary

- Records relating to tax must be maintained to satisfy tax authority requirements.
- There is usually a minimum retention period for which records relating to tax must be kept.
- There are deadlines for reporting and paying outstanding tax to the tax authorities.

3 Tax enforcement

Introduction

This section looks at the enforcement of tax and the powers of tax authorities to deal with non-compliance with tax legislation. We then move on to look at the important distinction between tax avoidance and tax evasion.

3.1 Enforcement

Tax authorities have the power to enforce compliance with the tax rules. These powers generally include the following:

(a) **Power to review and query filed returns.** Tax legislation will usually specify a deadline for the tax authorities to open an enquiry into a filed tax return.

(b) **Power to request special reports or returns.** A special report or return is usually requested when the tax authorities believe that an entity may not be providing full information.

(c) **Power to examine records** (generally extending back some years). This is generally carried out by appointment with the company. In the UK, the tax authorities can go back 20 years in cases where fraud is suspected.

(d) **Powers of entry and search.** When the tax authority believes that fraud has occurred, it can obtain a search warrant to enter a business's premises and seize the records.

(e) **Exchange of information with tax authorities in other jurisdictions.** This has become very important as a counter-terrorism measure in recent years. One tax authority may become aware of funds being moved to another country in suspicious circumstances. It will then warn the tax authority in that other jurisdiction.

3.2 Tax avoidance and tax evasion

KEY TERMS

TAX AVOIDANCE is a way of arranging your affairs to take advantage of the tax rules to pay as little tax as possible. It is legal and is often referred to as tax planning.

TAX EVASION is a way of paying less tax by **illegal methods,** for example by not declaring income or claiming fictitious expenses.

Tax avoidance and evasion tend to be most common where the following situations apply:

- High tax rates, making it more worthwhile to avoid tax and to spend money on tax advice
- Imprecise wording of the tax laws, leaving loopholes to be exploited
- Insufficient penalties for tax evasion
- Perceived inequity in the tax laws, which makes evasion/avoidance seem more justified

When a tax authority becomes aware that so many businesses are avoiding tax by using a perceived loophole in the law, it may bring in **anti-avoidance legislation** to close the loophole. However this takes time and so modern laws usually include general anti-avoidance clauses in new tax bills to cover any loopholes. In other tax regimes, the tax authority may have to take the case to court to obtain a legal ruling as to whether a scheme is against the spirit of the law.

However, in the long term, if it wishes to minimise avoidance and evasion, a tax authority has to concentrate on the following:

(a) reducing opportunity by deducting tax at source whenever possible

(b) keeping the tax system as simple as possible

(c) increasing the risk of detection by having an efficient system of checking tax returns

(d) developing good communications between tax authorities and enterprises

(e) maximising penalties for evasion and making sure that this is well publicised

(f) making sure that the tax system is perceived as equitable and that the tax administration deals fairly and courteously with taxpayers

Section summary

- Tax authorities have the power to enforce compliance with the tax rules via various means.

- **Tax avoidance** is a way of arranging your affairs to take advantage of the tax rules to pay as little tax as possible. It is legal.

- **Tax evasion** is a way of paying less tax by **illegal methods**, eg not declaring the income or money laundering.

Chapter Summary

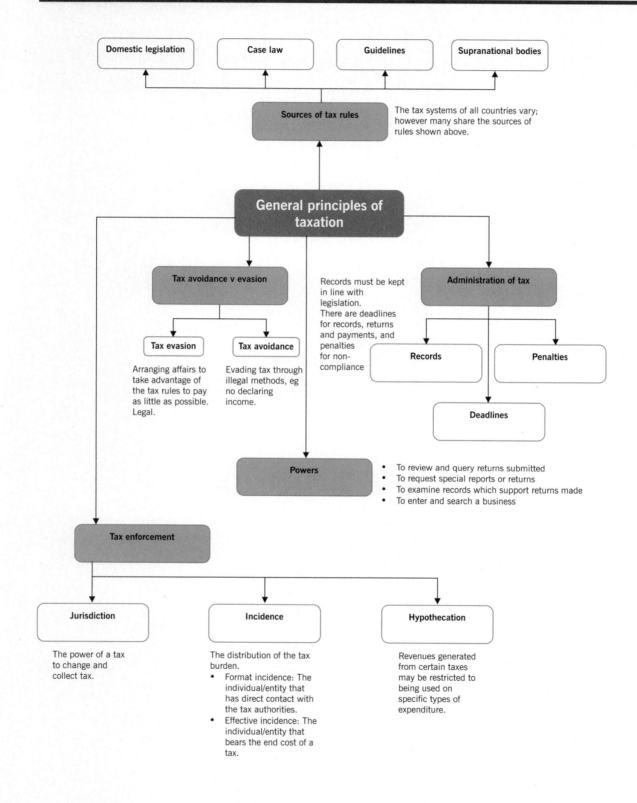

Domestic legislation   Case law   Guidelines   Supranational bodies

Sources of tax rules

The tax systems of all countries vary; however many share the sources of rules shown above.

General principles of taxation

Tax avoidance v evasion

Records must be kept in line with legislation. There are deadlines for records, returns and payments, and penalties for non-compliance

Administration of tax

Tax evasion   Tax avoidance

Arranging affairs to take advantage of the tax rules to pay as little as possible. Legal.

Evading tax through illegal methods, eg no declaring income.

Records   Penalties

Deadlines

Powers

- To review and query returns submitted
- To request special reports or returns
- To examine records which support returns made
- To enter and search a business

Tax enforcement

Jurisdiction

Incidence

Hypothecation

The power of a tax to change and collect tax.

The distribution of the tax burden.
- Format incidence: The individual/entity that has direct contact with the tax authorities.
- Effective incidence: The individual/entity that bears the end cost of a tax.

Revenues generated from certain taxes may be restricted to being used on specific types of expenditure.

Quick Quiz

1   Value added tax is an example of which kind of tax?

    A   Indirect tax

    B   Capital gains tax

    C   Direct tax

    D   Income tax

2   List Adam Smith's characteristics of a 'good' tax.

3   Define tax evasion in no more than 15 words.

4   A system of taxation in which a higher proportion is paid in tax as income rises is known as:

    A   A progressive system

    B   A regressive system

    C   Hypothecation

    D   Direct tax

5   List four powers that tax authorities have to ensure companies comply with tax legislation.

Answers to Quick Quiz

1   A   Indirect tax

2   Equity, certainty, convenience and efficiency

3   **Tax evasion** is a way of paying less tax by **illegal methods**.

4   A   A **progressive** system

5   Review and query tax returns; request special reports; enter and search a company's premises; examine records of previous years.

Now try this question from the OTQ Question Bank

Number

Q10

DIRECT TAXATION

In this chapter we look at some of the different types of direct taxation which are relevant to corporations and employees.

topic list	learning outcomes	syllabus references
1 Direct taxes on company profits and gains	D3	D3 (a)
2 Interaction of corporate and personal income tax	D3	D3 (a)
3 Employee taxation	D1	D1 (a)

Chapter Overview

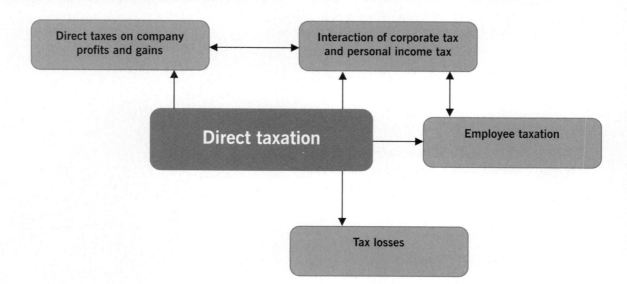

1 Direct taxes on company profits and gains

Introduction

There are two types of direct taxes on companies that you need to be aware of:

- Company income tax on profits from trading income

- Capital gains tax on gains made on disposals of assets and investments

In this section, we look in detail at the principles and calculation of these taxes. Your syllabus covers the general principles of tax which should be applicable across most countries. In this chapter, we have used the UK tax system to illustrate the principles.

1.1 Company income tax on profits

A company pays company income tax on the **taxable profits** it generates. Company income tax is charged on the **trading income** of the company.

KEY TERM

TAXABLE PROFIT is the accounting profit adjusted according to the tax rules and is the amount on which tax is actually paid.

The financial statements provide the starting point for calculating taxable profits, however some items included in the accounting profit may not be allowed for tax purposes.

The following items are often specifically disallowed:

- Entertaining
- Depreciation and amortisation
- Taxes paid to other public bodies
- Donations to political parties

The company income tax charge is calculated as **taxable profit × tax rate**.

Exam alert

Rules for allowed and disallowed items vary according to the tax regime. In the exam you will be told what rules to apply. The tax rules are also released on the CIMA website prior to the exam. Make sure you check the website to see what they are:

www.cimaglobal.com/Students

1.1.1 Adjustments to accounting profit

The following statement shows the types of adjustments to accounting profit needed to arrive at taxable profit.

	$'000	$'000
Accounting profit per financial statements		5,000
Add back items of expense that are not tax allowable:		
Entertaining	50	
Amortisation	75	
Donations to political parties	50	
Depreciation	125	
Balancing charge (see section 1.1.3)	100	
		400
		5,400

	$'000	$'000
Deduct items of income that are not taxable or tax allowances given:		
Non-taxable income (eg government grants)	70	
Tax depreciation	60	
Balancing allowance (see section 1.1.3)	20	
		(150)
Taxable profit		5,250

Here the accounting profit is $5m, but the tax will be paid on the taxable profit of $5.25m. If the tax rate is 30%, the tax due is $1,575,000 (30% × $5,250,000).

The depreciation added back here is the **accounting depreciation** charged in the statement of profit or loss and other comprehensive income. This is not normally an allowable expense for tax purposes and so must be added back to taxable profits. Instead, most tax regimes have rules for '**tax depreciation**'. In the UK this allowable tax depreciation is known as **capital allowances**.

Question 19.1

Taxable profit

Learning outcome D3

Talbot is resident in Country X for tax purposes. Country X has the following rules for taxation of corporate profits:

(a) Accounting rules on recognition and measurement are followed for tax purposes.

(b) All income other than grants received from government bodies is taxable.

(c) All expenses other than depreciation, amortisation, entertaining, taxes paid to other public bodies and donations to political parties are tax deductible.

(d) The corporate tax on profits is at a rate of 25%.

Talbot has prepared the following statement of profit or loss for the year ended 31 December 20X3.

STATEMENT OF PROFIT OR LOSS FOR THE YEAR ENDED 31 DECEMBER 20X3

	$'000	$'000
Revenue		1,150
Cost of sales		(700)
Gross profit		450
Income from government grant		100
		550
Expenses:		
Client entertaining	75	
Telephone costs	10	
Donation to Green Party (political party)	25	
Stationery costs	30	
Travel expenses	35	
Rent and utilities	50	
Depreciation	80	
Amortisation of intangible asset	50	
		(355)
Profit before tax		195

Talbot is entitled to tax depreciation of $100,000 for the year.

Required

Calculate Talbot's taxable profit and tax due for the year ended 31 December 20X3.

1.1.2 Tax depreciation

Accounting depreciation is not an allowable expense for tax purposes. Instead, **tax depreciation** is given to compensate entities for the fall in value of their assets. Tax depreciation is calculated in a similar way to accounting depreciation, but following the specific tax rules. Tax depreciation can be used by the government to encourage businesses to invest in particular assets (eg environmentally friendly cars) or to generally boost the economy. This is done by giving **accelerated tax depreciation**, for example a **100% first year allowance**, on these assets in the year they are purchased.

Most countries allow tax depreciation on plant and machinery, including computer equipment and motor vehicles, and on buildings; however other types of non-current assets may also be included. Many countries do not allow tax depreciation on land.

1.1.3 Calculating tax depreciation

Exam alert

The rules for calculating tax depreciation vary according to the tax regime. In your exam you will be told which rules apply. The tax rules are also released on the CIMA website prior to the exam. Make sure you check the website to see what they are:

www.cimaglobal.com/Students

It is possible that these rules will be based on the UK system which is discussed below.

In the UK, similar assets are grouped together and put into a 'pool' of expenditure. A tax depreciation allowance (called the '**writing down allowance**') is given on the **tax written down value** (ie cost less previous allowances) of the pool. The writing down allowance is usually given as a percentage of the written down value.

Over the life of an asset, the tax depreciation should equal the purchase price of the asset less any amount realised on disposal. Therefore, when disposal takes place, there is often a '**balancing charge**' or '**balancing allowance**' to account for any difference.

A balancing charge occurs when the disposal value deducted exceeds the balance remaining in the pool for the asset. The balancing charge equals the excess and is effectively a negative tax depreciation allowance as the entity has been over compensated for the fall in value of the asset.

For instance:

	$
Purchase price of asset	50,000
Tax depreciation allowed	(40,000)
Remaining value for tax purposes	10,000
Amount realised on disposal	(15,000)
Balancing charge	(5,000)

If the asset had realised $7,000 on disposal, the company would have received a balancing allowance of $3,000 – this is effectively an additional tax depreciation allowance to make sure the entity is fully compensated for the fall in value of the asset.

Question 19.2

Tax depreciation

Learning outcome D3

Winton is resident in country Y. In Country Y, tax depreciation is deductible as follows: 50% of additions to plant and machinery in the accounting period in which they are recorded; 25% per year of the written down value in subsequent accounting periods except that in which the asset is disposed of.

Winton makes up accounts 31 December each year. At 31 December 20X7, the tax written down value of plant and machinery is $100,000. During the year to 31 December 20X8, Winton purchases a machine for $20,000 and a van for $10,000. During the year to 31 December 20X9, Winton disposed of the van for $7,000.

Required

Calculate the tax depreciation Winton will claim for the years to 31 December 20X8 and 31 December 20X9.

1.1.4 Treatment of trading losses

When a company makes a loss instead of a taxable profit, no tax will be payable for that year, instead tax relief will be given according to the rules of the tax regime.

Exam alert

The rules for relieving losses vary according to the tax regime. In your exam you will be told what rules to apply. The tax rules are also released on the CIMA website prior to the exam. Make sure you check the website to see what they are:

www.cimaglobal.com/Students

Possible ways of getting tax relief for a trading loss are:

- Carry the loss forward against future **trading profits** of the **same trade**
- Offset the loss against other income or **capital gains** of the same period
- Carry the loss back against profits of previous periods
- Offset the loss against the profits of another group company ('group loss relief')

Some countries do not allow **capital gains/losses** to be offset against **trading gains/losses** and vice versa.

Some countries do not allow losses to be carried back and some restrict the number of years for which they can be carried forward.

Example: Trading losses

In Country S, trading losses can be carried back and offset against trading profits in the previous year. Any unrelieved losses can be carried forwards indefinitely and offset against trading profits of future periods.

Entity A started trading in 20X6 and had the following results:

	Trading profits/losses $'000
20X6	50
20X7	(100)
20X8	45
20X9	30

Required

Calculate the taxable profits for all years.

Solution

	Note	Taxable profits
		$'000
20X6	1	-
20X7		-
20X8	2	-
20X9	3	25

Notes

1   $50,000 of the trading loss made in 20X7 is carried back and offset against the $50,000 trading profits made in 20X6. The remaining unrelieved trading loss of $50,000 is carried forwards.

2   $45,000 of the unrelieved trading loss carried forwards is offset against the $45,000 trading profits made in 20X8. This leaves $5,000 of unrelieved trading losses carried forwards.

3   The remaining $5,000 unrelieved trading loss is offset against the $30,000 trading profits generated in 20X9 to give taxable profits of $25,000.

The losses carried back or forwards must be used to their maximum extent, it is not possible to partially relieve profits if the losses available could relieve more of the profits. For example, in 20X6, $50,000 from the £100,000 loss in 20X7 must be used as relief, it is not possible to just offset, say, just $40,000 of losses and leave taxable profits of $10,000.

1.1.5 Cessation of trading

When a business ceases trading, there may be provision for carrying back any losses generated in the last year of trading (sometimes known as **terminal losses**) against previous years' taxable profits. In the UK, a business calculates the losses for the last twelve months ending on the day trade ceases. These terminal losses can then be carried back and offset against the final year of assessment and the three previous tax years.

Question 19.3	Cessation of trading

Learning outcome D3

In Country Y, terminal losses can be carried back two years and offset against trading profits on a last in first out (LIFO) basis.

Entity F ceased trading in 20X9 and had the following results:

	Trading profits/losses
	$'000
20X6	100
20X7	50
20X8	25
20X9	(80)

Required

What is the effect of terminal loss relief on taxable profits for each year?

1.2 Capital gains tax

A company pays capital gains tax on capital gains it makes. When an asset is disposed of for more than its original cost, a '**capital gain**' arises.

KEY POINT

A distinction is made between '**trading income**' that arises from the trade of the business and which is subject to company income tax, and '**capital gains**' which result when an asset is disposed of for more than its cost which are subject to capital gains tax.

Most tax regimes have **separate rules** covering the taxation of capital gains. In the UK, capital gains are included in the total profits chargeable to corporation tax (along with taxable profits from trading activities) and so are taxed at the corporate income tax rate.

Different tax jurisdictions have different rules concerning the taxation of capital gains. In the UK, the largest capital gains made by individuals are probably made on the sales of residential property, but these are exempt from taxation as long as the property constitutes a 'main residence'. Other items are also excluded, such as cars, boats and caravans. The UK government probably makes most of its capital gains tax revenue from gains made on transfers of shares in companies listed on the Stock Exchange.

Some countries have an annual exemption from capital gains which means that only gains in excess of the annual exemption will be subject to tax.

The capital gain is usually calculated as the **disposal proceeds less the cost of the asset** being disposed of. Other costs that can be deducted from the disposal proceeds include any **initial purchase costs** incurred, the cost of any **improvements** and **enhancements** to the asset (but **not repairs**), and **any costs incurred to sell** the asset.

Some countries also allow the original cost of the asset to be adjusted up to current prices by the use of an index, such as the Retail Price Index, before calculating the capital gain. This prevents the taxpayer from having to pay tax on a gain which is simply the result of inflation.

1.2.1 Indexation allowance

This relief for inflation is known as the **indexation allowance** in the UK. Companies are entitled to indexation allowance from the date of acquisition until the date of disposal of an asset. It is based on the movement in the Retail Price Index (RPI) between those two dates and is calculated as follows.

LEARN

> **Indexation allowance** = acquisition cost × indexation factor

Example: Indexation allowance

An asset is acquired by a company in February 20X0 at a cost of $15,000. The asset is sold for $25,500 in December 20X9. The indexation factor from February 20X0 to December 20X9 was 30%. Gains are taxed at 25%.

Required

Calculate the capital gain arising and the tax payable. Work to the nearest $1.

Solution

	$	$
Proceeds of sale		25,500
Cost	15,000	
Indexation allowance (15,000 × 30%)	4,500	
Total allowable cost		(19,500)
Capital gain		6,000
Tax payable (6,000 × 25%)		1,500

KEY POINT

Indexation allowance **cannot create or increase a capital loss**. If there is a gain before the indexation allowance, the allowance can reduce that gain to zero but no further. If there is a loss before the indexation allowance, there is no indexation allowance.

Question 19.4

Capital gains

Learning outcome D3

Company A bought an asset on 1 January 20X0 for $80,000 and incurred buying costs of $1,000. In June 20X2 enhancements were made to the asset which cost $10,000, along with repairs to fix damage which cost $4,000.

On 1 March 20X5, the asset was sold for $150,000 and selling costs of $2,500 were incurred.

The indexation factor from January 20X0 to March 20X5 was 20% and from June 20X2 to March 20X5 was 10%. Capital gains are taxed at 30%.

Required

What is the capital gains tax to be charged on the disposal of the asset?

1.2.2 Capital losses

Capital losses can be relieved in the following ways:

(a)   Carried back against previous capital gains
(b)   Carried forward against future capital gains
(c)   Offset against current or future trading profits

However, many countries do not allow capital gains to be carried back against previous capital gains or to be offset against trading profits. In your exam the rules for offsetting capital losses will be given.

Question 19.5

Learning outcome D3

In Country S, capital losses can be offset against capital gains in the same period or can be carried forward and offset against capital gains in future years. Unrelieved capital losses cannot be carried back.

Entity E had the following results:

	Capital gains $m	Capital losses $m
20X6	100	(150)
20X7	75	-
20X8	5	(10)

Required

Calculate the taxable gains for all years.

1.2.3 Rollover relief

An entity may sell an asset and realise a capital gain. However, it may then need to replace the asset. If the entity pays tax on the capital gain, this will reduce the proceeds available for reinvestment. Therefore, some countries allow the tax charge on the disposal of a business asset to be **deferred** until the replacement asset is disposed of. If this is a type of asset that will have to be continuously replaced (such as manufacturing machinery), then this deferral could go on indefinitely. In some tax jurisdictions, this is known as **rollover relief**.

Question 19.6

Learning outcome D3

Country R has the following tax regulations:

- Trading losses in any year can be carried back and offset against trading profits in the previous year, and any unrelieved trading losses can be carried forwards indefinitely to offset against trading profits in future years.
- Capital losses can be offset against capital gains in the same tax year and carried forward and offset against capital gains of future periods. Unrelieved capital losses may not be carried back.
- Capital gains/losses cannot be offset against trading profits/losses or vice versa.

Entity A had the following results:

	Trading profits/losses $	Capital gains/losses $
20X6	10,000	7,000
20X7	(15,000)	(5,000)
20X8	35,000	14,000

Required

Calculate the taxable gains and profits for all years.

1.3 Group loss relief

Tax rules are also necessary to deal with tax losses in groups. In the UK, losses of one group subsidiary may be set against the profits of another group subsidiary. When assets are transferred between group companies, capital gains tax is deferred until the asset is sold outside the group. In effect, UK group relief rules treat the group as one entity for tax purposes.

This UK treatment is an example of **tax consolidation.** In general, if a group of enterprises are recognised as a **tax group**, it is possible for them to gain relief for trading losses by offsetting the losses of one group member against the profits of another group member. The rules for group relief will vary from country to country, as will the rules for recognition of a tax group (which may differ from the rules under which groups are recognised for financial reporting purposes).

Some countries also have their own regulations for recognising **tax groups for capital gains purposes**. It is not usually possible to offset capital losses and gains between the group members. However, there are usually provisions that allow the transfer of assets between group members without recognising a capital gain or loss. The calculation of the gain and the payment of the tax are usually **deferred** until the asset is sold outside the tax group. Good tax planning is needed to ensure that all asset sales to third parties take place through just one group member. These provisions can then be used to accumulate all the group's capital gains and losses in that member, thereby effectively obtaining offset.

Group relief may be used to save tax as the group company surrendering the loss may pay tax at a lower rate than the company receiving the loss. It also may enable tax relief to be gained earlier as instead of the company making the loss having to carry that loss forward, it can instead surrender it to a group company which can utilise it in the current year.

Section summary

- Entities are subject to **direct taxes** on the **trading profits** and **capital gains** they generate.

- **Company income tax** is paid on the **taxable profit** of an entity. Taxable profit is the accounting profit adjusted according to the tax rules.

- Depreciation is not normally allowable for tax purposes. Instead, entities are allowed to deduct **tax depreciation** which is calculated based on the rules of the tax regime.

- When an asset is disposed of for more than its original cost, a **capital gain** arises that is subject to corporate income tax. An **indexation allowance** may be given to counter the effects of inflation and reduce the gain chargeable to tax.

- **Trading losses** and **capital losses** can usually be **relieved** against profits and gains according to the rules of the tax regime.

2 Interaction of corporate tax and personal income tax

Introduction

The interaction of the corporate and personal tax systems in a country depends on the system of tax that operates in that country. When a company pays a dividend to its shareholders, it is paid out of the company's taxed profits and therefore has already been subject to tax. If the dividend income received by the individual is then taxed again under personal income tax, the dividend will effectively have been taxed twice. The system of tax which is in operation in a country determines whether this will happen as it specifies the interaction between corporate and personal tax. There are four main systems of tax, which we cover in this short section.

2.1 Classical system

Under the classical system of taxation, company income tax is charged on all of the profits of the entity, whether distributed or not. Dividends are paid out of taxed profits and are then chargeable to personal income tax in the hands of the shareholder. This system is simple to administer but gives rise to **double taxation** of dividends. This system could result in entities being less likely to distribute dividends as it leads to double taxation.

2.2 Imputation system

Under the imputation system, the underlying company income tax that has already been paid is **imputed** to the shareholder as a tax credit. He pays income tax on the dividend but deducts the tax credit. This avoids the problem of double taxation.

2.3 Partial imputation system

It is also possible to have a system of **partial imputation**, where the taxpayer receives a tax credit of only part of the underlying company income tax.

2.4 Split rate system

Some tax jurisdictions operate a **split rate system** in which distributed profits are taxable at a lower rate than retained profits. This avoids double taxation of dividends. This can function under the classical, imputation or partial imputation system.

Example: classical versus imputation system

Cadis Co supplies the following information.

	$
Year to 30 June 20X8	
Taxable profits	100,000
Dividend paid for the year (net)	24,500

The corporate income tax rate is 30% and shareholders pay income tax at 40% on dividends received.

Required

Calculate the total tax payable by Cadis Co and its shareholders as at 30 June 20X8 under:

(a) the classical system,
(b) the imputation system; and
(c) a partial imputation system where a tax credit of 20% is allowed

Solution

(a) **Classical system**

	$
Corporate income tax paid by Cadis Co (100,000 × 30%)	30,000
Tax on dividends paid by shareholders (24,500 × 40%)	9,800
Total tax paid	39,800

(b) **Imputation system**

	$	$
Corporate income tax paid by Cadis Co		30,000
Shareholders:		
Dividend received	24,500	
Tax credit (24,500/70 × 30)	10,500	
Gross dividend	35,000	
Tax at 40% (35,000× 40%)	14,000	
Less tax credit	(10,500)	
		3,500
Total tax paid		33,500

(c) **Partial imputation system**

	$	$
Corporate income tax paid by Cadis Co		30,000
Shareholders:		
Dividend received	24,500	
Tax credit (24,500/70 × 20)	7,000	
Gross dividend	31,500	
Tax at 40% (31,500× 40%)	12,600	
Less tax credit	(7,000)	
		5,600
Total tax paid		35,600

You can see that the classical system does not encourage the payment of dividends.

Section summary

- There are four main systems of taxing corporate income: **classical, imputation, partial imputation** and **split rate**.
- The classical system is much **simpler** but most countries do not use it.

3 Employee taxation

Introduction

Employees are liable to income tax on their employment income and are responsible for dealing with their own tax liabilities.

3.1 Taxable income

The amount of tax paid depends on the way that earnings are measured. In the UK, an employee is taxed on all income actually received from the employment in tax year including 'non-cash' items (called

benefits in kind). Cash income includes basic and overtime pay, bonuses, commission and redundancy pay. Examples of benefits in kind include company cars, private health insurance, free accommodation and cheap loans from the employer.

3.2 Deductible expenses

Tax regimes often allow employees to deduct expenses from their earnings before the tax rate is applied. In the UK an employee can claim that expenses were incurred **wholly, exclusively and necessarily**, in the course of his or her employment. Examples of these expenses include professional subscriptions, business travel, charitable donations through a payroll deduction scheme and contributions to pension plans.

3.3 Social security contributions

Some taxes are called **social security** contributions because they are used to pay for social security items such as pensions and public heath services. In the UK the social security contribution is National Insurance. It is paid by both the employee and the employer.

3.4 Employer as a tax collector (PAYE)

Many tax regimes require the employer to deduct employee tax in instalments directly from the employee's pay and pay it over to the tax authorities. In the UK, this system is called 'PAYE' or 'Pay As You Earn'.

If the employee feels that he or she has paid too much tax, it is up to the individual to deal with the tax authority to obtain a refund. The employer merely acts as a tax collector.

While placing a burden on employers, a PAYE system has major advantages for the tax authorities:

- The tax authorities only have to deal with the employer, rather than all the individual employees.

- It makes it easier for governments to forecast tax revenues as they receive regular payments from employers.

- It allows the tax to be collected earlier than would be the case if it were assessed on the employee's earnings at the end of the year, improving cash flows for the government.

- The costs of administering the system are borne by employers, rather than by the government.

- It greatly reduces the risks of default or late payment as tax is collected at source, helping the government to minimise the tax gap.

It also makes tax payment easier for individuals, who do not have to deal with a large bill once or twice a year.

3.5 Calculating employee tax

Calculating how much income tax is due for an employee is very similar to calculating how much company income tax is due for a company. However, individuals are usually given a 'personal allowance' which is an amount they can earn before they have to start paying tax.

A standard proforma for calculating employee income tax is shown below.

	$
Salary	X
Plus: Bonuses, commission, benefits in kind	X
Less:	
Personal allowance	(X)
Professional subscriptions	(X)
Business travel	(X)
Charitable donations	(X)
Taxable income	X

The tax due is calculated as **taxable income × tax rate**.

There are usually various rates of tax depending on the amount of taxable income. For example:

- all amounts up to $10,000 – taxed at 10%
- all amounts from $10,001 - $30,000 – taxed at 20%
- all amounts above $30,000 – taxed at 40%.

Question 19.7

Employee tax

Learning outcome D1

Khalid earns $45,000 per year. During the tax year, he also received a bonus of $1,000 and Khalid's company paid an additional 2% of his salary into a pension scheme. Khalid received taxable benefits in kind with a value of $750 from his employer and made charitable donations of $300.

The personal allowance for the tax year is $6,600 and the tax rates on taxable income are as follows:

- 20% on the first $32,000
- 40% on all income above $32,000

Required

Calculate how much employee tax is payable by Khalid for the year.

Section summary

Employee taxation is personal tax; the employer acts as a tax collector.

set.

- **Prudence** dictates that deferred tax assets can only be recognised when **sufficient future taxable profits** exist against which they can be utilised.

Chapter Summary

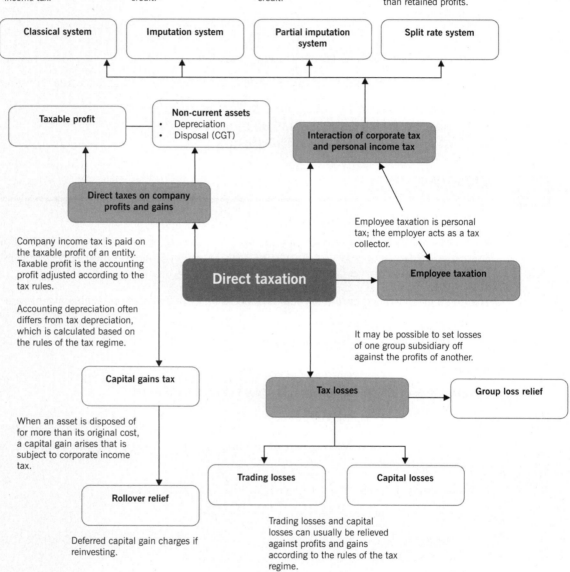

Company income tax is charged on all profits. Dividends are paid out of taxed profits and are then chargeable to personal income tax.

The underlying company income tax paid is imputed to the shareholder as a tax credit.

Part of the underlying company income tax paid is imputed to the shareholder as a tax credit.

Distributed profits are taxable at a lower rate than retained profits.

Classical system

Imputation system

Partial imputation system

Split rate system

Taxable profit

Non-current assets
- Depreciation
- Disposal (CGT)

Interaction of corporate tax and personal income tax

Direct taxes on company profits and gains

Company income tax is paid on the taxable profit of an entity. Taxable profit is the accounting profit adjusted according to the tax rules.

Accounting depreciation often differs from tax depreciation, which is calculated based on the rules of the tax regime.

Direct taxation

Employee taxation is personal tax; the employer acts as a tax collector.

Employee taxation

It may be possible to set losses of one group subsidiary off against the profits of another.

Capital gains tax

When an asset is disposed of for more than its original cost, a capital gain arises that is subject to corporate income tax.

Tax losses

Group loss relief

Trading losses

Capital losses

Rollover relief

Deferred capital gain charges if reinvesting.

Trading losses and capital losses can usually be relieved against profits and gains according to the rules of the tax regime.

Quick Quiz

1   Complete the sentence:

Taxable profit is the .... adjusted according to the tax rules and is the amount on which .... is actually paid.

2   A withholding tax is:

A   A tax withheld from the tax authorities
B   The amount of tax paid by a company on its underlying profits
C   A tax deducted at source before payment of a dividend
D   A tax for which relief is not usually given

3   Name **three** advantages to government of employee income tax deducted at source by employers.

4   Under the OECD Model Tax Convention an entity is considered to be resident in the country:

A   Of its incorporation

B   Where its main trading activities occur

C   Of its effective management and control

D   In which it has a permanent establishment

5   Complete the sentence:

A classical system of company income tax is one where an entity is taxable on all of its .... and .... whether they are .... or not.

Answers to Quick Quiz

1   Accounting profit; tax

2   C   A tax deducted at source before payment of a dividend.

3   •   It allows the tax to be collected earlier than would be the case if it were assessed on the employee's earnings at the end of the year.

    •   The costs of administering the system are borne by employers, rather than by the government.

    •   It greatly reduces the risks of default or late payment, helping government to minimise the tax gap.

4   C   Of its effective management and control

5   Income; gains; distributed.

Answers to Questions

19.1 Taxable profit

		$'000	$'000
Accounting profit			195
Add: disallowable expenditure:	entertaining	75	
	depreciation	80	
	amortisation	50	
	political donation	25	
			230
Less: non-taxable income		100	
tax depreciation		100	
			(200)
Taxable profit			225

The tax rate is 25%, so the tax due is **$56,250** ($225,000 × 25%)

19.2 Tax depreciation

	Plant and machinery pool $'000	Total tax depreciation for the year $'000
Year ended 31 December 20X8		
Opening written down balance	100	
Writing down allowance @25%	(25)	(25)
Additions	30	
First year allowance at 50%	(15)	(15)
Closing written down balance	90	(40)
Year ended 31 December 20X9		
Opening written down balance	90	
Disposal	(7)	
Balancing charge (working)	2	2
	85	
Writing down allowance @25%	(21)	(21)
Closing written down balance	64	(19)

Working

	$
Purchase price of van	10,000
Tax depreciation allowed	(5,000)
Remaining value for tax purposes	5,000
Amount realised on disposal	(7,000)
Balancing charge (added to taxable profit)	(2,000)

Note that the balancing charge increases taxable profit and therefore decreases the amount of tax depreciation allowed in the year.

19.3 Cessation of trading

	20X6 $'000	20X7 $'000	20X8 $'000	20X9 $'000
Trading profits	100	50	25	–
Loss relief	–	(50)	(25)	
Taxable profits	100	=	=	=

The final year's trading losses (terminal losses) are carried back on a LIFO basis, so the losses are offset against the most recent trading profits first. The losses must be used to the maximum extent in each year. The tax rules in Country Y only allow terminal losses to be carried back two years, so the remaining unrelieved terminal losses ($80,000 – $25,000 – $50,000 = $5,000) cannot be used.

19.4 Capital gains

		$
Sales proceeds		150,000
Less selling costs		(2,500)
Net proceeds		147,500
Less cost to purchase	(80,000)	
Less enhancements	(10,000)	
Less purchase costs	(1,000)	
		(91,000)
		(56,500)
Less indexation allowance:		
On cost ((80,000 + 1,000) × 20%)		(16,200)
On enhancements (10,000 × 10%)		(1,000)
Capital gain		39,300
Capital gains tax (39,300 × 30%)		11,790

Note that the cost of repairs cannot be deducted as they are not an enhancement or improvement to the asset.

19.5 Capital losses

	Notes	Taxable gains $m
20X6	1	-
20X7	2	25
20X8	3	-

Notes

1   The capital loss of $150m can be offset against the capital gain of $100m, leaving $50m of unrelieved losses to carry forward.

2   The unrelieved losses of $50m is offset against the gain of $75m.

3   The capital loss of $10m can be offset against the capital gain of $5m. The remaining unrelieved losses of $5m can be carried forward against any future gains, but cannot be carried back against the gain made in 20X7.

19.6 Loss relief

	Trading profits $	Capital gains $
20X6	–	7,000
20X7	–	–
20X8	30,000	9,000

The trading loss of $15,000 in 20X7 can be carried back and offset against the $10,000 trading profits made in 20X6. The remaining $5,000 unrelieved loss can be carried forwards and offset against the trading profits of $35,000 in 20X8.

The capital loss of $5,000 in 20X7 cannot be offset against the capital gains in 20X6, but can be carried forward to be offset against the capital gains of $14,000 made in 20X8.

19.7 Employee tax

		$	$
Salary		45,000	
Plus:	Bonus	1,000	
	Pension contribution (2% × 45,000)	900	
	Benefits in kind	750	
			47,650
Less:	Personal allowance	(6,600)	
	Charitable donations	(300)	
			(6,900)
Taxable income			40,750
Tax payable:			
@20%: 20% × 32,000		6,400	
@40%: 40% × (40,750 – 32,000)		3,500	
Total tax due			9,900

Now try these questions from the OTQ Question Bank	Number
	Q1
	Q12
	Q26
	Q29
	Q54
	Q55

INTERNATIONAL AND INDIRECT TAXATION

 This chapter considers international and indirect taxation.

topic list	learning outcomes	syllabus references
1 International taxation	D2	D2 (a)
2 Indirect taxes	D1	D1 (a)
3 Value Added Tax (VAT)	D1	D1 (a)

Chapter Overview

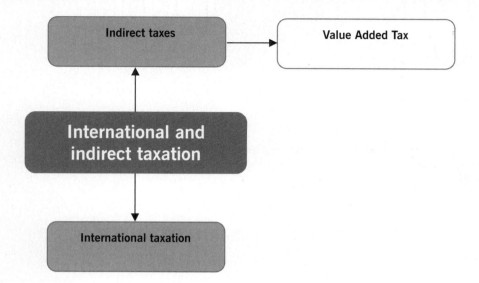

1 International taxation

Introduction

This section introduces some key concepts in international taxation and looks at double taxation treaties and the OECD Model Tax Convention.

1.1 Corporate residence

Entities usually pay company income tax on their worldwide income in the country they are resident in for tax purposes. Therefore determining an entity's **country of residence** is important. There are different ways to determine the residence of an entity, including its:

(a) **Place of incorporation (domicile)**
(b) **Place of effective management** and control
(c) **Place of permanent establishment**

A **permanent establishment** means a fixed place of business through which the business of an entity is wholly or partly carried on.

There must be a degree of permanence, for example:

(i) Place of management
(ii) Branch
(iii) Office
(iv) Factory
(v) Workshop
(vi) Mine, oil or gas well, quarry
(vii) A building site or construction or installation project if it lasts more than 12 months

A warehouse is not a permanent establishment, it is just a storage area. A permanent establishment is somewhere where trade is carried out or decisions are made.

1.2 Double tax and OECD deemed residence

Each tax authority will have its own rules on how residence is determined. This can sometimes lead to entities being resident in two countries. For example, suppose a company is incorporated in country X, where residency is determined on the basis of incorporation only. However, the company conducts most of its activities in country Y, where its board of directors meet. In country Y, residency is determined based on the place of management and control. In this situation, the company will be deemed to be resident in both country X and country Y. The company is therefore theoretically subject to tax in both of those countries and may have to pay tax twice on its income. This is known as **double tax**.

The OECD Model Tax Convention addresses the issue of double residence.

KEY POINT

In the case where an entity is resident in more than one country, the OECD Model Tax Convention suggests that the entity will be **deemed** to be **resident only in the country of its effective management**.

A place of effective management is:

- the place where **key management and commercial decisions are made**
- the place where the **board or senior management meet**

An entity can only have one place of effective management, so using the OECD Model Tax Convention rules means that the entity would only be taxed in that country, which solves the problem of double tax.

1.3 Payments remitted from overseas subsidiaries

A group may have overseas subsidiaries which will from time to time pay dividends to the parent company. In this situation, two types of tax become relevant: withholding tax and underlying tax.

1.3.1 Withholding tax

If a company makes payments to an individual or another company or an individual resident in a different country, it may first have to pay **withholding tax (WHT)** to the local tax authority. A withholding tax ensures that the local government gains some income from the dividend payment so that not all of the money earned by the company in that country is remitted overseas.

The rate of withholding tax varies depending on the country. Withholding tax also applies to other types of payment, such as interest payments, royalties, capital gains and rents.

Example: Withholding taxes

P owns 30% of the equity shares in A, an entity resident overseas. P receives a dividend of $40,000 from A, after the deduction of withholding tax at 15%.

Required

Calculate the amount of withholding tax paid by A to the nearest $1.

Solution

P receives $40,000 net of withholding tax at 15%.

Therefore, withholding tax = 40,000 × 0.15/0.85 = $7,059

1.3.2 Underlying tax

Underlying tax (ULT) is the tax which has already been suffered by the profits from which a dividend is paid. This happens when an entity receives a dividend from a foreign entity when the dividend has been paid out of taxed profits. Under some tax systems, the entity can obtain relief for the tax levied in the foreign country on the amount out of which their dividend was paid.

Underlying tax is calculated as follows.

Underlying tax = gross dividend × $\dfrac{\text{tax actually paid by foreign company}}{\text{foreign company's profit after tax}}$

The gross dividend is the dividend paid by the foreign entity before withholding tax.

Example: underlying tax

Continuing the example from above, A had profits after tax for the year of $450,000 and paid corporate income tax of $150,000.

Required

Calculate the amount of ULT that relates to the dividend received by P to the nearest $1.

Solution

Gross dividend = 40,000+ 7,059 = $47,059

ULT = 47,059 × $\frac{150,000}{450,000}$ = $15,686

1.3.3 Double tax

When a parent company receives a dividend payment from an overseas subsidiary, that dividend will often already have been subject to underlying tax and withholding tax. Because that dividend now forms part of the income of the parent company, it will also be subject to corporate income tax in the country in which the parent is resident. In effect the dividend has been **taxed twice**.

To relieve this burden, **double tax relief** is often available for the overseas tax paid.

1.4 Double tax relief

There are three main methods for giving double tax relief.

1.4.1 Exemption method

In the Exemption method, the dividend received is exempted from tax in the receiving company's country. So, if income is taxed in Country A, then it will not be taxed in Country B.

1.4.2 Tax Credit method

In the Tax Credit method, the dividend received is subject to tax in the receiving company's country, but the foreign tax already paid is credited against the tax due in the receiving company's country. So the tax paid in Country A is credited against (ie deducted) from the tax due in Country B. No refund of tax is given if the tax already paid in Country A is higher than that due in Country B.

Example: Tax Credit method I

RH, a company resident in Country Y, is a 100% owned subsidiary of APH, a company resident in Country X. At the year end, RH paid a dividend of $54,000, after deduction of a withholding tax of 10%, to APH. RH had reported a profit after tax of $450,000 and paid a corporate income tax bill of $90,000 in Country Y. In Country X:

- Corporate income tax is 40%
- Double tax relief is given by the Tax Credit method

Required

How much tax is payable by APH in Country X?

Solution

Tax paid in Country Y

WHT = 54,000 × 10/90 = $6,000

$$\text{Underlying tax} = \text{gross dividend} \times \frac{\text{tax actually paid by foreign company}}{\text{foreign company's profit after tax}}$$

Gross dividend = 54,000 + 6,000 = $60,000

$$\text{Underlying tax} = 60,000 \times \frac{90,000}{450,000} = \$12,000$$

Tax payable by APH in Country X

	$
Net dividend	54,000
Add back WHT	6,000
Add back ULT	12,000
Gross dividend	72,000
Taxed at 40% (72,000 × 40%)	28,800
Less: Double tax relief for WHT	(6,000)
Less: Double tax relief for ULT	(12,000)
Tax due in Country X	10,800

Example: Tax Credit method II

SW, a company resident in Country Y, is a 100% owned subsidiary of LR, a company resident in Country X. At the year end, SW paid a dividend of $130,000, before deduction of a withholding tax of 15%, to LR. SW had reported a profit after tax of $200,000 and paid a corporate income tax bill of $50,000 in Country Y. In Country X:

• Corporate income tax is 20%

• Double tax relief is given by the Tax Credit method.

Required

How much tax is payable by LR in Country X?

Solution

Tax paid in Country Y

WHT = 130,000 × 15% = $19,500

$$\text{Underlying tax} = \text{gross dividend} \times \frac{\text{tax actually paid by foreign company}}{\text{foreign company's profit after tax}}$$

$$\text{Underlying tax} = 130,000 \times \frac{50,000}{200,000} = \$32,500$$

Tax payable by LR in Country X

	$	$
Net dividend (130,000 – 19,500)	110,500	54,000
Add back WHT	19,500	6,000
Add back ULT	32,500	12,000
Gross dividend	162,500	72,000
Taxed at 20%	32,500	
Less: Double tax relief for WHT	(19,500)	
Less: Double tax relief for ULT (relief restricted to $13,000)	(13,000)	
Tax due in Country X	Nil	

1.4.3 Deduction method

This is where only the **income after tax** in Country A is taxable in Country B. The example below illustrates the **deduction** method.

Example: Deduction method

RH, a company resident in Country Y, is a 100% owned subsidiary of APH, a company resident in Country X. At the year end, RH paid a dividend of $54,000, after deduction of a withholding tax of 10%, to APH. RH had reported a profit after tax of $450,000 and paid a corporate income tax bill of $90,000 in Country Y.

In Country X:

- Corporate income tax is 40%

- Double tax relief is given by the Deduction method.

Required

How much tax is payable by APH in Country X?

Solution

Tax payable by APH in Country X	$
Net dividend received	54,000
Tax payable at 40%	21,600

1.4.4 Double taxation treaties

Often two countries will establish a **double tax treaty** between them to determine which country will tax income and what method of double tax relief will be available to entities that have taxable income in both countries. The starting point for double taxation treaties is often the **OECD's Model Tax Convention**. The Model Tax Convention recommends the use of the Tax Credit method for double tax relief.

You do not need to know the OECD model tax convention in detail. However, it does make good background reading. www.oecd.org

1.5 Types of overseas operations

A business trading abroad will have to decide whether it should do so through a **subsidiary** or a **foreign branch**. This decision will not be made principally on the basis of tax considerations, but the following tax issues will be taken into consideration.

Subsidiary

- The overseas subsidiary will be treated as a separate company for tax purposes. The parent company will be liable to tax on foreign dividends received from the subsidiary.

- Losses made by a non-resident subsidiary are not available for group relief.

- The parent company will not normally be subject to capital gains tax on gains made by a non-resident subsidiary.

- Any assets transferred to the parent from the non-resident subsidiary may become subject to capital gains tax on transfer.

- Transfer pricing arrangements between parent and foreign subsidiary will be subject to scrutiny from the tax authorities.

Branch

- The branch will be treated as an extension of the main entity and all of the branch's profits will be included in the main entity's tax calculations.

- Money transferred from a branch to the main entity will not be treated as a dividend.

- Losses sustained by a branch are usually immediately available for group relief.

- The main entity will be subject to capital gains tax on any capital gains made by a branch.

- Assets can usually be transferred to the main entity without triggering capital gains tax.

Section summary

- Where a company pays corporate income tax is determined by which country it is **resident** in.

- An entity's country of residence for tax purposes can be determined by its **place of incorporation, place of effective management** or by its **place of permanent establishment.**

- If an entity operates in several countries, it could be deemed resident in all of those countries, leading to **double taxation**.

- In such circumstances, the OECD Model Tax Convention deems companies to be resident in their **place of effective management**.

- Overseas subsidiary companies often remit dividends to their parent company. These payments will often have been subject to **withholding tax** and **underlying tax**. When the dividend is subsequently taxed as part of the parent company's income, it will have been **taxed twice.**

- **Double tax relief**, is often available in this situation. Relief may be given by **deduction, exemption** or **tax credit.**

2 Indirect taxes

Introduction

This section looks at the different types of indirect taxes. As we saw in Chapter 18, an indirect tax is a tax on expenditure (or 'consumption'), rather than on income.

2.1 Types of indirect taxes

2.1.1 Unit taxes

Unit taxes are based on the number or weight of items, eg excise duties on cigarettes or tobacco.

2.1.2 Ad valorem taxes

Ad valorem taxes are based on the value of the items, eg a sales tax or value added tax.

2.2 Excise duties

Excise duties are a 'unit' tax – they are levied on the **amount** of the commodity.

Governments apply excise duty to goods that have large sales volumes and are easy to **control**, ie there are a few large producers and products covered by the duty are easily defined.

Excise duty tends to be levied on four major commodities – **alcohol, tobacco, oil products and motor vehicles**. The tax is collected earlier in the supply chain than sales taxes. By the time the product reaches the final consumer the price will already include excise duty. For instance, each brewery will have an excise officer assigned to it, who will know exactly what quantities are being produced. Because they are collected early in the supply chain from a limited number of products, excise duties yield large amounts of revenue for low collection cost and are therefore popular with governments.

Governments may apply excise duties to increase the cost of drinking, smoking and motoring as a way of discouraging the consumption of these products and to raise revenue to pay for extra costs that may be incurred as a result, such as increased healthcare costs.

Excise duties, unlike sales taxes, are not refundable and so are usually treated as part of the cost of the asset when calculating the amount of sales tax due.

2.3 Wealth and property taxes

Some countries tax individuals and companies on the value of land and buildings or other valuable property or on 'total wealth' – for a company this would be its asset value.

2.3.1 Property taxes

Some countries operate systems under which people are taxed on their property – usually land and buildings, but sometimes including other assets. The UK has a system whereby individuals and businesses are taxed at a local level on the basis of the value of their property.

2.3.2 Wealth taxes

A number of countries levy wealth taxes, either on individuals or on entities or on both. This will involve measurement and valuation of assets each year. The tax is usually a straight percentage, for example 2%, of total net worth (total assets less total liabilities).

Section summary

There are two types of indirect taxes: **unit taxes** and **ad valorem taxes**.

3 Value Added Tax (VAT)

Introduction

In this section we examine VAT and its administration. VAT is a consumption tax, the amount paid depends on the consumption of goods by the consumer and is added to the purchase price.

3.1 Single-stage versus multi-stage sales taxes

A sales tax can be single-stage or multi-stage.

Single-stage sales taxes are applied at one stage in the supply chain, either at the manufacturing, wholesale or retail level. Most sales taxes tend to be applied at the retail level (such as the retail sales tax applied in the USA), so the end user will bear the tax burden.

Multi-stage sales taxes are applied at several stages in the supply chain. A multi-stage sales tax is usually **chargeable and deductible** at different points in the supply chain (such as **VAT**), so the business deducts the tax it pays on purchases and pays over the balance to the government. The incidence of tax is therefore on the final consumer of the goods or services. A multi-stage sales tax can also be **cumulative** (known as a **cascade** tax) where no refund is received for tax paid in the previous stage and so the tax is a business cost at each stage in the supply chain.

3.2 Multi-stage sales tax: VAT

VAT is a multi-stage sales tax that is charged by a business each time a product is sold. However, the business can claim back the VAT it has paid on purchasing products or raw materials to make the product, which is known as 'input VAT'. So the effect in the end is that the final consumer suffers the full VAT amount on the final purchase price, but this amount has been paid to the tax authorities in several slices by the various businesses in the supply chain along the way. The following example shows how VAT works.

Example: VAT (1)

		Price net of VAT $	VAT @ 20% $	Total price $
(a)	Manufacturer buys raw materials	40	8	48
	Manufacturer makes and sells television to wholesaler	200	<u>40</u>	240
	Manufacturer pays VAT		<u>32</u>	
(b)	Wholesaler buys television	200	40	240
	Wholesaler sells television to retailer	320	<u>64</u>	384
	Wholesaler pays VAT		<u>24</u>	
(c)	Retailer buys television	320	64	384
	Retailer sells television	480	<u>96</u>	576
	Retailer pays VAT		<u>32</u>	
(d)	Customer buys television	480	96	576

KEY POINT

The total tax of $96 is suffered by the customer (the end user) who cannot claim back any VAT paid. The tax amounts paid by the manufacturer, the wholesaler and the retailer will all have been reclaimed.

	$
Supplier of raw materials	8
Manufacturer	32
Wholesaler	24
Retailer	32
Total VAT paid	96

3.3 VAT business liability

VAT on sales is called **output tax**, while VAT on purchases is called **input tax**. A business owes the tax authority the output tax it collects but deducts from this liability the input tax it pays.

Output tax	−	Input tax	=	Amount paid to tax authority

Example: VAT (2)

Carrying on the example from above, how much VAT is paid over to the tax authorities by the Manufacturer, Wholesaler and Retailer?

Solution

		Output VAT	Input VAT	Amount paid to tax authority
		$	$	$
(a)	Manufacturer	40	(8)	32
(b)	Wholesaler buys television	64	(40)	24
(c)	Retailer buys television	96	(64)	32
				96

3.4 Registering for VAT

In most countries, entities are required to register for VAT when their taxable sales (also known as 'taxable supplies') exceed a certain level. Only entities registered for VAT can charge output VAT on their sales and reclaim input VAT on their purchases.

- Once an entity is registered for VAT, it must:
- Charge VAT on its sales
- Reclaim VAT on its purchases
- Keep records relating to VAT
- Complete a quarterly VAT return and pay any VAT owed to the tax authorities.

3.5 Rates of VAT

Some activities may be **exempt from VAT**, eg banking services. Traders who carry on exempt activities cannot charge VAT on those activities and cannot reclaim VAT on inputs relating to those activities.

Transactions which are not exempt from VAT will be taxable at one of three rates:

(a)   Standard rate. In the UK this is currently 20%.

(b)   Higher or reduced rate. For example in the UK, domestic fuel is taxable at 5%.

(c)   Zero rate (0%). For example, in the UK children's clothing and protective clothing, such as cycle helmets, are taxable at 0%.

Exam alert

In the exam you will be told the rates of VAT to apply. The tax rules are also released on the CIMA website prior to the exam. Make sure you check the website to see what they are:

www.cimaglobal.com/Students

You will not be expected to know the types of goods or services that are zero rated or exempt from VAT. This information will be provided in the exam.

If you are given a figure **excluding VAT**, the VAT charged is calculated as:

exclusive price × VAT rate

If you are given a figure **including VAT**, the VAT charged is calculated as:

inclusive price × VAT rate
(100 + VAT rate)

Question 20.1   VAT

Learning outcome D1

In country X, VAT is charged at the following rates:

Standard rate – 20%

Lower rate – 5%

Zero rate – 0%

BB Co is resident in country X and has made the following sales (including VAT) during the last VAT period.

Product X (zero rated)	$350,000
Product Y (standard rated)	$240,000

Product X and Product Y are both made from the same raw material, Z, of which BB Co purchased $160,000 (excluding VAT) during the period. Raw material Z is a lower rated product for VAT purposes. There was no opening or closing inventories of Z.

Required

(a)   Calculate BB Co's gross profit for the period

(b)   Calculate the amount of VAT to be paid to or received from the tax authorities for this VAT period

Section summary

- VAT is a **multi-stage sales tax**. It is chargeable and deductible at different points in the supply chain.

- VAT on sales is output tax. VAT on purchases is input tax.

- There are usually three rates of VAT. These are **standard rate, higher or reduced rate** and **zero rate**.

Chapter Summary

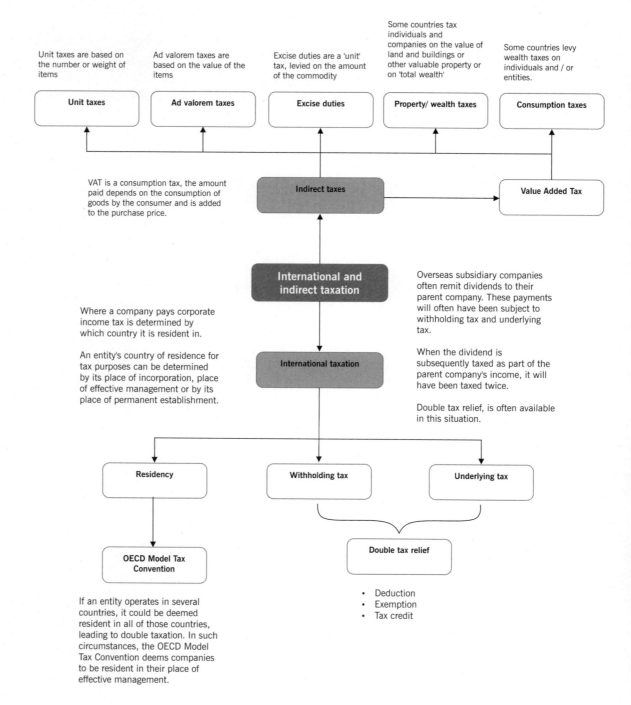

Unit taxes are based on the number or weight of items

Ad valorem taxes are based on the value of the items

Excise duties are a 'unit' tax, levied on the amount of the commodity

Some countries tax individuals and companies on the value of land and buildings or other valuable property or on 'total wealth'

Some countries levy wealth taxes on individuals and / or entities.

Unit taxes

Ad valorem taxes

Excise duties

Property/ wealth taxes

Consumption taxes

VAT is a consumption tax, the amount paid depends on the consumption of goods by the consumer and is added to the purchase price.

Indirect taxes

Value Added Tax

International and indirect taxation

Where a company pays corporate income tax is determined by which country it is resident in.

An entity's country of residence for tax purposes can be determined by its place of incorporation, place of effective management or by its place of permanent establishment.

Overseas subsidiary companies often remit dividends to their parent company. These payments will often have been subject to withholding tax and underlying tax.

When the dividend is subsequently taxed as part of the parent company's income, it will have been taxed twice.

Double tax relief, is often available in this situation.

International taxation

Residency

Withholding tax

Underlying tax

OECD Model Tax Convention

Double tax relief

If an entity operates in several countries, it could be deemed resident in all of those countries, leading to double taxation. In such circumstances, the OECD Model Tax Convention deems companies to be resident in their place of effective management.

- Deduction
- Exemption
- Tax credit

Quick Quiz

1   The tax expense related to the profit from ordinary activities should be shown in the statement of profit or loss.

True ☐

False ☐

2   Current tax is the amount of income tax payable in respect of the .... for a period.

3   Value added tax (VAT) is an example of which kind of tax?

A   Unit tax
B   Ad valorem tax
C   Direct tax
D   Income tax

4   Peter is a VAT registered trader. In the quarter to 31 March 20X5 Peter sold goods for $40,000 (excluding VAT). During the same period he made purchases of $15,330 (including VAT).

Required

Calculate Peter's output and input VAT for the quarter and his liability to the tax authorities. The rate of VAT is 15%. Work to the nearest $.

Answers to Quick Quiz

1   True

2   Taxable profit

3   B   Ad valorem tax

4

	$
Output tax ($40,000 × 15%)	6,000
Input tax ($15,330 × 15/115)	(2,000)
Net VAT payable	4,000

Answers to Questions

20.1 VAT

(a)   Gross profit is calculated using sales and purchases *net of VAT*

	$'000	$'000
Sales - Product X (zero rated)	350	
- Product Y (240,000 × 100/120)	200	
		550
Cost of sales		
- Raw material Z		(160)
Gross profit		390

(b)

	$'000	$'000
Output VAT - Product X (zero rated)	0	
- Product Y (240,000 × 20/120)	40	
		40
Input VAT		
- Raw material Z (160,000 × 5%)		(8)
		32

VAT due to the tax authorities = $32,000

Now try these questions from the OTQ Question Bank	Number
	Q2
	Q25
	Q27
	Q52
	Q53
	Q56
	Q57

MANAGEMENT OF WORKING CAPITAL, CASH AND SOURCES OF SHORT-TERM FINANCE

Part D

WORKING CAPITAL AND THE OPERATING CYCLE

In this chapter we consider functions of the management accountant relating to the **management of working capital** in general terms, including how much working capital the business requires and the impact on working capital of changes in the business.

topic list	learning outcomes	syllabus references
1 Working capital	C2	C2 (b)
2 Working capital ratios	C2	C2 (b)
3 Working capital requirements	C2	C2 (b)

Chapter Overview

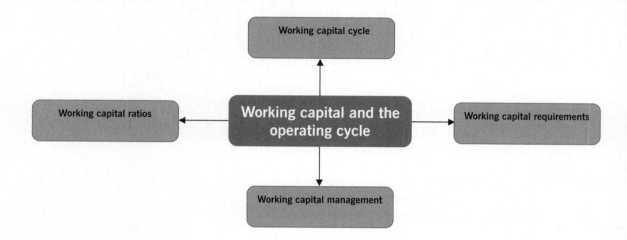

1 Working capital

1.1 What is working capital?

> ### Introduction
>
> Every business needs adequate **liquid resources** to maintain **day-to-day cash flow**. It needs enough to pay wages and salaries as they fall due and enough to pay suppliers if it is to keep its workforce and ensure its supplies. Maintaining adequate working capital is not just important in the short term. Sufficient liquidity must be maintained in order to ensure the **survival** of the business in the **long term** as well. Even a profitable company may fail if it does not have adequate cash flow to meet its liabilities as they fall due.

KEY TERM

WORKING CAPITAL is the capital available for conducting the day-to-day operations of an organisation; normally the excess of current assets over current liabilities. (CIMA *Official Terminology*)

1.2 Working capital characteristics of different businesses

Different businesses will have different working capital characteristics. There are three main aspects to these differences.

(a) Holding inventories (from their purchase from external suppliers, through the production and warehousing of finished goods, up to the time of sale)

(b) Taking time to pay suppliers and other payables

(c) Allowing customers (receivables) time to pay

The current assets of a business can be subdivided into **permanent current assets** (the core levels of inventory and receivables) and **fluctuating current assets**, which vary from period to period.

1.3 Examples

(a) Supermarkets and other retailers receive much of their sales in cash or by credit card or debit card. However, they typically buy from suppliers on credit. They may therefore have the advantage of significant cash holdings, which they may choose to invest.

(b) A company which supplies to other companies, such as a wholesaler, is likely to be selling and buying mainly on **credit**. Co-ordinating the flow of cash may be quite a problem. Such a company may make use of short-term borrowings (such as an overdraft) to manage its cash.

(c) Smaller companies with a limited trading record may face particularly severe problems. Lacking a long track record, such companies may find it difficult to obtain credit from suppliers. At the same time, customers will expect to receive the length of credit period that is normal for the particular business concerned. The firm may find itself squeezed in its management of cash.

1.4 What is working capital management?

Ensuring that **sufficient liquid resources** are **maintained** is a matter of working capital management. This involves achieving a balance between the requirement to **minimise** the risk of **insolvency** and the requirement to **maximise** the **return** on assets (or profit). Efficient working capital management is vital if the organisation is to stay in business. Profitable businesses can go under very quickly if liquidity is not maintained. The business must decide what level of cash and inventories are to be maintained and how they are to be funded.

A business pursuing an **aggressive** working capital policy will hold **minimal cash** and inventories and use short-term financing to fund both permanent and fluctuating current assets. This policy carries the **highest risk** of insolvency and the highest level of financial return.

A business pursuing a **conservative** policy will hold **large levels** of ready **cash** and safety inventory and use long-term funding for both non-current and most current assets. This is the **least risky** option but results in the **lowest expected return**.

An excessively conservative approach to working capital management resulting in high levels of cash holdings will harm profits because the opportunity to make a return on the assets tied up as cash will have been missed.

A **moderate** policy will match short-term finance to fluctuating current assets and non-fluctuating current (and non-current) assets will be matched by long-term funding.

1.5 The working capital cycle

WORKING CAPITAL CYCLE is the period of time which elapses between the point at which cash begins to be expended on the production of a product and the collection of cash from a purchaser.

(CIMA *Official Terminology*)

KEY TERM

The connection between investment in working capital and cash flow may be illustrated by means of the **working capital cycle** (also called the **cash cycle, operating cycle** or **trading cycle**).

The working capital cycle in a manufacturing business equals:

The average time that raw materials remain in inventory	X
Less the period of credit taken from suppliers	(X)
Plus the time taken to produce the goods	X
Plus the time finished goods remain in inventory after production is completed	X
Plus the time taken by customers to pay for the goods	X
	X

If the turnover periods for inventories and receivables lengthen, or the payment period to payables shortens, then the operating cycle will lengthen and the investment in working capital will increase.

Example: working capital cycle

Wines Co buys raw materials from suppliers that allow Wines 2.5 months credit. The raw materials remain in inventory for 1 month, and it takes Wines 2 months to produce the goods. The goods are sold within a couple of days of production being completed and customers take on average 1.5 months to pay.

Required

Calculate Wines's working capital cycle.

Solution

We can ignore the time finished goods are in inventory as it is no more than a couple of days.

	Months
The average time that raw materials remain in inventory	1.0
Less: The time taken to pay suppliers	(2.5)
The time taken to produce the goods	2.0
The time taken by customers to pay for the goods	1.5
	2.0

The company's working capital cycle is 2 months. This can be illustrated diagrammatically as follows.

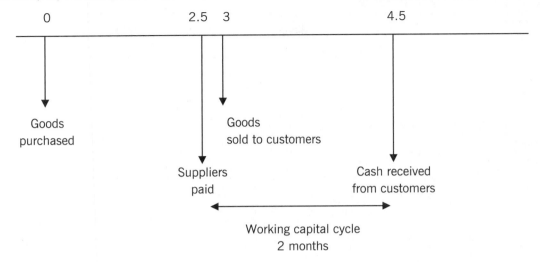

The working capital cycle is the period between the suppliers being paid and the cash being received from the customers.

1.6 Managing the cycle

A **longer** working capital cycle requires **more financial resource**, so management will seek whenever possible to **reduce** the length of the cycle. Their possible options are as follows.

(a) **Reduce** levels of **raw materials inventory**. This may be done by the introduction of some type of just-in-time system, which will necessitate more efficient links with suppliers. Production delays due to running out of inventory must be avoided.

(b) **Reduce work in progress** by reducing production volume or improving techniques and efficiency.

(c) **Reduce finished goods inventory**, perhaps by improving distribution. This may lead to delays in fulfilling customer orders.

(d) **Delay payments to suppliers**. This can lead to loss of discounts and of supplier goodwill.

(e) **Reduce** period of **credit given to customers**. This may mean offering discounts and more aggressive credit control may lead to loss of customers.

1.7 Cash flow planning

Since a company must have adequate cash inflows to survive, management should plan and control cash flows as well as profitability. **Cash budgeting** is an important element in short-term cash flow planning.

The purpose of cash budgets is to make sure that the organisation will have **enough cash inflows** to meet its cash outflows. If a budget reveals that a short-term cash shortage can be expected, steps will be taken to meet the problem and **avoid the cash crisis** (perhaps by arranging a bigger bank overdraft facility).

Cash budgets and cash flow forecasts on their own do not give full protection against a cash shortage and enforced liquidation of the business. There may be unexpected changes in cash flow patterns. When unforeseen events have an adverse effect on cash inflows, a company will only survive if it can maintain adequate cash inflows despite the setbacks.

Question 21.1   Cash flow patterns

Learning outcome C2

Give examples of unforeseen changes which may affect cash flow patterns.

Section summary

The amount tied up in **working capital** is equal to the value of all inventory and receivables less payables. This amount directly affects the liquidity of the organisation.

Working capital cycle is the period of time which elapses between the point at which cash begins to be expended on the production of a product and the collection of cash from a purchaser.

(CIMA *Official Terminology*)

2 Working capital ratios

Introduction

Working capital ratios may help to indicate whether a company has too much working capital (over-capitalised) or too little (overtrading).

2.1 The current ratio and the quick ratio

The standard test of liquidity is the **current ratio**. It can be obtained from the statement of financial position.

KEY TERM

$$\text{CURRENT RATIO} = \frac{\text{Current assets}}{\text{Current liabilities}}$$

A company should have enough current assets that give a promise of 'cash to come' to **meet its commitments** to **pay its current liabilities**. Obviously, a ratio **in excess of 1** should be expected; an ideal is probably about 2. Otherwise, there would be the prospect that the company might be unable to pay its debts on time. In practice, a ratio comfortably in excess of 1 should be expected, but what is 'comfortable' varies between different types of businesses.

Some manufacturing companies might hold large quantities of raw material inventories, which must be used in production to create finished goods. Finished goods might be warehoused for a long time, or sold on lengthy credit. In such businesses, where **inventory turnover is slow**, most inventories are **not very easy** to **turn into liquid assets**, because the cash cycle is so long. For these reasons, we calculate an additional liquidity ratio, known as the **quick ratio** or acid test ratio.

KEY TERM

$$\text{QUICK RATIO, or ACID TEST RATIO} = \frac{\text{Current assets less inventories}}{\text{Current liabilities}}$$

This ratio should ideally be at least 1 for companies with a slow inventory turnover. For companies with a fast inventory turnover, a quick ratio can be less than 1 without suggesting that the company is in cash flow difficulties.

The current ratio and the quick ratio are known as liquidity ratios.

2.2 The receivables collection period

A rough measure of the average length of time it takes for a company's customers to pay is the '**receivable days**' ratio.

KEY TERMS

$$\text{RECEIVABLE DAYS RATIO} = \frac{\text{Average trade receivables}}{\text{Average daily sales on credit terms}}$$ (CIMA *Official Terminology*)

An equivalent measure is the receivables turnover period.

$$\text{RECEIVABLES TURNOVER PERIOD} = \frac{\text{Average trade receivables}}{\text{Credit sales for the year}} \times 365 \text{ days}$$

The trade receivables are not the **total** figure for receivables in the statement of financial position, which includes prepayments and non-trade receivables. The trade receivables figure will be itemised in an analysis of the total receivables, in a note to the accounts.

The estimate of receivables days is only approximate.

(a)   The statement of financial position value might be used instead of the average. However, don't forget that the statement of financial position value of receivables might be abnormally high or low compared with the 'normal' level the company usually has.

(b)   Sales revenue in the statement of profit or loss excludes sales tax, but the receivables figure in the statement of financial position includes sales tax. We are not strictly comparing like with like. If the figures are too distorted by sales tax, adjustment will be needed.

(c)   Average receivables may not be representative of year-end sales if sales are growing rapidly.

2.3 The payables payment period

Similar measures can be used for payables.

The payables payment period indicates the average time taken, in calendar days, to pay for supplies received on credit.

KEY TERMS

$$\text{PAYABLES DAYS RATIO} = \frac{\text{Average trade payables}}{\text{Average daily purchases on credit terms}}$$ (CIMA *Official Terminology*)

$$\text{PAYABLES PAYMENT PERIOD, or PAYABLES TURNOVER PERIOD} = \frac{\text{Average trade payables}}{\text{Purchases on credit terms for year}} \times 365 \text{ days}$$

If the credit purchases information is not readily available, cost of sales can be used instead. Don't forget however that some elements of cost of sales (for example, labour costs) are not relevant to trade payables. Note also that credit purchases in the statement of profit or loss do not include sales tax.

2.4 The inventory turnover period

The inventory turnover period shows **how long goods are being kept** in inventory.

Another ratio worth calculating is the inventory turnover period. This is another estimated figure, obtainable from published accounts, which indicates the average number of days that items of inventory are held for. As with the average receivable collection period, it is only an approximate figure; there may be distortions caused by seasonal variations in inventory levels. However it should be reliable enough for finding changes over time.

KEY TERMS

$$\text{INVENTORY TURNOVER} = \frac{\text{Inventory}}{\text{Average daily cost of sales in period}} \text{ or } \frac{\text{Average inventory}}{\text{Cost of sales}}$$

The inventory turnover period can also be calculated:

$$\text{INVENTORY TURNOVER PERIOD} = \frac{\text{Inventory}}{\text{Cost of sales}} \times 365 \text{ days}$$

A lengthening inventory turnover period indicates:

(a)   A slowdown in trading, or

(b)   A build-up in inventory levels, perhaps suggesting that the investment in inventories is becoming excessive

Where a business is manufacturing goods for resale, inventory turnover will have three components:

Raw materials: $\dfrac{\text{average materials inventory}}{\text{purchases of raw materials}} \times 365$

WIP: $\dfrac{\text{average work in progress}}{\text{manufacturing cost}} \times 365$

Finished goods: $\dfrac{\text{average finished goods}}{\text{cost of sales}} \times 365$

Where average values are not available, closing values can be used.

Where no breakdown of inventories is supplied, just use the overall ratio: $\dfrac{\text{average inventory}}{\text{cost of sales}}$

If we add together the inventory days and the receivable days, this should give us an indication of how soon inventory is convertible into cash, thereby giving a further indication of the company's liquidity.

All the ratios calculated above will **vary industry by industry**; hence **comparisons** of ratios calculated with other similar companies in the same industry are important. There are organisations which specialise in **inter-firm comparison**. A company submits its figures to one of these organisations and receives an analysis of the average ratios for its industry. It can then compare its own performance to that of the industry as a whole.

The receivables turnover period, payables turnover period and inventory turnover period are known as **efficiency ratios**.

The working capital cycle (covered in Section 1) can be calculated using the following formulae.

		Days
$\dfrac{\text{Raw materials inventory}}{\text{Raw materials purchases}} \times 365 =$		X
$\dfrac{\text{Work in progress}}{\text{Manufacturing cost}} \times 365 =$		X
$\dfrac{\text{Finished goods}}{\text{Cost of sales}} \times 365 =$		X
$\dfrac{\text{Trade receivables}}{\text{Sales}} \times 365 =$		X
$\dfrac{\text{Trade payables}}{\text{Purchases}} \times 365 =$		(X)
		$\overline{\overline{X}}$

Note that if you are provided with the statement of financial position figures for the start and end of a year (top line in each formula), you should calculate the average for the year. You add the two figures together and divide by two.

Exam skills

Another term you may come across is **capital employed**. This usually means non-current assets + current assets – current liabilities.

Section summary

Working capital ratios may help to indicate whether a company has too much working capital (over-capitalised) or too little (overtrading).

$$\text{Current ratio} = \frac{\text{Current assets}}{\text{Current liabilities}}$$

$$\text{Quick ratio} = \frac{\text{Current assets less inventories}}{\text{Current liabilities}}$$

$$\text{Receivable days ratio} = \frac{\text{Average trade receivables}}{\text{Average daily sales on credit terms}} \qquad \text{(CIMA } \textit{Official Terminology}\text{)}$$

$$\text{Receivables turnover period} = \frac{\text{Average trade receivables}}{\text{Credit sales for the year}} \times 365 \text{ days}$$

$$\text{Payables days ratio} = \frac{\text{Average trade payables}}{\text{Average daily purchases on credit terms}} \qquad \text{(CIMA } \textit{Official Terminology}\text{)}$$

$$\text{Payables payment period, or payables turnover period} = \frac{\text{Average trade payables}}{\text{Purchases on credit terms for year}} \times 365 \text{ days}$$

$$\text{Inventory turnover} = \frac{\text{Inventory}}{\text{Average daily cost of sales in period}} \quad \text{or} \quad \frac{\text{Average inventory}}{\text{Cost of sales}}$$

3 Working capital requirements

Introduction

Current assets may be financed either by long-term funds or by current liabilities.

Liquidity ratios are a **guide** to the risk of **cash flow problems** and insolvency. If a company suddenly finds that it is unable to renew its short-term liabilities (for example, if the bank suspends its overdraft facilities, or suppliers start to demand earlier payment), there will be a **danger of insolvency** unless the company is able to turn enough of its **current assets** into **cash quickly**.

3.1 The need for funds for investment in current assets

Current liabilities are often a **cheap method of finance** (trade payables do not usually carry an interest cost) and companies may therefore consider that, in the interest of higher profits, it is worth accepting some risk of insolvency by increasing current liabilities, taking the maximum credit possible from suppliers.

3.2 The volume of current assets required

The **volume of current assets** required will depend on the **nature** of the company's business. For example, a manufacturing company may require more inventories than a company in a service industry. As the **volume of output** by a company **increases**, the **volume of current assets** required will **also increase**.

Even assuming efficient inventory holding, receivable collection procedures and cash management, there is still a certain degree of choice in the total volume of current assets required to meet output requirements. Policies of low inventory-holding levels, tight credit and minimum cash holdings may be contrasted with policies of high inventories (to allow for safety or buffer inventories) easier credit and sizeable cash holdings (for precautionary reasons).

3.3 Over-capitalisation and working capital

If there are **excessive** inventories, receivables and cash, and very few payables, there will be an **over-investment** by the company in current assets. **Working capital** will be **excessive** and the company will be in this respect **over-capitalised**. The return on investment will be lower than it should be, and long-term funds will be unnecessarily tied up when they could be invested elsewhere to earn profits.

Over-capitalisation with respect to working capital should not exist if there is good management, but the warning signs of excessive working capital would be unfavourable accounting ratios, including the following.

(a) **Sales/working capital**

The volume of sales as a multiple of the working capital investment should indicate whether, in comparison with previous years or with similar companies, the total volume of working capital is too high.

(b) **Liquidity ratios**

A current ratio greatly in excess of 2:1 or a quick ratio much in excess of 1:1 may indicate over-investment in working capital.

(c) **Turnover periods**

Excessive turnover periods for inventories and receivables, or a short period of credit taken from suppliers, might indicate that the volume of inventories or receivables is unnecessarily high, or the volume of payables too low.

Example: working capital ratios

Calculate liquidity and working capital ratios from the following accounts of a manufacturer of products for the construction industry, and comment on the ratios.

	20X8 $m	20X7 $m
Sales revenue	2,065.0	1,788.7
Cost of sales	1,478.6	1,304.0
Gross profit	586.4	484.7

	20X8 $m	20X7 $m
Current assets		
Inventories	119.0	109.0
Receivables (note 1)	400.9	347.4
Short-term investments	4.2	18.8
Cash at bank and in hand	48.2	48.0
	572.3	523.2
Payables: amounts falling due within one year		
Loans and overdrafts	49.1	35.3
Income taxes	62.0	46.7
Dividend	19.2	14.3
Payables (note 2)	370.7	324.0
	501.0	420.3
Net current assets	71.3	102.9

Notes

	20X8 $m	20X7 $m
1 Trade receivables	329.8	285.4
2 Trade payables	236.2	210.8
3 We are not given a breakdown of inventories		

Solution

	20X8	20X7
Current ratio	$\dfrac{572.3}{501.0} = 1.14$	$\dfrac{523.2}{420.3} = 1.24$
Quick ratio	$\dfrac{453.3}{501.0} = 0.90$	$\dfrac{414.2}{420.3} = 0.99$
Receivables' turnover period	$\dfrac{329.8}{2,065.0} \times 365 = 58 \text{ days}$	$\dfrac{285.4}{1,788.7} \times 365 = 58 \text{ days}$
Inventory turnover period	$\dfrac{119.0}{1,478.6} \times 365 = 29 \text{ days}$	$\dfrac{109.0}{1,304.0} \times 365 = 31 \text{ days}$
Payables turnover period	$\dfrac{236.2}{1,478.6} \times 365 = 58 \text{ days}$	$\dfrac{210.8}{1,304.0} \times 365 = 59 \text{ days}$

The company is a manufacturing group serving the **construction industry**, and so would be expected to have a **comparatively lengthy receivables turnover period**, because of the relatively **poor cash flow** in the construction industry. It is clear that the company **compensates** for this by ensuring that they do **not pay** for raw **materials** and other costs before they have **sold** their **inventories** of finished goods (hence the similarity of receivables and payables turnover periods).

The company's **current ratio** is a little **lower** than **average** but its **quick ratio** is **better** than average and very little less than the current ratio. This suggests that **inventory** levels are **strictly controlled**, which is reinforced by the low inventory turnover period. It would seem that working capital is **tightly managed**, to avoid the poor liquidity which could be caused by a high receivables turnover period and comparatively high payables.

3.4 Overtrading

OVERTRADING is the condition of a business which enters into commitments in excess of its available short-term resources. This can arise even if the company is trading profitably, and is typically caused by financing strains imposed by a lengthy operating cycle or production cycle.   (CIMA *Official Terminology*)

In contrast with over-capitalisation, **overtrading** happens when a business tries to do **too much too quickly** with **too little long-term capital**, so that it is trying to support too large a volume of trade with the capital resources at its disposal.

Even if an overtrading business operates at a **profit**, it could easily run into serious **trouble** because it is **short of money**. Such liquidity troubles stem from the fact that it does not have enough capital to provide the **cash** to pay its **debts** as they fall due.

Example: overtrading

Great Ambition appoints a new managing director who has great plans to expand the company. He wants to increase revenue by 100% within two years, and to do this he employs extra sales staff. He recognises that customers do not want to have to wait for deliveries, and so he decides that the company must build up its inventory levels. There is a substantial increase in the company's inventories. These are held in additional warehouse space which is now rented. The company also buys new cars for its extra sales representatives.

The managing director's policies are immediately successful in boosting sales, which double in just over one year. Inventory levels are now much higher, but the company takes longer credit from its suppliers, even though some suppliers have expressed their annoyance at the length of time they must wait for payment. Credit terms for receivables are unchanged, and so the volume of receivables, like the volume of sales, rises by 100%.

In spite of taking longer credit, the company still needs to increase its overdraft facilities with the bank, which are raised from a limit of $40,000 to one of $80,000. The company is profitable, and retains some profits in the business, but profit margins have fallen. **Gross profit margins** are lower because some prices have been reduced to obtain extra sales. **Net profit margins** are lower because overhead costs are higher. These include sales representatives' wages, car expenses and depreciation on cars, warehouse rent and additional losses from having to write off out-of-date and slow-moving inventory items.

The statement of financial position of the company changed over time from (A) to (B).

	Statement of financial position (A) $	Statement of financial position (A) $	Statement of financial position (B) $	Statement of financial position (B) $
Non-current assets		160,000		210,000
Current assets				
Inventory	60,000		150,000	
Receivables	64,000		135,000	
Cash	1,000		–	
		125,000		285,000
Total assets		285,000		495,000
Current liabilities				
Bank	25,000		80,000	
Payables	50,000		200,000	
		75,000		280,000
Share capital	10,000		10,000	
Retained earnings	200,000		205,000	
		210,000		215,000
Total equity/liabilities		285,000		495,000

Sales revenue	$1,000,000	$2,000,000
Gross profit	$200,000	$300,000
Net profit	$50,000	$20,000

In situation (B), the company has reached its overdraft limit and has four times as many payables as in situation (A) but with only twice the sales revenue. Inventory levels are much higher, and inventory turnover is lower.

This is an example of overtrading. If Great Ambition had to pay its next trade payable, or salaries and wages, before it received any income, it could not do so without the bank allowing it to exceed its overdraft limit. The company is profitable, although profit margins have fallen, and it ought to expect a prosperous future. But if it does not sort out its cash flow and liquidity, it will not survive to enjoy future profits.

Solution

Suitable solutions to the problem would be measures to reduce the degree of overtrading. **New capital** from the shareholders could be injected. Short-term finance could be converted to longer-term finance. **Better control** could be applied to inventories and receivables. The company could **abandon ambitious plans** for increased sales and more non-current asset purchases until the business has had time to consolidate its position, and build up its capital base with retained profits. It partly requires the business to take a long-term view of future prospects, and **avoid short-termism**.

KEY TERM

SHORT-TERMISM is a bias towards paying particular attention to short-term performance, with a corresponding relative disregard to the long term. (CIMA *Official Terminology*)

3.5 Symptoms of overtrading

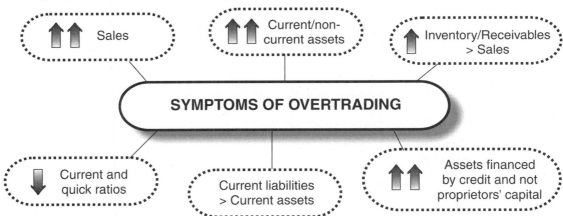

When business seeks to increase its sales too rapidly without an adequate capital base, there is a danger of overtrading. Overtrading may also be caused by the following.

(a) When a business repays a loan, it often replaces the old loan with a new one. However a business might **repay a loan** without **replacing it**, with the consequence that it has **less long-term capital** to finance its current level of operations.

(b) A business might be profitable, but in a period of inflation, its **retained profits** might be **insufficient** to pay for replacement non-current assets and inventories, which now cost more because of inflation. The business would then rely increasingly on credit, and find itself eventually unable to support its current volume of trading with a capital base that has fallen in real terms.

3.6 The working capital requirement

Computing the working capital requirement is a matter of calculating the value of current assets less current liabilities, perhaps by taking averages over a one year period.

Example: working capital requirements

The following data relate to Corn Co, a manufacturing company.

Sales for the year	$1,500,000

Costs as percentages of sales

	%
Direct materials	30
Direct labour	25
Variable overheads	10
Fixed overheads	15
Selling and distribution	5

On average:

(a)   Receivables take 2½ months before payment.

(b)   Raw materials are in inventory for three months.

(c)   Work-in-progress represents two months' worth of half produced goods.

(d)   Finished goods represent one month's production.

(e)   Credit is taken as follows.

(i)	Direct materials	2 months
(ii)	Direct labour	1 week
(iii)	Variable overheads	1 month
(iv)	Fixed overheads	1 month
(v)	Selling and distribution	½ month

Work-in-progress and finished goods are valued at material, labour and variable expense cost.

Compute the working capital requirement of Corn assuming the labour force is paid for 50 working weeks a year.

Solution

(a)   The annual costs incurred will be as follows.

		$
Direct materials	30% of $1,500,000	450,000
Direct labour	25% of $1,500,000	375,000
Variable overheads	10% of $1,500,000	150,000
Fixed overheads	15% of $1,500,000	225,000
Selling and distribution	5% of $1,500,000	75,000

(b)   The average value of current assets will be as follows.

		$	$
Raw materials	3/12 × $450,000		112,500
Work-in-progress			
Materials (50% complete)	1/12 × $450,000	37,500	
Labour (50% complete)	1/12 × $375,000	31,250	
Variable overheads (50% complete)	1/12 × $150,000	12,500	
			81,250
Finished goods			
Materials	1/12 × $450,000	37,500	
Labour	1/12 × $375,000	31,250	
Variable overheads	1/12 × $150,000	12,500	
			81,250
Receivables	2.5/12 × $1,500,000		312,500
			587,500

(c)   Average value of current liabilities will be as follows.

		$	$
Materials	2/12 × $450,000	75,000	
Labour	1/50 × $375,000	7,500	
Variable overheads	1/12 × $150,000	12,500	
Fixed overheads	1/12 × $225,000	18,750	
Selling and distribution	0.5/12 × $75,000	3,125	
			116,875

(d)   Working capital required is ($(587,500 – 116,875)) = <u>470,625</u>

It has been assumed that all the direct materials are allocated to work-in-progress when production starts.

Question 21.2	Overtrading

Learning outcome C2

Define what is meant by the term 'overtrading' and describe some of the typical symptoms.

Question 21.3	Quick ratio

Learning outcome C2

The figures below have been extracted from the accounts of Premier Co.

	$
Sales revenue	750,000
Cost of sales	500,000
Gross profit	250,000
Current assets	
Inventories	75,000
Trade receivables	100,000
Other receivables	10,000
Cash at bank and in hand	5,000
	190,000

	$
Current liabilities	
Overdraft	30,000
Dividend	40,000
Trade payables	80,000
Other payables	10,000
	160,000
Net current assets	30,000

What is the quick ratio?

A   0.69
B   0.72
C   0.82
D   1.19

Section summary

Over-capitalisation means that the organisation has an excess of working capital.

Overtrading means that the organisation has too little working capital.

Chapter Summary

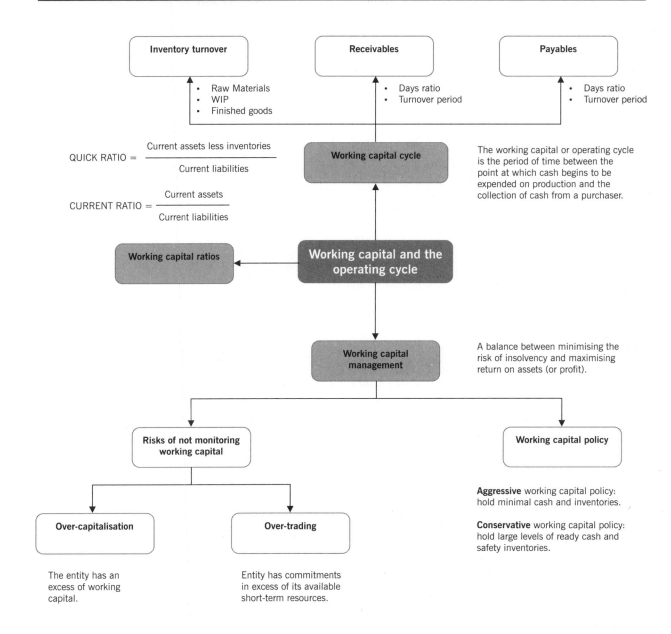

Inventory turnover
- Raw Materials
- WIP
- Finished goods

Receivables
- Days ratio
- Turnover period

Payables
- Days ratio
- Turnover period

$$\text{QUICK RATIO} = \frac{\text{Current assets less inventories}}{\text{Current liabilities}}$$

$$\text{CURRENT RATIO} = \frac{\text{Current assets}}{\text{Current liabilities}}$$

Working capital cycle

The working capital or operating cycle is the period of time between the point at which cash begins to be expended on production and the collection of cash from a purchaser.

Working capital ratios

Working capital and the operating cycle

Working capital management

A balance between minimising the risk of insolvency and maximising return on assets (or profit).

Risks of not monitoring working capital

Working capital policy

Aggressive working capital policy: hold minimal cash and inventories.

Conservative working capital policy: hold large levels of ready cash and safety inventories.

Over-capitalisation

Over-trading

The entity has an excess of working capital.

Entity has commitments in excess of its available short-term resources.

Quick Quiz

1   Which of the following is the most likely to be a symptom of overtrading?

    A   Static levels of inventory turnover   C   Increase in the level of the current ratio
    B   Rapid increase in profits   D   Rapid increase in sales

2   The operating cycle is:

	A The time	
Less	B The time	
Plus	C The time	
Plus	D The time	
Plus	E The time	

    Fill in the blanks.

3   Fill in the blanks with the following:

    Current liabilities; current assets; inventories; 1.

    Quick ratio = $\dfrac{\text{less}}{\rule{4cm}{0.4pt}}$ (This should be at least ....)

4   Which of the following describes *overcapitalisation* and which describes *overtrading*?

    A   A company with excessive investment in working capital
    B   A company trying to support too large a volume of trade with the capital resources at its disposal

5   Which of the following statements best defines the current ratio?

    A   The ratio of current assets to current liabilities.
        For the majority of businesses it should ideally be about 2.

    B   The ratio of current assets to current liabilities.
        For the majority of businesses it should ideally be about 1.

    C   The ratio of current assets excluding inventory to current liabilities.
        For the majority of businesses it should ideally be about 1.

    D   The ratio of current assets excluding inventory to current liabilities.
        For the majority of businesses it should ideally be about 2.

6   The receivables payment period is a calculation of the time taken to pay by all receivables.

    True   ☐

    False ☐

7   What is the working capital requirement of a company with the following average figures over a year?

	$
Inventory	3,750
Trade receivables	1,500
Cash and bank balances	500
Trade payables	1,800

8   WHB Co has the following year end balances.

	$		$
Sales	879,000	Raw material inventory	123,000
Cost of production	690,000	WIP inventory	90,600
Cost of sales	771,000	Finished goods	101,400
Purchases of raw materials	533,400	Receivables	187,800
		Payables	102,000

Using efficiency ratios, calculate the length of the working capital cycle to the nearest day.

Answers to Quick Quiz

1   D   Rapid increase in sales

2   A   The time raw materials remain in inventory
      B   The time period of credit taken from suppliers
      C   The time taken to produce goods
      D   The time finished goods remain in inventory after production is completed
      E   The time taken by customers to pay for goods

3   Quick ratio $= \dfrac{\text{Current assets less inventories}}{\text{Current liabilities}}$ (This should be at least 1)

4   A   Overcapitalisation
      B   Overtrading

5   A   The ratio of current assets to current liabilities. For the majority of businesses it should ideally be about 2.

6   False. The calculation normally only includes trade receivables.

7   Working capital requirement = current assets less current liabilities = 3,750 + 1,500 + 500 – 1,800
                                                        = \$3,950

8   188 days

			Days
$\dfrac{\text{Raw materials inventory}}{\text{Raw materials purchases}}$	$\times\ 365 = \dfrac{123,000}{533,400} \times 365 =$		84
$\dfrac{\text{Work in progress}}{\text{Manufacturing cost}}$	$\times\ 365 = \dfrac{90,600}{690,000} \times 365 =$		48
$\dfrac{\text{Finished goods}}{\text{Cost of sales}}$	$\times\ 365 = \dfrac{101,400}{771,000} \times 365 =$		48
$\dfrac{\text{Trade receivables}}{\text{Sales}}$	$\times\ 365 = \dfrac{187,800}{879,000} \times 365 =$		78
$\dfrac{\text{Trade payables}}{\text{Purchases}}$	$\times\ 365 = \dfrac{102,000}{533,400} \times 365 =$		(70)
			$\overline{188}$

Answers to Questions

21.1 Cash flow patterns

Your list probably included some of the following.

(a)   A **change** in the **general economic environment**. An economic recession will cause a slump in trade.

(b)   A **new product**, launched by a competitor, which takes business away from a company's traditional and established product lines.

(c)   **New cost-saving product technology**, which forces the company to invest in the new technology to remain competitive.

(d)   **Moves by competitors** which have to be countered (for example a price reduction or a sales promotion).

(e)   **Changes in consumer preferences**, resulting in a fall in demand.

(f)   **Government action** against certain trade practices or against trade with a country that a company has dealings with.

(g)   **Strikes** or other industrial action.

(h)   **Natural disasters**, such as floods or fire damage, which curtail an organisation's activities.

21.2 Overtrading

'**Overtrading**' refers to the situation where a company is **over-reliant** on **short-term finance** to support its operations. This is **risky** because short-term finance may be **withdrawn** relatively **quickly** if suppliers lose confidence in the business, or if there is a general tightening of credit in the economy. This may result in a **liquidity crisis** and even bankruptcy, even though the firm is **profitable**. The fundamental **solution** to overtrading is to **replace short term finance** with **longer term finance** such as term loans or equity funds.

The term overtrading is used because the condition commonly arises when a company is **expanding rapidly**. In this situation, because of increasing volumes, more **cash** is needed to pay input costs such as **wages** or **purchases than** is currently being collected **from customers**. The result is that the company runs up its overdraft to the limit and sometimes there is insufficient time to arrange an increase in facilities to pay other payables on the due dates.

These problems are often **compounded** by a general **lack of attention** to **cost control** and **working capital management**, such as receivables collection, because most management time is spent organising selling or production. The result is an unnecessary **drop** in **profit margins**.

When the overdraft limit is reached the company frequently raises funds from **other expensive short term sources**, such as receivables factoring or receivables prompt payment discounts, and delays payment to suppliers, instead of underpinning its financial position with equity funds or a longer term loan. The consequent under-capitalisation delays investment in non-current assets and staff and can **further harm** the quality of the firm's operations.

21.3 Quick ratio

B   The quick ratio is the ratio of current assets excluding inventories to current liabilities.

In this case: $\dfrac{190,000 - 75,000}{160,000} = 0.72$

Now try this question from the OTQ Question Bank

Number

Q61

CASH FLOW FORECASTS

Survival in business depends on the ability to generate cash. **Cash flow information** directs attention towards this critical issue. Cash flow is a more comprehensive concept than 'profit' which is dependent on accounting conventions and concepts.

The **cash budget** is an extremely important mechanism for monitoring cash flows. Various complications about timing of cash flows or lack of particular figures may be included in cash budget exam questions.

At the heart of this chapter is the method for systematically preparing a cash budget. You must be able to set out a budget clearly, supported by appropriate workings.

Section 6 looks at why cash flow problems arise and methods for **easing cash shortages**.

Section 7 concentrates on **float**. Float is the time difference between when a payment is first initiated and when the funds become available for use.

topic list	learning outcomes	syllabus references
1 Cash flows and profit	C3	C3 (a)
2 The purpose of cash forecasts	C3	C3 (a)
3 Cash budgets in receipts and payments format	C3	C3 (a)
4 Cleared funds cash forecasts	C3	C3 (a)
5 Cash forecasts based on financial statements	C3	C3 (a)
6 The need for cash management	C3	C3 (a)
7 Cash management models	C3	C3 (a)
8 Cash management services	C3	C3 (a)

Chapter Overview

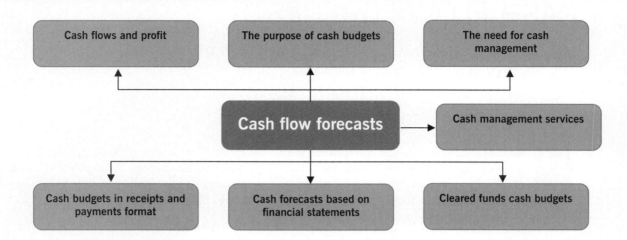

1 Cash flows and profit

1.1 Types of cash transaction

Introduction

There are many types of cash transaction. They can be distinguished by their **purpose** (ie what they are for), their **form** (how they are implemented), and their frequency.

Sometimes the following distinctions are made.

(a) **Capital** and **revenue** items

   (i) **Capital** items relate to the **long-term functioning** of the business, such as raising money from shareholders, or acquiring non-current assets.

   (ii) **Revenue** items relate to **day-to-day operations**, as in the operating cycle, including other matters such as overdraft interest.

(b) **Exceptional** and **unexceptional** items

   (i) **Exceptional** items are **unusual**. An example would be the costs of closing down part of a business.

   (ii) **Unexceptional** items include **everything else**. You have to be careful using this distinction, as the phrase 'exceptional item' has a precise meaning in the preparation of a company's financial statements.

(c) **Regular** and **irregular** items

   (i) **Regular** items occur at **predictable intervals**. Such intervals might be frequent such as the payment of wages every week or month, or relatively infrequent, such as the disbursement of interim and final dividends twice a year. A capital item might be the regular repayment of principal and interest on leased property. Annual disbursements are sums of money paid at yearly intervals.

   (ii) **Irregular** items **do not occur at regular intervals**.

1.2 Cash flows and profit

Trading profits and **cash flows** are different. A company can make losses but still have a net cash income from trading. A company can also make profits but have a net cash deficit on its trading operations.

(a) Cash may be obtained from a transaction which has **nothing** to do with **profit or loss**. For example, an issue of shares or loan stock for cash has no immediate effect on profit but is obviously a source of cash. Similarly, an increase in bank overdraft provides a source of cash for payments, but it is not reported in the statement of profit or loss.

(b) Cash may be paid for the **purchase of non-current assets**, but the charge in the statement of profit or loss is depreciation, which is only a part of an asset's cost.

(c) When a non-current asset is sold there is a profit or loss on sale **equal to the difference** between the **sale proceeds** and the '**net book value**' of the asset in the statement of financial position at the time it is sold.

(d) Cash flows also differ from trading profits due to changes in the amount of the company's inventories, receivables and payables.

   (i) **Profit** is sales minus the cost of sales.

   (ii) **Operational cash flow** is the difference between cash received and cash paid from trading.

(iii) Cash received differs from sales because of changes in the amount of receivables.

	$
Customers owing money at the start of the year	X
Sales during the year	X
Total money due from customers	X̄
Less customers owing money at the end of the year	(X)
Cash receipts from customers during the year	X

(iv) Cash paid differs from the cost of sales because of changes in the amount of inventories and payables.

	$
Closing inventories at the end of the year	X
Add cost of sales during the year	X
	X
Less opening inventories at the start of the year	(X)
Equals purchases	Y

	$
Payments owing to suppliers at the start of the year	X
Add purchases	Y
	X
Less payments still owing to suppliers at the end of the year	(X)
Equals **cash payments** to suppliers during the year	X

(v) Operational cash flow therefore differs from profit because of changes in the amount of receivables, inventories and payables between the start and end of a period.

Question 22.1   Profits and cash flow

Learning outcome C3

Assume that Beta achieved sales revenue in a particular year of $200,000 and the cost of sales was $170,000. Inventories were $12,000, payables $11,000 and receivables $15,000 at the start of the year. At the end of the year, inventories were $21,000, payables were $14,000 and receivables $24,000.

Required

Calculate the profits and the operational cash flow resulting from the year's trading.

The difference between profit and cash flow has important implications.

(a) If a company is profitable but short of cash, one reason could be an increase in the other elements of working capital. Instead of seeking credit from a bank to finance the growth in working capital, management may consider whether **operational cash flows could be improved** by squeezing working capital, and:

(i) Reducing receivables
(ii) Reducing inventories
(iii) Taking more trade credit from suppliers

Better control over working capital could remove the need to borrow.

(b) If a company is making losses, it could try to maintain a positive operational cash flow by **taking more credit** (ie by increasing its payables and so reducing working capital). (Supplier companies would then consider whether to give the extra credit required, or whether to refuse because the risk would be too great.)

Question 22.2

Profits compared with cash flow

Learning outcome C3

Write brief notes on why the reported profit figure of a business for a period does not normally represent the amount of cash generated in that period.

1.3 Benefits of holding cash

(a) **Transactions motive**. Cash is needed for every-day expenses such as wages and payments to suppliers.

(b) **Precautionary motive**. This is cash held 'just in case' to cover unexpected expenditure.

(c) **Investment motive**. This is cash held to take advantage of any unforeseen profit-making opportunities.

Obviously when a business is holding cash, it is not getting as high returns as it might if it invested the cash instead.

Section summary

Trading profits and **cash flows** are different. A company can make losses but still have a net cash income from trading. A **company** can also make profits but have a net cash deficit on its trading operations.

2 The purpose of cash forecasts

Introduction

Cash forecasting ensures that sufficient funds will be available when they are needed to sustain the activities of an enterprise. Efficient financial planning also minimises interest payments and maximises the return from any spare cash. Interest rates will differ according to whether money is being lent to, or borrowed from, the bank. The **time value of money** is another important factor. The bank will charge a higher rate of interest on a long-term loan than on a short term loan and will pay a higher rate of interest on an account subject to a longer notice of withdrawal than on an account that requires only 24 hours notice.

All of these factors must be considered when forecasting cash requirements.

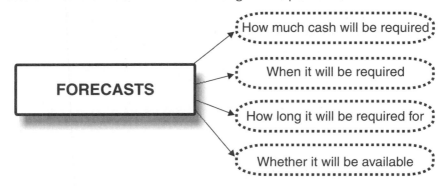

Banks have increasingly insisted that customers provide cash forecasts (or a business plan that includes a cash forecast) as a precondition of lending. A newly established company wishing to open a bank account will also normally be asked to supply a **business plan**. The cash and sales forecasts will also allow the bank to **monitor** the **progress** of the new company, and control its lending more effectively.

2.1 Deficiencies

Any forecast **deficiency** of cash will have to be funded.

(a)   If **borrowing** arrangements are not already secured, a source of funds will have to be found. If a company cannot fund its cash deficits it could be wound up.

(b)   The firm can make arrangements to **sell any short-term financial investments** to raise cash.

(c)   The firm can delay payments to suppliers, or pull in payments from customers. This is sometimes known as **leading and lagging**.

Because cash forecasts cannot be entirely accurate, companies should have **contingency funding**, available from a surplus cash balance and liquid investments, or from a bank facility.

Forecasting gives management time to arrange its funding. Planning in advance, instead of a panic measure to avert a cash crisis, gives a business more choice on **when to borrow**, and will probably mean obtaining a **lower interest rate**.

2.2 Forecasting a cash surplus

If a **cash surplus** is forecast, having an idea of both its **size** and **how long** it will exist could help decide how **best to invest it**.

In some cases, the amount of interest earned from surplus cash could be significant for the company's earnings. The company might then need a forecast of its interest earnings in order to indicate its prospective earnings per share to stock market analysts and institutional investors.

2.3 Types of forecast

KEY TERM

A CASH BUDGET is a detailed budget of estimated cash inflows and outflows, incorporating both revenue and capital items.   (CIMA *Official Terminology*)

In companies that use cash flow reporting for control purposes, there will probably be:

- A cash budget divided into monthly or quarterly periods
- A statement comparing actual cash flows against the monthly or quarterly budget
- A revised cash forecast
- A statement comparing actual cash flows against a revised forecast

Revised forecasts should be prepared to keep forecasts **relevant** and **up-to-date**. Examples would be a revised three-month forecast every month for the next three-month period, or a revised forecast each month or each quarter up to the end of the annual budget period.

A **rolling forecast** is a forecast that is **continually updated**. When actual results are reported for a given time period (say for one month's results within an annual forecast period) a further forecast period is added and forecasts for intermediate time periods are updated. A rolling forecast can therefore be a 12-month forecast which is updated at the end of every month, with a further month added to the end of the forecast period and with figures for the intervening 11 months revised if necessary.

Cash flow control with budgets and revised forecasts

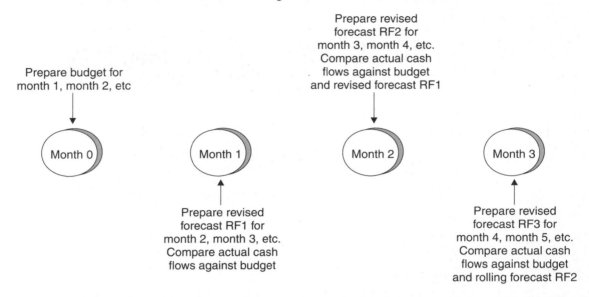

Section summary

Cash flow forecasts provide an early warning of liquidity problems and funding needs. Banks often expect business customers to provide a cash forecast as a condition of lending.

Cash budgets and forecasts can be used for **control reporting**.

3 Cash budgets in receipts and payments format

Introduction

A cash budget is a detailed forecast of cash receipts, payments and balances over a planning period. It is formally adopted as part of the business plan or master budget for the period.

3.1 Assumptions

For each item of cash inflow or outflow, assumptions must be made about the **quantity** and timing of the flow. The total amount of receipts and payments will be derived from other budgets, such as the company's operating budgets and capital expenditure budget. Assumptions will already have been made for these to prepare the profit or loss budget. Assumptions about the **time to pay** must be introduced for cash forecasting.

The forecasting method can be either one or a combination of the following.

- Identifying a particular cash flow, and scheduling when it will be received or paid
- Projecting future trends and seasonal cycles in business activity and cash flows
- Analysing historical payment patterns of regular repeat payments

3.2 Preparing the cash budget

Cash budgets are prepared by taking **operational budgets** and converting them into forecasts as to when receipts and payments occur. The forecast should indicate the highest and lowest cash balance in a period as well as the balance at the end.

The steps in preparing the cash budget are as follows:

Preparation

1   Set up a proforma cash budget

	Month 1 $	Month 2 $	Month 3 $
Cash receipts			
Receipts from customers	X	X	X
Loan etc	X	X	X
	X̲	X̲	X̲
Cash payments			
Payments to suppliers	X	X	X
Wages etc	X	X	X
	X̲	X̲	X̲
Opening balance	X	X	X
Net cash flow (receipts – payments)	X	X	X
Closing balance	X̲	X̲	X̲

Sort out cash receipts

2   Establish budgeted sales month by month

3   Establish the length of credit period taken by customers

$$\text{Receivables collection period (no. of days credit)} = \frac{\text{average (or year-end) receivables during period}}{\text{total credit sales in period}} \times \text{no. of days in period}$$

4   Determine when budgeted sales revenue will be received as cash (by considering cash receipts from total receivables)

5   Establish when opening receivables will pay

6   Establish when any other cash income will be received

Sort out cash payments

7   Establish production quantities and material usage quantities each month

8   Establish material inventory changes and hence the quantity and cost of materials purchases each month

9   Establish the length of credit period taken from suppliers and calculate when cash payments to suppliers will be made

$$\text{Payables payment period (no. of days credit)} = \frac{\text{average (or year-end) payables during period}}{\text{total purchases on credit in period}} \times \text{no. of days in period}$$

10   Establish when amount due to opening payables will be paid

11   Establish when any other cash payments (excluding non-cash items such as depreciation) will be made

12   Show clearly on the bottom of the budget opening position, net cash flow and closing position

If an overdraft is shown, suggest delaying payments to suppliers, speeding up payments from customers, reducing production volumes or arranging further overdraft facilities

3.3 Cash payments

Assumptions about payments are easier to make than assumptions about income. Assumptions about payments to suppliers can take account of:

(a) The **credit terms** given by suppliers (or groups of suppliers), company policy on purchase orders and the administration of cheque payments

(b) Any **specific supply arrangements**, (such as a delivery once every two months, with payment for each delivery at the end of the following month)

(c) **Past practice** (eg the proportion of invoices (by value) paid in the month of supply and invoice, the proportion paid in the month following, and so on)

(d) **Predictable dates** for certain payments, such as payments for rent, business rates, telephones, electricity and company tax

As a guideline, assumptions about payments should lean towards caution, ie if in doubt, budget for earlier payments.

3.4 Fixed cost expenditures

Some items of expenditure will be regarded as **fixed costs** in the operating budget. Salaries, office expenses and marketing expenditure are three such items. With some fixed costs, it could be assumed that there will be an **equal monthly expenditure** on each item, with cash payment in the month of expenditure perhaps, or in the month following. Other costs may not be monthly. If annual building rental is payable quarterly in advance, the budget should plan for payments on the specific dates.

3.5 Receipts

Assumptions about receipts might be more difficult to formulate than assumptions about payments.

(a) For a company that depends almost entirely on consumer sales by cash, credit card and debit card, the major uncertainty in the cash flow forecast will be the **volume of sales**. The timing of receipts from a large proportion of those sales will be predictable (payment with sale).

(b) Companies that have a **mixture of cash and credit sales** must attempt to **estimate** the **proportion** of **each** in the total sales figure, and then formulate assumptions for the timing pattern of receipts from credit sales.

(c) There are several ways of estimating when receipts will occur.

   (i) If the company has **specific credit terms**, such as a requirement to pay within 15 days of the invoice date, it could assume that:

   (1) Invoices will be sent out at the time of sale

   (2) A proportion, say 25%, will be paid within 15 days (½ month)

   (3) A proportion, say 65%, will be paid between 16 days and 30 days (one month after invoice)

   (4) A proportion (say 9%) will pay in the month following

   (5) There will be some bad debts (say 1%, a proportion that should be consistent with the company's budgeted expectations)

   (ii) If there is a policy of cash discounts for early payment, the **discounts allowed** should be provided for in the forecasts of receipts.

   (iii) The time **customers take to pay** can be estimated from past experience. Care should be taken to allow for seasonal variations and the possibility that payments can be slower at some times of the year than at others (for example, delays during holiday periods).

(iv) **Payment patterns** can also vary from one country to another. Companies in France and Italy for example will often take several months after the invoice date to pay amounts due.

3.6 Calendar variations

Assumptions could be required to take account of calendar variations.

(a) **Days-in-the-month effect**. It could be assumed that receipts will be the same on every day of the $20^{th}/21^{st}/22^{nd}/23^{rd}$ etc working day each month. Alternatively, it could be assumed that receipts will be twice as high in the first five days of each month. Assumptions should generally be based on past experience.

(b) **Days-in-the-week effect**. Where appropriate, assumptions should be made about the cash inflows on each particular day of the week, with some days regularly producing higher cash inflows than other days. Such forecasts should be based on historical analysis.

Receipts for some companies, particularly retailers, follow a **regular weekly pattern** (with some variations for holidays and seasons of the year). Companies should be able to estimate total weekly takings in cash (notes and coins), cheques and credit card vouchers, the number of cheques and credit card vouchers handled and the deposit spread (for each day, the percentage of the total takings for the week, eg 10% on Monday, 15% on Tuesday).

3.7 Time periods and overdraft size

Dividing the forecast period into time periods should coincide as closely as possible with significant cash flow events, to provide management with information about the **high or low points for cash balances**. In other words, as well as predicting the **month end surplus or overdraft**, the **maximum overdraft *during* the month** should be predicted.

Example: timing of cash flows

Oak Tree Villa operates a retail business. Purchases are sold at cost plus $33^1/3$%. Or put another way, purchases are 75% of sales.

(a)

	Budgeted sales $	Labour cost $	Expenses incurred $
January	40,000	3,000	4,000
February	60,000	3,000	6,000
March	160,000	5,000	7,000
April	120,000	4,000	7,000

(b) It is management policy to have sufficient inventory in hand at the end of each month to meet sales demand in the next half month.

(c) Payables for materials and expenses are paid in the month after the purchases are made or the expenses incurred. Labour is paid in full by the end of each month.

(d) Expenses include a monthly depreciation charge of $2,000.

(e) (i) 75% of sales are for cash.
     (ii) 25% of sales are on one month's interest-free credit.

(f) The company will buy equipment for cash costing $18,000 in February and will pay a dividend of $20,000 in March. The opening cash balance at 1 February is $1,000.

Required

(a) Prepare a statement of profit or loss for February and March.
(b) Prepare a cash budget for February and March.

Solution

(a)   STATEMENT OF PROFIT OR LOSS

	February		March		Total	
	$	$	$	$	$	$
Sales		60,000		160,000		220,000
Cost of purchases (75%)		45,000		120,000		165,000
Gross profit		15,000		40,000		55,000
Less: labour	3,000		5,000		8,000	
expenses	6,000		7,000		13,000	
		9,000		12,000		21,000
		6,000		28,000		34,000

(b)   *Workings*

(i)   *Receipts:*

		$
in February	75% of Feb sales (75% × $60,000)	45,000
	+ 25% of Jan sales (25% × $40,000)	10,000
		55,000
in March	75% of Mar sales (75% × $160,000)	120,000
	+25% of Feb sales (25% × $60,000)	15,000
		135,000

(ii)

	Purchases in January $		Purchases in February $
Purchases:			
For Jan sales (50% of $30,000) *	15,000		
For Feb sales (50% of $45,000)	22,500	(50% of $45,000)	22,500
For Mar sales	–	(50% of $120,000)	60,000
	37,500		82,500

These purchases are paid for in February and March.

* Remember that the question says that it is management policy to have sufficient inventory
on hand for 50% of next month's sales. You can also use the formula: Purchases = Closing
inventory + sales demand – opening inventory. So for January we have (45,000 × 50%) +
(40,000 × 75%) – (30,000 × 50%) = 37,500.

(iii)   *Expenses.* Cash expenses in January ($4,000 – $2,000) and February ($6,000 – $2,000)
are paid for in February and March respectively. Depreciation is not a cash item.

CASH BUDGET

	February $	March $	Total $
Receipts from sales	55,000	135,000	190,000
Payments			
Trade payables	37,500	82,500	120,000
Expenses payables	2,000	4,000	6,000
Labour	3,000	5,000	8,000
Equipment purchase	18,000	–	18,000
Dividend	–	20,000	20,000
Total payments	60,500	111,500	172,000
Receipts less payments	(5,500)	23,500	18,000
Opening cash balance b/f	1,000	(4,500)*	1,000
Closing cash balance c/f	(4,500)*	19,000	19,000

* The cash balance at the end of February is carried forward as the opening cash balance for March.

Notes

1   The profit in February and March means that there is sufficient cash to operate the business as planned.

2   Steps should be taken either to ensure that an overdraft facility is available for the cash shortage at the end of February, or to defer certain payments so that the overdraft is avoided.

3.8 Cash budgets and opening receivables and payables

One situation which can be problematic is if you are required to analyse an **opening statement of financial position** to decide how many outstanding receivables will pay what they owe in the first few months of the cash budget period, and how many outstanding payables must be paid.

Example: receivables and payables

For example, suppose that a statement of financial position as at 31 December 20X4 shows that a company has the following receivables and payables.

Receivables	$150,000
Trade payables	$ 60,000

You are informed of the following.

(a)   Customers are allowed two months to pay.
(b)   1½ months' credit is taken from trade suppliers.
(c)   Sales and materials purchases were both made at an even monthly rate throughout 20X4.

Required

Determine in which months of 20X5 the customers will eventually pay and the suppliers will be paid.

Solution

(a)   Since customers take two months to pay, the $150,000 of receivables in the statement of financial position represent credit sales in November and December 20X4, who will pay in January and February 20X5 respectively. Since sales in 20X4 were at an equal monthly rate, the cash budget should plan for receipts of $75,000 each month in January and February from the receivables in the opening statement of financial position.

(b)   Similarly, since suppliers are paid after 1½ months, the statement of financial position payables will be paid in January and the first half of February 20X5, which means that budgeted payments will be as follows.

	$
In January (purchases in second half of November and first half of December 20X4)	40,000
In February (purchases in second half of December 20X4)	20,000
Total payables in the statement of financial position	60,000

(The payables in the statement of financial position of $60,000 represent 1½ months' purchases, so that purchases in 20X4 must be $40,000 per month, which is $20,000 per half month.)

Example: a month-by-month cash budget in detail

Now you have some idea as to the underlying principles, let us put these to work. From the following information which relates to George and Zola, prepare a month by month cash budget for the second half of 20X5 and make brief comments as you consider might be helpful to management.

(a)   The company's only product, a leather bag, sells at $40 and has a variable cost of $26 made up as follows.

Material	$20
Labour	$4
Variable overhead	$2

(b)   Fixed costs of $6,000 per month are paid on the 28th of each month.

(c)   *Quantities sold/to be sold on credit*

	May	*June*	*July*	*Aug*	*Sept*	*Oct*	*Nov*	*Dec*
	1,000	1,200	1,400	1,600	1,800	2,000	2,200	2,600

(d)   *Production quantities*

	May	*June*	*July*	*Aug*	*Sept*	*Oct*	*Nov*	*Dec*
	1,200	1,400	1,600	2,000	2,400	2,600	2,400	2,200

(e)   Cash sales at a discount of 5% are expected to average 100 units a month.

(f)   Customers are expected to settle their accounts by the end of the second month following sale.

(g)   Suppliers of material are paid two months after the material is used in production.

(h)   Wages are paid in the same month as they are incurred.

(i)   70% of the variable overhead is paid in the month of production, the remainder in the following month.

(j)   Company tax of $18,000 is to be paid in October.

(k)   A new delivery vehicle was bought in June, the cost of which, $8,000 is to be paid in August. The old vehicle was sold for $600, the buyer undertaking to pay in July.

(l)   The company is expected to be $3,000 overdrawn at the bank at 30 June 20X5.

(m)   The opening and closing inventories of raw materials, work in progress and finished goods are budgeted to be the same.

Solution

CASH BUDGET FOR 1 JULY TO 31 DECEMBER 20X5

	July $	Aug $	Sept $	Oct $	Nov $	Dec $	Total $
Receipts							
Credit sales	40,000	48,000	56,000	64,000	72,000	80,000	360,000
Cash sales	3,800	3,800	3,800	3,800	3,800	3,800	22,800
Sale of vehicles	600						600
	44,400	51,800	59,800	67,800	75,800	83,800	383,400
Payments							
Materials	24,000	28,000	32,000	40,000	48,000	52,000	224,000
Labour	6,400	8,000	9,600	10,400	9,600	8,800	52,800
Variable overhead (W1)	3,080	3,760	4,560	5,080	4,920	4,520	25,920
Fixed costs	6,000	6,000	6,000	6,000	6,000	6,000	36,000
Company tax				18,000			18,000
Purchase of vehicle		8,000					8,000
	39,480	53,760	52,160	79,480	68,520	71,320	364,720
Excess of receipts over payments	4,920	(1,960)	7,640	(11,680)	7,280	12,480	18,680
Balance b/f	(3,000)	1,920	(40)	7,600	(4,080)	3,200	(3,000)
Balance c/f	1,920	(40)	7,600	(4,080)	3,200	15,680	15,680

Working

Variable overhead

	June $	July $	Aug $	Sept $	Oct $	Nov $	Dec $
Variable overhead production cost	2,800	3,200	4,000	4,800	5,200	4,800	4,400
70% paid in month		2,240	2,800	3,360	3,640	3,360	3,080
30% in following month		840	960	1,200	1,440	1,560	1,440
		3,080	3,760	4,560	5,080	4,920	4,520

Comments

(a)   There will be a small overdraft at the end of August but a much larger one at the end of October. It may be possible to delay payments to suppliers for longer than two months or to reduce purchases of materials or reduce the volume of production by running down existing inventory levels.

(b)   If none of these courses is possible, the company may need to negotiate overdraft facilities with its bank.

(c)   The cash deficit is only temporary and by the end of December there will be a comfortable surplus. The use to which this cash will be put should ideally be planned in advance.

Question 22.3

Cash forecast

Learning outcome C3

Tom Ward has worked for some years as a sales representative, but has recently been made redundant. He intends to start up in business on his own account, using $15,000 which he currently has invested. Tom maintains a bank account showing a small credit balance, and he plans to approach his bank for the necessary additional finance. Tom asks you for advice and provides the following additional information.

(a)   Arrangements have been made to purchase non-current assets costing $8,000. These will be paid for at the end of September and are expected to have a five-year life, at the end of which they will possess a nil residual value.

(b) Inventories costing $5,000 will be acquired on 28 September and subsequent monthly purchases will be at a level sufficient to replace forecast sales for the month.

(c) Forecast monthly sales are $3,000 for October, $6,000 for November and December, and $10,500 from January 20X7 onwards.

(d) Selling price is fixed at the cost of inventory plus 50%.

(e) Two months' credit will be allowed to customers but only 1 month's credit will be received from suppliers of goods.

(f) Running expenses, including rent, are estimated at $1,600 per month, all paid in cash.

(g) Tom intends to make monthly cash drawings of $1,000.

Required

Prepare a forecast cash budget for the 6 months October 20X6 to March 20X7.

Question 22.4

Cash budget

Learning outcome C3

You are presented with the following budgeted data for your organisation for the period November 20X1 to June 20X2. It has been extracted from functional budgets that have already been prepared.

	Nov X1 $	Dec X1 $	Jan X2 $	Feb X2 $	Mar X2 $	Apr X2 $	May X2 $	June X2 $
Sales	80,000	100,000	110,000	130,000	140,000	150,000	160,000	180,000
Purchases	40,000	60,000	80,000	90,000	110,000	130,000	140,000	150,000
Wages	10,000	12,000	16,000	20,000	24,000	28,000	32,000	36,000
Overheads	10,000	10,000	15,000	15,000	15,000	20,000	20,000	20,000
Dividends		20,000						40,000
Capital expenditure			30,000			40,000		

You are also told the following.

(a) Sales are 40% cash, 60% credit. Credit sales are paid two months after the month of sales.
(b) Purchases are paid the month following purchase.
(c) 75% of wages are paid in the current month and 25% the following month.
(d) Overheads are paid the month after they are incurred.
(e) Dividends are paid three months after they are declared.
(f) Capital expenditure is paid two months after it is incurred.
(g) The opening cash balance on 1 January 20X2 is $15,000.

The managing director is pleased with the above figures as they show sales will have increased by more than 100% in the period under review. In order to achieve this he has arranged a bank overdraft with a ceiling of $50,000 to accommodate the increased inventory levels and wage bill for overtime worked.

Required

(a) Prepare a cash budget for the six month period January to June 20X2.

(b) Comment upon your results in the light of your managing director's comments and offer advice.

(c) If you have access to a computer spreadsheet package and you know how to use it, try setting up the cash budget on it. Then make a copy of the budget and try making changes to the estimates to see their effect on cash flow.

Section summary

Cash budgets are prepared by taking **operational budgets** and converting them into forecasts as to when receipts and payments occur. The forecast should indicate the highest and lowest cash balance in a period as well as the balance at the end.

4 Cleared funds cash forecasts

Introduction

Knowing what **cleared funds** are likely to be has a direct and immediate relevance to cash management in the **short-term**. If a company expects to have insufficient cleared funds in the next few days to meet a payment obligation, it must either borrow funds to meet the obligation or (if possible) defer the payment until there are cash receipts to cover it.

4.1 Cleared funds

Float refers to the amount of money tied up between the time a payment is initiated and **cleared funds** become available in the recipient's bank account for immediate spending.

A **cleared funds cash forecast** is a short-term cash forecast of the cleared funds available to a company in its bank accounts, or of the funding deficit that must be met by **immediate borrowing**. Cleared funds forecasts should be reviewed and updated regularly, *daily* for companies with large and uncertain cash flows. Uncertainty might be caused by the internal organisation of the recipient.

(a)   The recipient might delay the banking of cheques.
(b)   Cheques do sometimes get held up by bureaucracy.

4.2 Preparing a cleared funds forecast

There should be relatively few items in a cleared funds forecast, and each forecast should generally relate to a **particular bank account** unless balances can be netted against each other.

A cleared funds forecast can be prepared by a combination of three methods.

(a)   **Obtaining information** from the **company's banks**.

(b)   **Forecasting for other receipts and payments** that have occurred but have not yet been lodged with a bank. You should be already familiar with bank reconciliations.

(c)   **Adapting the cash budget**.

    (i)   Analyse the cash budget into suitable time periods.
    (ii)   Identify cash book payments and receipts.
    (iii)   Adjust these for float times.

Question 22.5   Types of forecast

Learning outcomes C3

Kim O'Hara runs an import/export retail business, largely on a cash basis. He likes to negotiate the best possible deals from his suppliers and this generally means a strict adherence to any payment terms so as to benefit from any settlement discounts. He also orders his supplies at the last possible moment, as he is a firm believer in 'just-in-time' philosophy. On the other hand Creighton, a listed company, is a large software house, dealing with major clients. Which type of forecast would be most appropriate to each business?

Section summary

Cleared funds are used for short-term planning. They take clearance delays into account.

5   Cash forecasts based on financial statements

Introduction

A statement of financial position based forecast is an estimate of the company's statement of financial position at a future date. It is used to identify either the cash surplus or the funding shortfall in the company's statement of financial position at the **forecast date**.

5.1 The statement of financial position

The statement of financial position is produced for **financial accounting purposes. It is not an estimate of cash inflows and outflows.** However a number of sequential forecasts can be produced, for example a forecast of the statement of financial position at the end of each year for the next five years.

5.2 Estimating a future statement of financial position

A statement of financial position estimate calls for some prediction of the amount/value of each item in the company's statement of financial position, **excluding cash and short-term investments**, as these are what we are trying to predict. A forecast is prepared by taking each item in the statement of financial position, and estimating what its value might be at the future date. The assumptions used are critical, and the following guidelines are suggested.

(a)   Intangible **non-current assets** (gross book value) and long term investments, if there are any, should be taken at their current value unless there is good reason for another treatment.

(b)   Some estimate of **non-current asset purchases** (and disposals) will be required. Revaluations can be ignored as they are not cash flows.

(c)   **Current assets**. Statement of financial position estimates of inventories and receivables can be based on fairly simple assumptions. The estimated value for inventories and receivables can be made in any of the following ways.

    (i)   **Same as current amounts**. This is unlikely if business has boomed.

    (ii)   **Increase by a certain percentage**, to allow for growth in business volume. For example, the volume of receivables might be expected to increase by a similar amount.

    (iii)   **Decrease by a certain percentage**, to allow for tighter management control over working capital.

    (iv)   **Assume to be a certain percentage** of the company's estimated **annual sales revenue** for the year.

    (v)   The firm can assume that the operating cycle will more or less **remain the same**. In other words, if a firm's customers take two months to pay, this relationship can be expected to continue.

(d)   **Current liabilities**. Some itemising of current liabilities will be necessary, because no single set of assumptions can accurately estimate them collectively.

    (i)   **Trade payables and accruals** can be estimated in a similar way to current assets, as indicated above.

(ii)   Current liabilities include **bank loans** due for repayment within 12 months. These can be identified individually.

(iii)   **Bank overdraft facilities** might be in place. It could be appropriate to assume that there will be no overdraft in the forecast statement of financial position. Any available overdraft facility can be considered later when the company's overall cash requirements are identified.

(iv)   **Taxation.** Any company tax payable should be estimated from anticipated profits and based on an estimated percentage of those profits.

(v)   **Dividends payable.** Any ordinary dividend payable should be estimated from anticipated profits, and any preferred dividend payable can be predicted from the coupon rate of dividend for the company's preferred shares.

(vi)   **Other payables** can be included if required and are of significant value.

(e)   **Long-term payables.** Long-term payables are likely to consist of long-term loans, and any other long-term finance debt. Unless the company has already arranged further long-term borrowing, this item should include just existing long-term debts, minus debts that will be repaid before the statement of financial position date.

(f)   **Share capital and reserves.** With the exception of the retained earnings, the estimated statement of financial position figures for share capital and other reserves should be the same as their current amount unless it is expected or known that a new issue of shares will take place before the statement of financial position date.

(g)   An estimate is required of the change in the company's **accumulated profits** in the period up to the end of the reporting period date. This reserve should be calculated as:

(i)   The existing value of accumulated profits

(ii)   Plus further retained profits anticipated in the period to the statement of financial position date (ie post tax profits minus estimated dividends)

The various estimates should now be brought together into a statement of financial position. The figures on each side of the statement of financial position will not be equal, and there will be one of the following.

(a)   A surplus of share capital and reserves over net assets (total assets minus total liabilities). If this occurs, the company will be forecasting a **cash surplus**.

(b)   A surplus of net assets over share capital and reserves. If this occurs, the company will be forecasting a **funding deficit**.

Example: Extra funding

Alpha has an existing statement of financial position and an estimated statement of financial position in one year's time before the necessary extra funding is taken into account, as follows. (Note that for the purpose of this exercise liabilities have been deducted from assets.)

	Existing		Forecast after one year	
	$	$	$	$
Non-current assets		100,000		180,000
Current assets	90,000		100,000	
Short-term payables	(60,000)		(90,000)	
Net current assets		30,000		10,000
		130,000		190,000
Long-term payables		(20,000)		(20,000)
Deferred taxation		(10,000)		(10,000)
Total net assets		100,000		160,000

	Existing		Forecast after one year	
	$	$	$	$
Share capital and reserves				
Ordinary share capital		50,000		50,000
Other reserves		20,000		20,000
Retained earnings		30,000		50,000
		100,000		120,000

The company is expecting to increase its net assets in the next year by $60,000 ($160,000 − $100,000) but expects retained profits for the year to be only $20,000 ($50,000 − $30,000). There is an excess of net assets over share capital and reserves amounting to $40,000 ($160,000 − $120,000), which is a funding deficit. The company must consider ways of obtaining extra cash (eg by borrowing) to cover the deficit. If it cannot, it will need to keep its assets below the forecast amount, or to have higher short-term payables.

A revised projected statement of financial position can then be prepared by introducing these new sources of funds. This should be checked for realism (eg by ratio analysis) to ensure that the proportion of the statement of financial position made up by non-current assets and working capital, etc is sensible.

Main uses of statement of financial position-based forecasts

(a)   As longer-term (strategic) estimates, to assess the scale of funding requirements or cash surpluses the company expects over time

(b)   To act as a check on the realism of cash flow-based forecasts (The estimated statement of financial position should be **roughly** consistent with the net cash change in the cash budget, after allowing for approximations in the statement of financial position forecast assumptions)

5.3 Deriving cash flow from statement of profit or loss and statement of financial position information

The previous paragraphs concentrated on preparing a forecast statement of financial position, with estimated figures for receivables, payables and inventory. Cash requirements might therefore be presented as the '**balancing figure**'. However, it is possible to derive a forecast figure for cash flows using both the statement of financial position and the statement of profit or loss.

This is examined in the example below, which is based on the first question (Profits and cash flow) in this chapter. For the time being, assume that there is no depreciation to worry about. The task is to get from profit to operational cash flow, by taking into account movements in working capital.

	Profit $	Operational cash flow $
Sales	200,000	200,000
Opening receivables (∴ received in year)		15,000
Closing receivables (outstanding at year end)		(24,000)
Cash in		191,000
Cost of sales	170,000	170,000
Closing inventory (purchased, but not used, in year)		21,000
Opening inventory (used, but not purchased, in year)		(12,000)
Purchases in year		179,000
Opening payables (∴ paid in year)		11,000
Closing payables (outstanding at year end)		(14,000)
Cash out		176,000
Profit/operational cash flow	30,000	15,000

		Profit $	Operational cash flow $
Profit			30,000
(Increase)/Decrease in inventories	Opening	12,000	
	Closing	(21,000)	
			(9,000)
(Increase)/Decrease in receivables	Opening	15,000	
	Closing	(24,000)	
			(9,000)
Increase/(Decrease) in payables	Closing	14,000	
	Opening	(11,000)	
			3,000
Operational cash flow			15,000

In practice, a business will make many other adjustments. The profit figure includes items which **do not involve** the **movement of cash**, such as the annual **depreciation** charge, which will have to be **added back** to arrive at a figure for cash.

Both 'receipts and payments' forecasts and forecasts based on financial statements could be used alongside each other. The cash management section and the financial controller's section should reconcile differences between forecasts on a continuing basis, so that the forecast can be made more accurate as time goes on.

All cash forecasts can now be prepared quickly and easily on **spreadsheets**. This enables revised figures to be calculated whenever assumptions are changed.

Section summary

A cash flow forecast can be prepared by projecting the movement in the statement of financial position or the statement of profit or loss.

6 The need for cash management

Introduction

This section looks at why cash flow problems arise and methods of easing shortages.

6.1 Cash flow problems

We have already used the concept of the **operating cycle**, which connects investment in working capital with cash flows. Cash flow problems can arise in several ways.

CASH FLOW PROBLEMS	
Making losses	Continual losses will eventually mean problems, whose timing depends on the size of losses and whether depreciation is significant; if it is, problems arise on replacement of assets
Inflation	Ever-increasing cash flows required just to replace used-up and worn out assets
Growth	Growth means business needs to support more receivables and inventory
Seasonal business	Cash flow difficulties may occur at certain times when cash inflows are low and outflows high, as inventories are being built up

CASH FLOW PROBLEMS	
One-off items of expenditure	Large items such as a loan repayment or the purchase of expensive non-current asset such as freehold land
Poor credit control procedures	A long average time for credit customers to pay may cause problems

6.2 Methods of easing cash shortages

6.2.1 Improving the business

Cash deficits can arise out of **basic trading factors** underlying the business such as falling sales or increasing costs. Clearly, the way to deal with these items is to take normal business measures, rectifying the fall in sales by marketing activities or, if this cannot be achieved, by cutting costs.

6.2.2 Controlling the operating cycle: short-term deficiencies

Cash deficits can also arise out of the business's management of the operating cycle and from timing differences. The following are possibilities.

(a)   **Borrowing** from the bank. This is only a short-term measure. It is possible that a bank will convert an overdraft into a long-term loan, or perhaps new overdraft limits can be set up.

(b)   **Raising capital.** This is likely to be expensive and should be generally used for long-term investment, not short term cash management.

(c)   **Different sources of finance** (such as leasing) might be used.

When a company cannot obtain resources from any other source such as a loan or an increased overdraft, it can take the following steps.

(a)   **Postponing capital expenditure**

    (i)   It might be imprudent to postpone expenditure on non-current assets which are needed for the **development** and **growth** of the business.

    (ii)   On the other hand, some **capital expenditures** might be **postponable** without serious consequences. The routine replacement of motor vehicles is an example. If a company's policy is to replace company cars every two years, it may decide, if cash is short, to replace cars every three years.

(b)   **Accelerating cash inflows which would otherwise be expected in a later period**

    The most obvious way of bringing forward cash inflows would be to press receivables for earlier payment (leading and lagging receivables).

(c)   **Reversing past investment decisions by selling assets previously acquired**

    Some assets are less crucial to a business than others and so if cash flow problems are severe, the option of selling short-term investments or even property might have to be considered.

(d)   **Negotiating a reduction in cash outflows, so as to postpone or even reduce payments**

    There are several ways in which this could be done.

    (i)   **Longer credit** might be taken from suppliers (leading and lagging payables).

    (ii)   **Loan repayments** could be rescheduled by agreement with a bank.

    (iii)   A **deferral of the payment of tax** could be agreed with the taxation authorities.

    (iv)   **Dividend payments** could be **reduced**. Dividend payments are discretionary cash outflows, although a company's directors might be constrained by shareholders' expectations.

    (v)   **Inventory levels** could decrease to reduce the amount of money tied up in their production cost.

Example: leading and lagging

Assume that Gilbert Gosayne sells Nullas. Each Nulla costs $50 to make and is sold for $100. The bank has refused an overdraft to Gilbert Gosayne. Suppliers are normally paid at the end of Month 1; the Nullas are sold on the 15th of Month 2. Payment is received on the first day of Month 3.

(a)   Under this system we have the following forecast.

	Inflows $	Outflows $	Balance $
Month 1 (end)	–	50	(50)
Month 2	–	–	(50)
Month 3 (beginning)	100	–	50

In other words the cash cycle means that the firm is in deficit for all of Month 2. As the bank has refused an overdraft, the suppliers will not be paid.

(b)   If, however, Gilbert Gosayne persuades its suppliers to wait for two weeks until the 15th of Month 2 and offers a settlement discount of $5 to customers to induce them to pay on the 15th of Month 2, the situation is transformed.

	Inflows $	Outflows $	Balance $
Month 1	–	–	–
Month 2	95	50	45
Month 3	–	–	45

In practice, it is not that simple.

(a)   Suppliers can object to their customers taking extra credit and it can also harm their businesses, thus jeopardising their ability to make future supplies. The customer also loses the possibility of taking advantage of trade discounts.

(b)   Customers might refuse to pay early, despite the inducement of a discount.

In fact, a firm's customers and suppliers might be 'leading and lagging' themselves.

A firm might be in a position to choose which of its suppliers should be paid now rather than later. Certain suppliers have to be paid early, if they are powerful. The bank is a powerful supplier: it is worth keeping the bank happy even if the firm loses out on a few trade discounts in the process.

Shortening the operating cycle is helpful in dealing with **short-term deficiencies** and saving interest costs, but it is not necessarily a long term solution to the business's funding problems. This is because a shorter operating cycle time will **reduce the amount of cash** that a company needs to invest in its operating activities.

Section summary

Cash shortages can be eased by postponing capital expenditure, selling assets, taking longer to pay suppliers and pressing customers for earlier payment (leading and lagging).

7 Cash management models

Introduction

Optimal cash holding levels can be calculated from formal models, such as the **Baumol** model and the **Miller-Orr** model.

A number of different cash management models indicate the **optimum amount of cash** that a company should hold.

7.1 The Baumol model

The **Baumol model** is based on the idea that deciding on optimum cash balances is like deciding on optimum inventory levels. It assumes that cash is steadily consumed over time and a business holds a stock of marketable securities that can be sold when cash is needed. The cost of holding cash is the opportunity cost, ie the interest foregone from not investing the cash. The cost of placing an order is the administration cost incurred when selling the securities.

The Baumol model uses an equation of the same form as the EOQ formula for inventory management which wewill look at in Chapter 25.

Costs are minimised when:

$$Q = \sqrt{\frac{2CS}{i}}$$

Where S = the amount of cash to be used in each time period

   C = the cost per sale of securities

   i = the interest cost of holding cash or near cash equivalents

   Q = the total amount to be raised to provide for S

Example: The Baumol model

Assum Finder Co faces a fixed cost of $4,000 to obtain new funds. There is a requirement for $24,000 of cash over each period of one year for the foreseeable future. The interest cost of new funds is 12% per annum; the interest rate earned on short-term securities is 9% per annum. How much finance should Finder raise at a time?

Solution

The cost of holding cash is 12% – 9% = 3%

The optimum level of Q (the 'reorder quantity') is:

$$\sqrt{\frac{2 \times 4,000 \times 24,000}{0.03}} = \$80,000$$

The optimum amount of new funds to raise is $80,000. This amount is raised every 80,000 ÷ 24,000 = $3^{1}/_{3}$ years.

7.1.1 Drawbacks of the Baumol model

The inventory approach illustrated above has the following drawbacks.

(a)   In reality, it is unlikely to be **possible** to **predict amounts required** over future periods with much certainty.

(b)   No **buffer inventory** of cash is allowed for. There may be costs associated with running out of cash.

(c)   There may be other **normal costs** of holding cash which increase with the average amount held.

7.2 The Miller-Orr model

In an attempt to produce a more realistic approach to cash management, various models more complicated than the inventory approach have been developed. One of these, the **Miller-Orr model**, manages to achieve a reasonable degree of realism while not being too elaborate.

We can begin looking at the Miller-Orr model by asking what will happen if there is no attempt to manage cash balances. Clearly, the cash balance is likely to 'meander' upwards or downwards. The Miller-Orr model imposes limits to this meandering.

If the cash balance reaches an **upper limit** (point A) the firm **buys sufficient securities** to return the cash balance to a normal level (called the 'return point'). When the cash balance reaches a lower limit (point B), the firm sells securities to bring the balance back to the return point.

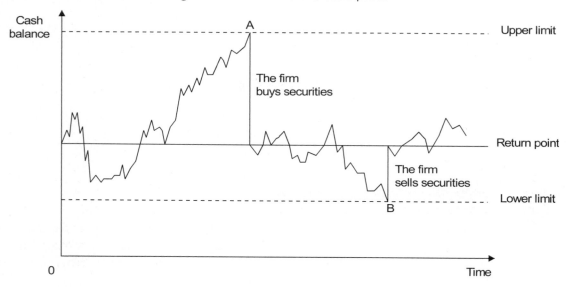

How are the upper and lower limits and the return point set? Miller and Orr showed that the answer to this question depends on the **variance of cash flows**, **transaction costs** and **interest rates**. If the day-to-day variability of cash flows is high or the transaction cost in buying or selling securities is high, then wider limits should be set. If interest rates are high, the limits should be closer together.

To keep the interest costs of holding cash down, the return point is set at one-third of the distance (or 'spread') between the lower and the upper limit.

$$\text{Return point} = \text{Lower limit} + \left(\frac{1}{3} \times \text{spread}\right)$$

$$\text{Spread} = 3\left(\frac{3}{4} \times \frac{\text{Transaction cost} \times \text{Variance of cash flows}}{\text{Interest rate}}\right)^{\frac{1}{3}}$$

To use the Miller-Orr model, it is necessary to follow the steps below.

Step 1   Set the **lower limit** for the **cash balance**. This may be zero, or it may be set at some minimum safety margin above zero.

Step 2   **Estimate** the **variance** of **cash flows**, for example from sample observations over a 100-day period.

Step 3   **Note the interest rate** and the **transaction cost** for each sale or purchase of securities (the latter is assumed to be fixed).

Step 4   **Compute the upper limit** and the **return point** from the model and implement the limits strategy.

You may be given the information to help you through the early steps, as in the example below.

Example: The Miller Orr model

The following data applies to a company.

1   The minimum cash balance is $8,000.

2   The variance of daily cash flows is 4,000,000, equivalent to a standard deviation of $2,000 per day.

3   The transaction cost for buying or selling securities is $50. The interest rate is 0.025 per cent per day.

How would we formulate a decision rule using the Miller-Orr model?

Solution

The spread between the upper and the lower cash balance limits is calculated as follows.

$$\text{Spread} = 3\left(\frac{3}{4} \times \frac{\text{Transaction cost} \times \text{Variance of cash flows}}{\text{Interest rate}} \right)^{\frac{1}{3}}$$

$$= 3\left(\frac{3}{4} \times \frac{50 \times 4,000,000}{0.00025} \right)^{\frac{1}{3}} = 3 \times \left(6 \times 10^{11}\right)^{\frac{1}{3}} = 3 \times 8,434.33$$

$$= \$25,303, \text{ say } \$25,300$$

The upper limit and return point are now calculated.

Upper limit   = lower limit + $25,300 = $8,000 + $25,300 = $33,300

Return point = lower limit + 1/3 × spread = $8,000 + 1/3 × $25,300 = $16,433, say $16,400

The decision rule is as follows. If the cash balance reaches $33,300, buy $16,900 (= 33,300 – 16,400) in marketable securities. If the cash balance falls to $8,000, sell $8,400 of marketable securities for cash.

Variance = standard deviation^2 so if you are given the standard deviation, you will need to square it to calculate the variance. If you are given the annual interest rate, you will need to divide it by 365 to obtain the daily interest rate.

The **usefulness of the Miller-Orr model** is limited by the assumptions on which it is based. In practice, cash inflows and outflows are unlikely to be entirely **unpredictable** as the model assumes: for example, for a retailer, seasonal factors are likely to affect cash inflows.

However, the Miller-Orr model may save management time which might otherwise be spent in responding to those cash inflows and outflows which cannot be predicted.

Section summary

Optimal cash holding levels can be calculated from formal models such as the **Baumol model** and the **Miller-Orr model**.

8 Cash management services

Introduction

This section looks at measures to reduce the amount of time between payment initiation and the availability of the fund.

8.1 Computerised cash management

A relatively recent development in banking services is that of cash management services for corporate customers. A company with many different bank accounts can obtain information about the cash balance in each account through a computer terminal in the company's treasury department linked to the bank's computer. The company can then arrange to move cash from one account to another and so manage its cash position more efficiently.

8.2 Float

As already mentioned, the term 'float' is sometimes used to describe the amount of time between:

(a)   The time when a **payment** is **initiated** (for example, when a debtor sends a cheque in payment, probably by post), and

(b)   The time when the **funds** become **available** for use in the recipient's bank account.

REASONS FOR LENGTHY FLOAT	
Transmission delay	Postal delays of a day, maybe longer
Lodgement delay	Delay in banking payments received, payee delaying presentation to bank of cash/cheques received
Clearance delay	Time for bank to clear cheque, payment not available for use by recipient until clearance (2-3 days in UK)

There are several measures that could be taken to reduce the float.

(a) The payee should ensure that the **lodgement delay** is kept to a minimum. **Cheques** received should be presented to the bank on the day of receipt.

(b) The payee might, in some cases, arrange to **collect cheques** from the payer's premises. This would only be practicable, however, if the payer is local. The payment would have to be large to make the extra effort worthwhile.

(c) The payer might be asked to pay through his own branch of a bank. The payer can give his bank detailed payment instructions, and use the credit clearing system of the bank giro. The **bank giro** is a means of making credit transfers for customers of other banks and other branches. The payee may include a bank giro credit slip on the bottom of his invoice, to help with this method of payment.

(d) **BACS** (Bankers' Automated Clearing Services), a system which provides for the computerised transfer of funds between banks, could be used. BACS is available to corporate customers of banks for making payments.

(e) For regular payments **standing orders** or **direct debits** might be used.

(f) **CHAPS** (Clearing House Automated Payments System) is a computerised system for banks to make same-day clearances (that is, immediate payment) between each other. Each member bank of CHAPS can allow its own corporate customers to make immediate transfers of funds through CHAPS. However, there is a large minimum size for payments using CHAPS.

Example: cash management

Ryan Coates owns a chain of seven clothes shops. Takings at each shop are remitted once a week on Thursday evening to the head office, and are then banked at the start of business on Friday morning. As business is expanding, Ryan Coates has hired an accountant to help him. The accountant gave him the following advice.

'Sales revenue at the seven shops totalled $1,950,000 last year, at a constant daily rate, but you were paying bank overdraft charges at a rate of 11%. You could have reduced your overdraft costs by banking the shop takings each day, except for Saturday's takings. Saturday takings could have been banked on Mondays.'

Comment on the significance of this statement, stating your assumptions. The shops are closed on Sundays.

Solution

(a) A bank overdraft rate of 11% a year is approximately 11/365 = 0.03% a day.

(b) Annual takings of $1,950,000 would be an average of $1,950,000/312 = $6,250 a day for the seven shops in total, on the assumption that they opened for a 52 week year of six days a week (312 days).

(c) Using the approximate overdraft cost of 0.03% a day, the cost of holding $6,250 for one day instead of banking it is 0.03% × $6,250 = $1.875.

(d) Banking all takings up to Thursday evening of each week on Friday morning involves an unnecessary delay in paying cash into the bank. The cost of this delay would be either:

    (i) The opportunity cost of investment capital for the business, or
    (ii) The cost of avoidable bank overdraft charges

It is assumed here that the overdraft cost is higher and is therefore more appropriate to use. It is also assumed that, for interest purposes, funds are credited when banked.

Takings on	Could be banked on	Number of days delay incurred by Friday banking
Monday	Tuesday	3
Tuesday	Wednesday	2
Wednesday	Thursday	1
Thursday	Friday	0
Friday	Saturday	6
Saturday	Monday	4
		16

In one week, the total number of days delay incurred by Friday banking is 16. At a cost of $1.875 a day, the weekly cost of Friday banking was $1.875 × 16 = $30.00, and the annual cost of Friday banking was $30.00 × 52 = $1,560.

(e)   *Conclusion*. The company could have saved about $1,560 a year in bank overdraft charges last year. If the overdraft rate remains at 11% and sales continue to increase, the saving from daily banking would be even higher next year.

Section summary

Reasons for a lengthy float include transmission delay, lodgement delay and clearance delay. There are several measures which can be taken to reduce the float.

Chapter Summary

A company can make losses but still have a net cash income from trading.

A company can also make profits but have a net cash deficit on its trading operations.

Cash flow forecasts provide an early warning of liquidity problems and funding needs.

Banks often require a cash forecast as a condition of lending.

Cash budgets and forecasts can help control cash use.

Cash management aims to prevent cash shortages and to ensure effective cash utilisation.

Cash shortages can be eased by postponing capital expenditure, selling assets, taking longer to pay suppliers and pressing customers for earlier payment (leading and lagging).

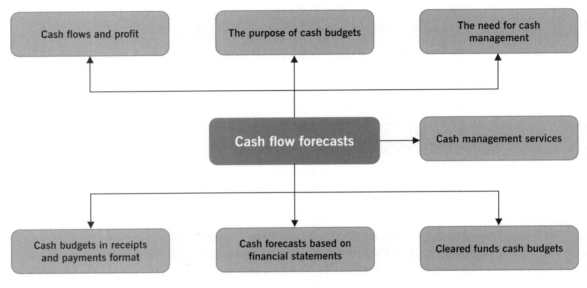

Cash budgets are usually prepared by taking operational budgets and converting them into forecasts as to when receipts and payments occur.

A cash flow forecast can be prepared based on movements in the forecast statement of financial position and statement of profit or loss.

A cleared funds cash forecast is a short-term cash forecast of the cleared funds available to a company in its bank accounts, or of the funding deficit that must be met by immediate borrowing.

Quick Quiz

1   Operational cash flows of a business could be improved directly by:

- **Reducing/Increasing** receivables
- **Reducing/Increasing** inventories
- **Reducing/Increasing** the credit period for the company's trade payables

Delete the word that does not apply.

2   Explain what a rolling forecast is in not more than 20 words.

3   The 'float' is the time between (A) .... and (B) .... (Fill in the blanks)

4   List the twelve main steps involved in preparing a cash budget.

5   Heavy Metal is preparing its cash flow forecast for the next quarter. Which of the following items should be excluded from the calculations?

   A   The receipt of a bank loan that has been raised for the purpose of investment in a new rolling mill

   B   Depreciation of the new rolling mill

   C   A tax payment that is due to be made, but which relates to profits earned in a previous accounting period

   D   Disposal proceeds from the sale of the old rolling mill

6   What are the main uses of forecasts based on the statement of financial position?

7   The cash flow forecast prepared by Heavy Metal suggests that the overdraft limit will be exceeded during the second month of the forecast period due to the timing of the asset purchase. However, by the end of the quarter the overdraft should be back to a level similar to that at the start of the period. Which of the following courses of action would you recommend to overcome this problem?

   A   Acquire the asset using a finance lease rather than by outright purchase
   B   Seek help from a venture capital company
   C   Make a rights issue to raise the additional funds
   D   Negotiate with the bank for a short-term loan to cover the deficit

8   Possible reasons for a lengthy float are:

   (A) .... delay

   (B) .... delay

   (C) .... delay

9   In the Miller–Orr cash management model:

   Return point = Lower limit +...................... × Spread

10   Hallas is a small manufacturing business that uses a large number of suppliers, many of which are located outside the UK. The accountant has suggested that Hallas could improve its cash position by sending payments out using surface mail rather than airmail as at present. If Hallas did this, which of the following would it be taking advantage of?

   A   Lodgement delay
   B   Clearance delay
   C   Transmission delay
   D   Collection delay

Answers to Quick Quiz

1   Cash flows could be improved by:

- Decreasing receivables
- Decreasing inventories
- Increasing the credit period for the company's trade payables

2   A forecast that is continually updated

3   (A)   Initiation of a payment
     (B)   When cleared funds become available in the recipient's bank account

4   *Step*

1	Set up a proforma cash budget
2	Establish budgeted sales month by month
3	Establish the length of credit period taken by customers
4	Determine when budgeted sales revenue will be received as cash
5	Establish when opening receivables will pay
6	Establish when any other cash income will be received
7	Establish production quantities and material usage quantities each month
8	Establish material inventory changes and quantity and cost of month-by-month materials purchases
9	Establish length of credit period taken from suppliers and calculate when cash payments to suppliers will be made
10	Establish when amount due to opening payables will be paid
11	Establish when any other cash payments will be made
12	Show clearly on the bottom of the budget opening position, net cash flow and closing position

5   B   This is a non-cash item and should therefore be excluded.

6   • As longer-term estimates, to assess the scale of funding requirements or cash surpluses the company expects over time

     • To act as a check on the realism of cash flow-based forecasts

7   D   Since the cash flow problems appear to be temporary in nature, it is appropriate to use a short-term solution. Additional long-term capital should not be required.

8   (A)   Transmission delay
     (B)   Lodgement delay
     (C)   Clearance delay

9   One third

10   C   Transmission delay

Answers to Questions

22.1 Profits and cash flow

	Profit $	Operational cash flow $
Sales	200,000	200,000
Opening receivables (∴ received in year)		15,000
Closing receivables (outstanding at year end)		(24,000)
Cash in		191,000
Cost of sales	170,000	170,000
Closing inventory (bought, but not used, in year)		21,000
Opening inventory (used, but not bought, in year)		(12,000)
Purchases in year		179,000
Opening payables (∴ paid in year)		11,000
Closing payables (outstanding at year end)		(14,000)
Cash out		176,000
Profit/operational cash flow	30,000	15,000

22.2 Profits compared with cash flow

The principal reasons why profit will not equal cash flow are as follows.

(a) The **'matching concept'** means that costs and revenues do not equal payments and receipts. Revenue is recognised in the statement of profit or loss when goods are sold, and any revenue not received is recorded as a receivable. Similarly, costs are incurred when a resource is acquired or subsequently used, not when it happens to be paid for.

(b) **Some items appearing** in the statement of profit or loss do not **affect cash flow**. For example, depreciation is a 'non-cash' deduction in arriving at profit.

(c) Similarly, items may **affect cash flow** but not profit. Capital expenditure decisions (apart from depreciation) and inventory level adjustments are prime examples.

22.3 Cash forecast

The opening cash balance at 1 October will consist of Tom's initial $15,000 less the $8,000 expended on non-current assets purchased in September, ie the opening balance is $7,000. Cash receipts from credit customers arise two months after the relevant sales.

Payments to suppliers are a little more tricky. We are told that cost of sales is 100/150 × sales. Thus for October cost of sales is 100/150 × $3,000 = $2,000. These goods will be purchased in October but not paid for until November. Similar calculations can be made for later months. The initial inventory of $5,000 is purchased in September and consequently paid for in October.

The forecast budget can now be constructed.

CASH FORECAST FOR THE SIX MONTHS ENDING 31 MARCH 20X7

	October $	November $	December $	January $	February $	March $
Payments						
Suppliers	5,000	2,000	4,000	4,000	7,000	7,000
Running expenses	1,600	1,600	1,600	1,600	1,600	1,600
Drawings	1,000	1,000	1,000	1,000	1,000	1,000
	7,600	4,600	6,600	6,600	9,600	9,600
Receipts						
Customers	–	–	3,000	6,000	6,000	10,500
Surplus/(shortfall)	(7,600)	(4,600)	(3,600)	(600)	(3,600)	900
Opening balance	7,000	(600)	(5,200)	(8,800)	(9,400)	(13,000)
Closing balance	(600)	(5,200)	(8,800)	(9,400)	(13,000)	(12,100)

22.4 Cash budget

(a)

	January $'000	February $'000	March $'000	April $'000	May $'000	June $'000
Sales revenue						
Cash (40%)	44	52	56	60	64	72
Credit (60%, 2 months)	48	60	66	78	84	90
	92	112	122	138	148	162
Purchases	60	80	90	110	130	140
Wages 75%	12	15	18	21	24	27
25%	3	4	5	6	7	8
Overheads	10	15	15	15	20	20
Dividends			20			
Capital expenditure			30			40
	85	114	178	152	181	235
b/f	15	22	20	(36)	(50)	(83)
Net cash flow	7	(2)	(56)	(14)	(33)	(73)
c/f	22	20	(36)	(50)	(83)	(156)

(b)   The overdraft arrangements are quite inadequate to service the cash needs of the business over the six-month period. If the figures are realistic then action should be taken now to avoid difficulties in the near future. The following are possible courses of action.

(i)   **Activities** could be **curtailed**.

(ii)   Other **sources of cash** could be **explored**, for example a long-term loan to finance the capital expenditure and a factoring arrangement to provide cash due from receivables more quickly.

(iii)   Efforts to **increase the speed of debt collection** could be made.

(iv)   **Payments to suppliers** could be **delayed**.

(v)   The **dividend payments** could be **postponed** (the figures indicate that this is a small company, possibly owner-managed).

(vi)   Staff might be **persuaded to work at a lower rate** in return for, say, an annual bonus or a profit-sharing agreement.

(vii)   **Extra staff** might be taken on to reduce the amount of overtime paid.

(viii)   The **inventory holding policy** should be **reviewed**. It may be possible to meet demand from current production and minimise cash tied up in inventories.

22.5 Types of forecast

Kim O'Hara would be best served by a **cleared funds forecast**, Creighton by a **cash book based forecast**.

Now try this question from the OTQ Question Bank	Number
	Q62

CASH MANAGEMENT

 In this chapter, we discuss **short- and medium-term finance**. This involves looking at the use of **bank loans** and **overdrafts**. The choice between taking out a loan or overdraft is often very important. You should concentrate on understanding **when different forms of borrowing** might be **most appropriate** for a business.

We also look at different methods of **financing foreign trade**.

In the second part of this chapter, we look at the ways in which **cash can be invested** in the short-term, and identify the purpose and main features of various types of short-term investment. The characteristics of different types of instrument may be tested in an MCQ. Alternatively in a longer question you might be asked to explain which types of investment an investor might choose.

topic list	learning outcomes	syllabus references
1 Budgeting for borrowings	C1	C1 (a)
2 Overdrafts	C1	C1 (a)
3 Loans	C1	C1 (a)
4 Trade payables as a source of finance	C1	C1 (a)
5 Export finance	C1	C1 (a)
6 Cash surpluses	C1	C1 (a)
7 Cash investments: bank and building society accounts	C1	C1 (a)
8 Marketable securities: prices and interest rates	C1	C1 (a)
9 Other types of investment	C1	C1 (a)
10 Risk and exposure	C1	C1 (a)

Chapter Overview

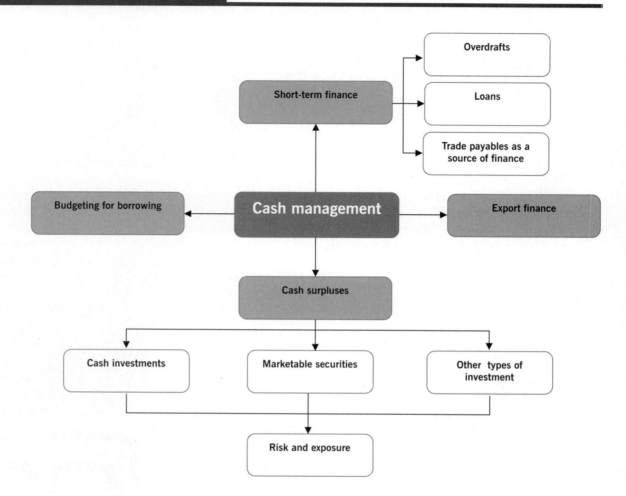

1   Budgeting for borrowings

Introduction

As far as borrowing is concerned, there are three aspects to the **maintenance of liquidity**. These are controlling timing differences, minimising risk and providing against contingencies.

1.1 Maintaining liquidity

(a)   An entity needs enough money to function operationally, pay salaries, suppliers and so on. Of course, eventually it will receive funds from customers, but the length of the cash cycle can mean reliance on **overdraft finance** at times.

(b)   An entity needs to minimise the **risk** that some of its sources of finance will be removed from it.

(c)   An entity also needs to provide against the **contingency** of any sudden movements in cash. Contingency measures can take the form of special arrangements with the bank, insurance policies and so on.

Some of these needs are more pressing than others.

(a)   **Working capital**

Working capital is often financed by an overdraft – this is a result of lagged payments and receipts as discussed earlier and the willingness of businesses to offer credit.

(b)   **Long-term finance**

This is used for major investments. Capital expenditure is easier to put off than, say, wages in a crisis, but a long-term failure to invest can damage the business and reduce its capacity.

(c)   **Overseas finance**

The borrowing might be required to finance **assets overseas**, in which case the **currency** of the borrowing might be important.

KEY TERMS

Bank borrowing can be obtained in the following ways.

(a)   OVERDRAFT FACILITY. A company, through its current account, can borrow money on a short-term basis up to a certain amount. Overdrafts are repayable on demand.

(b)   TERM LOAN. The customer borrows a fixed amount and pays it back with interest over a period or at the end of it.

(c)   COMMITTED FACILITY. The bank undertakes to make a stipulated amount available to a borrower, on demand.

(d)   A REVOLVING FACILITY is a facility that is renewed after a set period. Once the customer has repaid the amount, the customer can borrow again.

(e)   UNCOMMITTED FACILITY. The bank, if it feels like it, can lend the borrower a specified sum. The bank has no obligation to lend.

Section summary

Maintenance of **liquidity** is an important corporate objective. Organisations may have problems due to **timing differences**, **risk** and **contingencies**.

2 Overdrafts

Introduction

Where payments from a current account exceed the balance on the account for a temporary period, the bank finances the deficit by means of an **overdraft**.

Overdrafts are a form of short-term lending, technically repayable on demand. Businesses may not need to use the overdraft facilities that they have been granted.

OVERDRAFTS	
Amount	Should not exceed limit, usually based on known income
Margin	Interest charged at base rate plus margin on daily amount overdrawn and charged quarterly. Fee may be charged for large facility
Purpose	Generally to cover short-term deficits
Repayment	Technically repayable on demand
Security	Depends on size of facility
Benefits	Customer has flexible means of short-term borrowing; bank has to accept fluctuation

2.1 Overdraft as short-term borrowing

By providing an overdraft facility to a customer, the bank is committing itself to provide an overdraft to the customer whenever the customer wants it, up to the agreed limit. The bank will earn interest on the lending, but only to the extent that the customer uses the facility and goes into overdraft. If the customer does not go into overdraft, the bank cannot charge interest.

The bank will generally charge a **commitment fee** when a customer is granted an overdraft facility or an increase in the overdraft facility. This is a fee for granting an overdraft facility and agreeing to provide the customer with funds if and whenever needed.

2.2 Overdrafts and the operating cycle

Many businesses require their bank to provide financial assistance for normal trading over the **operating cycle**.

For example, suppose that a business has the following operating cycle.

	$	$
Inventories and receivables		10,000
Bank overdraft	1,000	
Payables	3,000	
		4,000
Working capital		6,000

The business now buys inventories costing $2,500 for cash, using its overdraft. Working capital remains the same, $6,000, although the bank's financial stake has risen from $1,000 to $3,500.

	$	$
Inventories and receivables		12,500
Bank overdraft	3,500	
Payables	3,000	
		6,500
Working capital		6,000

A bank overdraft provides support for normal trading finance. In this example, finance for normal trading rises from $(10,000 – 3,000) = $7,000 to $(12,500 – 3,000) = $9,500 and the bank's contribution rises from $1,000 out of $7,000 to $3,500 out of $9,500.

A feature of bank lending to support normal trading finance is that the amount of the overdraft required at any time will depend on the **cash flows of the business**: the timing of receipts and payments, seasonal variations in trade patterns and so on. An overdraft will increase in size if the customer writes more cheques, but will reduce in size when money is paid into the account.

There should be times when there will be no overdraft at all, and the account is in credit for a while. In other words, the customer's account may well **swing** from overdraft into credit, back again into overdraft and again into credit, and so on. The account would then be a **swinging account**. The purpose of the overdraft is to bridge the gap between cash payments and cash receipts.

When a business customer has an overdraft facility, and the account is always in overdraft, then it has a **solid core** (or **hard core**) instead of swing. For example, suppose that the account of Blunderbuss has the following record for the previous year:

Quarter to	Average balance $	Range $		$	Debit turnover $
31 March 20X5	40,000 debit	70,000 debit	–	20,000 debit	600,000
30 June 20X5	50,000 debit	80,000 debit	–	25,000 debit	500,000
30 September 20X5	75,000 debit	105,000 debit	–	50,000 debit	700,000
31 December 20X5	80,000 debit	110,000 debit	–	60,000 debit	550,000

These figures show that the account has been permanently in overdraft, and the hard core of the overdraft has been rising steeply over the course of the year (from a minimum overdraft of $20,000 in the first quarter to one of $60,000 in the fourth quarter).

If the hard core element of the overdraft appears to be becoming a **long-term feature** of the business, the **bank** might wish, after discussions with the customer, to **convert** the hard core of the overdraft into a **medium-term loan**, thus giving formal recognition to its more permanent nature. Otherwise annual reductions in the hard core of an overdraft would typically be a requirement of the bank.

2.3 The purpose of an advance for day-to-day trading

The purpose of a bank overdraft for normal day-to-day trading is to help with the financing of current assets. However, there are a number of different reasons why a business might need an overdraft facility. Only **some** of these reasons will be sound and acceptable to a bank.

Borrowing by a business will either **increase the assets** of the business or **decrease its liabilities**.

2.4 Increasing business assets

If borrowing is to increase the business assets, a bank will first check whether the purpose is to acquire more **non-current assets** or more **current assets**. A customer might ask for an overdraft facility to help with day to day trading finance, when the *real* cause of his shortage of liquidity is really a decision to purchase a new non-current asset. There is nothing wrong with asking a bank for financial assistance with the purchase of non-current assets. But borrowing to purchase a non-current asset **reduces the liquidity** of the business, and might even make it illiquid.

Question 23.1

Bank overdraft

Learning outcome C1

The directors of Wrong Wreason have asked their bank for a $50,000 overdraft which they say will be used for normal trading operations. They present two statements of financial position, one indicating the firm's position before the loan and one after. What do you think the bank's response will be?

WRONG WREASON – STATEMENT OF FINANCIAL POSITION (BEFORE)

	$	$
Non-current assets		200,000
Current assets	120,000	
Current liabilities: trade payables	60,000	
Working capital		60,000
		260,000
Share capital and reserves		260,000

WRONG WREASON – STATEMENT OF FINANCIAL POSITION (AFTER)

	$	$	$
Non-current assets (200,000 + 50,000)			250,000
Current assets		120,000	
Current liabilities: bank overdraft	50,000		
trade payables	60,000		
		110,000	
Working capital			10,000
			260,000
Share capital and reserves			260,000

An overdraft facility for **day-to-day trading** should therefore be either to **increase total current assets**, or to **reduce other current liabilities.**

2.5 Increasing total current assets

A request for an overdraft facility to increase total current assets can be pinpointed more exactly, to a wish by the company:

- To increase its **inventory** levels
- To increase its overall **receivables**
- To increase its overall sales **turnover**

The underlying guide to a bank's attitude to lending (in addition to avoiding risk) is whether the finance will be temporary (and 'swinging') or longer term. There might be a number of reasons for a business **increasing its inventory levels** without increasing its total sales.

REASONS FOR INCREASING INVENTORY LEVELS	
Large order	Overdraft suitable, temporary finance to enable business to fulfil order
Inventory build up anticipating seasonal peak	Overdraft suitable, temporary finance to support cost of inventory
Speculative purchase, eg buying raw materials	Overdraft suitable, provided finance temporary and not unacceptably risky
Permanent increase without increase in sales	Overdraft probably not suitable; need for review of finance facilities; inventory may be unsaleable

Reasons for a business wanting to **increase its total receivables** without increasing its sales turnover might be:

(a)   A loss of efficiency in the credit control, invoicing and debt collection procedures of the business, or

(b)   The inability of existing customers to pay without being allowed more credit

In both cases, the bank will be cautious about agreeing to an increased overdraft facility. Delays in invoicing should be eliminated by the business; however, if more credit must be allowed to maintain sales, a bank might agree to an overdraft facility for this purpose.

When a business **increases its sales turnover**, it will almost certainly have to increase its investment in inventories and receivables. It will probably be able to obtain more credit from trade payables, but the balance of the extra finance required will have to be provided out of extra proprietors' capital or other lending. A danger with business expansion is **overtrading**, and a bank will be wary of requests to support ambitious expansion schemes.

2.6 Using an overdraft to reduce other current liabilities

A bank might be asked to provide an overdraft facility to enable a business to pay its tax bills, or to reduce its volume of trade payables. The payment of tax might be sales tax (generally every quarter) or year end corporation tax. An overdraft facility to help a business to pay tax when it falls due is a 'legitimate' and acceptable purpose for an overdraft, although the bank might wish to know why the business had not set funds aside to pay the tax. A bank should be able to expect that the overdraft would soon be paid off out of profits from future trading.

An **extension** to an overdraft in order to pay trade suppliers must be for the purpose of **reducing the overall average volume of trade payables**, which in turn implies a significant change in the trade payables position of the business, all other things being equal. Why might such a reduction in total trade payables be required?

(a)   **To take advantage of attractive purchase discounts offered by suppliers for early settlement of debts**. This should be an acceptable purpose for an extra overdraft to a bank, because taking the discount would reduce the costs and so increase the profits of the business.

(b)   **To pay suppliers who are pressing for payment**. A bank will deal **cautiously** with such a request. It might be because the supplier is desperate for money. If the business *customer* is getting into difficulties, and is falling behind with paying their debts, a banker would take the view that agreeing to an increased overdraft would simply mean taking over debts that might one day never be paid, and so may not agree to such a proposition.

Section summary

Overdrafts are a form of short-term lending, technically repayable on demand. Businesses may not need to use the overdraft facilities that they have been granted.

3 Loans

Introduction

Bank loans tend to be a **source** of **medium-term finance**, linked with the purchase of specific assets. Interest and repayments will be set in advance.

3.1 When a loan is appropriate

A customer might ask the bank for an overdraft facility when the bank would wish to suggest a loan instead; alternatively, a customer might ask for a loan when an overdraft would be more appropriate.

(a)   In most cases, when a customer wants finance to help with 'day to day' trading and cash flow needs, an **overdraft** would be the **appropriate method** of financing. The customer should not be

short of cash all the time, and should expect to be in credit in some days, but in need of an overdraft on others.

(b) When a customer wants to borrow from a bank for only a **short period of time**, even for the purchase of a major non-current asset such as an item of plant or machinery, an overdraft facility might be more suitable than a loan, because the customer will stop paying interest as soon as the account goes into credit.

(c) When a customer wants to borrow from a bank, but cannot see their way to repaying the bank except over the course of a few years, the **medium- or long-term nature** of the financing is best catered for by the provision of a loan rather than an overdraft facility.

3.2 Advantages of an overdraft over a loan

(a) The customer only pays interest when overdrawn.

(b) The bank has the flexibility to review the customer's overdraft facility periodically, and perhaps agree to additional facilities, or insist on a reduction in the facility.

(c) An overdraft can do the same job as a loan: a facility can simply be renewed every time it comes up for review.

(d) Being short-term debt, an overdraft will not affect the calculation of a company's gearing.

Bear in mind, however, that overdrafts are normally **repayable on demand**.

3.3 Advantages of a loan

(a) Both the customer and the bank **know exactly** what the repayments of the loan will be and how much interest is payable, and when. This makes planning (budgeting) simpler.

(b) The customer does not have to worry about the bank deciding to reduce or **withdraw** an overdraft facility before being in a position to repay what is owed. There is an element of 'security' or 'peace of mind' in being able to arrange a loan for an agreed term.

(c) Loans normally carry a **facility letter** setting out the precise terms of the agreement.

For purchases of a non-current asset it is important, however, that the **term of the loan should not exceed** the **economic or useful life** of the asset purchased with the money from the loan. A business will often expect to use the revenues earned by the asset to repay the loan, and obviously, an asset can only do this as long as it is in operational use.

Section summary

Bank loans tend to be a **source** of **medium-term finance**, linked with the purchase of specific assets. Interest and repayments will be set in advance.

There are advantages and disadvantages to having an overdraft instead of a loan.

4 Trade payables as a source of finance

Introduction

Trade credit from suppliers is another possible short-term source of finance.

4.1 Trade payables as a source of short-term finance

Taking credit from suppliers is a normal feature of business and nearly every company has at any time a number of suppliers waiting for payment.

It may be thought that this is a form of interest free borrowing, but:

(a)   Any available settlement discounts will be lost
(b)   It will lead to a loss of supplier goodwill
(c)   If the supplier resorts to legal action, this may affect the organisation's future credit rating.

The organisation must weigh up the cost of lost discounts against the value of the number of days borrowing obtained. It may be more financially worthwhile to pay the supplier early and obtain the discount than to hang onto the funds and invest them for the additional days.

Section summary

Trade credit from suppliers is another possible short-term source of finance, but it has its disadvantages.

---

5 Export finance

5.1 Finance for foreign trade

Introduction

Foreign trade raises special **financing problems**.

Foreign trade financing problems include the following.

(a)   When goods are sold abroad, the customer might ask for credit. The period of credit might be 30 days or 60 days, say, after receipt of the goods; or perhaps 90 days after shipment. Exports take time to arrange, and there might be **complex paperwork**. Transporting the goods can be slow, particularly if they are sent by sea. These delays in foreign trade mean that exporters often build up large investments in inventory and receivables.

(b)   The risk of irrecoverable debts can be greater with foreign trade than with domestic trade. If a foreign customer refuses to pay a debt, the exporter must pursue the debt in the customer's own country, where procedures will be subject to the laws of that country.

There are various measures available to exporters to overcome these problems. (Apart from credit risks, there are other risks, including the risk of currency (exchange rate) fluctuations and political risks.)

5.2 Reducing the investment in foreign receivables

A company can reduce its **investment in foreign receivables** by insisting on earlier payment for goods. Another approach is for an exporter to **arrange for a bank to give cash for a foreign debt**, sooner than the exporter would receive payment in the normal course of events. There are several ways of controlling the risk of financing exports. These include **bills of exchange, export factoring, forfaiting** and **documentary credits.**

5.3 Advantages of using bills of exchange in international trade

Bills of exchange are similar to an advance against collection, used when the bill is payable outside the exporter's country (eg in foreign buyer's country).

(a)   They provide a **convenient method** of **collecting payments** from foreign buyers.

(b) The exporter can seek **immediate finance**, using term bills of exchange, instead of having to wait until the period of credit expires (ie until the maturity of the bill). At the same time, the foreign buyer is allowed the full period of credit before payment is made.

(c) On payment, the foreign buyer keeps the bill as **evidence of payment**, so that a bill of exchange also serves as a receipt.

(d) If a bill of exchange is dishonoured, it may be used by the drawer to **pursue payment** by means of legal action in the drawee's country.

(e) The buyer's bank might add its name to a term bill, to indicate that it **guarantees payment** at maturity. On the continent of Europe, this procedure is known as **'avalising'** bills of exchange.

5.4 Reducing the irrecoverable debt risk

Methods of minimising irrecoverable debt risks are broadly similar to those for domestic trade. An exporting company should vet the creditworthiness of each customer, and grant credit terms accordingly. Methods of reducing the risks of irrecoverable debts in foreign trade are described below.

5.5 Export factoring

Export factoring relates to export trade and is similar to the factoring of domestic trade debts.

KEY TERM

FACTORING is the sale of debts to a third party (the factor) at a discount, in return for prompt cash. A factoring service may be with recourse, in which case the supplier takes the risk of the debt not being paid, or without recourse when the factor takes the risk.   (CIMA *Official Terminology*)

5.6 Main aspects of factoring

(a) **Administration** of the **client's invoicing**, **sales accounting** and debt collection services are generally involved.

(b) The arrangement is likely to provide **credit protection** for the client's debts, whereby the factor takes over the risk of loss from irrecoverable debts and so 'insures' the client against such losses.

(c) The factor will **make payments** to the client **in advance** of collecting the debts. This is sometimes referred to as 'factor finance' because the factor is providing cash to the client against outstanding debts.

A factoring service typically offers prepayment of up to 80% against approved invoices. Service charges vary between around 0.75% and 3% of total invoice value, plus finance charges at levels comparable to bank overdraft rates for those taking advantage of prepayment arrangements.

Factoring, as compared with forfaiting (which we discuss below), is widely regarded as an appropriate mechanism for trade finance and collection of receivables for **small to medium-sized exporters**, especially where there is a flow of **small-scale contracts**.

5.7 Forfaiting

KEY TERM

FORFAITING is a method of export finance whereby a bank purchases from a company a number of sales invoices or promissory notes, usually obtaining a guarantee of payment of the invoices or notes.

Forfaiting is the most common method of providing **medium-term** (say, three to five years) export finance. It has normally been used for export sales involving **capital goods** (machinery etc), where payments will be made over a number of years.

Forfaiting works as follows.

(a) An exporter of capital goods finds an overseas buyer who wants medium-term credit to finance the purchase. The buyer must be willing to pay **some of the cost** (perhaps 15%) at once and to pay the balance in **regular instalments** normally for the next five years.

(b) The buyer will either issue a **series** of **promissory notes**, or accept a **series of drafts** with a final maturity date, say, **five years ahead** but providing for regular payments over this time. In other words, a series of promissory notes maturing every six months, usually each for the same amount.

(c) In most cases, however, the buyer will be required to find a bank which is willing to guarantee **(avalise)** the notes or drafts.

(d) At the same time, the exporter must find a bank that is willing to be a **'forfaiter'**.

(e) The exporter will deliver the goods and receive the avalised promissory notes or accepted bills. They will then sell them to the forfaiter, who will purchase them **without recourse to the exporter.** The forfaiter must now bear the risk, ie:

    (i) Risks of non-payment

    (ii) Political risks in the buyer's country

    (iii) Transfer risk, the buyer's country not meeting its foreign exchange obligations

    (iv) Foreign exchange risk

    (v) The collection of payment from the avalising bank

The diagram below should help to clarify the procedures.

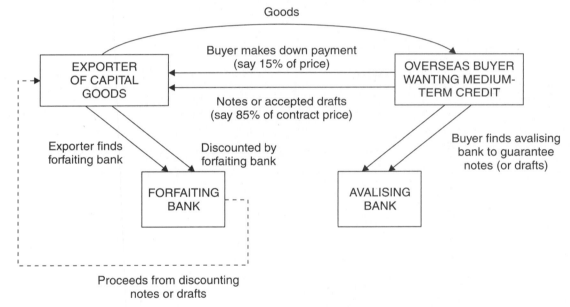

Forfaiting can be an expensive choice, and arranging it takes time. However, it can be a useful way of enabling trade to occur in cases where other methods of ensuring payment and smooth cash flow are not certain, and in cases where trade may not be possible by other means.

5.8 Documentary credits

Documentary credits ('letters of credit') provide a method of payment in international trade which gives the exporter a risk-free method of obtaining payment.

(a) The exporter receives **immediate payment** of the amount due to him, less the discount, instead of having to wait for payment until the end of the credit period allowed to the buyer.

(b) The buyer is able to get a **period of credit** before having to pay for the imports.

The process works as follows:

(a) The buyer and the seller first of all agree a contract for the sale of the goods, which provides for payment through a documentary credit.

(b) The **buyer** then requests a bank in his country to issue a **letter of credit** in favour of the exporter. This bank which issues the letter of credit is known as the **issuing bank.**

(c) The issuing bank, by issuing its letter of credit, guarantees payment to the beneficiary.

Documentary credits are **slow** to arrange, and **administratively cumbersome**; however, they might be considered essential where the **risk of non-payment is high**, or when **dealing** for the **first time** with an **unknown buyer**.

Section summary

It is worth remembering that the **exporter** can obtain finance from the foreign buyer by insisting on **cash with order** and the **importer** can obtain finance from the foreign supplier by means of normal trade credit, perhaps evidenced by a term bill of exchange.

Export factoring provides all the advantages of factoring generally and is especially useful in assessing credit risk.

Forfaiting provides medium-term finance for importers of capital goods.

6 Cash surpluses

Introduction

Many companies have temporary cash surpluses which they need to manage so as to earn a return. **Banks** provide one avenue for investment, but larger firms can invest in other forms of financial instrument in the money markets. Generally speaking, the greater the return offered, the riskier the investment.

6.1 Managing cash

Cash is an asset of a business; if it is to be invested, it must be invested profitably, and the investment must be secure.

6.2 Liquidity

We need to consider what we mean by surplus. Take the following example.

Example: liquidity

(a) Drif Co receives money every month from cash sales and from trade receivables for credit sales of $1,000. It makes payments, in the normal course of events of $800 a month. In January, the company uses an overdraft facility to buy a car for $4,000.

	Jan $	Feb $	March $
Brought forward	–	(3,800)	(3,600)
Receipts	1,000	1,000	1,000
Payments	(800)	(800)	(800)
Car	(4,000)	0	0
Overdrawn balance	(3,800)	(3,600)	(3,400)

The company has been left with a persistent overdraft, even though, in operating terms it makes a monthly surplus of $200.

(b)   Guide Co on the other hand has monthly cash receipts of $1,200 and monthly cash payments of $1,050. The company sets up a special loan account: it borrows $5,000 to buy a car. This it pays off at the rate of $80 a month.

	Jan $	Feb $	March $
Brought forward	–	70	140
Receipts	1,200	1,200	1,200
Payments	(1,050)	(1,050)	(1,050)
Loan repayment	(80)	(80)	(80)
Operating surplus	70	140	210

Which do you consider has the healthier finances? Clearly Drif Co produces an operating surplus (before the car purchase) of $200 ($1,000 – $800) a month, which is more than Guide Co ($150, ie $1,200 – $1,050). Furthermore Guide Co has a much higher net debt, the loan for the car being $5,000 as opposed to $4,000.

Yet, in effect the financing arrangements each has chosen has turned the tables. Drif Co is relying on normal overdraft finance which will be **repayable on demand**. Its normal **operating surplus** of receipts from sales and receivables over payments to suppliers has been completely swamped by the long-term financing of a car.

On the other hand, Guide Co, by arranging a separate term loan, which is more secure from Guide Co's point of view, is able to run an **operating surplus** of $70 a month. It has effectively separated an operating surplus arising out of month to month business expenses from its cash requirements for capital investment (in the car), leaving a **financial inflow**.

This shows the following.

(a)   A 'surplus' can sometimes be created by the way in which **financial information** is **presented**.

(b)   It is often necessary to distinguish **different kinds** of cash transaction (eg capital payments).

(c)   Different types of debt have **different risks** for the company attached to them.

Cash surpluses may arise from **seasonal factors**, so that surpluses generated in good months are used to cover shortfalls later. In this case, the management of the business needs to ensure that the surpluses are big enough to cover the later deficits. The mere existence of a surplus in one or two months in a row is no guarantee of liquidity in the long term.

6.3 Safety

Considerations of **safety** are also important. Cash surpluses are rarely hoarded on the company's premises, where they can be stolen: but what should be done with them, in the short term?

(a)   They are assets of the company, and do need to be **looked after** as well as any other asset.

(b)   In time of inflation, money effectively **falls in value**.

(c)   Any surplus must be kept **secure**: as depositors in the collapsed Icelandic banks must be painfully aware, some banks are not as secure as others. Some investments are riskier than others.

Question 23.2   Investing cash

Learning outcome C1

Compare the following two situations. Steve and Andy are both in the car repair business. Both own equipment worth $4,000 and both owe $200 to suppliers. Steve, however, has accumulated $1,000 in

BPP
LEARNING MEDIA

cash which is deposited in a non interest bearing current account at his bank. Andy has $100 in petty cash.

	Steve $	Andy $
Non-current assets	4,000	4,000
Cash at bank	1,000	100
Payables	(200)	(200)
Net assets	4,800	3,900
Profit for the year	1,200	1,200

Which would you say is the more profitable?

There is the other question about cash surpluses: what do you do with them, to make a profit? They are business assets like any other.

(a)   In the long term, a company with an ever increasing cash balance can:

    (i)   **Invest it in new business opportunities** for profit

    (ii)   **Return it to owners/shareholders** by way of increased drawings/dividends

(b)   In the short term, surplus funds need to be invested so that they can earn a return when they are not being used for any other purpose.

    (i)   A return can be earned perhaps by an earlier payment of business debts. The return is the **'interest' saved**.

    (ii)   Otherwise, there is a variety of deposit accounts and financial instruments which can be used to earn a return on the cash surpluses until they are needed. These are discussed in the next section of this chapter.

6.4 Guidelines for investing

Any business will normally have a number of guidelines as to how the funds are invested. A firm will try and maximise the return for an **acceptable** level of risk. What is acceptable depends on the preferences of the firm in question.

To maintain liquidity, it is often company policy that the surplus funds should be **invested** in financial instruments which are **easily converted** into cash; in effect, enough of the surplus funds should be invested to maintain liquidity.

There have been a number of reported incidents where a firm's corporate treasury department took too many risks with the firm's funds, investing them in risky financial instruments to gain a profit. These went sour, and firms have been left with high losses, arising solely out of treasury operations, with little relevance to the firm's main business.

Guidelines can cover issues such as the following examples.

(a)   Surplus funds can only be invested in **specified types of investment** (eg no equity shares).

(b)   All investments must be **convertible into cash** within a set number of days.

(c)   Investments should be **ranked**: surplus funds to be invested in higher risk instruments only when a sufficiency has been invested in lower risk items (so that there is always a cushion of safety).

(d)   If a firm invests in certain financial instruments, a **credit rating** should be obtained. Credit rating agencies, issue gradings according to risk.

6.5 Legal restrictions on investments

The type of investments an organisation can make is restricted by law in certain special cases:

(a)   Where public (ie taxpayers') money is invested by a **public sector** (central or local government) institution

(b)   Where the money is invested by a company on behalf of personal investors in cases such as **pension schemes**

(c)   In the case of **trusts** (as determined by the relevant Act)

Section summary

A company has a variety of opportunities for using its **cash surpluses**, but the choice of obtaining a return is determined by considerations, of **profitability**, **liquidity** and **safety**.

Surplus funds can be deposited in **interest bearing accounts** offered by banks, finance houses or building societies. Generally speaking:

*   These are for a fixed period of time
*   Early withdrawal may not be permitted, or may result in a penalty
*   The principal does not decline in monetary value

7 Cash investments: bank and building society accounts

Introduction

Banks and building societies offer various different facilities for earning interest on cash deposits.

7.1 High street bank deposits

Commercial banks in most countries offer a wide range of different types of interest earning account. The main banks and many building societies may also pay interest on some types of **current account** (for day-to-day transactions). Some of these may be of limited relevance to large corporations, but for sole traders and small businesses, high street bank products are important.

For someone who wishes to invest a small sum for a short period, **deposit account** facilities may be available from the banks.

Features of deposit accounts

*   Usually seen as very low risk (although in current climate it is possible for banks to be unable to repay the deposit)

*   Some accounts are instant access (therefore high liquidity)

*   High liquidity and low risk mean that rates of return are low

7.2 High interest deposit accounts and high interest cheque accounts

If you have a larger amount of money to invest, you may be able to place the money in a high interest account. Access is usually still immediate, but the rate of interest offered will be higher.

7.3 Option deposits

These arrangements are offered in many countries for predetermined periods of time ranging from 2 to 7 years with minimum deposits. The interest rates, which may be linked to base rates, reflect the longer term nature of the arrangement and the corresponding lack of withdrawal facilities before the expiry of the agreed term. For businesses, these might be of limited relevance.

7.4 Other facilities

Banks may offer special facilities for very large amounts.

(a)   With very large amounts, it may be possible to get fixed rate quotes for **money market deposits** for varying intervals such as seven days up to eighteen months or longer.

(b)   For still larger amounts it is possible to arrange for the money to be deposited with the bank's finance company at better rates than that available for normal deposits. Alternatively the business can go direct to a finance company itself.

CASE STUDY

EUROZONE DEBT CRISIS – BAILOUT BLUES – Russians join locals as big losers in Cyprus levy

By Kerin Hope in Nicosia, Charles Clover in Moscow and Michael Steen in Frankfurt.

Cypriots clustered around bank cash machines in Nicosia's old town yesterday afternoon to pick up a few hundred euros amid rumours that banks may stay closed tomorrow and perhaps even longer.

The mood was angry as islanders digested the news they were to lose up to a tenth of their deposits in a levy imposed as a condition for a €10bn bailout by international lenders.

"I withdrew four hundred [euros] yesterday and the same today," said Angeliki, a teacher who declined to give her full name. "I'm not so worried about a bank collapse but I'm furious that I'm going to lose some of my savings."

A white-haired man who gave his name as Haralambos said he felt cheated because his bank told him that deposits up to €100,000 were fully guaranteed.

"I feel certain there are grounds for bringing a lawsuit against whoever did this," he said. "They have no right to take money from a pensioner."

Source: Financial Times 18 March 2013

Section summary

Banks offer several different facilities for earning interest on cash deposits.

8 Marketable securities: prices and interest rates

Introduction

In the cash investments discussed in the previous section, the investor's initial capital is secure. The investor cannot get back less than they put in. Another common feature is that such investments are not marketable.

8.1 Marketable securities

However, there are also **marketable securities**, such as gilts, bonds and certificates of deposit. Such securities are bought and sold, and they earn interest. What determines their price?

8.2 Prices of fixed interest stocks

The price of marketable securities is affected by the following.

(a) The **interest rate** (known as the **coupon rate**) on a stock is normally fixed at the outset, but it may become more or less attractive when compared with the interest rates in the money markets as a whole. Let us take an example. Suppose that investors in the market expect a return of 6.47%.

(i) $2^1/2$% Consolidated Stock pays $2.50 interest for every $100 of the stock's nominal value. However, the increased return means that:

$$\frac{\$2.50}{\text{Price of }\$100\text{ nominal}} = 6.47\%$$

therefore, the **expected** price is $\frac{\$2.50}{0.0647} = \$38.64$

Where general interest rates rise, the price of stocks will fall.

(ii) Where general interest rates fall, the price of stocks will rise. For example, if the market required a return of 6%, the price of $100 nominal of a non-redeemable $2\frac{1}{2}$% stock would be:

$\frac{\$2.50}{\text{Price}} = 6\%$ therefore, the expected price is $41.67.

Both these examples ignore two other features affecting prices of stocks.

(b) The **risk** associated with the payment of interest and the **eventual repayment of capital**. Some Government securities are considered virtually risk-free but other fixed interest stocks may not be.

(c) The **length of time to redemption** or **maturity**. Suppose the following market values were quoted on 25 March 20X2.

9% Treasury Stock 20X5 $113.8029
9% Treasury Stock 20X9 $142.6311

The first stock is due to be redeemed in 20X5, whereas the second will not be redeemed until the year 20X9. In both cases, as with all government securities except those that are index-linked, the stocks will be redeemed at their nominal value of $100. The closer a stock gets to its redemption date the closer the price will approach $100. This is known as the **pull to maturity**.

8.3 Yields on fixed interest stocks

The paragraphs below concentrate on gilts (government securities) but the principles involved apply equally to any other fixed interest stocks including, for example company loan stock.

8.4 Interest yield

The yield for a particular gilt is an expression for the return on the stock if it was bought at the price ruling and held for one year.

KEY TERM

INTEREST YIELD (also known as the flat yield or running yield) is the interest or coupon rate expressed as a percentage of the market price.

$$\text{Interest yield} = \frac{\text{Gross interest}}{\text{Market price}} \times 100\%$$

| Question 23.3 | Interest yield |

Learning outcome C1

On 19 March 20X0 the market price of 9% Treasury Stock 20X9 is $134.1742. What is the interest yield?

The interest yield in practice is influenced by two other factors.

(a) **Accrued interest**

The interest on 10% Treasury Stock 20X3 is paid in two equal instalments on 8 March and 8 September each year. Thus, if an investor were to sell their stock on 1 June 20X0, in the absence of any other rules they would be forgoing a considerable amount of interest which will be received on 8 September 20X0 by the purchaser. **The price paid by the purchaser must reflect this amount of accrued interest**, and this type of calculation is tested in Question 3.4: Cost of purchase.

(b) **Cum int** and **Ex int**

For administrative reasons, issuers of securities (eg the government) must close their books some time before the due date for the payment of interest, so that they can prepare and send out the necessary documentation in time for it to reach the registered owners of securities before the due dates. Any person who buys stocks **ex int** will not receive the next interest payment. This will be sent to the former owner.

8.5 Redemption yields

KEY TERM

REDEMPTION YIELD is the rate of interest at which the total of the discounted values of any future payments of interest and capital is equal to the current price of a security.   (CIMA *Official Terminology*)

The interest yield takes no account of the fact that most Government stocks are redeemable (ie that their face value will be repaid) nor of the proximity of the redemption date although we have seen how the pull to maturity can affect the price. A more realistic measure of the overall return available from a stock is the **gross redemption yield**. This takes account of both the **interest payable until redemption** and the **redemption value**.

| Example: redemption yield (yield to maturity) |

A bond with a coupon rate of 8% is redeemable in 9 years time for $100. Its current market price is $91. What is the percentage yield to maturity?

Solution

This is an internal rate of return calculation. We will take two discount rates and see where the IRR is likely to fall.

Nine annual receipts of $8 and the final receipt in 9 years' time of $100, discounted at the IRR, will give us the current market price of $91.

We will begin by taking 10% as the discount rate.

t = 9, r = 10

($8 × 5.759) + ($100 × 0.424) = $46.07 + $42.40 = $88.47

This is very close to $91. Now we will try 9%.

t = 9, r = 9

($8 × 5.995) + ($100 × 0.46) = $47.96 + $46 = $93.96

We can see that the IRR must be midway between 10% and 9%.

(88.47 + 93.96)/2 = 91.22

So the percentage yield to maturity is 9.5%.

Note: You may need to refer to your CIMA C3 knowledge for this question.

Yields are determined by **market prices** which in turn reflect the **demand for particular stocks**. Thus, if a yield is relatively low it can be concluded that the price is relatively high and that the demand for the stock is also relatively high. Conversely, a high yield means that a stock is relatively unpopular.

The major factors affecting choice are these.

(a)   Whether the investor is looking for **income or capital appreciation**

(b)   The investor's **tax position**

(c)   The investor's **attitude to the risk** inherent in gilts resulting from changes in interest rates. (It is important to remember that although the eventual repayment of a gilt is not in doubt, the market price may fluctuate widely between the date of purchase and the eventual redemption)

(d)   **Other aspects** of the **investor's business**. (The banks and building societies tend traditionally to concentrate on holding short-dated stocks (redeemable soon) while the insurance companies and pension funds which have long-term liabilities often match these with long-dated gilts (redeemable further in the future)).

Section summary

The **yield** (profitability) of a money market instrument depends on:

- Its face value
- The interest rate offered
- The period of time before it is redeemed (ie converted into cash) by the issuer

9 Other types of investment

Introduction

This section looks at other types of investment such as treasury bills and certificates of deposit.

9.1 Government securities: example – gilts

KEY TERM

The term GILTS is short for 'gilt-edged securities' and refers to marketable British Government securities. These stocks, although small in number (around 100), dominate the fixed interest market in the UK.

The *Financial Times* classifies gilts according to the length of their lives.

(a)   Shorts – lives up to five years (Stock Exchange up to seven years)

(b)   Mediums – lives from five to fifteen years (Stock Exchange seven to fifteen years)

(c)   Longs – lives of more than fifteen years

(d)   Undated stocks (Issued many years ago these are sometimes known as irredeemable or one-way option stocks. These include *War Loan 3^1/$_2$%, Conversion Loan 3^1/$_2$%, Consolidated Stock 2^1/$_2$%.* Each has certain other peculiarities)

(e)   Index-linked stocks

By 'life' is meant the **number of years** before the issuer repays the principal amount.

9.1.1 Fixed interest gilts

Most gilts are fixed interest, and their prices and yields follow the principles outlined in Section 8 above.

9.1.2 Treasury bills

KEY TERM

A TREASURY BILL is government short-term debt, maturing in less than one year, and generally issued at a discount.
(CIMA *Official Terminology*)

TREASURY BILLS are issued weekly by the government to finance short-term cash deficiencies in the government's expenditure programme. The holder is paid the full value of the bill on maturity. Since they are negotiable, they can be re-sold, if required, before their maturity date. This means they have high liquidity.

Treasury bills do not pay interest, but the purchase price of a Treasury bill is less than its face value, the amount that the government will eventually pay on maturity. There is thus an **implied rate of interest** in the price at which the bills are traded. They are therefore subject to interest rate risk. They have minimal capital risk as they are backed by government.

9.1.3 Index-linked stocks

There are various **index-linked Treasury stocks** in issue. The first such stock, 2% Treasury Stock 1996, was issued in March 1981. Both the interest and the eventual redemption value are linked to inflation.

These gilts offer a **guaranteed real return** equal to the **coupon rate**. Many investment fund managers would have considered such a return highly satisfactory over the last fifteen years.

9.1.4 Gilt prices in the Financial Times

Gilt prices are to be found in the *Financial Times* (in £). For all categories other than index-linked gilts, the information is presented as follows.

Monday edition

Notes	Price (£)	Wk% +/–	Amount £m	Interest due	Last xd
Treas 10pc 20X3	121.0801	0.4	2,506	Mr 8 Se 8	22.2

Tuesday to Saturday editions

| | Yield | | | | 52 week | |
Notes	Int	Red	Price (£)	+ or –	High	Low
Treas 10pc 20X3	8.27	4.72	120.9273	+0.0600	123.52	115.44

The first (Monday) example above shows that:

(a)   10% Treasury Stock 20X3 was quoted at £121.0801 at the close of business on the previous Friday, a change of +0.4% in the week.

(b)   £2,506 million of the stock was in issue.

(c)   Interest is due on 8 March and 8 September.

(d)   The stock last went **ex-interest** on 22 February. In other words, if you bought the stock after 22 February, you will not receive the interest due on 8 March. This interest will be paid to whoever held the stock up to 22 February.

The second (Tuesday to Saturday) example shows that:

(a)   The current price of the same stock was £120.9273 at the close of business on the previous day, which is £0.06 higher than the price on the day before.

(b)   The highest quoted price in the 52 weeks to date is £123.52; the lowest is £115.44.

(c)   The gross interest yield and the gross redemption yield are given in the first two columns.

9.1.5 Purchase, sale and issue of gilts

Question 23.4	Cost of purchase

Learning outcome C1

Suppose that a client wishes to purchase 13¾% UK Treasury Stock 2002-05 with a nominal value of £5,000. The transaction is executed by a stockbroker, who charges commission of 0.8%, in March 2001 at a price of £111.5064. Accrued interest is 56 days. What will be the total cost?

Gilts can be dealt in any amount down to 1p. It is therefore quite possible to buy, say, £13,456.83 nominal value of a particular stock. This facility is often useful to investors who wish to round up an existing holding to some convenient figure. Similarly, it is quite possible to spend an exact amount on a particular stock. For example, an investor might ring up his stockbroker and ask him to buy £5,000 worth of the 13¾% Treasury Stock on the day referred to in the Question above. The broker would then buy stock with a nominal value of:

$$£5,000 \times \frac{£100}{£111.5064} = £4,484.05$$

9.2 Local authority stocks

We have already mentioned that it is possible for investors to deposit their money with local authorities. In addition to these investments there are a very large number of marketable local authority securities.

These stocks may, in most respects, be considered as being very similar to British Government Stocks. The main differences are as follows.

(a)   The security of a local authority is not considered quite as **good** as that of the central government.

(b)   The market in most of the stocks is **much thinner** (ie there are not many transactions) than for gilts, since the amounts involved are smaller and the stocks tend to be held by just a few institutions.

As a result of the points listed above, the yield on local authority stocks tends to be rather higher than on gilts.

9.3 Certificates of deposit

KEY TERM

A CERTIFICATE OF DEPOSIT is a negotiable instrument that provides evidence of a fixed term deposit with a bank. Maturity is normally within 90 days, but can be longer.   (CIMA *Official Terminology*)

9.3.1 Issue of CDs

Certificates of deposit (CDs) are issued by an institution (bank or building society), certifying that a specified sum has been deposited with the issuing institution, to be repaid on a specific date. The term may be as short as seven days, or as long as five years. Since CDs are negotiable, if the holder of a CD cannot wait until the end of the term of the deposit and wants cash immediately, the CD can be sold. The appeal of a CD is that it offers an attractive rate of interest, *and* can be easily sold. CDs are sold on the market at a discount which reflects prevailing interest rates. This means that they are subject to interest rate risk and capital risk since the value of the investment will change depending on market interest rates.

CDs have one major advantage over a money-market time deposit with the same bank or building society, namely **liquidity**. Unlike a money market deposit which cannot be terminated until it matures, CDs can be liquidated **at any time** at the prevailing market rate. In return for this liquidity, the investor must, however, accept a lower yield than a money market deposit would command.

9.4 Bills of exchange

KEY TERM

A BILL OF EXCHANGE is a negotiable instrument, drawn by one party on another, for example by a supplier of goods on a customer, who by accepting (signing) the bill, acknowledges the debt, which may be payable immediately (a sight draft) or at some future date (a time draft). The holder of the bill can, thereafter, use an accepted time draft to pay a debt to a third party, or can discount it to raise cash.
         (CIMA *Official Terminology*)

9.4.1 Definitions

(a)   The **bill** is **drawn** on the company or person who is being ordered to pay.
(b)   The **drawer** orders payment of the money.
(c)   The **drawee** is the party who is to pay, and to whom the bill is addressed.
(d)   The **payee** receives the funds.

Using the example of a cheque. A (the drawer), writes out a cheque to B (the payee). The cheque instructs A's bank (the drawee), to pay B a sum of money. The drawee of a bill of exchange does not have to be a bank, and the payment date does not have to be immediate.

A bill is an unconditional order to pay, and it will always include the word 'pay' and be phrased so as to make it clear that the order is unconditional. The bill must also specify the name of the payee, which might be the drawer ('Pay... to our order') or a third party ('Pay.... to XYZ or order....').

For a term bill with a future payment date, the **drawee** signs their acceptance of the order to pay (**accepts the bill** in other words, agrees to pay) and returns the bill to the drawer or the drawer's bank. When a bill is accepted, it becomes an IOU or promise to pay. If the bill is dishonoured the drawer can take legal action against the drawee. Bills of exchange are therefore subject to default risk depending on the credit worthiness of the drawee.

9.4.2 Discounting bills

As an IOU, an accepted bill of exchange is a form of debt. It is a **negotiable instrument**.

(a) The holder of the bill can hold on to the bill until maturity, then present it to the specified bank for payment.

(b) Alternatively, the bill holder can **sell the bill** before **maturity**, for an amount below its payment value (ie at a discount). The **buyer** of a bill expects to make a profit by purchasing the bill at a discount to its face value and then either receiving full payment at maturity on presenting the bill for payment, or reselling the bill before maturity. The buyer could be a bank or a supplier with which the seller has a debt.

The seller obtains immediate cash from the buyer of the bill, but in effect is borrowing short-term funds, with the interest rate for borrowing built into the discount price. The size of the discount will reflect the interest rate that the buyer of the instrument wishes to receive, and the term to the instrument's maturity. To calculate the discounted amount to be paid the following formula is used.

$$\text{Discounted price} = F \times \left[1 - \frac{RT}{Y} \right]$$

Where F = Face value
R = Discount rate
T = Number of days
Y = Number of days in year

For example, a bill of exchange with a face value of $50,000 payable in 60 days where the buyer requires a discount rate of 5%.

$$\text{Discounted price} = \$50,000 \times \left[1 - \frac{60 \times 0.05}{365} \right] = \$49,589$$

Bills of exchange are also used to finance domestic and international trade, because they are tradeable instruments for short-term credit.

Money market instruments are traded on either an interest rate basis or a discount basis.

(a) When an **interest rate** basis applies, a **principal sum** is lent and the borrower repays the **principal plus interest** at maturity. The interest rate is specified and applied to the principal amount for the term of the loan to calculate the amount of interest payable. Bank loans are made on this basis.

(b) When a **discount basis** applies, a **specified sum** is **payable at maturity** to the holder of a money market instrument. If the instrument is purchased before maturity, the price will be less than the amount payable at maturity.

9.5 Other commercial stocks

9.5.1 Bonds

KEY TERMS

A BOND is a debt instrument normally offering a fixed rate of interest (coupon) over a fixed period of time, with a fixed redemption value.

COUPON is the annual interest payable on a bond, expressed as a percentage of the nominal value.

(CIMA *Official Terminology*)

BOND is a term given to any fixed interest (mostly) security, whether it be issued by the government, a company, a bank or other institution. (Gilts are therefore **UK government bonds**.) Businesses also issue bonds. They are usually for the long term. They may or may not be secured.

Example: Bond selling price

An unquoted bond has a coupon rate of 6%. It will repay its face value of $1,250 at the end of 10 years. The yield to maturity is 12%. What is the selling price of the bond?

Solution

You may need your old CIMA C3 notes to remind you of the net present value (NPV) technique.

The selling price of the bond is the **net present value** of the **interest** received every year for 10 years **and the $1,250** which we receive **at the end** of 10 years.

- The **coupon rate** of 6% determines **the amount of** interest received annually

- However, the amounts received are then discounted at the **discount factor** of 12% (the **yield to maturity**)

Interest = $1,250 × 6% = $75 (each year)

As the interest is received **each year**, it is an **annuity**. We need to look at the **cumulative present value tables** (at the back of this book) for 12% for 10 years. This gives us 5.650.

The $1,250 is received after 10 years so we need to look at the **present value tables** for 12% for 10 years. This gives us 0.322.

The net present value is therefore

$(75 × 5.650) + $(1,250 × 0.322) = $826

This is the **selling price** for the bond.

9.5.2 Commercial paper

KEY TERM

COMMERCIAL PAPER is unsecured short-term loan notes issued by companies, and generally maturing within three months.

Like a gilt, CP is traded often at a discount reflecting the yield required. It is a type of promissory note, and companies find them useful for short term borrowing (usually 3 months), and is unsecured. It is therefore risky. Although formal **credit ratings** are not required in some countries, they do help investors make rational choices. A firm's CP is therefore given a credit rating by third party agencies to assess its risk.

Loan stocks are issued in return for loans **secured on a particular asset of the business**. The factory, for example, may be offered as **security**. The loan is for the long term. Loan stock holders take priority over other payables when a business is wound-up. They can force a liquidation.

9.6 Money-market accounts

These are similar in principle to a bank deposit account. Here funds are deposited with a bank or other financial institution for a fixed period of time and cannot be accessed until the term has ended. Terms range from overnight to 12 months.

Section summary

Gilts are securities issued by the UK government. Other fixed interest marketable securities include **local authority bonds**, and **corporate debt**.

A **certificate of deposit** is a certificate indicating that a sum of money has been deposited with a bank and will be repaid at a later date. As CDs can be bought and sold, they are a liquid type of investment.

A **bill of exchange** is like a cheque, only it is not drawn on a bank. It orders the drawee to pay money.

Commercial paper and **loan stock** are debt instruments issued by companies: commercial paper is unsecured.

10 Risk and exposure

Introduction

Businesses should have guidelines in place covering **what sort of investments** are **allowed** and how much should be **invested** in **lower risk** securities.

10.1 Risk

Risk can be considered under the following headings:

(a) **Default risk**. The risk that payments of interest or capital will not be received on schedule.

(b) **Price risk**. The risk that the value of a fixed interest investment will be adversely affected by a rise in interest rates.

(c) **Foreign exchange risk**. The risk that value of foreign investment may be adversely affected by movement in exchange rates.

(d) **Tax and regulation risk**. The risk that legal or tax charges at home or abroad impact upon the value of investments.

10.2 The relationship between risk and return

The return expected by an investor will depend on the level of risk. The higher the risk, the higher the required return. This can be illustrated as in the diagram below.

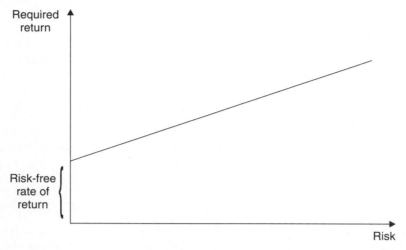

Marketable UK securities can be ranked in order of increasing risk and increasing expected return.

- Government securities   *Low risk*
- Local authority stocks
- Other 'public' corporation stocks
- Company loan stocks
- Other secured loans
- Unsecured loans
- Convertible loan stocks
- Preference shares
- Equities   *High risk*

(a) **Government stock**

The risk of default is negligible and hence this tends to form the base level for returns in the market. The only uncertainty concerns the movement of interest rates over time, and hence longer dated stocks will tend to carry a higher rate of interest.

(b) **Company loan stock**

Although there is some risk of default on company loan stock (also called corporate bonds), the stock is usually secured against corporate assets.

(c) **CDs and Bills of Exchange**

The riskiness of CDs and bills of exchange varies with the creditworthiness of the issuers. They are riskier than government (and probably local government) securities, but less risky than shares.

10.3 Diversification and holding a portfolio

Holding more than one investment always carries less risk than holding only one. If only one investment is held, the investor could lose a lot if this one investment fails. The extent to which risk can be reduced will depend on the relationship which exists between the different returns. The process of reducing risk by increasing the number of separate investments in a portfolio is known as **diversification**.

Section summary

Businesses should have guidelines in place covering **what sort of investments** are **allowed** and how much should be **invested** in **lower risk** securities. The relative attractiveness of investing in any of these securities derives from their **return** and the **risk**. **Diversification** across a range of separate investments can reduce risk for the investor.

Chapter Summary

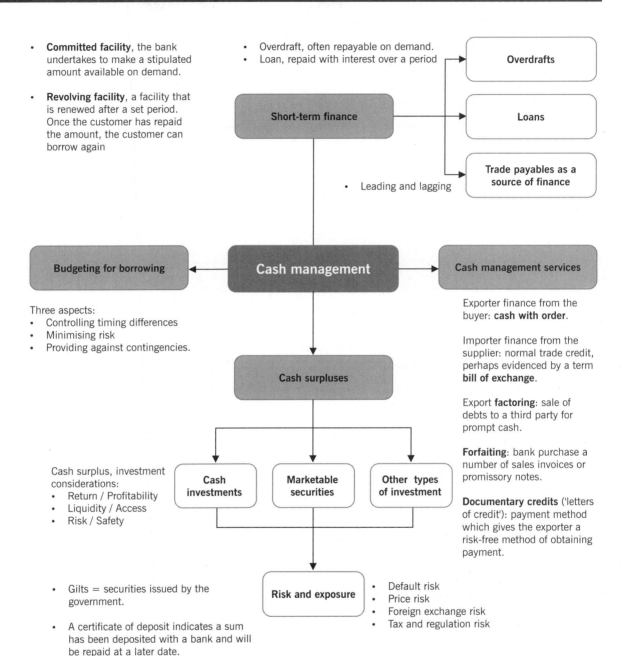

- **Committed facility**, the bank undertakes to make a stipulated amount available on demand.

- **Revolving facility**, a facility that is renewed after a set period. Once the customer has repaid the amount, the customer can borrow again

- Overdraft, often repayable on demand.
- Loan, repaid with interest over a period

Overdrafts

Loans

Trade payables as a source of finance

Short-term finance

- Leading and lagging

Budgeting for borrowing

Cash management

Cash management services

Three aspects:
- Controlling timing differences
- Minimising risk
- Providing against contingencies.

Exporter finance from the buyer: **cash with order**.

Importer finance from the supplier: normal trade credit, perhaps evidenced by a term **bill of exchange**.

Export **factoring**: sale of debts to a third party for prompt cash.

Cash surpluses

Forfaiting: bank purchase a number of sales invoices or promissory notes.

Cash surplus, investment considerations:
- Return / Profitability
- Liquidity / Access
- Risk / Safety

Cash investments

Marketable securities

Other types of investment

Documentary credits ('letters of credit'): payment method which gives the exporter a risk-free method of obtaining payment.

- Gilts = securities issued by the government.

- A certificate of deposit indicates a sum has been deposited with a bank and will be repaid at a later date.

- A bill of exchange is like a cheque, but not drawn on a bank.

- Commercial paper and loan stock = debt instruments issued by companies.

Risk and exposure

- Default risk
- Price risk
- Foreign exchange risk
- Tax and regulation risk

Quick Quiz

1   Which of the following is **not** a type of bank borrowing?

     A   Term loan
     B   Certificate of deposit
     C   Revolving facility
     D   Uncommitted facility

2   Match the name of the bank borrowing facilities detailed below with the relevant description.

     Facility   *Description*

     A   Overdraft   1   Renewable after a set period.

     B   Revolving facility   2   Borrowing of a fixed amount for a fixed period.

     C   Term loan   3   Borrowing through the customer's current account up to a certain limit. Repayable on demand.

3   What reasons may make a business ask for an overdraft to reduce trade payables?

4   Which of the following is normally an advantage of an overdraft over a term loan?

     A   No risk of the bank withdrawing the facility
     B   Interest only paid to the extent that funds are required
     C   Better for borrowing to finance purchase of non-current assets
     D   Planning and budgeting are simpler

5   Banks are generally likely to grant an overdraft facility when a business is building up its inventory.

     True   ☐

     False   ☐

6   Which of the following methods could *not* be used to reduce the risk of irrecoverable debts in foreign trade?

     A   Export factoring
     B   Forfaiting
     C   Advances against collections
     D   Documentary credits

7   Apart from liquidity, what are the other two key considerations which a business should bear in mind in managing cash?

8   …………………………… ……………………………… is an unsecured short-term loan note issued by companies, and generally maturing within three months.

9   Interter yield $= \dfrac{\boxed{}}{\boxed{}} \times 100\%$. Fill in the boxes.

10   On a particular day, 9% Treasury Stock 2012 is quoted at a price of $141. What is the coupon rate?

11   The market prices of gilts will generally fall if interest rates rise.

     True   ☐

     False   ☐

12   Rank the following in order of risk (1 for the lowest risk).

	Preferred shares
	Government securities
	Company loan stock
	Ordinary shares
	Local authority stocks

13   Ms Archer is intending to purchase 8% Treasury Stock 2003-06 with a nominal value of $10,000. The transaction is executed by a broker, who charges commission of 0.8%, at a price of $105.50. Accrued interest is 30 days. What will be the total cost?

A $10,700
B $10,634
C $10,616
D $10,550

Answers to Quick Quiz

1   B   This is a type of investment, not a debt.

2   A3; B1; C2

3   (a)   To take advantage of early settlement discounts
    (b)   To pay suppliers who are pressing for payment

4   B   Interest only paid to the extent funds are required

5   False. Some reasons for building up inventories (coping with seasonal demand, taking advantage of favourable purchase terms) will probably be acceptable to the bank, but generally such build-ups will be temporary. Banks are less likely to grant an increase to support a permanent increase in inventory level.

6   C   This can reduce the investment in foreign receivables, but it does not reduce the risk of irrecoverable debts.

7   Safety; profitability

8   Commercial paper

9   Interest yield $= \dfrac{\text{Coupon rate}}{\text{Market price}} \times 100\%$

10 9%

11 True

12 Preferred shares, 4; Government securities, 1; Company loan stock, 3; Ordinary shares, 5; Local authority stocks, 2.

13 A

	$
Purchase consideration: $10,000 @ $105.50 per $100	10,550
Accrued interest: 30 days at 8% ($10,000 × 0.08 × 30/365)	66
Broker's commission: $10,550 × 0.8%	84
	10,700

 ## Answers to Questions

23.1 Bank overdraft

Although the directors might believe that they are asking the bank to help with financing their current assets, they are really asking for assistance with the purchase of a non-current asset, because the bank lending would leave the total current assets of the company unchanged, but will increase the current liabilities. Consequently, bank borrowing on overdraft to buy a non-current asset would reduce the working capital of Wrong Wreason from $60,000 to $10,000. In contrast, borrowing $50,000 to finance extra current assets would have increased current assets from $120,000 to $170,000, and with current liabilities going from $60,000 to $110,000, total working capital would have remained unchanged at $60,000 and liquidity would arguably still be adequate.

23.2 Investing cash

(a)   Both obviously have made the same amount of profit in the year in question. In absolute terms they are equal.

(b)   However, if we examine more closely, we find that the relative performance of Steve and Andy differs.

	Steve	*Andy*
$\dfrac{\text{Profit}}{\text{Net assets}}$	$\dfrac{\$1,200}{\$4,800} = 25\%$	$\dfrac{\$1,200}{\$3,900} = 30.8\%$

In other words, Andy is making the same amount out of more limited resources. Steve could have easily increased his profit if he had invested his spare cash and earned interest on it.

23.3 Interest yield

$$\text{Interest yield} = \frac{\text{Gross interest}}{\text{Market price}} \times 100\%$$

$$= \frac{9}{134.1742} \times 100\% = 6.71\%$$

23.4 Cost of purchase

	£
Purchase consideration £5,000 @ 111.5064 per £100	5,575.32
Accrued interest: 56 days at 13¾% (£5,000 × 0.1375 × 56/365)	105.48
Broker's commission on consideration 0.8% on £5,575.32	44.60
Total purchase cost	5,725.40

Now try these questions from the OTQ Question Bank	Number
	Q63
	Q64

RECEIVABLES AND PAYABLES

 The previous chapters have discussed some of the issues of managing cash, and you will have noted the **time lag** between the provision of goods and services and the receipt of cash for them. This time lag, as we have seen, can result in a firm making considerable demands on its bank to finance its working capital. Any increase in the time lag can make it significantly more difficult for a business to pay **its** own debts as they fall due.

This chapter introduces receivables management by considering the policy decisions that a business has to take in relation to **all** receivables.

An important decision in this area is whether to offer **settlement discounts** in return for quicker payment.

The credit controller also has to monitor the ongoing creditworthiness of customers and the **aged receivables listing** is a principal instrument used.

Section 7 deals with ways of limiting or managing the risk from bad debts.

In sections 8 and 9 we look at the need to monitor payables and describe payment methods and procedures. As with receivables, the effect of discounts is important.

topic list	learning outcomes	syllabus references
1 What is credit control?	C1	C1 (a)
2 Total credit	C1	C1 (a)
3 The credit cycle	C1	C1 (a)
4 Payment terms and settlement discounts	C1	C1 (a)
5 Maintaining information on receivables	C1	C1 (a)
6 Collecting debts	C2	C2 (c)
7 Credit insurance, factoring and invoice discounting	C1	C1 (a)
8 Managing payables	C1	C1 (a)
9 Methods of paying suppliers	C2	C2 (c)

Chapter Overview

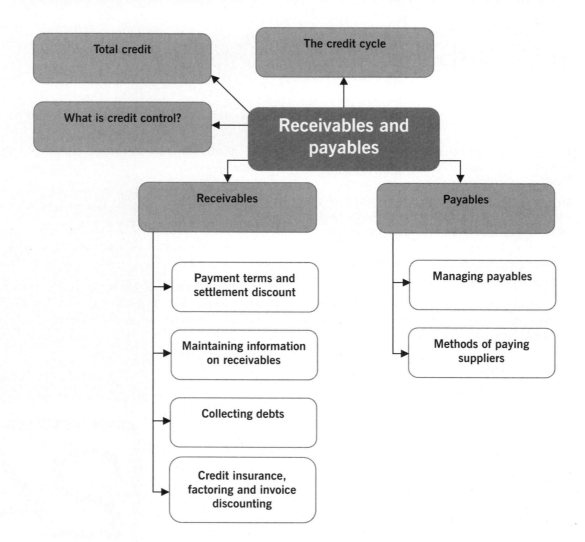

1 What is credit control?

Introduction

Credit control deals with a firm's management of its working capital. **Trade credit** is offered to business customers. **Consumer credit** is offered to household customers.

1.1 Credit

There are two aspects to **credit** we shall consider here.

(a) **Trade credit**

This is credit issued by a business to another business. For example, many invoices state that payment is expected within thirty days of the date of the invoice. In effect this is giving the customer thirty days credit. The customer is effectively borrowing at the supplier's expense.

(b) **Consumer credit**

This is credit offered by businesses to the end-consumer.

(i) Many businesses offer **hire purchase terms**, whereby the consumer takes out a loan to repay the goods purchased. Failure to repay will result in the goods being repossessed.

(ii) In practice, much of the growth in consumer credit has been driven not so much by retailers as by banks. **Credit cards** are largely responsible for the explosive growth in consumer credit.

Credit control issues are closely bound up with a firm's management of liquidity, discussed in earlier chapters. Credit is offered to enhance sales and profitability, but this should not be to the extent that a company becomes illiquid and insolvent.

Credit is also vital in securing orders in certain specified situations.

(a) **Economic conditions** can influence the type and amount of credit offered. In 'boom times, when customers are queuing with orders' (Bass, in *Credit Management Handbook*), new customers can be asked for security, and risk can be minimised. In other times, credit must be used to entice customers in, and so the credit manager's job is to control risk.

(b) **High-risk or marginal customers** require flexible payment arrangements. High risk customers are often profitable, but the risk has to be managed. The customer may require a credit limit of $50,000, on standard terms, but may only deserve $35,000. The supplier might choose instead to offer a $30,000 credit limit, together with a discount policy to encourage early payment.

Just as there is a relationship between offering credit and securing sales, there must also be a suitable working relationship between credit control personnel and sales and marketing staff. Some say that, 'a sale is not complete until the money is in the bank' and the cost of chasing after slow payers and doubtful debts is considerable.

1.2 A firm's credit policy

A firm should have policies for credit and credit control.

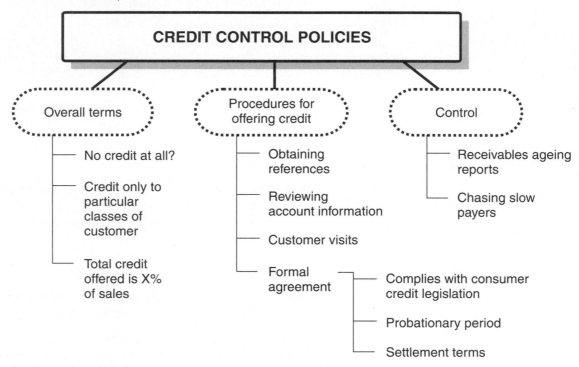

When a new customer applies for credit, their credit status will be assessed in a number of ways:

(a)   References. Standard practice is to require a banker's reference and two trade references.
(b)   The company's published accounts.
(c)   The use of credit reference agencies such as Dun and Bradstreet.

Section summary

Credit control deals with a firm's management of its working capital. **Trade credit** is offered to business customers. **Consumer credit** is offered to household customers.

2 Total credit

Introduction

Total credit can be measured in a variety of ways. Financial analysts use days sales in receivables, but as this is an annualised figure it gives no idea as to the make-up of total receivables.

2.1 The cost of credit

A bank's decision to lend money to a customer is determined by many factors over which the customer has little control. The bank, for example, might only wish to extend so much credit to firms in a particular industry.

Similarly, the firm itself has to maintain a 'global' approach to credit control in the light of the firm's objectives for **profit**, **cash flow**, **asset use** and **reducing interest costs**.

Finding a **total level of credit** which can be offered is a matter of finding the least costly balance between enticing customers, whose use of credit entails considerable costs, and refusing opportunities for profitable sales.

Firstly it helps to see what receivables, which often account for 30% of the total assets of a business, actually represent.

2.2 Measuring total receivables

The **days sales in receivables ratio**, sometimes called **receivables payment period** represents the length of the credit period taken by customers.

$$\frac{\text{Total receivables} \times 365}{\text{Sales in 365 days}} \quad \text{Days sales}$$

For example, in 20X4 X Co made sales of $700,000 and at 31 December 20X4, receivables stood at $90,000. The comparable figures for 20X3 were $600,000 (annual sales) and $70,000 (receivables at 31 December 20X3).

	20X4	*20X3*
Receivables represent	$\dfrac{\$90,000 \times 365}{\$700,000} = 47$ days	$\dfrac{\$70,000 \times 365}{\$600,000} = 43$ days

In 20X4, the company is taking longer to collect its debts.

2.3 Effect on profit of extending credit

The main cost of offering credit is the interest expense. How can we assess the effect on profit?

Let us assume that the Zygo Company sells widgets for $1,000, which enables it to earn a profit, after all other expenses except interest, of $100 (ie a 10% margin).

(a) Aibee buys a widget for $1,000 on 1 January 20X1, but does not pay until 31 December 20X1. Zygo relies on overdraft finance, which costs it 10% pa. The effect is:

	$
Net profit on sale of widget	100
Overdraft cost $1,000 × 10% pa	(100)
Actual profit after 12 months credit	Nil

In other words, the entire profit margin has been wiped out in 12 months.

(b) If Aibee had paid after six months, the effect would be:

	$
Net profit	100
Overdraft cost $1,000 × 10% pa × $^6/_{12}$ months	(50)
	50

Half the profit has been wiped out. (*Tutorial note.* The interest cost might be worked out in a more complex way to give a more accurate figure.)

(c) If the cost of borrowing had been 18%, then the profit would have been absorbed before seven months had elapsed. If the net profit were 5% and borrowing costs were 15%, the interest expense would exceed the net profit after four months.

A second general point is the relation of **total credit to irrecoverable debts**. Burt Edwards argues that there is a law of 10-to-1: 'Experience in different industries shows that the annual interest expense of borrowings to support overdue debts, ie those in excess of agreed payment terms, is at least ten times the total lost in irrecoverable debts'. This is not a 'law', but has been observed to be the case over a variety of UK businesses.

Question 24.1

Cost of credit

Learning outcome C2

Winterson Tools has an average level of receivables of $2m at any time representing 60 days outstanding. (Their terms are thirty days.) The firm borrows money at 10% a year. The managing director is proud of the credit control: 'I only had to write off $10,000 in irrecoverable debts last year,' she says proudly. Is she right to be proud?

The level of total credit can therefore have a significant effect on **profitability**. That said, if credit considerations are included in pricing calculations, extending credit can, in fact, increase profitability. If offering credit generates extra sales, then those extra sales will have additional repercussions on:

(a) The **amount of inventory** maintained in the warehouse, to ensure that the extra demand must be satisfied

(b) The **amount of money** the company **owes** to its **suppliers** (as it will be increasing its supply of raw materials)

This means an increase in **working capital**. Working capital is an **investment**, just as a non-current asset (eg new machinery) is, albeit of a different kind.

To determine whether it would be profitable to extend the level of total credit, it is necessary to assess the following.

- The additional sales volume which might result
- The profitability of the extra sales
- The extra length of the average debt collection period
- The required rate of return on the investment in additional receivables

Question 24.2

Increase in credit period

Learning outcome C2

A company is proposing to increase the credit period that it gives to customers from one calendar month to one and a half calendar months in order to raise sales from the present annual figure of $24 million representing 4m units per annum. The price of the product is $6 and it costs $5.40 to make. The increase in the credit period is likely to generate an extra 150,000 unit sales. Is this enough to justify the extra costs given that the company's required rate of return is 20%? Assume no changes to inventory levels, as the company is increasing its operating efficiency. Assume that existing customers will take advantage of the new terms.

Example: total investment in receivables

RB Co is considering a change of credit policy which will result in a slowing down in the average collection period from one to two months. The relaxation in credit standards is expected to produce an increase in sales in each year amounting to 25% of the current sales volume.

Sales price per unit	$10.00
Profit per unit (before interest)	$1.50
Current sales revenue per annum	$2.4 million

The required rate of return on investment is 20%.

Assume that the 25% increase in sales would result in additional inventories of $100,000 and additional payables of $20,000. Advise the company on whether or not it should extend the credit period offered to customers, in the following circumstances.

(a)   If all customers take the longer credit of two months

(b)   If existing customers do not change their payment habits, and only the new customers take a full two months' credit

Solution

The change in credit policy would be justifiable, in the context of this question, if the rate of return on the additional investment in working capital exceeds 20%.

Extra profit

Profit margin $^{\$1.50}/_{\$10}$ =	15%
Increase in sales revenue $2.4m × 25%	$0.6 million
Increase in profit (15% × $0.6m)	$90,000

The total sales revenue is now $3m ($2.4m + $0.6m)

(a)   *Extra investment, if all customers take two months credit*

	$
Average receivables after the sales increase (2/12 × $3 million)	500,000
Current average receivables (1/12 × $2.4 million)	200,000
Increase in receivables	300,000
Increase in inventories	100,000
	400,000
Increase in payables	(20,000)
Net increase in 'working capital'	380,000

Return on extra investment $\dfrac{\$90,000}{\$380,000} = 23.7\%$

(b)   *Extra investment, if only the new customers take two months credit*

	$
Increase in receivables (2/12 × $0.6 million)	100,000
Increase in inventories	100,000
	200,000
Increase in payables	(20,000)
Net increase in working capital investment	180,000

Return on extra investment $\dfrac{\$90,000}{\$180,000} = 50\%$

In both case (a) and case (b) the new credit policy appears to be worthwhile.

Furthermore, the cost profile of the product can also support extra sales. If the firm has high fixed costs but low variable costs, the extra production and sales could provide a substantial contribution at little extra cost.

2.4 Receivables quality and liquidity

Another objective of any credit control system is to minimise any risks to **cash flow** arising from insolvent customers. The **quality** of receivables has an important impact on a firm's overall liquidity. Receivable quality is determined by their **age** and **risk**.

Some **industries** have a higher level of risk than others, in other words, there is a higher probability that customers will fail to pay. Some markets are riskier than others. Selling goods to a country with possible payment difficulties is riskier than selling them in the home market.

For many customers, delaying payment is the cheapest form of finance available and there has been much publicity recently about the difficulties that delayed payments cause to small businesses. There is no easy answer to this problem.

2.5 Policing total credit

The total amount of credit offered, as well as individual accounts, should be policed to ensure that the senior management policy with regard to the total credit limits is maintained. A **credit utilisation report** can indicate the extent to which total limits are being utilised. An example is given below.

Customer	Limit $'000	Utilisation $'000	%
Alpha	100	90	90
Beta	50	35	70
Gamma	35	21	60
Delta	250	125	50
	435	271	
		62.3%	

This might also contain other information, such as days sales outstanding and so on.

Reviewed in aggregate, this can reveal the following.

- The number of customers who might want more credit
- The extent to which the company is exposed to receivables
- The 'tightness' of the policy
- Credit utilisation in relation to total sales

It is possible to design credit utilisation reports to highlight other trends.

- The degree of exposure to different countries
- The degree of exposure to different industries

Trade receivables analysis as at 31 December

Industry	Current credit utilisation $'000	% of total receivables %	Annual sales $ million	As a % of total sales %
Property	9,480	25.0	146.0	19.2
Construction	7,640	20.2	140.1	18.4
Engineering	4,350	11.5	112.6	14.8
Electricals	4,000	10.6	83.7	11.0
Electricity	2,170	5.7	49.2	6.5
Transport	3,230	8.5	79.9	10.5
Chemicals, plastics	1,860	4.9	43.3	5.7
Motors, aircraft trades	5,170	13.6	105.8	13.9
	37,900	100.0	760.6	100.0

2.6 Analysis

(a) An industry analysis of credit exposure shows in this case that over 45% of the company's trade receivables (about $17 million) are in the property and construction industries. Management should have a view about this exposure to industry risk.

(b) The size of the exposure to property and construction could seem excessive, in view of the cyclical nature of these industries, the current economic outlook, and the comparatively slow payment rate from these customers. (These industries account for only 37.6% of annual sales, but 45.2% of trade receivables.) Management might wish to consider whether the company should try to reduce this exposure.

(c) A decision might also be required about whether the company should be willing to accumulate trade receivables in these sectors, in order to sustain sales, or whether the credit risk would be too high.

2.7 Conclusion

The amount of **total credit** that a business offers is worthy of consideration at the highest management levels. Two issues are:

- The firm's working capital needs and the investment in receivables
- The management responsibility for carrying out the credit control policy

| Question 24.3 | Inflation |

Learning outcome C2

Your company is concerned about the effect of inflation, which (you should suppose) currently stands at 6%, on its credit control policy. Outline the main points to consider, for discussion with your manager.

Section summary

Total credit can be measured in a variety of ways. Financial analysts use days sales in receivables, but as this is an annualised figure it gives no idea as to the make-up of total receivables.

The **total investment in receivables** has to be considered in its impact on the general investment in working capital.

3 The credit cycle

Introduction

The **credit control department** is responsible for those stages in the collection cycle dealing with the offer of credit, and the collection of debts.

3.1 The credit cycle

The credit control function's jobs occupy a number of stages of the **order cycle** (from customer order to invoice despatch) and the **collection cycle** (from invoice despatch to the receipt of cash), which together make up the **credit cycle.** The job of the credit control department can comprise all those activities within the dotted line **in the Collection Cycle diagram**.

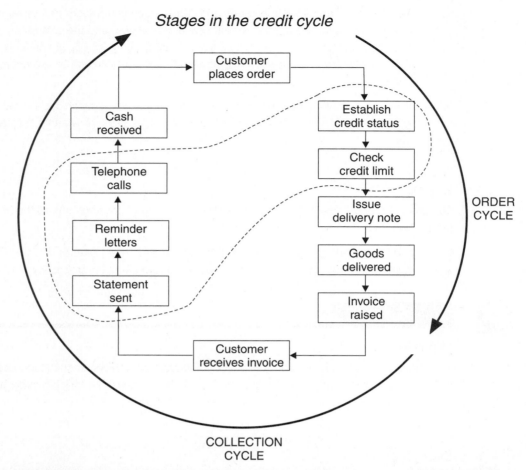

(a) **Establish credit status for new customers or customers who request a credit extension.** This might include references from the customer's bank or from a credit reference agency.

(b) **Check credit limit**

If the order is fairly routine, and there is no problem with credit status, then credit control staff examine their records or at least the sales ledger records to see if the new order will cause the customer to exceed the credit limit. There are a number of possible responses, as follows.

(i) **Authorisation**

If the credit demanded is within the credit limit, and there are no reasons to suspect any problems, then the request will be authorised.

(ii) **Referral**

It is possible that the credit demanded will exceed the limit offered in the agreement.

(1) The firm can simply **refuse the request for credit**, at the risk of damaging the business relationship. However, credit limits are there for a reason – to protect the business's profitability and liquidity.

(2) The firm can offer a **revised credit limit**. For example, the customer may be solvent and a regular payee, therefore a low risk. The company might be able to offer a higher credit limit to this customer.

(3) The firm can **contact the customer**, and request that some of the outstanding debt be paid off before further credit is advanced.

(c)   **Issuing documentation**

Issuing the delivery note, invoicing and so on is not the job of the credit control department, but the credit control department will need to have **access to information** such as invoice details to do its job.

(d)   **Settlement**

The credit control department takes over the collection cycle, although the final payment is ultimately received by the accounts department. Collection involves reviewing overdue debts, and chasing them.

Question 24.4	Credit control and working capital

Learning outcome C2

See if you can explain the likely effects of a company's credit control policy on the control of working capital in general.

Section summary

The **credit control department** is responsible for those stages in the collection cycle dealing with the offer of credit, and the collection of debts.

4   Payment terms and settlement discounts

Introduction

A firm must consider suitable **payment terms** and **payment methods**. **Settlement discounts** can be offered, if cost effective and if they improve liquidity.

4.1 Payment terms

An important aspect of the credit control policy is to devise suitable **payment terms**, covering when should payment be made and how this should be achieved.

(a)   Credit terms have to take into account the **expected profit** on the sale and the seller's cash needs.

(b)   Credit terms also establish when **payment is to be received**, an important matter from the seller's point of view.

> **TERMS AND CONDITIONS OF SALE**
> *   Nature of goods to be supplied
> *   Price
> *   Delivery
> *   Date of payment
> *   Frequency of payment
> *   Discounts

The credit terms the seller offers depend on many factors.

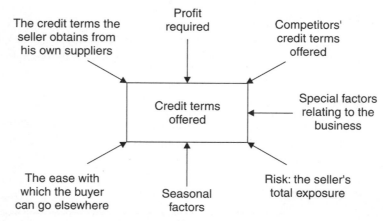

The terms must be simple to understand and easily enforceable. If the seller does not enforce his terms he is creating a precedent.

All sale agreements are **contracts**, as described earlier: credit terms are part of the contract. Although contracts do not have to be in writing, it helps if they are, and these are confirmed by the invoice.

PAYMENT TERMS	
Payment a specified number of days after delivery	Eg Net 10 (10 days)
Weekly credit	All supplies in a week must be paid for by a specified date in the next week
Half monthly credit	All supplies in one half of month must be paid for by a specified date in the next
10th and 25th	Supplies in first half of the month must be paid for by 25th, supplies in second half must be paid for by 10th of next month
Monthly credit	Payment for month's supplies must be paid by specified date in next month; if date 7th might be written Net 7 prox. Some monthly credit called Number MO; 2MO means payment must be in next month but one
Delivery	Certain payment terms geared to delivery • CWO Cash with order • CIA Cash in advance • COD Cash on delivery • CND Cash on next delivery

4.2 Methods of payment

Payment can be accepted in a variety of forms.

- Cash
- BACS
- Cheques
- Banker's draft
- Standing order
- Direct debit
- Credit card
- Debit card
- Bills of exchange, promissory notes
- Internet transfers

4.3 Payment times: settlement discounts

Some firms offer settlement discounts if payment is received early.

(a) If sensibly priced, they encourage customers to pay earlier, thereby avoiding some of the financing costs arising out of the granting of credit. Thus they can affect **profitability**.

(b) The seller may be suffering from cash flow problems. If settlement discounts encourage earlier payment, they thus enable a company to **maintain liquidity**. In the short term, liquidity is often more important than profitability.

(c) Settlement discounts might, conceivably, **affect the volume of demand** if, as part of the overall credit terms offered, they encourage customers to buy.

However discounts can have certain disadvantages.

(a) If a discount is offered to **one customer**, the company may have to offer it to other customers.
(b) **Discounts** may be **difficult to withdraw**.
(c) They establish a **set settlement period**, which might otherwise be lowered in the future.

To consider whether the offer of a discount for early payment is financially worthwhile it is necessary to compare the **cost** of the discount with the **benefit** of a reduced investment in receivables.

Example: settlement discounts

Wingspan currently has sales of $3m, with an average collection period of two months. No discounts are given. The management of the company are undecided as to whether to allow a discount on sales of 2% to settle within one month. The company assumes that all customers would take advantage of the discount. The company can obtain a return of 30% on its investments.

Advise the management whether or not to introduce the discount.

Solution

In this example the offer of a discount is not expected to increase sales demand. The advantage would be in the **reduction of the collection period**, and the resulting saving in the working capital investment required.

Our solution will value receivables at sales value.

(a) *Change in receivables*

	Receivables valued at sales price $
Current value of receivables (2/12 × $3m)	500,000
New value of receivables (1/12 × $3m)	250,000
Reduction in investment in receivables	250,000

(b) The cost of reducing receivables is the cost of the discounts, ie

2% × $3 million = $60,000

(c) The reduction in receivables of $250,000 would cost the company $60,000 per annum. If the company can earn 30% on its investments, the benefit is:

30% × $250,000 = $75,000

The discount policy would be worthwhile, since the benefit of $75,000 exceeds the cost of $60,000.

The percentage cost of an early settlement discount to the company giving it can be estimated by the formula:

$$\left(\frac{100}{100-d}\right)^{\frac{365}{t}} - 1$$

Where: d is the discount offered (5% = 5, etc)

t is the reduction in payment period in days

In the example above, the formula can be applied as follows.

$$\text{Cost of discount} = \left(\frac{100}{100-2}\right)^{\frac{365}{30}} - 1$$

$$= 27.9\%$$

Stages in the calculation:

STAGE 1   100/98 = 1.0204

STAGE 2   365/30 = 12.1666

STAGE 3   1.0204 ^ (or y^x) 12.1666

STAGE 4   = 1.2785

STAGE 5   –1 = 27.85%, say 27.9

Since 27.9% is less than the 30% by which the company judges investments, offering the discount is worthwhile.

Example: discount for early payment

CF Co needs to improve its cash flow and has therefore offered customers a 1.5% discount if they pay within 10 days, instead of the agreed 30 days. Calculate the effective annual interest rate to CF Co of offering the discount (to one decimal place), assuming that customers currently pay their invoices at the end of the 30 day period.

Solution

The payment will be made 20 days earlier than usual so t = 20.

$$\text{Cost of discount} = \left(\frac{100}{100-1.5}\right)^{\frac{365}{20}} - 1$$

$$= 31.8\%$$

| Question 24.5 | Discount |

Gamma grants credit terms of 60 days net to customers, but offers an early settlement discount of 2% for payment within seven days. What is the cost of the discount to Gamma?

Exam skills

Make sure you learn the formula for the percentage cost of an early settlement discount.

As far as an **individual customer** is concerned, the principles are similar. For example, assume Boris has an average $10,000 outstanding, representing two months sales. You offer Boris a 1% settlement discount which would reduce the average amount outstanding to $5,000 (before discounts). You borrow money at 5%. A 1% discount on annual sales of $60,000 would cost you $600. Overdraft interest saved is $250 ($5,000 × 5%) so it is not worth offering the discount.

4.4 Late payment

It has been suggested that businesses should charge interest on overdue debts, however:

(a)   **Charging for late payment** might be misconstrued (The supplier might assume that charges for late payment give the customer the authority to pay late.)

(b)   A statutory **rate for interest** on overdue debts may not have been established in the country.

(c)   Charging for payments relates only to the effect of the late payment on **profitability**, not on liquidity

| Question 24.6 | Good cash management |

Thinking back to topics covered in earlier chapters, explain how good cash management may realise each of the following benefits.

(a)   Better control of financial risk
(b)   Opportunity for profit
(c)   Strengthened statement of financial position
(d)   Increased confidence with customers, suppliers, banks and shareholders

| Question 24.7 | Credit control policy |

Your company has been growing rapidly over the last two years and now wishes to introduce a more formal credit control policy. You are asked to give a brief presentation on the factors involved in setting up such a policy.

Section summary

A firm must consider suitable **payment terms** and **payment methods**. **Settlement discounts** can be offered, if cost effective and if they improve liquidity.

5 Maintaining information on receivables

Introduction

For control purposes, **receivables** are generally analysed by age of debt.

5.1 Receivables age analysis

An **aged receivables listing** will probably look very much like the schedule illustrated below. The analysis splits up the total balance on the account of each customer across different columns according to the dates of the transactions which make up the total balance. Thus, the amount of an invoice which was raised 14 days ago will form part of the figure in the column headed 'up to 30 days', while an invoice which was raised 36 days ago will form part of the figure in the column headed 'up to 60 days'. (In the schedule below, 'up to 60 days' is used as shorthand for 'more than 30 days but less than 60 days'.)

Account number	Customer name	Balance	Up to 30 days	Up to 60 days	Up to 90 days	Over 90 days
B004	Brilliant	804.95	649.90	121.00	0.00	34.05
E008	Easimat	272.10	192.90	72.40	6.80	0.00
H002	Hampstead	1,818.42	0.00	0.00	724.24	1,094.18
M024	Martlesham	284.45	192.21	92.24	0.00	0.00
N030	Nyfen	1,217.54	1,008.24	124.50	0.00	84.80
T002	Todmorden College	914.50	842.00	0.00	72.50	0.00
T004	Tricorn	94.80	0.00	0.00	0.00	94.80
V010	Volux	997.06	413.66	342.15	241.25	0.00
Y020	Yardsley Smith & Co	341.77	321.17	20.60	0.00	0.00
Totals		6,745.59	3,620.08	772.89	1,044.79	1,307.83
Percentage		100%	53.6%	11.5%	15.5%	19.4%

HEATH CO
AGE ANALYSIS OF RECEIVABLES AS AT 31.1.X2

An age analysis of receivables can be prepared manually or, more easily, by computer. In theory this should represent actual invoices outstanding, but there are problems, which we shall discuss later in this chapter, of unmatched or 'unallocated' cash and payments on account.

The age analysis of receivables may be used to help decide what action to take about older debts. Going down each column in turn starting from the column furthest to the right and working across, we can see that there are some rather old debts which ought to be investigated.

A number of **refinements** can be suggested to the aged receivables listing to make it easier to use.

(a)   A report can be printed in which **overdue accounts** are seen first: this highlights attention on these items.

(b)   It can help to aggregate data by **class of customer**.

(c)   There is no reason why this should not apply to individual receivable accounts as below. You could also include the date of the last transaction on the account (eg last invoice, last payment).

Account number	Customer name	Balance	Up to 30 days	Up to 60 days	Up to 90 days	Over 90 days	Sales revenue in last 12 months	Days sales outstanding
B004	Brilliant	804.95	649.90	121.00	0.00	34.05	6,789.00	43

We can see from the age analysis of Heath's receivables given earlier that the relatively high proportion of debts over 90 days (19.4%) is largely due to the debts of Hampstead. Other customers with debts of this age are Brilliant, Nyfen and Tricorn.

Additional ratios which might be useful in management of receivables, in addition to days sales outstanding, are as follows.

(a) **Overdues as a percentage of total debt.** For example, assume that Heath offers credit on 30 day terms. Brilliant's debt could be analysed as:

$$\frac{\$121.00 + \$34.05}{\$804.95} = 19.3\% \text{ overdue.}$$

(b) **If debts are disputed**, it is helpful to see what proportion these are of the total receivables and the total overdue. If, of Heath's total receivables of $6,745.59, an amount of $973.06 related to disputed items, the ratio of disputed debts to total outstanding would be:

$$\frac{\$973.06}{\$6,745.59} = 14.4\%$$

As a percentage of total items *over* 30 days old:

$$\frac{\$973.06}{\$6,745.59 - \$3,620.08} = 31\%$$

An increasing disputes ratio can indicate:

(i)   Invoicing problems
(ii) Operational problems

5.2 Receivables' ageing and liquidity

Also of interest to the credit controller is the *total* percentage figure calculated at the bottom of each column. In practice the credit controller will be concerned to look at this figure first of all, in order to keep the ageing figures consistent. Why might a credit controller be worried by an increase in the **ageing**? If the credit controller knows the customers are going to pay, should it matter?

Think back to your work on cash forecasting. This is based on the expectation that a company's debts will be paid within, say, 30 days after receipt of goods. In other words revenue booked in Month 1 would be followed up by cash in Month 2. The cash forecast also has an outflow side. Any reduction in the inflow caused by an overall increase in the receivables period affects the company's ability to pay its debts and increases its use of overdraft finance: unauthorised overdrafts carry a hefty fee as well as interest.

5.3 Delays in payments by specific customers

It may be the case that an increase in the overall receivables ageing is caused by the activities of one customer, and there is always the possibility that cut-off dates for producing the report can generate anomalies. (For example, a customer might pay invoices at the end of every calendar month, whereas the receivables ageing analysis might be run every 30 days.)

However, the credit controller should try and avoid situations where a customer starts to delay payment. He or she should review information from:

- Sales staff regarding how the company is doing
- The press for any stories relevant to the company

- Competitors
- The trade 'grapevine'

These can supply early warning signals.

If, however, there is a persistent problem, the credit controller might have to insist on a **refusal of credit**.

(a) This is likely to be resented by sales staff who will possibly receive less commission as a result of lower sales.

(b) However, if there is a possibility of default, the loss of a *potential* sale is surely less severe than the failure of *actual* money to arrive.

Section summary

For control purposes, **receivables** are generally analysed by age of debt.

Some customers are **reluctant** to pay. The debt collector should keep a record of every communication. A **staged process** of reminders and demands, culminating in debt collection or legal action, is necessary.

6 Collecting debts

Introduction

There should be efficiently organised procedures for ensuring that **overdue debts** and **slow payers** are dealt with effectively.

6.1 Collecting debts

Collecting debts is a two-stage process.

(a) Having agreed credit terms with a customer, a business should issue an invoice and expect to receive payment when it is due. **Issuing invoices** and **receiving payments** is the task of sales ledger staff. They should ensure that:

   (i) The **customer is fully aware** of the terms.
   (ii) The **invoice is correctly drawn up** and issued promptly.
   (iii) They are aware of any **potential quirks** in the customer's system.
   (iv) **Queries** are **resolved quickly**.
   (v) **Monthly statements** are **issued promptly**.

(b) If payments become overdue, they should be 'chased'. Procedures for pursuing overdue debts must be established, for example:

   (i) **Instituting reminders or final demands**

      These should be sent to a named individual, asking for repayment by return of post. A second or third letter may be required, followed by a final demand stating clearly the action that will be taken. The aim is to goad customers into action, perhaps by threatening not to sell any more goods on credit until the debt is cleared.

   (ii) **Chasing payment by telephone**

      The telephone is of greater nuisance value than a letter, and the greater immediacy can encourage a response. It can however be time-consuming, in particular because of problems in getting through to the right person.

(iii) **Making a personal approach**

Personal visits can be very time-consuming and tend only to be made to important customers who are worth the effort.

(iv) **Notifying debt collection section**

This means not giving further credit to the customer until he has paid the due amounts.

(v) **Handing over debt collection to specialist debt collection section**

Certain, generally larger, organisations may have a section to collect debts under the supervision of the credit manager.

(vi) **Instituting legal action to recover the debt**

Premature legal action may unnecessarily antagonise important customers.

(vii) **Hiring an external debt collection agency to recover the debt**

This is an expense which must be justified.

6.2 Special cases

6.2.1 'Key account' customers

In most businesses, major **'key account' customers** will receive special treatment in the sales effort, and it is appropriate that special treatment is also given in managing the debts in these cases. In such circumstances, a more personal approach to debt collection is advisable, with the salesman or a debt collection officer (perhaps the credit manager himself) making an approach to the customer to request payment.

6.2.2 Reconciliation and 'on account' payments

A problem you might encounter is a customer who pays a round sum to cover a variety of invoices. The round sum may be a **payment 'on account'**: in other words, the customer might not state which invoices the payment refers to. This might occur because the customer is having liquidity problems. Unallocated payments on account, which have not been agreed, should be investigated.

Section summary

There should be efficiently organised procedures for ensuring that **overdue debts** and **slow payers** are dealt with effectively.

7 Credit insurance, factoring and invoice discounting

Introduction

The earlier **customers** pay the better. **Early payment** can be encouraged by good administration and by **discount policies**. The risk that some **customers** will never pay can be partly guarded against by **insurance**.

7.1 Credit insurance

Companies might be able to obtain **credit insurance** (**default insurance**) against certain approved debts going bad through a specialist credit insurance firm.

When a company arranges credit insurance, it must submit specific proposals for credit to the insurance company, stating the name of each customer to which it wants to give credit and the amount of credit it wants to give. The insurance company will accept, amend or refuse these proposals, depending on its assessment of each of these customers.

Credit insurance is normally available for only up to about 75% of a company's potential bad debt loss. The remaining 25% of any bad debt costs are borne by the company itself. This is to ensure that the company does not become slack with its credit control.

7.2 Domestic credit insurance

Credit insurance for **domestic** (ie not export) businesses is available from a number of sources.

Insurance companies are prepared to assume for themselves the risk of the debt going bad, and they hope to profit from this. Furthermore, they are less vulnerable, as institutions, to the possibility that debt will ruin their business.

There are several types of credit insurance on offer. These are briefly described below.

7.2.1 'Whole turnover' policies

Whole turnover policies can be used in two ways.

(a) It can **cover** the **firm's entire receivables ledger**, although, normally speaking, the actual amount paid out will rarely be more than 80% of the total loss for any specific claim.

(b) Alternatively, the client **can select** a **proportion of its receivables** and insure these for their entire amount.

In other words, perhaps 80% of each debt is insured; or the entire amount of the debts incurred, say, by perhaps 80% of the customers.

Premiums on a whole turnover policy are usually **1% of the insured sales**.

Question 24.8	Compensation

Learning outcome C2

Gibbony Whey has a whole turnover policy for its debts. The policy is underwritten by Broaken Amis Assurance and is on a whole turnover basis, whereby 80% of the receivables ledger is covered, provided that the total credit offered to customers does not exceed $1m. In the first quarter of 20X4, the company made total sales of $4m: at the end of the quarter receivables for credit sales stood at $1.4m. Gibbony Whey has traded with Sloe Pears: the underwriters approved a credit limit for Sloe Pears of $1,700. At the end of the quarter, Sloe Pears had outstanding debts of $2,100. Sloe Pears turns into a 'bad receivable' when the company's buildings are completely destroyed by a falling asteroid.

Gibbony Whey writes to Broaken Amis claiming for the bad debt. How much will Gibbony Whey be entitled to as compensation?

7.2.2 Annual aggregate excess of loss

Under an **annual aggregate excess of loss policy**, the insurer pays 100% of debts above an agreed limit. This is similar to motor insurers requiring that the first amount (eg $50) of a loss is borne by the insured.

7.2.3 Specific account policies

Insurance can be purchased to cover a **specific customer account** in the event of some contingency. For example, a policy might depend on the customer being formally declared insolvent.

7.3 Factoring

KEY TERM

FACTORING is an arrangement to have debts collected by a factor company, which advances a proportion of the money it is due to collect.

Some businesses might have difficulties in financing the amounts owed by customers. There are two main reasons for this.

(a)   If a business's **sales** are rising **rapidly**, its **total receivables** will **rise quickly too**. Selling more on credit will put a strain on the company's cash flow. The business, although making profits, might find itself in difficulties because it has too many receivables and not enough cash.

(b)   If a business grants **long credit** to its customers, it might run into **cash flow difficulties** for much the same reason. Exporting businesses must often allow long periods of credit to foreign buyers, before eventually receiving payment, and their problem of financing receivables adequately can be a critical one.

Factors are organisations that offer their clients a financing service to overcome these problems. They are prepared to advance cash to the client against the security of the client's receivables. The business will assign its receivables to the factor and will typically ask for an advance of funds against the debts which the factor has purchased, usually up to 80% of the value of the debts.

For example, if a business makes credit sales of $100,000 per month, the factor might be willing to advance up to 80% of the invoice value (here $80,000) in return for a commission charge, and interest will be charged on the amount of funds advanced. The balance of the money will be paid to the business when the customers have paid the factor, or after an agreed period.

This service gives the business immediate cash in place of a debt (which is a promise of cash in the future). If the business needs money to finance operations, borrowing against trade debts is therefore an alternative to asking a bank for an overdraft.

The main aspects of factoring

These are as follows.

(a)   Administration of the client's invoicing, sales accounting and debt collection service.

(b)   Credit protection for the client's debts, whereby the factor takes over the risk of loss from irrecoverable debts and so 'insures' the client against such losses. Factoring is often **with recourse**, which means that the client carries the risk of irrecoverable debts. However the arrangement can be made **without recourse**, which means that the risk of irrecoverable debts has been transferred to the factor.

(c)   Making payments to the client in advance of collecting the debts. This is sometimes referred to as '**factor finance**' because the factor is providing cash to the client against outstanding debts.

The appeal of factor financing to **growing firms** is that factors might advance money when a bank is reluctant to consider granting a larger overdraft. Advances from a factor are therefore particularly useful for companies needing more and more cash to expand their business quickly.

7.4 The advantages of factoring

Benefits of factoring for a business customer

(a)   The business can **pay** its **suppliers promptly**, and so be able to take advantage of any early payment discounts that are available.

(b)   **Optimum inventory levels** can be **maintained**, because the business will have enough cash to pay for the inventories it needs.

(c)   **Growth** can be **financed** through **sales** rather than by injecting fresh external capital.

(d)   The business gets **finance linked** to its **volume of sales**. In contrast, overdraft limits tend to be determined by historical balance sheets.

(e)   The managers of the business do **not** have to **spend their time** on the **problems of slow paying receivables.**

(f)   The business does **not incur** the **costs** of running **its own receivables ledger** department.

An important **disadvantage of factoring** is that customers will be making payments direct to the factor, which is likely to present a **negative picture of the firm**.

7.5 Invoice discounting

KEY TERM

INVOICE DISCOUNTING is the sale of debts to a third party at a discount, in return for prompt cash. The administration is managed in such a way that the debtor is unaware of the discounter's involvement and continues to pay the supplier.   (CIMA *Official Terminology*)

Invoice discounting is related to factoring and many factors will provide an invoice discounting service. For example, if your business had just redecorated the Town Hall it might have sent the Council an invoice for $5,000. This would be an easy invoice to sell on for cash because the Council are very likely to pay. An invoice for $5,000 sent to 'A Cowboy & Co' would not be so easy to sell for immediate cash!

The invoice discounter does **not** take over the administration of the client's sales ledger, and the arrangement is purely for the **advance of cash**. A business should only want to have some invoices discounted when it has a temporary cash shortage.

Confidential invoice discounting is an arrangement whereby a debt is confidentially assigned to the factor, and the client's customer will only become aware of the arrangement if he does not pay his debt to the client.

Question 24.9	Factoring

Learning outcome C2

The Managing Director, the Chief Accountant and the Chief Internal Auditor were meeting to discuss problems over debt collection recently identified in the Forward Company. One point made strongly by the Chief Internal Auditor was that his staff should be involved in much more than the routine verification tasks normally undertaken. It is, therefore, agreed that the internal audit section should look at the problem and consider the possibility of using the services of a factor to take over some, or all, of the work of the receivables credit section.

Required

Outline the advantages and disadvantages of using the services of a factor.

Section summary

The earlier customers pay the better. **Early payment** can be encouraged by good administration and by **discount policies**. The risk that some **customers** will never pay can be partly guarded against by **insurance**.

Credit insurance can be obtained against some irrecoverable debts. However, the insurers will rarely insure an entire bad debt portfolio – as they are unwilling to bear the entire risk. Also the client's credit control procedures should be of a suitable standard to avoid any unnecessary exposure.

Some companies use **factoring** and **invoice discounting** to help short-term liquidity or to reduce administration costs.

Factoring involves **debt collection** by the **factoring company** which advances a proportion of the monies due. **Invoice discounting** is the sale of debts at a discount in return for cash.

8 Managing payables

Introduction

Effective management of **trade payables** involves seeking satisfactory credit terms from suppliers, getting credit extended during periods of cash shortage, and maintaining good relations with suppliers.

8.1 Trade credit

Trade payables are those suppliers who are owed money for goods and services which they have supplied for the trading activities of the enterprise. For a manufacturing company, trade payables will be raw materials suppliers.

The **management of trade payables** involves:

- Attempting to obtain satisfactory credit from suppliers
- Attempting to extend credit during periods of cash shortage
- Maintaining good relations with regular and important suppliers

Question 24.10

Obtaining credit

Learning outcome C2

What might your firm have to do to obtain credit from a supplier?

Taking credit from suppliers is a normal feature of business. Nearly every company has some trade payables waiting for payment. Trade credit is a source of short-term finance because it helps to keep working capital down. It is usually a cheap source of finance, since suppliers rarely charge interest. However, trade credit *will* have a cost, whenever a company is offered a discount for early payment, but opts instead to take longer credit.

8.1.1 Trade credit and the cost of lost early payment discounts

Trade credit from suppliers is particularly important to small and fast growing firms. The costs of making maximum use of trade credit include:

(a)   The loss of suppliers' goodwill
(b)   The loss of any available cash discounts for the early payment of debts

The cost of lost cash discounts can be estimated by the formula:

$$\left(\frac{100}{100-d}\right)^{\frac{365}{t}} - 1$$

where d is the size of the discount. For a 5% discount, d = 5.

　　t is the reduction in the payment period in days which would be necessary to obtain the early payment discount

Example: trade credit

X has been offered credit terms from its major supplier of 2/10, net 45. That is, a cash discount of 2% will be given if payment is made within ten days of the invoice, and payments must be made within 45 days of the invoice. The company has the choice of paying 98c per $1 on day 10 (to pay before day 10 would be unnecessary), or to invest the 98c for an additional 35 days and eventually pay the supplier $1 per $1. The decision as to whether the discount should be accepted depends on the opportunity cost of investing 98c for 35 days. What should the company do?

Solution

If the company refuses the cash discount, and pays in full after 45 days, the implied cost in interest per annum would be approximately:

$$\left(\frac{100}{100-2}\right)^{\frac{365}{35}} - 1 = 23.5\%$$

Suppose that X can invest cash to obtain an annual return of 25%, and that there is an invoice from the supplier for $1,000. The two alternatives are as follows.

	Refuse discount $	Accept discount $
Payment to supplier	1,000.0	980
Return from investing $980 between day 10 and day 45:		
$\$980 \times \dfrac{35}{365} \times 25\%$	(23.5)	
Net cost	976.5	980

It is cheaper to refuse the discount because the investment rate of return on cash retained, in this example, exceeds the saving from the discount.

Although a company may delay payment beyond the final due date, thereby obtaining even longer credit from its suppliers, such a policy would be inadvisable (except where an unexpected short-term cash shortage has arisen). Unacceptable delays in payment will worsen the company's credit rating, and additional credit may become difficult to obtain.

8.2 Other payables

There is usually less scope for flexibility with other types of short-term payables. Things like rent and tax and dividends have to be paid out in full on certain specific dates.

'Management' in such cases is a matter of ensuring that what is due gets paid on time and that the finance is available when needed.

Age analysis of payables

You will be able to appreciate what an age analysis of payables is, having looked at the age analysis of receivables earlier in the chapter.

Example: age analysis of payables

Here is an age analysis of payables for Heath Co.

HEATH CO						
AGE ANALYSIS OF TRADE PAYABLES AS AT 31.1.X2						
Account code	Supplier name	Balance	Up to 30 days	Up to 60 days	Up to 90 days	Over 90 days
V001	Vitatechnology	3,284.00	2,140.00	1,144.00	–	–
P002	Prendergast Tubes	1,709.50	1,010.50	699.00	–	–
G072	Gerald Printers	622.64	622.64	–	–	–
P141	Plates of Derby	941.88	510.92	290.75	–	140.21
P142	Plates of Derby	604.22	514.42	–	–	89.80
G048	Greenlands Centre	34.91	–	–	–	34.91
Totals		7,197.15	4,798.48	2,133.75	–	264.92
Percentage		100%	66.7%	29.6%	0.0%	3.7%

Various points of analysis and interpretation could arise from an age analysis of payables.

(a)   Is the company **paying its suppliers earlier** than it needs to?

(b)   Is the company taking **advantage of suppliers' discounts** where this is advantageous?

(c)   Do older amounts represent **disputes**, disagreements or accounting errors that ought to be looked into?

(d)   In the case of Heath Co, is it possible that the fact that there are two accounts for Plates of Derby has led to confusion, perhaps resulting in the older unsettled items?

8.3 The purchasing cycle

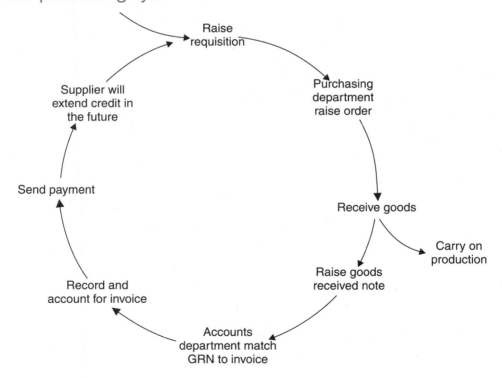

The purchasing business is now the customer, which has its credit status checked, takes delivery of goods and invoice, and pays for the goods or services.

8.4 Payment terms as part of the order

The **payment terms** offered by or agreed with the supplier form part of the contract with the supplier.

8.5 Controls over purchasing

In the same way as controls are maintained over receivables, controls should also be in place over purchase commitments. The **documentation** in the diagram above is an important control. In addition, there should be restrictions on who is allowed to place an order; perhaps only a **centralised purchasing function** should be permitted to order goods. When goods arrive the goods received department should check they **agree to the order** and are of **acceptable quality**. The details of invoices should be **carefully checked**, and the purchasing department should confirm that the goods have been received.

Businesses with several sites should decide whether purchasing should be **centralised** in one location or devolved to each site. A central location may be able to **co-ordinate inventory holdings better, obtain better prices or bulk discounts**, and have access to a **wider range of suppliers**. Local ordering may be more **flexible** to **individual locations'** needs, and local purchasing managers may form **stronger relationships** with **local suppliers**.

Section summary

Effective management of **trade payables** involves seeking satisfactory credit terms from suppliers, getting credit extended during periods of cash shortage, and maintaining good relations with suppliers.

9 Methods of paying suppliers

Introduction

Trade payables are a useful and cheap **source of finance,** but a successful business needs to ensure that it is seen as a good credit risk by its suppliers. Some suppliers must be paid on specific dates. This must be remembered and cash must be available.

We should bear in mind that the methods that a business uses to **make payments** for goods and services, wages and salaries, rent and rates and so on are broadly the same as the methods of **receiving payments**. However, a business is likely to use some methods of payment much more often than others, and the most commonly used are **cheque** and **BACS** (especially for salaries and wages). **Other payment methods** are cash, banker's draft, standing order, direct debit, mail transfer, telegraphic transfer and online payment.

9.1 Payments by cash

Cash payments are used quite often by a business:

(a)   For **small payments** out of petty cash
(b)   For **wages**

Using cash to pay large amounts of money to suppliers ought to be very rare indeed.

(a)   Cash needs to be kept **secure**: it is easily stolen.

(b)   Cash can get **lost in the post**.

(c)   It will be difficult to keep **control over cash** if it is used often for making payments.

(d)   Unless a supplier issues a **receipt**, there will be no evidence that a cash payment has been made. This is bad for record keeping.

9.2 Advantages and disadvantages of paying by cheque

Cheques are widely used in business to pay for supplies and other expenses. It is worth thinking briefly about the advantages and disadvantages of using cheques as a method of payment.

Advantages of cheque payments	Disadvantages of cheque payments
Cheques are **convenient to use** for payments of any amount (provided sufficient money is in the bank, or the organisation has a large enough overdraft facility).	There are **security problems** with keeping cheques safe from theft and misuse (forged signatures), although cheques are certainly more secure than cash as a method of payment.
The cheque **counterfoil** and cheque number can be used to provide a useful method for tracing past payments whenever any queries arise.	Cheques can be a **slow method of payment**, and a supplier might insist on a different method that is more prompt and reliable, such as standing order.
They are commonly used and **widely accepted**.	

9.3 Bank giro credits

Bank giro credits (**credit transfers**) are a means by which payments might be **received** from customers. Bank giro credits can also be used by businesses to **make payments**.

In practice, bank giro credits are rarely used by businesses to pay suppliers, except in cases where the supplier sends an invoice with a detachable pre-printed bank giro credit transfer paying-in slip. Suppliers who use their own pre-printed bank giro credit transfer forms include the various utility companies.

Bank giro credit transfers are sometimes used by small companies to pay monthly salaries.

9.4 Payments by banker's draft

A supplier might sometimes ask a customer to pay by **banker's draft**. Banker's drafts are not used for small value items, but might be used when a large payment is involved, such as for the purchase of a company car.

9.5 Standing orders

Standing order payments might be used by a business to make regular payments of a fixed amount.

(a)   **Hire purchase (HP) payments** to a hire purchase company (finance house), where an asset has been bought under an HP agreement

(b)   **Rental payments** to the landlord of a building occupied by the business

(c)   Paying **insurance premiums** to an insurance company

9.6 Direct debits

Payments by direct debit **might** be made by some companies for regular bills such as telephone, gas, electricity and water bills. The company being paid by direct debit will inform the payer of the amount and date of each payment in a printed statement.

Question 24.11   Payment methods

Learning outcome C2

Libra has to make the following payments.

(a) $6.29 for office cleaning materials bought from a nearby supermarket.

(b) $231.40 monthly, which represents hire purchase instalments on a new van. The payments are due to Marsh Finance over a period of 36 months.

(c) $534.21 to Southern Electric for the most recent quarter's electricity and standing charge. A bank giro credit form/payment counterfoil is attached to the bill. There is no direct debiting mandate currently in force.

(d) $161.50 monthly for ten months, representing the business rates payable to Clapperton District Council, which operates a direct debiting system.

(e) $186.60 to Renton Hire for a week's hire of a car on company business by the Sales Director. The Sales Director must pay on the spot, and does not wish to use a personal cheque or cash.

(f) $23,425.00 to Selham Motors for a new car to be used by the Finance Director. Selham Motors will not accept one of the company's cheques in payment, since the Finance Director wishes to collect the vehicle immediately upon delivering the payment in person and Selham Motors is concerned that such a cheque might be dishonoured.

Recommend the method of payment which you think would be most appropriate in each case, stating your reasons.

9.7 BACS

When a business uses **Bankers' Automated Clearing Services (BACS)**, it sends information (which will be input into the books of the business) to BACS for processing. Many different businesses use BACS; even small businesses can do so because their bank will help to organise the information for BACS. To give examples, BACS is widely used for monthly salaries by an employer into employees' bank accounts, as already mentioned, and for standing order payments, as well as for payments to suppliers.

9.8 Internet payments

Many organisations now have access to online banking and use this to pay employees and suppliers. Funds can be transferred between accounts with a few clicks. It is very important to prevent unauthorised access to the system and to keep records, such as printouts, of all transactions.

KEY POINT

Don't neglect payables management, as a business can gain cash flow advantages from careful management of payables.

Section summary

Trade payables are a useful and cheap **source of finance,** but a successful business needs to ensure that it is seen as a good credit risk by its suppliers. Some suppliers must be paid on specific dates. This must be remembered and cash must be available.

The most common and convenient methods of payment are by **cheque**, **BACS** and **Internet transfer**. Other payment methods are often arranged at the insistence of the supplier, and this explains much of the use of banker's drafts, standing orders and telegraphic transfers.

Chapter Summary

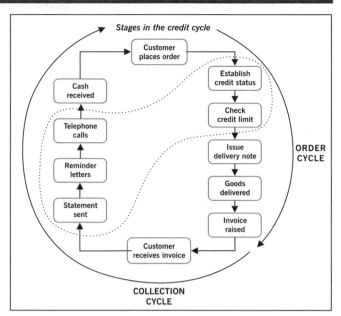

Stages in the credit cycle

Considerations when **adding to
the total credit offered**:

- Additional sales generated

- Profitability of extra sales

- Addition to the average
  receivables collection period

- Required rate of return on
  the investment

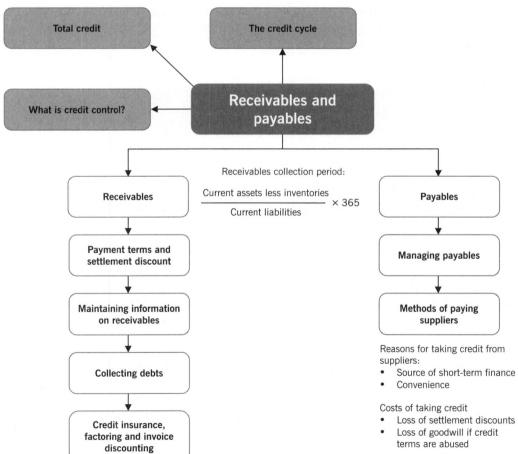

Total credit

The credit cycle

What is credit control?

**Receivables and
payables**

Receivables collection period:

$$\frac{\text{Current assets less inventories}}{\text{Current liabilities}} \times 365$$

Receivables

Payables

**Payment terms and
settlement discount**

Managing payables

**Maintaining information
on receivables**

**Methods of paying
suppliers**

Collecting debts

Reasons for taking credit from
suppliers:
- Source of short-term finance
- Convenience

Costs of taking credit
- Loss of settlement discounts
- Loss of goodwill if credit
  terms are abused

**Credit insurance,
factoring and invoice
discounting**

Credit is offered to attract customers,
secure orders, enhance revenue and
improve profitability.

The management of receivables will have
an impact on working capital and liquidity.

Quick Quiz

1   Goods and Chattels are considering increasing the period of credit allowed to customers from one calendar month to two months. Annual sales are currently $2.4m, and annual profits are $120,000. It is anticipated that allowing extended credit would increase sales by 20%, while margins would be unchanged. The company's required rate of return is 15%. What is the financial effect of the proposal?

    A   Reduction in profit of $102,000   C   Increase in profit of $102,000
    B   Reduction in profit of $18,000   D   Increase in profit of $18,000

2   The .... cycle and the .... cycle together make up the .... cycle. Fill in the blanks, using the following words: credit; collection; order.

3   How can we calculate the number of days sales represented by receivables?

4   What matters should the terms and conditions of sale cover?

5   What is meant by COD?

6   Which of the following would be the last document issued to a customer in the order processing and debt collection cycle?

    A   Statement   C   Advice note
    B   Reminder   D   Invoice

7   List typical column headings that you would expect to see in an aged analysis of receivables.

8   List three types of credit insurance policy.

9   What service involves collecting debts of a business, advancing a proportion of the money it is due to collect?

10   What service involves advancing a proportion of a selection of invoices, without administration of the receivables ledger of the business?

11   Which of the following is likely to be the most effective way of obtaining payment from a difficult customer?

    A   Personal visit   C   Sending a fax reminder
    B   Telephone request   D   Sending an e-mail reminder

12   In what order would a company normally undertake the following actions to collect a debt?

    A   Hiring an external debt collection agency to recover the debt
    B   Notifying the debt collection service
    C   Sending a reminder
    D   Instituting legal action to recover the debt

13   The premium for whole turnover policies is usually ....% of insured sales, and whole turnover policies rarely cover more than ......% of the total loss.

14   Cost of lost cash discount $= \left(\dfrac{100}{100-d}\right)^{\frac{365}{t}} - 1$. What do d and t represent?

15   Avery has been offered a cash discount of 2% by one of its suppliers if it settles its accounts within 10 days. Avery currently takes 60 days credit from the supplier. What is the implied cost in interest per annum to the nearest whole % if Avery decides not to take the discount?

    A   2%   C   16%
    B   12%   D   24%

16   What is the difference between trade credit and consumer credit?

17   Name three ways a company could pay for goods and services.

Answers to Quick Quiz

1	B	Existing receivables	$2.4m ÷ 12	$200,000
		New level of receivables	$2.4m × 1.2 ÷ 6	$480,000
		Increase in receivables		$280,000
		Additional financing cost	$280,000 × 15%	$42,000
		Additional profit	$2.4m × 20% × 5%	$24,000
		Net decrease in profit	$42,000 – $24,000	$18,000

2   The order cycle and the collection cycle together make up the credit cycle.

3    $\dfrac{\text{Total receivables}}{\text{Annual credit sales}} \times 365 = \text{Days sales}$

4   Nature of goods to be supplied, price, delivery, date of payment, frequency of payment (if instalments), discount

5   Cash On Delivery

6   B   The normal sequence is advice note, invoice, statement, reminder.

7
- Account number
- Customer name
- Total balance
- Up to 30 days
- Up to 60 days
- Up to 90 days
- Over 90 days

8   Whole turnover; excess of loss; specific account

9   Factoring

10   Invoice discounting

11   A   Personal visit is the most expensive option, but is the most likely to obtain results. It is therefore recommended in the case of high value receivables.

12   C   Sending a reminder
        B   Notifying the debt collection service
        D   Instituting legal action to recover the debt
        A   Hiring an external debt collection agency to recover the debt

13   The premium for whole turnover policies is usually **1%** of insured sales, and whole turnover policies rarely cover more than **80%** of the total loss.

14   d is the percentage discount given.
       t is the reduction in payment period to obtain this discount (in days).

15   C   In this case:

$$\left(\frac{100}{100-2}\right)^{\frac{365}{50}} - 1 = 15.9\%, \text{ say } 16\%$$

16   Trade credit is offered to business customers whereas consumer credit is offered to household customers.

17   Any three from cash, cheque, bank giro credits, banker's draft, standing order, direct debit, BACS, or online payment.

Answers to Questions

24.1 Cost of credit

At the moment, Winterson Tools is paying $10\% \times \$1m$ (ie $^{30}/_{60}$ days $\times$ $2m) = $100,000 in interest caused by customers taking the extra month to pay. The credit control could therefore be much improved.

24.2 Increase in credit period

The existing value of receivables is:

$$\frac{\$24\,m}{12\,months} = \$2m$$

If sales increased by 150,000 units, the value of receivables would be:

$$1\tfrac{1}{2} \times \frac{\$24m + (150{,}000 \times \$6)}{12\,months} = \$3{,}112{,}500.$$

The receivables have to be financed somehow, and the additional $1,112,500 will cost $1,112,500 $\times$ 20% = $222,500 in financing costs.

The profit on the extra sales is: 150,000 units $\times$ ($6 – $5.40) = $90,000

The new credit policy is not worthwhile, mainly because existing customers would also take advantage of it.

24.3 Inflation

Inflation accentuates the importance of credit control, because the cost of the investment in receivables, in real terms, is higher. If a company grants credit of $100,000 for 3 months, and the rate of inflation is 6% per annum, the value in 'today's money' of the eventual receipts in 3 months' time would be about $1\tfrac{1}{2}\%$ less – ie about $1,500 less. If the rate of inflation went up to, say, 12%, the value of the same receipts in 3 months' time would be about $3,000 less. In other words, the cost of granting credit increases as the rate of inflation gets higher. Also, with higher inflation, customers have an increased incentive to pay late.

24.4 Credit control and working capital

Working capital includes inventory, receivables, payables and cash. The effect of credit policy on working capital is that if **more credit** is granted, there will be a **slowdown** in the **inflow of cash** (unless the extension of credit also results in an increase in sales). **Discounts** for **early payment** would also affect cash flows. Similarly, **tightening up on credit** and so granting less credit will result in a **speeding up** of **cash inflows**, provided that there is no reduction in sales as a consequence of the restriction of credit.

The total amount of working capital should be kept under control because the investment in working capital must be financed, and so excessive receivables are unnecessarily costly and would reduce the organisation's return on capital employed.

Credit policy is therefore significant both from the point of view of **liquidity** (cash flow) and the **management of finance** (investment).

24.5 Discount

Gamma is offering customers the option of paying $98 after seven days per $100 invoiced, or payment in full after 60 days.

Using the formula

$$\text{Cost of discount} = \left(\frac{100}{100-d}\right)^{\frac{365}{t}} - 1$$

$$= \left(\frac{100}{100-2}\right)^{\frac{365}{53}} - 1$$

$$= 14.9\%$$

24.6 Good cash management

(a) **Better control of financial risk.** By determining and maintaining the proper level of cash within a company in accordance with the organisation's financial procedures and within defined authorisation limits.

(b) **Opportunity for profit**. By reducing to a minimum the opportunity cost associated with maintaining cash balances in excess of company's operating needs. Earnings (or surpluses) are improved by freeing up surplus cash for investment purposes while reducing interest charged through minimising borrowing.

(c) **Strengthened statement of financial position**. By reducing or eliminating cash balances in excess of target balances and putting surplus cash to work by investing it (eg in the overnight money market); by reducing or eliminating cash borrowing and keeping interest costs as low as possible.

(d) **Increased confidence with customers, suppliers, banks and shareholders**. By having access to funds to disburse to suppliers (creditors), banks (interest, fees and principal payments) and shareholders (dividends) when due. By providing good instructions to customers (receivables) to enable the organisation to convert receipts into usable bank deposits.

24.7 Credit control policy

The factors involved in establishing a credit control policy are as follows.

(a) **A total credit policy** must be **decided**, whereby the organisation decides how much credit it can and should allow to customers in total. Receivables should not be excessive in relation to total sales revenues, and the cost of financing receivables should also be considered. The receivables policy that is established will include maximum periods for payment.

(b) A **credit policy** must be **set** for deciding credit terms for individual customers. This will include establishing a system of credit rating, and procedures for deciding the maximum credit limit and terms for the payment period.

(c) The **purpose of allowing credit** is to **boost sales demand**. Management must consider how 'generous' credit terms should be to encourage sales, whilst at the same time avoiding excessive increases in irrecoverable debts, and problems with chasing payment from slow payers.

(d) Granting credit will inevitably mean that **problems will arise with slow payers** and irrecoverable debts. Procedures must be established for collecting debts from slow payers and writing off irrecoverable debts.

(e) **Discounts** might be **offered** for **early payment of debts**, and a decision should be taken as to how much discount, if any, should be offered to encourage early payment, thereby reducing the volume of receivables.

24.8 Compensation

$1,700 × 80% = $1,360.

Gibbony Whey gave more credit than was underwritten by the insurance company.

24.9 Factoring

The decision to factor the debts should only be taken once a wide ranging assessment of the costs and benefits of so doing has been carried out. This will involve the following steps.

(a) Find out **which organisations** provide debt factoring services. These may include the firm's own bankers, but there might be specialist agencies available who could also do the job.

(b) **Some assessment** of the **services provided** should also be made. Factors take on the responsibility of collecting the client firm's debts. There is a variety of factoring services.

    (i) **With recourse factoring**. This is the most basic service, whereby the bank undertakes to collect the debts and offer an advance, perhaps 80% thereon. The remainder is paid over once the cash has been received from customers. If the debt cannot be collected, the bank can claim back the advance from the client firm.

    (ii) **No recourse factoring**. The bank undertakes to pay the debts, but cannot claim the advance back from the client if the debt does not prove collectable.

    (iii) Some factors are willing to **purchase a number of invoices**, at a **substantial** discount. The factor would not be taking responsibility for the client's overall credit administration. In a way, this is like receiving an advance from a debt collector.

(c) The **costs of the factoring** service can then be assessed. The cost is often calculated as a percentage of the book value of the debts factored, so that if the factor took over $1,000,000 of debt at a factoring cost of 1.5%, then the client would pay a fee of $15,000. Moreover interest might also be charged on the advance, in some cases before the debt was recovered.

(d) This can then be compared with the **costs of doing nothing**. If the choice is between either employing a factor or leaving things as they are, then the costs included in the decision include administration, salaries, interest costs on the overdraft, and other cash flow problems (eg delayed expenditure on purchases owing to irrecoverable debts, might mean that the company cannot take advantage of settlement discounts offered).

(e) However, before any final decision is taken, the organisation can try to ensure that factoring is still better value than other choices. These can include:

    (i) The **introduction** of **settlement discounts** as an inducement to pay early might improve the collection period, and hence reduce the outstanding debt

    (ii) The **use** of **credit insurance** in some cases

    (iii) A **stronger credit control policy**

    (iv) Perhaps **appointing more credit control staff** might in the long run be cheaper than factoring if the collection rate increases

There may well be operational or management solutions to this problem. These should be investigated first as customers might not like dealing with a third party.

24.10 Obtaining credit

A firm would have to provide good references, maintain a good payment record, allow the supplier to pay a visit, and generally be *known* to be a successful business and a good credit risk.

24.11 Payment methods

(a)   This is a small business payment which should be paid out of petty **cash** for the sake of convenience.

(b)   A **standing order** is convenient for regular fixed payments. Once the standing order instruction is made, the bank will ensure that all payments are made on the due dates and will stop making payments at the date specified in the instruction. Some finance companies may insist on a standing order being set up, as it is convenient for them to receive instalments regularly without having to issue payment requests or reminders.

(c)   **Pay by cheque at the bank**, accompanied by the bill and completed bank giro credit form. The bank clerk will stamp the bill as evidence that the payment was made. Paying by cheque is safer than paying by cash and is more usual for such a large payment. Handing the cheque over at the bank will be convenient and evidence of payment will be obtained. If the payment is made at a bank other than that at which Libra holds an account, the bank receiving the payment will probably make a small charge for processing it. An alternative method is to send a **crossed cheque by post**, enclosing the payment counterfoil.

(d)   The **direct debit mandate** will allow the Council to debit the amounts due direct from Libra's bank account on the due dates. The mandate will be effective until it is cancelled. The Council must inform Libra in advance of the amounts it will be debiting.

(e)   Payment by **credit card** or **charge card** avoids the need to pay immediately by cash or cheque. The amount paid will appear on the monthly statement for the card used. If the Sales Director's personal card is used, he will claim payment later from the company, which may pay him by cheque or with his monthly salary payment. If a company credit or charge card is used, the company will be responsible for paying the amounts shown on the monthly statement.

(f)   A **banker's draft** cannot be stopped or cancelled once it is issued. Being effectively like a cheque drawn on the bank itself, it is generally accepted as being as good as cash. It is therefore most likely to be accepted by Selham Motors.

Now try this question from the OTQ Question Bank

Q65

MANAGING INVENTORY

 You should be able to apply the **EOQ** model for inventory ordering; it is likely to feature somewhere in every paper. As well as doing the calculations, you need to explain its assumptions and the components of inventory costs.

We also discuss in overview the impact of **lean manufacturing** and **just-in-time** on inventory control and other important aspects of purchasing.

topic list	learning outcomes	syllabus references
1 IAS 2 (revised) *Inventories*	B2	B2 (b)
2 Managing inventories	C2	C2 (b)
3 Purchasing	C2	C2 (b)

Chapter Overview

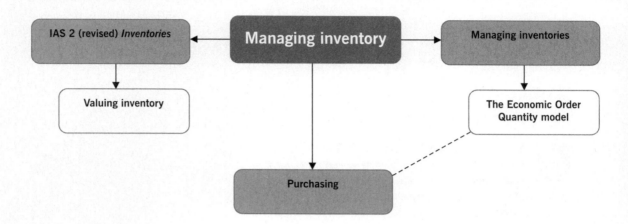

1 IAS 2 (revised) *Inventories*

Introduction

In this section we develop the knowledge on inventories you have accumulated in previous papers. We will examine IAS 2 (revised) *Inventories,* specifically how the value of inventory should be measured and disclosed.

1.1 Valuing inventory

In most businesses the value put on inventory is an important factor in the determination of profit. Inventory valuation is, however, a highly subjective exercise and consequently there is a wide variety of different methods used in practice.

1.2 Accounting treatment

IAS 2 lays out the required accounting treatment for inventories (sometimes called stocks) under the historical cost system. The major area of contention is the cost **value of inventory** to be recorded. This is recognised as an asset of the entity until the related revenues are recognised (ie the item is sold) at which point the inventory is recognised as an expense (ie cost of sales). Part or all of the cost of inventories may also be expensed if a write-down to **net realisable value** is necessary. The IAS also provides guidance on the cost formulas that are used to assign costs to inventories.

1.3 Definitions

The standard gives the following important definition.

KEY TERM

INVENTORIES are assets:

- Held for sale in the ordinary course of business;

- In the process of production for such sale; or

- In the form of materials or supplies to be consumed in the production process or in the rendering of services

Inventories can **include** any of the following:

- **Goods purchased and held for resale**, eg goods held for sale by a retailer, or land and buildings held for resale

- **Finished goods** produced

- **Work in progress** being produced

- Materials and supplies awaiting use in the production process (**raw materials**)

1.4 Measurement of inventories

KEY POINT

Inventories should be measured at the **lower** of **cost** and **net realisable value.**

1.5 Cost of inventories

The cost of inventories will consist of all:

(a)   **Costs of purchase**
(b)   **Costs of conversion**
(c)   **Other costs** incurred in bringing the inventories to their **present location** and **condition**

1.5.1 Costs of purchase

The standard lists the following as comprising the costs of purchase of inventories:

(a)   **Purchase price** *plus*

(b)   **Import duties** and other taxes *plus*

(c)   Transport, handling and any other costs **directly attributable** to the acquisition of finished goods, services and materials *less*

(d)   **Trade discounts**, rebates and other similar amounts

1.5.2 Costs of conversion

Costs of conversion of inventories consist of two main parts.

(a)   Costs **directly related** to the units of production, eg direct materials, direct labour

(b)   Fixed and variable **production overheads** that are incurred in converting materials into finished goods, allocated on a systematic basis

You may have come across the terms 'fixed production overheads' or 'variable production overheads' elsewhere in your studies. The standard defines them as follows.

KEY TERMS

FIXED PRODUCTION OVERHEADS are those indirect costs of production that remain relatively constant regardless of the volume of production, eg the cost of factory management and administration.

VARIABLE PRODUCTION OVERHEADS are those indirect costs of production that vary directly, or nearly directly, with the volume of production, eg indirect materials and labour.   *(IAS 2)*

The standard emphasises that fixed production overheads must be allocated to items of inventory on the basis of the **normal capacity of the production facilities**. This is an important point.

(a)   **Normal capacity** is the expected achievable production based on the average over several periods/seasons, under normal circumstances.

(b)   The above figure should take account of the capacity lost through **planned maintenance**.

(c)   If it approximates to the normal level of activity then the **actual level of production** can be used.

(d)   **Low production** or **idle plant** will *not* result in a higher fixed overhead allocation to each unit.

(e)   **Unallocated overheads** must be recognised as an **expense** in the period in which they were incurred.

(f)   When production is **abnormally high**, the fixed production overhead allocated to each unit will be reduced, so avoiding inventories being stated at more than cost.

(g)   The allocation of variable production overheads to each unit is based on the **actual use** of production facilities.

1.5.3 Other costs

Any other costs should only be recognised if they are incurred in bringing the inventories to their **present location and condition**. Borrowing costs can be included in the cost of inventory provided the requirements of IAS 23 *Borrowing costs* are met.

The standard lists types of cost which **would not be included** in cost of inventories. Instead, they should be recognised as an **expense** in the period they are incurred.

- **Abnormal amounts** of wasted materials, labour or other production costs

- **Storage costs** (except costs which are necessary in the production process before a further production stage)

- **Administrative overheads** not incurred to bring inventories to their present location and condition

- **Selling and distribution costs**

1.6 Determining cost

The cost of inventory used should be the actual unit cost of an item. However, if there are a large number of interchangeable (ie identical or very similar) items, it will be virtually impossible to determine costs on an individual item basis. Therefore IAS 2 allows the following **cost estimation** techniques.

(a) **FIFO** (first in, first out). Using this technique, we assume that components are used in the order in which they are received from suppliers, ie we assume the oldest items are sold first. So closing inventory will consist of the most recently purchased items and will be valued as such.

(b) **Weighted Average Cost** (AVCO). As purchase prices change with each new purchase of inventories from suppliers, the average price of items in inventory is constantly changed. Under the AVCO method, each item in inventory at any moment is assumed to have been purchased at the average price of all items in inventory at that moment. A recalculation of the weighted average cost can be made after each purchase, **or alternatively only at the period end**.

The same technique should be used by the entity for all inventories that have a similar nature and use.

Note that the LIFO formula (last in, first out) is **not permitted** by the revised IAS 2.

Example: FIFO and AVCO

On 1 November 20X2 a company held 300 units of finished goods item No 9639 in inventory. These were valued at $12 each. During November 20X2 three batches of finished goods were received into store from the production department, as follows.

Date	Units received	Production cost per unit
10 November	400	$12.50
20 November	400	$14
25 November	400	$15

Goods sold out of inventory during November were as follows.

Date	Units sold	Sale price per unit
14 November	500	$20
21 November	500	$20
28 November	100	$20

What was the profit from selling inventory item 9639 in November 20X2, applying the following principles of inventory valuation?

(a) FIFO

(b) AVCO (using cumulative weighted average costing)

Ignore administration, sales and distribution costs.

Solution

(a)   *FIFO*

		Issue cost Total $	Closing inventory $
Date	Issue costs		
14 November	300 units × $12 plus		
	200 units × $12.50	6,100	
21 November	200 units × $12.50 plus		
	300 units × $14	6,700	
28 November	100 units × $14	1,400	
Closing inventory	400 units × $15		6,000
		14,200	6,000

(b)   *AVCO (cumulative weighted average cost)*

			Unit cost $	Balance in inventory $	Total cost of issues $	Closing inventory $
1 November	Opening inventory	300	12.000	3,600		
10 November	400		12.500	5,000		
	700		12.286	8,600		
14 November	500		12.286	6,143	6,143	
	200		12.286	2,457		
20 November	400		14.000	5,600		
	600		13.428	8,057		
21 November	500		13.428	6,714	6,714	
	100		13.428	1,343		
25 November	400		15.000	6,000		
	500		14.686	7,343		
28 November	100		14.686	1,469	1,469	
30 November	400		14.686	5,874	14,326	5,874

Summary: profit

	FIFO $	AVCO $
Opening inventory	3,600	3,600
Cost of production	16,600	16,600
	20,200	20,200
Closing inventory	6,000	5,874
Cost of sales	14,200	14,326
Sales (1,100 × $20)	22,000	22,000
Profit	7,800	7,674

Different inventory valuations have produced different cost of sales figures, and therefore different profits.
In our example opening inventory values are the same, therefore the difference in the amount of profit
under each method is the same as the difference in the valuations of closing inventory.

The profit differences are only temporary. In our example, the opening inventory in December 20X2 will
be $6,000 or $5,874, depending on the inventory valuation used. Different opening inventory values will
affect the cost of sales and profits in December, so that in the long run inequalities in cost of sales each
month will even themselves out.

1.7 Net realisable value (NRV)

KEY TERM

NET REALISABLE VALUE is the estimated selling price in the ordinary course of business less the estimated costs of completion and the estimated costs necessary to make the sale.

As we noted earlier, a key principle in IAS 2 is that inventories should be carried at the **lower of cost and NRV**.

We can identify the principal situations in which **NRV is likely to be less than cost**, ie where there has been:

(a)   An **increase in costs** or a **fall in selling price**
(b)   A **physical deterioration** in the condition of inventory
(c)   **Obsolescence** of products
(d)   A decision as part of the company's marketing strategy to manufacture and sell products at a **loss**
(e)   **Errors in production or purchasing**

Question 25.1

Cost vs NRV

Learning outcome B2

The following figures relate to inventory held at the year end.

	A	B	C
	$	$	$
Cost	20	9	12
Selling price	30	12	22
Modification cost to enable sale	–	2	8
Marketing costs	7	2	2
Units held	200	150	300

Required

Calculate the value of inventory held.

1.8 Disclosure

The financial statements should disclose the following.

(a)   **Accounting policies** adopted in measuring inventories, including the cost formula used

(b)   **Total carrying amount of inventories** and the carrying amount in classifications appropriate to the entity (eg raw materials, work in progress, finished goods)

(c)   **Carrying amount** of inventories carried at NRV

(d)   The amount of inventories recognised as an expense during the period

(e)   The amount of any write-down to NRV of inventories during the period.

Question 25.2

Inventory valuation

Learning outcome B2

You are the accountant at Water Pumps Co, and you have been asked to calculate the valuation of the company's inventory at cost at its year end of 30 April 20X5.

Water Pumps manufactures a range of pumps. The pumps are assembled from components bought by Water Pumps (the company does not manufacture any parts).

The company does not use a standard costing system, and work in progress and finished goods are valued as follows.

(a)   Material costs are determined from the product specification, which lists the components required to make a pump.

(b)   The company produces a range of pumps. Employees record the hours spent on assembling each type of pump, this information is input into the payroll system which prints the total hours spent each week assembling each type of pump. All employees assembling pumps are paid at the same rate and there is no overtime.

(c)   Overheads are added to the inventory value in accordance with IAS 2 *Inventories*. The financial accounting records are used to determine the overhead cost, and this is applied as a percentage based on the direct labour cost.

For direct labour costs, you have agreed that the labour expended for a unit in work in progress is half that of a completed unit.

The draft accounts show the following materials and direct labour costs in inventory.

	Raw materials	Work in progress	Finished goods
Materials ($)	74,786	85,692	152,693
Direct labour ($)		13,072	46,584

The costs incurred in April, as recorded in the financial accounting records, were as follows.

	$
Direct labour	61,320
Selling costs	43,550
Depreciation and finance costs of production machines	4,490
Distribution costs	6,570
Factory manager's wage	2,560
Other production overheads	24,820
Purchasing and accounting costs relating to production	5,450
Other accounting costs	7,130
Other administration overheads	24,770

For your calculations assume that all work in progress and finished goods were produced in April 20X5 and that the company was operating at a normal level of activity.

Required

Calculate the value of overheads which should be added to work in progress and finished goods in accordance with IAS 2 *Inventories*.

Note. You should include details and a description of your workings and all figures should be calculated to the nearest $.

Section summary

Inventories should be measured at the **lower** of **cost** and **net realisable value**.

The cost of inventories includes the **costs of purchase**, **costs of conversion** and **other costs** incurred in bringing the inventories to their present location and condition.

The cost of interchangeable inventories should be estimated using **FIFO** (first in, first out) or **Weighted Average Cost**. LIFO (last in, first out) is not allowed under IAS 2.

Net realisable value is the estimated selling price less the estimated costs of completion and the estimated costs necessary to make the sale.

2 Managing inventories

Introduction

Business should consider at what level of inventory orders should be made, taking account of demand levels, delivery times and any uncertainties. **Safety inventory** may be held if uncertainties are particularly large.

2.1 Controlling inventory

Almost every company carries inventories of some sort, even if they are only inventories of consumables such as stationery. For a manufacturing business, inventories, in the form of **raw materials**, **work in progress** (goods or projects on which work has been carried out but which are not yet ready for sale) and **finished goods**, may amount to a substantial proportion of the total assets of the business.

Some businesses attempt to control inventories on a scientific basis by balancing the costs of inventory shortages against those of inventory holding.

(a)   The **economic order quantity (EOQ) model** can be used to decide the optimum **order size** for inventories which will minimise the costs of ordering inventories plus inventory holding costs.

(b)   If **discounts** for **bulk purchases** are **available**, it may be cheaper to buy inventories in **large order sizes** so as to obtain the discounts.

(c)   Uncertainty in the demand for inventories and/or the supply lead time may lead a company to **decide to hold buffer inventories** or **safety inventories** (thereby increasing its investment in working capital) in order to reduce or eliminate the risk of running out of inventory.

KEY TERM

SAFETY INVENTORY is the quantity of inventories of raw materials, work in progress and finished goods which are carried in excess of the expected usage during the lead time of an activity. The safety inventory reduces the probability of operations having to be suspended due to running out of inventories.

(CIMA *Official Terminology*)

2.2 Inventory costs

Inventory costs can be conveniently classified into four groups.

(a)   **Holding costs** comprise the cost of capital tied up, warehousing and handling costs, deterioration, obsolescence, insurance and pilferage.

(b)   **Procuring costs** depend on how the inventory is obtained but will consist of **ordering costs** for goods purchased externally, such as clerical costs, telephone charges and delivery costs.

(c)   **Shortage costs** may be:

   (i)   The loss of a sale and the contribution which could have been earned from the sale

   (ii)   The extra cost of having to buy an emergency supply of inventories at a high price

   (iii) The cost of lost production and sales, where the stock-out (running out of inventory) brings an entire process to a halt

(d)   The **cost of the inventory** itself, the supplier's price or the direct cost per unit of production, will also need to be considered when the supplier offers a discount on orders for purchases in bulk.

Businesses need to be aware of rates of **consumption/usage, and lead times**, the time between placing an order with a supplier and the inventory becoming available for use.

Note that inventory demand is sometimes classed as **dependent demand** or **independent demand**. For example, a computer would have an independent demand whereas its accessories such as antivirus software, mouse, monitor and so on, have a dependent demand. We will look at independent demand only.

2.3 Re-order quantities: the basic EOQ model

KEY TERM

ECONOMIC ORDER QUANTITY (EOQ) is the most economic inventory replenishment order size, which minimises the sum of inventory ordering costs and inventory holding costs. EOQ is used in an 'optimising' inventory control system. (CIMA *Official Terminology*)

Let
D = the usage in units for one year (the demand)

C_o = the cost of making one order

C_h = the holding cost per unit of inventory for one year $\Big\}$ relevant cost only

Q = the reorder quantity

Assume that:

(a) Demand is constant
(b) The lead time is constant or zero
(c) Purchase costs per unit are constant (ie no bulk discounts)

LEARN

The **total annual cost** of having inventory is:

Holding costs + **ordering** costs

$$\frac{QC_h}{2} + \frac{C_oD}{Q}$$

The order quantity, Q, which will minimise these total costs is given by the following formula. (You do not need to know how this formula is derived.)

EXAM

Economic Order Quantity $EOQ = \sqrt{\dfrac{2C_oD}{C_h}}$

Where C_o = cost of placing an order
C_h = cost of holding one unit in inventory for one year
D = annual demand

Example: economic order quantity

The demand for a commodity is 40,000 units a year, at a steady rate. It costs $20 to place an order, and 40c to hold a unit for a year. Find the order size to minimise inventory costs, the number of orders placed each year, and the length of the inventory cycle.

Solution

$$Q = \sqrt{\frac{2C_oD}{C_h}} = \sqrt{\frac{2 \times 20 \times 40,000}{0.4}} = 2,000 \text{ units. This means that there will be}$$

$\dfrac{40,000}{2,000}$ = 20 orders placed each year, so that the inventory cycle is once every 52 ÷ 20 = 2.6 weeks.

Total costs will be (20 × $20) + $\left(\dfrac{2,000}{2} \times 40c\right)$ = $800 a year.

2.4 The effect of discounts

The solution obtained from using the simple EOQ formula may need to be modified if bulk discounts (also called quantity discounts) are available.

To decide mathematically whether it would be worthwhile taking a discount and ordering larger quantities, it is necessary to minimise the total of:

- Total material costs
- Ordering costs
- Inventory holding costs

The total cost will be minimised:

- At the pre-discount EOQ level, so that a discount is not worthwhile, or
- At the minimum order size necessary to earn the discount

Example: bulk discounts

The annual demand for an item of inventory is 45 units. The item costs $200 a unit to purchase, the holding cost for one unit for one year is 15% of the unit cost and ordering costs are $300 an order. The supplier offers a 3% discount for orders of 60 units or more, and a discount of 5% for orders of 90 units or more. What is the cost-minimising order size?

Solution

(a)   The EOQ ignoring discounts is:

$$\sqrt{\frac{2 \times 300 \times 45}{15\% \text{ of } 200}} = 30 \text{ units}$$

	$
Purchases (no discount) 45 × $200	9,000
Holding costs 15 units × $30 (Ch)	450
Ordering costs 1.5 orders × $300	450
Total annual costs	9,900

(b)   With a discount of 3% and an order quantity of 60 units costs are as follows.

	$
Purchases $9,000 × 97%	8,730
Holding costs 30 units × 15% of 97% of $200	873
Ordering costs 0.75 orders × $300	225
Total annual costs	9,828

(c)   With a discount of 5% and an order quantity of 90 units costs are as follows.

	$
Purchases $9,000 × 95%	8,550.0
Holding costs 45 units × 15% of 95% of $200	1,282.5
Ordering costs 0.5 orders × $300	150.0
Total annual costs	9,982.5

The cheapest option is to order 60 units at a time.

Note that the value of C_h varied according to the size of the discount, because C_h was a percentage of the purchase cost. This means that total holding costs are reduced because of a discount. This could easily happen if, for example, most of C_h was the cost of insurance, based on the cost of inventory held.

Question 25.3

Order quantity

Learning outcome C2

A company uses an item of inventory as follows.

Purchase price:	$96 per unit
Annual demand:	4,000 units
Ordering cost:	$300
Annual holding cost:	10% of purchase price
Economic order quantity:	500 units

Should the company order 1,000 units at a time in order to secure an 8% discount?

2.5 Criticisms of the EOQ model

Criticism	Comment
Assumes a constant unit stockholding cost	Costs might have steps or be curvilinear
Assumes a known, constant ordering cost	ABC might help to determine the cost of placing an order
Assumes a constant rate of demand	So that inventory reduces steadily
Assumes zero lead time, ie an order is placed when inventory reaches zero and is received immediately	So that inventory can be assumed to fluctuate evenly between zero and the reorder quantity, Q. Hence average inventory $= Q/2$

Question 25.4

EOQ

Learning outcome C2

Maurice sells one product for which the annual demand is 50,000 units. Ordering costs are $40 per order, holding costs $0.50 per item per year.

Required

Calculate the economic order quantity.

2.6 Uncertainties in demand and lead times: the re-order level system

KEY TERM

RE-ORDER LEVEL = maximum usage × maximum lead time.

It is the measure of inventory at which a replenishment order should be placed. Use of the above formula builds in a measure of safety inventory and minimises the possibility of the organisation running out of inventory.

The EOQ model assumes a level of stability which does not always apply in business.

When the volume of demand is uncertain, or the supply lead time (time taken for the supplier to deliver) is variable, there are problems in deciding what the re-order level should be. By holding a **safety inventory**, a company can reduce the likelihood that inventories run out during the re-order period (due to high demand or a long lead time before the new supply is delivered). The **average annual** cost of such a safety inventory would be:

Quantity of safety inventory (in units) × Inventory holding cost per unit per annum

The diagram below shows how the inventory levels might fluctuate with this system. Points marked 'X' show the re-order level at which a new order is placed. The number of units ordered each time is the EOQ. Actual inventory levels sometimes fall below the safety inventory level, and sometimes the re-supply arrives before inventories have fallen to the safety level, but on average, extra inventory holding amounts to the volume of safety inventory. The size of the safety inventory will depend on whether running out of inventory is allowed.

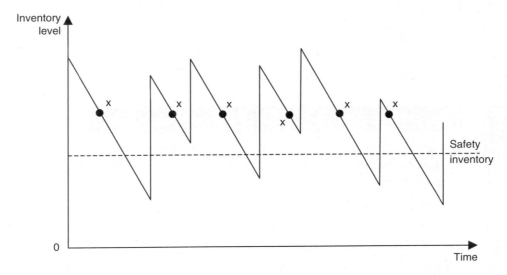

In the modern manufacturing environment running out of inventory can have a disastrous effect on the production process. Nevertheless you may encounter situations where the risk of running out is assumed to be worth taking. In this case the re-order level may not be calculated in the way described above.

2.7 Periodic review

An alternative to the re-order level system is a periodic review system. Using this system, inventory levels are reviewed at fixed intervals, for instance the same day each month. Orders are then put through to top inventory up to pre-set levels.

2.8 Finite number of re-order levels

You may see a question where you are given a list of the re-order levels from which the business will select one. For each **possible re-order level**, and therefore each level of buffer inventory, **calculate**:

- The **costs of holding buffer inventory** per annum

- The **costs of running out of inventory** (Cost of running out of inventory × expected number of times running out per order × number of orders per year)

The expected number of times running out per order reflects the various levels by which demand during the lead time could exceed the re-order level.

Example: possibility of running out of inventory (1)

If re-order level is 4 units, but there was a probability of 0.2 that demand during the lead time would be 5 units, and 0.05 that demand during the lead time would be 6 units, then expected number of times running out = $((5 - 4) \times 0.2) + ((6 - 4) \times 0.05) = 0.3$.

Demand normally distributed

Alternatively you may be told that demand is normally distributed. If this is the case you need to know:

- Average weekly demand
- Standard deviation of demand
- Lead time
- Acceptable risk levels

Re-order level = (Average weekly demand × lead time) + $x\sigma$

Where x =   number of standard deviations that correspond to the chance the business wishes to have of avoiding running out of inventory

        σ =   standard deviation of demand

Example: possibility of running out of inventory (2)

Average weekly demand is 200 units, the standard deviation of demand (σ) is 40 units and demand is normally distributed. Lead time for orders is one week. What re-order levels should the business set if it wishes to have

(a)   A 90% chance
(b)   A 95% chance
(c)   A 99% chance

of avoiding running out of inventory. The relevant values from normal distribution tables are respectively:

(a)   1.28
(b)   1.65
(c)   2.33

Solution

Re-order level = (Average weekly demand × lead time) + $x\sigma$

(a)   Re-order level   = (200 × 1) + (1.28 × 40)
                           = 251.2 units

(b)   Re-order level   = 200 + (1.65 × 40)
                           = 266 units

(c)   Re-order level   = 200 + (2.33 × 40)
                           = 293.2 units

2.9 Maximum and minimum inventory levels

KEY TERMS

MAXIMUM INVENTORY LEVEL = re-order level + re-order quantity – (minimum usage × minimum lead time)

It is the inventory level set for control purposes which actual inventory holding should never exceed.

The maximum level acts as a warning signal to management that inventories are reaching a potentially wasteful level.

MINIMUM INVENTORY LEVEL or SAFETY INVENTORY = re-order level – (average usage × average lead time)

It is the inventory level set for control purposes below which inventory holding should not fall without being highlighted.

The minimum level acts as a warning to management that inventories are approaching a dangerously low level and that inventory may run out.

$$\text{Average inventory} = \text{Minimum level} + \frac{\text{re-order quantity}}{2}$$

This formula assumes that inventory levels fluctuate evenly between the minimum (or safety) inventory level and the highest possible inventory level (the amount of inventory immediately after an order is received, safety inventory and reorder quantity).

Section summary

Business should consider at what **level** of inventory orders should be made, taking account of demand levels, delivery times and any uncertainties. **Safety inventory** may be held if uncertainties are particularly large.

Inventory holding and ordering costs can be minimised using the **economic order quantity** model. If **discounts** are offered for bulk purchases, the higher holding costs should be weighed against the lower ordering and purchasing costs.

3 Purchasing

Introduction

Purchasing may be centralised or decentralised. The optimal mix of quantity, quality, price and delivery arrangements should be sought.

3.1 The purchasing function

Purchases can account for a major part of a company's expenditure, but rarely get subjected to the planning and control constraints that are experienced by other business functions. This comment is not true of all branches of industry and commerce. In high street stores, 'buying' is recognised as one of the most important functions of the business.

The effectiveness of the purchasing function affects profit in three ways.

(a) Effective purchasing ensures the best **value for money** is obtained by the firm.

(b) Effective purchasing assists in **meeting quality targets**. Again this has an impact on a firm's long-term marketing strategy, if quality is an issue.

(c) An effective purchasing strategy minimises the amount of purchased **material held in inventory**.

3.2 The purchasing mix

The purchasing manager has to obtain the best purchasing **quantity**, **quality**, **price**, and **delivery arrangements**. Purchasing may be **centralised** or **decentralised**.

PURCHASING MIX	
Quantity	Size and timing of orders dictated by balance between delays in production caused by insufficient inventory and costs of inventory-holding
Quality	Quality of goods required for the manufacturing process, and the quality of goods acceptable to customers
Price	Short-term trends may influence, but best value over period of time is most important
Delivery	Lead time between placing and delivery of an order and reliability of suppliers' delivery arrangements

3.3 Building supplier relationships

Many companies are seeking to build up **long-term relationships with suppliers**, often offering them advice and help with product development, manufacturing processes and quality. This often leads to a reduction in the number of suppliers a firm deals with. This policy is a means of **ensuring consistency** of bought-in component quality.

3.4 Centralised versus decentralised purchasing

There are advantages to both centralised and decentralised purchasing. Each organisation will make this decision on the basis of their own business and their own business environment.

3.4.1 Advantages of centralised purchasing

- The firm will be buying in larger quantities and so will be able to negotiate more substantial discounts.

- The organisation as a whole should be able to arrange more favourable credit terms than an individual branch.

- Inventory handling functions will be mainly centralised, which should save costs – but some handling will still have to be done at branch level.

- It should be possible to hold lower overall levels of inventory than if inventory was being held at each branch.

- Only one buying department will be needed, which will save costs.

3.4.2 Advantages of decentralised purchasing

- Local branches will be more in control of their production and sales if they have local control of purchasing.

- The purchasing requirements of individual branches may vary. For instance, some lines of inventory may sell better in some areas than others.

- Local branches will be able to form their own relationships with suppliers. There may be more mutual co-operation between a smaller organisation and its supplier than between a large purchasing department and a supplier.

- A local branch can be made more accountable for its own profitability and cash management if it has control of its own purchasing function.

Section summary

Purchasing may be **centralised** or **decentralised**. The optimal mix of **quantity, quality, price** and **delivery arrangements** should be sought.

Chapter Summary

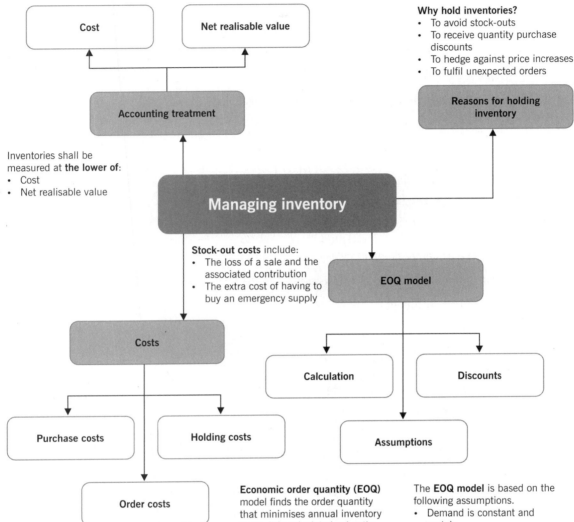

Why hold inventories?
- To avoid stock-outs
- To receive quantity purchase
  discounts
- To hedge against price increases
- To fulfil unexpected orders

Inventories shall be
measured at **the lower of**:
- Cost
- Net realisable value

Stock-out costs include:
- The loss of a sale and the
  associated contribution
- The extra cost of having to
  buy an emergency supply

Holding costs: capital tied up, warehousing
and handling costs, deterioration,
obsolescence, insurance and pilferage.

Purchase costs: the cost of the inventory itself

Order (or procuring) costs include:
administration and clerical costs, telephone
charges and delivery costs.

Economic order quantity (EOQ)
model finds the order quantity
that minimises annual inventory
costs. It is calculated using the
formula:

$$EOQ = \sqrt{\frac{2CoD}{Ch}}$$

The **EOQ model** is based on the
following assumptions.
- Demand is constant and
  certain
- Delivery is instantaneous or lead
  time is constant
- Purchase costs are constant (no
  discounts for bulk purchases)
If **discounts** are offered, additional
calculations are required.

Quick Quiz

1   The basic EOQ formula for inventories indicates whether bulk discounts should be taken advantage of.

True   ☐

False ☐

2   What are the elements of the purchasing mix?

3   The Economic Order Quantity can be expressed as follows:

$$\sqrt{\frac{2C_o D}{C_h}}$$

What does C_h describe in this formula?

A   The cost of holding one unit of inventory for one year
B   The cost of placing one order
C   The cost of a unit of inventory
D   The customer demand for the item

4   Calculate the maximum level of inventory using the following information:

Max lead time = 5 days
Min lead time = 2 days
Average lead time = 3 days
Reorder level = 100 units
Reorder quantity = 150 units
Maximum usage = 60 units per day
Average usage = 30 units per day
Minimum usage = 20 units per day

5   Calculate the minimum level of inventory, using the information in question 4.

Answers to Quick Quiz

1   False. It may be necessary to modify the formula to take account of bulk discounts.

2   Quantity, quality, price, delivery arrangements.

3   A   The cost of holding one unit of inventory for one year

4   Maximum   = re-order level + re-order quantity – (minimum usage × minimum lead time)
     level of inventory = 100 + 150 – (20 × 2)
                        = 210 units

5   Minimum   = re-order level – (average usage × average lead time)
     level of inventory = 100 – (30 × 3)
                        = 10 units

Answers to Questions

25.1 Cost vs NRV

Item	Cost $	NRV $	Valuation $	Quantity Units	Total value $
A	20	23	20	200	4,000
B	9	8	8	150	1,200
C	12	12	12	300	3,600
					8,800

25.2 Inventory valuation

Calculation of overheads for inventory

Production overheads are as follows.

	$
Depreciation/finance costs	4,490
Factory manager's wage	2,560
Other production overheads	24,820
Accounting/purchase costs	5,450
	37,320

Direct labour = $61,320

$$\therefore \text{ Production overhead rate} = \frac{37,320}{61,320} = 60.86\%$$

Inventory valuation

	Raw materials $	WIP $	Finished goods $	Total $
Materials	74,786	85,692	152,693	313,171
Direct labour	–	13,072	46,584	59,656
Production overhead (at 60.86% of labour)	–	7,956	28,351	36,307
	74,786	106,720	227,628	409,134

Variable overheads will be included in the cost of inventory.

25.3 Order quantity

The total annual cost at the economic order quantity of 500 units is as follows.

	$
Purchases 4,000 × $96	384,000
Ordering costs $300 × (4,000/500)	2,400
Holding costs $96 × 10% × (500/2)	2,400
	388,800

The total annual cost at an order quantity of 1,000 units would be as follows.

	$
Purchases $384,000 × 92%	353,280
Ordering costs $300 × (4,000/1,000)	1,200
Holding costs $96 × 92% × 10% × (1,000/2)	4,416
	358,896

The company should order the item 1,000 units at a time, saving $(388,800 − 358,896) = $29,904 a year.

25.4 EOQ

$$\text{EOQ} = \sqrt{\frac{2C_0 D}{C_h}}$$

$$= \sqrt{\frac{2 \times 40 \times 50,000}{0.50}}$$

$$= 2,828 \text{ units}$$

Now try these questions from the OTQ Question Bank	Number
	Q49
	Q66

APPENDIX

MATHS TABLES AND FORMULAE

Present value table

Present value of $1, that is $(1 + r)^{-n}$ where r = interest rate; n = number of periods until payment or receipt.

Periods (n)	Interest rates (r)									
	1%	2%	3%	4%	5%	6%	7%	8%	9%	10%
1	0.990	0.980	0.971	0.962	0.952	0.943	0.935	0.926	0.917	0.909
2	0.980	0.961	0.943	0.925	0.907	0.890	0.873	0.857	0.842	0.826
3	0.971	0.942	0.915	0.889	0.864	0.840	0.816	0.794	0.772	0.751
4	0.961	0.924	0.888	0.855	0.823	0.792	0.763	0.735	0.708	0.683
5	0.951	0.906	0.863	0.822	0.784	0.747	0.713	0.681	0.650	0.621
6	0.942	0.888	0.837	0.790	0.746	0.705	0.666	0.630	0.596	0.564
7	0.933	0.871	0.813	0.760	0.711	0.665	0.623	0.583	0.547	0.513
8	0.923	0.853	0.789	0.731	0.677	0.627	0.582	0.540	0.502	0.467
9	0.914	0.837	0.766	0.703	0.645	0.592	0.544	0.500	0.460	0.424
10	0.905	0.820	0.744	0.676	0.614	0.558	0.508	0.463	0.422	0.386
11	0.896	0.804	0.722	0.650	0.585	0.527	0.475	0.429	0.388	0.350
12	0.887	0.788	0.701	0.625	0.557	0.497	0.444	0.397	0.356	0.319
13	0.879	0.773	0.681	0.601	0.530	0.469	0.415	0.368	0.326	0.290
14	0.870	0.758	0.661	0.577	0.505	0.442	0.388	0.340	0.299	0.263
15	0.861	0.743	0.642	0.555	0.481	0.417	0.362	0.315	0.275	0.239
16	0.853	0.728	0.623	0.534	0.458	0.394	0.339	0.292	0.252	0.218
17	0.844	0.714	0.605	0.513	0.436	0.371	0.317	0.270	0.231	0.198
18	0.836	0.700	0.587	0.494	0.416	0.350	0.296	0.250	0.212	0.180
19	0.828	0.686	0.570	0.475	0.396	0.331	0.277	0.232	0.194	0.164
20	0.820	0.673	0.554	0.456	0.377	0.312	0.258	0.215	0.178	0.149

Periods (n)	Interest rates (r)									
	11%	12%	13%	14%	15%	16%	17%	18%	19%	20%
1	0.901	0.893	0.885	0.877	0.870	0.862	0.855	0.847	0.840	0.833
2	0.812	0.797	0.783	0.769	0.756	0.743	0.731	0.718	0.706	0.694
3	0.731	0.712	0.693	0.675	0.658	0.641	0.624	0.609	0.593	0.579
4	0.659	0.636	0.613	0.592	0.572	0.552	0.534	0.516	0.499	0.482
5	0.593	0.567	0.543	0.519	0.497	0.476	0.456	0.437	0.419	0.402
6	0.535	0.507	0.480	0.456	0.432	0.410	0.390	0.370	0.352	0.335
7	0.482	0.452	0.425	0.400	0.376	0.354	0.333	0.314	0.296	0.279
8	0.434	0.404	0.376	0.351	0.327	0.305	0.285	0.266	0.249	0.233
9	0.391	0.361	0.333	0.308	0.284	0.263	0.243	0.225	0.209	0.194
10	0.352	0.322	0.295	0.270	0.247	0.227	0.208	0.191	0.176	0.162
11	0.317	0.287	0.261	0.237	0.215	0.195	0.178	0.162	0.148	0.135
12	0.286	0.257	0.231	0.208	0.187	0.168	0.152	0.137	0.124	0.112
13	0.258	0.229	0.204	0.182	0.163	0.145	0.130	0.116	0.104	0.093
14	0.232	0.205	0.181	0.160	0.141	0.125	0.111	0.099	0.088	0.078
15	0.209	0.183	0.160	0.140	0.123	0.108	0.095	0.084	0.079	0.065
16	0.188	0.163	0.141	0.123	0.107	0.093	0.081	0.071	0.062	0.054
17	0.170	0.146	0.125	0.108	0.093	0.080	0.069	0.060	0.052	0.045
18	0.153	0.130	0.111	0.095	0.081	0.069	0.059	0.051	0.044	0.038
19	0.138	0.116	0.098	0.083	0.070	0.060	0.051	0.043	0.037	0.031
20	0.124	0.104	0.087	0.073	0.061	0.051	0.043	0.037	0.031	0.026

Cumulative present value of $1 per annum, Receivable or Payable at the end of each year for n years $\frac{1-(1+r)^{-n}}{r}$

Periods (n)	Interest rates (r)									
	1%	2%	3%	4%	5%	6%	7%	8%	9%	10%
1	0.990	0.980	0.971	0.962	0.952	0.943	0.935	0.926	0.917	0.909
2	1.970	1.942	1.913	1.886	1.859	1.833	1.808	1.783	1.759	1.736
3	2.941	2.884	2.829	2.775	2.723	2.673	2.624	2.577	2.531	2.487
4	3.902	3.808	3.717	3.630	3.546	3.465	3.387	3.312	3.240	3.170
5	4.853	4.713	4.580	4.452	4.329	4.212	4.100	3.993	3.890	3.791
6	5.795	5.601	5.417	5.242	5.076	4.917	4.767	4.623	4.486	4.355
7	6.728	6.472	6.230	6.002	5.786	5.582	5.389	5.206	5.033	4.868
8	7.652	7.325	7.020	6.733	6.463	6.210	5.971	5.747	5.535	5.335
9	8.566	8.162	7.786	7.435	7.108	6.802	6.515	6.247	5.995	5.759
10	9.471	8.983	8.530	8.111	7.722	7.360	7.024	6.710	6.418	6.145
11	10.368	9.787	9.253	8.760	8.306	7.887	7.499	7.139	6.805	6.495
12	11.255	10.575	9.954	9.385	8.863	8.384	7.943	7.536	7.161	6.814
13	12.134	11.348	10.635	9.986	9.394	8.853	8.358	7.904	7.487	7.103
14	13.004	12.106	11.296	10.563	9.899	9.295	8.745	8.244	7.786	7.367
15	13.865	12.849	11.938	11.118	10.380	9.712	9.108	8.559	8.061	7.606
16	14.718	13.578	12.561	11.652	10.838	10.106	9.447	8.851	8.313	7.824
17	15.562	14.292	13.166	12.166	11.274	10.477	9.763	9.122	8.544	8.022
18	16.398	14.992	13.754	12.659	11.690	10.828	10.059	9.372	8.756	8.201
19	17.226	15.679	14.324	13.134	12.085	11.158	10.336	9.604	8.950	8.365
20	18.046	16.351	14.878	13.590	12.462	11.470	10.594	9.818	9.129	8.514

Periods (n)	Interest rates (r)									
	11%	12%	13%	14%	15%	16%	17%	18%	19%	20%
1	0.901	0.893	0.885	0.877	0.870	0.862	0.855	0.847	0.840	0.833
2	1.713	1.690	1.668	1.647	1.626	1.605	1.585	1.566	1.547	1.528
3	2.444	2.402	2.361	2.322	2.283	2.246	2.210	2.174	2.140	2.106
4	3.102	3.037	2.974	2.914	2.855	2.798	2.743	2.690	2.639	2.589
5	3.696	3.605	3.517	3.433	3.352	3.274	3.199	3.127	3.058	2.991
6	4.231	4.111	3.998	3.889	3.784	3.685	3.589	3.498	3.410	3.326
7	4.712	4.564	4.423	4.288	4.160	4.039	3.922	3.812	3.706	3.605
8	5.146	4.968	4.799	4.639	4.487	4.344	4.207	4.078	3.954	3.837
9	5.537	5.328	5.132	4.946	4.772	4.607	4.451	4.303	4.163	4.031
10	5.889	5.650	5.426	5.216	5.019	4.833	4.659	4.494	4.339	4.192
11	6.207	5.938	5.687	5.453	5.234	5.029	4.836	4.656	4.486	4.327
12	6.492	6.194	5.918	5.660	5.421	5.197	4.988	7.793	4.611	4.439
13	6.750	6.424	6.122	5.842	5.583	5.342	5.118	4.910	4.715	4.533
14	6.982	6.628	6.302	6.002	5.724	5.468	5.229	5.008	4.802	4.611
15	7.191	6.811	6.462	6.142	5.847	5.575	5.324	5.092	4.876	4.675
16	7.379	6.974	6.604	6.265	5.954	5.668	5.405	5.162	4.938	4.730
17	7.549	7.120	6.729	6.373	6.047	5.749	5.475	5.222	4.990	4.775
18	7.702	7.250	6.840	6.467	6.128	5.818	5.534	5.273	5.033	4.812
19	7.839	7.366	6.938	6.550	6.198	5.877	5.584	5.316	5.070	4.843
20	7.963	7.469	7.025	6.623	6.259	5.929	5.628	5.353	5.101	4.870

Formulae

Annuity

Present value of an annuity of $1 per annum, receivable or payable for n years, commencing in one year, discounted at r% per annum:

$$PV = \frac{1}{r}\left[1 - \frac{1}{[1+r]^n}\right]$$

Perpetuity

Present value of $1 per annum, payable or receivable in perpetuity, commencing in one year, discounted at r% per annum:

$$PV = \frac{1}{r}$$

OBJECTIVE TEST QUESTION AND ANSWER BANK

1   A company makes an accounting profit of $300,000 during the year. This includes non-taxable income of $50,000 and book depreciation of $30,000. In addition, expenses of $25,000 are disallowable for tax purposes. If the tax allowable depreciation totals $24,000, what is the taxable profit?

    A $279,000
    B $281,000
    C $319,000
    D $321,000

2   A company has sales of $200,000, excluding sales tax, in a period. Its purchases, excluding sales tax, total $150,000. It has no zero-rated sales but 20% of its purchases are zero-rated. Sales tax is 17.5%. What is the sales tax payable for the period?

    A $7,447
    B $8,750
    C $14,000
    D $29,750

3   Which of the following are the fundamental qualitative characteristics of financial information?

    A   Timeliness and comparability
    B   Understandability and verifiability
    C   Timeliness and verifiability
    D   Relevance and faithful representation

4   When carrying out an audit an external auditor must satisfy himself of a number of matters. Which one of the following is not one of those matters?

    A   The accounts have been prepared by a qualified accountant
    B   Adequate accounting records have been kept
    C   The accounts have been prepared in accordance with the legislation
    D   The accounts are in agreement with accounting records

5   According to the IASB *Framework* the enhancing qualitative characteristics of financial statements are:

    A   Verifiability, consistency, reliability and going concern
    B   Understandability, prudence, reliability and relevance
    C   Understandability, timeliness, verifiability and comparability
    D   Prudence, consistency, relevance and accruals

6   T purchases production machinery costing $200,000 and having an estimated useful life of 20 years with a residual value of $4,000. After being in use for 6 years the remaining useful life of the machinery is revised and estimated to be 25 years, with an unchanged residual value. The annual depreciation charge after these events is $....................

7   Fill in the two series of missing words.

An asset is a resource controlled by an entity as a result of .... and from which .... are expected to flow to the entity.

8   Which of the following statements is NOT correct?

    A   IFRIC prepares interpretations of IFRSs for approval by the IASB

    B   IOSCO gives advice to the IASB on priorities and on major standard-setting projects

    C   IFRIC provides timely guidance on financial reporting issues not specifically addressed by IFRSs

    D   IFRS Foundation trustees appoint IASB members

9   A company purchases a new machine and the costs involved in this are given below.

	$
Purchase price	680,000
Delivery costs	30,000
Installation costs	80,000
Cleaning costs after first production run	4,000

At what figure would the machine initially be included in the statement of financial position?

$.........................

10   Which of the following is a source of tax rules?

A   International accounting standards
B   Local company legislation
C   Local tax legislation
D   Domestic accounting practice

11   H has prepared its financial statements for the year ending 30 June 20X8. On 15 July a major fraud was uncovered by the auditors which had taken place during the year to 30 June. On 31 July the company made a large loan stock issue which has significantly increased the company's gearing level.

In accordance with IAS 10 *Events after the reporting period*, how should the two events be treated in the financial statements?

	Fraud	Loan stock issue
A	Accrued in accounts	Disclosed in notes
B	Accrued in accounts	Accrued in accounts
C	Disclosed in notes	Disclosed in notes
D	Disclosed in notes	Accrued in accounts

12   F Co estimates its tax due for the year ended 30 June 20X8 to be $520,000. Tax for the year ended 30 June 20X7 was estimated at $475,000 and eventually settled at $503,000. A taxable temporary difference of $76,000 has arisen during the year due to accelerated tax allowances. The tax rate is 30%.

What is the tax charge in the statement of profit or loss and other comprehensive income for the year ended 30 June 20X8?

A $520,000
B $542,800
C $548,000
D $570,800

13   According to IAS 36 *Impairment of assets* what is the recoverable amount of a non-current asset?

A   Net selling price
B   Value in use
C   The higher of net selling price and value in use
D   The lower of net selling price and value in use

14   Which of the following types of research and development expenditure must be written off in the year it is incurred?

A   Market research costs confirming the ultimate commercial viability of a product
B   Legal costs in connection with registration of a patent
C   Costs of searching for possible alternative products
D   Costs of research work which are to be reimbursed by a customer

15   If an auditor believes an item in the financial statements is materially misstated and he considers that the effect on the financial statements is *material,* but not *pervasive*, what type of audit opinion would be issued?

    A   Unmodified opinion
    B   Qualified opinion
    C   Disclaimer of opinion
    D   Adverse opinion

16   Which of the following statements are true with regards to an ethical code.

    1   A code based on a set of principles rather than rules is more flexible in a rapidly changing environment

    2   The CIMA *Code of ethics for professional accountants* is principles based

    3   A code based on a set of rules requires accountants to evaluate and address threats to independence

    A   2 only
    B   1 and 2 only
    C   2 and 3 only
    D   1, 2 and 3

17   What is the **main** objective of the external audit?

    A   To prevent and detect fraud and error

    B   To provide assistance to a client's management in preparing accounts

    C   To ensure that an adequate system of internal controls is maintained

    D   To provide a report on the truth and fairness of the view given by the accounts

18   According to IAS 36 *Impairment of assets*, how often should assets be tested for impairment?

    A   Every year
    B   Every 3 years
    C   Every time non-current assets are revalued
    D   When there is an indication that impairment may have occurred

19   G has revalued one of its buildings to $1,200,000 at 31 December 20X8. The building was purchased 8 years ago at a cost of $840,000 and is being depreciated over a period of 40 years.

    The depreciation charge for the year ending 31 December 20X9 will be $.........................

20   A company had the following transactions and results for the period to 31 December 20X6.

	$m
Profit for the period	18
Revaluation surplus of property	2
Dividends	6
Issue of share capital	4

    What is the net change in equity?

    A $12m
    B $24m
    C $18m
    D $14m

21   Which of the following items must be disclosed on the face of the statement of profit or loss (classification of expense by function format)?

(i)   Revenue
(ii)   Dividends
(iii)   Depreciation
(iv)   Profit before tax

A   (i) only
B   (i) and (iv)
C   (i), (ii) and (iv)
D   All of the above

22   State the definition of a non-adjusting event in no more than twenty-five words.

23   Which of the following events constitutes a change in accounting policy?

A   Reducing the warranty provision from 5% of sales to 2% of sales

B   Reducing the useful life of items of plant and equipment from 15 years to 10 years

C   Changing depreciation of plant and equipment from 15% reducing balance to 10% straight-line

D   Changing the basis of measurement of inventories from FIFO to average cost basis

24   Which of the following does not accurately describe 'true and fair view'?

A   It is a dynamic concept that evolves in response to changes in accounting and business practice

B   Even reasonable business people and accountants may not share a consensus as to the degree of accuracy and completeness required

C   Courts are likely to examine the meanings of the word 'true' and the word 'fair' in interpreting the meaning of 'true and fair'

D   Courts are likely to look to the ordinary practices of professional accountants

25   A company is resident in Country Z. It has a branch in Country Y. The branch has taxable profits of $100,000, on which tax of $5,000 is paid. The tax rate in Country Z is 20% and there is a double taxation treaty between Countries Y and Z that allows tax relief on the full deduction basis. If the company has total taxable profits including those of the branch of $200,000, how much tax will it pay in Country Z?

A $20,000
B $25,000
C $35,000
D $40,000

26   Where is employee tax recorded in a set of financial statements?

A   Charged to employee costs in the statement of profit or loss and other comprehensive income
B   Not included in the financial statements at all
C   Included as a payable in the statement of financial position
D   Included as a receivable in the statement of financial position

27 A company has sales of $800,000, excluding sales tax, in a period. Its purchases, including sales tax, total $550,000. The rate of sales tax is 10%. If 25% of all sales are zero rated, what is the sales tax payable for the period?

A $10,000
B $20,000
C $22,500
D $30,000

28 A professional accountant in business has an immediate manager who is a very forceful, domineering individual. The manager has stated work in progress has increased by 200% during the current reporting period and instructed the professional accountant to report this level in the financial statements. Evidence is available which indicates that the work in progress has not increased by anywhere near the rate advised by the manager. What kind of threat to compliance with the fundamental principles for accountants in business is this?

29 A company has an accounting profit of $200,000 for the year. This includes depreciation of $25,000 and disallowable expenses of $10,000. If the tax allowable depreciation totals $30,000 and the tax rate is 30%, what is the tax payable?

A $55,500
B $58,500
C $60,000
D $61,500

30 Which of the following must be presented in the statement of profit or loss according to IAS 1 (revised) *Presentation of Financial Statements*?

1 Tax expense
2 Revenue
3 Finance costs
4 Depreciation expense

A 1, 2, 3 and 4
B 1, 2 and 3 only
C 1, 3 and 4 only
D 2 and 4 only

31 When considering IFRS 5 *Non-current Assets Held for Sale and Discontinued Operations*, which of the following statements is true?

1 A discontinued operation must have been disposed of by the end of the reporting period.

2 A discontinued operation must be a separate major line of business or geographical area of operation.

3 A discontinued operation must be clearly distinguished operationally and for financial reporting purposes.

A 1, 2 and 3
B 1 and 2 only
C 2 and 3 only
D 1 and 3 only

32 Which of the following does the IASB's *Conceptual Framework* deal with?

1 The objective of financial statements

2 The qualitative characteristics that determine the usefulness of information in financial statements

3 The definition, recognition and measurement of the elements from which financial statements are constructed

4 Concepts of capital and capital maintenance

5 Directly with the definition of true and fair presentation

6 The proforma financial statements

A 2, 3 and 4
B 1, 2, 5 and 6
C 1, 2, 3 and 4
D 1, 5 and 6

33 Information from the statement of cash flows and related notes of Gresham Co for the year ended 31 December 20X9 can be found in the table below.

	$
Depreciation	30,000
Profit on sale of non-current assets	5,000
Proceeds from sale of non-current assets	20,000
Purchase of non-current assets	25,000

If the carrying amount of property, plant and equipment was $110,000 on 31 December 20X8, what was it on 31 December 20X9?

A $85,000
B $90,000
C $70,000
D $80,000

34 The following information relates to the non-current assets of Lundy Ltd.

	$
Carrying amount at 1 January 20X6	1,200
Carrying amount at 31 December 20X6	3,000
Carrying amount of non-current assets disposed of during 20X6	250
Depreciation charge for the year ended 31 December 20X6	500
Loss arising on disposal of non-current assets during 20X6	75

In the statement of cash flows for the year ended 31 December 20X6, what will be the figures for disposals of and additions to non-current assets?

	Disposals	Additions
A	$175	$2,550
B	$325	$2,550
C	$175	$1,050
D	$325	$1,050

35 Define a subsidiary in no more than 15 words.

36   Vaynor Co acquired 100% of the ordinary shares in Weeton Co and Yarlet Co some years ago. Extracts from the statements of financial position of the three companies as on 30 September 20X7 were as follows.

	Vaynor Co $'000	Weeton Co $'000	Yarlet Co $'000
Retained earnings	90	40	70

At acquisition Weeton Co had retained losses of $10,000 and Yarlet Co had retained earnings of $30,000.

The consolidated retained earnings of Vaynor Co on 30 September 20X7 were:

A $160,000
B $180,000
C   200,000
D $220,000

37   Milton Co owns all the share capital of Keynes Co. The following information is extracted from the individual company statements of financial position as on 31 December 20X1.

	Milton Co $	Keynes Co $
Current assets	500,000	200,000
Current liabilities	220,000	90,000

Included in Milton Co's purchase ledger is a balance in respect of Keynes Co of $20,000. The balance on Milton Co's account in the sales ledger of Keynes Co is $22,000. The difference between those figures is accounted for by cash in transit.

If there are no other intra-group balances, what is the amount of current assets less current liabilities in the consolidated statement of financial position of Milton Co and its subsidiary?

A $368,000
B $370,000
C $388,000
D $390,000

38   Oxford Co owns 100% of the issued share capital of Cambridge Co, and sells goods to its subsidiary at a profit margin of 20%. At the year end their statements of financial position showed inventories of:

Oxford Co $290,000
Cambridge Co $160,000

The inventory of Cambridge Co included $40,000 of goods supplied by Oxford Co and there was inventory in transit from Oxford to Cambridge amounting to a further $20,000. At what amount should inventory be carried in the consolidated statement of financial position?

A $438,000
B $442,000
C $458,000
D $462,000

Using the following information answer questions 39 and 40

Patience Co has a wholly owned subsidiary, Bunthorne Co. During 20X1 Bunthorne Co sold goods to Patience Co for $40,000 which was cost plus 25%. At 31 December 20X1 $20,000 of these goods remained unsold.

39   In the consolidated statement of profit or loss for the year ended 31 December 20X1 the revenue will be reduced by

A $20,000
B $30,000
C $32,000
D $40,000

40   In the consolidated statement of profit or loss for the year ended 31 December 20X1 the profit will be reduced by

A $4,000
B $6,000
C $8,000
D $10,000

41   The following figures related to Sanderstead Co and its 100% subsidiary Croydon Co for the year ended 31 December 20X9.

	Sanderstead Co $	Croydon Co $
Revenue	600,000	300,000
Cost of sales	(400,000)	(200,000)
Gross profit	200,000	100,000

During the year Sanderstead Co sold goods to Croydon Co for $20,000, making a profit of $5,000.

These goods were all sold by Croydon Co before the year end.

What are the amounts for total revenue and gross profit in the consolidated statement of profit or loss of Sanderstead Co for the year ended 31 December 20X9?

	Revenue	Gross profit
A	$900,000	$300,000
B	$900,000	$295,000
C	$880,000	$300,000
D	$880,000	$295,000

42   Extracts from the statement of profit or loss of Pik Co and its subsidiaries and Wik Co, its associate, for the year ended 31 March 20X6 are as follows.

	Pik Co (inc subsidiaries) $'000	Wik Co $'000
Gross profit	2,900	1,600
Administrative expenses	(750)	(170)
Distribution costs	(140)	(190)
Dividends from Wik Co	20	–
Profit before tax	2,030	1,240
Income tax expense	(810)	(440)
Profit for the year	1,220	800

Pik Co acquired 25% of the ordinary shares in Wik Co on 1 April 20X3 when the retained earnings of Wik Co were $80,000.

At what amount should the profit before tax be shown in the consolidated Statement of profit or loss of Pik Co for the year ended 31 March 20X6?

A $2,010,000
B $2,210,000
C $2,340,000
D $3,270,000

43 Austen Co has owned 100% of Kipling Co and 30% of Dickens Co, an associate, for many years. At 31 December 20X5 the trade receivables and trade payables shown in the individual company statements of financial position were as follows.

	Austen Co $'000	Kipling Co $'000	Dickens Co $'000
Trade receivables	50	30	40
Trade payables	30	15	20
Trade payables included amounts owing to			
Austen Co	–	–	–
Kipling Co	2	–	4
Dickens Co	7	–	–
Other suppliers	21	15	16
	30	15	20

The inter-company accounts agreed after taking into account the following.

(1) An invoice for $3,000 posted by Kipling Co on 31 December 20X5 was not received by Austen Co until 2 January 20X6.

(2) A cheque for $6,000 posted by Austen Co on 30 December 20X5 was not received by Dickens Co until 4 January 20X6.

What amount should be shown as trade receivables in the consolidated statement of financial position of Austen Co?

A $75,000
B $79,000
C $87,000
D $115,000

44 The following information was disclosed in the financial statements of Maine for the year ended 31 December 20X6:

	20X6 $	20X5 $
Plant and equipment, cost	735,000	576,000
less accumulated depreciation	265,000	315,000
Carrying amount	470,000	261,000

During 20X6:

Expenditure on plant and equipment was	$512,000
Loss on the disposal of old plant was	$107,000
Depreciation charge on plant and equipment was	$143,000

What were the sales proceeds received on the disposal of the old plant?

A $ 53,000
B $160,000
C $246,000
D $267,000

45 The following information relates to Elton for the year ending 31 December 20X6.

	$
Income tax liability on 1 January 20X6	21,000
Over provision in respect of 20X5	1,000
Income tax charge on profits for the year ended 31 December 20X6	35,000
Income tax liability on 31 December 20X6	28,000

The tax paid to be included in Elton's statement of cash flows for the year ending 31 December 20X6 is

A $27,000
B $29,000
C $30,000
D $32,000

46 An intangible asset held at historical cost has been impaired in value. The fair value of the intangible asset is $10,000, the cost of selling is $500. The present value of the value in use of the intangible asset is estimated to be $9,000.

The carrying amount of the intangible asset is $10,500.

The value of the impairment and account where the impairment will be recorded is:

A $1,500, income statement
B $1,000, income statement
C $1,500, revaluation reserve
D $1,000, revaluation reserve

47 A firm with a year end of 31 December buys a non-current asset at the beginning of 2003 for $1,200. The estimated useful life is 10 years, with a scrap value of $200. The firm uses the straight-line method of depreciation. On 1 January 20X6 the estimated useful life is shortened to a total of eight years. The appropriate depreciation charge for 20X6 is:

A $125
B $140
C $150
D $168

48 Which of the following conditions would prevent any part of the development expenditure to which it relates from being capitalised?

A The development is incomplete

B The development expenditure capitalised to date has been reviewed and written down to its recoverable amount.

C Funds are unlikely to be available to complete the development

D The development is expected to give rise to more than one product

49   Beans Co has prepared the following schedule of its inventory:

Item	Purchase price of raw materials	Attributable production overheads incurred	Attributable distribution overheads to be incurred	Expected selling price
	$	$	$	$
X	80	10	12	85
Z	20	5	10	40
	100	15	22	125

What is the aggregate amount at which inventory that should be stated in the statement of financial position of Beans Co?

A $98
B $103
C $120
D $125

50   The following events took place between the reporting date and the date on which the directors approved the accounts. Which event should be classified as an adjusting event in accordance with IAS 10?

A   The settlement of a court case confirming the cost of damages against which a provision had been made

B   The acquisition of a subsidiary

C   A rights issue

D   A dramatic fall in the value of an overseas investment due to exchange rate movement

51   Nasty is a wholly owned subsidiary of Ugly. Inventories in their individual statements of financial position at the year end are shown as:

Ugly $40,000
Nasty $20,000

Sales by Ugly to Nasty during the year were invoiced at $15,000 which included a profit by Ugly of 25% on cost. Two thirds of these goods were included in inventories at the year end.

At what value should inventories appear in the consolidated statement of financial position?

A $50,000
B $57,000
C $57,500
D $58,000

52   A company is resident in Country X and pays interest of $72,000 net of withholding tax to a company resident in Country Y. If the rate of withholding tax is 10%, how much withholding tax is due?

A $8,000
B $8,500
C $8,888
D $9,000

53 A company has made sales in a period of $400,000, excluding sales tax. Its purchases including sales tax were $276,000. If the rate of sales tax is 15%, how much is payable to the tax authorities?

    A $10,772
    B $16,172
    C $18,600
    D $24,000

54 Current liabilities include accrued expenses with a carrying amount of $3,000. The related expense will be deducted for tax purposes on a cash basis.

Interest receivable has a carrying amount of $1,400. The interest revenue will be taxed on a cash basis.

What are the tax bases of these items?

A	Accrued expenses	Nil	Interest receivable	Nil
B	Accrued expenses	$3,000	Interest receivable	Nil
C	Accrued expenses	Nil	Interest receivable	$1,400
D	Accrued expenses	$3,000	Interest receivable	$1,400

55 A company has profits of $20m after deducting depreciation of $4m. The tax allowance for non-current assets is $3m and there are tax disallowable expenses of $1.5m. Non-taxable income included in profit is $0.5m. What is the taxable profit?

    A $20m
    B $20.5m
    C $22m
    D $22.5m

56 A company has made sales of $230,000 inclusive of sales tax in a period. The rate of sales tax is 15%. The purchases during the same period were $150,000 excluding tax and $35,000 of these were for exempt goods. How much sales tax is payable to the tax authorities?

    A $12,750
    B $15,000
    C $17,250
    D $19,500

57 A company is resident in country A, but has a branch in country B. The branch has taxable profits of $100,000 on which it pays tax of $40,000 in country B. The tax rate in country A is 30%. There is a double taxation treaty between countries A and B giving relief under the credit basis. How much double tax relief is available in country A?

    A   None
    B $30,000
    C $40,000
    D   The income is exempt in country A

58   The following figures relate to Sanderstead and its subsidiary Croydon for the year ended 31
      December 20X9.

	Sanderstead	Croydon
	$	$
Revenue	600,000	300,000
Cost of sales	(400,000)	(200,000)
Gross profit	200,000	100,000

During the year, Sanderstead sold goods to Croydon for $20,000 making a profit of $5,000.
These goods were all sold by Croydon before the year end.

What are the amounts for revenue and gross profit in the consolidated statement of profit or loss of
Sanderstead for the year ended 31 December 20X9?

	Revenue	Gross Profit
A	$900,000	$300,000
B	$900,000	$295,000
C	$880,000	$300,000
D	$880,000	$295,000

59   Northumberland Co is the sole subsidiary of Beauchamp Co. The cost of sales figure for 20X4 for
      Beauchamp Co and Northumberland Co are $28.8 million and $21.6 million respectively. During
      20X4 Beauchamp sold goods which had cost $4.8 million to Northumberland for $7.2 million.
      Northumberland has not yet sold any of these goods.

What is the consolidated costs of sales figure for 20X4?

A $43.2 million
B $45.6 million
C $50.4 million
D $52.8 million

60   Eagle acquired 25% of the ordinary share capital of Hawk on 1 January 20X5 for $640,000 when
      the retained earnings of Hawk stood at $720,000. Eagles appointed two directors to the board of
      Hawk and the investment is regarded as long term. The summarised balance sheet of Hawk on 31
      December 20X9 is as follows:

	$'000
Assets	4,000
Equity	
Share capital	800
Share premium	450
Retained earnings	1,140
	2,390
Liabilities	1,610
	4,000

Hawk has made no new issues of shares nor has there been any movement in the share premium
account since Eagle acquired its holding.

At what amount will the investment in Hawk be shown in the consolidated statement of financial
position of the Eagle group as on 31 December 20X9?

A $745,000
B $640,000
C $597,500
D $839,500

61   The master budget of PQ reveals the following information.

Statement of financial position extracts

	$'000
Current assets (including inventory 1,950)	3,470
Current liabilities	1,790

Budgeted income statement extracts

	$'000
Revenue	7,550
Profit from operations	1,240
Return on capital employed	24%

What is the quick or acid test ratio to assess PQ's liquidity?

A   0.5
B   0.6
C   0.7
D   0.8

62   A business has production overheads of $347,000 in December 20X8 but it is anticipated that these will increase by 1.25% per month for the next few months. Overheads are paid the month after they are incurred.

What is the cash outflow for overheads that is paid during the month of March 20X9 (to the nearest whole $)?

A $347,000
B $355,729
C $351,338
D $360,176

63   You work for a manufacturing company that is facing a short-term liquidity problem. Which of the following assets would you recommend that it sells in order to bridge the cash deficit while doing the minimum damage to its core activities? Explain the reasons for your decision.

A   10% of its fleet of delivery vehicles
B   Some of its plant and machinery
C   The patent on a new design
D   Its 60% equity stake in the company that supplies a scarce raw material for the manufacturing process

64   Which of the following best describe the main features of overdraft finance?

(i)   High interest rate
(ii)   Repayable in instalments
(iii)   Useful for capital expenditure
(iv)   Low interest rate
(v)   Short-term form of finance
(vi)   Repayable on demand
(vii)   Available as long as required

A   (i), (ii), (iii)
B   (i), (v), (vi)
C   (iii), (iv), (vii)
D   (ii), (iv), (v)

65 A company's trade receivables balance at the beginning of the year was $22,000. The statement of profit or loss showed revenue from credit sales of $290,510 during the year. The trade receivables days at the end of the year were 49 days.

Assume that:

- Sales occur evenly throughout the year
- All balances outstanding at the start of the year were received
- All sales are on credit and there were no irrecoverable debts
- No trade discount was given

How much cash did the company receive from its customers during the year?

A $290,510
B $273,510
C $268,510
D $234,510

66 Product G has an annual demand of 32,000 units which is spread out evenly throughout the year. The materials for Product G are received 3 weeks after placing the order. Other information is as follows.

Material cost per product G $15 per unit Ordering cost $180 per order
Annual holding cost 10% of purchase price
What is the economic order quantity for the material?

A 1,960 B 800 C 2,771 D 10,733

1   B

		$	$
Accounting profit			300,000
Add:	depreciation	30,000	
	disallowed expenses	25,000	
			55,000
			355,000
Less:	non-taxable income	50,000	
	tax allowable depreciation	24,000	
			74,000
Taxable profit			281,000

2   C

	$
Output tax (200,000 × 17.5%)	35,000
Input tax ((150,000 × 80%) × 17.5%)	21,000
Payable	14,000

3   D   Relevance and faithful representation are the two fundamental qualitative characteristics. Comparability, verifiability, timeliness and understandability are the enhancing qualitative characteristics.

4   A   In order to state that the financial statements show a true and fair view the auditor must satisfy himself that the other three matters are valid.

5   C

6    $5,488

	$
Cost	200,000
Depreciation $6 \times \left(\dfrac{200,000 - 4,000}{20} \right)$	58,800
Carrying amount end year 6	141,200
Depreciation year 7 $\dfrac{141,200 - 4,000}{25}$	$5,488

7   An asset is a resource controlled by an entity as a result of **past transactions or events** and from which **future economic benefits** are expected to flow to the entity.

8   B   IOSCO (The International Organisation of Securities Commissions) is the representative of the world's securities markets regulators. IOSCO has been active in encouraging and promoting the improvement and quality of international standards. The IFRS Advisory Council) gives advice to the IASB on priorities and on major standard setting projects.

9    $790,000. The cost to appear initially in the statement of financial position is the cost of getting the machine ready for production. This will include the delivery and installation costs but not the cleaning costs after the first production run.

10   C   Local tax legislation forms the basis of local taxation and so is a source of tax rules. The other options are all sources of accounting rules.

11   A   The fraud is an adjusting event as it took place during the year to 30 June although it was not discovered until after the year end. The loan stock issue is a non-adjusting event but due to its materiality should be disclosed in the notes.

12   D

	$'000
Estimated charge 20X8	520,000
Underprovision 20X7	28,000
Transfer to deferred tax (76,000 × 30%)	22,800
	570,800

13   C   The higher of net selling price and value in use.

14   C   Items A and B are costs incurred in the *development* of a product. Note that while market research costs are not normally development costs, they *may be* treated as such when confirming ultimate commercial viability.

           C is research and therefore must be written off.

           D is work in progress (inventory) which you are being paid to do.

15   B   Qualified opinion.

16   B   A rules based system tends to remove the need to evaluate, as accountants can just check whether certain rules are being met or not, rather than applying the principles to given situations.

17   D

18   D

19   Depreciation charge $= \dfrac{\$1,200,000}{32 \text{ years}} = \$37,500$

20   C

	$m
Profit for the period	18
Dividends	(6)
Revaluation	2
Issue of shares	4
	18

           Retained profit is profit after deducting dividends.

21   A   Although some companies present dividends at the foot of the statement of profit or loss, the IAS 1 formats only require them to be shown in the statement of changes in equity. Only final profit or loss for the period is required to be shown.

22   Non-adjusting events **arise after the end of the reporting period** and concern **conditions** which did **not exist** at that time.

23   D   A change in the method of valuing inventory is a change of accounting policy.

24   C   Courts are **not likely** to examine the individual meanings of the word 'true' and the word 'fair' in interpreting the meaning of 'true and fair'. The courts are likely to use an approach that applies the **concepts implied** by the **expression** '*true and fair*'.

25   C   Total tax due is $40,000 ($200,000 x 20%) less double taxation relief for $5,000, leaves $35,000 to pay.

26   C   The company acts as a tax collector on behalf of the tax authority. Therefore any tax deducted is put in a payable account until the money is actually paid to the tax authority. The balance on the payable account represents the amount collected but not yet paid over.

27   A

	$
Output tax (800,000 x 75% x 10%)	60,000
Input tax (550,000/110 x 10)	50,000
Payable	10,000

           The important point to remember is that zero rated sales are still taxable supplies; they just pay tax at 0%. Therefore input tax does not need to be restricted.

28   Intimidation. The professional accountant is being intimidated by a dominant personality.

29 D

	$	$
Accounting profit		200,000
Add: depreciation	25,000	
disallowed expenses	10,000	
		35,000
		235,000
Less: tax allowable depreciation		30,000
Taxable profit		205,000

Tax payable = $205,000 x 30% = $61,500.

30 B All these items should be shown in the statement of profit or loss except depreciation which may be disclosed in a note as per IAS 1 (revised)

31 C In order to be classified as discontinued, a component must either have been disposed of or be held for sale (provided that it is highly probable that it will be sold within 12 months of classification.

32 C The IASB's *Conceptual Framework* deals with 1, 2, 3 & 4. It does not attempt to define the concept of true and fair directly, although it states that the application of the principal 'qualitative' characteristics and the application of appropriate IASs will result in financial statements which show a true and fair view. Proforma financial statements are given in IAS 1 and not the *Conceptual Framework*.

33 B $90,000

NON-CURRENT ASSETS (CARRYING AMOUNT)

	$		$
Balance b/d	110,000	Depreciation	30,000
Additions	25,000	Disposals (Carrying amount)	15,000
		Balance c/d	90,000
	135,000		135,000

34 A

Non current assets – carrying amount

	$		$
B/d	1,200	Disposals	250
		Depreciation charge	500
∴ Additions	2,550	c/d	3,000
	3,750		3,750

Disposal

	$		$
Carrying amount	250	Loss on disposal	75
		∴ Proceeds	175
	250		250

35 A subsidiary is an entity that is controlled by another entity (known as the parent).

36 B

	$'000
Vaynor Co	90
Weeton Co (40+10)	50
Yarlet Co (70-30)	40
	180

37 D

	Milton Co $'000	Keynes Co $'000	Adjustment $'000	Consolidated $'000
Current assets	500	200	-22+2	680
Current liabilities	(220)	(90)	20	(290)
	280	110		390

38 C

	$'000
Oxford Co	290
Cambridge Co	160
In transit to Cambridge Co	20
Less: PURP ((40 + 20) × 20%)	(12)
	458

39 D Reduce revenue by intra-group sales of $40,000.

40 A Reduce consolidated profit by provision for unrealised profit.

$$20,000 \times \frac{25}{125} = \$4,000$$

41 C

	Sanderstead Co $	Croydon Co $	Adj $	Consol $
Revenue	600,000	300,000	(20,000)	880,000
Cost of sales	(400,000)	(200,000)	20,000	(580,000)
Gross profit				300,000

42 B

	$'000
Pik Co (incl subsidiaries)	
Gross profit	2,900
Less Administrative expenses	(750)
Distribution costs	(140)
Share of profit of associates (25% × 800)	200
	2,210

43 A

	$'000	$'000
Austen Co		50
Kipling Co	30	
Less Intra group (2 + 3)	(5)	
		25
		75

44 A

Plant and equipment – cost

	$		$
B/d	576,000	∴ disposals	353,000
Additions	512,000	C/d	735,000
	1,088,000		1,088,000

Accumulated depreciation

	$		$
		B/d	315,000
∴ disposals	193,000	Charge for year	143,000
C/d	265,000		
	458,000		458,000

Disposals

	$		$
Cost	353,000	Depreciation	193,000
		Loss	107,000
		∴ proceeds	53,000
	353,000		353,000

45　A

Income tax payable

	$		$
		B/d	21,000
Overprovision	1,000	Charge for year	35,000
∴ paid	27,000		
C/d	28,000		
	56,000		56,000

46　B　Fair value less costs to sell

　　=　$10,000 – $500

　　=　$9,500

Value in use = $9,000

∴ Recoverable amount = $9,500

Impairment	=	carrying amount – recoverable amount
	=	$10,500 – $9,500
	=	$1,000

If an asset is held at historical cost, the impairment is always charged to the statement of profit or loss.

47　B

	$	
Cost 2003	1,200	
Depreciation per annum	$\dfrac{1,200-200}{10}$	= 100
Carrying amount 31.12.05	$1,200 - (100 \times 3)$	= 900
Depreciation charge 2006	$\dfrac{900-200}{5}$	= 140

48　C　A　is clearly nonsense. You capitalise costs during the development and therefore the development is incomplete.

　　B　the capitalised development expenditure should be reviewed annually and written down to its recoverable amount. As long as the other criteria are satisfied this should not be a problem.

　　C　adequate financial resources to complete the project are not available. The intangible with therefore not be completed for use or sale. It is important not to carry cost forward.

　　D　this is obviously not a problem as long as the products can be specifically identified and development expenditure reliably attributed to each.

49 A

	Cost	NRV	Cost & NRV
X	90	73	73
Z	25	30	25
			98

50 A B, C and D are standard non-adjusting events

51 D Cost + Profit = Selling price

100   25   125

PUP = (25/125 × 15,000) × 2/3 = $2,000

Inventories = $40,000 + $20,000 − $2,000 = $58,000

52 A The net interest paid is $72,000. This represents 90% of the interest. Therefore the tax is $8,000 (72,000 × $\frac{10}{90}$).

53 D

	$
Output tax ($400,000 × 15%)	60,000
Input tax ($276,000 × $\frac{15}{115}$)	(36,000)
	24,000

54 A The accrued expenses will all be deductible for tax purposes, so the tax base is nil.

When the interest is received, it will all be subject to tax, so the tax base is nil.

55 C Taxable profit = $20m + $4m − $3m + $1.5m − $0.5m

56 A

	$
Output tax ($230,000 × $\frac{15}{115}$)	30,000
Input tax ($150,000 − $35,000) × 15%	(17,250)
	12,750

57 B $100,000 × 30%

58 C

59 B 28.8 + 21.6 − 7.2 (intragroup) + 2.4 (PUP) = 45.6

60 A An investment in an associate will be valued at the equity valuation less impairment losses on the investment in associate in the consolidated statement of financial position.

No mention is made in the question of any impairment losses, therefore the valuation is:

	$
Cost of associate	640,000
Share of post acquisition retained earnings ((1,140 − 720) × 25%)	105,000
	745,000

61 D

Acid test ratio $= \dfrac{(3,470 - 1,950)}{1,790}$

$= \dfrac{1,520}{1,790}$

$= 0.8$

62   B

March cash outflow for overheads = £347,000 × 1.0125 × 1.0125
                                   = £355,729

63   A

The company should sell 10% of its delivery vehicles. It will keep the majority of its delivery vehicles, and it is safe to assume that reasonably priced alternatives are available. This sale should not damage the long term profitability of the company.

Assuming that the plant and machinery is in use and not redundant, selling this would impact a core activity of the business. In addition the likely sale proceeds may not reflect the actual value in use to the business. The plant should not be sold in these circumstances.

The patent is likely to be a key to securing the long-term future profitability of the company. It should not be sold to meet short-term needs as this will damage the company's competitive advantage.

A 60% stake constitutes a controlling interest in the supplier. Given that this supplier provides a scarce raw material to the company, selling this shareholding could damage the supply of this raw material.

64   B

(i), (v), (vi)

65   B

Closing receivables = 290,510/365 × 49 = $39,000

Cash received is therefore:

	$
Opening receivables	22,000
Credit sales	290,510
Closing receivables	(39,000)
Cash received	273,510

66   C

$$EOQ = \sqrt{\frac{2C_oD}{C_h}}$$

$$= \sqrt{\frac{2 \times 180 \times 32,000}{1.50}}$$

$$= \sqrt{7,680,000}$$

$$= 2,771$$

PRACTICE QUESTION AND ANSWER BANK

What the examiner means

The very important table below has been prepared by CIMA to help you interpret exam questions.

Learning objectives	Verbs used	Definition
1 Knowledge What are you expected to know	• List • State • Define	• Make a list of • Express, fully or clearly, the details of/facts of • Give the exact meaning of
2 Comprehension What you are expected to understand	• Describe • Distinguish • Explain • Identify • Illustrate	• Communicate the key features of • Highlight the differences between • Make clear or intelligible/state the meaning of • Recognise, establish or select after consideration • Use an example to describe or explain something
3 Application How you are expected to apply your knowledge	• Apply • Calculate/ compute • Demonstrate • Prepare • Reconcile • Solve • Tabulate	• Put to practical use • Ascertain or reckon mathematically • Prove with certainty or to exhibit by practical means • Make or get ready for use • Make or prove consistent/compatible • Find an answer to • Arrange in a table
4 Analysis How you are expected to analyse the detail of what you have learned	• Analyse • Categorise • Compare and contrast • Construct • Discuss • Interpret • Prioritise • Produce	• Examine in detail the structure of • Place into a defined class or division • Show the similarities and/or differences between • Build up or compile • Examine in detail by argument • Translate into intelligible or familiar terms • Place in order of priority or sequence for action • Create or bring into existence
5 Evaluation How you are expected to use your learning to evaluate, make decisions or recommendations	• Advise • Evaluate • Recommend	• Counsel, inform or notify • Appraise or assess the value of • Propose a course of action

1 Convex

Convex is a limited liability company incorporated in Switzerland. However its board are all English and board meetings are held regularly in London. Head office is in Switzerland but the main accountancy offices are in London and the chairman and the chief executive are based in London.

Required

(a) Where is the place of management of Convex?

(b) Would your answer to part (a) change if the following were the case?

    (i) The Board are all Swiss nationals?

    (ii) Board meetings are held in Switzerland with the main accounts offices in London and the chairman and chief Executive based in Switzerland?

2 Tax and dividends

(a) Company A has an accounting profit of $750,000. This total is after charging book depreciation of $300,000, formation expenses of $15,000 and entertaining expenses of $75,000. The figure also includes government grants received of $25,000.

The tax rate is 25%. Under A's tax regime, government grants are tax-free and formation and entertaining expenses are disallowable. If the tax allowable depreciation is $350,000, calculate the tax due for the current period.

(b) Company A has paid a net dividend during the accounting period of $1,500,000. It operates in a country where a full imputation system applies. Corporate income tax is 25% and personal income tax is 30%.

How much tax will be paid by its shareholders?

3 VAT

A company has sales of $570,000 including VAT. Its purchases for the same period were $300,000 excluding VAT. The sales tax rate is 17.5%. Calculate the tax payable to the tax authorities if 20% of sales are zero-rated but only 15% of its purchases are zero-rated.

4 Regulatory influences

State three different regulatory influences on the preparation of the published accounts of quoted companies and briefly explain the role of each one. Comment briefly on the effectiveness of this regulatory system.

5 Accounting standards

There are those who suggest that any standard setting body is redundant because accounting standards are unnecessary. Other people feel that such standards should be produced, but by the government, so that they are legislated.

Required

Discuss the statement that accounting standards are unnecessary for the purpose of regulating financial statements.

6 IASB

Consider to what extent the IASB has succeeded in its aims and what problems it still faces.

7 External auditors

Describe the external auditors' responsibilities with respect to the financial statements.

8 Audit report

Explain what is meant by a 'modified' audit report and describe the differences between a 'modified' and an 'unmodified' report.

9 New project

A professional accountant in business has recently been put in charge of a new project by the finance director. However, the accountant does not have the required level of expertise for this project. The accountant is uncomfortable carrying out the work and is uncertain about what to say to the finance director.

Required

Identify the ethical issues in this situation and describe the action the accountant should take.

10 IFRS 5

At 30 November a manufacturing company decided to sell one of its processing plants and steps were taken to locate a buyer. After consultation with a property agent, who advised that prices in the area were expected to rise sharply over the next twelve months, senior management decided to raise the price of the building in anticipation of this. The buyers who were interested have now withdrawn due to the price rise but the directors are confident that in the new year, when property prices rise, they will obtain the price required. In the meantime, the processing plant is continuing to operate and handle customers orders.

At 31 December, will this plant be classified as 'held for sale' under IFRS 5? Explain your answer.

11 CEC

After its end of year physical inventory count and valuation, the accounts staff of CEC have reached a valuation of $153,699 at cost for total inventories held at the year end.

However, on checking the figures, the chief bookkeeper has come across the following additional facts.

(a) The count includes damaged goods which originally cost $2,885. These could be repaired at a cost of $921 and sold for $3,600.

(b) The count excludes 300 units of item 730052 which were sold to a customer SC on a sale or return basis, at a price of $8 each. The original cost of the units was $5 each. SC has not yet indicated to CEC whether these goods have been accepted, or whether they will eventually be returned.

(c) The count includes 648 units of item 702422. These cost $7.30 each originally but because of dumping on the market by overseas suppliers, a price war has flared up and the unit cost price of the item has fallen to $6.50. The price reduction is expected to be temporary, lasting less than a year or so, although some observers of the market predict that the change might be permanent. CEC has already decided that if the price reduction lasts longer than six months, it will reduce its resale price of the item from $10.90 to about $10.

Required

Calculate the closing inventory figure for inclusion in the financial statements of CEC, making whatever adjustments you consider necessary in view of items (a) to (c). Explain your treatment of each item.

12 Plant and equipment

A business's plant and equipment account and depreciation account at 31 December 20X8 show the following:

Year of purchase	Cost $	Accumulated depreciation $
20X5	100,000	80,000
20X6	70,000	42,000
20X7	50,000	20,000
20X8	30,000	6,000
	250,000	148,000

Depreciation is calculated at 20% on a straight line basis with a full year's charge in the year of acquisition and none in the year of disposal.

During 20X9 the following transactions took place:

(a) Purchases of plant and equipment amounted to $150,000
(b) Plant that had been bought in 20X5 for $40,000 was sold for $5,000
(c) Plant that had been bought in 20X7 for $10,000 was damaged and had to be scrapped

Required

Prepare the following ledger accounts as at 31 December 20X9:

Plant and equipment – cost
 – accumulated depreciation
 – disposals

13 IT

The accounts of IT at 1 January 20X6 include capitalised development costs of $26,500. During the year ended 31 December 20X6 IT purchased a new business. The consideration paid to the proprietor included $4,800 in respect of goodwill. The company also spent $7,900 in research and $3,500 on development activities.

The directors of IT intend to write off $1,200 in respect of impairment of goodwill. They believe that $22,600 of development costs should be carried forward at 31 December 20X6, in accordance with IAS 38.

Show the ledger accounts for goodwill and research and development in the books of IT.

14 F

F, an engineering company, makes up its financial statements to 31 March in each year. The financial statements for the year ended 31 March 20X1 showed revenue of $3m and trading profit of $400,000.

Before approval of the financial statements by the board of directors on 30 June 20X1 the following events took place.

(a) The financial statements of P for the year ended 28 February 20X1 were received which indicated a permanent decline in that company's financial position. F had bought shares in P some years ago and this purchase was included in unquoted investments at its cost of $100,000. The financial statements received indicated that this investment was now worth only $50,000.

(b) There was a fire at the company's warehouse on 30 April 20X1 when inventory to the value of $500,000 was destroyed. It transpired that the inventory in the warehouse was under-insured by some 50%.

(c) It was announced on 1 June 20X1 that the company's design for tank cleaning equipment had been approved by the major oil companies and this could result in an increase in the annual revenue of some $1m with a relative effect on profits.

Required

You are required to explain how, if at all, items (a) to (c) above should be reflected in the accounts of F for the year ended 31 March 20X1.

15 B

The draft financial statements for B, a limited liability company, are set out below.

STATEMENT OF PROFIT OR LOSS AND OTHER COMPREHENSIVE INCOME FOR THE YEAR ENDED 30 SEPTEMBER 20X1

	$'000
Revenue	600
Cost of sales	(410)
Gross profit	190
Profit on sale of non-current asset	10
	200
Depreciation	(30)
Other expenses	(70)
Interest expense	(15)
Profit for the year	85

STATEMENT OF FINANCIAL POSITION AS AT 30 SEPTEMBER

	20X1		20X0	
	$'000	$'000	$'000	$'000
Non-current assets (see note)		450		520
Current assets				
Inventory	65		50	
Receivables	80		30	
Bank and cash	30		15	
		175		95
Total assets		625		615
Equity and liabilities				
Share capital		400		400
Retained earnings		145		95
Non-current liability				
Loan		20		100
Current liabilities				
Payables		60		20
		625		615

Notes

The company purchased non-current assets for $40,000 during the year ended 30 September 20X1.

Dividends of $35,000 were paid during the year.

Ignore taxation.

Required

(a) Prepare a statement of cash flows for B for the year ended 30 September 20X1.

(b)   In the year to 30 September 20X2 B had the following results:

	$'000
Revenue	640
Cost of sales	(400)
Gross profit	240
Depreciation	(30)
Other expenses	(35)
Interest expense	(15)
Profit for the year	160

Notes

1   Interest was paid up to date and the remaining loan paid off
2   There were no purchases or sales of non-current assets
3    $615,000 was received from customers and $390,000 paid to suppliers.
4   Cost of sales was:

	$'000
Opening inventory	65
Purchases	410
Closing inventory	(75)
	400

Required

Prepare the statement of financial position as at 30 September 20X2

16 Cat

Set out below are the statements of financial position of Cat Co as at 30 June 20X1 and 20X2.

CAT CO
STATEMENT OF FINANCIAL POSITION AS AT 30 JUNE

	20X1		20X2	
	$	$	$	$
Assets				
Non-current assets				
Cost	85,000		119,000	
Depreciation	26,000		37,000	
		59,000		82,000
Current assets				
Inventories	34,000		40,000	
Receivables (trade)	26,000		24,000	
Cash at bank	10,000		13,500	
		70,000		77,500
Total assets		129,000		159,500
Equity and liabilities				
Equity				
Ordinary $1 shares	26,000		28,000	
Share premium	12,000		13,000	
Retained earnings	44,000		70,500	
		82,000		111,500
Non-current liabilities				
10% loan stock		20,000		10,000
Current liabilities				
Payables (trade)	15,000		23,000	
Taxation	12,000		15,000	
		27,000		38,000
Total equity and liabilities		129,000		159,500

Notes

1   No non-current assets were disposed of during the year.
2   Of the 10% loan stock, $10,000 was redeemed at par on 31 December 20X1.
3   Dividends of $13,000 were paid during the year.

Required

(a)   Prepare a statement of cash flows for the year to 30 June 20X2, using the format specified in IAS 7.

(b)   The 20X2 statement of financial position was drafted without taking account of the following adjustments:

(i)   Capital allowances were received during 20X2 which exceeded depreciation by $15,000. The tax rate is 30%.

(ii)   Inventory valued at $9,000 has been damaged. It can be sold for $6,000 following $2,000 remedial work.

(iii)   A provision of $8,000 was made for possible costs following a legal case. This was incorrectly included in trade payables. The case has now been decided and only $3,000 is payable.

Required

Redraft the 20X2 statement of financial position to take account of these adjustments.

Note. This does **not** affect your answer to (a)

17 ABA

The directors of ABA, a limited liability company, are reviewing the draft financial statements for the year ended 30 June 20X9. The profit for the year before tax currently stands at $923,000. The auditors have drawn their attention to the following matters:

(a)   An announcement was made on 4 July that one of their customers, IMX, had gone into liquidation. The liquidator is estimating that suppliers will receive 30c in the $. The receivable in ABA's accounts regarding IMX is $325,000 at 30 June.

(b)   A line of inventory valued at cost of $150,000 has become obsolete. It can only be disposed of for $200,000 via an agent who will require 20% of selling price as commission for selling it. Other disposal costs will amount to $25,000.

(c)   An outstanding claim for damages by an ex-employee who was injured in the warehouse is likely to amount to $50,000. No provision has been made for this as it was expected to be covered by insurance. However the insurance company are now claiming that certain safety procedures were not in place, rendering the cover invalid.

Required

Explain how each of these issues should be dealt with and show the effect on the profit for the year before tax.

18 International tax

J has an overseas branch L, which made a profit adjusted for tax purposes of $8 million for the year ended 30 June 20X6. This figure is included in the financial statements to 30 June 20X6. Taxable profits of the overseas branch have suffered local tax at a rate of 15%. J calculates that its tax liability for the year to 30 June 20X6 will be $1.5m. Overseas tax has not been taken into account in computing this tax liability. The liability for the year ended 30 June 20X5 has been agreed at $970,000. The deferred tax

payable needs to be reduced to $290,000 at 30 June 20X6. J has the following balances brought forward: Current tax: $976,000; Deferred tax: $300,000.

Required

Prepare the notes in respect of current and deferred tax as they would appear in the financial statements of J for the year ended 30 April 20X6.

19 A Co, B Co and C Co

The statements of profit or loss and statements of financial position for the year 20X2 for A Co, B Co and C Co are given below.

STATEMENTS OF PROFIT OR LOSS FOR THE YEAR ENDED 31 DECEMBER 20X2

	A Co $'000	B Co $'000	C Co $'000
Revenue	10,000	7,000	9,000
Cost of sales	(6,000)	(2,000)	(4,500)
Gross profit	4,000	5,000	4,500
Expenses	(2,200)	(1,200)	(1,900)
Profit before taxation	1,800	3,800	2,600
Taxation	(800)	(800)	(600)
Profit for the year	1,000	3,000	2,000

STATEMENTS OF FINANCIAL POSITION AT 31 DECEMBER 20X2

	A Co $'000	B Co $'000	C Co $'000
Assets			
Non-current assets			
Property, plant and equipment	25,300	9,000	10,000
Investment in B Co at cost	4,000	–	–
Investment in C Co at cost	1,000	–	–
	30,300	9,000	10,000
Current assets	21,500	7,000	4,000
Total assets	51,800	16,000	14,000
Equity and liabilities			
Equity			
Ordinary share capital	10,000	4,000	3,000
Share premium account	4,000	–	–
Retained earnings	2,800	7,000	4,000
Total equity	16,800	11,000	7,000
Non-current liabilities	10,000	2,000	3,000
Current liabilities	25,000	3,000	4,000
Total equity and liabilities	51,800	16,000	14,000

Additional information

(a) A Co has owned 100% of B Co since incorporation.

(b) A Co purchased 25% of the shares in C Co for $1 million on 1 January 20X2. Pre-acquisition retained earnings were $2 million.

(c) During the year, A Co sold goods to C Co for $1.5 million at cost plus a 20% mark-up. These goods were still in the inventories of C Co at year-end.

Required

Prepare, for A Co, the consolidated statement of profit or loss for the year ended 31 December 20X2 and the consolidated statement of financial position at that date.

20 Fallowfield and Rusholme

Fallowfield acquired a 100% holding in Rusholme three years ago when Rusholme's retained earnings balance stood at $16,000. Both businesses have been very successful since the acquisition and their respective statements of profit or loss for the year ended 30 June 20X8 are as follows:

	Fallowfield $	Rusholme $
Revenue	403,400	193,000
Cost of sales	(207,400)	(92,600)
Gross profit	196,000	100,400
Other income	6,000	–
Distribution costs	(16,000)	(14,600)
Administrative expenses	(24,250)	(17,800)
Dividends from Rusholme	25,000	–
Profit before tax	186,750	68,000
Income tax expense	(61,750)	(22,000)
Profit for the year	125,000	46,000

STATEMENT OF CHANGES IN EQUITY (EXTRACTS)

	Fallowfield Retained earnings $	Rusholme Retained earnings $
Balance at 1 July 20X7	163,000	61,000
Dividends	(40,000)	(25,000)
Total comprehensive income for the year	125,000	46,000
Balance at 30 June 20X8	248,000	82,000

(a) During the year Rusholme sold some goods to Fallowfield for $40,000, including 25% mark up. Half of these items were still in inventories at the year-end.

(b) Fallowfield sold plant costing $22,000 to Rushholme during the year. The profit on the sale has been shown as other income. Depreciation on plant is charged at 25%.

Required

Produce the consolidated statement of profit or loss of Fallowfield Co and its subsidiary for the year ended 30 June 20X8, and an extract from the statement of changes in equity, showing retained earnings. Goodwill is to be ignored.

1 Convex

(a) Although the head office is in Switzerland, board meetings are held in London and the chairman and chief executive are based in London. **Therefore the place of management is London.**

(b) (i) The nationality of the Board Members is irrelevant to the place of management. Therefore the place of management is London.

   (ii) As board meetings are held in Switzerland and the chairman and chief executive are based in Switzerland, **the place of management is Switzerland**. Although the accounting offices are in London, this does not affect the place where management decisions are made.

2 Tax and dividends

> **Top tips.** Remember that the dividend is a **net** amount.

(a)

		$'000	$'000
Accounting profit			750
Add: disallowable expenditure:	entertaining	75	
	formation expenses	15	
	book depreciation	300	
			390
			1,140
Less: non-taxable income		25	
tax allowable depreciation		350	
			(375)
Taxable profit			765

The tax rate is 25%, so the tax due is $191,250 (25% × $765,000).

(b)

	$'000
Net dividend received	1,500
Tax credit (1,500 / 75 × 25)	500
Gross dividend	2,000
Tax at 30% (2,000 × 30%)	600
Less tax credit	(500)
Tax payable by shareholders	100

3 VAT

	$
Output tax (see note)	70,000
Input tax (300,000 x 85%) x 17.5%	44,625
Tax payable	25,375

Note

Assume sales excluding VAT are Y.

Then zero-rated sales are 20% x Y and standard rated gross sales are Y x 80% x 1.175%.

So:

(20% x Y) + (Y x 80% x 1.175%) = 570,000

0.2Y + 0.94Y = 570,000

1.14Y = 570,000

Y = 500,000

Check: Net sales are $500,000, so VAT due is $500,000 x 80% x 17.5% ($70,000). This gives sales including VAT of $570,000.

4 Regulatory influences

> **Top tips.** Do not omit the requirement to **explain**. It is best to use **headings** to divide your answer.

Stock Exchange

A quoted company is a company whose shares are bought and sold on a stock exchange. This involves the signing of an agreement which requires compliance with the rules of that stock exchange. This would normally contain amongst other things the stock exchange's detailed rules on the information to be disclosed in listed companies' accounts. This, then, is one regulatory influence on a listed company's accounts. The stock exchange may enforce compliance by monitoring accounts and reserving the right to withdraw a company's shares from the stock exchange: ie the company's shares would no longer be traded through the stock exchange. In many countries there is, however, no statutory requirement to obey these rules.

Local legislation

In most countries, companies have to comply with the local companies legislation, which lays down detailed requirements on the preparation of accounts. Company law is often quite detailed, partly because of external influences such as EU Directives. Another reason to increase statutory regulation is that listed companies are under great pressure to show profit growth and an obvious way to achieve this is to manipulate accounting policies. If this involves breaking the law, as opposed to ignoring professional guidance, company directors may think twice before bending the rules - or, at least, this is often a government's hope.

Standard-setters

Professional guidance is given by the national and international standard-setters. Prescriptive guidance is given in accounting standards which must be applied in all accounts intended to show a 'true and fair view' or 'present fairly in all material respects'. IFRSs and national standards are issued after extensive consultation and are revised as required to reflect economic or legal changes. In some countries, legislation requires details of non-compliance to be disclosed in the accounts. 'Defective' accounts can be revised under court order if necessary and directors signing such accounts can be prosecuted and fined (or even imprisoned).

The potential for the IASB's influence in this area is substantial.

5 Accounting standards

The users of financial information – shareholders, suppliers, management, employees, business contacts, financial specialists, government and the general public - are entitled to this information about a business entity to a greater or lesser degree. However, the needs and expectations of these groups will vary.

The preparers of the financial information often find themselves in the position of having to reconcile the interests of different groups in the best way for the business entity. For example whilst shareholders are looking for increased profits to support higher dividends, employees will expect higher wage increases; and yet higher profits without corresponding higher tax allowances (increased capital allowances for example) will result in a larger tax bill.

Without accounting standards to prescribe how certain transactions should be treated, preparers **would be tempted to produce financial information which meets the expectations of the favoured user group**.

For example creative accounting methods, such as off balance sheet finance, could be used to enhance a company's statement of financial position to make it more attractive to investors/lenders.

The aim of accounting standards is that they should regulate financial information in order that it shows the following characteristics, amongst others.

(a) Objectivity
(b) Comparability
(c) Completeness
(d) Consistency

6 IASB

The main aims of the IASB, operating under the oversight of the IFRS Foundation, are:

(a) to develop a single set of high quality, understandable, enforceable and globally accepted international financial reporting standards

(b) to promote the use and rigorous application of those standards

(c) to take account of the financial reporting needs of emerging economies and small and medium-sized entities

(d) to bring about convergence of national accounting standards and IFRSs to high quality solutions

The tendency of the IASB has been to concentrate on the development of standards, leaving the others, which are slightly more vague aims to follow behind.

One of IASB's targets has been to produce a set of 'core standards' which the worldwide body representing stock exchanges, IOSCO, can accept for all cross-border listings. In theory, this would mean that, say, a German company that prepares its accounts using IFRSs would be accepted for a listing on the Tokyo Stock Exchange.

IOSCO has given the core standards qualified endorsement and with the new standards and improvements to existing standards issued in 2003 and 2004, the IASB claims to have now established a 'stable platform' of standards.

However, individual stock exchanges may still make life difficult for foreign companies by insisting on substantial additional disclosures. The IASB is facing an uphill struggle, but there have been substantial successes, notably the EU decision that the consolidated accounts of listed companies must comply with IFRS from 2005.

In recent years the IASB has also been pursuing the convergence of IFRSs and standards produced in the US by the FASB. There is now a timetable for convergence between IFRS and US GAAP. When this is achieved it will greatly increase the influence of the IASB.

7 External auditors

The external auditors' responsibilities with respect to the financial statements are concerned with deciding whether the accounts show a **true and fair view** of the affairs of the company for the year. The auditors must express an **opinion** on the financial statements to this effect.

The auditors conduct an audit which examines the figures in the financial statements and agrees them back to the underlying accounting information. They are required to satisfy themselves that the directors have prepared the accounts correctly and that there is no materially misleading information within them. To this end the auditors have a statutory right to all information and explanations deemed necessary to perform the audit.

The external auditors report to the members of the company and their responsibility is limited to the expression of this opinion.

They are not responsible for the accounting systems, or for the detection of all fraud and error. While auditors will report on whether or not the accounting system is satisfactory, and will design their tests in order to have **a good chance of detecting any material fraud or error**, these issues are the responsibility of the directors.

8 Audit report

If the auditor's work leads them to conclude that the financial statements are free from material error or misstatement and that they give a true and fair view of the financial affairs of the company then they will issue an **unmodified opinion**. This opinion covers the statement of profit or loss and other comprehensive income, the statement of financial position, the statement of changes in equity, the statement of cash flows and the notes to the accounts. They also review the directors report to ensure that this does not contain information which is materially misleading or which conflicts with elements of the financial statements. The auditor's report is the statement of their opinion on these elements of the financial statements. They state explicitly that the statement of financial position reflects the state of the company's affairs at the year end and that the statement of profit or loss and other comprehensive income gives the company's profit or loss for the year. The report also covers a number of other elements, such as the fact that adequate accounting records were kept, by exception.

A modified report contains a modified opinion because the auditors are concerned that the financial statements do not or may not give a true and fair view. This may occur due to the auditor concluding that the financial statements are as a whole are not free from material misstatements or because the auditor cannot obtain sufficient appropriate audit evidence to conclude that the financial statements as a whole are free from material misstatement.

The extent of the modification is determined by whether the misstatement or inability to obtain sufficient appropriate audit evidence is merely **material** or is **pervasive**.

When the auditors issue a modified report it must contain a full explanation of the reasons for the modification and, where possible, a quantification of the effects on the financial statements. This means that a modified report will contain at least one more paragraph than an unmodified report.

The modified report should leave the reader in no doubt as to its meaning and the implications it has on an understanding of the financial statements.

9 New project

Ethical issues

The accountant has been asked to manage a project for which he or she does not have sufficient expertise. This is a threat to the fundamental principle of **professional competence and due care**. The CIMA *code of ethics for professional accountants* specifically requires accountants to only undertake tasks for which they have sufficient experience.

The finance director may be unaware that the accountant does not possess the requisite knowledge for the project in question. It may be tempting for the accountant to ignore the issue, especially if he or she is concerned that their reputation is discredited or they are hoping for a promotion within the business. This is a threat to the fundamental principle of **professional behaviour**. Under the CIMA Code, accountants in business should not intentionally mislead employers as to their level of expertise.

Action to take

Initially, the accountant should inform the finance director of his or her concerns and discuss an appropriate course of action. The problem may be alleviated by the accountant attending further training or if there are only specific areas where he or she lacks expertise, consulting with others on these areas. If

none of these safeguards are appropriate then the management of the project should be reassigned to a member of staff with the correct experience.

If the finance director insists the accountant manages the project after being made aware of his or her lack of expertise, the accountant should raise the matter with the next level of management, if this exists.

The accountant should only contact external parties if a satisfactory response cannot be obtained internally. It may be appropriate to contact CIMA or an independent professional advisor. As confidentiality rules apply, legal advice should be sought before contacting an external party.

The accountant should only refuse to manage the new project as a last resort.

10 IFRS 5

Top tips. Read this question carefully. The definition of 'held for sale' is quite specific.

The plant will not be classified as 'held for sale'.

For this to be the case, the asset must be available for immediate sale and its sale must be **highly probable**. For the sale to be highly probable, the asset must be actively marketed for sale at a price that is reasonable in relation to its current fair value.

This property is being marketed at a price which is **above** its current fair value. It is improbable that it will be sold at that price until property prices rise. This delay has been imposed by the seller, so it cannot be said that his intention is to sell the plant immediately. Therefore it cannot be classified as 'held for sale'.

11 CEC

Top tips. This is a fairly easy question. Remember to **explain** each item.

		Adjustment	
		Add to inventory value $	Subtract from inventory value $
Item	Explanation		
(a)	Cost $2,885. Net realisable value $(3,600 – 921) = $2,679. The inventory should be valued at the lower of cost and NRV. Since NRV is lower, the original valuation of inventories (at cost) will be reduced by $(2,885 – 2,679)		206
(b)	Inventory issued on sale or return and not yet accepted by the customer should be included in the valuation and valued at the lower of cost and NRV, here at $5 each (cost)	1,500	
(c)	The cost ($7.30) is below the current and foreseeable selling price ($10 or more) which is assumed to be the NRV of the item. Since the current valuation is at the lower of cost and NRV, no change in valuation is necessary		
		1,500	206

	$	$
Original valuation of inventories, at cost		153,699
Adjustments and corrections:		
To increase valuation	1,500	
To decrease valuation	(206)	
		1294
Valuation of inventories for the financial statements		154,993

12 Plant and equipment

> **Top tips.** Do not forget the annual depreciation charge.

PLANT AND EQUIPMENT – COST

	DR $		CR $
Balance b/f	250,000	Plant 20X5 disposal	40,000
Purchases	150,000	Plant 20X7 disposal	10,000
		Balance c/d	350,000
	400,000		400,000
Balance b/d	350,000		

PLANT AND EQUIPMENT – ACCUMULATED DEPRECIATION

	DR $		CR $
Plant 20X5 disp	32,000	B/f	148,000
Plant 20X7 disp	4,000	Current year chg – 350,000 x 20%	70,000
Balance c/d	182,000		
	218,000		218,000
		Balance b/d	182,000

PLANT AND EQUIPMENT – DISPOSALS

	DR $		CR $
Plant 20X5	40,000	Plant 20X5 depn	32,000
Plant 20X7	10,000	Plant 20X7 depn	4,000
		Plant 20X5 proceeds	5,000
		Losses on disposals	9,000
	50,000		50,000

13 IT

> **Top tips.** The important point is to distinguish between the amounts actually spent during the year and the amounts taken to profit or loss.

PURCHASED GOODWILL

	$		$
Cash	4,800	Statement of profit or loss: impairment loss	1,200
		Balance c/d	3,600
	4,800		4,800
Balance b/d	3,600		

RESEARCH AND DEVELOPMENT EXPENDITURE

	$		$
Balance b/f	26,500	∴ Statement of profit or loss (7,900 + (26,500 + 3,500 – 22,600))	15,300
Cash: research	7,900		
development	3,500	Development costs c/d	22,600
	37,900		37,900
Balance b/d	22,600		

14 F

> **Top tips.** Remember that some events after the end of the reporting period, while not adjusting events, may still require disclosure.

The treatment of the events arising in the case of F would be as follows.

(a) The fall in value of the investment in P has arisen over the previous year and that company's financial accounts for the year to 28 February 20X1 provide additional evidence of conditions that existed at the end of the reporting period. The loss of $50,000 is material in terms of the trading profit figure and it should therefore be reflected in the financial statements of F. Due to the size and nature of the loss, it should be disclosed separately either in profit or loss or in the notes, according to IAS 1.

(b) The destruction of inventory by fire on 30 April (one month after the end of the reporting period) must be considered as a new condition which did not exist at the end of the reporting period. Since the loss is material, being $250,000, it should be disclosed separately, by way of a note describing the nature of the event and giving an estimate of its financial effect.

(c) The approval on 1 June of the company's design for tank cleaning equipment creates a new condition which did not exist at the end of the reporting period. This is, therefore, an event which does not require adjustment under IAS 10.

15 B

> **Top tips.** This is very likely to be examined. Make sure you know the format. Do not neglect part (b).

(a) STATEMENT OF CASH FLOWS FOR THE YEAR ENDED 30 SEPTEMBER 20X1

	$'000	$'000
Profit before tax (85 + 15)		100
Adjustment for non-cash-flow items		
Profit on sale of non-current asset		(10)
Depreciation		30
Adjustment for working capital		120
Inventory		(15)
Receivables		(50)
Payables		40
Cash generated from operations		95
Interest paid		(15)
Net cash from operating activities		80
Cash flows from investing activities		
Sale of non-current asset (W2)	90	
Purchase of non-current assets	(40)	
Net cash from investing activities		50
Cash flows from financing activities		
Dividends paid	(35)	
Loan repaid	(80)	
Net cash used in financing activities		(115)
Net increase in cash and cash equivalents		15
Cash and cash equivalents at beginning of period		15
Cash and cash equivalents at end of period		30

Working

Sale of non-current assets

	$'000
Carrying amount (520 + 40 − 30 − 450)	80
Profit from sale	10
Proceeds from sale	90

Alternative working using T account

NON-CURRENT ASSETS DISPOSAL

	$'000		$'000
Carrying amount	80	Proceeds from sale	90
Profit from sale	10		
	90		90

(b)   STATEMENT OF FINANCIAL POSITION AS AT 30 SEPTEMBER 20X2

	$'000	$'000
Non-current assets (450 − 30)		420
Current assets		
Inventory	75	
Receivables (80 + 640 − 615)	105	
Bank and cash (W)	220	400
Total assets		820
Equity and liabilities		
Share capital		400
Retained earnings (145 + 160)		305
Current liabilities (60 + 410 + 35 − 390)		115
		820

Working

Bank and cash

	$'000
Balance at 30 September 20X1	30
Received from customers	615
Paid to suppliers	(390)
Interest paid	(15)
Loan paid off	(20)
	220

Alternative working using T account

BANK AND CASH

	$'000		$'000
Balance at 30 Sept 20X1	30	Paid to suppliers	390
Received from customers	615	Interest paid	15
		Loan paid off	20
		Balance c/d	220
	645		645

16 Cat

> **Top tips.** This question is easier than it looks. Work through it methodically.

(a)   CAT CO
     STATEMENT OF CASH FLOWS FOR THE YEAR ENDED 30 JUNE 20X2

	$	$
Cash flows from operating activities		
Profit before tax (W1)	54,500	
Interest expense	1,500	
Depreciation (37,000 – 26,000)	11,000	
Increase in inventories	(6,000)	
Decrease in receivables	2,000	
Increase in payables	8,000	
Interest paid	(1,500)	
Dividends paid	(13,000)	
Income tax paid (W2)	(12,000)	
Net cash from operating activities		44,500
Cash flows from investing activities		
Payments to acquire non-current assets (W3)		(34,000)
Net cash used in investing activities		10,500
Cash flows from financing activities		
Issue of ordinary share capital	3,000	
Redemption of loan stock	(10,000)	
Net cash used in financing activities		(7,000)
Net increase in cash and cash equivalents		3,500
Cash and cash equivalents at beginning of year		10,000
Cash and cash equivalents at end of year		13,500

Workings

1   *Profit before tax*

	$
Retained earnings b/f 1.7.X1	44,000
Profit before tax	**54,500**
Taxation	(15,000)
Dividends	(13,000)
Retained earnings c/f 30.6.X2	(70,500)

Profit for the year is after charging loan interest of 10% × 10,000 for 12 months and 10% × 10,000 for 6 months.

Alternative working using T account

RETAINED EARNINGS

	$		$
Taxation	15,000	Balance b/f 1.7.X1	44,000
Dividends	13,000	Profit before tax (bal fig)	54,500
Balance c/f 30.6.X2	70,500		
	98,500		98,500

2   *Tax paid*

	$
Balance b/f 1.7.X1	12,000
Tax charge	15,000
	27,000
Tax paid *	**(12,000)**
Balance c/f 30.6.X2	15,000

Note. The tax paid will be last year's year-end provision

Alternative working using T account

TAXATION

	$		$
Tax paid*	12,000	Balance b/f 1.7.X1	12,000
Balance c/f 30.6.X2	15,000	Tax charge	15,000
	27,000		27,000

3   *Non-current assets*

	$
Balance b/f 1.7.X1	85,000
Purchases	**34,000**
Balance c/f 30.6.X2	119,000

Alternative working using T account

NON-CURRENT ASSETS

	$		$
Balance b/f 1.7.X1	85,000		
Purchases (bal fig)	34,000	Balance c/f 30.6.X2	119,000
	119,000		119,000

(b)   STATEMENT OF FINANCIAL POSITION AS AT 30 JUNE 20X2

	$	$
Assets		
Non-current assets		
Cost	119,000	
Depreciation	(37,000)	
		82,000
Current assets		
Inventories (40,000 – 3,000 – 2,000)	35,000	
Receivables	24,000	
Cash	13,500	
		72,500
Total assets		154,500

Equity and liabilities
Equity

Ordinary $1 shares	28,000	
Share premium	13,000	
Retained earnings (W)	66,000	
		107,000
Non-current liabilities		
10% loan stock	10,000	
Deferred tax	4,500	
		14,500
Current liabilities		
Provision for legal costs	3,000	
Trade payables (23,000 – 8,000)	15,000	
Taxation	15,000	
		33,000
Total equity and liabilities		154,500

Working: Retained earnings

	$'000
As per draft statement of financial position	70,500
Transfer to deferred tax (15,000 x 30%)	(4,500)
Inventory adjustment	(5,000)
Reduction in provision	5,000
	66,000

17 ABA

> **Top tips.** Do not forget to show effect of these adjustments on the net profit before tax.

(a) The value of the IMX receivable will have to be written down. If, as appears likely, something can be recovered, then the debt will not need to be written off entirely. It can be written down to 30c in the $. The write-down needed will be $227,500.

(b) NRV of this inventory is now:

	$
Sales proceeds	200,000
Less agents commission 20%	(40,000)
Less disposal costs	(25,000)
	135,000

As this is less than cost, the inventory should be written down by $15,000.

(c) It currently looks probable that this liability will not be met by the insurance company, so it should be provided for in full in accordance with IAS 37.

Effect on profit for the year before tax

	$
Draft profit for the year	923,000
IMX write-down	(227,500)
Inventory write-down	(15,000)
Provision for damages	(50,000)
Adjusted profit for the year	630,500

(b) '1 for 2' rights issue at 80c

37.5m shares are now issued at 80c.

	$'000
Share capital (37,500 + 18,750)	56,250
Share premium (37.5m × 30c)	11,250
Retained earnings	7,500
	75,000

18 International tax

> **Top tips.** This question covers a number of issues. Deal with each one separately.

Tax on profit on ordinary activities – note to statement of profit or loss and other comprehensive income

	$'000
Current tax	
Tax on profit for the year	1,500
Overseas tax paid (note)	(1,200)
Overprovision for previous period ($976,000 - $970,000)	(6)
Deferred tax	
Decrease in provision ($300,000 - $290,000)	(10)
Total tax charge	284

Note: Tax paid by overseas branch = $8m x 15% = $1.2m.

STATEMENT OF FINANCIAL POSITION

	$m
Non-current liabilities	
Deferred tax	290
Current liabilities	
Current tax	300

19 A Co, B Co and C Co

> **Top tips.** Write out your proforma statements before working methodically down the given information in this question.

A CO
CONSOLIDATED STATEMENT OF PROFIT OR LOSS FOR THE YEAR ENDED 31 DECEMBER 20X2

	$'000
Revenue (10,000 + 7,000)	17,000
Cost of sales (6,000 + 2,000 + 63 (W1))	(8,063)
Gross profit	8,937
Expenses (2,200 + 1,200)	(3,400)
Share of profit of associate (2,000 × 25%)	500
Profit before taxation	6,037
Taxation (800 + 800)	(1,600)
Profit for the year	(4,437)

A CO
CONSOLIDATED STATEMENT OF FINANCIAL POSITION AT 31 DECEMBER 20X2

	$
Assets	
Non-current assets	
Property, plant and equipment (25,300 + 9,000)	34,300
Investment in associate (W2)	1,437
Current assets (21,500 + 7,000)	28,500
Total assets	64,237
Equity and liabilities	
Ordinary share capital	10,000
Share premium account	4,000
Retained earnings (2,800 + 7,000 + 500 – 63 (W2))	10,237
Total equity	24,237
Non-current liabilities (10,000 + 2,000)	12,000
Current liabilities (25,000 + 3,000)	28,000
Total equity and liabilities	64,237

Points to note

1   A Co has owned the shares in B Co since incorporation and the shares were acquired at nominal value (4,000 shares for $4 million). There is therefore no difference between the value of the consideration transferred by A Co and the value of the assets it acquired.

Workings

1   *Unrealised profit*

$$1,500 \times \frac{20}{120} \times 25\% = 63$$

2   *Investment in associate*

	$'000
Cost of investment	1,000
Share of post-acquisition retained earnings ((4,000 – 2,000) × 25%)	500
Unrealised profit (W1)	(63)
	1,437

20 Fallowfield and Rusholme

CONSOLIDATED STATEMENT OF PROFIT OR LOSS FOR THE YEAR ENDED 30 JUNE 20X8

	$
Revenue (403,400 + 193,000 – 40,000)	556,400
Cost of sales (207,400 + 92,600 – 40,000 + 4,000)	(264,000)
Gross profit	292,400
Distribution costs (16,000 + 14,600)	(30,600)
Administrative expenses (24,250 + 17,800 – (6,000 × 25%))	(40,550)
Profit before tax	221,250
Income tax expense (61,750 + 22,000)	(83,750)
Profit for the year	137,500

STATEMENT OF CHANGES IN EQUITY (EXTRACT)

	Retained earnings $
Balance at 1 July 20X7 (W1)	208,000
Dividends	(40,000)
Total comprehensive income for the year	137,500
Balance at 30 June 20X8 (W2)	305,500

Workings

1 *Retained earnings brought forward*

	Fallowfield $	*Rusholme* $
Per question	163,000	61,000
Pre-acquisition retained earnings	–	(16,000)
Share of Rusholme	163,000	45,000
	45,000	
	208,000	

2 *Retained earnings carried forward*

	Fallowfield $	*Rusholme* $
Per question	248,000	82,000
PUP	–	(4,000)
Pre-acquisition retained earnings		(16,000)
Disposal of plant		
Profit	(6,000)	
Depreciation (6,000 x 25%)	1,500	
	243,500	62,000
Share of Rusholme post-acquisition earnings	62,000	
	305,500	

INDEX

Note: **Key Terms** and their references are given in **bold**.

Notes

Notes

Notes

Notes

Notes

Review Form – Paper F1 Financial Reporting and Taxation (6/15)

Please help us to ensure that the CIMA learning materials we produce remain as accurate and user-friendly as possible. We cannot promise to answer every submission we receive, but we do promise that it will be read and taken into account when we up-date this Study Text.

Name: _____ Address: _____

_____

_____

How have you used this Study Text?
(Tick one box only)

☐ Home study (book only)

☐ On a course: college _____

☐ With 'correspondence' package

☐ Other _____

Why did you decide to purchase this Study Text? *(Tick one box only)*

☐ Have used BPP Texts in the past

☐ Recommendation by friend/colleague

☐ Recommendation by a lecturer at college

☐ Saw information on BPP website

☐ Saw advertising

☐ Other _____

During the past six months do you recall seeing/receiving any of the following?
(Tick as many boxes as are relevant)

☐ Our advertisement in *Financial Management*

☐ Our advertisement in *Pass*

☐ Our advertisement in *PQ*

☐ Our brochure with a letter through the post

☐ Our website www.bpp.com

Which (if any) aspects of our advertising do you find useful?
(Tick as many boxes as are relevant)

☐ Prices and publication dates of new editions

☐ Information on Text content

☐ Facility to order books off-the-page

☐ None of the above

Which BPP products have you used?

Text ☑   Passcard ☐

Kit ☐   i-Pass ☐

Your ratings, comments and suggestions would be appreciated on the following areas.

	Very useful	Useful	Not useful
Introductory section	☐	☐	☐
Chapter introductions	☐	☐	☐
Key terms	☐	☐	☐
Quality of explanations	☐	☐	☐
Case studies and other examples	☐	☐	☐
Exam skills and alerts	☐	☐	☐
Questions and answers in each chapter	☐	☐	☐
Fast forwards and chapter roundups	☐	☐	☐
Quick quizzes	☐	☐	☐
Question Bank	☐	☐	☐
Answer Bank	☐	☐	☐
OT Bank	☐	☐	☐
Index	☐	☐	☐

	Excellent	Good	Adequate	Poor
Overall opinion of this Study Text	☐	☐	☐	☐

Do you intend to continue using BPP products?   Yes ☐   No ☐

On the reverse of this page is space for you to write your comments about our Study Text. We welcome your feedback.

The BPP Learning Media author of this edition can be e-mailed at: helenajones@bpp.com

Please return this form to: Valli Rajagopal, CIMA Product Manager, BPP Learning Media Ltd, FREEPOST, London, W12 8BR

TELL US WHAT YOU THINK

Please note any further comments and suggestions/errors below. For example, was the text accurate, readable, concise, user-friendly and comprehensive?